Do Institutions Matter?

Do Institutions Matter?

Government Capabilities in
the United States and Abroad

R. KENT WEAVER *and* BERT A. ROCKMAN
editors

The Brookings Institution
Washington, D.C.

Copyright © 1993
THE BROOKINGS INSTITUTION
1775 Massachusetts Avenue, N.W., Washington, D.C. 20036

Library of Congress Cataloging-in-Publication data:

Do institutions matter? : government capabilities in the United
  States and abroad / R. Kent Weaver and Bert A. Rockman,
  editors.
      p.   cm.
  Includes biographical references and index.
  ISBN 0-8157-9256-5 (alk. paper) — ISBN 0-8157-9255-7
  1. Separation of powers—United States.   2. Cabinet system.
3. Policy sciences.   4. Public institutions. I. Weaver, R. Kent,
1953–   II. Rockman, Bert A.
  JK305.D6   1992
  320.4'04'0973—dc20   92-35665
                                                                CIP

9 8 7 6 5 4 3 2 1

The paper used in this publication meets the minimum requirements
of the American National Standard for Information Sciences—Per-
manence of paper for Printed Library Materials, ANSI Z39.48-1984.

THE BROOKINGS INSTITUTION

The Brookings Institution is an independent organization devoted to nonpartisan research, education, and publication in economics, government, foreign policy, and the social sciences generally. Its principal purposes are to aid in the development of sound public policies and to promote public understanding of issues of national importance.

The Institution was founded on December 8, 1927, to merge the activities of the Institute for Government Research, founded in 1916, the Institute of Economics, founded in 1922, and the Robert Brookings Graduate School of Economics and Government, founded in 1924.

The Board of Trustees is responsible for the general administration of the Institution, while the immediate direction of the policies, program, and staff is vested in the President, assisted by an advisory committee of the officers and staff. The by-laws of the Institution state: "It is the function of the Trustees to make possible the conduct of scientific research, and publication, under the most favorable conditions, and to safeguard the independence of the research staff in the pursuit of their studies and in the publication of the results of such studies. It is not a part of their function to determine, control, or influence the conduct of particular investigations or the conclusions reached."

The President bears final responsibility for the decision to publish a manuscript as a Brookings book. In reaching his judgment on the competence, accuracy, and objectivity of each study, the President is advised by the director of the appropriate research program and weighs the views of a panel of expert outside readers who report to him in confidence on the quality of the work. Publication of a work signifies that it is deemed a competent treatment worthy of public consideration but does not imply endorsement of conclusions or recommendations.

The Institution maintains its position of neutrality on issues of public policy in order to safeguard the intellectual freedom of the staff. Hence interpretations or conclusions in Brookings publications should be understood to be solely those of the authors and should not be attributed to the Institution, to its trustees, officers, or other staff members, or to the organizations that support its research.

Foreword

*T*he 1992 election brought at least a temporary end to divided party control of the U.S. government, a phenomenon that has been blamed for the inability of America to meet many domestic and foreign policy challenges. Even under a unified government, however, many questions are likely to persist about the effectiveness of American governing institutions to meet such challenges. Although reformers bemoan the weaknesses of the American system, surprisingly little attention has been devoted to systematic comparisons of the policymaking capacities of American political institutions with those of other advanced industrial democracies.

This volume, edited by R. Kent Weaver and Bert A. Rockman, moves significantly toward filling that gap. Systematically crafted case studies compare the governing capacity of America's separation-of-powers system with that of various types of parliamentary systems. These cases draw upon policymaking in the United States and other countries in areas including energy, trade, military security, pensions, and the budget to illustrate how institutional arrangements affect governing capacities, such as the abilities to innovate, to impose losses, and to target resources effectively. From these studies, the editors derive important conclusions about how institutions affect policymaking capacity. They then suggest reforms of American government designed to increase that capacity.

Weaver and Rockman find that differences among parliamentary regimes are at least as important as differences between parliamentary and presidential regimes. Political institutions create both opportunities and risks for policymaking capacities, and whether the risks or opportunities dominate frequently depends on the social and political conditions in specific countries. Moreover, strengthening some governmental capacities often requires sacrificing others. The editors therefore caution against viewing any single set of institutions as optimal for all times and countries and against making institutional arrangements too difficult to reform.

R. Kent Weaver is a senior fellow in the Brookings Governmental Studies program, and Bert A. Rockman is university professor of political science at the University of Pittsburgh and a nonresident senior fellow in the Governmental Studies program at Brookings.

The editors wish to thank the many people who helped produce the book. Renuka D. Deonarain organized the conference at which initial drafts of papers were presented. Sandra Z. Riegler, Susan A. Stewart, Eloise C. Stinger, and Elizabeth O. Toy provided administrative assistance. Helen Hall, Susan J. Thompson, and Antoinette T. Williams provided word processing assistance. Nancy Davidson directed the editing of the manuscript, and individual chapters were also edited by Rozlyn Coleman and James R. Schneider. Todd L. Quinn and Alison M. Rimsky verified its factual content. Susan L. Woollen prepared the manuscript for publication, and Gerald Van Ravenswaay prepared the index.

Brookings would like to acknowledge support provided by the Dillon Fund. The interpretations and conclusions presented here are solely those of the authors and should not be ascribed to the persons whose assistance and funding support is acknowledged above or to the trustees, officers, or other staff members of the Brookings Institution.

BRUCE K. MACLAURY
President

January 1993
Washington, D.C.

Contents

Tables

Figures

R. Kent Weaver and Bert A. Rockman

Assessing the Effects of Institutions

T he final decade of the twentieth century is witnessing a stunning tide of democratization sweeping across much of the world. Whether the democratic politics of the moment achieves a lasting stability will largely depend on how the newly democratized countries are able to cope with problems such as economic development, political and social integration, and a high volume of public demand on scarce resources. How effective they are at responding to these problems will depend on many factors, including their choice of political institutions.[1]

These issues of institutional choice are also pertinent to the world's oldest democracy, the United States. Is the American institutional framework an example to follow or to avoid? How well does the American institutional framework actually function?

The last question has been recurrent at least since the time of Woodrow Wilson's extraordinary analyses of the state of American governing institutions.[2] Yet it also is very current. Indeed, these times of triumph for the democratic idea abroad seem to have coincided with concerns about the incapacity of democratic institutions at home. American political reformers frequently are critical of the system of separation of powers for failing to give anybody clear authority to govern or, alternatively, giving different authorities competing powers to govern.[3] Be-

The authors would like to thank participants in the project, and especially James L. Sundquist, Harvey Feigenbaum, and Sven Steinmo, for detailed and helpful comments on earlier versions of this chapter.

1. James MacGregor Burns, "U.S., Model for Eastern Europe?" *New York Times,* February 8, 1990, p. A29.

2. See Woodrow Wilson, *Congressional Government: A Study in American Politics* (Houghton Mifflin, 1900).

3. Richard E. Neustadt refers to the American system as one that is not a system of

1

cause no one has exclusive authority to govern, no one can be held exclusively accountable, and that leaves plenty of room to point fingers. The outcome, according to critics, is division and deadlock. There are powerful inducements for politicians, in either the White House or Congress, to avoid dealing with difficult problems, which then fester until the costs of coping with them become extraordinary. Parochialism and logrolling in Congress, the critics also charge, lead to incoherent and inefficiently targeted policies. Some would add that the separation of powers also prevents the country from speaking with a single voice in foreign policy.[4] Some political scientists have gone even further, charging that separation of presidential and legislative powers is inherently unstable.[5] Expressions of frustration with federal institutions are also endemic in the popular press.[6]

The constitutional order bequeathed by the Framers of the American Constitution was not designed for efficient government. It was designed to counter ambition with ambition and to inhibit tyranny. But the potential shortcomings of the constitutional design have been magnified in recent times by increasing demands on government and by the continuing partisan division of governmental power, with Republicans generally controlling the presidency and Democrats the Congress. Former Treasury Secretary C. Douglas Dillon has argued that divided government causes both policymaking and accountability to suffer because, instead

---

separated powers but instead a system of separate authorities sharing power. See Neustadt, *Presidential Power and the Modern Presidents: The Politics of Leadership from Roosevelt to Reagan* (Free Press, 1990).

4. See, for example, Lloyd N. Cutler, "To Form a Government," *Foreign Affairs,* vol. 59 (Fall 1980), pp. 126–43; Donald L. Robinson, ed., *Reforming American Government: The Bicentennial Papers of the Committee on the Constitutional System* (Westview, 1985); James L. Sundquist, *Constitutional Reform and Effective Government,* rev. ed. (Brookings, 1992), chap. 1; and James MacGregor Burns, *The Deadlock of Democracy: Four-Party Politics in America* (Prentice-Hall, 1963). See also the discussion in James Q. Wilson, "Does the Separation of Powers Still Work?" *Public Interest,* no. 86 (Winter 1987), pp. 36–52.

5. See Juan J. Linz, "The Perils of Presidentialism," *Journal of Democracy,* vol. 1 (Winter 1990), pp. 51–69; and Fred W. Riggs, "The Survival of Presidentialism in America: Paraconstitutional Practices," *International Political Science Review,* vol. 9 (October 1988), pp. 247–78.

6. A cover article in *Newsweek,* for example, argued that Congress is "a fortress of unreality, with its own laws, logic and codes of behavior." See Jonathan Alter, Howard Fineman, and Eleanor Clift, "The World of Congress," *Newsweek,* April 24, 1989, p. 28. *Time* was even more downbeat, asking on its cover, "Is Government Dead?" with the subtitle, "Unwilling to Lead, Politicians are Letting America Slip into Paralysis." Stanley W. Cloud, "The Can't Do Government," *Time,* October 23, 1989, pp. 28–32. For a critique of popular views and a defense of Congress, see Nelson W. Polsby, "Congress-Bashing for Beginners," *Public Interest,* no. 100 (Summer 1990), pp. 15–23.

of avoiding stalemate, "the president blames the Congress, the Congress blames the president, and the public remains confused and disgusted with government in Washington."[7]

Although American political reformers often disagree on the particulars of the institutional remedies they seek, they generally share the view that governing in the modern era requires some changes to counteract the inefficiencies of governing capability that inhere in the current constitutional design. Increasing the collective capacity, responsibility, and accountability of the federal government has been the thread that ties together the various strands of reform proposals. Few critics propose adoption of a parliamentary system in the United States, in part because such a drastic institutional change is highly unlikely. Nevertheless, a parliamentary model—and more specifically, the British "party government" model—serves as the implicit, if unattainable, ideal for many critics of existing American political institutions.

Belief that the institutional grass is greener somewhere else is not limited to the United States, however. In the Netherlands, Dutch political analysts have criticized their country's electoral system of at-large proportional representation for giving rise to multiparty coalitions. The fragility of these coalitions induces internal jockeying leading to the breakup and reformation of governments between elections, which in turn may cause changes in the ideological balance of government without popular ratification. These outcomes are viewed as weakening both executive power and democratic accountability.[8] Italians have criticized their system for promoting weak governments dominated by patronage-oriented parties and for failing to produce alternation in government by competing coalitions.[9] Israelis recently adopted a series of electoral reforms, including direct popular election of the prime minister, in response to repeated governmental and coalitional crises and political deadlocks.[10] Critics in

---

7. C. Douglas Dillon, "The Challenge of Modern Governance (1982)," in Robinson, ed., *Reforming American Government*, p. 26. See also Dom Bonafede, "Reform of U.S. System of Government Is on the Minds and Agendas of Many," *National Journal*, June 29, 1985, pp. 1521–24; and James L. Sundquist, "Needed: A Political Theory for the New Era of Coalition Government in the United States," *Political Science Quarterly*, vol. 103 (Winter 1988–89), pp. 613–35.

8. For a review of critiques of the Dutch system, see Hans Daalder, "Changing Procedures and Changing Strategies in Dutch Coalition Building," *Legislative Studies Quarterly*, vol. 11 (November 1986), pp. 507–31.

9. The latter criticism is made especially by the Communists. For a review of critiques of the Italian system and proposals for change (including direct election for political executives), see Gianfranco Pasquino, "That Obscure Object of Desire: A New Electoral Law for Italy," *West European Politics*, vol. 12 (July 1989), pp. 280–94.

10. Dan Izenberg, "Against All Odds: Knesset Votes for Direct Election of P.M.,"

Britain have argued that their electoral and governmental system exacerbates cleavages, underrepresents third parties, gives excessive power to the government of the day, and undermines policy stability.[11]

Postwar European experience suggests that a change in institutional arrangements can make a difference for governmental stability and effectiveness but does not always do so. Hopeful news comes from France, where the establishment of a semipresidential system under the Fifth Republic in 1958 ended a prolonged period of unstable coalition governments, and from the Federal Republic of Germany, where toughened procedures for bringing down governments similarly put an end to the political instability of the Weimar Republic.[12] Less hopeful news comes from Northern Ireland, where instituting an electoral system of proportional representation did not succeed in promoting a coalition government across the Catholic-Protestant religious divide (see the chapter by Richard Gunther and Anthony Mughan).

Experience in the United States and abroad also suggests that there is enormous flexibility to work within and around most nations' basic constitutional structures. For example, the U.S. Federal Reserve Board enjoys a level of autonomy from both the legislative and executive branches that causes it to stand outside the standard American checks-and-balances model. Central banks in many parliamentary systems also enjoy great autonomy. And many pieces of U.S. legislation include automatic triggers that change policy outputs without action by either the president or Congress, let alone requiring both of them to act in concert.[13]

Despite widespread interest in the influence of political institutions on governmental effectiveness, basic issues remain unanswered:

Jerusalem Post, March 19, 1992, p. 1. For background, see Bernard Susser, "'Parliadential' Politics: A Proposed Constitution for Israel," *Parliamentary Affairs*, vol. 42 (January 1989), pp. 112–22.

11. See S. E. Finer, ed., *Adversary Politics and Electoral Reform* (London: Anthony Wigram, 1975); and Geoffrey Debnam, "Adversary Politics in Britain 1964–1979: Change of Government and the Climate of Stress," *Parliamentary Affairs*, vol. 42 (April 1989), pp. 213–29.

12. On France, see, for example, Philip M. Williams, *The French Parliament: Politics in the Fifth Republic* (Praeger, 1968); and Ezra N. Suleiman, "Presidential Government in France," in Richard Rose and Ezra N. Suleiman, eds., *Presidents and Prime Ministers* (Washington: American Enterprise Institute for Public Policy Research, 1980), pp. 94–138. On Germany, see Renate Mayntz, "Executive Leadership in Germany: Dispersion of Power or 'Kanzlerdemokratie'?" in Rose and Suleiman, eds., *Presidents and Prime Ministers*, pp. 139–70.

13. R. Kent Weaver, "Setting and Firing Policy Triggers," *Journal of Public Policy*, vol. 9 (July–September 1989), pp. 307–36.

— What are the effects of differences in institutional arrangements for governmental effectiveness, if any? *Which* institutions matter and how do they affect governmental performance?

— If political institutions do facilitate differences in policymaking capabilities, how do these differences come about?

— How, if at all, can knowledge about institutional consequences be applied? Are differences in institutional effectiveness so severe that reforms are called for in the United States or in other countries?

This volume seeks answers to these questions.

Evaluating Governmental Effectiveness

Before proceeding with an investigation of institutional influences on governmental effectiveness, it is essential to have a working definition of effective government. What is seen as desirable and effective by one observer, after all, may be viewed in precisely opposite terms by another. Governmental effectiveness can be measured according to several standards.[14] One common standard is that of democratic rule. Government should be responsive to the will of the populace. Citizens should be able to hold their elected officials accountable for their actions. The likelihood that elected officials will abuse power should be minimized. While these concerns are undeniably legitimate, they are quite different from concerns that have been raised about parochialism, policy incoherence, and deadlock. Indeed, some writers have argued that it is precisely an overabundance of democracy that produces ineffective government.[15]

A second common standard for assessment is that of particular policy outputs—for example, whether one state spends more on public services than another or promotes faster economic growth. These specific outputs are matters of political choice, however. Countries may vary in the extent to which they provide welfare services because their citizens have dif-

---

14. On the evaluation of governmental performance, see, for example, Harry Eckstein, *The Evaluation of Political Performance: Problems and Dimensions* (Beverly Hills: Sage, 1971); Giuseppe Di Palma, *Surviving Without Governing: The Italian Parties in Parliament* (University of California Press, 1977), chap. 1; and G. Bingham Powell, Jr., "Party Systems and Political System Performance: Voting Participation, Government Stability and Mass Violence in Contemporary Democracies," *American Political Science Review*, vol. 75 (December 1981), pp. 861–79.

15. See Samuel Brittan, "The Economic Contradictions of Democracy," *British Journal of Political Science*, vol. 5 (April 1975), pp. 9–159; and Michel Crozier, Samuel Huntington, and Joji Watanuki, *The Crisis of Democracy: Report on the Governability of Democracies to the Trilateral Commission* (New York University Press, 1975).

ferent preferences for these services rather than because one type of political institution was more effective than another in translating public preferences into policy outcomes.

This book assesses governmental performance from a different perspective, and does so in a manner more consistent with current concerns about the effectiveness of U.S. institutions. It focuses on a specific set of tasks, and on capabilities that governments, regardless of their specific policy objectives, need in order to perform those tasks. By a capability, we mean a pattern of government influence on its environment that produces substantially similar outcomes across time and policy areas. A high level of any specific capability increases, but does not guarantee, a high level of performance in a government's interactions with its environment.

Ten specific capabilities that all governments need will be examined here: to *set and maintain priorities* among the many conflicting demands made upon them so that they are not overwhelmed and bankrupted; to *target resources* where they are most effective; to *innovate* when old policies have failed; to *coordinate conflicting objectives* into a coherent whole; to be able to *impose losses* on powerful groups; to *represent diffuse, unorganized interests* in addition to concentrated, well-organized ones; to *ensure effective implementation* of government policies once they have been decided upon; to *ensure policy stability* so that policies have time to work; to *make and maintain international commitments* in the realms of trade and national defense to ensure their long-term well-being; and, above all, to *manage political cleavages* to ensure that the society does not degenerate into civil war. These capabilities are the dependent variables for this study. The individual chapters in this volume examine specific policy problems that require the use of one or more of these capabilities.

Several caveats should be noted about using this list of capabilities as a standard for government effectiveness. First, capabilities are inherently situational: they involve a relationship among government objectives, efforts, and perceived problems that are never completely comparable across individual countries. Capabilities cannot be observed and measured directly; judgments about a government's capabilities can only be imputed. One should not assume that any specific capability for an individual country is highly uniform across a large number of policy areas or over time. A country may have a strong capability for innovating in social policy, for example, but a weak capability for innovating in agricultural or energy policy. Or a country may appear to have strong capabilities for imposing losses on unions or ethnic minorities, but little capability for imposing losses on corporations or farmers. At a minimum, these possibilities show that capabilities in any specific situation are likely to be strongly influenced by the nature of the groups supporting and opposing a government, by ideologies concerning the legitimacy of certain kinds of government action, and by a variety of other environmental factors. Indeed, one should not assume without investigation that it is productive to speak of capabilities as general patterns of government action across a variety of policy areas.

Second, the list is not exhaustive. The capabilities listed above are fundamental to the effectiveness of governing, however. Third, effectiveness even at a broad range of tasks is not the sole purpose of government. The notion of effectiveness employed here is focused more on policy management than on the legitimacy of government institutions and leaders. We do not think that values such as legitimacy are unimportant. But we believe that government capabilities merit sustained attention because governing institutions, especially in the United States, have been strongly criticized as lacking in effectiveness.

Fourth, although we believe that effectiveness at these tasks should be an important consideration in judging governmental institutions, effectiveness was not the exclusive or perhaps even central objective for the Framers of the American Constitution. Effectiveness may not necessarily be a high priority for current policymakers, either. Davis Bobrow points out in his chapter on defense policy that conflict management is a more important objective for both Japanese and American governing elites than is an efficient targeting of resources.

These caveats about the notion of governmental capabilities should not, however, mute the central issue of institutional design and choice that we pose here: if some types of institutional arrangements do lead to systematically lower capabilities than others when dealing with similar problems, and if these arrangements result in recurrent crises of effectiveness, then institutional reforms clearly need to be considered.

A General Model of Government Capabilities

What is it that enhances or detracts from a government's ability to perform specific tasks? The hypothesis being tested in this study is that political institutions shape the processes through which decisions are made and implemented and that these in turn influence government capabilities. Features such as the extent to which decisionmaking is centralized, the degree to which decisions are subject to multiple vetoes, and the extent to which elites are stable and share common values and objectives may affect specific capabilities. However, not all processes are equally relevant to all capabilities. This general model is summarized in figure 1. A first analytical task, then, is to specify causal linkages between political institutions and decisionmaking processes and then to show how decisionmaking processes in turn influence government capabilities.

There are many possible institutions to examine, however (for example, federalism, bureaucratic structures, electoral rules, or number of legislative chambers), even if one draws the definition of "institutions" fairly narrowly.[16] To make the task more manageable, we have chosen in this book to employ three layers or tiers of explanation (see figure 2). Our initial focus is a comparison of how the U.S. checks-and-balances system and other countries' parliamentary institutions influence governmental performance on a variety of tasks. This is a subject about which there is much accepted wisdom, but surprisingly little systematic research.

Highlighting the consequences of parliamentary-presidential differences is, however, not the end point of analysis, but rather a place to begin what is inevitably a more complex and subtle analysis of institutional influences on governmental effectiveness. A second tier of explanation focuses on variations within parliamentary and presidential systems (regime and government types). There is no "typical" parliamentary system that can be compared with the U.S. presidential system: differences are especially pronounced between parliamentary systems using proportional representation and single-member-district plurality systems as typified by the Westminster model. Moreover, the way that power is distributed in individual parliamentary systems may change over time even when basic institutional arrangements do not change. Thus an individual parliamentary system may be governed in some periods by a single-party majority, at other times by a minority governing with the consent of other parties, and at still others by a multiparty coalition. James Sundquist has similarly argued that the United States has functioned under two different models of governance: unified party control of Congress and the presidency, and divided government.[17] If the operations of institutions can vary substantially across countries and over time, then presumably the effectiveness of those institutions can vary as well. This calls into question the usefulness of a simple distinction between parliamentary systems and separation-of-powers systems.

A third tier of explanation takes an even broader cut at explaining governmental effectiveness. Not all important institutional differences

16. Some scholars have stretched the definition of "institutions" far beyond governmental structures and even political parties to include things as diverse as the structure of labor-capital relations and the position of a country within the international economy. See Peter A. Hall, *Governing the Economy: The Politics of State Intervention in Britain and France* (Cambridge: Polity Press, 1986).

17. Sundquist, "Needed: A Political Theory."

Figure 1. *Determinants of Government Policymaking Capabilities*

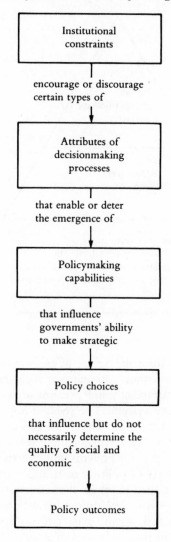

Figure 2. *Tiers of Explanations of Differences in Government Capabilities*

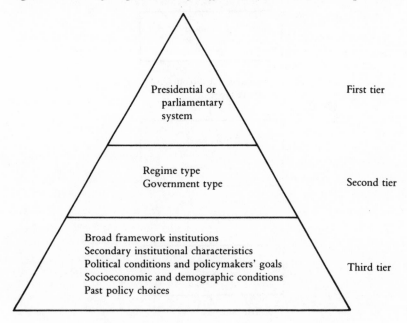

between nations stem from the nature of executive-legislative relations. For example, whether a state is unitary or federal in its governmental structure is a matter completely independent of whether it has a presidential or parliamentary system. The relative importance and scope of the judiciary is, at least to some extent, independent of the presidential-parliamentary distinction. But both of these institutional arrangements have potential implications for government effectiveness.

In addition, the effects of political institutions can be mediated both by the broader social milieu in which those institutions function and by their historical development. Institutions reflect not just legal forms but also normative understandings and expectations. The legal forms, moreover, may not always be their most crucial aspects.[18] Although it is likely

18. On this point, see Theda Skocpol, "Bringing the State Back In: Strategies of Analysis in Current Research," in Peter B. Evans, Dietrich Rueschemeyer, and Theda Skocpol, eds., *Bringing the State Back In* (Cambridge: Cambridge University Press, 1985), especially pp. 17–20. For a critique of the "new institutionalism," see Gabriel A. Almond, "The Return to the State," *American Political Science Review*, vol. 82 (September 1988), pp. 853–74, and the responses by Eric A. Nordlinger, Theodore J. Lowi, and Sergio Fabbrini, pp. 875–901.

that formalized structures affect the way interest groups form, the methods of aggregating political majorities, and bargaining processes, they are not likely to fully determine them. Here, such factors as the histories of programs, successful responses in the past, dominant beliefs among leaders, and the political culture of the society may be especially vital in determining how institutions actually function.[19]

Testing a fully elaborated model of institutional effects on governmental performance is beyond our scope here. As more variables are included, a larger number of cases are needed to sort out alternative causes. We begin with the parliamentary-presidential distinction because that distinction is taken seriously in discussions of political reform (particularly in the United States) and because it leads to a discussion of more complex, but clearly related, influences on governmental performance.

In view of their greater complexity, the second and third layers of explanation are developed less fully in this introduction. The individual case study chapters that follow and our penultimate chapter offer limited assessments of institutional effects from each tier in our effort to address as comprehensively as possible the question "Do institutions matter?"

Parliamentary and Presidential Systems

One simple explanation of differences in policymaking capabilities focuses on the decisionmaking structures and processes of democratic parliamentary systems and of separation-of-powers systems. Many of the standard arguments made on behalf of parliamentary systems can be broken down into a set of four steps, following the schematic representation in figure 1:

1. Institutional rules regarding the separation or fusion of executive and legislative power lead to differing decisionmaking processes in parliamentary systems and the U.S. checks-and-balances system, with parliamentary systems featuring stronger party discipline, greater recruitment of ministers from the legislature, greater centralization of legislative power in the cabinet, and greater centralization of accountability.

2. These differences in decisionmaking processes give governments

19. For critiques of formalism in the analysis of the influence of political institutions, see Robert Dahl, *A Preface to Democratic Theory* (University of Chicago Press, 1956); and Harry Eckstein, "Constitutional Engineering and the Problem of Viable Rrepresentative Government," in Harry Eckstein and David E. Apter, eds., *Comparative Politics: A Reader* (Free Press, 1963), pp. 97–104.

in parliamentary systems greater capabilities to perform a variety of policymaking tasks.

3. The greater capabilities of governments in parliamentary systems in controlling their environments allows them to make superior policy choices.

4. The greater capabilities of governments in parliamentary systems give them a better prospect of turning their policy choices into policy outcomes consistent with those choices.

We begin by outlining basic structural differences between parliamentary and presidential systems, and then contrast their decisionmaking processes and the implications of these differences for government capabilities.

Institutional Constraints

The central difference between parliamentary and separation-of-powers systems lies in the relationship between the executive and legislative branches. In parliamentary systems, the head of government is chosen by the legislature and is dependent for continuation in office on maintaining the confidence of the legislature.[20] In separation-of-powers systems, the chief executive is chosen independently of the legislature—usually by direct election—and serves a fixed term of office. The chief executive can neither dismiss the legislature and call for new elections nor be dismissed by the legislature without cause (in the U.S. case, through impeachment for "high crimes and misdemeanors"). There are also a few hybrid systems, most notably that of France.[21]

Decisionmaking Processes

These basic differences in institutional rules suggest that there are likely to be some consistent differences in policymaking processes between parliamentary systems and the U.S. system of separation of powers.

STRONG PARTY DISCIPLINE. Political parties in parliamentary systems tend to be much more cohesive in the legislature than in a separation-of-powers system. If they were not, the executive would be constantly

20. In most cases, the formal selection of the prime minister is made by the head of state, but only when it becomes clear which party or coalition commands the largest bloc in the legislature and can effectively form a government.

21. In France the president is elected independently of the legislature for a fixed term. However, the president does not have a true veto power in the American sense, but he can dissolve the legislature.

threatened with ouster from office.[22] In the American system, on the other hand, it is not necessary for the executive to win in the legislature on all important votes to stay in office. As a result, control over individual legislators is not as important, and legislators are much freer to vote their constituency interests or beliefs.

Party cohesion in parliamentary systems is no happy accident. To keep parties cohesive without constantly having to buy party members' support on each measure coming before the legislature, parties in parliamentary systems almost always have greater mechanisms of control over their legislators than do parties in the United States.[23] Legislators in proportional representation systems typically are selected from party lists developed by the central party organizations. Those who deviate from the party line on important votes may find themselves dropped from the list in the next election. Those in single-member-constituency systems generally are dependent upon the central party organization for ratification, campaign financing, or both. Equally important, in virtually all parliamentary systems, legislators' career advancement requires co-operation with party leaders.

In the United States central party organizations play a weaker role in candidate recruitment and campaign financing. Legislators therefore have much more leeway to build a "personal vote" for themselves through constituency service and by voting the interests of their district over that of the party.[24] Legislators' job security and career advancement (both

22. A number of parliamentary systems have moved away from the requirement that governments must win all votes to stay in power, but most still require a majority on crucial pieces of legislation such as the budget. In Germany, a cabinet can be dismissed only by a "constructive" vote of no confidence, that is, one that simultaneously elects a successor to the sitting chancellor (prime minister). See Arend Lijphart, *Democracies: Patterns of Majoritarian and Consensus Government in Twenty-One Countries* (Yale University Press, 1984), pp. 74–76. Only once, in 1982, has a sitting chancellor been unseated by a constructive nonconfidence vote. See A. Bruce Boenau, "Changing Chancellors in West Germany," *West European Politics,* vol. 11 (July 1988), pp. 24–41.

23. Of course, party members themselves have an incentive not to overturn a government since they would then have to stand for reelection. But this alone presumably would not be sufficient to dissuade legislators from voting against their party on matters where their constituents feel very strongly about a specific issue and thus expect deviation from the party line. Party discipline provides legislators with political cover to deviate from their constituents' opinions. See David M. Olson, *The Legislative Process: A Comparative Approach* (Harper and Row, 1980), pp. 255–65; and Michael L. Mezey, *Comparative Legislatures* (Duke University Press, 1979), pp. 77–81, 102–03, for a discussion of factors influencing the degree of party cohesion.

24. However, legislators may engage in constituency casework even where the political advantages are at best marginal, as they appear to be in Israel, where the nation is a single electoral district with party-list proportional representation. See Eric M. Uslaner, "Case-

within the legislature and in seeking other offices) also depend much less on cooperation with party leaders. As a result, incentives to cooperate are lower.[25]

RECRUITMENT OF MINISTERS FROM THE LEGISLATURE. In most parliamentary systems, all, or nearly all, heads of executive departments are drawn from the elected members of the national legislature.[26] They thus tend to bring to their jobs political experience and savvy, and they are more often policy generalists than specialists. In the United States, members of Congress are constitutionally prohibited from serving in executive positions. Although a number bring congressional experience or experience in other elected posts (governorships or mayoralties) to the cabinet, a cabinet member is not necessarily a professional politician— indeed, most are not.[27]

CENTRALIZATION OF LEGISLATIVE POWER IN THE CABINET. In parliamentary systems, party discipline can turn the legislature into a rubber stamp for executive actions. There is usually a tremendous difference in power between cabinet members and backbenchers, and legislative committees (if they exist at all) have limited power to amend

work and Institutional Design: Redeeming Promises in the Promised Land," *Legislative Studies Quarterly,* vol. 10 (February 1985), pp. 35–52.

25. See Bruce Cain, John Ferejohn, and Morris Fiorina, *The Personal Vote: Constituency Service and Electoral Independence* (Harvard University Press, 1987), pp. 12–13. Cain, Ferejohn, and Fiorina argue that Britain's single-member-district system also offers some resources for electoral independence, but the career advancement incentives for cooperation with party leaders are still quite high.

26. Exceptions to this rule include France, Switzerland, Luxembourg, the Netherlands, and Norway, where cabinet members cannot be members of the legislature. See Lijphart, *Democracies,* pp. 71–72. In Austria, about half of cabinet ministers have not had parliamentary experience before appointment to the cabinet in the postwar period. See J. Blondel, "Ministerial Careers and the Nature of Parliamentary Government: The Cases of Austria and Belgium," *European Journal of Political Research,* vol. 16 (January 1988), pp. 51–71. In Finland's quasi-presidential system, "most ministers—about two-thirds of them after the Second World War—have always been members of Parliament, but there is no binding behavioural norm prescribing that even the most important ministers should be drawn from among the MPs." See Jaakko Nousiainen, "Bureaucratic Tradition, Semi-Presidential Rule and Parliamentary Government: The Case of Finland," *European Journal of Political Research,* vol. 16 (March 1988), p. 252. See also Mattei Dogan, ed., *Pathways to Power: Selecting Rulers in Pluralist Democracies* (Westview, 1989).

27. Within the U.S. executive branch, unity is further undercut by the fact that the system "vests executive branch leadership in a president and department heads whose personal and political fates are not closely tied together." Hugh Heclo, "One Executive Branch or Many?" in Anthony King, ed., *Both Ends of the Avenue: The Presidency, the Executive Branch, and Congress in the 1980s* (Washington: American Enterprise Institute for Public Policy Research, 1983), p. 27.

government legislation or propose their own.[28] The potential for concentration of power can be especially high in those parliamentary systems where a prime minister has a firm majority in the legislature, has no constitutional requirement for cabinet consultation, and is surrounded with weak and compliant ministers. Under these circumstances, a prime minister may simply choose not to consult. This possibility has raised fears in some parliamentary systems that cabinet government is being replaced by "presidential government," unchecked by an independent legislature.[29]

In the American system, the cabinet rarely serves as a collective decisionmaking body. Presidents do not often see it as worthwhile to consult members of the cabinet in areas outside their department's jurisdiction unless the cabinet member has a special personal relationship with the president. Moreover, congressional committees and individual legislators have considerably greater opportunities to influence legislation and the behavior of bureaucracies, both through committee actions and floor amendments, than do legislators in parliamentary systems. Department heads concerned with their department's welfare are thus dependent upon good relations with Congress. This weakens their allegiance to presidential priorities.[30]

CENTRALIZATION OF ACCOUNTABILITY. One of the most obvious differences between parliamentary systems and the U.S. system lies in the way that governments and politicians are held accountable for their actions. In parliamentary systems, governments are held accountable to the legislature through parliamentary debate and questioning by opposition parties, and ultimately (though very rarely) by the threat of a vote of no confidence. They also are held accountable through the retrospective judgments of voters at the next election. Usually it is not possible to prevent a government from acting once it has decided on a course of action, but it is clear that the governing party or parties and their leaders are the ones who should be held accountable. Because cabinet solidarity and party discipline are expected to be binding, members of the cabinet or rank-and-file members of a governing party cannot stray from the party fold and stay within the cabinet or party. Because defection

28. There are, of course, exceptions. For an extreme case, see Mildred Schlesinger, "Legislative Governing Coalitions in Parliamentary Democracies: The Case of the French Third Republic," *Comparative Political Studies,* vol. 22 (April 1989), pp. 33–65.

29. See, for example, R. H. S. Crossman, "Prime Ministerial Government," in Anthony King, ed., *The British Prime Minister,* 2d ed. (Duke University Press, 1985), pp. 175–94.

30. Heclo, "One Executive Branch or Many?" p. 27.

is possible only under unusual circumstances, individual legislators are likely to incur little constituent pressure to defect from party positions on controversial matters.

In the U.S. system, accountability is more diffuse because power is shared and decisions are bargained between the branches. Knowing that legislators are not bound by party discipline makes it easier for constituents to put pressure on their representatives. Yet because power and responsibility are so diffuse, it is often difficult for voters and interest groups to know whom to hold accountable for specific decisions—a process that one political scientist has referred to as the "institutionalization of buck-passing."[31]

Policymaking Capabilities

Critics of the U.S. system argue that the decisionmaking processes associated with the separation-of-powers system—notably the fragmentation of legislative power—are less effective for policymaking than those in parliamentary systems.[32] An alternative perspective suggests that most shortcomings in governmental effectiveness are inherent in governing complex societies with a high level of demands on government, rather than the consequence of any particular set of institutions. Moreover, this latter perspective suggests, presidential systems may have offsetting advantages and parliamentary systems may have offsetting infirmities. This view is understandably skeptical as to whether the parliamentary-presidential difference is a key variable in determining policymaking capabilities.[33]

Throughout this study, we will contrast these positions in two unadulterated, "ideal type" forms that are intended merely to highlight the issues in dispute rather than to reflect the views of any individual. The first position, which we will refer to as the "parliamentarist view," holds

31. See William S. Livingston, "Britain and America: The Institutionalization of Accountability," *Journal of Politics,* vol. 38 (November 1976), p. 882.

32. These critics do not view separation of powers only in negative terms, it should be noted. They agree that it has such positive effects as inhibiting overly rapid change and limiting the ability of majorities to ride roughshod over minorities. But they argue that the costs associated with the separation-of-powers system simply have grown too large in an era when problems require timely and forceful government action.

33. See, for example, R. Kent Weaver, "Are Parliamentary Systems Better?" *Brookings Review,* vol. 3 (Summer 1985), pp. 16–25. For overviews of advantages and disadvantages of presidential and parliamentary government, see Arend Lijphart, "Introduction," in Lijphart, ed., *Parliamentary versus Presidential Government* (Oxford University Press, 1992), pp. 1–27; and Matthew Soberg Shugart and John M. Carey, *Presidents and Assemblies: Constitutional Design and Electoral Dynamics* (Cambridge University Press, 1992), chap. 1.

that in any given situation the marginal effects of parliamentary institutions on governmental performance are likely to be strongly and consistently positive relative to those of the U.S. separation-of-powers system. The second position, which we will call the "presidentialist view," holds that across the range of tasks outlined above the advantages of parliamentary systems over the U.S. separation-of-powers system are likely to be weak, intermittent, nonexistent, or outweighed by disadvantages.

The case studies in the chapters that follow develop the presidentialist-parliamentarist contrast in some detail for each of the ten capabilities we explore in this book. Here we will attempt simply to illustrate the implications of these contrasting views for several capabilities. For example, a parliamentarist position stresses that concentration of legislative power and party discipline is likely to enhance governmental capacity to impose losses and to innovate in policy by removing veto points. A determined parliamentary government can then do as it wishes, so long as it has a legislative majority. A presidentialist position, while conceding that concentrated legislative power gives parliamentary systems an advantage in imposing losses, suggests that this advantage concentrates accountability and makes for reluctance to impose losses, since voters can clearly blame the governing party or parties for their losses. A presidentialist argument would also stress that multiple sources of policy proposals in a separation-of-powers system increase the capacity to innovate.

Similar contrasts between presidentialist and parliamentarist arguments can be drawn for other capabilities. Concerning priority setting among objectives, coordination among directly conflicting objectives, and effective targeting of resources, a parliamentarist perspective argues that centralization of legislative power in the cabinet provides a centralized forum in which alternatives can be directly compared and efficient trade-offs made. A parliamentarist perspective would also note that the independence and decentralization of legislative power make Congress highly susceptible to outside pressures, thereby heightening proclivities to micromanage at the expense of policy stability.

Presidentialist responses are possible for each of these arguments. A presidentialist perspective might hold, for example, that cabinets in a parliamentary system have very high work loads, which result in decisions being driven downward into cabinet committees and individual departments.[34] Thus cabinets in parliamentary systems are unlikely in practice to set firm priorities or coordinate objectives. With respect to

34. See Thomas T. Mackie and Brian W. Hogwood, "Decision-making in Cabinet Government," in Mackie and Hogwood, eds., *Unlocking the Cabinet: Cabinet Structures in Comparative Perspective* (Beverly Hills: Sage, 1985), pp. 1–15.

Table 1. Regime Types among Parliamentary Systems in Selected Countries

Regime type and country	Modal government type	Modal pattern of decisionmaking structures and processes	Secondary government types	Facilitating electoral rules
Multiparty coalition Netherlands Belgium Denmark Norway Federal Republic of Germany Israel Weimar Germany	Two or more parties govern in minimum winning coalition, with partners changed after elections	Highly variable elite cohesion Variable veto points Highly variable elite stability Highly variable interest group access	Minority single-party government Oversized coalition Majority single-party government	Proportional representation with low hurdles
Party government United Kingdom Canada Australia	Two major parties alternate majority control of government	Generally high elite cohesion Few veto points High elite stability between elections Generally limited interest group access	Minority government Multiparty coalition government	Single-member-district plurality
Single-party-dominant Japan Sweden (pre-1976) Italy (pre-1970s)	Dominant party rules alone or as dominant coalition partner for prolonged periods	Generally high elite cohesion Few veto points High elite stability Selective interest group access	Minority government by dominant party Coalition government by opposition parties	Proportional representation or multimember districts that encourage large parties and discourage small parties

targeting resources, a presidentialist perspective suggests that there is little reason to believe that allocations in parliamentary systems will be more economically efficient than in the United States. Instead, their centralized process may promote a "politically efficient" allocation of resources to the districts of cabinet ministers, to localities favoring the governing party or parties, or to tightly contested electoral districts. (Indeed, in coalition cabinets, cabinet posts often are awarded to parties closely allied to particular interests, notably agrarian ones, as a payoff for their support.) Regarding policy stability, the presidentialist perspective views the separation of powers as inhibiting substantial changes in a policy once in place, while in a parliamentary system, a change in the governing party can lead to policy reversal and stop-and-go government.

Variations among Parliamentary and Presidential Systems

A simple contrast between parliamentary and presidential systems suggests substantial homogeneity within each type of system. A closer examination, however, reveals that policymaking structures and processes in parliamentary systems can vary tremendously across countries and over time. Indeed, comparing parliamentary systems and the American separation-of-powers system is less a matter of comparing apples and oranges than of comparing apples with all other fruits.

Variations in Types of Parliamentary Regimes

Perhaps the most important difference among parliamentary systems is the modal pattern of government formation, what we will call the *regime type*. The regime type for any individual country tends to be durable over time, but it is not immutable. Table 1 shows three parliamentary regime ideal-types, with examples of each listed in declining order of how closely each fits the type.[35]

In most parliamentary systems, electoral competition involves three or more parties, usually resulting in coalition governments that include

35. Characterizations of many marginal cases are inevitably contentious. For example, T. J. Pempel sees Sweden as an example of a single-party-dominant system, while Kaare Strom views it as an example of a distinctive "Scandinavian pattern of government formation" in which minority governments are the norm. See T. J. Pempel, "Introduction," in Pempel, ed., *Uncommon Democracies: The One-Party Dominant Regimes* (Cornell University Press, 1990), pp. 1–32; and Kaare Strom, "Deferred Gratification and Minority Governments in Scandinavia," *Legislative Studies Quarterly*, vol. 11 (November 1986), p. 585.

several parties. In a few countries—primarily Britain and its former colonies—two large parties (and sometimes one or more smaller ones) compete in elections, and one of the two large parties generally forms a majority government. This is commonly referred to as the "party government" model. And in a very few countries—postwar Japan is the clearest case—a single party dominates government policymaking for prolonged periods, ruling either alone or as a dominant coalition partner.[36]

Which of these regime types emerges depends especially on the link between electoral rules and cleavage structures. We focus here on electoral rules.[37] Systems of proportional representation with a low or nonexistent hurdle (a small percentage of the vote that a party is required to reach if it is to be awarded any parliamentary seats) and no representational bonus to the largest parties tend to encourage fragmentation in the party system and multiparty coalition systems. Single-member constituencies, on the other hand, tend to overrepresent the largest parties in the political system and also those with a strong regional base, while severely punishing smaller parties. They create strong pressures for a two-party system.[38] In general, proportional representation systems lead to a more precise registration of voters' party preferences, and plurality systems are more apt to produce stable one-party rule.[39] The emergence of a

36. On single-party-dominant systems, see Pempel, "Introduction."

37. The literature on the consequences of electoral laws for representation and government formation is immense. See, for example, Maurice Duverger, *Political Parties: Their Organization and Activity in the Modern State,* trans. Barbara North and Robert North (Wiley, 1954); Douglas W. Rae, *The Political Consequences of Electoral Laws,* 2d ed. (Yale University Press, 1971); Bernard Grofman and Arend Lijphart, eds., *Electoral Laws and Their Political Consequences* (New York: Agathon Press, 1986); and Rein Taagepera and Matthew Soberg Shugart, *Seats and Votes: The Effects and Determination of Electoral Systems* (Yale University Press, 1989). The introduction to Grofman and Lijphart's *Electoral Laws* has a comprehensive list of election law provisions that may affect the makeup of a government (pp. 2–3).

38. A few countries (notably Germany) have hybrid systems. The German system provides that half of the members of the Bundestag are elected directly in single-member districts, and the rest of the seats are awarded based on total party vote to bring the total allocation of seats close to strict proportionality for all parties passing the hurdles of 5 percent of the national vote or three constituency seats. See Max Kaase, "Personalized Proportional Representation: The 'Model' of the West German Electoral System," in Arend Lijphart and Bernard Grofman, eds., *Choosing an Electoral System: Issues and Alternatives* (Praeger, 1984), pp. 155–64. Not surprisingly, this system has produced two large parties and, usually, one or two smaller ones—currently the Free Democrats and Greens. It has also usually produced coalitions of the Free Democrats and one of the large parties and has complicated electoral strategies for all parties. See Geoffrey K. Roberts, "The 'Second-Vote' Campaign Strategy of the West German Free Democratic Party," *European Journal of Political Research,* vol. 16 (May 1988), pp. 317–37.

39. Arend Lijphart and Bernard Grofman, "Choosing an Electoral System," in Lijphart and Grofman, eds., *Choosing an Electoral System,* p. 6. Proportional representation clearly

single dominant party is induced by electoral rules that (1) disproportionately reward the largest party, (2) allow factions to compete within that party without splitting off to form separate parties, (3) discourage the formation of a single alternative party, and (4) discourage the formation of small parties that might siphon votes away from the leading party. Such rules include proportional representation in relatively small districts (as in Sweden) or plurality elections in multimember districts (as in Japan). Significant hurdles, such as a 5 percent vote threshold for small parties to gain representation, also can contribute to single-party dominance.[40]

A country does not necessarily retain the same regime type indefinitely, however, especially if there are major shifts in electoral rules, cleavage structures, or constitutional arrangements.[41] Israel, for example, shifted from relatively weak one-party dominance to more fluid coalition arrangements as a cleavage based on source of migration became more salient.[42] In Sweden changes in electoral rules served to weaken the dominance of the Social Democratic party.[43]

---

makes it very unlikely that a single party will win a majority of seats in the legislature. Richard Rose's data for 1945–83 show that among fourteen Western parliamentary systems, only four Westminster-style systems with first-past-the-post electoral systems (Australia, Canada, New Zealand, and the United Kingdom) had single-party control of the dominant house in the legislature more than 55 percent of the time. Richard Rose, "The Capacity of the President: A Comparative Analysis," *Studies in Public Policy,* no. 130 (Glasgow: University of Strathclyde, 1984), p. 12.

40. For examples of rules favoring single-party dominance, see Pempel, "Introduction." As Pempel notes, however, favorable electoral rules are not enough to assure the emergence of one-party-dominant regimes: a dominant party must also "keep itself in power long enough so that it can continue enacting and implementing policies that reinforce its power base" (p. 16).

41. Shifts in electoral rules (such as more primaries) and the movement from unified government to divided government across the executive and legislative branches in the United States have also been characterized as a regime change. See especially Sundquist, "Needed: A Political Theory." Below we will consider united and divided party control of the executive and legislature in the United States as two alternative "government types" with a single regime type.

42. The Labor party (beginning in 1969, the Labor Alignment) never held an absolute majority of sets in the Knesset, but was always the dominant partner in any coalition before 1977.

43. The Swedish electoral law reform reduced the bonus in seats given to the largest party under a system of regional proportional representation, but it also provided incentives for the conservative opposition parties to remain divided and increased parliamentary representation for the Social Democrats' allies to the left, the Communists. See Olof Ruin, *Tage Erlander: Serving the Welfare State, 1946–1969,* trans. Michael F. Metcalf (University of Pittsburgh Press, 1990), pp. 89–95; and Jan Lanke and Bo Bjurulf, "En granskning av den svenska vallagen" (An examination of the Swedish election law), *Statsvetenskaplig Tidskrift,* vol. 89, no. 2 (1986), pp. 123–29.

Variations of Government Type within Regimes

The modal pattern of government formation—what we have called the "regime type"—can explain a lot about what decisionmaking processes and policy outcomes are likely to prevail in a society. In a party government system, for example, expectations and actions of the two parties and of interest groups are likely to be conditioned by their awareness that the party currently in power will eventually be out and the party currently out of power will eventually be in. In countries where multiparty coalitions are the norm, most parties are likely to moderate their programs and actions to make themselves acceptable coalition partners. Within any individual country, however, there may be alternation over time among several different *government types* (such as single-party majority, single-party minority, or minimal majority coalition). Table 1 lists secondary government types commonly associated with each parliamentary regime type. For example, in the postwar period, Sweden's dominant Social Democrats most often have governed with a minority government, occasionally have had a parliamentary majority, and also have acted as an opposition to bourgeois majority coalition and single-party minority governments.[44] In both Britain and Canada, there have been periods of minority government as well as single-party majority government. Governments in countries as diverse as Germany and Israel have occasionally featured oversized coalitions as well as "minimum winning coalitions" (the minimum size needed to have a parliamentary majority). The critical point here is that both the modal "regime type" and the "government type" in power at any given time may have important effects on a country's decisionmaking processes and its capabilities.

Important differences in government type also occur in the U.S. separation-of-powers system. For most of the country's history, unified government, in which the same party controls both the presidency and Congress, has been the predominant pattern of government—especially in the first two years of a presidential term. Since 1955, however, divided government, with the president and Congress controlled by different parties, has become much more common.[45]

Which types of governments emerge in a particular period, and how

44. For data, see Strom, "Deferred Gratification and Minority Governments in Scandinavia," p. 602.

45. See Sundquist, "Needed: A Political Theory." On the sources of divided government, see William A. Galston, "Putting a Democrat in the White House," *Brookings Review*, vol. 7 (Summer 1989), pp. 21–25; and Gary C. Jacobson, *The Electoral Origins of Divided Government: Competition in U.S. House Elections, 1946–1988* (Westview, 1990).

long they are sustained, obviously depends heavily on electoral rules and cleavage structures.[46] In parliamentary systems, the type of government formed also depends on rules and norms regulating government formation. In Denmark, for example, the lack of a requirement for an initial vote of confidence encourages the formation of minority governments, and those governments can survive until other parties in the Folketing vote to bring the government down.[47] Norms have developed in both Britain and Canada against use of formal coalitions when neither major party holds a majority of the seats, while the opposite norm—no use of minority governments—has developed in the Federal Republic of Germany.[48]

Decisionmaking Processes

We suggested earlier that there are a number of decisionmaking processes potentially relevant to policymaking capabilities that differ fairly consistently between parliamentary systems and the U.S. presidential system (for example, party discipline and centralization of legislative power in the cabinet). But the existence of multiple regime and government types in parliamentary systems and the possibility of both unified and divided government in the U.S. presidential system indicate that a simple model of the effects of parliamentary-presidential differences on

46. On the duration of governments, see Arend Lijphart, "Measures of Cabinet Durability: A Conceptual and Empirical Evaluation," *Comparative Political Studies,* vol. 17 (July 1984), pp. 265–79; Kaare Strom, "Party Goals and Government Performance in Parliamentary Democracies," *American Political Science Review,* vol. 79 (September 1985), pp. 738–54, and the exchange between Strom, Eric C. Browne, John P. Frendreis, Dennis W. Gleiber, and Claudio Cioffi–Revilla, "Contending Models of Cabinet Stability," *American Political Science Review,* vol. 82 (September 1988), pp. 923–41.

47. Similarly, a majority of the Swedish Riksdag must vote against a proposed or sitting prime minister to bring him down. If the major parties abstain, as they did in a vote to name Ola Ullsten as prime minister in 1978, a minority government can be maintained with a tiny plurality of support. See Vernon Bogdanor, "Introduction," in Bogdanor, ed., *Coalition Government in Western Europe* (London: Heinemann, 1983), pp. 1–15. As noted earlier, the West German system is even more restrictive than the Swedish and Danish systems in its requirements for unseating a sitting government.

48. See Bogdanor, "Introduction"; and Ferdinand Müller-Rommel, "The Centre of Government in West Germany: Changing Patterns under 14 Legislatures (1949–1987)," *European Journal of Political Research,* vol. 16 (March 1988), pp. 175–76. Other factors, such as a past history of working together by potential coalition partners, may also affect both the specific makeup of coalitions and the likelihood that particular types of coalitions will be able to form. See, for example, Mark N. Franklin and Thomas T. Mackie, "Familiarity and Inertia in the Formation of Governing Coalitions in Parliamentary Democracies," *British Journal of Political Science,* vol. 13 (July 1983), pp. 275–98.

policymaking capabilities has to be supplemented with a second tier of explanations. Such a model is outlined in figure 3. It incorporates several institutional determinants of decisionmaking structures and processes (specifically electoral rules and the rules and norms of government formation) in addition to constitutional provisions for a parliamentary or presidential system. It also incorporates important attributes of decisionmaking structures and processes that result from significant variation across regime and government types. These attributes include the following.

COHESION OF GOVERNMENT ELITES. While parliamentary systems generally centralize legislative power, they do not guarantee that the elites at the center of the political system will be cohesive—that is, share and act upon a common set of policy and political interests. Indeed, the need to build a majority coalition, either within one party or among several parties, can lead to strange bedfellows in parliamentary systems just as it has in the U.S. party system.

Governments made up of a single party holding a minority or bare majority of legislative seats are most likely to be cohesive because they are usually drawn from a relatively narrow spectrum of issue opinion.[49] Maintaining cohesion is likely to be especially difficult in multiparty coalition governments. Such coalitions join together in government parties that will be competing directly against one another in the next election. While coalitions provide incentives for elite cohesion—the governing parties do not want to be perceived as squabbling and ineffective—they also provide incentives to posture and to jockey for position and power. Cohesion of government elites in a multiparty coalition is likely to be especially low in the period leading up to an election, when parties may see an advantage in establishing a distinctive public profile.

Electoral laws that link legislators closely to local constituencies rather than to the national party may also decrease elite cohesion. In Japan's single-party-dominant system, for example, a system of multimember electoral districts and a decentralized system of campaign finance have contributed to a high degree of factionalism within the ruling Liberal Democratic party (LDP). Thus, although the LDP has dominated Japanese politics since the early 1950s, the Japanese prime minister has more often been a follower than a molder of consensus.[50]

49. Of course, single-party minority governments sacrifice susceptibility to legislative veto in return for gains in cohesiveness.

50. See, for example, Samuel Kernell, "The Primacy of Politics in Economic Policy," in Kernell, ed., *Parallel Politics: Economic Policymaking in Japan and the United States* (Brookings, 1991), pp. 325–78.

Figure 3. *A Two-Tier Model of Determinants of Government Policymaking Capabilities*

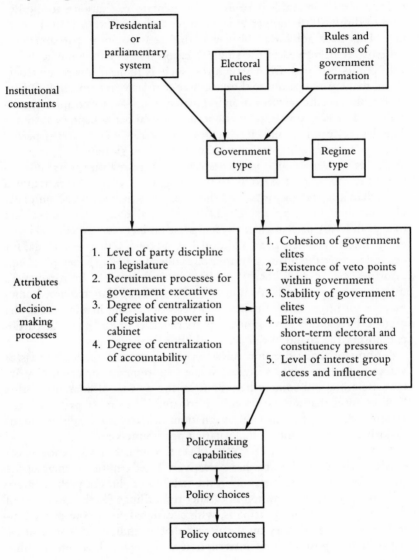

EXISTENCE OF EFFECTIVE VETO POINTS. The U.S. government has numerous veto points, many of which operate within the decentralized and bicameral legislature. Parliamentary institutions, ironically, tend to diminish the power of legislatures and concentrate it in the cabinet. This does not mean, however, that veto points in parliamentary systems are narrowed to the single decision point of the cabinet. Some veto points can arise from structures, such as judicial review or federalism, that are exogenous to the executive-legislative relationship. Others arise from specific features of individual systems—for example, bicameralism. But veto points also arise in unicameral parliamentary systems. The degree to which effective vetoes exist varies widely across parliamentary systems and even over time in the U.S. system.

The effectiveness of veto points can be measured on several dimensions: their number, the extent to which approval at each point requires more than a simple majority, and the extent to which a veto is complete, permanent, and nonappealable rather than partial, temporary, and subject to appeal. Many parliamentary systems use cabinet committees and inner or "political" cabinets as an additional veto point. Others—Canada, for example—give the finance minister or a collective body (policy planning, priorities, or treasury board) an effective, if sometimes informal, veto over ministry proposals. And in still others, such as Japan, party bodies exercise an important influence over decisionmaking in addition to the cabinet. In coalition governments, party caucuses or leaders of the parties composing the coalition can act as additional veto points.

Nonmajoritarian decision rules can also increase the effectiveness of vetoes in parliamentary systems. While requirements for unanimity are rare, Belgium and some other countries use a "rule of consensus" that "presupposes that any decision is negotiated."[51] In most parliamentary systems, threats of ministerial resignations can act as an additional nonmajoritarian constraint on majoritarian decisionmaking.

STABILITY OF GOVERNMENT ELITES. Cabinet and subcabinet officials in the United States have relatively brief tenures in their posts. But there also is wide variation in the stability of elites in parliamentary systems. It is not uncommon in cabinet reshufflings for the same cast of characters to exchange portfolios, with occasional moves out of the cabinet. Measuring stability by the period that an individual is in a single departmental post without interruption will suggest less elite stability

51. André-Paul Frognier, "The Mixed Nature of Belgian Cabinets between Majority Rule and Consociationalism," *European Journal of Political Research,* vol. 16 (March 1988), p. 216.

than measuring by the individual's total tenure in the cabinet.[52] Whatever the measure used, the stability of government elites is likely to be related to regime type. Countries where a single dominant party repeatedly governs alone are likely to have relatively stable elites (though there may be substantial individual circulation among posts). Where coalition governments are the norm, there is likely to be a stable core elite, with more rotation at the margins. Party government systems are likely to have wholesale turnover at election time whenever the governing party is defeated.

SHORT-TERM AUTONOMY OF ELITES. There is also substantial variation across parliamentary and presidential government types in the degree to which governmental elites need to be responsive to short-term group pressures and electoral considerations. A single-party majority government in a parliamentary system is best able to resist such pressures. It may not actually do so, however, if it senses that the political costs of doing so are too high. Minority parliamentary governments, or those with tenuous parliamentary coalitions, do not have the luxury of choice. They must generally tailor their positions in the short run to maintain majority support. Failure to do so risks, at a minimum, the defeat of their proposals, and at worst, a collapse of their government. Political elites in the United States are in an intermediate position: they do not need to be concerned with losing their posts by bringing on premature elections, but they do need to build coalitions if they wish to get their policy preferences enacted. Moreover, these legislators face a stronger individual accountability for their actions than those in systems where party discipline is strong. The absence of elite short-term autonomy is especially likely to affect government capability to impose losses on powerful groups. It is also likely to inhibit effective targeting by making logrolling coalitions more necessary.

INTEREST GROUP ACCESS AND INFLUENCE. In the U.S. system, interest groups of many kinds can gain access and exercise influence at numerous points in the policymaking process. One strong tradition in the literature on American politics argues that "iron triangles" tend to develop between interest groups, bureaucracies that service those groups, and congressional oversight committees. Others, however, claim that because access is relatively open in the United States, interest group influence may be broadly dispersed and variable over time.[53]

52. See discussions in Jean Blondel, *Government Ministers in the Contemporary World* (Beverly Hills: Sage, 1985); and Frognier, "The Mixed Nature of Belgian Cabinets."
53. Hugh Heclo, "Issue Networks and the Executive Establishment," in Anthony

In parliamentary systems, centralization of legislative power presumably decreases the alternatives open to interest groups, and party discipline makes appeals to individual legislators an almost hopeless strategy in terms of changing policy outcomes.[54] The bureaucracy and cabinet ministers are the main points of access open to interest groups. Moreover, it is usually impossible to reverse a government's position (if it has a majority) once that position has been taken. And open campaigns against the government, the bureaucracy, or the governing party may be risky, since the interest group will have to deal with the same actors repeatedly.

This characterization of parliamentary systems should not be exaggerated or overgeneralized, however. To take the most obvious example, relations between Labour governments and the trade union movement in Britain are generally close, if often tense.[55] The structural relationships between interest groups and political parties and cabinet members are often even more direct in countries characterized by multiple parties and coalition governments. Labor unions and business organizations, agrarian groups, and environmentalists are often represented directly by individual parties. Moreover, these interests are often granted privileged access to government through corporatist arrangements.[56]

In the few countries with single-party-dominant systems, the pattern is perhaps best described as one of high but somewhat biased access. In Sweden, for example, the close ties between the Social Democratic party and the blue-collar labor confederation give the latter privileged access, but do not guarantee that it will always win. In Japan's LDP, Japanese business and agricultural groups have close relationships to relevant ministries, but organized labor's access has been much more limited.

In short, interest group access in parliamentary systems is often more structured and executive-centered than in the United States. But this does not mean that interest groups are less influential. In many parliamentary systems, interest groups may be less well placed than their American counterparts to overturn government decisions that conflict

King, ed., *The New American Political System* (Washington: American Enterprise Institute for Public Policy Research, 1978), pp. 87–124; and David Vogel, *Fluctuating Fortunes: The Political Power of Business in America* (Basic Books, 1989).

54. See, for example, David Arter, *The Nordic Parliaments: A Comparative Analysis* (St. Martin's, 1984), pp. 31–41.

55. See Stephen Bornstein and Peter Gourevitch, "Unions in a Declining Economy: The Case of the British TUC," in Peter Gourevitch and others, *Unions and Economic Crisis: Britain, West Germany and Sweden* (London: Allen and Unwin, 1984), pp. 15–88.

56. See, for example, Suzanne Berger, *Organizing Interests in Western Europe: Pluralism, Corporatism, and the Transformation of Politics* (Cambridge: Cambridge University Press, 1981); and Gerhard Lehmbruch and Phillippe C. Schmitter, *Patterns of Corporatist Policymaking* (Beverly Hills: Sage, 1982).

with their goals, but they also may be better placed to ensure that such decisions are never made to begin with.

Policymaking Capabilities

Differences in the modal pattern of a country's government—what we have referred to as regime type—clearly can have an important effect on governmental capabilities. If all major actors in a political system expect a single party to play a dominant role in that system for the foreseeable future, they are likely to act differently than if they think a government's initiatives might be reversed after the next election, an expectation commonly associated with the party government model. If the governing pattern requires negotiation among coalition partners on a routine basis, a different pattern of behavior and interaction is likely to result.

The party government model, in which one party generally holds a majority of legislative seats and changes in the partisan makeup of the cabinet usually occur only after an election, is generally seen as especially capable of developing coherent policies and imposing losses on powerful organized groups. However, where one-party majority government has to deal with strong issue disagreements along party lines and there is alternation of parties in office, policy reversals across terms of office result.[57] Although a government's ability to produce dramatic innovations and impose losses is likely to be weaker under a multiparty coalition norm, this regime type may generate a stronger capacity to implement incremental change and produce a greater degree of policy stability once policies are in place.[58] Some analysts associate oversized and inclusive coalitions in particular with the successful management of extraordinarily difficult cleavages.[59]

Within a single country, differences over time in government type

57. See Sven Steinmo's discussion of British tax policy in "Political Institutions and Tax Policy in the United States, Sweden, and Britain," *World Politics*, vol. 41 (July 1989), pp. 500–35. For a skeptical view on this issue, see Richard Rose, *Do Parties Make A Difference?* 2d ed. (Chatham, N.J.: Chatham House, 1984).

58. Ronald Rogowski, "Trade and the Variety of Democratic Institutions," *International Organization*, vol. 41 (Spring 1987), pp. 203–23; and Nouriel Roubini and Jeffrey Sachs, "Government Spending and Budget Deficits in the Industrial Countries," *Economic Policy*, vol. 4 (April 1989), pp. 100–32.

59. Arend Lijphart, *The Politics of Accommodation: Pluralism and Democracy in the Netherlands* (University of California Press, 1968); and Lijphart, *Democracies*. For a recent discussion of the Dutch case, see the special issue of *West European Politics*, vol. 12 (January 1989), especially Hans Daalder, "The Mould of Dutch Politics: Themes for Comparative Inquiry," pp. 1–20.

may also lead to changes in government capabilities. In a parliamentary system, a minimum winning coalition might be in a better position than an oversized coalition to impose losses on powerful interest groups, because more of those groups will be outside the coalition's base of support. Minority governments may be most reluctant to impose losses for fear of losing a confidence vote.[60] We have already noted that divided government in the United States has been widely associated with a variety of policymaking infirmities in comparison with unified party control of the executive and legislature, especially with respect to setting and maintaining priorities, coordinating conflicting objectives, and imposing losses on powerful groups.

Other Influences on Governmental Capacity

"Third-tier" influences on governmental capabilities and policies can be categorized into five broad groups. Two concern governmental institutions. They are broad framework political institutions unrelated to the distribution of executive to legislative power, such as judicial review and federalism; and secondary features of legislatures, such as bicameralism. Three other groups—political conditions and policymakers' goals, socioeconomic and demographic conditions, and past policy choices—reflect an even broader array of noninstitutional influences on capabilities.

Third-tier factors may influence the real and apparent linkage between first- and second-tier institutional factors and government capabilities in two distinct ways. First, they may interact with and modify the real effects of first- and second-tier factors, either facilitating these effects (that is, making them stronger or more likely) or limiting them (making them weaker or less likely). For example, Ellis Krauss and Jon Pierre argue in their chapter that parliamentary institutions are insufficient to carry out an effective industrial policy; a political culture that supports the idea of an industrial policy is necessary as well. Effective bicameralism, which is especially strong in the U.S. system, may strengthen the tendency for separation-of-powers arrangements to undercut centralization of power in the executive.

Alternatively, third-tier factors may operate independently from first-

---

60. Arriving at unbiased judgments about the performance of particular government types is particularly tricky, however. As Kaare Strom has noted, certain government types (notably minority governments) "might perform poorly because they form in situations where no government could expect to be successful." Strom, "Party Goals and Government Performance in Parliamentary Democracies," p. 739.

and second-tier effects, but in ways that mask or exaggerate their effects on government capabilities. Weaknesses in one or more U.S. government capabilities, for example, might be due to judicial review or federalism, neither of which are necessarily related to the separation of executive and legislative powers. We focus here briefly on the effects that some important third-tier factors are likely to have on decisionmaking structures and processes and, in turn, on government capabilities.

Broad Framework Institutions

Institutional features other than the structure of executive-legislative relationships, notably the extent to which courts exert independent power and the extent to which power is devolved to subnational governments, can exercise a powerful independent effect on policymaking capabilities. On the whole, judicial review and federalism, like the separation of powers, tend to diffuse power and add veto points.

JUDICIAL REVIEW. The strength or weakness of judicial review of executive and legislative actions vary substantially across parliamentary systems. In the classic Westminster model, the parliament is supreme, bound only by convention and traditional rights rather than by a written constitution. But even in some of Britain's former colonies, such as Canada, powers of the government of the day have begun to be limited by charters of rights and by activist courts. Constitutional courts have increased their power in several West European countries, and the growing role of the European Community's Court of Justice ultimately may be the most important development of all.[61]

By adding an additional intragovernmental veto point, judicial review may influence a number of governmental capabilities, for example, decreasing government's ability to impose losses, raising obstacles to rapid innovation, and inhibiting coherence among policies. The effects of judicial review are by no means unidirectional, however. In the United States, for example, while the courts have sometimes inhibited legislative innovation, they also have helped to resolve fundamental deadlocks at the federal level on issues such as racial segregation.

FEDERALISM. Sharing of power between national and subnational governments is a feature of such parliamentary systems as Germany,

---

61. On constitutional courts in Western Europe, see, for example, Alec Stone, "In the Shadow of the Constitutional Council: The 'Juridicisation' of the Legislative Process in France," *West European Politics*, vol. 12 (April 1989), pp. 12–34; and Paul Furlong, "The Constitutional Court in Italian Politics," *West European Politics*, vol. 11 (July 1988), pp. 7–23.

Canada, and Australia. The precise nature of federal relationships varies widely, however, and so do its effects on government capabilities. Where two levels of government with different goals have substantial autonomy to develop and implement policies in the same or overlapping policy jurisdictions, federalism may lead to policy incoherence. Where one government is dependent on another for implementation, as in Germany, the implementing level may pursue its own goals at the expense of the principal's goals. Where two levels of government share jurisdiction and must negotiate agreements in many policy areas (for example, in Canada), the result is to add veto points and presumably to increase the difficulty of achieving policy innovation and loss imposition.[62] The growth of supranational governments, notably the European Community, may have similar effects on government capabilities.

BUREAUCRATIC STRENGTH AND AUTONOMY. Countries also differ in the extent to which their government bureaucracies are highly professionalized and unified or possess a monopoly on expertise. They differ as well in the degree of discretionary authority that their bureaucracies wield. Strong bureaucracies have been linked to a number of government capabilities, such as policy stability, effective priority setting, and effective targeting of industries for promotion or phasing out.[63] Traditionally, the United States has been seen as having a relatively weak bureaucracy heavily penetrated by political appointees at the top, subject to political interference at all levels, and prodded in inconsistent directions.[64] This makes it difficult to target resources effectively and to implement legislative mandates.

Secondary Characteristics of Legislatures

While differences in regime and government types are likely to have a strong influence on governmental capabilities, individual countries make

62. One scholar has referred to this negotiation process as "federal-provincial diplomacy." Richard Simeon, *Federal-Provincial Diplomacy: The Making of Recent Policy in Canada* (University of Toronto Press, 1972).

63. See, for example, Chalmers Johnson, *MITI and the Japanese Miracle: The Growth of Industrial Policy, 1925–1975* (Stanford University Press, 1982); and John Zysman, "The French State in the International Economy," in Peter J. Katzenstein, ed., *Between Power and Plenty: Foreign Economic Policies of Advanced Industrial States* (University of Wisconsin Press, 1978), pp. 255–93.

64. See, for example, Stephen Skowronek, *Building A New American State: The Expansion of National Administrative Capacities, 1877–1920* (Cambridge University Press, 1982); and Hugh Heclo, *A Government of Strangers: Executive Politics in Washington* (Brookings, 1977).

additional institutional choices about organizing their legislatures that may further affect policymaking capabilities.

ORGANIZATION AND VOTING RULES. Legislative voting may be recorded or secret and may require either simple majorities or supermajorities.

Requirements that legislators openly declare their position in roll call votes may have powerful effects on governmental capabilities in both parliamentary and presidential systems, but the effects are quite different in the two types of systems. Almost all parliamentary systems have party whips to determine how legislators have voted and thus enforce party discipline by punishing defectors. Without party discipline, deference to cabinet proposals cannot be maintained, and the government might fall, which also means that legislators might have to run again. The effects of not having an open voting rule can be seen in Italy, where until recently the final legislative vote on all bills was secret.[65] As a result, party cohesion in Italy was lower and government coalitions were less stable than in most other parliamentary systems. This, in turn, threatened capabilities to obtain both policy stability and policy coherence.

In the United States, sanctions for breaking party discipline are weak because the tenure of the executive does not depend on maintaining support of the legislature, legislators' electoral fates are largely independent of the executive's, and legislators can stand for office independent of party organization through primary elections. Not surprisingly, then, U.S. parties are much less cohesive than those in most parliamentary systems. Moreover, local constituency interests provide powerful incentives to defect when national party positions and salient constituency concerns conflict. Increased party discipline would not in any case necessarily increase deference to the executive in periods of divided government. Open voting tends to decrease legislators' short-term autonomy from constituent pressures and increase interest groups' abilities to monitor legislators' behavior. Open voting (as exemplified in the increased use of recorded votes in the U.S. House of Representatives since 1970), by increasing legislators' exposure, is likely to diminish institutional capacity to impose losses and target resources effectively.[66]

Voting rules that require supermajorities for legislative action may affect government capabilities similarly in both presidential and parliamentary systems. In parliamentary systems, such requirements apply

65. See Clyde Haberman, "Italy 'Snipers' in Legislature May Now Fall," *New York Times,* October 2, 1988, p. 9.

66. See R. Kent Weaver, "The Politics of Blame Avoidance," *Journal of Public Policy,* vol. 6 (October–December 1986), pp. 371–98.

mostly to constitutional changes,[67] and they tend to restrict policy and institutional innovation by the governing parties. Requirements for legislative supermajorities are more common in the United States. Presidents need to get two-thirds approval from senators to ratify treaties and can sustain vetoes with only one-third plus one of the members voting in either chamber of Congress. The first requirement limits presidential power and the second adds to it, but both tend to restrain innovation and create a bias toward the policy status quo.

The power and privileges afforded legislative committees may also affect government capabilities: the more resources, expertise, and authority committees have, the harder it is to set central priorities and coordinate conflicting policies—especially if committee members hold views different from those of the entire chamber.[68] A multistage process adds further veto points, which may make policy innovation and loss imposition more difficult.

While the U.S. Congress is certainly the paradigmatic decentralized legislature, diffusion of authority within Congress has varied greatly over time.[69] Legislatures in parliamentary systems also differ in the extent to which specialized working groups are able to modify government proposals.[70]

67. In Sweden, for example, changes to fundamental laws require identical decisions by two successively elected parliaments; a minimum of ten months must also pass between these votes in most cases. See the Swedish Riksdag, *Constitutional Documents of Sweden* (Stockholm: Norstedts Tryckeri, 1981), pp. 61–62. Belgium requires both special majorities and an intervening election for constitutional revision. See Maureen Covell, "Possibly Necessary but not Necessarily Possible: Revision of the Constitution in Belgium," in Keith G. Banting and Richard Simeon, eds., *Redesigning the State: The Politics of Constitutional Change in Industrialized Nations* (University of Toronto Press, 1985), pp. 71–94. Many federal countries (for example, Canada and Switzerland) require the approval of a majority or special majorities of subnational units. See also Lijphart, *Democracies*, pp. 188–91.

68. See, for example, Kenneth A. Shepsle and Barry R. Weingast, "The Institutional Foundations of Committee Power," *American Political Science Review*, vol. 81 (March 1987), pp. 85–104; and Richard L. Hall and Bernard Grofman, "The Committee Assignment Process and the Conditional Nature of Committee Bias," *American Political Science Review*, vol. 84 (December 1990), pp. 1149–66.

69. Indeed, James Q. Wilson argues that the diffusion of power within Congress in the 1970s was more debilitating to American government than the separation of powers per se. Wilson, "Does the Separation of Powers Still Work?" On changes over time in the degree of centralization in the U.S. Congress, see, for example, Roger H. Davidson, "Committees as Moving Targets," *Legislative Studies Quarterly*, vol. 11 (February 1986), pp. 19–33; and Davidson, "The New Centralization on Capitol Hill," *Review of Politics*, vol. 50 (Summer 1988), pp. 345–64.

70. The standing committees of the Italian parliament, for example, exercise full legislative authority in some cases. See Francesco D'Onoforio, "Committees in the Italian Parliament," in John D. Lees and Malcolm Shaw, eds., *Committees in Legislatures: A Com-*

BICAMERALISM. Most parliamentary systems have essentially uni-cameral legislatures, but a few are genuinely bicameral. Most of these second chambers, as in Britain and Canada, have atrophied to a vestigial policymaking role. Where they retain power, it is often because they have a distinct electoral base; for example, they represent the Länder governments in Germany's Bundesrat. In these cases, second chambers can significantly inhibit some of the capabilities often attributed to par-liamentary systems, such as the ability to innovate rapidly and to achieve consistency in policy goals.

Policymakers' Goals and Political Opposition

Whether a government has a secure and cohesive legislative majority strongly affects its capabilities. But the willingness of government leaders to take risks (by imposing losses on powerful constituencies, for example) is also a function of the goals and commitment of party leaders and the condition of the opposition forces. The ability of Margaret Thatcher's government to reshape British policy for more than a decade derived from a combination of the sturdiness and clarity of her vision and the division within and among the opposition parties. Had the opposition not been so self-destructive, Conservative backbenchers might have steeled themselves to inhibit some of Thatcher's more severe initiatives.[71] But defining clear goals is important for many capabilities to be fully realized. It is relatively rare, however, to get stability in a government and clarity of direction at the same time.

Social Conditions

Social conditions and organizations can affect governmental capabil-ities and policy outcomes in several ways. The strength and structure of cleavages, for example, help determine the challenges that governments face and affect the cohesion of governing elites. If some governments are less successful in managing political cleavages than others, this may

---

parative Analysis (Duke University Press, 1979), pp. 61–101; and Frederic Spotts and Theo-dor Wieser, Italy: A Difficult Democracy (Cambridge: Cambridge University Press, 1986), chap. 6. On legislatures in parliamentary systems, see the special issue of West European Politics, vol. 13 (July 1990), especially Philip Norton, "Legislatures in Perspective," pp. 143–52.

71. See, for example, Ivor Crewe and Donald D. Searing, "Ideological Change in the British Conservative Party," American Political Science Review, vol. 82 (June 1988), pp. 361–84.

be due to the intensity of the cleavages they confront rather than the institutions through which they govern.

Features of social organization may also directly influence governmental capabilities. Some societies (notably in Scandinavia) have a high level of social organization, with peak associations that facilitate elite bargaining and compel compliance among individual firms, unions, or other interests. A system with such a high degree of social and political organization generally leads to a stable elite environment and potentially increases elite cohesion as well. Such a high level of organization facilitates government bargaining with interests and makes it easier to impose losses on some issues by aiding the negotiation of side payments to make those losses more tolerable. Similarly, Mancur Olson has argued that in a society where encompassing rather than narrow interest groups are dominant, those interests will "internalize much of the cost of inefficient policies and accordingly have an incentive to redistribute income to themselves with the least possible social cost, and to give some weight to economic growth and to the interests of society as a whole."[72] On the other hand, if some sectors of society—labor, for example—are poorly organized, the government may be more able to impose losses on those sectors.

The size of a country and its place in the international trading system also can affect both its governmental capabilities and its policy choices. Peter Katzenstein, for example, argues that the smaller West European states have made highly adaptive choices in industrial and trade policy because their small size and dependence on an open international trading system precluded many of the policy options open to the larger states.[73]

Past Policy Choices

Policy inheritances also constrain future policy outcomes and governmental capabilities.[74] Expenditure commitments to pensions and health

72. Mancur Olson, *The Rise and Decline of Nations: Economic Growth, Stagflation, and Social Rigidities* (Yale University Press, 1982), p. 92. See also Olson, "A Theory of the Incentives Facing Political Organizations: Neo-Corporatism and the Hegemonic State," *International Political Science Review,* vol. 7 (April 1986), pp. 165–89. For Olson's argument to hold, however, leaders of "encompassing" interest groups must enjoy substantial autonomy to aggregate and reject interests from subunits and the rank and file.

73. Peter J. Katzenstein, *Small States in World Markets: Industrial Policy in Europe* (Cornell University Press, 1985).

74. On policy inheritances, see Richard Rose, "Inheritance Before Choice in Public Policy," paper prepared for Harvard Business School Conference on Socio-Economics, March 31–April 2, 1989; and Paul D. Pierson, *Dismantling the Welfare State? Reagan, Thatcher and the Politics of Retrenchment* (Cambridge: Cambridge University Press, forthcoming).

care, both by their magnitude and by the constituencies they create, inhibit new commitments. Current policies also may make loss imposition and policy innovation easier or more difficult, depending on whether they conceal losses or make them highly visible.

Comparing Capabilities

As noted earlier, one can think of each of a government's capabilities as a pattern of performance across many policy areas and over time. A government's performance in innovating and imposing losses, for example, may be more or less consistent across policy areas, and its average level of performance also may be better or worse than the average level of other countries.

Comparing Individual Capabilities across Countries

Looking at differences in average levels and consistency of governmental performance can suggest answers to the questions of whether there are institutional effects on government capabilities, how great they are, and under what conditions they exist.

If countries with differing institutional arrangements (for example, separation versus fusion of powers) have both strong and consistent differences in a given capability, an obvious (if not always correct) conclusion is that institutions account for the difference. However, if countries with different institutions have similar capabilities and countries with similar institutions exhibit great inconsistency, then institutional effects probably are unimportant.[75]

Real institutional effects may be disguised by looking at only the first tier of explanation. Parliamentary systems allow for a range of regime types, some of which may be superior to the U.S. separation-of-powers

75. There also may be differences in decisionmaking processes or outcomes (for example, between parliamentary systems and the U.S. system) without one being clearly more or less capable than another. Pressures to target selective benefits to the politically powerful rather than to where they are most needed occur almost everywhere. Although these pressures may be channeled through a different arena (the cabinet in a parliamentary system and congressional committees in a separation-of-powers system), and the politicians who reap the rewards in each system (cabinet ministers or the government party in parliamentary systems, congressional committee members in the U.S. system) may be slightly different, observers might be warranted in concluding that the government's ability to target efficiently was relatively weak in each system.

system and some not.[76] Party government systems, for example, may have a capability to target resources that is superior to that of the United States, but few parliamentary systems produce party government. In comparing types of systems, it is important to keep in mind that the U.S. system cannot be compared with only the small minority of Westminster-style and single-party-dominant parliamentary systems, but must also be compared with the larger range of coalitional systems. Similarly, an individual government may have different policy capabilities over time. In the United States, movement between unified and divided government may influence capabilities to set and maintain priorities, to innovate in policymaking, and to impose losses. The 1992 election restored unified party control of the presidency and Congress after twenty-four years in which divided government had been the norm. How this change affects government capabilities—as well as how extended the period of unified government will be—remains to be seen.

Institutional effects also may be overlooked in examining aggregate patterns if these effects are dependent upon the presence of other, noninstitutional, factors. (In statistical parlance this would be called an interaction effect.) For example, David Vogel argues in his chapter that single-party-dominant systems may have some advantages of speed in responding to diffuse interests when public support for doing so is intense, but that at most times the U.S. system of separated powers is more likely to provide steady access for such interests. In this case, then, the strength and direction of institutional effects on the capability is dependent upon public opinion.

Comparing across Capabilities

The range of patterns and explanations that exists in discussing any single capability is equally evident in drawing comparisons *across* the set of capabilities. One possibility is that some institutional arrangements

---

76. Significant variation in decisionmaking processes and government capabilities across regime and government types does not necessarily invalidate either the parliamentarist or presidentialist argument. If all parliamentary regime and government types were at least equal to their U.S. counterparts in promoting specific governing capabilities and some were far superior, the case for the parliamentarist position would be strong even if parliamentary systems varied widely in their capabilities. A compelling case for the parliamentarist position would be lacking, however, if evidence suggested either that parliamentary systems differed widely in their capabilities and no single regime or government type was consistently superior to the U.S. system, or that the most capable parliamentary regime and government types were also the least common and their superior performance resulted from noninstitutional conditions that are unlikely to be present in the United States.

(for example, parliamentary systems) are strongly and consistently more effective for most or all capabilities. Another is that there is no consistent pattern of institutional superiority whatsoever. A third possibility is that specific institutional arrangements are more effective at some things but inferior at other things. Some systems may be effective at managing political cleavages, for example, but much weaker in their capability to impose losses. A fourth possibility, consistent with the third, is that there are important trade-offs in institutional capabilities. The reasons that an institutional arrangement allows a government to be more effective at some things may be the same reasons it is less effective at other things. For example, the same characteristics that are likely to allow for rapid policy innovation also may make for more policy mistakes or lead to instability in government policies. Finally, institutional effects may show up in a consistent direction across a variety of capabilities, but only when accompanied by other facilitating conditions—again emphasizing the contingent nature of institutional effects.

Capabilities as Opportunities and Risks

The case studies that follow will show that institutional effects on government capabilities are not uniform, direct, or unidirectional; neither are they nonexistent. Institutional effects are real and significant, but often indirect and contingent. Indeed, the case studies suggest that the terms institutional "advantages" and "disadvantages" are a misleading way of thinking about institutional effects on government capabilities. Political institutions are best thought of as creating risks and opportunities for effective policymaking. Whether these risks and opportunities are realized depends upon whether the specific conditions that facilitate or limit those institutional effects are present. Party government parliamentary arrangements, for example, provide an opportunity for governments to impose losses on powerful groups in society, but this capability is not likely to be realized in the absence of political will. Federalism provides an opportunity to manage political cleavages by allowing groups to conduct their own affairs without interference from others, but this opportunity will be fully realized only where groups are geographically separate; otherwise, federalism may increase the risk that regional majorities will oppress regional minorities.

In short, institutional arrangements that create opportunities for effective governance in one country may heighten risks of governmental failure in another because the latter government faces different facilitating and limiting conditions. Moreover, countries face different policy challenges that make certain capabilities more or less important. Thus it makes little sense to speak of one set of institutional arrangements as inherently more effective than another, with respect either to any single capability or to the range of capabilities. Increasing a government's capabilities involves finding the best fit among three factors: the nature of its policy challenges, its institutional arrangements, and the conditions that facilitate and limit institutional effects.

Research Strategy

The next ten chapters provide cross-national analyses of specific dimensions of governmental competence in order to assess the role of governmental institutions in influencing outcomes. Most of these chapters draw on case studies of particular policy areas. A chapter on the ability of institutions to innovate and adapt quickly to a changed environment, for example, looks at responses to a changing energy market after the 1973–74 oil embargo. The ability of governments to impose losses when needed will be discussed in chapters on pension policies and industrial adjustment. Chapters on trade policy and national security policy examine possible systemic differences in the capacity to negotiate and implement international agreements free from excessive interest group control. Most of the chapters compare the U.S. experience with that of at least two countries with parliamentary (or in the case of France, hybrid) institutions and highlight the role of institutional arrangements in determining outcomes. Each chapter not only addresses the simple presidential–parliamentary distinction, but also draws heavily on the other tiers of explanation to analyze the sources of governmental performance. Indeed, for most capabilities, the simple parliamentary-presidential distinction does not lead very far toward explaining differences in government performance. In the final chapters, we draw conclusions about the roots of governmental effectiveness across the cases and capabilities and derive some lessons for institutional reform.

The use of a comparative case study approach is dictated by the nature of our research problem. Capabilities cannot be observed directly, but must be inferred by looking at outcomes and comparing the constraints that governments faced in reaching those outcomes. Comparative case studies provide a richness of detail that permits a nuanced evaluation of the roots of governmental effectiveness.[77] The case studies in this volume,

77. Comparative case studies also have some limitations: they do not allow firm conclusions to be drawn about the consistency of government capabilities and institutional effects on those capabilities across policy areas, nor, in most cases, do they permit an

while not the definitive word on the complex subject of government capabilities, bring to bear important evidence on when and how institutions influence government effectiveness.

This study addresses a highly complex set of questions wrapped within a disarmingly simple one—whether parliamentary government is superior to the separation of powers. As with most simple questions, we find no simple answers. At the end of this volume, we suggest some general patterns of, and limitations to, institutional effects and draw some guidelines for would-be institutional reformers. The lessons we draw will not entirely satisfy either reformers who find America's political institutions to be the source of its policy problems or those who favor preservation of the status quo. Nor will they provide certain guidance for leaders in newly democratizing countries. Institutions do not provide panaceas, but they do have predictable risks and opportunities. Serious debate about institutional reform and design must be based on an understanding of the balance between those risks and opportunities.

---

analysis of the consistency of capabilities and institutional effects over an extended period. The need to draw tentative conclusions based on limited evidence and to compare things that are not strictly comparable is endemic to comparative studies, however.

Harvey Feigenbaum, Richard Samuels,
and R. Kent Weaver

Innovation, Coordination, and Implementation in Energy Policy

*I*n the aftermath of the oil shocks of the 1970s, every advanced industrial state confronted the possibility of future increases in real energy prices and further disruptions in supply. Issues involving energy reached the top of policy agendas almost everywhere. Governments scrambled to develop new and more secure sources of energy. In addition, many governments sought to adjust energy taxes and pricing structures to encourage domestic production, lower consumption, and shift consumption toward domestically produced energy sources.[1]

Such policy initiatives inevitably triggered conflicts with other valued objectives and other interests, however. Governments were called upon not only to develop new policies but also to implement old and new policies in more difficult circumstances. Residential and industrial consumers resisted paying higher prices. Environmentalists resisted extension of nuclear power, additional air pollution from coal-burning power plants, and increased exploration and production in environmentally sensitive regions. The Three Mile Island nuclear mishap in 1979 and the more serious Chernobyl accident in 1986 further increased resistance to nuclear power plants in many countries. Producers of specific energy sources sought to ensure that government initiatives did not disadvantage

The authors would like to thank John E. Chubb, James A. Desveaux, Neil Freeman, Kathryn Harrison, Jeffrey Henig, Maureen Appel Molot, Pietro Nivola, and Eric Uslaner for their helpful comments on earlier versions of all or part of this chapter. Harvey Feigenbaum would like to thank the Fulbright Western Europe Research Program for providing resources in support of the research presented here.

1. See the discussion in G. John Ikenberry, "The Irony of State Strength: Comparative Responses to the Oil Shocks in the 1970s," *International Organization*, vol. 40 (Winter 1986), pp. 105–37.

them vis-à-vis their competitors. And politicians in countries with substantial domestic energy sources—notably the United States and Canada—struggled to deal with the political and economic effects of income transfers from consuming regions to producing regions and disputes among producers, national governments, and local governments over how to allocate the revenues produced by higher prices.[2]

Moreover, all of this occurred in an environment of enormous fluctuations in oil prices. Policy responses that seemed sensible when Middle East supply disruptions drove prices up (for example, stimulating production of unconventional oil sources) seemed extravagant and wasteful when prices fell.

This chapter examines differing policy choices made by five industrialized countries—the United States, Canada, France, West Germany, and Japan—in this new environment. It uses the case of energy policy to explore how political institutions affected three government capabilities: innovation in policymaking, coordination of conflicting objectives, and effective implementation of adopted policies.

Energy policy choices cannot be explained entirely, or even primarily, by differences in political institutions and government capabilities. Resource endowments and historical usage patterns are particularly important constraints on energy policy options. Policy innovation aimed at increasing domestic production of fossil fuels, for example, would not be a feasible strategy in countries like Japan or France where there are minimal reserves of those fuels. Resource endowments also shape political coalitions: where there are domestic producers of a specific fuel, their interests will have to be taken into account in any political settlement. In addition, resource endowments and policy inheritances flowing from those endowments shape usage patterns: where an energy source has traditionally been cheap and abundant, expectations that this will continue get built into capital stocks (such as poorly insulated homes, gas-guzzling autos, and suburban sprawl), making it difficult to adapt quickly to changes in energy supply or price. Because the five countries began from very different starting points in resource endowments, usage patterns, and policy inheritances, their responses to the energy crisis would probably differ substantially even if the governments' capabilities were fairly similar.

2. See especially Franklin Tugwell, *The Energy Crisis and the American Political Economy: Politics and Markets in the Management of Natural Resources* (Stanford University Press, 1988); Pietro Nivola, *The Politics of Energy Conservation* (Brookings, 1986); and G. Bruce Doern and Glen Toner, *The Politics of Energy: The Development and Implementation of the NEP* (Toronto: Methuen, 1985).

While there were some specific differences in policy objectives, the five countries did share three common goals: reducing dependence on Middle Eastern oil and susceptibility to supply shocks, improving energy efficiency and conservation, and finding and bringing on-line new and more secure energy sources.[3] Successful policy responses required continued implementation of existing policies that furthered these goals, innovation to replace policies that did not, and coordination of these objectives with others (notably environmental protection) that were at least partially in conflict. The exact mix of capabilities required in individual countries varied, depending on resource endowments and policies already in place; countries that already had strong conservation-promoting policies, for example, did not need to innovate as much as implement those policies. But meeting their distinctive challenges of innovation, coordination, and implementation in reaching the goals of energy policy can serve as a common standard for evaluation for all five countries.

Institutions and Policy Capabilities

Before proceeding with the case studies, it is helpful to establish a baseline of expectations about how differences in political institutions are likely to affect each of the three capabilities examined here.

Policy Innovation

Differences between institutional arrangements that separate or fuse executive and legislative powers (Weaver and Rockman's first tier of explanation) can have several effects on governments' capacity to innovate in policy. From a parliamentarist perspective, parliamentary systems' centralization of legislative power in the cabinet and party discipline within the legislature are likely to facilitate policy innovation. So long as a government has a parliamentary majority, it presumably can force an initiative through the legislature. Hence parliamentary systems should adapt more quickly and completely to changed economic and geopolitical circumstances. Separation-of-powers systems, on the other hand, are prone to deadlock even in times of crisis. Because of multiple veto points

---

3. We do not claim that this set of goals exhausts national energy goals. In the United States, for example, keeping energy prices low is an important goal. France and Japan, on the other hand, tolerate high end-user prices to encourage conservation.

in the system, even a small minority of opponents can block bold innovative proposals. Thus nonincremental change is likely to occur only after "critical elections" that alter dramatically the distribution of power within Congress.[4]

A presidentialist perspective suggests three responses to these arguments. First, centralization of legislative power in the cabinet does not remove the need to secure agreement among contending factions of the governing party or parties, nor does it remove politicians' fear of offending those who favor the status quo (indeed, it may enhance it). Even under a single-party majority government, compromises are almost certain to be made to obtain the illusion of consensus. As Richard Neustadt put it in comparing Britain and the United States:

> Beneath the surface, this combine called "Cabinet" wrestles with diversities of interest, of perspective, of procedure, of personality, much like those we are used to witnessing above ground in the dealings of our separated institutions. Not only is the hidden struggle reminiscent of our open one, but also the results are often similar: "bold, new ventures" actually undertaken are few and far between. Whitehall dispenses with the grunts and groans of Washington, but both can labor mightily to bring forth mice.[5]

Moreover, the American system may give "policy entrepreneurs" in both Congress and the executive substantial opportunities and incentives to develop innovative policies that threaten the interests of existing departments by creating alternative power centers and giving greater access to interest groups. Such initiatives might never surface in a more centralized parliamentary system where the bureaucracy is likely to be the principal fountain of policy advice.[6] The checks-and-balances system of potentially competing executive and legislative branches also provides incentives for each branch to develop its own technical expertise. This limits the ability of the executive to demand blind obedience along party lines or mislead the legislature, as is possible in parliamentary regimes. Thus presidential regimes may produce not only more innovation but better policies, because bad ideas do not survive the gauntlet of committee staffs and legislators. Finally, parliamentary systems' ability to change

4. See, for example, David W. Brady, *Critical Elections and Congressional Policy Making* (Stanford University Press, 1988).

5. Richard E. Neustadt, "White House and Whitehall," *The Public Interest*, no. 2 (Spring 1966), p. 66.

6. See Don K. Price, "The Parliamentary and Presidential Systems," *Public Administration Review*, vol. 3 (Autumn 1943), p. 324.

policy more rapidly is a mixed blessing, for it may lead to policy error. As Hugh Heclo and Aaron Wildavsky put it: "The danger in Britain is [that] the government may agree all too quickly, before the major implications of the policy are understood or the affected interests realize what is about to happen to them, leaving all concerned agape and aghast as the machine implements the policy with its usual splendid impartiality, that is, with equal harm all around."[7]

These arguments suggest that multiple veto points and elite cohesion are important determinants of a government's capacity for innovation. But parliamentary systems and separation-of-powers systems vary greatly across regime and government types on both characteristics. The "first-past-the-post" electoral rules of Westminster systems tend to magnify the translation of swings in voter support into changes in legislative support, making policy innovation more likely; proportional representation tends to dampen those effects.[8] Reaching agreement on significant innovation is likely to be especially difficult under a minority government or a coalition government composed of parties with divergent goals and bases of support. In the American separation-of-powers system, divided party control of government between the executive and legislature may increase the prospects for deadlock, while large legislative majorities for a president's party may open windows of opportunity for innovation by overwhelming the effects of party fragmentation.[9]

Veto points that inhibit innovation can also arise from third-tier characteristics such as federalism and the courts. Federalism, with its multiple centers of decision and its array of access points, is porous to new ideas and offers a diverse set of "laboratories" for policy experiments and innovation. This may allow the best ideas to percolate to the top and be adopted at the national level.[10] But federalism may also provide additional

7. Hugh Heclo and Aaron Wildavsky, *The Private Government of Public Money: Community and Policy inside British Politics* (MacMillan, 1974), p. 12.

8. See David W. Brady, Charles S. Bullock III, and L. Sandy Maisel, "The Electoral Antecedents of Policy Innovations: A Comparative Analysis," *Comparative Political Studies*, vol. 20 (January 1988), pp. 395–422.

9. For a review and a critique of deadlock in divided government, see David R. Mayhew, *Divided We Govern: Party Control, Lawmaking, and Investigations, 1946–1990* (Yale University Press, 1991). On the window of opportunity, see John Keeler, "Opening the Window for Reform: Mandates, Crises and Extraordinary Policymaking," *Comparative Political Studies* (forthcoming). As Keeler notes, large legislative majorities may facilitate innovation in both parliamentary and presidential systems by conveying the sense of a public mandate for change, especially in the immediate postelection period.

10. Federal organization does not guarantee innovation, however. President Nixon's New Federalism, based on revenue sharing and major block grants to state and local governments, resulted in very little innovation at the subnational level, despite the increase

veto points in the innovation and implementation processes if provincial government cooperation is required at either stage. Judicial review is another possible veto point for policy innovation.

Policy Coordination

Coordination of conflicting objectives is perhaps the most difficult capability to conceptualize of those examined in this volume. Achieving more of one objective often means sacrificing (or trading off) some of another objective. Building new urban highways may improve mobility at the cost of increased air pollution and increased energy consumption. Most obviously for this chapter, increasing domestic energy production is likely to mean a decline in environmental quality. Conflicting goals are especially likely to need coordination when individual bureaucracies act as advocates for only a subset of those goals and view the rest as externalities.

Governments that differ greatly in their governing ideologies, political support bases, and policy inheritances should not be expected to make identical trade-offs. For example, France might prefer more nuclear energy production, while the United States might prefer projects favoring lower environmental risk.[11] But governments can be compared with one another in terms of their ability to make efficient trade-offs—that is, to minimize the sacrifice of one value needed to obtain a given level of a conflicting value. Their ability to obtain more of one or both values over time can also be compared.

Political institutions can have an important effect on how these decisions are made. The centralized decisionmaking forum of the cabinet may provide parliamentary systems with important opportunities to facilitate simultaneous consideration of—and efficient trade-offs between—conflicting policy objectives. Parliamentary systems' fewer veto points may also help to ensure that trade-offs can occur; interest groups

---

of untied federal monies to the latter. Richard P. Nathan and Charles F. Adams, Jr., *Revenue Sharing: The Second Round* (Brookings, 1977); and Donald Kettl, "Can the Cities Be Trusted? The Community Development Experience," *Political Science Quarterly*, vol. 94 (Fall 1979), pp. 437–51. Too much experimentation at the state level can also lead to problems of evaluation and coordination at the national level. John Randolph, "Implementation and Effectiveness of State-Administered, Federally Funded Energy Conservation Programs," *Energy Systems and Policy*, vol. 9, no. 1 (1985), p. 56.

11. Proponents of nuclear power argue that it is the least polluting form of electricity generation. This must be balanced against the potential for leakage of radiation into the environment at all stages in the fuel cycle, including waste storage, to get a true picture of environmental risk.

are less likely to be able to prevent any policy innovations that cause them to suffer losses. And parliamentary systems do not have to make room for accommodation between the legislature and the executive to allow each to protect the values it views as most important, even if it comes at very high cost to other values.

The presidentialist position suggests, however, that incrementalism and decentralization to departments and cabinet committees may wipe out any opportunities that parliamentary systems might have in coordinating conflicting objectives. As in the U.S. system, central elites in parliamentary systems are unlikely to succeed in challenging bureaucratic and interest group support for existing programs, so coordination of policymaking is likely to be minimal, especially when it crosses departmental lines.

Not all parliamentary and presidential systems are alike, however. Coalition governments may have more difficulty than single-party majorities in coordinating policies, for example, especially when policy conflicts cut across ministries controlled by different political parties. Even more important cross-national differences in capacity to coordinate are likely to stem from third-tier institutional variations. Decentralization of power to legislative committees may decrease policy coordination, especially when an issue cuts across committee jurisdictions and committees are controlled by members who are not representative of the chamber as a whole. In the United States, for example, fragmentation of authority across congressional committees means that legislation on such issues as transportation, pollution, and energy will be considered by different committees, and conflicts on those issues probably never will be explicitly addressed. Federalism may also contribute to a lack of coordination when differing levels of government pursue inconsistent objectives within overlapping jurisdictions. And characteristics of the bureaucracy may also influence coordination: for example, bureaucracies at the ministry level may be highly autonomous from central leadership and committed to their own goals.

Effective Implementation

Both new and existing policies to deal with policy problems may be undermined by ineffective implementation. The parliamentarist perspective stresses that implementers in parliamentary systems face fewer masters. They do not have to contend with legislators and political appointees who may have conflicting preferences that are entrenched in the legislation that guides bureaucratic action.[12] Hence they have a greater ability to implement policies effectively once parliament has decided upon them. Nor is a prime minister in a parliamentary system ever likely to face a situation comparable to a congressional override of a presidential veto, which gives the president strong incentives to undercut implementation of a policy that he vehemently opposes.[13] The American system may also provide interest groups with more avenues of access and appeal than parliamentary systems.

A presidentialist perspective suggests two possible problems with this analysis. First, greater reliance on career civil servants in most parliamentary systems can weaken implementation when those career officials oppose the governing parties' policies. In the absence of independent oversight, the bureaucracy may shirk from implementing what it perceives to be infeasible directives. Second, it is possible that hastily agreed-upon policies (facilitated by parliamentary institutions) may not allow time for problems to be worked out and may eventually lead to policy reversal.

Second-tier perspectives suggest some additional considerations. In the United States, for example, divided government might lead to particularly heavy intervention by Congress in administrative concerns and hence to muddled implementation. In party government parliamentary systems, the relatively high probability that a government of very different ideological stripe may come to power in the near future is likely to disrupt implementation in sectors where it is important to provide clear and consistent long-term signals and incentives to private-sector actors (for example, in the housing sector). These actors are unlikely to risk their own funds when policy initiatives (and hence long-term payoffs) may be altered.[14] This is much less likely to be a problem in single-party-dominant and coalitional systems, where the prospects for policy gyrations are lower. At the third level of explanation, bureaucratic autonomy may contribute to effective implementation, while highly independent courts are likely to increase the opportunities for opponents of a policy to block it. Reliance on subnational governments to implement the central government's policies—when the latter may have different objectives—is likely to increase implementation difficulties.

12. For an argument that "the most cherished structural features of American government pose obstacles to good administration," see Martha Derthick, *Agency under Stress: The Social Security Administration in American Government* (Brookings, 1990), p. 4ff.

13. Price, "Parliamentary and Presidential Systems," p. 321.

14. See Bruce Headey, *Housing Policy in the Developed Economy: The United Kingdom, Sweden and the United States* (London: Croom Helm, 1978), chap. 9.

The Cases

The five cases examined here offer a wide variety of institutional arrangements to test against hypotheses about institutional effects. The United States is of course a separation-of-powers system, while Canada (party government), Germany (coalitional), and Japan (single-party-dominant) offer a variety of parliamentary systems. Canada has also had periods of minority as well as majority government, and energy issues featured prominently in the former. France, as will be discussed further below, is a hybrid system. Significant differences also appear in the countries' third-tier characteristics. France and Japan are both highly centralized, while the other three countries have subnational governments with substantial autonomy. France and Japan also have the least active and independent judiciaries and the most autonomous bureaucracies.

Starting Points and Policy Responses: An Overview

As noted earlier, the five case study countries began responses to the energy crisis from very different starting points. In the United States and Canada, energy usage per capita and in relation to GNP was much higher than in any of the other three countries in 1973 (figure 1 and appendix table A-1). In part, this was due to energy taxes that were extremely low in comparison to those in other industrialized countries. The United States and Canada were also far less dependent on imported oil than the other countries for their total energy needs: imports were only about 17 percent of supply in the United States, and Canada was a net exporter, while Japan depended on imports for more than 80 percent of its needs (table A-1 and figure 2).

As might be expected from the differences in their starting points, the five countries' responses to the energy crises of 1973–74 and 1979 varied greatly. Changes in taxes on energy consumption are one good indicator of governments' seriousness in conservation efforts. The United States and Canada entered the postembargo world with taxes on gasoline consumption far lower than those of the other three countries. Canada's energy taxes did move significantly higher (although far lower than Japan's, France's, or Germany's) in the 1980s, but movement was much more modest in the United States. Indeed, U.S. gasoline taxes declined in real terms between 1980 and 1990.[15]

15. On trends in gasoline prices and taxes, see Organization of Petroleum Exporting Countries, *Petroleum Product Prices and their Components in Selected Countries, 1983: Statistical*

Figure 1. *Energy Intensity of Five OECD Countries, 1970–90*[a]

Metric tons of oil equivalent consumed per 1985 million U.S. dollars of GDP

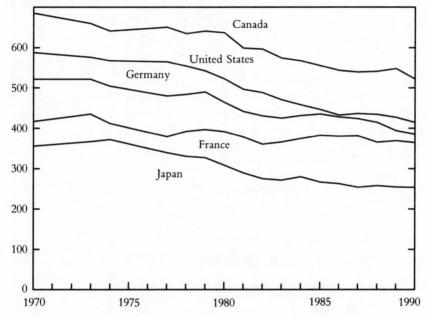

Source: International Energy Agency, *Energy Balances of OECD Countries, 1989–1990* (Paris: OECD 1992), pp. 90, 102, 106, 126, 170.

a. Data not available for 1971, 1972, 1975, 1976.

Ultimate performance—that is, progress toward the three goals of conservation, reduced dependence on Middle East oil imports, and new sources of supply—also varied. Only the United States succeeded in reducing its total energy use per capita, but it was beginning from a much larger base and still consumed far more than all of the other countries except Canada in 1990 (table A-1). The dependence of France, Germany, and Japan on imported oil, especially Middle East oil, fell dramatically after 1974, but in the United States it actually increased until the late 1970s, and, after a brief decline, reached new heights in 1990 (table A-1).[16] All five countries substantially reduced oil usage where there were alternatives, notably in generation of electricity (table A-2), and all five increased their overall domestic energy production (table A-3). The paths

Time Series 1960–1983 (Vienna: OPEC, 1984); and International Energy Agency, *Energy Prices and Taxes: Fourth Quarter 1990* (Paris: OECD, 1991).

16. Matthew L. Wald, "U.S. Imports Record 49.9% of Oil," *New York Times*, July 19, 1990, p. D1.

Figure 2. *Domestic Energy Production as Percentage of Energy Usage, Five OECD Countries, 1970–90*[a]

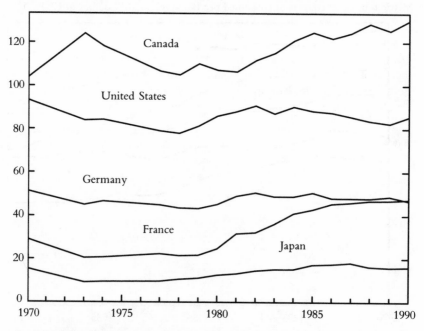

Source: International Energy Agency, *Energy Balances of OECD Countries*, pp. 90, 102, 106, 126, 170. Usage defined as total primary energy supply by OECD.
    a. Data not available for 1971, 1972, 1975, 1976.

they chose were different, however. France focused on increasing its nuclear energy output (table A-2). (Nuclear energy is considered domestic production even when the nuclear fuel is imported.) Germany and Japan also made major progress toward this goal, while nuclear energy development in the United States began to slow down in the mid-1970s and stalled completely after the Three Mile Island accident in 1979.[17]

Progress toward the three goals of reduced dependence on Middle Eastern oil, increased conservation and energy efficiency, and increased availability of domestic energy sources should not be seen as reliable indicators of government capabilities, however. Progress toward the three objectives depends on the policymaking environment itself as much as or more than on governmental capacity to influence the environment. Canada's improvement in energy self-sufficiency, for example, has more

17. New nuclear plants continued to come on-line as a result of previous orders, but new orders dried up completely.

to do with its energy resource base than with governmental capacity to innovate, coordinate conflicting objectives, and implement policies. To understand how governmental capacity—and political institutions—affected variations in countries' attainment of three common energy objectives, we must examine policymaking in the five countries in more detail. For each of the case study countries, we will first briefly review their policymaking "starting points"—resource endowments and utilization patterns, policy inheritances, and institutional arrangements at the time of the first oil shocks—and then examine policy responses to the energy crisis.

The United States

U.S. responses to the energy crisis have been marked largely by delays, compromise on modest innovation, stalemate, and occasional reversal. These outcomes reflect the way that political support coalitions are built and maintained in the United States, namely, domination by legislators rather than by bureaucrats, motivation by short-term electoral considerations (especially crises and swings in public moods) rather than by long-term policy considerations and bureaucratic values, multiple vetoes, and permeability to outside influences rather than a closed process.

Starting Points

The United States differs from most of the other case study countries in its resource endowments and policy inheritances. It historically has had large reserves of oil and did not become a net oil importer until 1948.[18] At the time of the first oil shock in 1973, the United States was still one of the world's largest oil producers, although domestic oil production peaked in 1970 and reserves of economically retrievable oil were declining. The United States also has large reserves of unconventional sources (notably oil-bearing shale rock), but oil could be produced profitably from these sources only at much higher prices or with subsidies, even if the enormous environmental problems could be solved. In addition, the United States has substantial (though declining) reserves of natural gas and enormous reserves of coal.

Reflecting its substantial and varied resource endowments, producer

18. See, for example, Robert Stobaugh, "After the Peak: The Threat of Hostile Oil," in Robert Stobaugh and Daniel Yergin, eds., *Energy Future: Report of the Energy Project of the Harvard Business School* (Ballantine, 1979), pp. 15–64.

interests in the American energy policy arena are well organized, powerful, and highly fragmented. The oil sector, for example, is dominated by large integrated producers, but independent producers and refiners are also well organized to defend their interests against the majors. In the natural gas sector different companies with conflicting interests engage in production, transportation, and distribution.[19] The electric utility sector is especially fragmented, with private and publicly owned (by federal, state, and local government) utilities involved in the generation, transmission, and distribution of electricity. Other stakeholders are also heavily involved in energy issues. Railroads, for example, lobby intensely against coal slurry pipelines; truckers oppose increased fuel taxes that will disadvantage them competitively vis-à-vis railroads. And a variety of environmental interests are concerned with issues such as offshore and wilderness oil drilling, coal slurry pipelines, nuclear reactor safety, and maintenance of clean air standards by power plants.

The U.S. government confronted the first energy crisis with a set of policymaking institutions that was also highly fragmented—even by U.S. standards. Within the federal government, congressional jurisdiction over energy was divided among a number of committees and subcommittees. Moreover, given the heavy regional stakes in energy policy, the House and Senate were unlikely to defer to their committees in energy matters. And representatives of producer regions tended to hold particularly powerful positions on energy matters in the Senate, generating interchamber conflict.

In the executive branch, a number of departments (such as Interior) and independent regulatory commissions (notably the Atomic Energy Commission and Federal Power Commission) had authority over energy issues. Policymaking tended to occur within distinct resource sectors (coal, oil, natural gas, and electricity) dominated largely by producer interests.[20] Retail prices of natural gas and electricity were regulated at the state level, while the federal government and state governments shared jurisdiction in other areas, notably approval of new energy facilities. There was, in short, neither a single coherent energy policy nor any policymaking mechanisms that would facilitate developing one at the time of the 1973 oil embargo.

19. Federal law prevents natural gas transmission companies from distributing natural gas.
20. See David Howard Davis, *Energy Politics,* 3d ed. (St. Martins, 1982); Tugwell, *The Energy Crisis and the American Political Economy,* chaps. 1–5; John E. Chubb, *Interest Groups and the Bureaucracy: The Politics of Energy* (Stanford University Press, 1983); and Don E. Kash and Robert W. Rycroft, *U.S. Energy Policy: Crisis and Complacency* (University of Oklahoma Press, 1984).

Policy inheritances in the United States increased problems of adapting to the postembargo energy environment. Transportation and housing policies encouraged low-density residential patterns and ownership of large cars while discouraging use of public transportation. Each of these raised the public's stakes in resisting higher energy prices. Perhaps most important in the short term, oil and gas price controls that exacerbated the effects of supply disruptions were already in place as a result of the wage and price freeze imposed by President Nixon in 1971. Dismantling such controls at a time of rapid price increases and hostility to energy producers was politically untenable; thus price controls set the parameters for future policy.

Policy Responses

The oil embargo and its aftermath spawned a succession of initiatives within the executive to centralize and coordinate energy policymaking. These efforts culminated in the creation of the Department of Energy in 1977.[21] But a number of important decisionmaking arenas, notably nuclear reactor safety regulation, remained outside the department. And while the president was centralizing authority, authority was being dispersed in Congress. Because of the increased salience of the energy issue, not only were more committees and subcommittees attempting to assert their jurisdiction over energy issues, but specialist committees were increasingly being challenged on the chamber floors. Several rounds of efforts to bring about a comprehensive realignment of congressional energy jurisdiction fell victim to committee efforts at turf protection.[22] In 1977 the House Democratic leadership resorted to a special Ad Hoc Committee on Energy to overcome the obstacles that multiple jurisdictions presented to consideration of President Carter's energy package, but the package was nevertheless defeated in the Senate. There were further upheavals in the 1980s in the executive branch: the Reagan administration entered office in 1981 with the professed aim of dismantling the Energy Department. Although this did not happen, budgetary strug-

21. For a brief overview of these initiatives, see Charles O. Jones and Randall Strahan, "The Effect of Energy Politics on Congressional and Executive Organization in the 1970s," *Legislative Studies Quarterly*, vol. 10 (May 1985), pp. 151–79, especially pp. 154–60.

22. See Jones and Strahan, "Effect of Energy Politics"; Eric M. Uslaner, *Shale Barrel Politics: Energy and Legislative Leadership* (Stanford University Press, 1979), chaps. 3, 6; and Bruce I. Oppenheimer, "Policy Effects of U.S. House Reform: Decentralization and the Capacity to Resolve Energy Issues," *Legislative Studies Quarterly*, vol. 5 (February 1980), pp. 5–30.

gles between Congress and the executive and high turnover were very disruptive for the department, especially in research programs.[23]

These organizational failures were reflected in substantive policy decisions. Nowhere was this more evident than in efforts to promote energy conservation. The simplest and most direct ways to promote conservation are to raise prices by deregulating them if they have been kept below world market levels and to impose additional taxes on energy consumption. Deregulation may also spark increased production if high-cost resources cannot be exploited profitably at the current price. Energy price increases are extremely unpopular with consumers, however. In addition, price decontrol may provide what the public perceives as "windfall" profits to oil and gas producers on their production from existing wells and may provoke massive regional redistributions of income.

PRICE CONTROL. Partisan and regional differences within Congress over how to allocate the benefits and costs of oil price decontrol, as well as disagreements over whether deregulation would really lead to major increases in production, were exacerbated by the dispersion of power within Congress, which made it harder to strike binding deals to trade off decontrol for a "windfall profits" tax. In the absence of ready-made legislative coalitions furnished by disciplined parties, coalitions had to be constructed; this proved particularly difficult where losses were being imposed and legislators feared being blamed for higher energy prices. Instead of deregulating oil prices, oil was divided into "tiers" based on when it had gone into production, and in the Energy Policy and Conservation Act of 1975, the price of "old" oil was actually reduced by a dollar a barrel. While Congress was formulating this act, the House of Representatives used its legislative veto authority to block two proposals for phased decontrol of oil prices put forward by President Gerald Ford.[24] In response to pressures from small refiners to ensure them access to oil, policies were also enacted that inadvertently encouraged the construction of new, inefficient refineries at a time when oil consumption was falling.[25] Oil prices were not fully decontrolled until the Reagan administration came into office in 1981, when the president used his authority to elim-

23. See David Narum, "A Troublesome Legacy: The Reagan Administration's Conservation and Renewable Energy Programs," *Energy Policy*, vol. 20 (January 1992), pp. 40–53.

24. See the discussion in Nivola, *Politics of Energy Conservation*, chap. 2, especially pp. 49–51.

25. See Richard Corrigan, "Without Federally Guaranteed Supplies, Small Refiners Are Scrambling for Oil," *National Journal*, April 18, 1981, pp. 636–40.

inate remaining controls eight months earlier than their scheduled demise under "sunset" provisions of the 1975 legislation.[26]

A similar pattern developed in the natural gas sector: Congress expanded both the scope and complexity of price controls under the Natural Gas Policy Act of 1978, contributing to supply and price disruptions and the creation of new vested interests in regulation. Producer interests were mollified with a phaseout of most controls in seven to nine years. Executive and legislative efforts to bring controls to an early end got bogged down in Congress.[27] Legislation fully freeing wellhead prices for natural gas was not passed until 1989—this time with little controversy, since phased decontrol under the 1978 act left little gas under regulation, and natural gas prices had in fact fallen rather than continuing to increase.[28]

The pattern for both oil and gas decontrol, in short, is one of substantially delayed adjustment to market forces, with eventual deregulation facilitated by real price declines in the preceding period, which lowered the salience of the energy issue; credible predictions that further deregulation would bring further price declines, thereby splitting consumer advocates and insulating legislators from blame that they had betrayed consumer interests; and sunset and phaseout provisions. Both phaseout and sunset provisions gradually shifted bargaining leverage to pro-deregulation forces—at least so long as energy prices were not rising—by making deregulation an eventual fait accompli unless proponents of continued regulation could overcome centripetal forces within Congress to pass new legislation. Ironically, then, the conclusion is that deregulation is most likely to succeed when it is least likely to lead to short-term price increases—and thus when it promises the least pain to consumers, the least blame for politicians, and the lowest incentives for conservation.

TAXATION. The story of energy taxation in the United States offers similar lessons about the difficulty of building legislative coalitions for policy innovations that impose substantial visible losses. The United States stands out in its low level of energy taxes, especially on gasoline. Congress has repeatedly rejected proposals for higher gasoline taxes by heavy bipartisan majorities in periods of both united and divided gov-

26. President Jimmy Carter had begun phased decontrol, and President Reagan's abolition of price controls eight months early was largely symbolic in nature. See Tugwell, *The Energy Crisis and the American Political Economy*, chap. 7, especially pp. 127–29.

27. See Nivola, *Politics of Energy Conservation*, chap. 3.

28. "Natural Gas Decontrol Bill Speeds through Congress," *Congressional Quarterly Almanac, 1989*, vol. 45 (1990), p. 675.

ernment. These actions reflected the broad impact and unpopularity of these taxes and the near-universality of politicians' fear of being identified with them. Moreover, any tax increase proposal raised difficult distributional issues that tended to fracture coalitions rather than build them. A gasoline tax, for example, was seen by rural legislators as discriminating against their constituents, while an oil import fee might disproportionately affect eastern states; a broad-based energy tax based on heat content would discriminate against less-efficient burning fuels (notably coal).

Thus Congress has avoided energy tax increases, except for gasoline tax increases of just five cents a gallon enacted in 1983 and 1990. In both of these cases, there were unusual conditions that significantly weakened politicians' fears of being held accountable. The first passed as part of the Surface Transportation Act of 1983. It benefited from occurring at a time of falling gasoline prices, strong presidential leadership, action in a lame duck Congress, and dedication of the funding to infrastructure improvements, allowing the bill to be sold as a jobs measure. It still passed by the slimmest of margins.[29] The 1990 increase was passed as part of that year's budget summit, which was much more closed to interest group policymaking than the normal legislative process; it nevertheless featured ferocious behind-the-scenes battles along regional lines that led to a broader energy tax being dropped from the package.[30] As a result of oil price fluctuations and a federal gasoline tax that declined in real terms, the real retail price of gasoline in the United States, after increasing more than 75 percent from 1973 to 1980, was by 1991 at its lowest point since 1947.[31]

Instead of raising energy taxes, politicians sought to limit consumption by indirect mechanisms. States were required to impose speed limits of fifty-five miles an hour or face a loss of highway funds (a measure that was partially repealed in 1987). In 1975 automakers were forced to gradually raise the corporate average fuel economy (CAFE) of the cars they produced or face fines, and "gas guzzler" excise taxes were imposed on

29. Other factors, such as strong concern over budget deficits, also increased support for the measure. For a comprehensive discussion of gasoline taxation in the United States, see Nivola, *Politics of Energy Conservation*, chap. 5.

30. See Phil Kuntz, "Energy Interests Try to Avoid Getting Burned by Congress," *Congressional Quarterly Weekly Report*, September 22, 1990, pp. 3004–07; and Kuntz, "Long-Anticipated Energy Taxes End in Rose Garden Surprise," *Congressional Quarterly Weekly Report*, October 6, 1990, pp. 3207–08.

31. See Matthew L. Wald, "Gasoline at Low Price, But Benefits May Fade," *New York Times*, July 26, 1991, p. D1; and Energy Information Administration, *Annual Energy Review, 1989* (Department of Energy, 1990).

cars that failed to meet CAFE standards.[32] But when American automakers had difficulty meeting the CAFE standards in 1986, they were relaxed.

INCREASING SUPPLY. An alternative to cutting consumption is increasing supply from conventional or high-cost sources. Again, price increases are the most direct route, because they make high-cost oil and gas wells economically feasible. Because this route has been largely foreclosed, prospective innovations have focused largely on proposals that pose particularly strong clashes between energy and environmental interests, such as President Bush's 1990 proposal to allow exploratory drilling in the Arctic National Wildlife Refuge. Environmentalists in Congress opposed the proposal, rallying instead around measures to require increased auto fuel efficiency. But this measure also faced strong opposition, notably from the beleaguered American auto industry. Both provisions were eventually stripped from congressional energy legislation as being too controversial.[33]

Perhaps the most ambitious U.S. policy innovation was in synthetic fuels to be manufactured from sources such as oil shale and coal.[34] Following a request from President Carter, Congress established a Synthetic Fuels Corporation in 1980 to help create a synthetic fuel industry through loans, loan guarantees, and price guarantees to the private sector. A phenomenal $88 billion was to be provided over five years from the windfall profits tax on oil. Additional (much lower) funding was provided for other nontraditional fuels (such as gasohol) to increase the geographic base of support for the program. But the corporation immediately faced political difficulties on a number of fronts. Oil prices began to decline, lowering the salience of the energy issue (and the desire on the part of legislators to be seen as "doing something" on energy) and making synthetic fuels even less price competitive with conventional oil. Many members of the Reagan administration, which came into office in 1981, were hostile to government intervention in energy mar-

32. See Robert W. Crandall and others, *Regulating the Automobile* (Brookings, 1986), chap. 6. Taxes on "gas guzzler" cars were doubled by the 1990 budget agreement.

33. See, for example, Margaret E. Kriz, "Going the Extra Mile," *National Journal*, May 11, 1991, pp. 1094–98, Kriz, "Arctic Showdown," *National Journal*, June 8, 1991, pp. 1341–44; and Matthew L. Wald, "Congress Expected to Pass Scaled-Down Energy Plan," *New York Times*, January 31, 1992, pp. D1, D4.

34. For a brief introduction to synthetic fuels, see Davis, *Energy Politics*, pp. 256–60. On earlier federal efforts to promote synthetic fuels, see Craufurd D. Goodwin, "Truman Administration Policies toward Particular Energy Sources," in Goodwin, ed., *Energy Policy in Perspective: Today's Problems, Yesterday's Solutions* (Brookings, 1981), pp. 146–67. This paragraph draws heavily on the account in Uslaner, *Shale Barrel Politics*, chap. 4.

kets.[35] The program was plagued with administrative problems (including allegations of incompetence and conflict of interest), while growing budget deficits made a program with few successes and many highly visible failures extremely vulnerable. Environmentalists used these openings to renew their attacks on the program. Support in Congress evaporated, and the corporation was abolished in 1986.

It is questionable whether the synthetic fuels program could have succeeded even if energy and political markets had been more favorable, however. By the late 1970s, it was clear that requiring multiple approvals from federal and state agencies for major energy projects like synfuels and nuclear power plants posed serious impediments to implementing those projects. To cope with this problem, President Carter proposed an energy mobilization board as a companion to his synfuels proposal. The board would have had the authority to set deadlines for other agencies' decisions and, if necessary, centralize and supplant them. The proposal was disliked by many interests (especially environmentalists and some oil companies) and ultimately rejected by the House of Representatives.[36]

NUCLEAR POWER. The problems of policy implementation and coordination were most evident in the nuclear power sector. There was a tremendous growth in nuclear power in the United States through the early 1970s. But a decline in the rate of increase in electricity consumption, combined with unfavorable changes in the regulatory and economic environments, put an end to construction of new nuclear power plants in the 1980s.

Several factors affected the cost of nuclear power in the United States. The multiplicity of American utilities made it difficult to standardize purchasing or reactor design.[37] All of these utilities are regulated by state

35. Budget Director David Stockman was prominent in this group. See Stockman, *The Triumph of Politics: Why the Reagan Revolution Failed* (Harper and Row, 1986), pp. 61, 110, 114–16.

36. The House had initially accepted the board but rejected it on a motion to recommit the conference committee report. On opposition to the energy mobilization board, see Christopher Madison, "New Board to Cut Red Tape May Cause Some Problems of Its Own," *National Journal*, May 10, 1980, pp. 760–64; and Uslaner, *Shale Barrel Politics*, pp. 88–89.

37. The United States has over three thousand utilities. Japan, with half the U.S. population, has ten. Only a few American utilities are large enough to consider nuclear generating stations, however. Most of the smaller utilities that considered nuclear power did so as part of consortia headed by large utilities. James Jasper argues that significant learning curve effects could have been achieved with as few as thirty reactors, and therefore a number of reactor types could have been accommodated in the U.S. market. However, the fact that any one utility rarely owned more than half a dozen nuclear plants made such

public utility commissions, as well as the Nuclear Regulatory Commission (NRC) in the case of the 112 nuclear plants.[38] Local public utilities are subject to the jurisdiction of federal and state courts. Construction time was also a problem. Reactor construction was frequently delayed because of court injunctions obtained by local residents objecting to the plants. In addition, except for the Tennessee Valley Authority, utilities were not allowed to increase charges before the reactors were constructed, so construction had to be financed by bonds or loans. Finally, the NRC's policy of requiring utilities to backfit plants with technologies developed after initial approval was a significant cause of delay and cost. Thus American nuclear power stations were increasingly delayed—generally four years or more for plants originally scheduled to open in 1977 or later—making those plants less competitive with domestic coal.[39] In addition, local governments had the power to scuttle plants entirely by refusing to cooperate on evacuation plans required before the NRC would grant an operating license, although this did not become a problem until the nuclear industry was already ceasing to expand. In such cases the federal government might preempt local governments, but such events were rare: federal preemption was legally possible, but politically risky, at least after the accident at Three Mile Island.[40]

A somewhat different pattern of political constraints resulting in prolonged stalemate is visible in the saga of the U.S. program to develop a fast breeder reactor on the Clinch River in Tennessee. Many scientists view breeder reactors as an almost inexhaustible source of energy because they burn uranium much more efficiently than standard fission reactors and produce plutonium that can be reprocessed for use as a nuclear fuel. But fast breeders also have disadvantages: the plutonium they create has a longer radioactive half-life than uranium and is much more easily usable

benefits less likely. See James M. Jasper, *Nuclear Politics: Energy and the State in the United States, Sweden and France* (Princeton University Press, 1990); and U.S. Council for Energy Awareness, *Electricity from Nuclear Energy* (Washington: USCEA, 1988), p. 2.

38. Roderick Oram, "The United States: A Slow Turnaround," *Financial Times*, July 4, 1989, Survey, p. IV. The NRC is the successor agency for the regulatory activity of the Atomic Energy Commission.

39. See John E. Chubb, "U.S. Energy Policy: A Problem of Delegation," in John E. Chubb and Paul E. Peterson, eds., *Can the Government Govern?* (Brookings, 1989), p. 85n; and Max Wilkinson, "Nuclear Economics: Brave New World Wakes Up to Financial Reality," *Financial Times*, July 4, 1989, Survey, p. II.

40. See Regina S. Axelrod, "Reagan's Conception of Federalism and Nuclear Power: Shoreham—A Case of Conflict," *Energy Policy*, vol. 19 (November 1991), pp. 841–48; and John L. Campbell, *Collapse of An Industry: Nuclear Power and the Contradictions of U.S. Policy* (Cornell University Press, 1988), p. 76.

in nuclear weapons. Hence widespread use of breeder reactors could facilitate the spread of nuclear weapons, and the transportation of re-processed fuels poses a potential target for terrorist attacks. Environmental groups used court challenges to delay the Clinch River project, but the major blow came in 1977, when President Carter, citing non-proliferation concerns, declared that the United States would not use plutonium as a nuclear fuel in commercial power plants and sought to cancel the Clinch River project. Project supporters in Congress refused to go along, however, and design work, site preparation, and purchase of components proceeded for several years. Ironically, positions of the two branches switched in the early 1980s: President Reagan supported the Clinch River project, while congressional support eroded. Escalating costs for the project and changing energy markets—notably lower world uranium prices and declining projections of future electricity demands—also worked against the project. An odd congressional coalition of en-vironmentalists and fiscal conservatives eventually killed the project in 1983, over the Reagan administration's objections, after the expenditure of more than $1.5 billion.[41]

Further barriers to both policy innovation and implementation are evident in U.S. policy toward the disposal of spent nuclear fuel from commercial power plants. Finding a permanent repository for these wastes poses a particularly obvious "not in my backyard" (NIMBY) loss-im-position problem. Currently, these wastes are stored on site at reactors because policymakers have not been able to agree on a permanent site. In 1982 Congress enacted legislation that provided an elaborate process for selection of two repository sites and gave states a veto that in turn could be overridden by Congress.[42] In 1987, a "negative log roll" was engineered in Congress to designate Yucca Mountain in Nevada as the first site and ratify a decision already made by the Energy Department to suspend site selection for a second repository, thereby removing other states from the risk of selection. But the state government of Nevada has denied the federal government permits needed to conduct fur-ther studies of the site and has also challenged the decision in the

41. See "Clinch River Project Scrapped by Congress," *Congressional Quarterly Almanac, 1983*, vol. 39 (1983), pp. 362–65; and Herbert Kitschelt, "Four Theories of Public Policy Making and Fast Breeder Reactor Development," *International Organization*, vol. 40 (Winter 1986), pp. 65–104.

42. The Nuclear Waste Policy Act of 1982 was approved on the expectation that one of these sites would be located east and one west of the Mississippi River, to assuage westerners' fear that they would be the sole nuclear dumping ground, but this distribution was not legally required.

courts.[43] As a result, it seems unlikely that a repository site will be ready until after 2010, meaning that spent fuel may continue to be stored at reactor sites until that time even though the reactors themselves may have been decommissioned.

Evaluating U.S. Performance

In short, the U.S. record is quite mixed on each of the three energy security goals outlined at the outset of this chapter and each of the capabilities needed to attain these goals. (Table 1 contains a rough summary of all five countries' progress toward each of these goals and a brief summary of the most important objectives the five governments were trying to reconcile with their energy security objectives.) Certainly little progress has been made in reducing oil imports, which were more than 20 percent higher in 1990 than in 1973 (table A-1). Some progress has been made in improving energy efficiency, especially in automobiles, but it is not clear whether government policy or changes in gasoline prices were responsible for these improvements.[44] Many efforts to promote new, more secure domestic energy sources were stymied by standoffs between environmental and energy interests and by fluctuations in real energy prices that made production from unconventional sources exceedingly risky and then unfeasible.

This relatively poor performance can be traced in part to weaknesses in government capabilities, which in turn can be traced in part to governmental structures. The U.S. system of decentralized and divided power at the national level proved capable of producing many innovations, but they were not comprehensive and were often indirect (and ineffective) in order to avoid imposing direct and highly visible losses. Rather than careful coordination of energy security objectives with conflicting goals (notably protecting the environment and keeping energy prices low), clear trade-offs were generally avoided, and interest groups used available veto points to avoid suffering any losses. The result was often policy stalemate or legislation that attempted to micromanage policy problems rather than give discretion to the executive. Policy implementation suffered both from numerous veto points (notably state and local govern-

43. See Rochelle L. Stanfield, "How Nevada Was Dealt a Losing Hand," *National Journal*, January 16, 1988, pp. 146–47; and Holly Idelson, "Nevada Prepares for Battle on Nuclear Waste—Again," *Congressional Quarterly Weekly Report*, September 7, 1991, pp. 2558–59.

44. See Crandall and others, *Regulating the Automobile*; and Kriz, "Going the Extra Mile."

Table 1. *Energy Policy Objectives and Achievements in Five OECD Countries*

Country	Progress toward energy objective			Competing and complementary objectives
	Reduce dependence on Middle East oil	Improve energy efficiency and conservation	Bring on-line new and more secure energy sources	
United States	Low	Medium	Medium	Keep energy prices low Protect environment Protect domestic auto industry Minimize risk of nuclear proliferation
Canada	. . .	Low	Medium	Promote regional economic development Protect environment Keep energy prices low (through 1984) Compete with provincial governments for allocation of resource rents Protect U.S. energy export markets
France	High	Low	Very high	Protect environment Minimize energy drain on balance of payments Maintain industrial competitiveness through low factor costs
Germany	High	High	Low	Reduce risks from nuclear power Reduce pollution from coal Maintain employment in domestic coal industry
Japan	High	Very high	High	Sustain rapid economic growth Protect environment Protect domestic coal industry

ments and the courts, in the case of nuclear power) and from poorly designed policies that created perverse results (natural gas shortages and a growth of inefficient refineries, for example).

Canada

Canada, like the United States, has substantial domestic energy resources. Indeed, Canada is a net exporter of energy, primarily natural gas and hydropower but also oil (table A-1 and figure 2). The existence of substantial domestic oil reserves made energy politics and policy agendas similar in Canada and the United States—and different from the other three countries considered here—in five ways. First, they contributed to a policy inheritance of low concern for conservation and hence low energy taxes and prices. Second, they meant that policymakers could maintain a domestic price for oil below the prevailing world price after the oil shocks, at least in the short term. This option promised significant political returns in nonproducing regions of the two countries. Third, politicians were tempted to pursue, at least rhetorically, policy initiatives promoting domestic "energy self-sufficiency" as a long-term goal rather than adjustment to continued dependency. Fourth, oil resources created strong differences in regional interests between producing and nonproducing regions. Canada's regional divisions are even stronger and more politically intractable than those in the United States. Finally, they meant that the roller coaster ride of rising and falling energy prices repeatedly threatened the viability of measures to increase high-cost production and threatened to undo accommodations between producer, consumer, and environmental interests and between governments.

Despite these parallels, energy policy in Canada has been marked much more than that in the United States by a bold initiative—the National Energy Program of 1980—and also by the reversal of that initiative. This difference in policy responses is due in large measure to differing political institutions, notably Canada's party government parliamentary system and its highly conflictual form of federalism.

Starting Points

In part because of its northern climate, Canada uses a lot of energy—the most, per capita, of the OECD countries (table A-1 and figure 1). Distributive issues also raise the political salience of energy policy in Canada. Conventional oil and gas resources are concentrated in western Canada, especially in the province of Alberta. Canadian policy before the oil shocks reserved the Canadian market west of Quebec for higher-cost Canadian oil, while Quebec and the Atlantic provinces were served by imports, making those provinces far more vulnerable to the oil price shocks and supply disruptions of the 1970s. As conventional oil reserves in the West declined, Canada became a net oil importer in the mid-1970s but returned to a net export position by 1982. Significant oil and gas discoveries have also been made off the Atlantic coast and in the Arctic, and Canada has enormous unconventional hydrocarbon resources, notably the oil sands in northern Alberta. But the offshore and unconventional resources can be extracted only at very high cost—and thus either at very high market prices or with government subsidies or government-imposed cross-subsidies.

At the time of the 1973 oil shock, ownership of petroleum production facilities was overwhelmingly American. This both limited and extended options for Canadian policymakers. On the one hand, it meant that both financial and physical capital (such as drilling rigs) were highly mobile and tended to move south if Canadian governments offered producers terms that were considered unacceptable. But it also meant that Canadian governments could play to nationalist impulses to justify policy decisions that could not be adopted in the United States.

Canada also has tremendous hydro and uranium resources for generating electricity. There is a strong tradition of public entrepreneurship in this sector, with generation and distribution of electricity largely under provincial ownership.[45]

Energy battles, especially over oil and gas, tapped into and reinforced existing cleavages between more industrialized central Canada (the provinces of Ontario and Quebec) and the peripheries that were already deeply imbedded in the party system. But regional conflicts are institutionalized in different ways in Canada and the United States. In the United States, decentralized congressional parties and strong committee systems mean that regional conflicts are often played out in prolonged congressional wrangling; in Canada's party government parliamentary system, legislators are constrained from acting openly as regional advocates against party positions, although such advocacy is endemic within the cabinet. Moreover, provincial governments' smaller number (ten), regional distinctiveness, and strong powers (for example, ownership of natural resources in Canada rests with the provinces, except on the "Canada lands" off the coasts and in the Yukon and Northwest Territories) have en-

---

45. For an overview, see Aidan R. Vining, "Provincial Hydro Utilities," in Allan Tupper and G. Bruce Doern, eds., *Public Corporations and Public Policy in Canada* (Montreal: Institute for Research on Public Policy, 1981), pp. 149–88.

couraged these governments to act as strong advocates of regional interests. As a result, so long as there is a single-party majority government in Ottawa, conflict usually is played out between the federal government and the provinces.[46] As in the United States, energy crisis led to conflict between industry and government over shares of increased oil and gas revenues, but in Canada there was almost equal salience for conflicts over which level of government—the producing province or the federal government—would reap the benefits.

Policy Responses

Perhaps the most striking feature of Canadian energy policy is the extent to which the energy policy objectives of decreasing susceptibility to supply shocks, improving energy efficiency and conservation, and bringing secure energy resources into production have been intertwined with, and in many cases subordinated to, other considerations. As one analysis put it, energy issues in Canada by 1980

> had long since ceased to be a matter of pure energy policy. They had acquired much of the political baggage inherent in Canadian politics. Energy policy was a summation of the Canadian body politic, embracing issues of nationalism, regionalism, foreign ownership of the economy, partisan conflict, theories and beliefs about Canada's resource heritage, bureaucratic growth and state intervention, and the realities of international independence and Canada-United States relations.[47]

While Canada's Westminster-style system of party government produces single-party majority governments most of the time, there were minority governments in Ottawa 30 percent of the time between the beginning of 1963 and the end of 1992. Both the first and second oil shocks occurred during periods of minority government in Ottawa, which had a significant impact on energy policymaking, especially for oil and gas. The 1973 oil shock occurred during an eighteen-month period in which a Liberal minority government headed by Pierre Trudeau was dependent upon the social democratic New Democratic party (NDP) to

46. On the impact of differing political institutions on management of regional conflict in Canada, see Roger Gibbins, *Regionalism: Territorial Politics in Canada and the United States* (Toronto: Butterworths, 1982). On federal-provincial conflict over energy, see David Milne, *Tug of War: Ottawa and the Provinces under Trudeau and Mulroney* (Toronto: James Lorimer, 1986), chap. 3.

47. Doern and Toner, *Politics of Energy*, p. 2.

68   *Harvey Feigenbaum, Richard Samuels, and R. Kent Weaver*

remain in power. The NDP pressed on the Liberals its agenda of increasing Canadian participation in the Canadian energy industry and protecting the standard of living of its constituents in heavily industrialized central Canada. To avoid defeat on a motion of no confidence, the Liberals extended a domestic oil price freeze and created Petro-Canada, a federal "crown corporation" (public enterprise) with a mandate to serve as a "window" for the federal government into the incredibly complex world of energy and as a vehicle to negotiate long-term agreements with foreign suppliers and to press for development of higher-risk energy projects.[48] The Liberals tried in the late 1970s to balance consumer interests with incentives to increase production by creating a two-price structure of "old" and "new" oil (as occurred in the United States). Domestic consumers were also protected by restrictions on exports of oil and natural gas to the United States.

The minority government at the time of the second oil shock was a Progressive Conservative government headed by Joe Clark. Despite its minority status, the Clark government proposed several bold energy initiatives. The Conservatives had supported privatization or dismantling of Petro-Canada while in opposition, but they gradually backed away from this policy while in office and in the face of another election campaign.[49] The most important Conservative initiative was a budget including a tax of eighteen cents a gallon on transportation fuels and increased federal taxes on other crude oil prices. These proposals were unacceptable to the opposition parties and unpopular with the electorate; the Clark government lost a motion of no confidence on them in the House of Commons and lost the ensuing general election.

The Liberals won a narrow victory in the general election of 1980 despite the fact that they won none of the sixty-three House of Commons seats in Canada's three westernmost energy-producing provinces. The new government's political base in the consuming regions of Ontario and Quebec was reflected in a new National Energy Program, one of the centerpieces of the last Trudeau government. The NEP stressed the objective of national energy self-sufficiency, along with increasing Ca-

48. On this period, see Fen Osler Hampson, *Forming Economic Policy: The Case of Energy in Canada and Mexico* (London: Frances Pinter, 1986), chap. 6; and Larry Pratt, "Petro-Canada," in Allan Tupper and G. Bruce Doern, eds., *Privatization, Public Policy and Public Corporations in Canada* (Halifax: Institute for Research on Public Policy, 1988), pp. 151–210. Pratt argues that the Liberals would likely have decided to create Petro-Canada anyway, but the NDP threat certainly influenced its timing.

49. On the Conservatives' Petro-Canada policy dilemmas, see Jeffrey Simpson, *Discipline of Power: The Conservative Interlude and the Liberal Restoration* (Toronto: Personal Library, 1980), pp. 159–74.

nadian ownership and "fairness" in energy pricing and revenue distribution, but it was as much about federal-provincial conflict over resource revenues and the Trudeau government's desire to raise the visibility of the federal government as it was about energy policy.[50] A new oil-pricing structure was imposed unilaterally by Ottawa to protect consuming regions by allowing oil prices to rise but to hold Canadian oil prices to 85 percent of the world price (or the U.S. price, if it was lower). It also included measures that increased the federal share of revenue from oil and gas production through a number of new taxes, largely at the expense of the producing provinces, and that increased Canadian ownership in the oil industry.[51] In addition, direct subsidies on the price of oil imported for eastern Canada were replaced by a cross-subsidy system for refiners similar to the American scheme. The politically sensitive issue of a gasoline tax was addressed by imposing a "Canadian ownership charge," at a level to be established later, on consumption, with the funds to be reserved for increasing Canadian ownership of the oil industry. This mechanism had three advantages: it avoided the "tax" label,[52] it established the principle in law without making clear how big the cost to consumers would be, and it established a popular rationale—Canadianization—for the charge.

Bitter opposition to the NEP by the producing provinces culminated in moves by Alberta to gradually shut down oil production in the province. Although Ottawa and Alberta eventually reached a pricing agreement, energy battles became one of the critical divisions in Canadian politics during the late 1970s and early 1980s. The bitterness of the conflict over the NEP was heightened by the fact that it coincided with a decline in the world price of oil and a severe depression in the western Canadian oil industry. Western Canadians placed most of the blame for these dislocations on the NEP.

50. See Government of Canada, *The National Energy Program* (Ottawa: Supply and Services, 1980), p. 2; and G. Bruce Doern, "The Mega-Project Episode and the Formulation of Canadian Economic Development Policy," *Canadian Public Administration*, vol. 26 (Summer 1983), pp. 219–38.

51. Most notably, the NEP replaced a tax-based system of incentives for oil and gas exploration with a grants system that was heavily weighted in favor of Canadian-owned companies and exploration on federally owned lands and offshore areas. The NEP also reserved for the Crown a 25 percent interest in oil and gas discoveries in the Canada lands, including those made before introduction of the NEP. The economic logic of encouraging development of the Canada lands was that only in these relatively unexplored areas were there likely to be substantial new finds that would make Canada self-sufficient in energy, but such a move also increased federal linkages to and control over the industry.

52. According to Doern and Toner, the "Ownership Charge became a 'charge' on consumers primarily because if it had been a tax it would, along with other NEP provisions, have quickly sent the total Liberal package well beyond the less than 18 cent election pledge of the Liberals." *Politics of Energy*, p. 55.

The Liberal party, under the new leadership of John Turner, was overwhelmingly defeated in the 1984 general election. And once again the Liberals were almost completely rejected in the three energy-producing westernmost provinces (the only Liberal seat there was won by Turner). The new Progressive Conservative government, under Prime Minister Brian Mulroney, saw increased reliance on market forces as the key to increased production, and it placed a high priority on lowering of tensions between the producing provinces and Ottawa.[53] Agreements were reached with producing provinces that moved Canadian oil prices to world levels, returned to a system of tax incentives for oil exploration, phased out many of the NEP taxes (despite Ottawa's huge budget deficits), eased restrictions on oil and gas exports to the United States, and gave provinces increased rights to offshore resources under Ottawa's jurisdiction. Other Liberal policies were altered more slowly. Mindful of the popularity of Petro-Canada, the Mulroney government did not sell the company outright, but reduced its access to public funds and sold a minority stake to the public in 1991. Restrictions on foreign takeovers of Canadian-owned oil companies were eased in 1992.[54] And while the federal government has retreated from promised support for oil sands development in Alberta, it has continued to support development of even more expensive oil from the Hibernia project off the coast of Newfoundland—a move that has further angered westerners.[55]

The NEP remains alive as a political issue, moreover: in the 1981-82 round of Canadian constitutional negotiations, the energy and resource-producing provinces insisted on clarification and extension of their jurisdiction over natural resources as a price of their consent.[56] The issue was reprised in 1992. During negotiations on a new package of constitutional reforms for Canada, Alberta acted as a potential deal breaker by

53. See the discussion in David Bercuson, J. L. Granatstein, and W. R. Young, *Sacred Trust? Brian Mulroney and the Conservative Party in Power* (Toronto: Doubleday Canada, 1986), chap. 8.

54. These changes were precipitated by the financial collapse of the giant Canadian developer Olympia and York, which owns Gulf Canada, Ltd., and was unable to find a domestic buyer for the company. See Drew Fagan, "Ottawa Set to Open Oil Patch to Further Foreign Investment," *Globe and Mail* (Toronto), March 21, 1992, pp. B1, B4; and Clyde H. Farnsworth, "Canada Lifts Oil Industry Investing Bar," *New York Times*, March 26, 1992, p. D3.

55. See Elaine Verbicky, "A Newfie White Elephant," *Petroleum Economist*, vol. 57 (December 1990), pp. 22–23.

56. See Marsha A. Chandler, "Constitutional Change and Public Policy: The Impact of the Resource Amendment (Section 92A)," *Canadian Journal of Political Science*, vol. 19 (March 1986), pp. 103–26.

insisting that any new constitution provide for a Canadian Senate that gives greater weight to the West and has greater power to block legislation passed by the House of Commons (currently the Senate is essentially a rubber stamp). A central reason for western support for this institutional change is the belief that it would be better able to prevent a repeat of what westerners see as the NEP's raid on provincial resources.[57]

Overlapping federal and provincial jurisdictions do not inevitably lead to conflict, however. The Canadian experience with nuclear power provides an important counterexample. The federal government regulates nuclear power plants, owns a crown corporation that designs and markets nuclear reactors (Atomic Energy of Canada, Ltd.), and has been heavily involved through crown corporations in uranium mining. Provincially owned electric utilities are Atomic Energy's main customers, since efforts to export the reactor design have met with limited success. The interests of the two levels of government have been largely symbiotic in this sector, because the federal government desperately needs a market for its reactors, while the provinces need the power—especially Ontario, where seventeen of twenty Canadian nuclear reactors operate, and dependence on nuclear power is greatest.[58] Although there have been serious delays and cost overruns in the licensing process, antinuclear activists have not been able to use the federal licensing process, pressure on provincial governments, or access to the courts to block nuclear power development in Canada. The greatest threat to the continued development of nuclear power in Canada has come not through direct pressure group activity but from electoral change at the provincial level: in 1990 the social democratic and "green-leaning" NDP won power in Ontario on a platform that included a phaseout of nuclear power in the province. Although the NDP government has been cautious in its statements since

57. On the connection between the NEP and Senate reform, see William Thorsell, "How Trudeau's Energy Policy Sowed the Seeds of Senate Reform," *Globe and Mail* (Toronto), May 30, 1992, p. D6. The package of constitutional reforms, including a more powerful Senate, was defeated in a national referendum on October 26, 1992.

58. Nuclear power also has the advantage over fossil fuel plants of not creating acid rain, an important environmental and political issue in the region. About half of Ontario's electricity is generated by nuclear power. On the nuclear industry in Canada, see generally G. Bruce Doern, *Government Intervention in the Canadian Nuclear Industry* (Montreal: Institute for Research on Public Policy, 1980); and G. Bruce Doern and Robert W. Morrison, eds., *Canadian Nuclear Policies* (Montreal: Institute for Research on Public Policy, 1980). On Atomic Energy's problems, see Matthew L. Wald, "Talking Deals: Help for Canada's Nuclear Industry," *New York Times*, January 10, 1991, p. D2; and Nicholas Hirst, "Candu's Market Meltdown," *Canadian Business*, vol. 64 (October 1991), pp. 56–61.

assuming office, it has ordered Ontario Hydro to emphasize conservation and restraints on demand rather than additional nuclear capacity.[59]

Nor has the issue of how to deal with spent nuclear fuel caused federal-provincial conflict. In this case, conflict has been avoided largely by keeping tough issues off the agenda. As in the United States, spent nuclear fuel is currently stored in pools of water at power plant sites. While planning for a deep underground long-term storage site in the vast and underpopulated Canadian Shield is under way, it has not yet gotten to the stage of identifying particular sites—the point at which the NIMBY problem sets in and "Ottawa-bashing" by the affected province or provinces can be expected to rise exponentially.[60]

However, nuclear power has faced a powerful competitor in Canada: hydro power. In Canada's second most populous province, Quebec, the two leading political parties split over whether to focus on nuclear or hydro development. The provincial Liberal party's vision of a vast hydro development in the James Bay region of northern Quebec as an engine of job creation—both in technology and construction and as a long-term lure for energy-intensive industry—won out over the Parti Québécois' preference for nuclear power in the early 1970s, and the PQ later converted to that strategy as well.[61] In recent years, Quebec and the federal government have sparred repeatedly over whether federal environmental reviews should apply to James Bay and other provincial hydro projects, while the Cree Indians who live in the region have tried to use Canadian courts and environmental review processes to delay or block the second phase of the project and force an earlier and more intensive environmental review.[62] Ironically, conflict *between* provinces has blocked a more effective trade-off of energy and environmental concerns through development of an alternative to the second phase of James Bay development

59. See Michelle Lalonde, "NDP Likely to Veto Nuclear Plants," *Globe and Mail* (Toronto), September 10, 1990, p. A1; and Elaine Verbicky, "Hydro's Nuclear Plans Frozen," *Petroleum Economist*, vol. 58 (March 1991), pp. 5–6.

60. See Atomic Energy of Canada, Ltd., *Managing Canada's Nuclear Fuel Wastes* (1989), especially pp. 17–18; and Ontario Hydro, *Radioactive Materials Management at Ontario Hydro: The Plan for Used Fuel* (May 1991), especially pp. 12–18.

61. See Elaine Verbicky, "Quebec's Hydro Plans at Risk," *Petroleum Economist*, vol. 59 (May 1992), pp. 7–9. Critics within the province have questioned whether energy-insensitive jobs in sectors such as aluminum smelting create as many economic benefits for the province as would the export of equivalent power to the United States. See, for example, Don McDonald, "Quebec Aluminum Jobs Costly, Study Finds," *Globe and Mail* (Toronto), September 3, 1991, p. B7.

62. See, for example, Rhéal Séguin, "Ottawa Being Totalitarian, Quebec Says," *Globe and Mail* (Toronto), March 18, 1992, p. A4; and Geoffrey York, "Quebec Senators Threaten Environmental Bill," *Globe and Mail* (Toronto), June 20, 1992, p. A10.

with much lower environmental costs, namely, expansion of the Churchill Falls hydro project in Labrador. Although the development is in the province of Newfoundland, most of the benefits of the first phase of the project have accrued to Hydro-Québec, which buys the power (the only route to major markets is through Quebec) and resells it at a much higher price. Arguing that it was cheated by the first Churchill Falls agreement, Newfoundland has refused to proceed with the next phase of that project until a more favorable deal can be struck for the second phase.[63]

If Canada's relatively closed, government-dominated decision arena has acted to exclude nongovernmental interests, its proximity and close trade ties to the United States have created new channels of policy access and constraint in recent years. Provisions of the Canada-U.S. free trade agreement of 1988 bar many of the NEP policies that discriminated against American firms and consumers while guaranteeing that Canadian producers will not be subject to any import tax imposed by the United States.[64] In addition, Canadian interests that find themselves excluded from the Canadian policymaking process increasingly find that they may be able to get leverage in the United States. The clearest case to date concerns the next phase of the James Bay hydro project, which will flood hundreds of thousands of acres that are the homeland of Cree Indians. Unable to block the development at the provincial level, the Cree took their lobbying to the New York State legislature. The governor of New York eventually canceled a huge contract to purchase power from Hydro-Québec, which the provincial utility had counted upon to win financing for the project.[65]

Evaluating Canadian Performance

Canada's combination of a party government parliamentary system and federalism has created a policymaking process in which governmental

63. See Barrie McKenna, "Power Strategy," Globe and Mail (Toronto), June 22, 1992, p. B1.

64. See Andre Plourde, "The NEP Meets the FTA," Canadian Public Policy, vol. 17 (March 1991), pp. 14–24; and Robert N. McRae, "Canadian Energy Development under the Free Trade Agreement," Energy Policy, vol. 19 (June 1991), pp. 473–79. American firms have also challenged Hydro-Quebec's policy of providing power at extremely low rates to industrial users in the province as an illegal subsidy.

65. While New York officials cited primarily economic factors in their decision, it was viewed in Quebec as a result of pressure from the Cree. Clyde H. Farnsworth, "Albany Cancellation Threatens Quebec Project," New York Times, March 29, 1992, p. 9; and Rhéal Séguin, "Crees Discredited Quebec 'All over the World,' Minister Says," Globe and Mail (Toronto), April 1, 1992, p. A8.

actors play a central role. Interest groups are especially likely to be excluded from policymaking during supply crises.[66] Relatively diffuse interests (notably consumers and environmentalists) have a particularly
hard time penetrating the process. The overall effect of party government
parliamentary institutions has been to minimize veto points and thus to
increase opportunities for policy innovation and implementation. These
capabilities are especially likely to be in evidence when the policy preferences of the federal and provincial governments coincide, but sometimes—notably with the NEP—when they do not. The NEP case also
illustrates, however, that these party government institutions and active
provincial governments also increase the risk of policy reversal and, when
costs and benefits differ along regional lines, destabilization of the political
system. Similarly, the absence of veto points at which interest groups
can hold policy hostage enhances governmental capability to coordinate
conflicting objectives so long as different levels of Canadian government
do not champion opposing values and defenders of one value cannot
utilize U.S. institutions or bilateral linkages to defend that value. The
associated risk, of course, is that values that do not have a government
as their defender will be ignored.

France

If any country, at first glance, seems the polar opposite of the United
States, it is France. Where the U.S. approach to energy was fragmented,
that of France was single minded. Where the U.S. policymakers were
prone to favor market-oriented solutions, the French were highly interventionist. Unlike Canada, however, in France an interventionist approach to energy policy was born of scarcity rather than abundance. All
three countries promoted domestic energy where possible. In the United
States and Canada, this meant coal, gas, oil, and (in Canada) hydro. In
France this meant nuclear power.

Starting Points

France is poorly endowed with energy resources, importing all but
the most minuscule amounts of petroleum. Domestic coal supplies are
small, low in quality, and expensive to mine (see table A-3). Hydro-

66. See Glen Toner and G. Bruce Doern, "The Two Energy Crises and Canadian Oil
and Gas Interest Groups: A Re-examination of Berry's Propositions," *Canadian Journal of
Political Science*, vol. 19 (September 1986), pp. 467–93.

electric sources are almost all utilized, and alternative energies such as solar, geothermal, and tidal power are all experimental.

Politically, France is a unitary state with a long tradition of state intervention in its domestic economy. French political institutions facilitated an interventionist energy strategy. The French president has a separate mandate from the legislature, but shares powers with the prime minister, who can be defeated by a motion of censure (a no-confidence vote) from the lower house of parliament, the National Assembly.[67] This quasi-parliamentary device tends to allow for more coherent energy policy than in the United States, but—as in Canada—reduces safeguards against policy mistakes.

As is the case in most party government parliamentary systems, the French legislature is much weaker than the executive. The French Constitution puts most levers in the hands of the executive, which can rule significantly by decree, controls the National Assembly's agenda, initiates budget changes, and controls amendments on all bills.[68] Moreover, members of the French legislature have no alternative sources of expertise.[69] In addition, France's system of two-ballot majority elections to the National Assembly creates much higher barriers to entry for "green" parties than Germany's system of modified proportional representation.

The French court system has only recently begun to exercise constraint on the government of the day. Principles of judicial review are enshrined in the French Constitution, and in some cases the Constitutional Council

67. Since the constitution is unclear on the division of powers between the president and prime minister, only a disciplined majority in the National Assembly allows the president to appoint a friendly (subservient) prime minister, permitting the former to exercise his full powers. Otherwise, executive power becomes a prize of coalition building in the parliament. If the coalition partners have strong links and are in opposition to the president, as was the case during "cohabitation" (1986–88), power is concentrated into the hands of the prime minister and his government. If, on the other hand, coalitions are loose and ad hoc, as during the Socialist minority governments of 1988–92, executive power is significantly constrained. For an analysis of the evolution of presidential powers under "cohabitation," see Harvey B. Feigenbaum, "Recent Evolution of the French Executive," *Governance*, vol. 3 (July 1990), pp. 264–78. See also Maurice Duverger, "A New Political System Model: Semi-Presidential Government," *European Journal of Political Research*, vol. 8 (1980), pp. 165–87. If, however, one equates presidential systems with a separation of powers, the cohabitation experience more closely resembles the conflict between the U.S. president and Congress when the two are dominated by opposing parties.

68. For an outline of the government's constitutional powers, see Colin Campbell and others, *Politics and Government in Europe Today* (Harcourt Brace Jovanovich, 1990), pp. 229–31. On the weakness of the parliament, see John Frears, "The French Parliament: Loyal Workhorse, Poor Watchdog," *West European Politics*, vol. 13 (July 1990), pp. 32–51.

69. Harvey B. Feigenbaum, *The Politics of Public Enterprise: Oil and the French State* (Princeton University Press, 1985), chap. 4.

may rule on constitutionality before a law is promulgated.[70] However, lower courts have tended to take the "public interest" as the superior value to individual rights, favoring government decisions over individual complaints on issues such as the siting of nuclear power stations.[71]

France is also highly centralized geographically. While local authorities in France often enjoy more autonomy than is usually assumed, Paris has more leverage over subnational governments than does Washington, Ottawa, or Bonn.[72] Yet even at the national level, the French system is not as highly centralized as it might appear. Examined closely, the highly touted French state is revealed to be a set of fragmented bureaucracies torn by rivalries of turf and clientelistic interest.[73] Overall, the French model is less removed from the American than one might think.

Not surprisingly, this institutional structure contributed to dominance of French energy policy decisions by line departments of the bureaucracy, acting in collusion with producer groups. The ministries involved in energy policy tend to vary according to the particular energy resource in question. The Ministries of Finance and Industry are always involved in nuclear energy matters as well as in "new energy" sources such as

70. The Constitutional Council was considered to be simply a political appendage of the Gaullists for the first two decades after 1958; see Henry W. Ehrmann, *Politics in France* (Little, Brown, 1983), pp. 329–30. John T. S. Keeler, however, has identified a recent trend toward judicial activism, but this may simply have been the result of Gaullist hold-overs ruling on Socialist reforms. See Keeler, "Toward a Government of Judges? The Constitutional Council as An Obstacle to Reform in Mitterrand's France," *French Politics and Society*, no. 11 (September 1985), pp. 12–24. For an analysis placing a heavier emphasis on judicial review, see Alec Stone, "In the Shadow of the Constitutional Council: The 'Juridicisation' of the Legislative Process in France," *West European Politics*, vol. 12 (April 1989), pp. 12–34.

71. Dorothy Nelkin and Michael Pollak, *The Atom Besieged* (MIT Press, 1981), pp. 155–56.

72. For a demystifying view of French local politics, see Jean-Pierre Worms, "Le Préfet et ses Notables," *Sociologie de Travail*, vol. 8, no. 3 (1966); and Mark Kesselman, *The Ambiguous Consensus: A Study of Local Government in France* (Knopf, 1967). Since the Deferred Law of 1982, French politics has become more decentralized in law as well as fact.

73. Harvey B. Feigenbaum, *The Politics of Public Enterprise* (Princeton University Press, 1985), chap. 4. The disappearance of the Gaullists as the dominant party of the Fifth Republic has tended to introduce a spoils system into the French bureaucracy. Whereas the Gaullists had a close relationship with the *hauts fonctionnaires* for over two decades, the successive governments of socialist Mitterrand (1981–86) and the cohabitation government with conservative Chirac (1986–88) made key positions in the bureaucracy overtly political. Changes in personnel at the top often made for cleavages between upper and lower ranks of the bureaucracy. On the close relationship between the Gaullists and the bureaucracy, see Ezra N. Suleiman, *Politics, Power and Bureaucracy in France* (Princeton University Press, 1974), chaps. 11, 13. On the politicization of the bureaucracy under cohabitation, see Feigenbaum, "Recent Evolution," pp. 271–72.

solar or geothermal. The nationalized utility, Electricité de France (EDF), and the Commissaréat á l'Energie Atomique (CEA), as producers, also play a role at the highest levels of decisionmaking.

There is an intimate relationship between state elites and the oil sector, where France has pursued an actively interventionist industrial strategy. The oldest state policy is linked to oil imports; legislation meant to encourage domestic refining dates to the 1860s.[74] The most enduring legislation, guaranteeing 50 percent of the French market to domestically owned importers, was the Law of 1928. The French state took a participatory interest in the Compagnie Française des Petroles (sometimes called the "Eighth Sister" during its heyday) and founded a second, wholly public firm, to search for oil in North Africa in 1939. The idea, if not always the practice, was that state-controlled companies would be more reliable importers of petroleum than foreign companies.[75]

Coal firms were nationalized after World War II. Charbonnages de France acted as a coordinator of nine major coal fields, which together constituted a monopoly of domestic coal production. The coal mines powered much of the postwar reconstruction effort, although France, like the rest of Western Europe, gradually replaced coal with oil for most uses.[76]

Gas and electricity utilities were also nationalized after the war. Gas production was minimal and dwindling, with the Société Nationale des Pétroles d'Aquitaine (later merged with Elf) managing domestic production. EDF, formed out of the merger and nationalization of the country's prewar utilities, became an increasingly important actor, especially as the government embarked on a domestic nuclear power program in the 1960s. Initially, the CEA took a leading role in the program, but lost to EDF as its home-grown graphite-gas reactors proved less economical than the Westinghouse light water design advocated by the national electric company.[77]

74. This was the relatively unsuccessful law of June 4, 1864. See Daniel Murat, *L'Intervention de l'Etat dans le secteur petrolier français* (Paris: Technip, 1969), chap. 1.

75. The public firm, partially privatized in 1977, is now the principal French national champion, marketing oil under the trade name Elf. Feigenbaum, *Politics of Public Enterprise*, pp. 54–86; see also pp. 37–42.

76. Nigel Lucas, *Western European Energy Policies: A Comparative Study of the Influence of Institutional Structure on Technical Change* (Clarendon Press, 1985), p. 10; and Dankwart A. Rustow, "Europe in the Age of Petroleum," in Stephen J. Warnecke and Ezra N. Suleiman, eds., *Industrial Policies in Western Europe* (Praeger, 1975), pp. 193–98.

77. The graphite-gas design originated in the French independent nuclear weapons program. It proved unstable as capacity was scaled up. For an analysis of the relationship of the weapons program to early nuclear reactors, see Lawrence Scheinman, *Atomic Energy Policy in France under the Fourth Republic* (Princeton University Press, 1965). The rivalry of

Conservation was a de facto product of French tax policy. Approximately 10 percent of general revenues were furnished by high taxes on refined petroleum products even before the oil crisis of 1973–74, and autarchic polices made oil at least 10 percent more expensive before taxes than in other European countries. Both of these considerations tend to explain the relatively efficient use of energy before 1973.[78]

Policy Responses

France has dramatically lowered both its overall oil dependence and its dependence on Middle Eastern oil since 1973 (table A-1). But one should be careful in attributing too much of this success to the capacity of the French state or to a coordinated energy policy. French oil companies moved away from their traditional dependence on Middle Eastern supplies primarily as a result of their own desire to rely less on mercurial OPEC governments rather than as a result of government policy. And although energy taxation has been an important vehicle for oil conservation, the fiscal concerns of the Treasury Ministry were more important than energy concerns in promoting this policy.[79] Although the French government has shown some interest in conservation, manifested primarily in the creation of an Agency for Energy Economies by President Giscard d'Estaing, the new agency had a very modest budget.

The major thrust of French energy policy since 1973 has not been on improving energy efficiency, and France's overall record in this area has been poor (table A-1). Instead, France has stressed acceleration of the development of nuclear power and has increased its nuclear power generation far more than any of the other countries discussed here (table

---

EDF, champion of light water technology and CEA, developer of France's original gas-graphite design, was intense. Once the decision was made in favor of light water, CEA settled into its role as a research institute and a fuel cycle provider through its affiliate, COGEMA. See Philippe Simonnot, *Les Nucléocrates* (Grenoble: Presses Universitaires de Grenoble, 1977).

78. Feigenbaum, *Politics of Public Enterprise*, p. 48. On prices relative to other EC countries, see Farid Saad, "France and Oil: A Contemporary Economic Study," Ph.D. dissertation, Massachusetts Institute of Technology, 1969, p. 171ff. For per capita energy use before 1973 in France and five other industrial countries, see Petroleum Finance Company, Ltd., *World Energy Markets: A Framework for Reliable Projections*, World Bank Technical Paper 92 (Washington: World Bank, 1988), pp. 49–52.

79. Gasoline taxes were increased twenty times between 1981 and 1991, and since 1983 gasoline taxes have been indexed for inflation, making tax increases politically easier to accomplish. See James A. Dunn, Jr., "Governing the Automobile in France and the U.S.: The Politics of Motor Fuel Taxes and Infrastructure Funds," paper prepared for the 1992 annual meeting of the American Political Science Association.

A-3). Indeed, the French government has encouraged converting business and residential heating to electricity, which is the least technically efficient method (table A-2). The reason for this shift to *tout électrique* was to conserve foreign exchange, as nuclear-sourced electricity could be paid for in French francs.[80] Unlike the United States, France pressed ahead with a breeder reactor project despite opposition from antinuclear groups.[81]

This implementation success can be attributed to a number of factors, notably a strong bureaucracy with weak legislative and judicial checks, combined with careful strategies of courting local regions by EDF. The bureaucracy in France was able to opt for nuclear power because the decision processes were relatively insulated from public opinion. Although there was considerable resistance to nuclear energy in France, the incapacity of local governments to influence energy decisions in France meant that there were few paths open to the opposition to nuclear power.[82] While frustrated extremists went so far as to launch missiles at a facility, opposition was so localized as to pose little threat to politicians with national constituencies, who simply let bureaucracy's nuclear choice stand. Parliamentary deputies from vociferous regions such as Brittany, lacking real oversight over energy policy, had no place to go and could do nothing but let the government run roughshod over nuclear opposition.[83]

Centralized control of decisionmaking processes also facilitated the cooptation of dissent. The French Socialists renamed the Agency for Energy Economies the Energy Conservation Agency and populated it with energy experts from the Confederation Française et Démocratique de Travail, a Socialist-leaning labor confederation oriented toward environmentalism and quality-of-life issues rather than the more bread-and-butter concerns of other labor unions. This effectively decapitated the chief opposition group to nuclear power while compartmentalizing dissent within the administration.[84] This strategy of cooptation also worked

80. There is considerable loss of energy in converting heat from a nuclear reaction to steam to electricity to heat. Using nuclear power reduces the overall foreign exchange content compared to fossil fuel alternatives because only the unprocessed nuclear fuel is imported. Although France has significant natural uranium reserves, preference was given to imports, primarily from Gabon, in the interests of conserving this natural resource. Gabon, a former French colony, accepts payment in francs.

81. Kitschelt, "Four Theories of Public Policy Making and Fast Breeder Reactor Development."

82. Herbert P. Kitschelt, "Political Opportunity Structures and Political Protest: Anti-Nuclear Movements in Four Democracies," *British Journal of Political Science*, vol. 16 (January 1986), pp. 57–85. For a detailed examination of the public consultation procedures in France (and Germany), see Nelkin and Pollak, *Atom Besieged*.

83. Jasper, *Nuclear Politics*, pp. 247–49.

84. We are grateful to Veronique Maurus for making this point.

at the local level. In France, the prolonged recession of the 1980s had its own effect on local dissent: by 1984 economically depressed Brittany, the only region to succeed in rejecting a nuclear power station, had a change of heart and demanded construction of a reactor to create jobs in the region.[85] When the state controls the principal source of funds for the economic rejuvenation of a depressed region, nuclear energy policy faces few obstacles.

Finally, the centralized French system helped to lower the costs of nuclear power relative to other energy sources and to the costs of nuclear power in other countries. Having a single purchaser of nuclear power plants allowed early standardization of reactor design and construction costs. Centralized licensing systems sped the construction process, reducing interest payments on construction loans.[86]

The French experience with the nuclear waste issue is marked by both similarities and differences with the other countries examined in this chapter. Initially, there was little trouble developing and implementing a solution to the waste storage problem. The first phase of the plan was to establish a waste reprocessing facility at La Hague, which reduced the amount of high-level radiation emitting residues but did not entirely eliminate the problem of storage. This is because reprocessing converts some, but not all, waste into reusable fuel. Although there was significant public criticism of the La Hague facility, the government built it as planned. Union protests over unsafe working conditions led to some stoppages after the plan was completed, but no other public protests made a dent.[87]

Gradually, however, public disaffection grew. Where the underdeveloped regions chosen as potential storage sites were initially receptive, especially to the possibilities for job creation, later the NIMBY syndrome began to take hold. It is interesting that virtually none of the opposition

85. "Bretagne: retour au 'tout electrique,' " *Libération*, April 29, 1984.

86. Standardization produced both economies of scale and learning curve effects allowing each new reactor to benefit from the experience of the old. See J. J. Taylor and G. Moynet, "Effects of Plant Standardization on Investment and Production Costs," in International Atomic Energy Agency, *Nuclear Power and Performance: Conference Proceedings 28 September-2 October, 1987* (Vienna: IAEA, 1988), vol. 1. pp. 211–30; Remy Carl, "Improvements to LWR Technology," paper prepared for the International Meeting on Further Improvements of LWR Technologies, Tokyo, April 1986, pp. (I)-1–2; and W. David Montgomery and James P. Quirk, "Cost Escalation in Nuclear Power," in Lon C. Ruedisili and Morris W. Firebaugh, eds., *Perspectives on Energy: Issues, Ideas, and Environmental Dilemmas* (Oxford University Press, 1978), pp. 347–51.

87. John L. Campbell, *Collapse of an Industry: Nuclear Power and the Contradictions of U.S. Policy* (Cornell University Press, 1988), pp. 172–73.

became politicized along party lines. Because the Socialists were a minority government in a parliament of disciplined parties, this would have
been the only way to block the parliament's designation of sites. Although France's tiny ecological parties were disaffected, the country's
two-ballot majority electoral system ensured that they would be underrepresented in the National Assembly.[88] The only opposition expressed
in parliament was from a few Socialist deputies, and the government
carefully underlined the fact that a final site would be voted on again in
ten to fifteen years by the National Assembly.[89] Thus the French dilatory
solution to waste storage ultimately resembled that of other countries.
Even a government relatively insulated from popular pressures is unlikely
to completely ignore opposition to its policies. Under such conditions
the temptation for policymakers is uniform: delay the decision.

Institutions alone cannot explain the French government's success in
implementing its push for nuclear power, however. The relative scarcity
of domestic energy sources made the atom a logical choice for a focus
of French energy policy. Had there existed a viable competing domestic
energy source, centrifugal forces within the policymaking establishment,
fostered by clientelism, would have been greater. Competition from
foreign energy sources is less significant politically. Importers tend to
make up a very small constituency.[90]

In fact, the only constituency that might have exerted enough influence
over French energy policy to deflect it from the nuclear path was the
coal unions. Initially, coal interests were often placated by government
intervention, ostensibly to promote "national" sources of energy. More
recently, France has acted to phase out subsidies for national coal.[91] It
was able to do so not so much because of insulated policymaking institutions as because of the political characteristics of coal's principal constituency. Miners' unions were a key constituency in the northern Socialist
Federation and benefited from their symbolic long association with French
socialism. When the Socialists first came to power, the government did

88. The increase in support for France's two minuscule green parties in the local elections of March 1992 might be seen as a sign of increased resistance to French energy policy,
but local governments still have little power to interfere with national policies.

89. William Dawkins, "French to Make Cleaner Job of Nuclear Waste," *Financial Times*,
May 15, 1991, p. 3.

90. However, should imported energy be significantly cheaper than domestic sources,
one would expect energy consumers to ally with importers. This is a significant issue in
North Rhine–Westphalia, Germany, where industrial consumers have put pressure on the
state's utility, RWE, to purchase electricity from France.

91. On the decline of coal in France, see Ministère de l'Industrie, des PTT et du
Tourisme, *Les Chiffres Cles de l'Energie* (Paris: Dunod, 1987), pp. 88–91.

what it could to maintain production. However, the austerity programs introduced after the failure of the 1982 reflation forced a reconsideration of all state subsidies, and Charbonnages de France, the nationalized coal company, was forced to shed personnel with minimal resistance from organized labor. This was because politically the unions had nowhere to go. They could not credibly threaten to move to the left, as the Communist party was electorally marginalized. Nor could the unions threaten to support the Conservatives, who advocated the same cost-cutting measures as the Socialists.[92] In short, not only did French policymaking institutions facilitate the nuclear option, but so did the political conditions that might otherwise have influenced French decisionmakers in the direction of coal. Constituency politics is not unknown in France, but, as in the United States, constituencies must have credible alternatives to make their influence felt.

Evaluating French Performance

The French experience in energy policy illustrates both the advantages and dangers of policymaking structures with few veto points. The executive's dominance of the legislature meant that a relatively limited number of insulated individuals could direct their energies to the development of a coherent policy with few encumbrances. Nuclear plant construction rose dramatically after 1974, coal was phased out, and dependence on imported oil was greatly reduced. But energy policy in France was a high-stakes gamble, betting on both the viability of a controversial technology and on continuing high world energy prices, for France's fixed energy cost structure (the construction costs of nuclear plants) would have been a severe competitive disadvantage if world energy prices had collapsed. In a sense, French policymakers traded dependence on mercurial OPEC countries for dependence on still-experimental technologies. A more porous set of policymaking institutions might have forced a diversified approach and, with diversity, a reduction in risk. By contrast, as will become clearer below, Germany's proportional representation electoral rules, federalism, and independent courts, and Japan's Liberal Democratic party's dependence on clients with diverse interests constrained both of these countries from putting all of their eggs in the nuclear basket.

---

92. On this last point, see Harvey B. Feigenbaum, "Democracy at the Margins: The International System and Policy Change in France," in Richard E. Foglesong and Joel D. Wolfe, eds., *The Politics of Economic Adjustment: Pluralism, Corporatism, and Privatization* (New York: Greenwood, 1989), pp. 87–106.

Germany

Germany, like the United States, has tended to leave energy problems to the private (or para-private) sector, intervening sparingly and only at the behest of key constituencies.[93] Not only was there a market bias to German preferences, but German federalism meant that even when government intervention was likely (for example, in licensing nuclear plants), the intervention would come at the state (Land) level. This meant that the German policy communities were more porous to new ideas than in France but less able to implement them.

Starting Points

Germany's level of energy resources is in between that of the United States and France. Economically retrievable coal in Germany has declined substantially (see table A-3). The significant coal deposits in the Ruhr cannot compete with imported coal (principally from China and South Africa) or with nuclear power (if one takes at face value nuclear industry cost estimates on waste storage and plant decommissioning).[94] Germany has no other major energy resources on or under its soil.

Germany's parliamentary political institutions at the national level encourage policy continuity over time through the constitutional mechanism of the constructive vote of confidence or no confidence, which reinforces the stability of the executive by forcing the opposition to agree on a new government in order to replace a sitting chancellor. But Germany's hybrid electoral system also encourages a diversity of interests and ideas by inhibiting single-party majority government.[95] Thus policy debates tend to take place between parties, as well as within them, at least during the period when the governing coalition is constructed. While there may be differences over policy questions between the parties forming the majority, the threat of dissolving a government is usually enough

93. This section focuses on German energy policy before unification with the former East Germany. For a discussion of East German energy problems and the problems posed by unification, see International Energy Agency, *Energy Policies of IEA Countries: 1990 Review* (Paris: OECD, 1991), pp. 213–45.

94. China's coal quality is considered more erratic than South Africa's. Eastern Germany has large deposits of high-sulphur "brown" coal. The reliance by the former East German Communist regime on this source of energy proved environmentally devastating. In addition, the dubious safety of Soviet-built reactors made energy supply a serious problem after reunification.

95. Although half the seats in the German Bundestag are single-member districts, the overall effect is the same as proportional representation, with a relatively high threshold of 5 percent of the vote needed to gain seats.

to keep the coalition partners in line. The same sanction concentrates the minds of recalcitrant backbenchers as well.

German courts have the power of judicial review, and activist judges are willing to make use of their authority. Although activism in Germany is normally associated with the Constitutional Court, where judicial review is a postwar phenomenon, administrative courts have been sensitive to procedural issues regarding energy policy, especially the location of nuclear power plants and radioactive waste storage sites.[96]

Like the United States, the German republic is a federal system. The federal bureaucracy in Bonn is small relative to the Länder bureaucracies, and most legislation must be implemented by the Länder. Regulation of nuclear plants, for example, is left to the Länder.[97] This leads to a diversity of policies and a multiplicity of access points, both of which affect the logic of national energy policy decisions.[98] Nationwide policies are harder to implement, while scale economies of policies conceived or implemented only at the Land level are more difficult to achieve.

Policy Responses

The overall thrust of German energy policy after the oil crises of the 1970s, excepting the subsidies for domestic coal, was market-oriented. Germany's oil policy, for instance, after the first oil crisis of 1973, was simply to allow prices to rise immediately and not to delay adjustment via subsidies or price controls.[99]

However, the German approach to energy is not entirely laissez-faire. The federal government subsidizes the German coal industry as a "national source of energy." The coal industry and unions put pressure on the pro-labor Social Democratic (SPD) government to impose a *Jahr-*

96. David P. Conradt, *The German Polity* (New York: Longman, 1982), pp. 197–200; and Nelkin and Pollak, *Atom Besieged*, pp. 158–66.

97. Peter J. Katzenstein, *Policy and Politics in West Germany: The Growth of A Semisovereign State* (Temple University Press, 1987), p. 20. In the former West Germany, there are ten states (plus Berlin) and over fifty utilities. The unification with the East added five states and one utility. A joint venture of three West German utilities—RWE, Preussenelektrika, and Bayernwerk—took over from the East German state electric grid in 1991. Most of the West German utility companies merely distribute power from the ten largest.

98. A report of the Federal Economics Ministry implied significant problems in this regard, as local governments often preferred subsidizing additional local energy concerns. Bundesministerium für Wissenschaft und Forschung, "Energy Report of the Government of the Federal Republic of Germany," no. 279 (Bonn, September 24, 1986), pp. 38–39.

99. Horst Mendershausen, *Coping with the Oil Crisis: French and German Experiences* (Johns Hopkins University Press, 1976), pp. 67–99.

hundertsvertrag ("century contract"), which requires the utilities to purchase a fixed amount of "national coal," the cost of which is passed along to consumers as the *Kohlepfennig*.[100] The subsidy to coal represents a significant burden, as domestic anthracite ("hard" coal) costs more than twice as much as imported coal. The European Commission has viewed the *Jahrhundertsvertrag* with a jaundiced eye.[101] There is also substantial prodding from France, which wants to sell its cheaper nuclear electricity to German industry. Consequently, subsidies are likely to be phased out after 1995, the end of the century contract.[102]

Electricity prices also rose after the oil crisis of 1973, reflecting fuel costs and encouraging conservation. At least part of the reason for this was the autonomy of the country's utilities. Even though most of the stock in these companies is owned by state and local governments, they operate essentially as private firms.[103] Utility policy is coordinated through their trade association, *Vereinigung Deutscher Elektrizitaetswerke* (VDEW), which facilitates noncoercive planning to avoid overcapacity, not unlike the French style lionized in Andrew Shonfield's classic work.[104] The importance of the VDEW in coordinating the industry's relations with the federal government also remarkably parallels that of trade associations in Japan (see below). Thus Germany's corporatist mode of organizing utilities in the otherwise unhindered market tended to protect them from the dislocations of supply disruption. German tolerance of such trade organizations contributed to a relatively efficient response to energy scarcity.

Germany's unusual system of modified proportional representation also affected energy policy by encouraging the movement away from nuclear power. Parties that garner at least 5 percent of the vote have the right to representation in the Bundestag, which gave representation to the Green party. Although the party collected less than 8 percent of the

100. The first "coal penny" agreement with utilities was signed in 1977. The SPD government also subsidized coal-fired generating plants. See Lucas, *Western European Energy Policies*, pp. 245–46.

101. The commission has allowed the subsidy to continue until 1995 but has gradually reduced the amount of coal qualified for subsidies. Forty million tons qualified in 1990, 36 million in 1991, and 30 million will be allowed in 1993. David Goodhart, "German Coal Subsidy May Be Reduced," *Financial Times*, May 28, 1991, p. 3.

102. Peter Bruce, "Old Friendships Burn Low," *Financial Times*, May 18, 1987, p. 25; and International Energy Agency, *Energy Policies of IEA Countries: 1990 Review*, pp. 214–17.

103. Some companies are privately owned and the largest, RWE, is mostly privately owned, but local governments have a disproportionate share of the voting rights, giving them a majority. See Lucas, *Western European Energy Policies*, p. 216.

104. Andrew Shonfield, *Modern Capitalism: The Changing Balance of Public and Private Power* (Oxford University Press, 1965), chap. 5.

vote in the last three elections, its ability to deprive the SPD of a plurality influenced the SPD's policies.[105] The SPD shifted toward the Green position on nuclear power and the environment to bring its youth vote back into the fold.[106] Thus proportional representation does, in a roundabout fashion, encourage policy innovation.

The SPD government's 1973 energy program initially envisioned nuclear power as the solution to energy supply disruption. This was also the position of the trade unions, which saw plant construction as a source of jobs. However, while nuclear protesters initially had trouble inserting their cause into a politics based on a capital-labor cleavage, they managed to convince Germany's administrative courts that the waste storage issue had not been solved. The courts imposed a de facto moratorium on new plant licenses from 1977 to 1982. After 1982, protest shifted to nuclear missiles rather than reactors, and reactors did not reignite as a public issue until the Soviet accident at Chernobyl.[107]

Like the United States, Germany had difficulty achieving learning-curve gains because of the multiplicity of nuclear plant designs. Initially, the market orientation of the federal government and the utilities fostered entry of several nuclear equipment supplier firms and delayed standardization of reactors. Moreover, the large number of electric utilities in Germany worked against the strategy pursued in the Canadian province of Ontario of minimizing public opposition to plant siting by concentrating new reactor capacity at the sites of existing plants.[108] The unpopularity of nuclear energy resulted in lawsuits and court-imposed cancellations. The SPD jumped on the bandwagon and even formed an

105. The West German Green party fell below the 5 percent threshold in the first postunification election, but the East German Green party, which ran separately in the East, did manage to break the 5 percent barrier.

106. The Soviet accident at Chernobyl also played a role. Moreover, the SPD advocated a ten-year transition period to phase out nuclear power, while the Greens urged immediate elimination of nuclear reactors from the electricity grid. See David Marsh, "The Consensus Lies in Tatters," *Financial Times*, January 14, 1987, p. 24. For a more scholarly discussion, see Christian Joppke, "Nuclear Power Struggles after Chernobyl: The Case of West Germany," *West European Politics*, vol. 13 (April 1990), pp. 178–91; and Joppke, "Models of Statehood in the German Nuclear Energy Debate," *Comparative Political Studies*, vol. 25 (July 1992), pp. 251–80.

107. Joppke, "Nuclear Power Struggles after Chernobyl," pp. 178–82. On the SPD policy change after Chernobyl, see the party's interim report, *Sichere Energieversorgung ohne Atomkraft: Die Lehren aus Tchernobyl: von der Empoerung zur Reform* (Bonn: Vorstand der SPD, Abt. Presse und Information, August 1986).

108. William E. Paterson, "Environmental Politics," in Gordon Smith, William E. Paterson, and Peter H. Merkl, eds., *Developments in West German Politics* (Duke University Press, 1989), pp. 267–88.

antinuclear alliance with the Greens in the state of Hesse. Although the federal government streamlined licensing procedures, the Länder (SPD-dominated) governments and the courts killed nuclear power. Moreover, the largest utilities (such as RWE in North Rhine–Westphalia) found it convenient and cheaper to import French nuclear power than to foster the domestic industry.[109]

The German experience with nuclear waste most approximates that of the United States. With privately owned utilities worried about the bottom line, federal and state governments responsible for licensing reprocessing sites for waste, and a legal system open to the easy intervention of private citizens, nuclear waste was an especially vulnerable issue.[110] Under public pressure, the Länder governments of Lower Saxony and Hesse refused to license reprocessing facilities. A site at Wackersdorf in Bavaria was found, but the Land government demanded federal compensation for the location. After construction delays and cost overruns made the German facility increasingly uncompetitive with the French reprocessing plant at La Hague, Wackersdorf was finally abandoned.[111] A similar fate befell German efforts to develop a fast breeder reactor: a breeder reactor was completed at Kalkar in North Rhine–Westphalia in 1985, but the SPD-led Land government refused to grant it an operating license. Moreover, changes in world uranium market have made it increasingly uneconomic; it will never be used.[112] The apparent end of a plutonium-based nuclear industry in Germany has made finding a long-term storage site for nuclear waste even more critical; the federal agency in charge of long-term storage selected sites at Konrad and Gorleben, but the prospects for avoiding the NIMBY syndrome are not promising.[113]

Germany has not been in the forefront of energy conservation efforts or promotion of nonnuclear technologies. Grant and subsidy schemes to promote energy savings in the residential and industrial sectors were phased out in the 1980s, although more direct measures may have to be reconsidered to implement a 1990 cabinet decision to reduce carbon diox-

109. David Marsh, "West Germany: Dashed Dreams," *Financial Times*, July 4, 1989, Survey, p. V.

110. Campbell, *Collapse of an Industry*, pp. 174–76.

111. Marsh, "West Germany: Dashed Dreams"; and Franz Berkhout and William Walker, "Spent Fuel and Plutonium Policies in Western Europe: The Non-nuclear Weapon States," *Energy Policy*, vol. 19 (July–August 1991), pp. 553–66.

112. Joppke, "Nuclear Power Struggles after Chernobyl," p. 188.

113. David Fishlock, "The Politics of Waste Disposal," *Financial Times*, July 4, 1989, Survey, p. II; Campbell, *Collapse of an Industry*, p. 176; and Joppke, "Models of Statehood," pp. 265–68.

ide emissions 25 percent by the year 2005.[114] Public research budgets have dwindled due to fiscal pressures, but the small government support for energy research and development is also at least partially due to a preference for allowing the market to dictate and supply research agendas. The money available finds its way to supply-increasing measures, especially to nuclear power.[115] A disproportionate share of research and development funding has gone to advanced reactor technologies (breeders, high-temperature gas reactors, reprocessing), all of which were eventually abandoned.

Evaluating German Performance

Germany's innovations in energy policy were left to the market to a much larger degree than in France. Conservation was achieved by letting prices rise, while the only major breach in the government's preference for a laissez-faire approach was to subsidize national sources of coal. Early interest in nuclear power was stymied by opposition groups who made their dissatisfaction known locally at nuclear plant and waste sites and nationally through the Green party and later the SPD. Courts and parties did form roadblocks to certain kinds of innovations. However, nongovernmental organizations such as the VDEW tended to substitute for government intervention in managing energy capacity. So although federalism and activist courts hindered the implementation of Bonn's policies, when they existed, the potential disasters that might have resulted from a wholly laissez-faire approach were frequently circumvented by the fact that the private sector was highly organized. Thus well-disciplined labor unions helped avoid the severe dislocations caused by energy price increases by moderating wage demands and facilitating adjustment,[116] while industry associations, like that of the utilities, coordinated their members' responses to reduce market uncertainties. From the German case one learns that institutional structures make a difference, but frequently their effectiveness can be judged only within a broad societal context.

114. See Eberhard Jochem, "Reducing CO2 Emissions—The West German Plan," *Energy Policy*, vol. 19 (March 1991), pp. 119–26.

115. For German research and development budgets, see International Energy Agency, *Energy Policies and Programs of IEA Countries: 1990 Review*, p. 236.

116. On this last point, see Fritz W. Scharpf, *Crisis and Choice in European Social Democracy*, trans. Ruth Crowley and Fred Thompson (Cornell University Press, 1991), chaps. 2, 7, 9.

Japan

Japanese responses to the oil crises of the 1970s have been largely successful: after a short recession and dizzying inflation in 1974, Japanese economic growth rates returned to the highest levels in the industrial world. While economic output more than doubled between 1973 and 1989, the energy intensity of the Japanese economy declined considerably. During this period Japan diversified its sources of primary energy. It reduced its dependence on petroleum from over 80 percent of its primary energy supply in 1973 to under 60 percent in 1990 (table A-1). Dependence on Middle Eastern sources, which had supplied 85 percent of Japan's petroleum in 1970, were reduced to about 70 percent by 1990.[117] As a proportion of primary energy supply, coal consumption increased slightly, while use of liquified natural gas (LNG) and nuclear power both increased more than tenfold during this period. In addition, despite slack oil prices, Japan has maintained a vigorous research and development program, and conservation has succeeded better in Japan than in any other industrial democracy.

Starting Points

Japan's success must be measured against its own meager resource endowments. Japan is more dependent upon imported energy than any other industrial nation. It imports more petroleum than any nation except the United States and accounts for more than 7 percent of global consumption. Including nuclear power (hardly a fully indigenous energy resource), less than 17 percent of Japan's primary energy is supplied from domestic sources (figure 2). Hydroelectric power, which today produces under 5 percent of Japan's primary energy supply, was fully installed by the 1950s; domestic supplies of coal, which today cover barely 8.5 percent of consumption, were insufficient by the 1960s; and Japanese oil fields do not produce enough petroleum to meet even 1 percent of total demand. There are no domestic uranium mines, and alternative energy sources such as geothermal and synthetic fuels do not yet provide more than 2 percent of Japan's energy consumption.

But resource poverty is just one of the inheritances that define the political economy of Japanese energy policy. A sectoral distribution of

117. It should be noted, however, that the volume of oil imports increased 26 percent from 1988 to 1991, while the percentage of imports from the Middle East increased from 67.6 percent to 72.8 percent over the same period. Derek Bamber, "Imports Heading for a New Record," *Petroleum Economist*, vol. 59 (May 1992), p. 25.

energy demand dominated by manufacturing is equally consequential. Nowhere else in the industrial world do household and commercial consumers consume as small a portion of total national consumption as in Japan. Partly as a result, public and private policies toward energy supplies, production, pricing, conservation, and fuel substitution are disproportionately arrived at by public officials and business leaders. Although homeowners, shopkeepers, and organized labor figure in the determination of these policies, they do so less systematically and less centrally than do capitalists and bureaucrats.

The structure of Japan's energy industries is distinctive in several ways, all of which are relevant to the politics of the energy policy process.[118] First, unlike in Europe, where each industrial state created a "national energy champion" (often as a state-owned monopoly), the Japanese oil, coal, and electric power industries have always been privately owned. Japanese economic policy consistently has been market-conforming, rather than market-displacing. It is easy (and mistaken) to imagine that this is because Japan's renowned bureaucracy presciently shunned state ownership as inefficient. To the contrary, finance and industrial capital in Japan successfully thwarted decades of efforts by the Ministry of International Trade and Industry (MITI) to create a national champion energy corporation in Japan built upon the French or Italian models.

The Japanese oil industry is divided in at least three politically relevant ways. Due to prewar agreements and battles among refiners, suppliers, and foreign interests, it has been truncated vertically for most of the twentieth century. Japanese refiners do not process their own crude oil, and there are virtually no Japanese oil fields at home and few abroad. Refiners downstream are organized as the Petroleum Association of Japan; they have different economic and political interests than the oil-producing firms upstream, organized as the Petroleum Development Association. They often have failed to coordinate their political support for oil policy and have each allied with different parts of a divided Japanese bureaucracy. Second, there are thirty-two separate refining firms in Japan, making oil the most fragmented heavy industry in the Japanese economy. Third, the oil industry is divided into firms that are affiliated with foreign capital and those that are wholly domestic. Although in 1990 there were only two Japanese refiners that were wholly owned by foreign majors (Esso Sekiyu and Mobil Sekiyu), firms with at least minority foreign equity account for half of Japan's refining capacity. The

118. See Richard J. Samuels, *The Business of the Japanese State: Energy Markets in Comparative and Historical Perspective* (Cornell University Press, 1987).

struggle to domesticate this industry has been a central theme in twentieth century Japanese energy policy, and it has divided the industry politically.

The coal industry was divided into large and small firms that frustrated energy policy for decades. The large mines were controlled by the prewar zaibatsu—most prominently Mitsui and Mitsubishi—that used the profits from mining to fund development of their industrial empires. They were confronted within the industry by small mine owners who often succeeded in nurturing local political support to block bureaucratic efforts to consolidate the industry and, in the last days of the industry, to create subsidy programs for coal as a declining sector. Long after the diversified interests of Mitsui and Mitsubishi sought to leave the industry in favor of oil and nuclear power (where they also had interests), the small mine owners used local politicians to slow Japan's energy revolution.

The electric power industry is rather more consolidated. The ten electric utilities are more uniform in size than the coal or oil companies. Since they enjoy regional monopolies, they do not compete with each other, except to attract industry to their region. It is not surprising, then, that the electric power industry is more coordinated in the articulation of its preferences. Indeed, it is one of the most powerful voices in Japanese politics. Fuel choices made by the electric utilities—coal in the 1950s, oil in the 1960s, and nuclear in the late 1970s—are carefully negotiated with suppliers and with the bureaucracy. The stability of these negotiations extends to the vendors of capital equipment as well. The utilities prefer to deal with the same set of "reliable" suppliers over a long period of time, rather than buying technology or fuel through competitive bidding. For example, Tokyo Electric Power has consistently purchased nuclear plants and components from General Electric, Toshiba, and Hitachi, while Kansai has done so from Mitsubishi and Westinghouse. This approach may have resulted in the relatively high capital cost of Japanese nuclear power stations (though financing rates that are low by international standards make this less apparent in the total cost).

There are two accepted forums for the reconciliation of energy policy preferences and for the adjustment of demands among vendors, suppliers, producers, and consumers. The primary forum for coordination within the private sector is the Federation of Economic Organizations (Keidanren), the peak business interest group in Japan that often is referred to as the boardroom for Japanese capital. The Keidanren helped the government develop its original comprehensive energy program, blocked many attempts to nationalize the energy industries, and has coordinated allocative decisions about energy supply and production.

MITI is often the more authoritative forum for this policy coordination, although it is not necessarily more powerful. As the central government agency responsible for the healthy development of Japanese industry, MITI serves both as trade gatekeeper and economic coordinator. MITI has access to detailed information about domestic market activities through its interactions with the Keidanren and the various industry associations. Through its formal advisory commissions that deliberate on matters of production, import, price, and market structure, the ministry is able to supervise Japan's complex and trade-dependent energy economy. Less formally, MITI enjoys power of "administrative guidance," whereby it cooperates with regulated parties (often accepting Keidanren compromises) to find ways to minimize the dislocations of "excessive competition" through coordinated action. In this way, negotiations among different segments of Japanese capital are institutionalized in the energy policy process. For example, steel firms can be enticed to accept more domestic coal than they would prefer and electric utilities can be induced to pay more for nuclear fuel in part because MITI is able to authorize the quids pro quo that policy comprises.

These bargains are also facilitated and enforced by the ruling Liberal Democratic party (LDP). Japan's unique system of multimember electoral districts provides a substantial bonus in seats to the LDP, while encouraging factionalism and localism within the party and discouraging partisan consolidation among the opposition.[119] In Japan's single-party-dominant system, the LDP is frequently required to adjust and coordinate disputes among its constituents, the most powerful of which are industrial and financial interests. The LDP has therefore worked diligently to preserve stable solutions to the wrenching effects of energy crises and industrial restructuring. Although LDP politicians are important players in the iterative negotiations among energy producers and consumers, they are more likely to become advocates than jurists in these negotiations. For example, virtually every prime minister in the postwar period had to impose costs on coal-consuming heavy industry in order to placate mine owners and workers who mobilized legions of local politicians.

The stability and efficacy of the parties to this process are reinforced by a carefully circumscribed but legitimate role for the state in the management of the economy. Through a process of "private ordering," Japanese firms are the principal architects of the regulatory process, not its objects. Administrative guidance is thus a tool both of the regulated

119. See, for example, T. J. Pempel, "Conclusion: One-Party Dominance and the Creation of Regimes," in Pempel, ed., *Uncommon Democracies: The One-Party Dominant Regimes* (Cornell University Press, 1990), pp. 333–60; and Steven R. Reed, "Japan's 1990 General Election: Explaining the Historic Socialist Victory," *Electoral Studies*, vol. 10 (1991), pp. 244–55.

industry and of the government.[120] Japanese firms use the state to enshrine bargains reached after extensive negotiations in a process of reciprocal consent by which state jurisdiction in markets is exchanged for private control. Moreover, in energy matters, these planners are joined by their embrace of the economic ideology of comprehensive security. The Japanese are willing to pay a premium to enhance their national security, which they define broadly to encompass access both to advanced technology and to energy resources. In this view, as many others have noted, economics *is* national security for the Japanese.

Policy Responses

Several institutional innovations in Japanese energy markets after the oil shocks of the 1970s illustrate the politics of reciprocal consent and the implementation of this economic ideology. One was the decision to accelerate the development of nuclear power in the early 1970s (table A-3). A program that had grown steadily since the mid-1950s was suddenly touted as the solution to Japan's dependence upon foreign fuels and rapidly depleting coal reserves. As in France, nuclear power was to become the single largest source of electric power; for much of the 1970s and 1980s, it was touted by public officials, utility executives, and vendors as the most promising avenue for achieving long-sought energy independence and an end to Japanese vulnerability to international political developments. The commitment to nuclear power was also the consequence of a larger national commitment to industrial and technological development.

However, there is no national electric utility in Japan like the French EDF. There are several vendors who build indigenized Japanese reactors, based originally on foreign designs, and are part of the same industrial and financial groups that had dominated the coal industry just decades earlier and now dominate Japanese financial markets. Each works through the Keidanren and with MITI to develop creatively the side payment system that provides incentives to the utilities to expand nuclear capacity and to quiet ecological political opposition at the grass roots. Statutes were passed in 1974 that imposed new taxes on electricity sales, with the revenues used to compensate (or bribe) communities and regions affected by new power plants; the compensation formula was especially generous

120. The term *private ordering* was first used to characterize administrative guidance by Michael R. Young, "Judicial Review of Administrative Guidance: Governmentally Encouraged Consensual Dispute Resolution in Japan," *Columbia Law Review*, vol. 84 (May 1984), pp. 923–83.

for nuclear projects.[121] Another part of this tacit agreement allows the utilities to pay more than the world market price for nuclear fuel and to treat stockpiled fuel as a capital expense. This expense generates a risk-free return to the utilities that is above market rates, facilitates investment in new nuclear capacity, and subsidizes industrial consumption, since the costs are borne disproportionately by households and commercial establishments.[122]

Japan is hardly immune from NIMBY problems in the nuclear industry, however. Domestic opposition to nuclear power has grown in recent years, spurred in part by several accidents at Japanese nuclear power plants, long considered the world's safest. Nuclear activists have not succeeded in shutting down any plants, and construction continues on new reactors at the site of current plants, which do not require new approvals by local governments. But it has become increasingly difficult, costly, and time consuming to find the new sites for nuclear reactors needed to meet the Japanese government's targets for growth of the nuclear industry. Lead times for construction of nuclear power plants increased to almost fifteen years in the 1980s, and government projections of the growth of nuclear plant capacity have repeatedly been cut back.[123]

Japan's long-term plans for dealing with nuclear waste have also encountered setbacks. Plans to develop a long-term storage site for nuclear waste have been delayed by public opposition in Hokkaido supported by Socialist party officials in the prefectural government. Japan proposes to solve its long-term waste disposal problem in part by reprocessing used fuel for use in plutonium reactors. This has the additional advantage of reducing dependence on uranium imports. But plans to increase domestic reprocessing capacity have been seriously delayed, and Japanese plans to ship waste fuel to Europe by sea for reprocessing have sparked concern from both the United States and the International Atomic Energy

---

121. See S. Hayden Lesbirel, "Implementing Nuclear Energy Policy in Japan: Top-down and Bottom-up Perspectives," *Energy Policy*, vol. 18 (April 1990), pp. 267–82, especially pp. 271–72; Samuels, *Business of the Japanese State*, pp. 246–47; and more generally, Thomas C. Lowinger, "Japan's Nuclear Energy Development Policies: An Overview," *Journal of Energy and Development*, vol. 15 (Spring 1990), pp. 211–30.

122. This argument is elaborated in Richard J. Samuels, "Consuming for Production: Japanese National Security, Nuclear Fuel Procurement, and the Domestic Economy," *International Organization*, vol. 43 (Autumn 1989), pp. 625–46.

123. See Lowinger, "Japan's Nuclear Energy Development Policies," pp. 226–27; Lesbirel, "Implementing Nuclear Energy Policy in Japan," p. 268; T. R. Reid, "Japanese Wrangling over Future Energy Policy," *Washington Post*, February 3, 1991, p. A18; David E. Sanger, "A Crisis of Confidence for Japan's Nuclear Power Strategy," *New York Times*, July 1, 1991, p. D1; and Tatsujiro Suzuki, "Japan's Nuclear Dilemma," *Technology Review*, vol. 94 (October 1991), pp. 41–49.

Agency that shipments of weapons-grade plutonium returning to Japan could be subject to terrorist attacks. Japanese utilities have been unenthusiastic about using plutonium in any case, since the world glut in uranium has made it a far cheaper fuel to use. As a result, Japan's nuclear industry faces a potentially huge glut of highly lethal plutonium in the next century.[124]

Fewer implementation problems have arisen in Japan's efforts to increase oil stockpiles to protect against a supply disruption. After the first oil shock, MITI sought to get Japanese oil companies to cooperate to develop ninety-day oil stocks. The companies resisted these pressures, arguing that the government should pick up the bulk of the costs for this effort, and it eventually did so.[125] Currently, Japanese private firms and public agencies together maintain the world's largest stockpile of petroleum (142 days).

Similar patterns are evident in policy for the development of alternative energy resources. After the Iranian revolution and the second oil shock in 1979, the Japanese began to take seriously alternative energy research and development. As in the United States, the preferred solution of the economic bureaucrats was the creation of a new public entity, a Japanese synthetic fuels corporation. MITI submitted legislation for a state-owned alternative energy public corporation in 1979. The Ministry of Finance (MOF) objected on fiscal grounds, and the Keidanren objected to this new form of state intervention in the economy. After business and MOF opposition had been vetted, the Diet passed legislation creating the New Energy Development Organization (NEDO). To placate MOF, new taxes were placed on petroleum and electricity consumption earmarked to support this new institution, and to satisfy business, the chairman of the Keidanren was made the chairman of NEDO.

Perhaps Japan's greatest success in energy policy is in promoting conservation. It has done so by sending a consistent set of signals—including energy price increases—to industrial consumers as well as residential consumers. The Japanese government introduced a variety of measures to encourage energy conservation after the first oil shock, including low-

124. See Suzuki, "Japan's Nuclear Dilemma"; David E. Sanger, "Japan's Quiet Plan to Import Plutonium Brings a Shudder of Nuclear Anxiety," *New York Times*, November 25, 1991, p. D8; T. R. Reid, "Tokyo Official Criticizes Nuclear Power Program; Expert Fears Proliferation of Plutonium," *Washington Post*, April 22, 1992, p. A24; and David E. Sanger, "Japan Is Cautioned on Plan to Store Tons of Plutonium," *New York Times*, April 13, 1992, p. A2.

125. Ronald A. Morse, "Japanese Energy Policy," in Wilfrid L. Kohl, ed., *After the Second Oil Crisis: Energy Policies in Europe, America and Japan* (Lexington, Mass.: Lexington Books, 1982), pp. 255–70; and Samuels, *Business of the Japanese State*, pp. 213–14.

interest loans, depreciation provisions, and tax incentives to encourage energy-efficiency in manufacturing. MITI has also encouraged Japanese companies to move away from traditional energy-intensive industries into less energy-intensive sectors.[126] As a result, while Japan increased its real GNP by 81 percent between 1973 and 1988, it increased energy demand by only about 16 percent. The trend was even more pronounced in the manufacturing sector: real value added increased by 64 percent in this period, while energy use fell by 12.5 percent—and oil use fell by 42 percent.[127]

Evaluating Japanese Performance

The Japanese case suggests generally high marks for each of the governmental capabilities assessed in this chapter: innovation, coordination of conflicting objectives, and policy implementation. But it also suggests that by focusing upon the formal institutions of governance, one runs the risk of understating the importance of the informal ones: the policy networks, subgovernments, regimes, and norms that govern elite interactions. Energy policy innovations, like those in other areas, are made not by single institutions for singular reasons, but by webs of individuals and institutions that negotiate and reciprocate in the expectation of future exchange. The stability of these players and of their network is more directly the product of bargains shaped by market structures than by constitutional forms.

Neither does "centralization" adequately convey the subtlety of these interactions. Japanese public administration is centralized but "vertically fractured." Policy innovation flourishes (indeed, may be nurtured) in a centralized system in which central institutions are mutually insular and where they must compete vigorously to maintain their power. Japanese energy politics is characterized by relentless competition among bureaucratic interests and their subgovernmental allies in the LDP and business.

126. See Shigeko N. Fukai, "Japan's Energy Policy," *Current History*, vol. 87 (April 1988), pp. 169–72; and Kenichi Yoda, "Japan's Energy Conservation Policy," *Industry and Environment*, vol. 13 (May–June 1990), pp. 8–11.

127. International Energy Agency, *Energy Policies of IEA Countries: 1990 Review*, p. 297; and Richard B. Howarth and Lee Schipper, "Manufacturing Energy Use in Eight OECD Countries: Trends Through 1988," *Energy Journal*, vol. 12 (April 1991), pp. 18–23. Additional data on Japanese energy consumption reported in this section are derived from British Petroleum, *Statistical Review of the World Energy Industry*, 1981, 1990; International Monetary Fund, *International Financial Statistics*, 1987, May 1990; *Japan Petroleum and Energy Trends*, August 10, 1990; and "Oil Prices and the Japanese Economy," *JEI Report*, no. 33A (August 24, 1990).

Finally, the Japanese energy policy regime is part and parcel of the ways in which market players and government officials develop economic priorities and strategies more generally in Japan. It cannot be explained without an understanding of Japanese resource dependency and without an appreciation of how the Japanese define their comprehensive security, and it cannot succeed without tolerance of higher domestic prices for goods and services by individual consumers. In the belief that value added at the doorstep of the consumer enhances economic security (and indeed technological development), the Japanese invested in high-cost oil refining and nuclear fuel for the same reason they invested in high-cost aluminum smelting, jet aircraft production, soda ash manufacturing, chemical fertilizers, and other inefficient and noncompetitive but import-substituting projects. If consumers are willing (or can be convinced) to defer consumption and subsidize production, Japanese industry will contribute over the longer run to a more secure, less dependent, and more technologically sophisticated economy that serves the interests of producers and consumers alike. Thus, what might otherwise be a simple economic story about prices is really a political story about the interaction of institutions, national security, and market ideology.

Patterns and Explanations

The differing policy environments confronted by governments seriously complicate the task of working back from an evaluation of energy policy outcomes to an assessment of government capabilities. Some of the Japanese government's success at innovation and policy implementation, for example, must be attributed less to high capabilities—a general ability to influence the environment—than to a societal environment that had a narrower range of producer interests and fewer viable options to consider. Implementing an ambitious program of expanding nuclear energy is likely to be much easier in a country like France, where there is a monopsonistic purchaser of power plants able to take advantage of economies of scale in plant design and construction.

It is also difficult to create an analytical level playing field for assessing capabilities of systems in which policymaking elites are drawn from a relatively narrow spectrum of opinion (notably party government parliamentary systems) versus those in which broader views are represented (the U.S. separation-of-powers system, for example). If innovative capacity is measured as the ability of central executive elites to enact their preferences, for example (as is true in most of the literature on strong

Table 2. Government Capabilities in the Energy Sector in Five OECD Countries

Country	Capability		
	Innovation	Coordination of conflicting objectives	Implementation
United States	*Mixed:* many programmatic innovations but difficulty adopting comprehensive and loss-imposing policies; repeated stalemate over energy pricing, exploration and taxation; reversal in case of synfuels; perverse results for some policies	*Low:* any changes from the status quo that would cause losses for most affected groups blocked by veto points	*Mixed:* reversal required in auto fuel economy; numerous nuclear plants delayed or canceled; legislative-executive sparring over Strategic Petroleum Reserve and breeder reactor
Canada	*High but unstable:* major innovation in NEP reversed by Mulroney government; disarray in energy sector created by NEP policies	*Mixed:* conflict and reversal over energy pricing and taxation; some disruption caused by intergovernmental conflicts over environment and pricing	*Fairly high:* conflicts between levels of government and between provinces causing some implementation problems
France	*Fairly high:* strengthened commitment to nuclear power; phasedown of coal; increased consumption taxes	*Fairly high:* environmental resistance to nuclear power development; energy efficiency concerns subordinated to development of nuclear industry	*High:* especially in siting nuclear power plants; less success in siting permanent nuclear waste disposal site
Germany	*Moderate:* phasedown of domestic coal successful	*Fairly high:* private-sector coordination substituted for activist national government	*Mixed:* courts and Länder governments used by nuclear protesters to delay program; successful policy of allowing energy prices to rise
Japan	*High:* strengthened commitment to nuclear power, conservation and new technologies; oil stockpile program created	*Very high:* continued high economic growth retained despite energy shocks; protests against nuclear power largely deflected	*Fairly high:* substantial success in conservation; expansion of nuclear power industry slowed but not stopped by protests

versus weak states), the success rate for energy policy innovations relative to the agenda of proposals seriously considered will almost certainly appear higher in systems where a unified government elite is able to monopolize agenda setting. In assessing innovative capacity, however, it is crucial to look not just at how successful a government is in adopting its own agenda, but also at whether those innovations represent plausible responses to the problems government is trying to address and whether they have in fact promoted those objectives or had perverse consequences. Similarly, in assessing capacity to coordinate objectives, a greater variety of objectives is almost inevitably visible in systems where there are contending centers of power, even if those objectives are not embodied in policy. In assessing coordination of objectives, it is necessary to analyze the conflicting objectives pursued not just by elected politicians but by all important actors in the society.

Keeping these analytical caveats in mind, it is possible to make rough assessments of each of the five governments' institutional capacity for innovation, coordination, and implementation as exhibited in the energy policymaking case. These assessments, summarized in table 2, suggest that governmental capacities do differ across countries in important ways.

The case studies also suggest that institutional structures can have important effects on each of these capabilities. The number and effectiveness of veto points and the porousness of governmental structures to interest group pressures are especially critical. Controversial tasks such as nuclear power plant construction and energy tax increases are easier to accomplish if naysayers are excluded from the process. But the institutional determinants of these three capabilities are not limited to the separation or fusion of executive and legislative power. The relationship of national to local governments, the independence of the courts, and the power and competence of the bureaucracy are also important institutional determinants of government capabilities. Noninstitutional factors play a critical role as well. The cases suggest the following conclusions.

1. *Policy and resource inheritances are more important in determining energy policy choices than are governmental capabilities or specific institutional arrangements.* What is most striking about the cases examined in this chapter are the broad similarities in energy policy debates and choices between the two countries with very large domestic energy resources—Canada and the United States—and their differences from the three countries that are much more dependent on energy imports. These basic differences led to differing coalitions, consumption patterns, and capital stocks, which in turn contributed to differences in matters such as gasoline pricing and taxation.

Differing policy and institutional inheritances also generate variations in policy response. It is not surprising that France, with its long history of public enterprise involvement in energy production, would choose a policy emphasizing state direction, while the United States, with its reliance primarily on regulation, would continue in a regulatory mode.[128]

2. *Party government parliamentary systems offer significant opportunities for policy innovation, but also pose significant risks of policy and political instability.* The absence of veto points that characterize party government systems— at least when they produce single-party majority governments—clearly enhances innovative capacity once government has decided on a preferred course of action, as the Canadian National Energy Program shows. A similar proposal almost certainly would have been delayed and watered-down in the United States, as President Carter's less dramatic energy proposals were. But the dangers of policy reversal are commensurately high, especially where policy interests and prescriptions of the two largest parties are radically different. Even more important, the NEP case suggests that dramatic central government actions that are strongly opposed by regional or other minorities may deepen political cleavages and increase the potential for constitutional or political instability.

3. *Minority government in parliamentary systems and divided government in the U.S. system can promote as well as hinder policy innovation.* The conventional wisdom on both of these types of government is that they are conducive to stalemate. For example, minority governments might be expected to be cautious about introducing policy innovations for fear of losing a vote of confidence in their legislatures. Of course, governments may sometimes be overly confident and miscalculate, as the Clark government in Canada did with its gasoline tax proposals in 1979. But minority governments may also need to trade specific policy innovations to obtain or ensure support from other parties. The creation of Petro-Canada by the Trudeau government in 1973 was at least in part a response to this political imperative.

In the United States, the cycle of supply crises and gluts has been a more important determinant of the timing of energy policy innovation than whether the government has been unified or divided. This is consistent with David Mayhew's finding that divided government has had little impact on the overall legislative output of the U.S. federal government—and by implication, little effect on policy innovation.[129] A large part of government's agenda and its legislative output is determined by forces that are not likely to vary between periods of united and divided government. Moreover, divided government may lead to more proposals

---

128. See Feigenbaum, *Politics of Public Enterprise*; and Ikenberry, "Irony of State Strength."
129. Mayhew, *Divided We Govern*, especially p. 179.

moving forward on the congressional agenda, as congressional leaders from the nonpresidential party seek to make a record for themselves and their party. Thus, even if the success rate of these proposals is lower, the legislative volume may be the same. Divided government may lead either to "stalemate" or to a "bidding up" phenomenon, depending on the political and policy calculations made by policymakers (see the chapters by Allen Schick and David Vogel).

Most of the major energy policy innovations in the United States occurred in the aftermath of the 1973 and 1979 oil shortages, but because these crises heightened consumer fears, they did not facilitate action on price deregulation. Much of the latter (for example, the 1989 natural gas act) occurred as "stealth" innovations during supply gluts, when consumer forces were often divided and the lower salience of the issue cooled politicians' fears of being identified with greedy producers.

4. *The U.S. system generates a lot of innovation that is not necessarily effective, coordinated, or stable.* The energy policy agenda in the United States has been crowded with a variety of conflicting proposals. Moreover, multiple veto points throughout the U.S. policymaking system did not prevent the creation of a huge array of new programs (for example, synfuels, CAFE standards, a windfall profits tax, national interstate speed limits, energy tax credits, low-income energy assistance) in the aftermath of the oil shocks. The sheer number of programs created— and in several cases later repealed or heavily modified—was far higher than in any of the other countries surveyed here. Nor have the seemingly endless debates on many proposals prevented the adoption of programs that had perverse effects (the oil refinery entitlements of the 1970s, for example); indeed, these debates have almost certainly enhanced the risks of such provisions by elevating political feasibility as a value over administrative feasibility.

What is particularly striking about most U.S. energy innovations, however, is that few of them imposed large, visible monetary costs on consumers; indeed, they were intended to avoid doing so. Bold market-conforming initiatives that would have enhanced conservation and energy security by raising consumer costs have almost always ended in stalemate or failed to get on the agenda altogether.

The reason for this pattern is that the U.S. system provides multiple points of influence or access for interest groups and politicians as well as veto points. This allows many legislators to press their own pet ideas or regional interests onto the policy agenda but makes it difficult to enact coherent multifaceted proposals in the absence of a policy consensus— which seldom exists. Putting together a winning coalition often requires both forgoing the most controversial changes and including projects that appeal to some set of legislators without threatening the interests of any. Logrolling and incrementalism displace broad and coordinated major policy change. And when programs provide disproportionate benefits to a few regions, they may be difficult to sustain, as occurred with Synfuels.

5. *Systems with different numbers of veto points are prone to different kinds of innovation errors.* Governments may err by enacting policies that have serious, often unforeseen, flaws or are less efficacious than potential alternatives. They may also err by innovating too little. The energy case makes clear that judgments about whether too much or too little innovation has occurred are time-bound. The benefits of natural gas deregulation in the United States are far more obvious in retrospect than they seemed to most participants in 1978, for example. And the French and Japanese decisions to press ahead with fast breeder reactor programs while the United States abandoned Clinch River before actual construction looked far wiser from the perspective of the late 1970s than they do from the perspective of the early 1990s. Judgments about policy "mistakes" are also likely to depend on what outcomes observers value.

Judgments about institutional proclivities for policy mistakes must therefore be made cautiously, but some tentative conclusions can be drawn. It will be recalled that a parliamentarist perspective suggests that the U.S. system is prone to insufficient policy innovation because those with a stake in the status quo will block policy changes that damage their interests. A presidentialist position, on the other hand, suggests that policy reversals and big mistakes are less likely to be made in less centralized systems. The case studies here suggest that each of these positions needs to be recast. The United States is less likely to undertake innovations involving major loss impositions or requiring effective geographic targeting and more likely to make big mistakes involving failure to adapt enough, quickly, or at all. But the United States is unlikely to engage in massive and costly reversals on the scale of Canada's National Energy Program. Both systems make major innovation errors, but they are different kinds.

6. *A wide variety of parliamentary arrangements present opportunities for significant and stable policy innovation.* Lasting energy policy innovation was achieved in Japan, France, and Germany (in rough descending order) despite enormous differences in their parliamentary institutions. However, there are important similarities in their decisionmaking attributes, notably limited access to policy formulation and relatively cohesive and stable elites. These decisionmaking attributes have been achieved through differing, and sometimes informal, institutional roots, however. In Japan, the institutional centers of these arrangements are a strong bureaucratic tradition and an electoral system that has facilitated the dominance of

the Liberal Democratic party. Although there are strong rivalries within both the LDP and the bureaucracy, repeated interaction among this relatively stable group of elites facilitates bargaining, compromise, and, if necessary, side payments needed to pave the way for policy innovation. In France, these mechanisms are centered on an expert and autonomous state bureaucracy with close ties to national champions (such as EDF or Elf). The French electoral system, meanwhile, makes it difficult for new parties to put issues on the agenda if the major parties and bureaucracy have reached a consensus. This system makes major policy gyration likely only on issues that coincide with the dominant left-right cleavage in French politics and upon which the major parties have not reached an accommodation. In Germany, the system is more porous to influence by new parties, especially at the Land level. But the prolonged pattern of majority coalitions in Bonn anchored by the centrist Free Democrats has also contributed to patterns of elite stability and limited access to policy formulation.

7. *Whether federalism promotes or inhibits policy innovation and implementation depends upon the structural relations between the levels of government and the nature of the policy change.* Federalism is often touted as a source of experimentation that can promote more policy innovation than is likely to be found in more centralized states. The energy policy case suggests that this is, at best, an overgeneralization. Federalism has many variants: for example, subnational governments may have exclusive jurisdiction over a policy sector, the national government may make policy decisions but rely on subnational governments for implementation, innovation may require the direct approval of both levels of government, or both the subnational and federal governments may have discretion to act without the approval of the other. These different types of federal relationships may all coexist within the same country: in the United States, for example, the federal government and the states can both levy gasoline taxes independently, and the federal government and individual states both play a role in granting permits for individual nuclear power plants.[130]

Whether federalism inhibits or promotes policy innovation depends on the distribution of costs and benefits of innovation as well as on the nature of relations between national and subnational governments. Federalism is most likely to stimulate innovation when subnational units can act autonomously and there are economic or political benefits that can be captured by acting early. Provincial government actions in Canada to stimulate development of their indigenous energy resources are a good

---

130. See, for example, Joseph F. Zimmermann, "Regulating Atomic Energy in the American Federal System," *Publius*, vol. 18 (Summer 1988), pp. 51–65.

example of this phenomenon.[131] But if innovation involves imposing losses (for example, imposing higher energy consumption taxes), there are strong incentives to be laggards, especially if those suffering losses can vote with their wheels (for example, by buying gasoline in another state or moving a business out of state). Policy innovation will be rejected unless the subnational units can find a way to act collusively (which gets more difficult as the number of such units rises) or the central government preempts action at the subnational level. If subnational governments hold veto power over central government decisions, policies that impose costs on a region or its citizens (such as siting of nuclear waste disposal sites) are less likely to be adopted and even less likely to be implemented; if the subnational government is responsible for implementation but has no veto, implementation will presumably be slower and less complete but will not be blocked entirely.[132]

8. *Formal or informal countervailing mechanisms can overcome some of the obstacles to innovation and implementation posed by multiple veto points, but only if there is acquiescence by most major interests.* Granting discretion to the president, executive departments, independent regulatory commissions, or special commissions established to break through an impasse can make decisions less susceptible to veto and provide political cover. Each of these options was used in the aftermath of the oil shocks in the United States, but they usually were given very little discretion or were not seen as providing sufficient cover. The Ad Hoc Energy Committee established in the House in 1977 failed to resolve the jurisdictional disputes and produce a comprehensive energy bill acceptable to the Senate. Congress gave Presidents Ford and Carter executive discretion to decontrol oil prices (thus getting the onus off legislators for doing so), but they were unwilling to pay the political price of doing so fully; as a result,

131. See, for example, H. V. Nelles, *The Politics of Development: Forests, Mines and Hydro-Electric Power in Ontario, 1849–1941* (Toronto: Archon, 1974); John Richards and Larry Pratt, *Prairie Capitalism: Power and Influence in the New West* (Toronto: McClelland and Stewart, 1979); and Robert Bourassa, *Power from the North* (Scarborough, Ont.: Prentice-Hall, 1985).

132. Federalism, and the form chosen, is often not endogenous in policy decisions. The distribution of potential costs and benefits from proposed innovations may strongly affect whether a federal regime is chosen to govern policy in a given policy area and, if so, what form of federalism is chosen. A federal policy regime is likely to be chosen when there are regional differences in the distribution of costs and benefits and thus uncertainty over the shape of choices made at the national level and binding on all subnational governments. Federalism appears to inhibit innovation in the energy sphere both because so many potential innovations involve imposition of concentrated costs and because fear of incurring costs has often led to the adoption of federal regimes that create multiple veto points. Examples include licensing of nuclear power plants and disposal of nuclear wastes.

prices remained below world market levels until President Reagan came into office. Independent regulatory commissions could have taken some of the pressure off Congress and the president to keep energy prices down, but instead of giving these bodies increased discretion, Congress increasingly interfered with their actions to control prices. And Congress almost created an energy mobilization board in 1980 that would have preempted other agencies' decisions and facilitated implementation of energy projects, but opposition from several quarters killed the idea.[133] The problem in the energy sector has been that there was too much disagreement—both over policy substance and policy control—to agree on effective countervailing mechanisms; doing so would have forced some current participants to sacrifice control over policymaking.

9. *Systems with different numbers of veto points are prone to different sorts of coordination errors.* Systems with many veto points and broad group access, like the United States, are prone to implement a number of different objectives in an uncoordinated manner. Systems with fewer veto points, and mechanisms in place to avoid policy gyrations, are likely to make more efficient trade-offs, but in so doing, tend to ignore completely the values held by some actors in the system, as the French, and to a lesser extent the Japanese, have done in their nuclear energy programs.

10. *Government capability to implement policy decisions depends more on bureaucracy, federalism, and judicial review than on the separation or fusion of executive and legislative power.* Multiple veto points and low elite cohesion inhibit governments' capacity for policy implementation as well as policy innovation. But because policy innovation and implementation often take place through different institutions, institutional capacity for these capabilities may vary significantly across countries and to a lesser extent across sectors within a single country. A good example is Germany, which has a relatively closed and centralized policy formulation process but a more open implementation process in many sectors.[134]

Legislative autonomy from the executive, made possible by the separation of powers in the United States, both permits and encourages

---

133. Another strategy is to limit potential blame by tying innovation or implementation to automatic triggers. President Carter's 1977 energy package, for example, would have triggered incremental increases in a "standby" gasoline tax if gasoline consumption passed specified levels. For this technique to succeed, policymakers need to be in agreement on desired outcomes but in need of a political fig leaf to cover their agreement. In addition, of course, there must be a policy trigger available that produces an acceptable outcome. See R. Kent Weaver, "Setting and Firing Policy Triggers," *Journal of Public Policy*, vol. 9, no. 3 (1991), pp. 307–36.

134. See Kitschelt, "Political Opportunity Structures and Political Protest."

Congress to directly affect the policy implementation process. In both the United States and countries with parliamentary systems, however, legislators are usually secondary players in implementation relative to bureaucrats (and in some systems, judges and subnational governments) once programs are set up. The major impact of the autonomous legislatures is probably in designing specific programs' implementation processes: who implements and how much discretion they have, who has access to the process, and what choke points are available to block implementation.

Bureaucracies that have a monopoly on expertise can aid implementation by disguising potential costs from affected interests, as in France. This is much harder in the United States because expertise is so broadly diffused among branches and among interest groups.

Implementation by subnational governments tends to generate conflict between the central government and state governments with different priorities. Even in highly centralized Japan, obstacles posed by subnational governments have been an important hindrance to implementation of the central government's nuclear power development strategy; these obstacles have been even more severe in Germany and the United States. An independent judiciary provides an additional point at which decisions may be challenged. Because political systems vary in so many ways in their access and veto points, it is impossible to generalize across political systems about which institutional obstacles to implementation are most important. Interest groups, understandably, try to utilize their limited resources where they think that it will do the most good, whether that be in court, before state and local agencies, or in election campaigns.[135]

11. *Government success in policy innovation, coordination of conflicting objectives, and policy implementation depends at least as much on the nature of social organization as on institutional structures.* Policy change usually means that someone will be made worse off, in either direct welfare or values. Elite cohesion and absence of institutional veto points can make it easier to compel losers to accept, but politicians generally seek alternatives (notably disguising or compensating) that incur less blame. It is easier to impose losses if winners and losers are within the same organization, giving organizational leaders mixed incentives and allowing them to impose losses and compensate losers internally, without the direct involvement of government. For example, the ability of Japanese interest groups to organize sectorwide mechanisms for allocating energy capac-

---

135. See the analysis in Kitschelt, "Political Opportunity Structures and Political Protest."

ities and supplies made it easier for their government to cooperate with them in doing so.

Conclusion

Political institutions play an important role in influencing government capabilities to innovate in policymaking, coordinate conflicting objectives, and implement policies. In particular, the number and effectiveness of veto points in the political system has a strong effect on each of these capabilities. However, the distinction between parliamentary systems and the U.S. separation-of-powers systems does not go very far in explaining differences in institutional capabilities. With respect to policy innovation and coordination, differing types of parliamentary systems display distinctive patterns of institutional capabilities. When it comes to implementing existing policies—notably in the area of nuclear power—federalism and an independent judiciary seem to have a greater effect on a government's capacity than does the separation or fusion of executive and legislative power.

Table A-1. *Changes in Energy Consumption Patterns in Five OECD Countries, 1973–90*

Country and energy use	1973	1990	1990 as percent of 1973
Energy consumption per capita[a]			
Canada	6.94	7.90	113.85
France	3.39	3.91	115.32
Germany	4.26	4.40	103.22
Japan	2.96	3.47	117.16
United States	8.13	7.58	93.22
Energy consumption in relation to GDP[b]			
Canada	0.66	0.52	79.14
France	0.44	0.37	83.79
Germany	0.53	0.39	73.93
Japan	0.37	0.25	69.11
United States	0.58	0.42	71.96
Net oil imports (millions of metric tons of oil equivalent)			
Canada	−14.18	−15.05	n.a.
France	131.44	87.93	66.90
Germany	147.06	110.07	74.85
Japan	271.59	255.13	93.94
United States	300.81	369.31	122.77
Net oil imports as percent of energy supply			
Canada	−9.26	−7.16	. . .
France	74.33	39.83	. . .
Germany	55.68	39.57	. . .
Japan	84.49	59.58	. . .
United States	17.46	19.38	. . .

n.a. Not available.

Sources: International Energy Agency, *Energy Balances of OECD Countries, 1989–1990* (Paris: Organization for Economic Cooperation and Development, 1992), pp. 90, 102, 106, 126, 170, 186.

a. Primary energy supply (measured in metric tons of oil equivalent) per capita.

b. Primary energy supply (measured in metric tons of oil equivalent) per million 1985 U.S. dollars.

Table A-2. *Inputs to Electricity Generation in Five OECD Countries, 1973 and 1990*

	Inputs									
	Oil		Gas		Solid fuels		Hydro		Nuclear	
Country	1973	1990	1973	1990	1973	1990	1973	1990	1973	1990
Canada	3	3	6	2	13	18	72	62	6	15
France	40	2	6	1	20	9	26	13	8	75
Germany	14	2	12	8	65	53	5	4	4	33
Japan	74	32	2	19	8	14	14	11	2	24
United States	17	4	19	9	45	56	14	10	5	21

Source: International Energy Agency, *Energy Balances of OECD Countries, 1989–1990*, pp. 91, 103, 107, 127, 171.

Table A-3. *Changes in Energy Production Patterns in Five OECD Countries, 1973–90*

Millions of metric tons of oil equivalent

Country and energy production	1973	1990	1990 as percent of 1973
Total energy			
Canada	190.11	274.73	144.51
France	36.30	104.67	288.35
Germany	118.79	130.17	109.58
Japan	29.50	69.00	233.90
United States	1,446.88	1,630.82	112.71
Crude oil, natural gas liquids, and natural gas			
Canada	157.69	183.74	116.52
France	8.40	5.99	71.31
Germany	21.03	16.65	79.17
Japan	3.42	2.49	72.81
United States	1,026.84	838.21	81.63
Coal			
Canada	11.70	37.93	324.19
France	18.04	8.24	45.68
Germany	92.34	71.51	77.44
Japan	17.90	4.57	25.53
United States	333.36	537.85	161.34
Nuclear energy			
Canada	3.98	11.13	279.65
France	3.84	81.85	2,131.51
Germany	3.06	38.35	1,253.27
Japan	2.53	52.71	2,083.40
United States	23.24	159.35	685.67

Source: International Energy Agency, *Energy Balances of OECD Countries, 1989–1990*, pp. 177, 179, 181, 182, 184.

Paul D. Pierson and R. Kent Weaver

Imposing Losses in Pension Policy

*I*mposing losses on powerful domestic groups is one of the most important and difficult challenges faced by modern governments. Given resource limitations and the scope of current public-sector activity, governments of any political complexion are likely to find that pursuing new priorities requires breaking some of their existing commitments. If they cannot, commitments will accumulate in such a way that choice becomes increasingly narrowed. Political analysts who would disagree heatedly over the desirability of particular cutbacks agree that the ability to impose losses is a critical governmental capacity.

Imposing losses is politically difficult, however, because doing so generally incurs costs that are concentrated, immediate, and highly visible, while the benefits are contingent, diffuse, and long term. Moreover, evidence suggests that voters possess a "negativity bias"—they are more aware of losses than of equivalent gains.[1]

Political structures are often thought to be an important determinant of governments' capacity to impose losses. One of the principal criticisms of the U.S. system is the alleged inability of its central government to impose losses on powerful interests. We evaluate that criticism by examining the loss-imposition process in a single policy area—cuts in old-age pensions. We will focus on pension-cutting initiatives in the United States, Canada, and Great Britain and will briefly consider the cases of Germany and Sweden. Our study suggests that parliamentary institutions offer risks as well as opportunities for loss imposition. Equally important, it suggests that noninstitutional factors, notably policy inheritances, play a critical role in mediating institutional effects.

---

1. See R. Kent Weaver, "The Politics of Blame Avoidance," *Journal of Public Policy*, vol. 6 (October–December 1986), pp. 371–98.

110

Institutional Structure and the Politics of Loss Imposition

Policymakers in democratic systems who propose loss-imposing initiatives must overcome their fellow politicians' fear of being punished by voters at a later date. Moreover, adoption and implementation of proposals usually requires approval at several points (department, cabinet, or legislature) within the government. Prospects for loss imposition are likely to be affected by factors related to each of the three tiers of explanation outlined in the introductory chapter to this volume.

The first tier is a simple dichotomy between parliamentary and separation-of-powers systems. The parliamentarist view suggests that because concentrated executive-legislative power in parliamentary systems lowers the number of effective veto points for loss-imposing initiatives, parliamentary systems will have a much greater capacity to impose losses than the U.S. system.[2] So long as the governing party has a majority, is able to prevent defections by rank-and-file legislators, and is willing to endure the possible future electoral consequences, the government can push through legislation even over heated opposition. Backbenchers' fear of punishment by party leaders (who control promotions) usually enforces discipline. In addition, members of parliament can offer to their constituents the excuse that party whips forced compliance with the party line. This further lowers incentives to defect in the face of blame-generating pressures. Moreover, governments may stick to their proposals out of fear that accepting major amendments will make them look weak and vacillating.

Supporters of parliamentary institutions contrast this concentration of power with the U.S. system of checks and balances, which they argue leads to deadlock and inaction, especially when Congress and the presidency are controlled by different political parties. Party lines in the legislature are much more fluid in the United States, and the executive branch has limited leverage to ensure passage of its proposals. There are, moreover, many points in the legislative process where potential losers can exercise effective influence to block policy changes. And U.S. legislators are more likely than those in a parliamentary system to be held individually accountable for their actions. All of these factors, the parliamentarist position suggests, make blame generating an effective mechanism for keeping loss-inducing policy proposals off the agenda in the United States and for weakening such proposals as they go through the policymaking process.

2. Lloyd N. Cutler, "To Form A Government," *Foreign Affairs*, vol. 59 (Fall 1980), pp. 126–43.

Not all analysts accept the idea that parliamentary systems will be more effective in imposing losses. While conceding that concentration of legislative power gives majority governments in parliamentary systems one important advantage in loss imposition, the presidentialist position suggests that concentration of accountability may weaken or offset much of this advantage. Because governmental power is more centralized in parliamentary systems, accountability is more centralized as well. The governing party or coalition can act to prevent groups from suffering losses (or to indemnify them for those losses). Equally important, the public knows that it can do so. Individual legislators in parliamentary systems are not immune from blame for party positions; they are, in fact, much more susceptible to swings in party support than their counterparts in the United States. This fact may, in turn, make governments in parliamentary systems even more reluctant to undertake any action that could offend an important constituency.[3] But this fear of negative political consequences will be felt not through the highly visible defection of individual legislators (as in the United States), but through behind-the-scenes pressure in the cabinet and party caucus.

Furthermore, although the centralization of parliamentary systems increases the government's accountability, it also decreases the accountability of the opposition. The costs of blame generating by opposition parties are likely to be low, since they are already excluded from governmental power. Opposition parties in parliamentary systems also have few alternatives to blame generating. They cannot hope to enact their own policy preferences while they are out of power; their only hope is to topple the current government by publicizing its misdeeds. Governments in parliamentary systems are likely to anticipate the high political cost of such actions by forgoing loss-imposing opportunities that concentrated power would have allowed them to undertake.

Accountability in the United States is a good deal more complex, but it is not inherently biased against loss imposition. Although individual politicians can be held accountable by voters for their actions, a number of mechanisms exist that allow politicians to diffuse and obscure blame for loss-imposing actions. Politically delicate decisions can be delegated to the courts, regulatory commissions, or ad hoc commissions or working groups that may be more insulated from blame-generating pressures. Committees and subcommittees can also be used to develop a bipartisan consensus that shields most legislators from blame when they sign on. And of course, the president and legislators can use each other as scape-

---

3. See R. Kent Weaver, "Are Parliamentary Systems Better?" *Brookings Review,* vol. 3 (Summer 1985), pp. 16–25; and Weaver, "Politics of Blame Avoidance."

goats. But many blame-avoiding mechanisms can be used only if presidents and legislators of both parties are willing to eschew blame-generating opportunities to provide political cover for each other.

A second tier of explanation stresses that not all parliamentary systems are alike. Electoral rules and the norms and rules relating to government formation are important determinants of whether two parties generally alternate in forming single-party majority governments, one party rules alone or as a dominant coalition partner for extended periods, or multi-party coalitions are the norm. Moreover, individual systems may have significant variations over time in government type—for example, majority versus minority government. Each of these variations may affect the capabilities of governing institutions. The coalition governments that characterize most proportional representation systems, for example, are likely to produce less cohesive government elites than a single-party majority government because the parties within the coalition will be competing against one another in the next election. Minority governments face the even more difficult task of getting an opposition party to back them in a potentially unpopular initiative. Thus there may be substantially less concentration of power in some parliamentary systems than the parliamentarist model suggests and less concentration of accountability than the presidentialist model suggests.

A third tier of explanation suggests additional factors that may strengthen or weaken the influence of executive-legislative relationships or mask their effects. Several third-tier effects are of particular importance for imposition of losses. The structure of existing policies, for example, may provide opportunities to lower the visibility of policy changes, thus lessening accountability and making it easier to impose losses.[4] Other governmental structures—for example, bicameralism in the legislature, an independent judiciary, or requirements for assent or cooperation from subnational governments—may lessen the concentration of power.

The following discussion of pension cases explores the relative influence of concentration of power effects and accountability effects. Determining the relative capability of parliamentary and checks-and-balances systems to impose losses revolves around an empirical question: is the opportunity to impose losses afforded by concentrated power outweighed in practice by the risks posed by increased accountability, that is, the governing party or coalition's fear that it will be identified with and punished for those losses? Our case studies suggest that both effects are present, that the former appears to be stronger, and that the relative

4. See, for example, Grattan Gray, "Social Policy by Stealth," *Policy Options,* vol. 11 (March 1990), pp. 17–29.

influence of these institutional effects in a given situation depends heavily on factors such as the structure of existing policy, the proximity of elections, and other institutional arrangements, such as federalism, that facilitate or limit governments' loss-imposing capabilities.

The Cases

The country and policy area case studies we have chosen have both advantages and disadvantages for the analysis. Canada and Britain are both Westminster or party government–style parliamentary democracies. Moreover, both have had single-party majority governments throughout the period we examine here. Thus they do not offer a full range of differences among parliamentary systems. But this choice of case studies does allow an in-depth analysis of the specific type of parliamentary arrangement most likely to provide the advantages associated with the "parliamentarist" position.

The advantage of examining pension policy is that the affected clientele is not closely identified with a single political party. All parties seek the electoral support of the elderly and are unlikely to view pension cutbacks as a politically costless action imposed on a constituency that would not vote for them anyway. But one should be cautious about generalizing too much from pension policy to other cases of governmental loss imposition. Pension cutbacks are a case of what might be called "redistributive" loss imposition, that is, losses imposed on a fairly large population group that is distributed fairly equally throughout the country. An increase in income tax rates is another example of redistributive loss imposition. There are, however, other types of losses. "Geographically distributive" losses, for example, might include closing state-owned facilities in a particular locality or placing a toxic-waste disposal site in a community, while "group distributive" losses involve costs borne by relatively narrow industries or occupational groups, such as doctors, dairy farmers, or truckers. It is possible that political institutions might have different effects on government capabilities to impose various types of losses.[5]

5. For example, "group distributive" losses might be easier to impose in parliamentary systems than in the U.S. system if the proposed initiative has broad popular support. When small groups of opponents are involved, concentrated accountability for loss imposition may be a relatively weak constraint on government action, while the effects of concentration of power in parliamentary systems may make group vetoes less feasible. The adoption of national health insurance is a good example. Although it is opposed by large segments of the medical community almost everywhere, governments in many parliamentary systems

The limitations of our case studies suggest that the conclusions derived from them should be viewed as quite preliminary. To increase our confidence in their validity, we would have to test them in additional policy areas, time periods, countries (notably in parliamentary systems where coalitions rather than single-party majorities are most common), and perhaps most important, with cases of different types of loss imposition.

Pension Policies, Program Structure, and Loss Imposition

Cutting pensions for the elderly is a difficult task for any government. The elderly are a large, politically active group, and they are viewed sympathetically by the rest of the electorate. Where pensions are based on a system of contributory social insurance, a sense that benefits have been "earned" adds to the perception of inviolability. Moreover, even those who are too young to receive old-age pensions may view themselves as being indirectly hurt by cutbacks, either because cuts will lower their benefits in the future, or because they will affect elderly relatives.

The enormous blame-generating potential of pension-cutting initiatives suggests that such initiatives will occur very rarely, if at all. But in Britain, Canada, and the United States, governments have confronted high budget deficits in recent years, and all face tremendous resistance to increased taxes. These constraints have forced consideration of pension cuts in all three countries. Moreover, administrations in both Britain and the United States have had a philosophical commitment to reducing the scope of the welfare state. All three governments have employed blame-reducing strategies in their pension-cutting initiatives, but each has been forced to back down on some initiatives.

United States

The United States has a two-tiered system of public old-age pensions for its residents. By far the larger of the two is old age and survivors insurance (OASI), more commonly known as social security. This is a contributory scheme, with benefits linked loosely to a worker's contribution history. In addition, there is a means-tested program, supplemental security income (SSI), which is financed from general government

---

have had sufficient authority—and, given favorable public opinion, sufficient incentives—to overcome that opposition. In the more fragmented institutional context of the United States, politicians have been unable to overcome concentrated opposition from the medical community despite broad popular support for national health insurance.

revenues. Benefit levels for both programs have been indexed since 1975. Because most cutback initiatives have centered on social security, our discussion will focus on that program.

Recent attempts to introduce social security cutbacks have stemmed both from repeated crises in the social security trust fund and from overall budgetary pressures. In Canada and Britain, the centralization of political authority means that a few distinct governmental initiatives produced battles over pensions, but in the United States struggles over pension cutbacks have emerged frequently and from a variety of sources in Congress as well as the executive branch. Not all assaults have been equally successful, however. Significant social security cutbacks took place in 1977 and 1983. There were also abortive initiatives in 1979, twice in 1981, in 1985, and in 1987. Social security cutback initiatives have been most successful when they occurred in the context of a trust fund crisis, when they gained the support of both the president and key congressional leaders, and when they were directed at a narrow and politically weak clientele. Efforts to enlist social security benefits in the battle to shrink the federal deficit have so far proven ineffective.

An impending trust fund crisis prompted the Carter administration's first major social security initiative, in the fall of 1977.[6] But neither the administration nor Congress was willing to impose substantial short-term losses on recipients. Instead, policymakers relied almost exclusively on injecting new revenues into the system for short-term improvements in the program's financial status. They eventually settled on sizable increases in payroll taxes and the wage base (the amount of wages subject to the social security tax), phased in after the next election to lessen their political repercussions.[7]

For the long term, the administration did propose major cuts in the initial benefits of most future beneficiaries. This proposal was prompted by the discovery that the method used to adjust workers' wage histories for inflation (and thus to establish their initial benefit) was faulty, giving newly retiring workers unexpected windfalls and rapidly depleting the OASI trust fund. There was strong agreement that some changes needed

6. See Joseph A. Califano, *Governing America: An Insider's Report from the White House and the Cabinet* (Simon and Schuster, 1981), chap. 19.

7. The administration had initially proposed the use of countercyclical general revenues, but this was unacceptable to congressional leaders and to business. For a detailed discussion of the 1977 legislation, see Califano, *Governing America*; Martha Derthick, *Policymaking for Social Security* (Brookings, 1979), chap. 19; and John Snee and Mary Ross, "Social Security Amendments of 1977: Legislative History and Summary of Provisions," *Social Security Bulletin*, vol. 41 (March 1978), pp. 3–20.

to be made.[8] The reforms were not widely perceived as imposing losses. Sponsors portrayed the change as a restoration of the always-intended benefit levels, and program supporters generally accepted this interpretation.

Even more important for blame minimizing was the decision to apply the change only to workers who reached age 62 beginning in 1979. Policymakers were reluctant to lower retroactively the real purchasing power of workers who had already retired or those who were about to become eligible to retire. Workers who became eligible to retire (reached age 62) for a five-year period after 1978 received an initial benefit based on a transitional formula that was lower than the old formula but higher than the new, corrected one. Congress thus attempted to correct a serious program flaw by not cutting the benefits of those who were most likely to notice and by delaying almost all benefit cuts until after the next election.[9]

The Carter administration proposed additional social security cuts in 1979, but President Carter sought to distance himself from his proposals even before they were issued as part of his fiscal year 1980 budget. In the absence of an immediate funding crisis, Congress took no action.[10]

In 1981 the incoming Reagan administration sought further cuts in OASI for several reasons. First, the 1977 changes had proven insufficient to make the OASI trust fund solvent; it was once again in danger of running dry as early as 1982. Additional funding problems faced the system in the long term when the "baby boom" generation retired in the twenty-first century. Second, because it constituted about one-sixth of all federal outlays, it was an obvious target for an admin-

8. An earlier decoupling proposal had been presented by the Ford administration. See *Decoupling the Social Security Benefit Structure*, Hearings before the Subcommittee on Social Security of the House Committee on Ways and Means, 94 Cong. 2 sess. (Government Printing Office, 1976).

9. This effort to avoid blame was not completely successful: as the benefit cuts phased in, a very active political movement (fueled by a direct mail campaign by one of the elder lobby groups) arose among retirees receiving lower benefits, the "notch babies." To date, however, the "notch babies" have failed to obtain congressional approval for remedial legislation. On the notch issue, see *Reductions in Social Security Benefits: The Notch*, Hearings before the House Select Committee on Aging, 99 Cong. 1 sess. (GPO, 1984–85); Julie Kosterlitz, "Mailouts to the Elderly Raise Alarms," *National Journal*, February 14, 1987, pp. 378–79; and General Accounting Office, *Social Security: The Notch Issue*, HRD-88-62 (March 1988).

10. As economist (and later Congressional Budget Office head) Rudolph Penner put it, "Congress held perfunctory hearings, primarily to give people a chance to berate the President for being so heartless." Rudolph G. Penner, "Cut Retirement Costs," *New York Times*, May 24, 1981, p. C3.

istration hoping to cut taxes without creating large deficits. Third, many Republicans felt that the role of the government in the social sector was already too large and saw Reagan's election as an opportunity to reduce it.

However, many of these same Republicans were convinced that seeking major cuts in social security was politically suicidal. President Reagan had complicated the already difficult task of cutting social security by promising in the 1980 presidential campaign that the program was part of a "social safety net" of programs that would be exempt from cuts; thus proposing cuts could lead to charges that the administration was not only hurting the elderly but also violating a promise. And, when considered along with the president's tax cut proposals, which heavily favored the well-to-do, cuts in social security could provide an opening for charges that the administration lacked a fundamental sense of fairness.

The Democrats were in an awkward position too, especially in the House of Representatives, where they still held a majority. The House Ways and Means Committee had traditionally exercised a strong leadership role on social security issues, and J. J. Pickle, chairman of the subcommittee with jurisdiction over social security, did not wish to surrender that role to the White House or the Senate, even if it meant taking the lead on politically unpleasant measures. Pickle knew, moreover, that some painful changes were necessary, and he feared that politicizing social security would lead to a stalemate.[11] House Democratic leaders, however, did not want to sacrifice opportunities to generate blame against the administration by proposing cuts themselves.

The administration initially proposed only minor changes in social security, notably elimination of the minimum benefit and benefits for college student survivors of social security–insured workers. Congressional Democrats quickly seized on the minimum benefit issue.[12] Clearly each side in the debate saw its significance not just in terms of the fate of minimum benefit recipients or the savings (just over $1 billion a year) from eliminating the benefit. The bigger stakes were the possibility that Democrats could portray the administration as heartless and unfair, tarnish the president's growing reputation as the invincible master of Congress, and perhaps derail some of the administration's domestic cuts. Even more important, Democrats were hoping to force congressional

11. See, for example, Pickle's conciliatory statement on the Reagan administration's May 1981 social security package in *Congressional Record*, May 21, 1981, p. 10584; and Steven V. Roberts, "In the Hurricane's Eye of Social Security Cuts," *New York Times*, June 6, 1981, p. A9.

12. See *Congressional Record*, March 30, 1981, pp. 5697, 5700.

Republicans to choose between supporting the administration and creating a record that could cost them dearly in the 1982 elections.[13]

Similar calculations surrounded emerging debates over more extensive social security cutbacks. Representative Pickle indicated in the spring of 1981 that he would like to address benefit indexation, for example, but that the White House would have to take the lead. The Pickle subcommittee did develop a package with a number of controversial measures that would lower social security benefits over the long term.[14]

The Pickle package might have become the focus of substantial blame-generating activity or provided the basis for a compromise package to cut projected trust fund deficits. Instead, Pickle's proposal was overtaken by events. The central actor at this critical juncture was director of the Office of Management and Budget, David Stockman. Given the overwhelming priority of deficit reduction, Stockman was concerned that the Ways and Means proposals did not produce enough short-term savings.[15] Based on this reasoning, Stockman sold an alternative package to the president in the spring of 1981.[16] By shifting the issue from one of solving the trust fund crisis to one of reducing the federal deficit, he precipitated the administration's first major setback.

Unlike Pickle's proposals, Stockman's alternative contained a large dose of immediate political pain. The administration's package included a three-month delay in the cost of living adjustment (COLA) and a change in calculating future retirees' initial benefits to eventually lower the "replacement rate" (percentage of prior earnings replaced by social security benefits) from 42 to 38 percent. It also lowered future payroll taxes. The most controversial cut, however, was a proposal to reduce benefits for future early retirees sharply (from 80 to 55 percent of full benefits) and almost immediately (in January 1982). Because a large proportion of

13. A compromise was eventually reached on the minimum benefit, continuing it for all recipients who became eligible before the end of 1981. Again, political pressures pointed toward a solution that exempted current beneficiaries from losses.

14. These included a cutback in early retirement benefits (from 80 percent of full benefits in current law to 64 percent) and a gradual increase from 65 to 68 in the age for receipt of full retirement benefits. Both changes were to be phased in over ten years beginning in 1990. Pickle's plan relied for the short term on a transfer of funds from the medicare hospital insurance trust fund. The latter funds would in turn be replaced by general revenues. See Warren Weaver, Jr., "New Rules Drafted for Social Security," *New York Times,* April 8, 1981, p. A25.

15. William Greider, *The Education of David Stockman and Other Americans* (Dutton, 1982), p. 43.

16. David A. Stockman, *The Triumph of Politics: Why the Reagan Revolution Failed* (Harper and Row, 1986), p. 183.

recipients take early retirement, the plan to cut these benefits without any phase-in was particularly hazardous.

The package immediately generated enormous criticism from congressional Democrats, and the American Association of Retired Persons and other groups in the "gray lobby" promised to mobilize their huge memberships to fight the cuts.[17] Even conservative Republicans complained that the decision to begin the early retirement changes almost immediately would upset the plans of older workers who had anticipated retirement under existing rules.[18]

As criticism mounted, the White House sought to distance the president from the proposals and to declare its openness to alternatives.[19] When it was clear that the White House was backing away, the administration's defenders on Capitol Hill deserted completely: Robert Dole, the Republican chairman of the Senate Finance Committee, proposed a resolution condemning immediate cuts in early retirement benefits. It passed by a 96–0 margin.

The cuts that were enacted in the 1981 budget reconciliation bill were more modest and less controversial than either the administration or Pickle proposals, cutting outlays by only about 2 percent in 1981–84.[20] Most of the cuts enacted in the reconciliation bill did not significantly affect the core retirement and survivors' benefits.[21] These cuts were not enough to solve social security's financial problems, but neither the president nor congressional Democrats wished to take the lead in proposing painful solutions. President Reagan's advisers had convinced him to propose a COLA delay in a new round of budget cuts announced in September, but this time the White House was more cautious: it floated the

17. The president's political advisers, aware of the potential dangers, unsuccessfully tried to protect Reagan by having the secretary of health and human services rather than the president announce the proposals. See Stockman, *Triumph of Politics*, chap. 7. See also David E. Rosenbaum, "First Major Cuts in Social Security Proposed in Detailed Reagan Plan," *New York Times*, May 13, 1981, p. A1; and Warren Weaver, Jr., "Coalition Plans Drive Against Move to Trim Social Security Benefits," *New York Times*, May 14, 1981, p. B15.

18. See, for example, the statement of Representative Carroll Campbell in *Congressional Record*, May 13, 1981, p. 9642; and Stockman, *Triumph of Politics*, pp. 190–91.

19. See Warren Weaver, Jr., "Eased Stand Hinted on Social Security," *New York Times*, May 29, 1981, p. A13.

20. See *Background Material and Data on Programs within the Jurisdiction of the Committee on Ways and Means, 1988 Edition*, Committee Print, House Committee on Ways and Means, 100 Cong. 2 sess. (GPO, 1988), pp. 24–25.

21. The major exception was the repeal of the social security minimum benefit for both current and future recipients, which became the subject of several bitter rounds of blame generating between the administration and congressional Democrats in the summer and fall of 1981.

proposed cuts a week in advance. When it became clear that a COLA delay would not gain the support of Republicans in Congress, the administration dropped the idea.[22] Representative Pickle tried to get the Ways and Means committee to address the long-term funding problem. Committee Democrats refused, however, following the House Democratic leadership, which feared that doing so would interfere with efforts to convince the public to hold the Republicans accountable for any cuts.[23]

Although the political dangers of proposing benefit cuts were evident, the issue refused to go away. As was the case in 1977, awareness of looming trust fund deficits forced a response. If imposing losses might be politically hazardous, so would be a failure to avert a financial crisis. Both sides in the dispute eventually agreed to entrust social security's financial problems to a bipartisan commission that was to report after the 1982 elections. An agreement was eventually reached, and Congress passed it in 1983 with some additions.[24] This time the changes in both taxes and benefits were more significant. But again a lot of attention was paid to minimizing blame.

In the short term, the most important change was a six-month delay in inflation adjustments for benefits. Because the period for calculating inflation adjustments was also changed, the result was that current (but not future) beneficiaries' benefits were permanently cut by the amount of inflation in that period. But nominal benefits were not cut. In addition, the benefits of high-income beneficiaries of social security became subject to income taxation for the first time.[25] The number subject to this tax will expand incrementally (because the income limits were not indexed), but only about one-sixth of social security recipients were subject to the tax in 1989.[26]

In the long term, the most dramatic effect of the 1983 legislation will be a gradual increase in the retirement age from 65 to 67, beginning in the year 2000 and ending in 2021. Although the reform was treated as a

22. See Stockman, *Triumph of Politics*, pp. 304–17; Warren Weaver, Jr., "Action on Major Pension Bill May Be Put Off," *New York Times*, September 21, 1981, p. A21; and Martin Tolchin, "Republicans Warn Reagan That Cuts Would Be Beaten," *New York Times*, September 22, 1981, p. A1.

23. See Warren Weaver, Jr., "O'Neill Said to Bar Pensions Hearing," *New York Times*, October 30, 1981, p. A25; and Weaver, "Plan for Pensions Lost in House Unit," *New York Times*, November 5, 1981, p. A21.

24. For a detailed discussion, see Paul Light, *Artful Work: The Politics of Social Security Reform* (Random House, 1985), pp. 117–228.

25. Individuals with incomes under $25,000 and couples with incomes under $32,000 remained exempt from taxation.

26. *Background Material and Data on Programs within the Jurisdiction of the Committee on Ways and Means, 1988 Edition*, Committee Print, p. 38.

change in eligibility rules, its result is likely to be a sizable reduction in benefits.[27] A recent analysis indicated the magnitude of the reductions involved. Between 1985 and 2030, replacement rates for 65-year-old retirees are projected to fall from 63.8 to 51 percent for low earners, and from 40.9 to 35.8 percent for medium earners.[28] Again, the measure lessened near-term blame generating by excluding current workers from its full effects. For workers who are affected, this increase in the retirement age is beyond the time horizon that most are likely to consider politically relevant.

The 1977 and 1983 social security reforms suggest that substantial loss imposition is possible in the U.S. pension system. However, an examination of unsuccessful efforts to include pensions in large "package" cuts to reduce the federal deficit suggests that trust fund crises have been a precondition for such actions. Although continued concern with the deficit and the recognition that large reductions were unlikely without a contribution from social security led politicians to return repeatedly to the topic of pension cutbacks, each attempt has confirmed social security's reputation as the "third rail" of American politics—to touch it would be deadly.

The Reagan administration's debacle of 1981, when Stockman shifted the issue from one of balancing trust funds to cutting spending, has already been described. Proposals to introduce major social security cuts as part of a deficit reduction plan resurfaced in 1985. This time Senate Republicans took the initiative. Having been burned on social security before, President Reagan was reluctant to pursue the matter, but leading Republican senators such as Robert Dole and Pete Domenici were worried about both the economic and political consequences of continued high deficits (twenty-two Republican senators were up for reelection in 1986).

After tortuous negotiations, Dole was able to steer a package through the Senate that included a one-year COLA freeze.[29] Hopes of generating a bandwagon effect that would diminish individual accountability rapidly dissipated. Reagan offered only lukewarm support; Senate Democrats expressed opposition. The proposed budget passed the Senate 50–49 almost entirely along party lines. Nor was the Democratically controlled

27. Most social security beneficiaries already retire before age 65. The estimated savings of the 1983 reforms were based on the assumption that individuals would not delay their retirement as a result of the changes but would instead accept reduced benefits.

28. Henry J. Aaron, Barry P. Bosworth, and Gary T. Burtless, *Can America Afford to Grow Old? Paying for Social Security* (Brookings, 1989), p. 28.

29. For a detailed discussion of this episode, see *Congressional Quarterly Almanac, 1985*, vol. 41 (1986), pp. 441–57.

House more obliging. Despite moments when a complex package that would have included defense and social security cuts and tax increases seemed possible, Reagan ultimately deserted the Senate Republican leadership to cut a deal with House Speaker Thomas P. (Tip) O'Neill, preserving social security in return for higher defense authorizations. The embittered senators had again discovered the dangers of tampering with such a popular program. Later in the year, when legislators and the president were negotiating the details of the Gramm-Rudman-Hollings deficit reduction mechanism, social security was specifically exempted from any automatic cuts.

Although the Reagan administration surely hoped it had heard the last of proposals for social security reductions, dramatic events produced a renewed struggle only two years later. On October 19, 1987, world financial markets collapsed, with the Dow Jones losing almost one-quarter of its paper value in a single day. With analysts arguing that the budget deficit was partly to blame, political pressures mounted rapidly for a governmental response. Those anxious for deficit reductions thought the crisis atmosphere might generate opportunities for broad changes, including cuts in social security.[30] The push for negotiations was given extra encouragement by the impending implementation of automatic cuts of about $23 billion under the terms of Gramm-Rudman-Hollings.

Reluctantly accepting the need for a "budget summit," Reagan excluded only one possible target for deficit reduction: social security. The mathematics of deficit reduction kept pushing social security back into negotiations, however. Early in the second week of discussions, word leaked that COLA limitations were being discussed. Even as the powerful lobbying apparatus of social security advocates moved into action, a growing sense that the financial markets were steadying stabilized what had been a crisis atmosphere. In this context, House Republicans signaled their unwillingness to go along with social security cuts. The president's initial decision to exclude bargaining over social security also militated against putting the program back on the negotiating table. As Leon Panetta, a key member of the House Budget Committee, noted, the president's initial stand "created a political situation where someone had to put it on [the table], and made it difficult for one party or the other to assume the responsibility. We had to have political leaders on both sides take the position, and that chemistry never came together."[31]

Although Senate Republicans continued to push for sweeping reforms

30. Elizabeth Wehr and John R. Cranford, "Crippled Market Spurs Budget Breakthrough," *Congressional Quarterly Weekly Report*, October 24, 1987, p. 2571.
31. Quoted in Tom Kenworthy, "The Narrow Road to Deficit Accord," *Washington Post*, November 22, 1987, p. A4.

that would include social security cuts, such open opposition within the party indicated the impossibility of creating the kind of consensus that would have permitted loss imposition. With social security excluded, broad contributions from tax increases, defense spending, and other domestic programs also proved elusive. The "budget summit" ultimately settled for a minimal package of new revenues and spending cuts, with social security left untouched.

Although the policy record in the United States reveals numerous defeats for those seeking pension cutbacks, it also suggests that success is obtainable. In the two cases where trust fund imbalances became central to the discussion, significant loss imposition took place. On the other hand, when this circumstance did not exist, or when policymakers failed to exploit it, developing the political consensus needed for significant pension cutbacks proved to be almost impossible.

Canada

Public pensions in Canada are based on a three-tier system, rather than a two-tier system as in the United States.[32] The oldest tier is a universal demogrant called old-age security (OAS), which provides a set amount to all Canadians aged 65 and over. A second tier, the guaranteed income supplement (GIS), supplements OAS payments to low-income senior citizens. Currently about 47 percent of OAS pensioners also receive at least some GIS payments.[33]

Both OAS and GIS are entirely within federal jurisdiction. But Ottawa does not have exclusive decisionmaking authority over the third tier, the Canada pension plan (CPP)—a contributory social insurance plan that pays benefits linked to an individual's contribution history. Provinces

32. In addition to the three tiers mentioned here, there is a smaller spouse's allowance program and a set of separate provincial and territorial supplements in some areas of Canada. Both of these programs aid poor senior citizens. A system of registered retirement savings plans (RRSPs), which allow contributors to defer taxation on income until they retire, primarily benefits middle- and upper-income Canadians. For general background on government pensions in Canada, see National Council on Welfare, *A Pension Primer: A Report by the National Council on Welfare* (Ottawa: Supply and Services, 1989); David W. Conklin, Jalynn H. Bennet, and Thomas J. Courchene, eds., *Pensions Today and Tomorrow: Background Studies* (Toronto: Ontario Economic Council, 1984); and Keith G. Banting, *The Welfare State and Canadian Federalism,* 2d ed. (Kingston: McGill-Queen's University Press, 1987). On the origins of Canadian pension policies, see Kenneth Bryden, *Old Age Pensions and Policy-Making in Canada* (Montreal: McGill-Queens University Press, 1974).

33. This figure is as of January 1989. National Council on Welfare, *A Pension Primer,* p. 8. The minimum income guaranteed by OAS and GIS is far higher than that provided by supplemental security income in the United States.

can opt out of the CPP to establish their own plans, although only Quebec has chosen to do so. (A separate Quebec pension plan [QPP], with contribution and benefit policies generally identical to those of the CPP, operates in Quebec.) As part of the federal-provincial bargaining that was required to allow Ottawa to establish the CPP, Ottawa agreed to allow the provinces to borrow CPP surpluses as they accrued in the early years of the program.[34] The provinces thus have resisted benefit increases because they did not want to have to pay back the funds they had borrowed. Moreover, changes in the Canada pension plan require approval of a "supermajority" of the Canadian provinces, making it a more difficult target for either expansionary or contractionary pension initiatives than the programs within exclusive federal jurisdiction.[35] Benefits in OAS, GIS, and CPP/QPP are all indexed for inflation. The guaranteed income supplement also has been increased on an ad hoc basis in three of the last four election years—1979, 1980, and 1984.

There have been three recent efforts to reduce pension costs in Canada. The first was part of the Trudeau government's "six and five" inflation-fighting package enacted in 1982. In that initiative, cost of living adjustments in old-age security, as well as previously negotiated public-sector wage increases, were limited to a maximum of 6 percent for 1983 and 5 percent for 1984. However, increases in the guaranteed income supplement were "superindexed," that is, increased more than inflation, to ensure that those at the very bottom of the income scale kept up with inflation. This concession, and the fact that pensioners were not singled out for cutbacks, helped to make the restraint package politically palatable, and it was adopted by Parliament. It ended up having little lasting effect, however, since inflation declined to levels close to the "six and five" guidelines.[36]

34. Negotiation with the provinces was required because supplementary benefits (for example, for widows and survivors) are within exclusive provincial jurisdiction, and thus federal entry required provincial assent to an amendment to the British North America Act. On the negotiations surrounding creation of the Canada pension plan, see Richard Simeon, *Federal-Provincial Diplomacy: The Making of Recent Policy in Canada* (University of Toronto Press, 1972), chap. 3; and Bryden, *Old Age Pensions and Policy-Making in Canada,* chap. 8.

35. Changes in the CPP must be approved by two-thirds of the Canadian provinces having two-thirds of the Canadian population. This means a veto can be exercised by any four provinces or Ontario alone. In practice, Quebec has a veto over major changes as well, since policymakers want to keep the Ontario and Quebec plans closely integrated. See Keith G. Banting, "Institutional Conservatism: Federalism and Pension Reform," in Jacqueline S. Ismael, ed., *Canadian Social Welfare Policy: Federal and Provincial Dimensions* (Kingston: McGill-Queens University Press, 1985), pp. 48–74, especially pp. 56–57.

36. See Ken Battle, "Indexation and Social Policy," *Canadian Review of Social Policy,* no. 16/17 (October 1986–January 1987), pp. 1–20.

The next initiative occurred as part of the Mulroney government's attempts to reduce the federal deficit shortly after it came into office in 1984. Despite its huge House of Commons majority, the new Progressive Conservative government wanted to proceed cautiously: the party had been out of power in Ottawa since 1963, except for a brief minority government under Joe Clark in 1979–80. Moreover, it was widely believed that disillusionment with the Liberals rather than enthusiasm for the Conservatives had won them the election. And the new prime minister, Brian Mulroney, was not a conservative ideologue.[37] His major interest was in building a political realignment favoring the Conservatives rather than advancing specific substantive goals. Attacking popular programs for the elderly is not a good way to promote such a realignment. While still in opposition, Mulroney had expressed willingness to reexamine the universality of OAS, but only with all-party agreement.[38]

These conditions were hardly auspicious ones for cutbacks in state pensions. But Canada's huge federal budget deficit, which reached 8.6 percent of GNP in the fiscal year ending in March 1985,[39] pushed the new government to consider pension cuts. In doing so, the government initially stumbled badly. News leaked in late 1984 that the government was considering cutting the universal demogrant programs—OAS and family allowances—as a way to reduce the deficit and target resources toward the needy. The government ultimately retreated from an attack on universality without ever articulating a clear proposal.[40] Indeed, Mulroney backed himself further into a fiscal corner by pledging to maintain universality.

Budget pressures remained strong, however, and the following spring Finance Minister Michael Wilson won cabinet approval for cutting social spending through an attack on indexing rather than universality. Under the government's proposal, adjustments would be made in OAS (as well

---

37. On the social philosophy of Mulroney and the Progressive Conservative party, see Michael J. Prince, "How Ottawa Decides Social Policy: Recent Changes in Philosophy, Structure, and Process," in Jacqueline S. Ismael, ed., *The Canadian Welfare State: Evolution and Transition* (Edmonton: University of Alberta Press, 1987), pp. 247–73; and Michael J. Prince, "What Ever Happened to Compassion? Liberal Social Policy 1980–84," in Alan M. Maslove, ed., *How Ottawa Spends 1984: The New Agenda* (Toronto: Methuen, 1984), pp. 112–14.

38. Prince, "What Ever Happened to Compassion?" p. 114.

39. Receiver General for Canada, *Public Accounts of Canada, 1987,* vol. 1; *Summary Report and Financial Statements* (Ottawa: Supply and Services, 1987), pp. 1–2.

40. Michael Clugston, "The Social Welfare Battle," *MacLean's,* January 7, 1985, p. 44. A full account of this episode is given in David Bercuson, J. L. Granatstein, and W. R. Young, *Sacred Trust? Brian Mulroney and the Conservative Party in Power* (Toronto: Doubleday Canada, 1986), chap. 6.

as family allowances and income tax brackets) only for inflation above 3 percent. Full indexing of the guaranteed income supplement was to be maintained, but since the latter is an add-on to OAS, poor seniors' benefits would also be cut.

While the idea was that cloaking restraint in the guise of fighting inflation would make it more politically palatable, the Mulroney-Wilson proposal played quite differently from the Trudeau government's "six and five" plan. It affected all recipients from the first dollar of inflation, whereas the "six and five" plan would have cut benefits only if inflation passed specified targets. Cuts were also concentrated on pensioners and families, rather than being shared throughout the public sector. And it did not (contrary to the advice of Finance Ministry public servants) protect the poorest elderly from cutbacks by "superindexing" the guaranteed income supplement. Moreover, the government's move contradicted Mulroney's campaign pledge to retain full indexation of OAS, leaving him open to criticism of his honesty and trustworthiness.[41]

Opposition was immediate and intense. The New Democratic and Liberal opposition in the House of Commons severely criticized the cuts.[42] There was also opposition outside the House of Commons. Both the Liberals and the New Democrats sent task forces across the country to hold hearings on—and publicize opposition to—the government's proposals. Senior citizens' organizations protested outside the Parliament building and mounted letter-writing campaigns.[43] The Quebec National Assembly unanimously passed a resolution asking the federal government to reconsider; Conservative premiers in the Maritime provinces were critical as well.[44] Even the business community's representatives questioned the initiative.[45] Within three weeks, the prime minister was

41. See Jeffrey Simpson, "Tangled Up in Pledges," *Globe and Mail* (Toronto), June 6, 1985, p. 6.

42. MPs of both parties called the prime minister a "liar" in Commons debates. This is a certain headline-grabber because the term is forbidden in parliamentary debate and MPs who use it are either forced to apologize or are ejected from the House for the remainder of the day. See " 'Baby' Copps Attacks Wilson," *Globe and Mail* (Toronto), June 8, 1985, p. 1.

43. See Barbara Yaffe, "Wilson Budget 'Stinks,' N.B. Seniors Contend," *Globe and Mail* (Toronto), June 7, 1985, p. 1; Yves Lavigne, "Elderly Urged to End PC Memberships as Pension Protest," *Globe and Mail* (Toronto), June 12, 1985, p. 1; and Charlotte Montgomery, "PM Faces Politician's Nightmare over Canadian Pension Furor," *Globe and Mail* (Toronto), June 20, 1985, p. 8.

44. See "Budget Concerns Maritime Premiers," *Globe and Mail* (Toronto), June 12, 1985, p. 5; and Barbara Yaffe, "Pension Cuts a 'Proposal,' PM Asserts," *Globe and Mail* (Toronto), June 13, 1985, p. 2.

45. "Business Joins Outcry Over Old-Age Security," *Globe and Mail* (Toronto), June 12, 1985, p. 8.

backtracking, saying that the cuts in OAS were only a proposal that would not take effect until the next year and might never be implemented if the economy performed well.[46] Two weeks later, the Mulroney government retreated completely, announcing that full indexing of OAS (but not family allowances and the personal income tax system) would be continued.[47]

After this debacle, it is not surprising that the Conservatives left the pension issue alone until after they won reelection in 1988, in a campaign that focused almost entirely on the issue of free trade with the United States.[48] Persistent federal budget deficits—still 4.9 percent of GNP in the fiscal year ending in March 1988—caused the issue to be rejoined. In his April 1989 budget, Finance Minister Wilson announced that there would be a special tax (known as a "clawback") on Canada's universal demogrants (OAS and family allowances) for upper-income families and individuals. This tax will phase out these benefits entirely for a small number of Canadians.[49] The finance minister estimated that the clawback would initially affect only 4.3 percent of the elderly population. But since the thresholds at which the clawback begins will be only partially indexed (to inflation over 3 percent, with additional adjustments on an ad hoc basis), the clawback will gradually affect more pensioners. Social policy advocates strongly criticized the erosion of universality in the clawback, but this time the finance minister stood firm, buoyed by a lack of substantial public protest. The proposals were so complicated, so selective in their short-term impact, and so gradual and uncertain in their long-term effect that it was difficult for the media or interest groups to present them in a way that was intelligible to the public.[50] Liberals used their majority in the appointive Senate to hold up passage of the clawback (and several other pieces of legislation) for more than a year, but it was

46. Yaffe, "Pension Cuts a 'Proposal,' PM Asserts," p. 1.

47. Charlotte Montgomery, "Tories Retreat on De-Indexing Pensions," *Globe and Mail* (Toronto), June 28, 1985, p. 1.

48. Social issues were not entirely absent from the debate, however, as the opposition parties charged that the free trade agreement threatened Canada's social programs. See Christopher Waddell, "Wilson Charges Foes with Lying to Elderly," *Globe and Mail* (Toronto), November 1, 1988, p. A1.

49. The "clawback" rate of 15 percent on OAS payments will phase in beginning at a net income of $50,000, and all OAS benefits will be taxed back at an income level of $76,332 when the system is fully in place. National Council on Welfare, *The 1989 Budget and Social Policy: A Report* (Ottawa: Supply and Services, September 1989), pp. 15–20.

50. See Gray, "Social Policy by Stealth," especially pp. 28–29. The opposition was also in disarray when the proposals were announced, with both the Liberals and the New Democrats in the midst of searches for new leaders.

finally adopted in October 1990. The Liberals have not pledged to repeal the clawback if they return to office.

Throughout each of these rounds of retrenchment, the Canada pension plan has remained untouched, protected by the difficulty of securing provincial agreement. It would be politically senseless to go out in front on an issue where resolution in the absence of a crisis is very doubtful, and where provincial ministers as well as the federal opposition parties would probably use the occasion to denounce the federal government in a high-profile setting. Ottawa and the provinces did negotiate a new CPP agreement in 1986, when the CPP faced a trust fund crisis that would soon force the debtor provinces to begin paying back the monies they had borrowed from the fund. Not surprisingly, given the nature of the bargainers, the agreement relied solely on increased payroll tax rates, and it will generate sufficient revenues so that the provinces do not have to pay back the money in the near future. The result, as one Canadian observer put it, was to reinforce the CPP's status as "essentially a typical, unfunded 'pay as you go' public pension plan, but one that has been burdened with a secondary role of generating revenue for the participating provinces."[51]

Great Britain

Like Canada, Britain has a three-tiered public pension system.[52] The basic pension has been the major component of state support. It is a flat-rate benefit for all who qualify through their contributions or their spouse's contributions. The state also provides a means-tested benefit for those who have not qualified for the contribution-based basic pension or who need a supplement to that pension to reach the poverty line. The third tier of the British system is an earnings-related component. After a number of false starts, a Labour government (with all-party support) introduced the state earnings-related pension scheme (SERPS) in 1975. SERPS provided for the gradual phase-in of parallel public and private earnings-related schemes. Individuals could either participate in SERPS, or, if

51. Bruce Kennedy, "Refinancing the CPP: The Cost of Acquiescence," *Canadian Public Policy*, vol. 15 (March 1989), p. 34.

52. For background on the development of the British pension system, see Hugh Heclo, *Modern Social Politics in Britain and Sweden: From Relief to Income Maintenance* (Yale University Press, 1974), chap. 4; and Michael O'Higgins, "Public/Private Interaction and Pension Provision," in Martin Rein and Lee Rainwater, eds., *Public/Private Interplay in Social Protection: A Comparative Study* (Armonk, N.Y.: M.E. Sharpe, 1986), pp. 99–148.

their employers so chose, "contract out" to a private, earnings-related plan backed by generous public subsidies.

When the Thatcher government came into power in 1979, this system must have struck it as a difficult target for reform. Since existing state pensions were ungenerous by international standards, cuts were hard to justify. The new SERPS scheme promised an expansion of future benefits, but it was the product of an agreement for which the Conservatives had repeatedly expressed support. Nonetheless, as Britain's second largest social expenditure (after the National Health Service), pensions remained an attractive target for a government committed to reducing state spending. Although Conservative efforts to change pension provision emerged slowly, they eventually produced major pension cutbacks.

The Thatcher government's efforts to reduce the public-sector role in pension provision followed two tracks. Initially, the government pursued an incremental strategy to limit the basic state pension. The 1980 Social Security Act changed the basis for uprating (indexing) the basic pension. From 1973 to 1980, benefits had generally been uprated in line with the higher of either prices or earnings. In practice, this usually meant earnings. Essentially, this formula ensured that pensioners would share in the benefits of economic growth. The 1980 act, however, provided for upratings only in line with prices. Although the act generated limited political controversy, it had substantial long-run implications.

Because earnings generally grow faster than prices, the new uprating formula meant that economic growth would gradually diminish the role of state pensions. Even in the short run, the real value of pensions has lagged far behind average earnings. In the long run, the effect would be dramatic. As the government actuary pointed out, in forty years the basic pension for a single pensioner (assuming 2 percent real annual earnings growth) would produce a replacement rate of less than one-half that provided in 1980.[53]

This change substantially reduced expenditure growth at a low political cost. A one-time shift in policy produced an annual cut of 1 or 2 percent in pension outlays. By 1988 the new upratings formula meant that a married pensioner received £65.90 a week rather than £79.90, a reduction of almost 20 percent. The change reduced annual government expenditures by £4 billion.[54] The low visibility of the change meant that an already weak opposition had trouble mobilizing against the measures.

---

53. *Report by the Government Actuary on the First Quinquennial Review,* HC Paper 445 (London: HMSO, 1982), p. 21.

54. "The Government Strikes It Rich by Mining the Poor," *The Guardian,* April 25, 1988, p. 8.

As long as the Thatcher government could claim that it was maintaining the basic pension's real value (and it did so repeatedly), it was difficult for program supporters to portray the new upratings formula as a major assault on state provision.[55]

Still, from the government's perspective the new upratings formula did nothing to alter the basic policy options open to future governments. Benefit growth would start from a significantly lower base, but both opposition parties were promising more generous basic pensions if they returned to government. More important, the government realized that SERPS would substantially increase long-term pension expenditures unless it was changed. Consequently, the government began to consider a second track of cutbacks directed at SERPS.

Yet an attack on SERPS was politically risky. The program had all the features that were supposed to make it untouchable: universal benefits, a relatively tight link between contributions and benefit entitlements, and a constituency that commanded widespread public support. Furthermore, the Conservatives had publicly backed the enactment of SERPS, and the Thatcher government had repeatedly promised to maintain it. During the preliminaries to the 1983 election, the prime minister denied having any "plans to change the earnings-related component of the state pension."[56]

Nonetheless, after the election it became clear that cuts in social security were under consideration. Apparently in an attempt to ward off immediate Treasury cuts in the social security budget, Social Services Secretary Norman Fowler agreed to launch what he dramatically termed "the most substantial examination of the social security system since the Beveridge report 40 years ago."[57] It was widely assumed that this examination was intended to produce significant expenditure cuts.

Fowler's report did not propose a sweeping restructuring of the British welfare state, but it did contain one bombshell: the proposal to abolish SERPS. The plan included some efforts to minimize blame. In a bow to political realities, Fowler's plan called for a lengthy transition. Those within fifteen years of retirement would stay in SERPS, while men under age 40 and women under 35 would lose all SERPS benefits. Those in

55. "Where We Are Going from Here," *Times* (London), March 28, 1986, p. 4.

56. Quoted in Sue Ward, "Pensions," in Richard Silburn, ed., *The Future of Social Security: A Response to the Social Security Green Paper* (London: Fabian Society, 1985), pp. 34–35.

57. *Parliamentary Debates* (Commons), 6th ser., vol. 57 (1984), col. 653. For a discussion of the Fowler reviews, see Nicholas Deakin, *The Politics of Welfare* (London: Methuen, 1987), pp. 119–54.

between would receive partial SERPS benefits since they would have limited time to build up new entitlements. In place of SERPS, employees would be required to make private contributions to either an employer-run pension plan or an employee's "personal pension" (similar to the individual retirement accounts developed in the United States).

These changes met the government's major ambitions for pension policy. SERPS would be eliminated, although reductions in anticipated expenditures were not expected until 2002. Yet by 2033 the plan would save an estimated 75 percent of the enormous projected SERPS expenditures.[58] It was hoped that the introduction of personal pensions would fill the gaps in private provision that previously had fueled demands for state pensions.

Virtually no one other than the government was pleased with the proposals, however. The Trades Union Congress called the plan a "colossal breach of faith on the Government's part."[59] Particular groups—especially advocates of women and the low-paid—argued that private alternatives would offer far less for them than SERPS.[60] More surprising was the harsh criticism of the proposals from ostensible government supporters: employers and the occupational pension funds. Both groups complained about the administrative headaches the scheme would create, since for at least fifteen years companies would have to run two schemes in tandem. Officials also worried that pensions would once again be a "political football." Even before Fowler's proposals were released, Labour Party leader Neil Kinnock announced that a Labour government would reverse any major modifications of SERPS. What was the advantage of introducing complex new arrangements if the next government would render them obsolete?

Employers also worried about the cost. In effect, the government planned to transform a public pay-as-you-go scheme into a private funded

58. "Fowler Unbowed," *The Economist*, June 22, 1985, p. 25.

59. "Campaign to Save Welfare State," *Financial Times*, September 4, 1985, p. 11.

60. An Institute for Fiscal Studies analysis confirmed this view. While a single man aged 40 could expect transitional SERPS payments and his private contributions to produce a pension equal to roughly 80 percent of what SERPS would have provided, a pension including benefits for a spouse would yield only 70 percent of what could have been received through SERPS. Although the IFS report offered no estimates, it noted that a single woman could expect to do significantly worse. Evan Davis and others, *1985 Benefit Reviews: The Effects of the Proposals* (London: Institute for Fiscal Studies, 1985), pp. 25–27. The Confederation of British Industry provided even more pessimistic projections. If, as seemed likely, most personal pension investments went into safe, short-term assets, the eventual pensions would be less than half those offered by SERPS. Michael Prowse, "Why Few Wish to Join the Fowler Bandwagon," *Financial Times*, September 20, 1985, p. 22.

scheme. Where SERPS had anticipated that future benefits would be paid from future contributions, the reforms called for the gradual accumulation of assets to pay retirement benefits. This produced a "double-payment" problem: employees (and employers) were asked to continue making national insurance contributions to pay for current retirees while making mandatory contributions to private schemes to fund their own retirement. The result, as the government acknowledged, was that the reforms would require higher contribution rates.[61]

The plan also promised to worsen the government's short-run fiscal position. The state would pay increased contributions for *its* employees, while the expansion of tax-free private pensions would lower government revenues. Concern for these budgetary implications had delayed the release of Fowler's proposals while the Treasury argued with Fowler over the budgetary costs of his plans. The social security review was intended to lower spending and allow Chancellor of the Exchequer Nigel Lawson to offer preelection tax cuts. Instead, higher tax expenditures would mean lower revenues and less room to reduce income taxes.[62]

Finally, the insurance companies that ran the occupational schemes saw their "expanded opportunities" as a decidedly mixed blessing. The erratic earnings patterns of many of the private sector's new clients made them expensive to include in plans. Administration might cost as much as 18 percent of contributions for personal pensions, compared with less than 2 percent for SERPS.[63] These schemes would also lose some of the state subsidization that had made the private sector's role in SERPS an attractive proposition. Furthermore, if the mandatory contributions produced meager pensions, insurers might face pressure to provide more generous benefits.

In short, Fowler's "fundamental examination" missed some important political ramifications. Prepared for complaints from the opposition parties, the government also drew sharp criticism from the Confederation of British Industry and major private insurers. Members of the pensions review team, including Stewart Lyon of Legal and General Assurance

61. For those already contracted out of SERPS to an employer-based scheme, rates were expected to increase from 13.2 percent of taxable wages to 16.5 percent, and this would be *before* the mandatory 4 percent payment to a private scheme. The *Financial Times* projected the increased annual cost to employers at roughly £1.5 billion to £2 billion. Eric Short and Peter Riddell, "Kinnock Warns on Pensions," *Financial Times,* March 1, 1985, p. 6; and Michael Prowse, "Pensions Move May Push Up NI Rates," *Financial Times,* May 13, 1985, p. 32.

62. Anthony Bevins, "Thatcher Calls in Fowler and Lawson in Effort to Repair Pensions Rift," *Times* (London), April 30, 1985, p. 2.

63. Ward, "Pensions," p. 38.

(Britain's largest pension fund), were highly critical of the proposals. Lyon argued that the review team had never considered a plan to phase out SERPS.[64]

By the fall of 1985, the government heard, in the words of a *Financial Times* correspondent, "a near-deafening chorus" to reconsider.[65] Faced with heavy opposition from interest groups and rising discomfort among backbench Conservative MPs, the government began to backpedal. When the government's legislative plan finally emerged in December's White Paper, the pension provisions had been substantially revised.[66]

The White Paper proposals, which became the Social Security Act of 1986, paid more attention to political realities. The government reversed the decision to abolish SERPS. Instead, the new plan substantially lowered benefits while continuing to encourage private alternatives.[67] As with Fowler's initial proposals, benefit cuts were to be phased in gradually, with the transition affecting those retiring between the years 2000 and 2010. The White Paper reaffirmed the earlier emphasis on expanding private provision through a combination of occupational schemes and personal pensions. Lower public pension benefits would increase the attractiveness of private alternatives. Finally, as an added incentive to contract out, the government offered an additional rebate of 2 percent of earnings to the standard rebate for newly contracted-out employees until 1993.

The White Paper was generally regarded as a significant retreat for the Thatcher government.[68] After all, it had failed to eliminate SERPS. Yet the reforms accomplished many of the government's objectives. By 2021, real SERPS expenditures are projected to drop by well over 50 percent compared with prereform estimates, from £16.4 billion to £7.1

64. Eric Short, "CBI Steps Up Attack on Pension Proposals," *Financial Times,* August 3, 1985, p. 4; Short, "Pension Plans Attacked by Legal and General," *Financial Times,* September 5, 1985, p. 7; and Short, "Serps Abolition Plan Opposed," *Financial Times,* September 12, 1985, p. 7.

65. Prowse, "Why Few Wish to Join the Fowler Bandwagon."

66. Department of Health and Social Security, *The Reform of Social Security: Programme for Action,* Cmnd. 9691 (London: HMSO, 1985).

67. SERPS benefits would now be based on average lifetime earnings, rather than a worker's best twenty years. SERPS pensions would be equal to 20 percent of qualifying earnings, rather than 25 percent. Widows and widowers would be entitled to 50 percent, rather than 100 percent, of a deceased spouse's pension.

68. See, for example, Rudolf Klein and Michael O'Higgins, "Defusing the Crisis of the Welfare State: A New Interpretation," in Theodore R. Marmor and Jerry L. Mashaw, eds., *Social Security: Beyond the Rhetoric of Crisis* (Princeton University Press, 1988), pp. 216–18.

billion.[69] The new arrangements will work against those with lower earnings and less stable work histories and will be particularly damaging to middle-aged workers, who will have less time to build up new entitlements.

Despite the major losses resulting from the revised pension proposals, political opposition weakened considerably. While other aspects of the social security revision met resistance, the reforms of SERPS emerged unscathed. What accounts for the dramatic reduction in the level of political blame attached to the revised proposals? Two factors were critical. First, the government took steps to minimize the number of immediate losers. Although the original proposal's transitional arrangements had mollified pensioners, the scheme had ignored two powerful losers: employers and the Treasury. In the revised proposals, the continuation of the existing pay-as-you-go state scheme and the more moderate extension of private alternatives reduced the short-run burdens on both these actors.

The second change was the greatly lowered visibility of cutbacks for those most affected, namely, those losing significant SERPS entitlements. Because of SERPS' immaturity, the loss involved to recipients must always have appeared somewhat abstract. The decision to "amend" rather than abolish the system made the loss even more elusive. By casting the reforms in a less dramatic, more technical fashion, Fowler recovered sufficiently to implement a successful package of pension cutbacks. In combination, the restriction of basic pension indexation and the modification of SERPS indicate the Thatcher government's substantial capacity to impose losses on current and future pensioners. However, there has also been evidence of substantial limitations. As noted, the first round of SERPS reforms resulted in a serious political setback. Thus the Thatcher government's mixed record suggests that even in a single policy area loss-imposing capabilities can vary from proposal to proposal.[70]

69. These figures are in 1988 prices. See Vanessa Fry, Stephen Smith, and Stuart White, *Pensioners and the Public Purse: Public Spending Policies and Population Ageing* (London: Institute for Fiscal Studies, 1990), p. 24.

70. The government stumbled again in 1988. Comments by Nigel Lawson in a casual press briefing were taken to indicate that the government was considering a move toward means-testing basic pension benefits. Opposition was immediate and intense, and the government was forced to hurriedly announce that it meant new spending, not a shift of resources from existing universal pension programs. As the government promised £200 million in new spending for the poor elderly, a senior conservative MP decried Lawson's blunder as possibly "the most expensive lobby briefing in history." Philip Webster, "Extra £200M for Poorest of Pensioners," *Times* (London), November 25, 1988, p. 1.

Pension Cuts in Proportional Representation Systems

Both Canada and the United Kingdom are party government systems, and in the time period considered here, both had single-party majority governments. These are probably the parliamentary regime and government types most conducive to loss imposition, because veto points and requirements for interparty negotiation are minimized. But they are not the normal condition in most parliamentary systems, which have proportional representation electoral rules. A brief review of pension cutback initiatives in two parliamentary systems with proportional representation electoral systems, West Germany and Sweden, reveals diverse experiences.[71] But many of the same patterns evident in the United States, Canada, and Britain were also present in these other countries, notably slow phase-ins for major cuts in replacement rates or eligibility and reliance on temporary freezes or changes in indexation mechanisms for short-term changes.[72] Each of these techniques makes loss imposition less visible.

Pension-cutting initiatives were quite successful in West Germany. Responding to slower economic growth, a decline in the working-age population relative to total population, and substantial deficits in both the overall budget and the pension program, the Social Democratic–led coalition under Helmut Schmidt initiated a series of cuts in pensions and other social programs beginning in 1977.[73] Christian Democratic–led coalitions after 1982 introduced further reductions. The cumulative effect of these changes was to lower the benefits of a "standard" new claimant by 15 percent over what they would had been under the pre-1977 formula.[74] Given the potential for controversy inherent in pension cuts and

71. Half of the seats in the West German Bundestag are elected from single-member constitutencies, but the remaining seats are awarded in such a way as to make the overall outcome quite similar to that for "pure" proportional representation systems.

72. See Organization for Economic Cooperation and Development, *Reforming Public Pensions* (Paris, 1988), pp. 65–99.

73. A new formula lowering all pension claims and delaying inflation adjustments for six months was enacted in 1977; this was promptly supplemented by 1978 legislation that canceled inflation adjustments in the benefit calculation for 1978 and capped them for 1979 through 1981, while raising employer-employee contribution rates. Because the freeze and caps were built into the basic benefit calculation, benefits were lowered for all future beneficiaries currently in the labor force.

74. Actual cuts in the standard of living of retirees were smaller. Jens Alber, "Germany," in Peter Flora, ed., *Growth to Limits: The Western European Welfare State since World War II*, vol. 2, *Germany, United Kingdom, Ireland, Italy* (New York: de Gruyter, 1988), p. 120. On pension cuts in Germany generally, also see Daniel Wartonick and Michael Packard, "Slowing Down Pension Indexing: The Foreign Experience," *Social Security Bulletin*, vol. 46 (June 1983), pp. 9–15.

the highly competitive nature of West Germany's party system, both Social Democratic and Christian Democratic–led governments have tried to attain all-party agreement for pension cut proposals. They have molded those proposals to obtain such assent, eschewing more radical alternatives.[75]

Pension-cutting efforts had a more mixed fate in Sweden, with significant initiatives but also significant reversals of those initiatives. In 1980–81 a coalition of the "bourgeois" parties, facing severe budget deficits and inflation that was pushing up indexed pensions faster than wages, changed the pension indexing system to reduce benefits.[76] These changes were very controversial, however, and the Social Democratic party pledged to restore the full value of pensions if it were returned to power. The Social Democrats formed a single-party minority government after the 1982 election and partially fulfilled their election pledge in 1983, but with a twist: 4 percent was deducted from the 1984 adjustment to compensate for the lost purchasing power of a 16 percent krona devaluation that the Social Democrats had also put in place after they returned to power. Most of the effects of the devaluation cut have since been restored,[77] and further Social Democratic austerity initiatives were resisted by the powerful blue-collar labor federation and the Left Party Communists, on whom the Social Democrats depended for support in the Riksdag.[78]

---

75. On recent pension policy in Germany, see Steen Mangen, "The Politics of Welfare," in Gordon Smith, William E. Paterson, and Peter H. Merkl, eds., *Developments in West German Politics* (Duke University Press, 1989), pp. 168–90.

76. Certain items that raised prices more than wages (indirect taxes, energy prices, food subsidies, and import duties) were henceforth to be excluded from the index used to adjust pensions, and adjustments would be made only once a year, rather than whenever inflation raised prices 3 percent over the level of the previous adjustment. The bourgeois coalition also trimmed the partial pension (*delpension*) available to individuals between the ages of 60 and 65 who chose partial early retirement: the replacement rate for their lost income cut was from 65 to 50 percent, but this was later reversed by the Social Democrats. For an introduction to indexing in Sweden, see Jan Granåson, *Index-använding och tolkning* (Indexes: Use and interpretation) (Lund: Studentlitteratur, 1984); and Åke Elmer, *Svensk socialpolitik* (Swedish social policy), 16th ed. (Stockholm: Liber, 1986), pp. 112–13. On recent pension reforms, see Sven E. Olsson, *Social Policy and Welfare State in Sweden* (Lund: Arkiv, 1990), pp. 222–28; Wartonick and Packard, "Slowing Down Pension Indexing"; and Sweden, Ministry of Finance, *The Swedish Budget 1987/88*, p. 74.

77. Adjustments continued to be made on the once-a-year schedule established by the bourgeois coalition, however.

78. For example, a government initiative to replace widows' pensions with a means-tested benefit was withdrawn before it came to a parliamentary vote. Olsson, *Social Policy and Welfare State in Sweden*, p. 227.

Patterns and Explanations

How have political institutions affected government loss-imposing capabilities in the pension sector? We first compare the outcomes of government loss-imposing initiatives in our three primary case study countries. Second, we evaluate the extent to which these patterns can be explained by factors other than institutional differences between parliamentary and checks-and-balances systems. Finally, we assess how political institutions interact with other factors—notably policy inheritances and electoral conditions—to affect a government's loss-imposing capabilities.

Evaluating Outcomes

Measuring differences in outcomes would seem to be the most straightforward part of an evaluation of institutional effects on governmental loss-imposing capability. But as the pension cases make clear, even this task is not so simple. No single indicator of outcomes will do, and each indicator must be interpreted with care.

If outcomes are measured by the success rate of publicly announced or acknowledged pension-cutting initiatives, for example, then the United States would clearly be rated as the least capable of the three countries examined here. There have been at least seven significant initiatives to cut social security since 1977, and only two of these—in 1977 and 1983— resulted in major changes.[79] But the success rate for pension-cutting initiatives is a misleading indicator. Because there are more potential proponents of policy initiatives in the United States who have at least some chance of seeing their proposals adopted, the number of initiatives is likely to be higher. Because interbranch collaboration is required to adopt losses, the success rate for these initiatives is likely to be lower, and failure in a first try is likely to lead to future attempts. Moreover, failed initiatives are easier to identify in the United States. In parliamentary systems, proposals that lack adequate support within the governing party usually will not see the light of day. In the United States such proposals might be leaked by proponents as trial balloons, leaked by opponents to embarrass and generate blame against proponents, or be presented by proponents as an opening bid from which some compromise is expected.

79. The 1981 reforms did eliminate the minimum benefit for future recipients, but this had a very minor effect on program spending. Moreover, the special minimum benefit was retained.

Another possible indicator of loss-imposing outcomes and capabilities is the magnitude of changes actually made. When one looks at the substance of the cuts enacted in the three countries, there are some striking similarities. In all three countries, short-term benefit cuts were made primarily through the low-visibility technique of manipulating indexation mechanisms; short-term cuts in nominal benefits were generally either minimal or nonexistent. And the overall pattern of short-term cuts was very modest: probably highest in Britain, lowest in Canada, with the United States in between.

The nature of long-term loss imposition is less clear because of some uncertainty in projecting future effects of programmatic changes. For example, one cannot know how the Canadian government will choose to make ad hoc adjustments in the trigger level for the OAS clawback or whether the scheduled increase in the social security retirement age in the United States will in fact be fully implemented. Nor can one predict the extent to which the Thatcher-era pension reforms would survive a future Labour government. The problem of a possible reversal of loss-imposing initiatives by a future government is especially salient for Britain because the Conservatives have held power for the entire period covered by this study.

If one excludes the possible effects of future policy changes, the rank order of long-term cuts is probably the same as for short-term changes, although the magnitude of change is different: quite substantial loss impositions in Great Britain, relatively modest ones in Canada, with the United States in between. But even here, there are important similarities among the countries. Long-term cuts (retirement age changes in the United States, the OAS "clawback" trigger in Canada, SERPS benefit cuts in Britain) were usually delayed or phased in to prevent dramatic differences in benefits for contiguous age cohorts. And in both the United States and Canada, changes were especially targeted at the better off (taxation of social security benefits in the United States, the OAS clawback in Canada). However, the absence of indexation in the income level at which benefits start being taxed in the United States and the incomplete indexation of this trigger in Canada mean that more and more senior citizens will eventually be affected. Regardless of the amount of losses actually imposed, successful loss-imposing efforts generally included substantial government efforts to disguise or diffuse those losses.

Using the size of cutbacks enacted as an indicator has some important shortcomings of its own, however. Differences in outcomes could result from the fact that proponents of retrenchment proposed loss-imposing actions of widely different amounts. Differing proposals, in turn, could stem from differences in ideology and goals of governmental elites (such as the more radical objectives of Thatcher's party than Mulroney's Conservatives), differences in the extent to which budgetary stress was driving policy, or differences in the political strength of opponents of retrenchment.

These problems suggest a third measure of success in loss-imposing actions: the ratio of final policy changes to initial cutback proposals. Here the results suggest a tremendous amount of variation among countries: proponents of retrenchment in the United States were relatively unsuccessful in most cases, for example, but the final 1983 retrenchment package contained even more long-term cuts than the social security reform commission had originally proposed. The Trudeau and second Mulroney proposals in Canada were largely successful, but the 1984–85 Mulroney initiative failed. Thatcher's government was more successful, but even it was forced to back down substantially with respect to SERPS. But this measure is not without problems either. Systems may vary in the extent to which retrenchment proposals reflect the true preferences of governmental elites. The U.S. system, in particular, may lead decision-makers to ask for more than they are likely to get on the assumption that some requests will have to be bargained away.

Sifting through the complexities of measuring successful loss imposition suggests a decidedly mixed assessment of institutional effects on government capabilities. The Thatcher government in Great Britain showed strong loss-imposing capabilities, but evidence from the Canadian case, where the Mulroney government backed away from cutbacks in 1984 and 1985 and has not touched CPP benefits, suggests a more ambiguous conclusion. Moreover, the U.S. system has on occasion, especially in the 1983 amendments, shown a significant capacity for imposing losses. Although the existence of parliamentary institutions—or at least the party government form of parliamentary institutions—provides important opportunities to governments when they wish to impose losses, parliamentarism is neither a necessary nor a sufficient condition for successful loss-imposing initiatives.

Alternative Explanations

The absence of a necessary or sufficient relationship between political institutions and loss-imposing outcomes need not lead one to conclude that the design of political institutions makes no difference. It may suggest instead that the relationship is a complex and mediated one. In order to identify the role played by institutions, it is helpful to establish the extent to which outcomes in the three cases can be explained by other factors, such as the nature of the policy problem or economic constraints facing governments.

One possible factor might be that the needs of the elderly in the three countries differ. Cutbacks might be greatest in Great Britain because the elderly there could best afford a decline in pension benefits. However, existing evidence suggests that a policy based on the needs of the elderly should have produced precisely the opposite outcome. Using a standardized poverty line, elderly poverty rates are lowest in Canada and highest in Great Britain—and the differences are substantial.[80]

A second plausible explanation for the distinctive outcomes would stress the role of economic pressures. The greater the pressure, one could argue, the greater the likelihood that loss-imposing policies will be successfully pursued. This pressure might be measured in either of two ways: general budgetary imbalances or the burden of pension spending in particular. In both respects, the differences among the three cases seem insufficient to explain the general outcome. General government deficits have fluctuated significantly in the three cases. Only in the case of the British pension reform of 1980 is there any fit between the timing of loss imposition and large budget deficits. The wide-ranging British reforms of 1986 came after budget problems were under control. In Canada, sizable deficits provided the justification for cutback efforts, but the attempts were largely unsuccessful at the time that deficits were greatest. In the United States, the major loss impositions of 1983 were quite emphatically separated from debates over the general budget deficits, and efforts to use budget deficits as a justification for social security cuts have been consistently ineffective.

Nor does the extent of pension costs appear to account for divergent outcomes. Affordability might appear to be a more pressing concern in the United States and Great Britain. Canada does in fact have the lowest pension expenditures of the three countries, but the differences are fairly small. In a broader comparative perspective, what stands out is that

80. Data recently gathered as part of the Luxembourg Income Study suggests that if the poverty line is defined as one-half of median adjusted national income, the poverty rate for the elderly was 17.2 percent in Canada (1981), 23.9 percent in the United States (1979), and 29.2 percent in Great Britain (1979). If the U.S. poverty line is used as a measure, the poverty rate for the elderly was 4.8 percent in Canada, 16.1 percent in the United States, and 37.0 percent in Great Britain in the same years. Timothy Smeeding, Barbara Boyle Torrey, and Martin Rein, "Patterns of Income and Poverty: The Economic Status of Children and the Elderly in Eight Countries," in John L. Palmer, Timothy Smeeding, and Barbara Boyle Torrey, eds., *The Vulnerable* (Washington: Urban Institute Press, 1988), pp. 96–97, tables 5.2, 5.3.

expenses of all three are similar and clustered at the low end among OECD countries.[81]

A third approach to accounting for divergent outcomes would stress the balance of resources between supporters and opponents of pension cutbacks.[82] A perspective focusing on the political resources of social groups would likely stress the role of three centers of opposition to cuts: program beneficiaries ("the gray lobby"), organized labor (which identifies pensions as part of the "social wage") and opposition parties (liberal or social democratic parties with a programmatic commitment to welfare state programs). The table below offers a rough summary of the resources available to each of these groups in the three cases. The table suggests some limits in the usefulness of a focus on political resources. The situations in the three countries do not vary in ways that easily fit with the policy outcomes reviewed here. Canada and Britain look fairly similar in this respect, yet the outcomes in the two cases were quite different. In the United States, pension cutbacks occurred despite the strong position of pensioners and the opposition party (Democrats had a substantial majority in the House during the entire period under review).

	Beneficiaries	*Trade unions*	*Opposition parties*
Canada	Low	Medium	Low
Britain	Low	Medium	Low
United States	High	Low	High

Another significant problem with a focus on the political resources of opponents stems from the fact that those trying to impose pension cutbacks in the three countries had only intermittent success. Since administrations in each country suffered major setbacks as well as occasional triumphs, despite the relative stability of opponents' resources, some other factors must have been operative as well.

81. Among ten OECD countries, the United States, Great Britain, and Canada ranked sixth, seventh, and ninth, respectively, in 1984 in the share of GNP allocated for pension expenditures. Michael O'Higgins, "The Allocation of Public Resources to Children and the Elderly in OECD Countries," in Palmer and others, eds., *The Vulnerable*, pp. 214–15, table 9.6.

82. Such an argument could be developed from either a traditional pluralist perspective emphasizing the role of interest group bargaining, or from a "power resources" perspective, emphasizing the balance of power between labor (unions and their social democratic allies) and business. For examples of the latter perspective, which has played a prominent role in recent comparative research on the determinants of welfare state development, see Walter Korpi, "Social Policy and Distributional Conflict in the Capitalist Democracies: A Preliminary Comparative Framework," *West European Politics,* vol. 3 (October 1980), pp. 296–316; and Michael Shalev, "Class Politics and the Western Welfare State," in Shimon E. Spiro and Ephraim Yuchtman-Yaar, *Evaluating the Welfare State: Social and Political Perspectives* (New York: Academic Press, 1983), pp. 27–50.

Institutions and Capabilities

The finding that parliamentary institutions sometimes, but not always, appear to be more capable of imposing losses than the U.S. system suggests two broad conclusions about institutional effects consistent with the analysis in the introductory chapter to this volume. First, institutional effects are not unidirectional: the concentration of power and accountability associated with parliamentary systems creates both opportunities and risks for governments attempting to impose losses, although the opportunities appear to outweigh the risks most of the time. Second, the strength of these opportunities and risks is heavily dependent upon other facilitating and limiting conditions.

The evidence presented in this comparison of loss-imposing initiatives in old-age pensions in the United States and two party government parliamentary systems suggests the following more specific (although tentative) conclusions about institutional effects on government loss-imposing capabilities.

1. *The centralization of legislative power and absence of veto points that characterize majority governments in party government parliamentary systems do offer important opportunities to impose losses that are lacking in the U.S. separation-of-powers system.* The existence of numerous veto points in the U.S. system has generally preempted loss-imposing reforms in social security, except when there was a trust fund crisis. Only when the alternative appears to be unthinkable—"insolvency" in the social security program—are losses successfully imposed. The British experience suggests a greater capacity for loss imposition, while the Canadian record is quite mixed. Whether the advantage enjoyed by single-party majority governments in party government systems also holds for minority governments in those systems is beyond the scope of the evidence presented here.

2. *Single-party majority parliamentary government does not ensure superior performance in imposing losses. Governments must also be willing to endure the political costs of such initiatives.* Even a government with a huge majority, like Mulroney's in 1984–85, may be unwilling to risk its electoral future on loss-imposing actions. The Thatcher government also moderated its initial SERPS proposals out of fear for their political consequences.

3. *The opportunities that single-party majority parliamentary governments provide for imposing losses may be eroded as the fears of accountability increase— for example, before elections or when opposition parties pose a viable political threat.* If the Thatcher government was more adept than the Mulroney government at imposing losses, it was also better placed to absorb blame.

The split of Thatcher's opposition into two relatively equal pieces, and bitter internal struggles within those parties, weakened their ability to project themselves as viable alternatives to the Conservatives.[83] As a result, Thatcher enjoyed a substantial electoral margin of safety during much of the period in question. The effective loss-imposing capability of single-party majority parliamentary governments may be high only when the hazards of accountability are low.

4. *Proportional representation systems vary widely in their loss-imposing capabilities, with political conditions playing a significant role in determining the level of capability.* The evidence presented here on pension cutbacks in systems with proportional representation (Sweden and Germany) is fragmentary. Again, however, it suggests that institutions by themselves do not determine outcomes, since coalition governments in West Germany's proportional representation system were more capable of achieving lasting pension cutbacks than were similar governments in Sweden. Political conditions (the electoral vulnerability of Swedish governments during this period) and the ability to mobilize all-party agreements (see point number 10 below), as was done in West Germany, interact with institutions to create differing capacities for loss imposition. Moreover, a major turnover of parties in the governing coalition, as in Sweden, may lead to a reversal of loss-imposing initiatives.

5. *The U.S. separation-of-powers system poses limited opportunities for loss imposition.* Governmental capabilities for loss imposition depend largely on concentrating power and diffusing or limiting accountability for those actions. The U.S. separation-of-powers system does neither. It is widely recognized that the diffusion of power in the U.S. system, requiring cooperation among political antagonists, is an obstacle to loss imposition. Equally important, however, individual legislators and the president usually can be held individually accountable—through roll call votes or proposals and vetoes—for their actions that contributed to loss imposition, if not for the final outcome. Unless there is near-unanimous agreement, accountability is neither concentrated nor diffused; instead it is divided and targeted at individual politicians through the American system of weak parties and candidate-centered politics.[84] And unanimity is

83. The specific geographic distribution of voter preferences combined with a system of first-past-the-post single-member legislative districts further strengthened the Conservative government's position vis-à-vis its electoral opponents. For an analysis of the Thatcher government placing significant weight on this factor, see Peter Jenkins, *Mrs. Thatcher's Revolution: The Ending of the Socialist Era* (Harvard University Press, 1988).

84. Indeed, blame generating has become a central feature of American electoral politics as resource constraints have limited opportunities to claim credit for new program initia-

hard to obtain, for there are always incentives for individual legislators to defect from any agreement reached by party leaders in order to lessen their own potential political liability.

While these institutional conditions pose serious obstacles to loss imposition, they are by no means insurmountable. But they do mean that strategies designed to counteract these obstacles, such as use of regulatory commissions or careful design of program rules, are likely to be a prerequisite for a major loss imposition in the United States.

6. *Divided government in the United States may weaken loss-imposing capabilities, but its effects are not unidirectional.* Variations in political conditions can also have some effect on loss-imposing capabilities in the United States. But somewhat surprisingly, the social security case does not reveal an unambiguously positive relationship between united party control of Congress and the presidency and the ability to impose losses. Certainly united government is neither necessary nor sufficient for loss imposition. Significant long-term cutbacks were made under both united (1977) and divided (1983) government; smaller cuts were also made under divided government (1981). Cutback initiatives failed under both modes of party control.

To understand why the relationship is so ambiguous, it is helpful to think in terms of the effects of united and divided government on both accountability and concentration of power. United government in the United States helps to concentrate power, but differing political bases and institutional jealousies mean that it is still difficult for Congress and the president to arrive at a mutually acceptable position. As for accountability, united government may increase the fears of the governing party that it will be held unambiguously accountable for losses imposed. It may also increase the incentives for the opposing party to make partisan attacks rather than share policymaking responsibility and accountability. Divided government makes it more difficult to concentrate power, but it also provides opportunities to diffuse party accountability, as was done in 1983. Partisan considerations may defeat blame-diffusing efforts—as they did in 1981 and 1985—where there is no action-forcing event such as a trust fund crisis. But the weak effects of divided government in the case of pensions suggest once again that accountability effects may offset concentration of power effects, at least in part.

7. *The effects of policy inheritances are often stronger than those of political institutions, and they may overwhelm parliamentary-presidential differences.* One

---

tives. See, for example, Michael Pfau and Henry C. Kanski, *Attack Politics: Strategy and Defense* (Praeger, 1990).

obvious factor influencing a government's ability to overcome accountability effects and impose losses is the ease with which immediate and
visible losses can be minimized. This in turn depends partly on the
opportunities provided by existing policy and partly on the government's
strategic skill in exploiting such opportunities (compare the Thatcher
government's first and second efforts to reform SERPS).

Existing policies can set the agenda for change both by highlighting
particular problems and by narrowing the range of feasible alternatives.[85]
Policies help to structure political interests, influencing both the form in
which constituencies coalesce and the political resources available to them.
How programs divide responsibilities between the public and private
sectors and between different units of government, whether eligibility
is determined by a means test or some more universal criteria, and whether
program funding derives from general revenues or an earmarked fund
are among the range of characteristics that might affect a program's
political health.

In all three countries, the structure of current policies had a clear
influence on the prospects for imposing losses. Program structures helped
to determine how issues were defined, the organizational strength of
opponents, and the prospects for shaping strategies to minimize the visibility and immediacy of prospective losses. In Britain, the immaturity
of SERPS minimized the need to impose immediate and painful cuts.
The extremely fragmented nature of British pension arrangements—with
different individuals relying to quite different extents on the basic pension, the state earnings-related scheme, and private "contracted-out"
schemes—also served to divide potential opponents. More important, it
created opportunities to lower the visibility of losses. Because there was
already a complex system of interdependence between public and private
provision, a major shift in pension policy could be cloaked in the language
of technical adjustment.

In the United States, by contrast, the state system already paid generous earnings-related benefits to an enormous number of people. Virtually all of the elderly shared a clear interest in maintaining social security.
Because the system had existed in roughly the same form for fifty years,
major change required a clear rupture with the status quo.[86] These pro-

85. Studies that stress the effects of the structure of existing policies on welfare state
development include Heclo, *Modern Social Politics in Britain and Sweden*; Margaret Weir,
Ann Shola Orloff, and Theda Skocpol, eds., *The Politics of Social Policy in the United States*
(Princeton University Press, 1988); and Paul Pierson, *Dismantling the Welfare State? Reagan,
Thatcher and the Politics of Retrenchment* (Cambridge University Press, forthcoming).

86. Another critical programmatic feature is the structure of indexation provisions.
The design of the U.S. social security system's provisions creates one additional barrier

gram features make social security pensions in the United States extremely resistant to cutbacks. However, the reliance of social security on a distinct financial apparatus of earmarked payroll taxes and a trust fund facilitated loss imposition. Social security trust fund crises created what Robert Behn has called an "overarching issue" that reshaped the political debate in ways conducive to cutbacks. The threat of financial shortages prevented program supporters from keeping cutbacks off the agenda and allowed retrenchment advocates to argue that reductions were necessary to save social security.[87]

That trust funds play an important role in structuring debates over programs is confirmed by the way that cutback efforts have lost force when surpluses have developed in programs. The growing social security surplus has undermined calls for cuts in the largest American social program, and the recent removal of the program from the unified budget is likely to reinforce its image as a separate entity, untouchable unless its own finances are precarious.

Neither Britain nor Canada's system of financing social insurance programs leaves room for this particular strategy. In Britain, the Treasury pays a flexible contribution to social insurance programs, ensuring that revenues and payments will balance. The result is that trust fund crises do not appear and provide no particular leverage for lowering benefits. In Canada, the complex requirements for provincial approval of changes in the Canada pension plan—the only tier financed by a trust fund— make it an unpromising target for cutbacks.

Program structures, then, significantly influence the prospects for successful loss imposition. Given the political difficulty of pursuing cutbacks, opportunities to obscure or delay the impact of cuts or to redefine the issue are essential. Whether such strategies are available depends heavily on how pension programs are organized.

8. *Other sorts of veto points—for example, requirements for agreement from geographic subunits, or an independent judiciary—may be as important as the separation of executive and legislative power in limiting loss-imposing capability.*

---

to cutbacks. Because the system is earnings-related, workers' initial benefit calculations are based on their past wages, adjusted for changes in average earnings over that time. This stabilization of "replacement rates" (benefits as a proportion of past earnings) built into the core structure of social security provides a major protection against the kind of gradual erosion of public pensions currently occurring in Great Britain. The Labour government of 1974–79 had tried to institutionalize a similar protection by adjusting the basic pension for the higher of earnings or prices. However, because this approach to protecting pensioners encouraged comparison with the less generous COLA arrangement of workers, it proved to be a relatively easy target for the Thatcher government.

87. Robert D. Behn, "Cutback Budgeting," *Journal of Policy Analysis and Management,* vol. 4 (Winter 1985), pp. 162–63.

The relationship between the executive and legislative branches is not the only determinant of whether government power and accountability are concentrated or diffused.[88] Federalism is one such factor. It is no accident that Canadian pension cuts have occurred only in one of the two tiers controlled exclusively by the national government. Long-term cuts in this single tier (old-age security) through the "clawback" will be similar in magnitude to those for social security in the United States, although the overall level of pension cuts will be lower. In the case of the Canada pension plan, concentration of power is inhibited not by checks and balances between branches (which are very slight in Canada's parliamentary system), but by the requirement for provincial consent to program changes; no cutbacks have been made. The overall lessons here are that many kinds of veto points can be important determinants of loss-imposing capability, and the effects of institutional arrangements may vary enormously not only across countries but also across individual programs and sectors. Subnational vetoes have had much more influence on recent pension policy in Canada than in the United States, and they have been much more important for pension policy than certain other issues because of the way that the CPP was designed.[89]

9. *Short electoral cycles may be as important a barrier to loss imposition as separation of executive and legislative powers.* Most of the major loss-imposing initiatives outlined above in all three countries occurred fairly soon after an election, usually just long enough for politicians to avoid being accused of cynicism for having failed to make the proposals public in the campaign. There is little reason to think that this timing is coincidental. Politicians like to leave a lot of time for the pain of loss-imposing initiatives to be forgotten (or counteracted by the beneficial effects of government actions) before they have to face the electorate again. If, as this chapter has suggested, accountability poses important risks for governmental loss-imposing capabilities, differences in the length of electoral cycles that increase or weaken accountability can be important. This suggests that the U.S. system has a much narrower window for such initiatives because elections are held every two years for the House and

88. For an extended discussion of this topic, see Keith Banting, "Two-Dimensional Institutions: A Commentary on 'Political Institutions and Loss-Imposition,' " presented at the Brookings conference on "Do Institutions Matter?" February 3, 1990; and Banting, "Institutional Conservatism."

89. Historically, however, federalism has had a very important influence on pension policy development in the United States. See, for example, Jill Quadagno, "From Old-Age Assistance to Supplemental Security Income: The Political Economy of Relief in the South, 1935–1972," in Weir and others, eds., *Politics of Social Policy in the United States*, pp. 235–63.

one-third of the Senate. (In Britain and Canada, elections must be called within five years and are normally called within four.) Moreover, U.S. legislators lack the protection from personal accountability for unpopular votes that party discipline affords British and Canadian MPs. Further, American legislators are highly dependent on political action committee financing from specific interest groups that are likely targets of any loss-imposing initiatives. And challengers to incumbents of both U.S. parties, who are also not bound by party discipline to defend agreements that their parties' leaders may have made, can pick or choose issues to embarrass incumbents.[90]

10. *Although basic institutional rules regarding executive-legislative relations set important parameters for decisionmaking, new and existing institutional arrangements can be manipulated to facilitate loss-imposing agreements.* Institutional countervailing mechanisms such as the Social Security Reform Commission and informal interbranch summits can help to overcome the multiple veto points that characterize the U.S. political system. Similar sorts of countervailing mechanisms (such as all-party agreements) can help to weaken accountability effects and potential veto points in parliamentary systems.

Indeed, the role of trust funds in U.S. social security and of federalism in the Canada pension plan suggests that one should be wary of statements about the capabilities of a particular set of institutional arrangements "all other things being equal." Implicit in such statements is an incorrect assumption that politicians do not or cannot compensate for perceived inadequacies of their institutional arrangements. But in the United States, conservatives concerned about the difficulty of mustering multiple approvals for loss-imposing initiatives have consistently rejected initiatives (notably the use of general revenues) that would remove the social security trust fund as an action-forcing mechanism for resisting program expansion. In Canada, provincial governments' concerns about the centralized power of a parliamentary system were reinforced by a series of unilateral social policy initiatives in the early 1960s by the federal government, for which they were expected to share in the costs. As a result, the provinces insisted that the Canada pension plan would include a direct provincial role in decisionmaking. The result has been to eliminate any "concentration of power" effect that Ottawa might have enjoyed in

---

90. Why then are reelection rates so high, especially in the House of Representatives? Two clear reasons are the advantages that incumbents enjoy in name recognition and campaign finance over their challengers. But evidence suggests that members have also become quite adept at tailoring their positions and votes to those of their constituents—and this almost certainly means avoiding positions that impose losses on them.

trimming CPP benefits. In short, politicians in both countries have done a lot to ensure that other things will rarely be equal.

Conclusion

For politicians seeking to impose losses on powerful groups, the structure of institutions matters, but it is by no means determinative. The ideal arrangement for imposing losses is one that concentrates power and limits or diffuses accountability. But such an institutional framework would not be a democratic one. In practice, democratic institutions vary in the ways that they distribute power and accountability and thus in the opportunities and risks that they create for loss-imposing initiatives. Party government parliamentary systems tend to concentrate both power and accountability, while the U.S. system diffuses power and divides and targets accountability among individual politicians. The former system generally creates more opportunities for loss imposition than the latter. The pattern in coalitional governments is much more variable, but it also creates important risks for loss imposition.

Political institutions are, moreover, only one of several factors that constrain politicians' strategic and policy choices, and they are often not the most important ones. Past policy choices are a particularly important source of opportunities and risks for imposing losses, as are opportunities to work around existing institutional structures. What the pension cases reveal most clearly, however, is that loss imposition is a difficult task for any government that can be held accountable by its populace.

Ellis S. Krauss and Jon Pierre

Targeting Resources for Industrial Change

Governments in many countries have created and implemented industrial policy: microeconomic policies that, by "the selection of the strategic industries to be developed or converted to other lines of work," attempt to promote their industries' adjustment, productivity, and international competitiveness, and thus the nation's economic growth.[1] An analysis of institutions and industrial policy primarily concerns governments' ability to target resources effectively, and the less central but related ability to impose losses, as industrial policy deals with "picking winners and losers" in sectors, firms, or technologies.

The U.S. trade deficit and declining competitiveness of American firms in major manufacturing sectors has stimulated a heated debate about whether the United States could and should create an industrial policy like Japan's. Much of this controversy—and the argument of many on both sides of it—appears to rest on the assumption that Japan's ability to formulate and implement an industrial policy depends primarily on the nature of its governmental institutions: a parliamentary system, centralized parties, and an autonomous and elitist bureaucracy.

Based on a comparative analysis of the development and operation of industrial policy in Sweden, Japan, and the United States, we argue that

The authors thank Richard Samuels, Peter Hall, and the participants in the conference for their helpful and insightful suggestions and criticisms of earlier versions of this paper. We are also grateful to the Swedish Information Service for a grant, and the Swedish Institute for their excellent local support, which enabled us to begin collaboration on this essay in 1989. The responsibility for this chapter, of course, is entirely our own.

1. We adopt here Chalmers A. Johnson's definition of industrial policy from his *MITI and the Japanese Miracle: The Growth of Industrial Policy, 1925–1975* (Stanford University Press, 1982), pp. 27–28. Our focus is thus more narrow than economic policies in general and does not include agriculture, transportation, or defense policies, for example, except those that target resources, intentionally or not, for industrial restructuring.

151

governmental institutions alone do not suffice to produce a particular industrial policy. Although specific governmental institutions indirectly affect the ability to target resources effectively and manage structural industrial change, outcomes depend more on the entire web of relations among many governmental and nongovernmental institutions and on the legacy of a nation's past historical choices.

Institutions and Industrial Policy

Many discussions of industrial policy assert or assume that there is a negative relationship between effective economic policy and political effectiveness. Policies intended to bring about economically rational outcomes may be distorted by decisions designed to satisfy political constituencies (such as diverting resources or avoiding the imposition of losses).[2] Political effectiveness, on the other hand, may be undermined by policies that target resources efficiently, impose necessary losses, and set and maintain economic growth priorities. As Hugh Heclo has argued, successful industrial policy may require steering between policies that are sound politics but questionable economics and those that are sound economics but questionable politics.[3]

The relationship between political and economic effectiveness in determining a government's ability to target resources and impose losses, however, is neither simple nor merely inverse. For example, responding to a political constituency in order to stay in power may have positive consequences for economic growth if those responses target resources to the right sectors or keep in power a governing party that provides political stability and formulates effective economic policies. Indeed, one supposed advantage of parliamentary systems over checks-and-balances systems is their capacity for policymaking for the collective good rather than for narrow sectarian or individual interests. Is this, however, an inherent capability of parliamentary systems, or is it due to other factors? Even if it is inherent, does that capacity guarantee the right policies and choices for economic growth?

2. On the perennial danger that industrial policy outcomes may be politicized, see Harold T. Gross and Bernard L. Weinstein, "A Second Look at the Industrial Policy Debate," *Policy Studies Journal*, vol. 14 (March 1986), p. 394.

3. Hugh Heclo, "Industrial Policy and the Executive Capacities of Government," in Claude E. Barfield, Jr., and William A. Schambra, eds., *The Politics of Industrial Policy* (Washington: American Enterprise Institute for Public Policy Research, 1986), p. 311.

Further, effective targeting involves not only the ability to formulate the right policies to promote economic efficiency, but also the ability to implement those policies effectively. Implementation may require satisfying diverse political constituencies in order to induce their cooperation or compliance with policies they may perceive to be against their self-interest (a classic collective action dilemma). Does any one type of political system necessarily produce both the capacity to formulate sound economic policies and the ability to implement them?

Our task, then, is to discover how political institutions affect the complicated synergistic relationships between political and economic objectives that may produce efficient targeting of resources. We seek to determine whether certain institutional arrangements (notably parliamentary institutions) are necessary or sufficient to produce efficient targeting, whether these effects simply make such efficiency more likely, or whether institutional effects are themselves dependent on other conditions.

Parliamentary versus Separation-of-Powers Systems?

As Weaver and Rockman argue, there are theoretical reasons to believe that parliamentary systems might be more capable of targeting resources efficiently than the U.S. system. From a parliamentarist perspective, the centralization of power in parliamentary systems offers major advantages in targeting resources effectively. In a single- or multiparty majority government, there are relatively few points at which parochial interests can gain access and make demands for resources. These governments do not have to be concerned with building ad hoc coalitions to get legislative approval for a package of government actions. Party discipline also limits the value of legislators' efforts to act as advocates for local or regional interests. The U.S. separation-of-powers system, however, offers many points of access and influence, notably in legislative committees and in the need to build coalitions on the floor of legislative chambers. Easy access also allocates disproportionate influence to those with leverage, such as members of legislative authorizing committees and appropriating subcommittees, either rewarding those members disproportionately or producing an overly broad distribution of benefits so as to ensure stable legislative majorities.[4]

4. Kenneth A. Shepsle and Barry R. Weingast, "Political Preferences for the Pork Barrel: A Generalization," *American Journal of Political Science*, vol. 25 (February 1981), pp. 96–111.

A presidentialist perspective need not dispute the claim that the United States does not target effectively. But it might question whether targeting in parliamentary systems is truly less politicized, or whether the politics simply is better concealed, resulting in a distribution of benefits that is different but not necessarily better. In parliamentary systems political influence on allocative activities can occur in the bureaucracy and within the cabinet. The lack of checks in many parliamentary systems may lead to a highly centralized allocation process that is used to favor the ruling party or coalition rather than promote economic efficiency.

Moreover, there are substantial variations among parliamentary and presidential systems. Differences among individual parliamentary systems in electoral rules and norms and in the way governments are formed may heavily influence targeting capabilities. Some of these effects are quite direct. For example, members of legislatures retain an interest in engaging in "pork barrel" behavior wherever their electoral districts are smaller than the entire country.[5] Thus electoral laws, rather than the separation of powers, may be the primary determinants of the extent and distribution of inefficient targeting behavior.[6]

Electoral laws can also give rise to a variety of government and regime types with differing capabilities. Multiparty coalitions, for example, may be subject to pressures to distribute resources among coalition partners, minority governments may have to build ad hoc coalitions, and party government regimes are thought to be especially prone to policy reversals. Each of these conditions is likely to work against maximizing economic efficiency in targeting. Differences across regime and government types make it more difficult to generalize about the targeting capability of parliamentary systems.

Finally, a number of conditions that have been hypothesized as contributing to a successfully targeted industrial policy are unrelated to the nature of executive-legislative relations. Some of these factors involve political institutions, notably the bureaucracy and judicial review. In particular, expert and autonomous bureaucracies are often seen as prerequisites for effective targeting. Other factors, such as the way that capital is allocated and the mode of industrial organization, do not involve

5. See, for example, Daniel I. Okimoto, *Between MITI and the Market: Japanese Industrial Policy for High Technology* (Stanford University Press, 1989).

6. See Thomas D. Lancaster, "Electoral Structures and Pork Barrel Politics," *International Political Science Review*, vol. 7 (January 1986), pp. 67–81; and Thomas D. Lancaster and W. David Patterson, "Comparative Pork Barrel Politics: Perceptions from the West German Bundestag," *Comparative Political Studies*, vol. 22 (January 1990), pp. 458–77.

political institutions at all.[7] These institutional arrangements are compatible with either parliamentary or presidential institutions.

Ideas, Institutions, and Instruments

There is a fair amount of consensus concerning the following ingredients for the formulation and execution of a successful industrial policy.[8]

— A political context in which there is a consensus on the importance of the goal of promoting economic growth through an economically rational industrial policy, that is, an ideology justifying the priority of the ends and means of an industrial policy.

— A relatively centralized and cohesive policymaking process, sufficient autonomy from partisan political pressures to enable executive agencies to formulate and implement policies based on rational economic efficiency, and the expertise of bureaucrats selected on professional rather than political criteria.

— A government's ability to gain the cooperation of societal actors through a variety of instruments and policies in order to implement industrial policy. The effectiveness of the state's instruments and policies will depend to a large extent on the organization of economic and social institutions.

Taking our cue from the institutional approach to political economy, we might divide these prerequisites into three general types: predominant ideas and ideology concerning industrial policy, the organization of state and nonstate institutions, and the state's instruments for relating to private interests.[9] We use this general framework to look at the development

7. See John Zysman, *Government, Markets, and Growth: Financial Systems and the Politics of Industrial Change* (Cornell University Press, 1983), chaps. 2, 6.

8. This discussion is based on Johnson, *MITI and the Japanese Miracle*, chap. 9; Zysman, *Governments, Markets, and Growth*, especially pp. 300–10; George C. Eads and Kozo Yamamura, "The Future of Industrial Policy," in Kozo Yamamura and Yasukichi Yasuba, eds., *The Political Economy of Japan*, vol. 1.: *The Domestic Transformation* (Stanford University Press, 1987), pp. 427–29; and R. Kent Weaver, *The Politics of Industrial Change: Railway Policy in North America* (Brookings, 1985), especially pp. 20–23. Most of these discussions are explicitly or implicitly based on the presumed successful Japanese model of industrial policy.

9. For example, see Peter A. Hall, *Governing the Economy: The Politics of State Intervention in Britain and France* (Cambridge, England: Polity Press, 1986), especially pp. 17–20 and also pp. 5, 276–80 for the shorthand expression of "institutions, interests, and ideas."

of industrial policy in our three countries. Unlike many other analyses of industrial policy, however, ours will pay particular attention to the linkages among these three sets of variables.

The Cases

The cases of Japan and Sweden provide a clear contrast with the U.S. system's diverse society, lack of dominant party, and supposedly weaker, more politicized bureaucracy. Both Japan and Sweden are parliamentary systems embedded in homogeneous societies, dominated by a single political party for long periods.[10] Both have a reputation for relatively strong, apolitical bureaucracies. In all of these senses, the two countries are unusual among parliamentary systems and probably have attributes most favorable to effective targeting (since the need to build interparty log-rolling coalitions is minimized, as is the likelihood of abrupt reversals after an election). These cases thus represent a best-case argument for the potential of parliamentary systems: finding that one or both of them did not exhibit better targeting capability than the United States would be a strong argument against the supposed inherent advantages of parliamentary institutions.

There are also variations between Japan's and Sweden's parliamentary systems that offer the opportunity to test whether it is the parliamentary-presidential distinction per se or other factors that may be determining the nature and outcomes of industrial policy. One might expect, for example, that leftist parties supported by labor unions (Sweden) will have different industrial policy goals and dissimilar types of political rationality than rightist parties supported by a coalition of big business and agriculture (Japan).

In addition, although the Liberal Democratic party (LDP) has monopolized or dominated the Japanese cabinet uninterruptedly since 1955, several majority and minority coalitions of nonsocialist parties held power in Sweden from 1976–82. This provides an opportunity to test the effect of differing government types on industrial policy and policymaking. The two countries also vary in their electoral systems. Japan has a bicameral Diet in which the more important House of Representatives is elected through a unique multimember constituency system. Sweden has a unicameral Riksdag elected through a proportional representation sys-

10. On single-party-dominant parliamentary regimes, see T. J. Pempel, ed., *Uncommon Democracies: The One-Party Dominant Regimes* (Cornell University Press, 1990).

tem in twenty-eight constituencies, plus thirty-nine national "adjustment seats" to lessen discrimination against smaller parties.

Finally, ties between political leadership and bureaucracy vary in the two parliamentary systems because of the unique Swedish system that formally separates policymaking functions in the ministries from implementation functions in the more technocratic and expert agencies (*ämbetsverk*).

If industrial policymaking and outcomes are similar in the two parliamentary systems and different from those in the United States, it suggests that the executive-legislative relationship is an important determinant of targeting capability. If all three systems are different from each other, it is likely that factors other than parliamentarism versus presidentialism are important.

Industrial Policy in Sweden

An explicit Swedish "industrial policy" arose rather late in the postwar period. Several state-related developments that predate this industrial policy, however, are important as background. One is the political stability provided by the fact that the Social Democratic party (SAP), committed to creating a social welfare state, had been in power continuously for thirteen years by the end of World War II. A working relationship had evolved between the SAP and the relatively elitist, autonomous bureaucracy. Second, the labor-supported SAP governments had actively pursued manpower and human resource policies well before the creation of a more explicit industry-targeted industrial policy. Third, capital and labor—especially the Swedish confederation of blue-collar unions (LO), which constitutes the major support base for the SAP—had developed a modus vivendi of mutual respect and recognition derived from an elaborate system of interest representation. Wage bargaining processes were highly institutionalized, wages were settled smoothly, and labor market disputes were relatively rare. Together, these features constitute what has often been referred to as "the Swedish model."[11]

11. See Erik Lundberg, "The Rise and Fall of the Swedish Model," *Journal of Economic Literature*, vol. 23 (March 1985), pp. 1–36; R. Kent Weaver, "Political Foundations of Swedish Economic Policy," in Barry P. Bosworth and Alice M. Rivlin, eds., *The Swedish Economy* (Brookings, 1987), pp. 289–317; Peter J. Katzenstein, *Small States in World Markets: Industrial Policy in Europe* (Cornell University Press, 1985); M. Donald Hancock, *Sweden: The Politics of Postindustrial Change* (Hinsdale, Ill.: Dryden Press, 1972); and Hugh Heclo and Henrik Madsen, *Policy and Politics in Sweden: Principled Pragmatism* (Temple University Press, 1987).

Origins and Development

In 1944 the SAP and the LO proposed a direct industrial policy with relatively radical goals, based on the forecast of a postwar recession. One reason the program was never implemented was that the recession failed to occur.[12] Instead Sweden—which had not suffered massive wartime destruction—found its businesses were in a good position to sell natural resources and heavy industrial goods such as steel and ships, sectors that took time to revive in the war-damaged countries.

The SAP and the LO also dropped their radical postwar industrial program because its potential for state control over industry and the market had generated great opposition from the business community and the bourgeois (nonsocialist) opposition parties. The SAP realized that the politics of nationalization would ultimately prove politically disastrous for the party: SAP voters's support for the development of a welfare state did not extend to public ownership of the means of production.[13] Business fear and resistance, and potential voter reaction, induced the SAP to reassure the private sector that nationalization and other radical changes were not on the agenda.[14] As a result, a "historical compromise" emerged between the Social Democrats and the Swedish Employers' Confederation: the SAP leadership offered private capitalism security from massive state intervention and nationalization in return for the tacit support for—or at least no overt opposition to—SAP social welfare policies. The social welfare state to a large extent would be financed through taxation on capital and income.[15]

Thus the controversy over the left's radical but aborted industrial policy paradoxically produced a consensus between the SAP and business that allowed the SAP to pursue its main goal, the building of the social

12. Leif Lewin, *Planhushållningsdebatten* (The debate on planned economy) (Stockholm: Almqvist and Wiskell, 1967), p. 133. See also Jon Pierre, *Partikongresser och regeringspolitik: En Studie ar den socialdemokratiska partikongressens beslutsfattande och inflytande 1948–1978* (Party congresses and governmental policies: A study of Social Democratic Party Congress decisionmaking and influence, 1948–1978) (Lund: Kommunfakta, 1986), pp. 108–10.

13. Björn von Sydow, "Socialdemokratisk politik och socialdemokratiska väljare" (Social Democratic politics and Social Democratic voters), *Statsvetenskaplig Tidskrift*, no. 3 (1982), pp. 165–69.

14. Sven Anders Söderpalm, *Direktörsklubben: Storindustrini svensk politik under 1930- och 40-talen* (The managers' club: Big business in Swedish politics in the 1930s and 1940s) (Stockholm: Rabén and Sjögren, 1976), p. 146ff.

15. Walter Korpi, *Arbetarklasse i välfärdskapitalismen: arbete, fackförening och politik i Sverige* (The labor class in welfare capitalism: Work, unions, and politics in Sweden) (Stockholm: Prisma, 1978), p. 350ff. See also Walter Korpi, *Den demokratiska klasskampen: Svenske politik i jämförande perspektiv* (The Democratic class struggle: Swedish politics in a comparative perspective) (Stockholm: Tiden, 1981), p. 23ff.

welfare state, and ignored an overtly targeted industrial policy. Both
ownership and economic decisions would be left to private firms. There
would be no state bureaucracy with responsibility for managing the
problems of industrial development. It was, as Gunnar Eliasson has called
it, "an almost 100 percent market policy solution."[16]

In the mid-1960s, however, Swedish industry confronted structural
problems and diminished comparative advantage as the sectors that had
been the backbone of Swedish industry—steel, mining, shipbuilding,
and pulp and paper—faced severe international competition.[17] Further,
the SAP leadership attributed an electoral setback in 1966 to voter discontent with rapid economic change, urbanization, and regional imbalance, with the government held responsible for not managing this change.[18]
This structural crisis, along with electoral results that gave more influence
to SAP party activists, triggered a reevaluation of the need for an active
industrial policy.

The LO had such a policy ready as the result of a lively internal debate
in the 1960s on how the basic goals of the unions—positive wage development, more equal distribution of wealth, full employment, and
social security—could be attained together with economic growth and
structural change. Their recipe called for a greatly expanded state role in
accelerating industrial adjustment. This was not to include a command
over the market, however; instead the importance of competition and
financial self-sufficiency for the individual firm was repeatedly emphasized.[19] The LO proposal called for targeting "sunrise industries" and
giving a larger role to public enterprises in these sectors. Its premise was
that business was too conservative to risk capital on the nascent industries
needed to keep Sweden internationally competitive in the future. The
program also created new administrative institutions, as will be described
below. In 1967–68 the SAP leadership adopted this program in response
to the country's industrial structural crisis and its potential for political instability, and then submitted it for parliamentary debate and
passed it.

Nevertheless, by the mid-1970s the structural problems that had man-

16. Gunnar Eliasson, "The Micro-Foundations of Industrial Policies," in Alexis Jac-
quemin, ed., *European Industry: Public Policy and Corporate Strategy* (Oxford University
Press, 1984), p. 322. Weaver, "Political Foundations," p. 298, makes a similar observation.

17. Jan Kuuse, *Strukturomvandlingen och Arbetsmarknadens Organisering* (Structural change
and the organization of the labor market) (Stockholm: Svenska Arbetsgivareföreningen,
1986), pp. 95, 108ff.

18. Pierre, *Partikongresser och regeringspolitik*, p. 113.

19. Pierre, *Partikongresser och regeringspolitik*, p. 117; and Weaver, "Political Foundations," p. 298.

ifested themselves in the mid-1960s worsened. The bold intentions of the 1967–68 industrial policy were geared for an expanding economy. Instead, a recession hit the Swedish economy, and the government reallocated resources to help terminate obsolete, uncompetitive firms.[20] The government found itself spending more money on sunset industries than sunrise sectors.

At this juncture, the 1976 general election put the SAP into opposition, and the first nonsocialist government in Sweden in forty-four years, a three-party coalition that held a bare majority of the Riksdag (51.6 percent), took power. But the three coalition partners were divided by inter- and intraparty conflicts, especially on the issues of nuclear energy and taxation. The first bourgeois coalition fell apart after two years. Nonsocialist governments—two minority and a one-seat majority—held power over the next four years. Not surprisingly, the successive politically vulnerable, nonsocialist governments, operating in a structural economic crisis and a political culture that placed a priority on labor market and welfare considerations, usually sacrificed long-term economic efficiency goals to short-term electoral objectives. Rather than altering the state-led industrial policy or shifting its altered priorities back to their original focus on sunrise industries, the nonsocialist governments actually expanded nationalization and subsidies for declining industries, fearing the political consequences of not doing so. By the second nonsocialist budget, subsidies for industry had more than tripled since the last SAP budget. Moreover, subsidies were now increasingly allocated to prevent unemployment rather than to stimulate new ventures.[21]

The nonsocialist governments argued that this policy produced structural change without any major negative social consequences such as rising unemployment. The overall result of the policy, however, was that long-term goals were lost, good money was thrown after bad, and the process of structural change was slowed. Furthermore, business strongly criticized the politicization of decisionmaking that resulted.

When the SAP returned to power in 1982, it claimed the expanded program of aid and nationalization by the nonsocialist government had been a failure, and it completely reoriented industrial policy. Direct financial aid to industry today is rare; instead, the government concentrates

20. Roger Henning, "Industripolitik eller sysselsättningspolitik" (Industrial policy or employment policy), in Axel Hadenius, Roger Henning, and Barry Holmström, eds., *Tre studier i politiskt beslutsfattande* (Three studies of political decisionmaking) (Stockholm: Almqvist and Wiksell International, 1984), p. 29.

21. Nils Lundgren and I. Ståhl, *Industripolitikens spelregler* (The rules of industrial policy) (Stockholm: Industriforbundets forlag, 1981), p. 154.

on infrastructure and coordination of research and development (R&D), and has devolved administration down to local bodies as well as making the regions the recipients of much of the aid.

Institutional Capacities and Instruments

When it came to the creation of industrial policy in Sweden, party policies clearly preceded public policy: state institutions originally were conceived in the late 1960s merely to enforce the joint policies of the SAP and the LO. These new institutions included the Ministry of Industrial Affairs (MIA) as well as an executive agency, *Statens Industriverk* (SIND).[22] At the same time, R&D-related state institutions were reorganized and merged to form the *Styrelsen för teknisk utveckling* (STU) to coordinate R&D. Additionally, a state-owned bank was created to provide more venture capital.

Once they became active in the 1970s, however, these new administrative institutions significantly altered the nature of the industrial policy process. The MIA increased the SAP leadership's discretion on industrial policy matters, and SAP congresses and activists now took a subordinate role. Policy initiative passed to the MIA and party leadership from the party itself.[23] In addition, the state apparatus acquired expertise and competence to develop various industrial policy instruments. Finally, there was now a bureaucracy to coordinate industrial policy and integrate it with related policy sectors such as labor policy. There was also an increase in the number and size of state enterprises in emerging industrial sectors that private companies feared to enter, and in 1969 an organization (*Statsföretag AB*) was established to coordinate these enterprises' activities and facilitate economies of scale within the group.[24]

The growth of R&D subsidies was at the heart of the future-oriented theme of those early years, as policymakers were convinced that Swedish industry would have to invest substantially in developing a production capability in line with future international demand. Direct R&D subsidies

22. There is a distinct separation of powers and jurisdiction between ministries, who are key in policy preparation but not implementation, and agencies (*ämbetsverk*), whose jurisdiction is confined to the execution of policy. Heclo and Madsen, *Policy and Politics in Sweden*, p. 10. This chapter discusses institutional arrangements as they were until July 1991, when STU, SIND, and the national energy board were merged into a new organization, NUTEK.

23. Pierre, *Partikongresser och regeringspolitik*, p. 122ff.

24. Pierre, *Partikongresser och regeringspolitik*, p. 138. See also Roger Henning, *Staten som företagare* (The state as entrepreneur) (Stockholm: Rabén and Sjögren, 1974).

were to be given both to sectors and to individual firms, but they were to be carefully targeted and directed toward the sunrise phase of the industrial life cycle.[25]

Just a few years after industrial policy began to be carried out by the MIA and SIND, however, it also became politicized: these organizations soon became attractive targets for constituency pressure. The targets of the expanded subsidies increasingly became individual firms, and the criteria by which they were targeted became more political. The private sector claimed that good access to politicians and bureaucrats and the ability to mobilize unions and constituencies had become more important in allocating state resources, and that political objectives had triumphed over economic effectiveness, distorting long-term industrial planning and implementation.[26]

The SAP government that returned to power after 1982 has rejected subsidies to firms but has increased the overall level of spending on R&D. Indeed, in 1987 Sweden had the world's highest level of R&D spending as a percentage of GNP, although, as is also true in Japan, privately financed R&D accounts for most of this total.[27] Government aid is not insubstantial, however: the Ministry of Industry's 1988 budget allocation totaled Skr 4.2 billion (almost $700 million at current exchange rates), a figure several times that of the comparable Japanese ministry's R&D budget. These funds generally go to three categories in the following order of magnitude: regional development, technical development (including STU), and small business and exports.[28]

Operating directly under the MIA, the STU is the key governmental organization for the coordination of R&D projects and the largest single allocator of R&D funds (Skr 779 million). It primarily sponsors research projects within universities but also coordinates regional R&D operations. A staff of some 270 employees has been reorganized into four major departments reflecting an emphasis on the development

25. "Firms whose future was uncertain should not be given subsidies." Proposal to the 1968 SAP Party Congress, "Program för aktiv näringspolitik" (Program for an active industrial policy), p. 52.

26. An evaluation of Swedish industrial policy done by the Boston Consulting Group criticized it as being too defensive and employing measures that did not facilitate the necessary structural change. *A Framework for Swedish Industrial Policy* (Stockholm: Liber Förlag, October 1978).

27. Approximately 70 percent is spent by the private sector. Per Dusing, "Sverige etta i världen i forskning" (Sweden number 1 in the world of research) *Göteborgsposten*, March 6, 1988.

28. Ministry of Industry, Government of Sweden, *Swedish Industry and Industrial Policy* (Industridepartementet, 1988), p. 5.

of broad and basic technologies rather than different industrial sectors.[29]

The unique division of functions between ministries and implementing agencies (*ämbetsverk*) in the Swedish system of government has generated problems of implementation in most policy areas, particularly in industrial policy. Although it is the *ämbetsverk* that are supposed to implement policies formulated by the ministries, in fact the relations between the STU, SIND, and the MIA are more complicated.

For example, although the STU as an agency is constitutionally protected from interference from the MIA, it must submit a budget proposal to the ministry every three years, and in its responses to this the MIA gains some influence on the STU's overall priorities. Nevertheless, within the parameters of its budget allocations, the STU enjoys a great deal of autonomy. The larger staff and technical expertise of STU personnel make it difficult for MIA officials to override STU priorities at budget time. Further, the STU funds that are channeled to regional development are relatively insulated from MIA pressure. Also, because the budget must then be approved by the Ministry of Finance, the MIA becomes more of a go-between for the STU with the Finance Ministry. Indeed, STU officials see the Finance Ministry as a more significant actor for R&D than the MIA.[30] This complicates policymaking further.

An interesting division of labor has developed between SIND and the MIA. The ministry deals primarily with the major companies, while SIND handles the small and medium-sized companies. Since Swedish industry to a large extent revolves around a few big companies that use many smaller and medium-sized companies as subcontractors, this division between the MIA and SIND has created substantial problems in implementing industrial policy.[31] Further, even the MIA has very limited leverage over large companies that do not yield to their suggestions. Swedish companies have a great deal of financial independence vis-à-vis the government and credit markets because they mobilize capital mainly from internal and equity sources.[32] The increasing internationalization

29. Interviews with Lennart Stenberg, administrative officer, Director General's Office for Policy Development, Evaluation and Coordination, STU, May 10, 1989; and interview with STU information official, December 11, 1989.

30. Interview with Stenberg, May 10, 1989.

31. Personal communication from Dan Hjalmarsson, Ministry of Industry senior official, May 8, 1989.

32. Swedish industry finances its investments primarily through internal profits, but a small percentage comes from equity markets. See Gunnar Eliasson, *Kreditmarknaden och Industrins Investeringar: En ekonometrisk studie av företagens Kortsiktiga invsterings beteende* (The

of many large Swedish companies also reduces the government's leverage.[33] Further, the small and medium-sized firms that are subcontractors can be assumed to take their primary cues from the big companies.

There also has been a functional decentralization within industrial policy: the largest component of MIA funds goes to four regional development programs. National government subsidies to smooth structural change are now targeted to regions rather than to companies. The government hopes to combine the termination of declining industries with the emergence of new industrial ventures.[34] Thus municipal industrial policy is one of the most important instruments for industrial development in Sweden. Much as in the United States, the municipalities seek various ways to attract new firms or to ensure that existing firms stay alive and well.[35]

The devolution of industrial policy is part of a more general trend in Sweden toward municipalities' growing autonomy and importance as implementers of national policies, but decentralization also can be seen as having a political goal—to manage or avoid conflicts at the national level. The SAP developed this strategy while in opposition during 1976–82 so that when it returned to office it would gain policy discretion and protect itself from pressures from constituencies facing industrial decline.[36]

As is often the case, however, policy diffused is also policy confused. The current division of labor leads to decreasing national coordination. R&D is more dispersed, and the termination of declining industries is conducted through a delicate bargaining process among the municipalities, the state bureaucracy, and private interests. By the 1980s the institutions created in the late 1960s had surrendered some of their leverage

credit market and industry's investments: An econometric study of companies' short-term investment behavior) (Stockholm: Almqvist and Wiksell, 1967), p. 18ff; Boston Consulting Group, *A Framework for Swedish Industrial Policy*, p. 70ff; and Industriens Utredningsinstitut, "Att rätt Värdera 90-talet: Slångstidsbedömning 1985" (A correct assessment of the 1990s: The IUI long-term assessment) (Stockholm: IUI, 1985), pp. 23ff, 351ff.

33. In the seventeen largest industrial groups in Sweden, which account for one-third of the country's industrial employment, more than half their total employees worked in foreign subsidiaries, and their overseas production exceeded their exports from Sweden. See Ministry of Industry, *Swedish Industry and Industrial Policy*, p. 61.

34. The so-called Uddevalla package, a set of subsidies given to a town facing the shutdown of a major shipyard, was the first time that this strategy was implemented. See Jon Pierre, "Public-private Partnerships in Industrial Structural Change," *Statsvetenskaplig Tidskrift*, no. 3 (1989), pp. 200–08.

35. Benny Hjern, *Kommunerna, naringslivet och sysselsattningen* (Municipalities, private industry, and employment) (Stockholm: Kommunforbundet, 1986).

36. Personal communication from Jan Carling, undersecretary, Ministry of Industry, May 8, 1989.

on industrial policy to local political bodies, partly to avoid the politicization of industrial policy that characterized the late 1970s.

Evaluating Swedish Industrial Policy

Sweden's attempt to introduce an industrial policy to nurture future industries has met with mixed results. Both the SAP and nonsocialist governments of the 1970s were able to initiate an industrial policy, mobilize a political consensus around it, and put it into effect; but those policies increasingly came to be used to forestall the political consequences of economic decline in key industries. The result was distortion of the original priorities and large economic inefficiencies in the targeting of resources.

The SAP-led governments of the 1980s attempted to reverse this by scaling back on the direct allocation of resources to business and devolving industrial policy toward the regions. R&D is well funded and administered by a relatively autonomous technocratic agency. These very changes, however, have resulted in major problems for the national government in coordination and capacity for implementation.

The parliamentary system of government may have facilitated the ability of Swedish governments to adopt, implement, or change the course of industrial policy when they desired. There is little evidence, however, that parliamentary institutions (even in tandom with an elite bureaucracy) have been a prime determinant of the content of industrial policy, have prevented its politicization, or have ensured its success. The dominant coalition of labor and the SAP and the historical consensus about employment policy, the welfare state, and compromise between business and government seem to have been the more crucial factors in the formation and direction of Sweden's industrial policy.

Industrial Policy in Japan

The idea that government should target resources to promote economic growth emerged in Japan during its nineteenth century modernization. In the 1920s a separate institution, the Ministry of Commerce and Industry, was created to formulate and implement industrial policy. Its involvement in the economy was expanded under the American occupation. In 1949 the ministry was transformed into the Ministry of International Trade and Industry (MITI), and it began to follow a path of public-private cooperation for structural change.[37]

37. Johnson, *MITI and the Japanese Miracle*, pp. 23–25, 196.

Postwar Development

The immediate postwar economic and political context in Japan contrasts starkly with that of Sweden. Devastation caused by the war, severe
shortages, high unemployment, and shortage of capital all constituted a
crisis that justified an activist approach to industrial policy. During the
late 1940s and early 1950s MITI gradually developed a comprehensive
and coordinated industrial policy that emphasized developing heavy industry through concentrated capital investment, importing foreign technology while offering protection from foreign competition, and expanding
exports to pay for the imported raw materials vital to the survival of
any Japanese industry.[38]

During this period, industrial policy operated in an environment of
unstable political leadership and politics polarized around left-right ideological issues, which culminated in 1960 in the intense crisis surrounding
the extension of the mutual security treaty with the United States. Following this, the leadership of the Liberal Democratic party, which had
become the majority party after its formation in 1955, needed a non-
conflictual issue that would buttress its support. Thus party leaders turned
their attention to economic growth with distributive benefits for the
population, lending further ideological support to industrial policy.

Prime Minister Hayato Ikeda presented an "income doubling" plan
in 1960 that in addition to the existing goal of heavy industrial development addressed concerns about social overhead capital and the improvement of national living standards. It also contained some elements
of liberalization of capital and trade that had been desired by both big
business and foreign governments.[39] Liberalization of direct government
controls on capital and trade accelerated after Japan joined the OECD in
1964. National income did more than double in the 1960s as GNP had
an average real annual growth rate exceeding 10 percent.[40]

However, the very high growth of the 1950s and 1960s soon produced
tremendous pollution, rapid urbanization, regional imbalance, and strains
on neglected infrastructure. By the late 1960s and early 1970s, there was
a nationwide protest movement against pollution, as well as an increased
awareness of the need to devote more attention to the quality of life. As
a result, MITI was forced to concentrate on goals other than economic
growth, and the LDP had to pass stringent antipollution laws and increase

38. Johnson, *MITI and the Japanese Miracle*, chap. 6.
39. On the political polarization before 1960 and its aftermath, see Michio Muramatsu
and Ellis S. Krauss, "The Conservative Policy Line and the Development of Patterned
Pluralism," in Yamamura and Yasuba, eds., *Political Economy of Japan*, pp. 522–25.
40. Johnson, *MITI and the Japanese Miracle*, p. 231.

social welfare. The oil shocks of 1973 and 1979, however, revitalized industrial policy and forced MITI to cope with the energy crisis and its consequences.

Other problems began to emerge in the 1970s. By rapidly creating heavy industry with great production overcapacity, the sunrise industries of the earlier postwar period quickly became sunset industries as the economy entered a recession and cheaper foreign competition from newly industrializing nations entered the international market in force. Now industrial policy had to deal with the orderly decline of depressed heavy industry, but without massive subsidies. There was also a new set of future-oriented policies: in the early 1970s, MITI, in collaboration with the private sector, embarked on developing knowledge-intensive, non-polluting industries that had a high value-added, high-technology component: advanced computers, semiconductors, information processing, and software.

Two further dimensions were added to the industrial policy agenda in the 1980s: developing greater strength in creating basic technology in order to decrease reliance on foreign technologies, and decentralizing emerging high-tech industries by creating "technopoli"—a working partnership of businesses, universities, and local governments—in many areas of Japan.[41]

Although the content and focus of industrial policy in Japan have varied over time, there has been little controversy throughout the postwar era about the existence of an industrial policy and the state's priority on intervening actively in specific sectors of the economy. Even when the antipollution movement criticized the flaws of existing industrial policy, the issue was not whether industrial policy was a legitimate function of government or had been effective, but rather that the state should have anticipated the consequences of its successful industrial policy and should also have been concerned with other values. Indeed, the response to the dual crises of the 1970s—environmental damage and energy shocks— was to add the management of these problems to the industrial policy agenda.

Governmental Capabilities

In a very short time after the war, MITI had developed a panoply of industrial policy tools, centering on foreign exchange and capital, cartels,

---

41. Sheridan Tatsuno, *The Technopolis Strategy: Japan, High Technology, and the Control of the Twenty-first Century* (Prentice-Hall, 1986), pp. 46–51, chap. 6, and *passim*.

and finance measures.[42] For example, MITI had approval powers over foreign technology licensing and all foreign currency transactions. It soon created the Japan Development Bank to provide capital to industries and instituted tax exemptions to stimulate targeted industries. Because Japanese firms acquired capital primarily from the credit market rather than equity markets, MITI could indirectly allocate capital to selective industries during this capital-poor early period by giving signals to the banks.[43]

Many of the more heavy-handed levers in the tool kit, such as approval of currency transactions, disappeared with liberalization in the 1960s, and the power of indicative credit allocation progressively declined as Japan acquired more capital. Since the 1960s MITI has had to rely more on "administrative guidance"—informal, persuasive, and more indirect methods of gaining industry cooperation and implementing policy.[44] For example, MITI has used leasing companies to stimulate economies of scale, and semiprivate associations whose revenue derives from sporting events provide funds for rationalizing industry or promoting technological development. These have been important but relatively neglected examples of MITI's indirect methods of stimulating demand for key industries.[45]

In dealing with declining industries, MITI has relied primarily on the creation of legal cartels to carry out the orderly reduction of capacity. The brunt of the implementation and cost of such policies falls on the firms themselves (and indirectly on consumers). However, the cartels prevent the cutthroat competition and decline in prices that would occur with an excess of supply over demand, and thus they indirectly help the companies to bear this burden. Policy toward declining industries nonetheless has not been as successful at solving the problems of overcapacity and decline as was originally expected.[46]

As was the case in Sweden in the late 1960s, the thrust of industrial policy in Japan has been primarily future-oriented and has involved tar-

42. Johnson, *MITI and the Japanese Miracle*, p. 227.

43. Some argue that this capacity alone has been key in implementing industrial policy in Japan. See Zysman, *Government, Markets, and Growth*, especially chaps. 2, 5.

44. Johnson, *MITI and the Japanese Miracle*, pp. 240–74.

45. Such strategies have been used in the development of robots and computers. See Ezra F. Vogel, *Comeback, Case by Case: Building the Resurgence of American Business* (Simon and Schuster, 1985), pp. 40, 90, 132, 149.

46. Merton J. Peck, Richard C. Levin, and Akira Goto, "Picking Losers: Public Policy Toward Declining Industries in Japan," *Journal of Japanese Studies*, vol. 13 (Winter 1987), pp. 79–88, 117–21. Also see Richard J. Samuels, "The Industrial Destructuring of the Japanese Aluminum Industry," in *Pacific Affairs*, vol. 56 (Fall 1983), pp. 495–509.

geting key industries. However, the two countries diverged greatly in the methods used to achieve these goals.[47] For example, MITI's prime means of implementing its industrial policy goals were not large subsidies to industry or the provision of generous R&D aid. After 1951 subsidies ceased to be a major method of industrial policy, and tax exemptions were used more extensively to manage private investment.[48] MITI's budgets, both generally and especially for aid to heavy and advanced technology industries, have been surprisingly small, considering the image of its power to direct the economy.[49] The government's share of R&D money has been consistently smaller, indeed close to half, that of the United States, Britain, or France.[50]

Another difference between Sweden and Japan is that Japanese industrial policy has not been oriented primarily to the level of the firm, but rather has focused on the selection and management of sectors, particularly sunrise sectors that fit the long-range visions of MITI's analysis of product cycles and international competitiveness. MITI never picks a single "national champion," as European industrial policy often does, and therefore it avoids reduced competition and increased dependence on government. Nor does it pick individual firms to survive and prosper and others to disappear. In many ways, MITI's approach to individual firms has been the opposite of the myth that it picks "winners and losers": rather, it has tended to ensure that all major firms in a priority sector are "winners" and has "socialized the risk" of any of them losing.[51]

47. The following discussion is based on Johnson, *MITI and the Japanese Miracle*, chaps. 6, 7; Edward J. Lincoln, *Japan's Industrial Policies* (Washington: Japan Economic Institute of America, April 1984); Ira C. Magaziner and Thomas M. Hout, *Japanese Industrial Policy* (Berkeley: University of California, Institute of International Studies, 1981); and Okimoto, *Between MITI and the Market*, chap. 2.

48. Johnson, *MITI and the Japanese Miracle*, pp. 232–33.

49. This continues to be true today. MITI's budget in fiscal year 1990 was only about 1 percent of the total budget for the eighteen major administrative agencies of the Japanese government. Keizai Koho Center (Japan Institute for Social and Economic Affairs), *Japan 1991: An International Comparison* (Tokyo: Keizai Koho Center, October 30, 1991), p. 80. Percentage calculated from raw data by authors. Further, MITI's total fiscal year 1985 R&D budget was about $250 million, about the same as the Japanese Science and Technology Agency spends just on nuclear power R&D. Of its R&D money, only $30 million was targeted to large-scale industries, $25 million to "next generation" industries, $19 million to electronics, and $8 million to machinery. Tatsuno, *The Technopolis Strategy*, app. E, p. 256.

50. Daniel I. Okimoto, "Political Context," in Daniel I. Okimoto, Takuo Sugano, and Franklin B. Weinstein, eds., *Competitive Edge: The Semiconductor Industry in the U.S. and Japan* (Stanford University Press, 1984), p. 107.

51. Richard J. Samuels uses the insightful term of the "state as guarantor." *The Business of the Japanese State: Energy Markets in Comparative and Historical Perspective* (Cornell Uni-

During the last few years, there have been new trends in the implementation of industrial policy. The increasing capital resources of Japanese firms and the expansion of Tokyo as an equity market have given the private sector more autonomy from both banks and the government. Further, as it has become difficult to keep the development of basic technologies confined within one ministerial jurisdiction, MITI has found itself in rivalry with other ministries for control of potential new industries.[52]

The Japanese Industrial Policy Puzzle

Japan has achieved international competitiveness and responded flexibly and well to the major changes required by industrial restructuring. Much of this is due to the strength and resilience of its firms, some—the exact extent indeterminable—to MITI's industrial policies. At the very least, Japan's industrial policy has been more successful than Sweden's at avoiding market-distorting intervention and in maintaining an orientation toward the future. Despite great politicization in other policy areas (see below), Japan's industrial policy toward large manufacturers and high-tech industries seems to have avoided the deep and pervasive forms of politicization that result in fragmented or market-adverse decisionmaking. This stands in marked contrast to Sweden and the United States—indeed to almost any other nation.

Many observers have attributed Japan's relative degree of success in industrial policy to the powerful, centralized, and autonomous MITI.[53] The national bureaucracy, according to this argument, was the only major governmental institution to survive both the war and the American occupation relatively unscathed, and thus in the political and economic

---

versity Press, 1987), p. 258. On specific techniques, also see Kozo Yamamura, "Success That Soured: Administrative Guidance and Cartels in Japan," in Yamamura, ed., *Policy and Trade Issues of the Japanese Economy: American and Japanese Perspectives* (University of Washington Press, 1982), pp. 80–86.

52. See, for example, the major conflict over telecommunications networks described in Chalmers Johnson, "MITI, MPT and the Telecom Wars: How Japan Makes Policy for High Technology," in Chalmers Johnson, Laura D'Andrea Tyson, and John Zysman, eds., *Politics and Productivity* (Ballinger, 1989), pp. 177–240. MITI shares the development of superconductivity with the Science and Technology Agency and the nurturing of biotechnology with four other ministries.

53. Johnson, *MITI and the Japanese Miracle*, is the most influential of this genre. For a concise summary of the academic debate between this "developmental state school" and its critics, see Gregory W. Noble, "The Japanese Industrial Policy Debate," in Stephan Haggard and Chung-in Moon, eds., *Pacific Dynamics: The International Politics of Industrial Change* (Westview Press, 1989), pp. 53–95.

leadership vacuum of the early postwar era MITI was the only actor capable of providing the goals and means of economic policymaking. Further, MITI has recruited the best and the brightest university graduates through a highly competitive examination system and has a reputation for expertise. Others stress the fact that MITI, by subsuming under its single organizational umbrella all the major aspects of industrial policy—manufacturing, natural resources, commerce, and trade—has continued to develop the capacity to form cohesive, centralized policy and decide relative priorities among sectors.[54]

There is merit to this explanation: MITI has been an influential and capable actor. We would argue, however, that bureaucratic power alone cannot provide a definitive answer to why industrial policy in Japan has been relatively effective and undistorted by partisan political interference. Since the 1960s political leadership has become more influential, and many of the formal powers MITI held in the early postwar period have been dismantled by liberalization. Bureaucracies elsewhere have had comparable jurisdiction and expertise (including Sweden's), but few have been able to maintain industrial policy in a future and market-conforming direction. Nor does the existence of a dominant party guarantee a lack of politicization of policymaking: the Social Democrats in Sweden, when faced with a challenge to their dominance and a structural crisis in the early 1970s, began to reorient industrial policy in less economically efficient directions.

Japan's relative ability to avoid disastrous partisan politicization and side-tracking of market-conforming policies is all the more remarkable given the Japanese electoral system, which provides incentives for legislative localism comparable with those in the U.S. Congress.[55] Japan's electoral system is relatively unusual. For the important House of Representatives, Japan has a system that involves neither proportional representation nor single-member constituencies: although the voter casts only one ballot, between two and six (usually three, four, or five) representatives are elected. This means that in most constituencies the LDP runs more than one candidate, and this intraparty competition has in turn encouraged candidate-centered vote mobilization. For example, the LDP uses *koenkai*, mass membership personal support organizations, to garner votes for individual candidates. Senior party faction leaders (who are the main competitors for the LDP party presidency, and thus the prime ministership) provide financial and political support for those seek-

54. Okimoto, *Between MITI and the Market*, pp. 113–14.

55. See Samuel Kernell, "The Primacy of Politics in Economic Policy," in Kernell, ed., *Parallel Politics: Economic Policymaking in Japan and the United States* (Brookings, 1991), pp. 325–78.

ing endorsement as official party candidates.[56] Once elected, a representative's parliamentary career is determined primarily by seniority within his faction and by the factional politics of cabinet appointments.[57]

The perennial dominance of the LDP as a majority party, combined with election bases somewhat independent of the central party organization, has produced a decentralized policymaking process. Although most government legislation is formulated in the ministries and agencies of the bureaucracy, it always passes through the LDP's Policy Affairs Research Council (PARC) before going to the party leaders and cabinet for final approval. PARC is a highly decentralized body with fifteen major divisions and hundreds of subcommittees on which LDP members serve depending on their policy or constituency interests. This allows individual members a great deal of input, and interest groups many points of access, to policy, and it is in PARC rather than the Diet that the real politics of the policy process occurs.

Therefore, although Japan's parliamentary system shares with others the characteristics of party discipline and recruitment of ministers from the legislature, it differs from those with proportional representation electoral systems in its less centralized party control of candidates and careers, greater access of interest groups, and greater incentive of politicians to represent interest groups and constituencies. In effect, Japan's system is a hybrid between the centralized decision functions of majority-party parliamentary leadership and the more independent and decentralized power base of American politicians.

The real puzzle of Japanese industrial policy is not how MITI became powerful enough to dictate and implement policy autonomously; it is rather how, given this electoral system, such potentially strong local pressures have been constrained and channeled to prevent industrial policy from being overwhelmed by parochial constituency interests.

Explaining Japan's Success

The ability of Japan's policymakers to avoid the centripetal, market-distorting effects of constituency pressures has been aided by the existence of a normative counterbalance to these pressures: the shared idea that economic growth is a priority and that large-scale manufacturing is essential to accomplish that growth. Consequently, both politicians and

56. The classic study of this phenomenon is Gerald L. Curtis, *Election Campaigning Japanese Style* (Columbia University Press, 1971), especially chaps. 1, 5, 6.

57. See Nathaniel B. Thayer, *How the Conservatives Rule Japan* (Princeton University Press, 1969), chap. 7.

bureaucrats have been sensitive to the possible harmful effects of placing parochial constituency demands ahead of large industry's needs.

Another important explanation lies in the policy instruments that have been used. By relying on sectoral rather than firm-specific aid, the Japanese government has avoided setting precedents for local bailouts. Third, despite decentralization in PARC, MITI still has a substantial degree of control over the policy agenda and is able to keep local initiatives from being actively considered. Ultimately, however, this policymaking environment depends on the organization of the private sector and its participation in industrial policymaking.

Japan's industrial organization encourages communication, negotiation, and cooperation between the public and private sectors. There are usually a few large firms in each major industrial sector—a "competitive oligopoly"—supported by many related small and medium-sized suppliers and subcontractors.[58] The hierarchical relationship of the smaller enterprises to the larger firms simplifies the politics of industrial policy: arrangements need be negotiated only with the larger firms, and small business will probably follow their lead. Further, large industry is highly organized into trade and peak associations, which provide information and aggregate and articulate business interests to MITI and gain firms' compliance with negotiated sector policy.[59]

Industrial policy is formulated with the established participation of the major actors affected by the policies. The most important vehicle for this is the Industrial Structure Council, an advisory body attached to MITI. Representatives of major industries and labor, academics, and former bureaucrats, meeting under the aegis of MITI, recommend policies and strategies. Thus this body and others play a major role in negotiating a preliminary consensus on the goals and means of industrial policy. Indeed, some analysts argue that the reason industry cooperates with industrial policy is this institutionalized negotiation process. Industry's opportunity to influence policymaking and the "reciprocal consent" it produces may be a primary characteristic of the Japanese state's relationship with industry.[60]

58. This industrial structure was created in part by MITI's cartel policy in the early postwar period and in part by the effects of Japanese firms' "lifetime employment" system. Okimoto, *Between MITI and the Market*, pp. 124–26; and Yamamura, "Success That Soured," p. 80.

59. On the importance and role of these networks, see Okimoto, *Between MITI and the Market*, pp. 152–61. Also see Leonard H. Lynn and Timothy J. McKeown, *Organizing Business: Trade Associations in America and Japan* (Washington: American Enterprise Institute for Public Policy Research, 1988) for a comparative treatment of such organizations.

60. Samuels, *Business of the Japanese State*, especially p. 260 and chap. 7.

Two additional factors have reinforced the close relationship between bureaucracy and business in industrial policy and helped avoid politicization by nonbusiness actors. Unions have been closely tied to the opposition parties, which have been excluded from power, and the Japanese system of "lifetime employment" makes layoffs the last resort of companies coping with difficult times. The former mitigates organized labor's political influence on policy, and the latter diminishes constituent pressure on the LDP to act on behalf of declining industry.

In this environment, the potentially negative relationship between industrial policy and an electoral system that creates great constituency pressures has been turned into a synergistic one. Because frequent microintervention in policy for large industry has few rewards and high costs, other policy areas that can bring constituents concrete benefits have become the primary targets of politicization. These include agriculture, construction, retailing, transportation, and postal services.[61] The ministries with jurisdictions in these areas are known as the "political ministries," as opposed to the more autonomous "economic ministries" of MITI and Finance.[62] "High policy" is left to the party and governmental leadership. As a result, MITI's relative autonomy, as John Campbell has argued, may be explained "by the lack of strong attempts at political intervention" as much as by bureaucratic capacity.[63]

In short, industrial policy in Japan has enjoyed an ideological consensus, has been flexible and future-oriented, has used a minimum of state resources, and most likely has contributed to managing structural change for international competitiveness. Its accomplishments have been made possible, however, not by any simple formula of an autonomous, technocratic state bureaucracy and centralized decisionmaking attributable to parliamentary government, but by a particular combination of conditions and institutions. These include the formation of a long-term political coalition of a conservative majority party, an elite bureaucracy, and big business; the weakness of organized labor; and the nature of industrial organization.

61. The politicization of agriculture has been enhanced by the great malapportionment of electoral districts—providing rural areas with many more seats than they would be entitled to by a "one man, one vote" distribution—and by the LDP's strength in rural areas.

62. On the politicization of these and other ministries and its consequences for industrial policy, see Okimoto, *Between MITI and the Market*, pp. 192–202; John Creighton Campbell, "Democracy and Bureaucracy in Japan," in Takeshi Ishida and Ellis S. Krauss, eds., *Democracy in Japan* (University of Pittsburgh Press, 1989), pp. 113–37; and Joel D. Aberbach and others, "Comparing Japanese and American Administrative Elites," *British Journal of Political Science*, vol. 20 (October 1990), pp. 461–88.

63. Campbell, "Democracy and Bureaucracy in Japan," p. 132.

Finally, both the conditions and the content of Japan's successful industrial policy have not been without costs: the diversion of resources to inefficient industries such as agriculture and construction, higher prices to consumers in declining industries because of reliance on cartels, and lack of attention to the consequences of making industrial change the highest priority of the state.

Industrial Policy in the United States

In the United States the very idea of an explicit, comprehensive industrial policy, such as that of Japan's, has been a matter of intense debate. The concept of an active government role in allocating resources has been controversial since the founding of the Republic. Historically this has been reflected in political conflicts about issues such as a national bank, government activism in the distribution of wealth, free trade versus protectionism, and laissez-faire versus Keynesian economic policies.

In the postwar period, U.S. presidents have been consistently committed to a liberal international trade regime.[64] However, this consensus did not come to be shared by societal actors (business and labor interests, reflected in congressional attitudes) until the late 1950s, reaching a peak during the early 1960s. After this period, as increasing foreign competition began to erode the support of various interests for a liberal trade regime, protectionist sentiments increased. Congress, under increasing pressure from domestic interests, reflected those pressures, but it was also reluctant to open the Pandora's box of protectionism again. One way it responded to this dilemma was to continue to let the president have discretion and authority, and thus responsibility, in the area of trade, but simultaneously to push him to respond more actively to domestic industry concerns.[65]

By the 1980s Japanese penetration of the American market and the declining competitiveness of U.S. firms in key sectors, combined with a burgeoning trade deficit, produced widespread concern among American political leaders and growing irritation over the seemingly closed nature of Japanese markets to U.S. exports in goods and services. Because they attributed the startling success of Japan to its industrial policy and

64. Stephen D. Krasner, "United States Commercial and Monetary Policy: Unravelling the Paradox of External Strength and Internal Weakness," in Peter J. Katzenstein, ed., *Between Power and Plenty: Foreign Economic Policies of Advanced Industrial States* (University of Wisconsin Press, 1978), pp. 54–56, 72–85.

65. Krasner, "United States Commercial and Monetary Policy," p. 84.

encouragement of specific key sectors, many American liberals, congressional Democrats, and academic Japan specialists began to call for a coherent, comprehensive U.S. industrial policy, including in some cases protection for American industry.

Many conservatives in the Reagan administration, Republicans, and academic economists viewed these proposals as unnecessary: either the changes occurring were no real problem, or they were caused by macroeconomic rather than microeconomic factors. They further perceived proposals for an explicit, coordinated industrial policy as stalking horses for protectionism and redistributive policies.

The content of the debate is less important, however, than the fact that although the "crisis" of American competitiveness and trade deficits put the idea of industrial policy explicitly on the policy agenda for the first time, it did not generate a consensus. Rather, it stimulated conflict and controversy as it became entangled in partisan agendas and traditional American cleavages over the role of government, the relationship between the private and public sectors, the distribution of economic resources, free trade versus protectionism, and the authority of Congress versus the president.

Policies and Resources for Industry

The lack of a long-term strategic component in the governmental targeting of resources, and of a consensus on the idea itself, makes it difficult to consider the United States as having an "industrial policy." Nevertheless the existence of many federal government policies with direct and indirect consequences for specific sectors indicates that the government does have a de facto approach to structural change in the economy, whatever the rhetoric or intent concerning those policies.[66]

Hugh Heclo and other writers have catalogued the range and variety of such policies.[67] The list constitutes an impressive argument that many

66. See, for example, Heclo, "Industrial Policy and the Executive Capacities of Government"; David McKay, "Industrial Policy and Non-Policy in the United States," *Journal of Public Policy*, vol. 3 (February 1983), pp. 29–48; and John Zysman and Laura D'Andrea Tyson, *U.S. and Japanese Trade and Industrial Policies* (Berkeley Roundtable on International Economy, 1984), pp. 78–111. A critical view of the approach taken here is found in Aaron Wildavsky, "Squaring the Political Circle: Industrial Policies and the American Dream," in Chalmers A. Johnson, ed., *The Industrial Policy Debate* (San Francisco: ICS Press, 1984), pp. 27–44, especially p. 41.

67. Heclo, "Industrial Policy and the Executive Capacities of Government," pp. 294–98; see also Zysman and Tyson, *U.S. and Japanese Trade and Industrial Policies*, pp. 83–96; and Lincoln, *Japan's Industrial Policies*, pp. 45–53.

federal government activities are involved with, and influence, the structure of the American economy: procurement and export promotion programs, import restrictions, trade adjustment assistance to workers, research and development support, information services, tax incentives, selective antitrust enforcement, promotion of regional economic development, emergency financial guarantees and loans for firms (such as Chrysler and Lockheed) and regions (New York City), and various attempts to institute tripartite negotiating forums among business, labor, and government. The cost of such programs is very difficult to ascertain, and estimates vary depending on whether they include agriculture, education, housing, and other "industries" we do not consider here as part of industrial structural change. The data nonetheless indicate substantial federal financial aid to business, mostly in the form of tax credits, loans, and loan guarantees.[68]

Furthermore, defense spending on R&D and procurement has been critical to the development of certain high-tech industries, especially semiconductors and aerospace.[69] Many critics, however, consider defense spending on technology to be more detrimental than helpful to U.S. competitiveness, because it drains funds, engineers, and product development away from the commercial sector.

Fragmented Policymaking

Although the U.S. government spends a great deal of money in many programs that explicitly or indirectly allocate resources to American industries, such aid has been totally uncoordinated and in no way part of a comprehensive strategy for industrial growth and change. It is U.S. political institutions that are usually seen as a major obstacle to more cohesive and comprehensive policies.

An electoral system that enables individual legislators to establish close ties independent of party organization to regional and functional groups, a decentralized congressional committee system, and the separation of the legislative, executive, and judicial branches provide multiple access and veto points for diverse interests. The lack of party discipline and the

68. Direct support for U.S. business (including agriculture) amounted to at least $130 billion in fiscal year 1984, not including all of defense spending. See Heclo, "Industrial Policy and the Executive Capacities of Government," p. 299. In 1980 alone the federal government made new loans to private business of $29 billion and new loan guarantees of $107 billion. See Lincoln, *Japan's Industrial Policies*, p. 47.

69. According to 1984–85 data, Pentagon spending on electronics R&D alone was several times the total R&D budget for the entire Japanese government. See Tatsuno, *Technopolis Strategy*, pp. 255–56.

Table 1. *U.S. Laws Related to Industrial Policy, 1977–88*[a]

Policy area	Carter administration 1977–80		Reagan administration 1981–88	
	Number	*Percent*	*Number*	*Percent*
Labor (employment, benefits, training, safety)	12	22	7	24
Energy, resources, environment	18	33	7	24
Technology and research	2	4	6	21
Declining industries	0	0	2	7
Transportation and communication	14	26	1	3
Commerce and commodities	3	6	4	14
Trade (tariffs, duties, overseas investment)	5	9	2	7
Total	54	100	29	100

Source: *Congressional Quarterly Weekly Report*, various issues, January 1977–December 1988. The authors wish to thank Zheya Gai for her assistance in gathering the data upon which this table is based.
a. Public laws passed by Congress and signed by the president related to industry and the economy.

separation of powers require the forming of coalitions to pass each bill, which makes it difficult to gain the requisite congressional majorities in two houses and presidential approval. The result is that few bills pass, and those that do tend to be either extremely specific ones for a narrow interest or extremely broad ones that distribute benefits widely—usually without discrimination or programmatic rationality—to attain passage.[70] The only exception may be when an externally derived crisis produces an unusual, and very temporary, consensus.

To show that this has been the pattern for policies to target resources to specific sectors, we categorized the laws related to economic policies passed during the Carter and Reagan administrations (see table 1). The number of bills in these policy areas on which both houses and the president could reach agreement is small—averaging about fourteen a year in the Carter administration and less than four a year in the Reagan years.

In addition, the majority of these laws under both administrations concerned infrastructure: energy and resources, labor, and transportation and communication. These affect many industries, rather than particular types of manufacturing or commercial industries. Those that did concern the latter were not general and comprehensive laws such as those the Japanese Diet passes to deal with problems facing declining or high-tech

70. See Weaver, *Politics of Industrial Change*, pp. 20–21.

industries. Instead most were narrowly focused, zeroing in on one or two particular problems in a particular sector. They ranged from extraordinarily trivial single-interest legislation—enabling honey producers to finance a research, promotion, and consumer information program (P.L. 98-590), for example—to legislation that was more important but targeted to a particular sector—such as promoting technology competitiveness and energy conservation in the steel industry (P.L. 100-697).[71]

Finally, it should be noted that the major change in categories across Democratic and Republican administrations is a relative decline in energy and transportation and an increase in technology. These probably represent each administration's major crises in industrial policy-related issues: energy and environmental problems in the Carter administration and the technology challenge from Japan under Reagan. The data indicate, therefore, that president and Congress can sometimes agree and cooperate across the institutional divide of the separation of powers, but it usually requires the unusual perception of crisis. Even then the policies produced are tailored to a particular problem, not a broad attack on the interrelated causes of the crisis.

Fragmented Administration

The narrow specificity and ad hoc nature of microeconomic policymaking in the checks-and-balances system has also resulted in a similar fragmentation of bureaucracy. As each new specific program is incrementally added, responsibility for it is grafted onto the myriad agencies administering dissimilar policies, or new agencies are created to administer that specific program, but often with jurisdiction that is unclear or shared with other agencies.

There is no cabinet-level equivalent to MITI, which can coordinate within one administrative unit the obviously related aspects of resources, energy, trade, manufacturing, commercial technology, and commerce. Nowhere has this administrative fragmentation become more obvious than in U.S. trade negotiations with the Japanese, in which conflicts between rival cabinet-level units have been endemic.[72] Below the cabinet

---

71. Quite exceptional is a law that comprehensively addressed a major industrial policy issue for a broad range of manufacturing sectors: the National Productivity and Innovation Act of 1984 to modify antitrust and intellectual property laws in order to enhance competitiveness of U.S. industries in foreign markets (P.L. 98-462).

72. See, for example, Clyde V. Prestowitz, Jr., *Trading Places: How We Allowed Japan to Take the Lead* (Basic Books, 1988), pp. 55–65, for the case of semiconductor negotiations. See also Ellis S. Krauss, *Under Construction: U.S.-Japan Negotiations to Open Japan's Construction Markets to American Firms, 1985–1988*, Pew Program in Case Teaching and Writing

level, administration is even more fragmented. There were 132 different economic policy units at the bureau level in the executive branch during the Carter administration, often with little coordination across units.[73]

Bureaucrats in these agencies also have little autonomy from the legislative process. Congress passes detailed legislation, keeps control over funding even for the most specific purposes,[74] and casts a watchful eye on administration by means of its large staff (much larger than in most parliamentary systems) and numerous committees and subcommittees.

Contrary to popular stereotypes, in parliamentary systems like Japan's much of the bureaucracy may be politicized, and American bureaucrats may have a great deal of expertise in their policy areas. However, the combination of Congress's specialized watchdog functions and each administration's ability to make new appointments at the entire upper level of the U.S. bureaucracy politicizes American administration in a different way. The Japanese bureaucracy tends to be divided vertically between ministries highly penetrated by LDP politicians and constituency concerns and economic ministries with more autonomy, such as MITI. The U.S. bureaucracy is politicized horizontally between politically appointed upper levels of leadership and lower-level career specialists, all watched over carefully by specialized units in the legislative branch.[75]

Capacity for Implementation

Even if the United States could formulate a comprehensive industrial policy, it would face major difficulties in implementing it because of a pluralistic market organization and a lack of established channels for business-government interaction. In many industries, particularly high-tech ones, market organization is fragmented among literally hundreds or thousands of firms. This impedes government-business relations and creates potential conflicts of interest among large and small firms. In comparison with their Japanese counterparts, American industry and trade associations are not as strong or hierarchically organized, and they have weaker control over their members. U.S. antitrust laws are a major

---

in International Affairs no. 145 (University of Pittsburgh, Graduate School of Public and International Affairs, 1989), pp. 8–10 and *passim.*

73. Heclo, "Industrial Policy and the Executive Capacities of Government," p. 303.

74. Weaver, *Politics of Industrial Change,* p. 22.

75. On U.S.-Japan differences, see Aberbach and others, "Comparing Japanese and American Administrative Elites." On the general institutional obstacles to industrial policy in the United States, see B. Guy Peters, "The Politics of Industrial and Regional Policy in the United States," paper prepared for conference on Regional Structural Change in International Perspective, October 1986, especially pp. 19–29.

obstacle to cooperation among firms in developing products (although they have become somewhat less so because of a 1984 revision of the law allowing cooperation under certain conditions).

Where industry is well organized, it is for the purpose of lobbying Congress, not negotiating with a bureaucracy. There are no institutionalized structures to allow business input into the process of policy formulation, which could result in reciprocal consent given by government and business to policies, as occurs in Japan. (The defense industry is an exception to almost all of the generalizations above: it has a more oligarchical market organization of large firms and long-established patterns of reciprocal bureaucracy-industry relations.)

Although American business is not as well organized as Japanese business for industrial policy, American labor is better organized for political influence than its Japanese counterpart. It is difficult to conceive of a broad-based industrial policy in the United States that would not have to include labor as a separate actor. This factor would complicate the development and implementation of an industrial policy and might introduce market-distorting effects like those that occurred in Sweden in the 1970s.

Finally, some analysts think that the greater dependence of American firms on equity, rather than credit markets, compared with those in Japan and Western Europe, deprives government of a major lever in implementing industrial policy. Credit-based markets allow government actors to target capital resources indirectly through the central bank's influence over other banks.[76]

The Consequences of the American System

There have been at least three major consequences of the federal government's inability to formulate and implement a coherent industrial policy for targeting resources to specific sectors. The first is that the American states and communities that have been most injured by deindustrialization have increasingly formulated their own regional industrial policies, as has occurred in Sweden. The U.S. context lacks the coordination and encouragement at the national level that Sweden has, however. Thus these subnational programs tend to be less successful in the larger and more diversified states, reflecting much of the same fragmentation and politicization that is characteristic at the federal level. They lack coordination within particular states, between states, and with

76. Zysman, Government, Markets, and Growth.

federal policies.[77] It is for this reason that B. Guy Peters suggests "rather than not having an industrial policy it could be argued that the United States suffers from *too many* industrial policies."[78]

The second consequence is that the federal policies that have been implemented for specific industries have been primarily reactive and a short-term response to the problems of industries in decline.[79] "Accelerationist" policies that anticipate future international markets and competition usually fail to gain the political consensus necessary under the American system to justify government intervention. Emerging high-tech industries, by their incipient nature, have traditionally lacked justification as a response to crisis, electoral or organized interest group constituencies, and an influential bureaucratic ally to mobilize sufficient support to have their needs translated into policies. It is only when the political consequences of international competition (such as unemployment or national security considerations) become obvious and a mature industry is in trouble that sufficient support can be mobilized for action to be taken.

The third consequence is that trade policy is increasingly the vehicle for such reactive responses. Because protectionism is contrary to the postwar consensus on free trade and there is a lack of consensus on activist government intervention on behalf of structure change, the policy options for coping with declining American industries are limited. Yet in the U.S. checks-and-balances system, for a president to do nothing invites partisan political criticism and congressional initiative.

Trade policy—where the executive has traditionally had great authority and there is a supporting consensus behind "free trade"—provides the president with a way out of this dilemma. By negotiating "temporary" and nominally voluntary restraints on offending imports and the opening of foreign markets with trading partners, the president satisfies calls for aid to uncompetitive American industries without adopting either overt protectionism or an explicit industrial policy. By so doing, he also maintains initiative in this area for the executive branch.[80]

77. Susan B. Hansen, "Industrial Policy and Corporatism in the American States," *Governance*, vol. 2 (April 1989), especially pp. 174–80, 191–94. See also Peter K. Eisinger, *The Rise of the Entrepreneurial State: State and Local Economic Development Policy in the United States* (University of Wisconsin, 1988).

78. Peters, "The Politics of Industrial and Regional Policy," p. 11. (Emphasis in the original.)

79. Okimoto, *Between MITI and the Market*, pp. 11–12.

80. For this argument based on a specific case, see Simon Reich, *Between Production and Protection: Reagan and the Negotiation of the VER for the Automobile Industry*, Pew Program

What should be recognized, however, is that such trade policies are a form of indirect targeting of resources to specific, threatened American industries and of government intervention in the domestic market structure. The American paradox is that what causes an incoherent industrial policy also leads to a trade policy that operates as an indirect, and possibly poor, substitute for the overt industrial policy that is ostensibly being avoided.

Governmental Institutions and Industrial Change

If two parliamentary systems, Japan and Sweden, could have such different experiences with targeting resources for industrial change, then parliamentary government does not explain patterns of industrial policy. Japan has had a relatively successful record in industrial policy toward manufacturing and technology, managing to keep economically effective policies from being distorted by political considerations; Sweden has not. Indeed, in its experience with politicization in the 1970s and current lack of coordination in its industrial policy, Sweden may resemble the United States more than Japan.

These experiences suggest that the distinction between parliamentary and checks-and-balances institutions is a less important determinant of industrial policy than the complex linkages among ideas, institutions, and instruments. More specific conclusions are the following.

1. *A political consensus on having an industrial policy is a prerequisite for a cohesive and coherent state approach to targeting resources for industrial change.* Japan developed such a consensus early, Sweden achieved it in the 1970s, and the United States is only now considering the need for a coherent policy, but is deeply divided. It is not even clear whether there is a widely shared perception that the United States' current economic and competitive problems constitute a crisis; and if such a shared perception did exist, the United States might not choose industrial policy as its response.

Historical development and past policy choices provide both the ratio-

---

in Case Teaching and Writing in International Affairs no. 119 (University of Pittsburgh, Graduate School of Public and International Affairs, 1989), especially "Teaching Material Supplement," p. 3. Also in the same series see Robert S. Walters' general argument in *U.S. Negotiation of Voluntary Restraint Agreements in Steel, 1984: Domestic Sources of International Economic Diplomacy,* no. 107 (1988), pp. 6–7 of "Teaching Material." See also Ellis S. Krauss and Simon Reich," "Ideology, Interests, and the American Executive: Toward a Theory of Foreign Competition and Manufacturing Trade Policy," *International Organization,* vol. 46 (Autumn 1992), pp. 857–97.

nale for and direction of a nation's response. Japan's commitment to economic development as one of the state's primary functions had been consistent since the late nineteenth century. It was not difficult, therefore, for the nation to choose industrial policy and create institutions to manage its immediate postwar economic crisis.

In Sweden, a consensus has existed since the 1930s on the need to sustain high employment levels and economic growth to provide the tax base for the prime goal of maintaining and expanding the welfare state. When the country was faced with a structural crisis in the late 1960s and early 1970s, industrial policy could be legitimized as an extension of this goal and new implementing institutions could be established. However, the consensus also led easily to the distortion of the original priorities of industrial policy by using it as a means to avoid unemployment and soften regional opposition to structural change.

Historically, there has been no consensus in the United States on state intervention, except for defense, trade, selected welfare programs, and macroeconomic policy. It is therefore not surprising that the federal government has targeted resources to industry through macroeconomic policy and the fragmented, indirect channels of interest group politics, defense policy, and trade negotiation. As long as a consensus on trade or defense was easier to reach than one on industrial policy, resources could be targeted through policies in these areas.

2. *Societal and political arrangements other than legislative-executive arrangements have also played a key role in determining the type of industrial policies adopted, the instruments used, and their effectiveness.* In Sweden, the political importance of organized labor in the dominant political coalition, the sources of capital and international nature of large industry, and the *ämbetsverk* system of administration have all helped to determine the content of industrial policy and the effectiveness and choice of instruments. For example, when industrial policy was implemented, direct subsidies and state enterprises had to be used because other kinds of leverage were lacking.

In postwar Japan, credit for financing, a hierarchical and oligopolistic concentration of industry in many sectors, and highly organized trade associations all provided MITI with indirect industrial policy instruments. A dominant political coalition in which big business was a major partner but organized labor was weak encouraged government-business ties. The institutionalized channels of information and influence from the private sector to government allowed industrial policies to maintain a future-oriented, market-conforming direction. Labor practices in large enterprises that made layoffs employers' last resort, and an electoral system that helped channel politicians' energy into policy areas other than industrial policy, reduced political pressures to deviate from that direction.

3. *Relationships among ideas, institutions, and instruments are not one-way; policies adopted affect institutions, and instruments and institutions feed back into consensus.* Sweden's use of direct subsidies and state enterprises to implement its policies helped to politicize the institutions of industrial policymaking, which in turn made the targeting of resources to industry a controversial issue. More recently, the devolution of industrial policy to regions as both the target and administrators of many programs has helped to depoliticize industrial policy and reestablish a consensus.

In the United States, the institutions that fragment industrial policy and give declining industries an advantage in mobilizing influence also encourage a disbelief in the viability of an American industrial policy.[81] That is, the nature of institutions can also facilitate or discourage a consensus concerning industrial policy.[82]

In Japan, by contrast, MITI's use of indirect means of implementation and low levels of direct financing has helped to keep industrial policy from being turned into a pork barrel for interest groups and politicians. Because decisions concerning industry have been until recently kept within MITI's jurisdiction and the well-established networks linking MITI and large industry, any conflicts over policy could be privatized and protected from distortion by narrow political interests.[83] This also helped preserve the consensus on industrial policy.

Conclusion

The outcome of state involvement in industrial change is highly dependent on a complex relationship among political consensus; the nature of existing societal, economic and political institutions; and the specific instruments and policies. Even single-party-dominant parliamentary institutions are neither a direct cause nor a sufficient condition for a particular kind of industrial policy, nor a guarantee of its success.

81. See, for example, Charles L. Schultze, "Industrial Policy: A Dissent," *Brookings Review*, vol. 2 (Fall 1983), pp. 9–11; and Peters, "The Politics of Industrial and Regional Policy in the United States," *passim* for academic examples of this linkage.

82. We are grateful to James L. Sundquist for this insight.

83. Richard Boyd argues this "privatization" of government-industry relations, and consequent depoliticization, is crucial. "Government-Industry Relations in Japan: Access, Communication, and Competitive Collaboration," in Stephen Wilks and Maurice Wright, eds., *Comparative Government-Industry Relations: Western Europe, the United States, and Japan* (Oxford University Press, 1987), pp. 64–65.

Does this mean that the type of governmental system has no effect on industrial policymaking? Not exactly. Governmental institutions do influence government capabilities, but they do so in ways that vary across parliamentary systems and even over time.

Because both Japan and Sweden are single-party-dominant systems, we are limited in our ability to generalize to other types of parliamentary systems, such as Britain's party government system or continental multi-party systems. But our comparison of this particular regime type and the United States does suggest the following effects of governmental institutions.

— Without a parliamentary system, the leaders of Japan's ruling party and MITI might not have had the centralizing powers to counteract the centrifugal tendencies of the Japanese electoral system, and Japanese policymaking would much more resemble the American case.

— Without the party leadership advantages of a parliamentary system, the Swedish SAP might not have been able to adopt an industrial policy so easily in the late 1960s nor change the existing policy so readily once it resumed power in the early 1980s.

— The fact that parliamentary systems allow for coalition and minority governments may also affect the targeting of resources: because of their political vulnerability in a proportional representation system, the non-socialist (and sometimes minority) governments of Sweden from 1976 to 1982 were impelled to maintain employment levels through whatever means necessary.

— The fragmented structure of the U.S. system probably also helps to fragment American interest groups and may discourage an ideological consensus on industrial policy. Further, Congress's role hinders the development of independent bureaucratic-industry channels like those MITI has been able to construct.

Parliamentary institutions are probably at least a necessary, if not sufficient, condition for having a coordinated industrial policy to target resources and impose losses. Governmental institutions alone do not produce an effective targeting of resources, but they do make a difference. They matter more by their indirect consequences on, and their linkage to, other key societal, economic, and political institutions than by their inherent individual properties.

Allen Schick

Governments versus Budget Deficits

Most industrialized democracies entered the 1980s with their public
finances in disarray. Two oil crises, stagflation, escalating debt
burdens, and the soaring costs of entitlements and other entrenched programs had generated huge deficits that destabilized the relationship between the government budget and the national economy. Fiscal stress
turned many governments from dispensers of political benefits into dis-
tributors of financial losses. This was a difficult adjustment; not every
country was able to make it.

This chapter compares the manner in which the United States and
two other countries—the Netherlands and Sweden—responded to fiscal
problems during the 1980s. All three countries experienced large public-
sector deficits in the early 1980s. The financial deficit peaked at 7.1 percent
of gross domestic product (GDP) in the Netherlands in 1982, 7.0 percent
in Sweden in 1982, and 3.8 percent in the United States in 1983.[1] Since
the mid-1980s, there has been general improvement in the fiscal balances
of OECD countries, but some have recovered much more substantially
than others. Sweden ended the decade with public-sector surpluses, but
the Netherlands and the United States still had sizable deficits.

Differences in fiscal performance may be partly due to economic circumstances, such as the effects of fluctuating natural gas prices in the
Netherlands. But a fuller explanation requires that political factors be
examined as well. Curbing budget deficits almost always requires two
governmental capabilities of central interest to this volume: setting and
maintaining priorities when policy objectives are in conflict and resources

1. The data cover the entire public sector, so that part of the deficit incurred by the
U.S. national government was offset by the surpluses accumulated by states and localities.
Organization for Economic Cooperation and Development, *OECD Economic Outlook*, no.
48 (December 1990), table R-14.

are limited, and imposing costs on concentrated interests. The argument advanced here is that differences in political institutions, especially electoral systems and the governments ensuing from them, have a major effect on governmental cohesion, which in turn affects governmental capabilities and performance in reducing deficits. If Sweden and the Netherlands have taken different fiscal paths, it is at least partly because beneath the surface similarity of their cabinet governments, one country has been much more politically cohesive than the other.

Government Capabilities and Government Deficits

Trying to reduce the deficit is at its core a political problem. It is not easy for elected politicians to vote for tax increases or benefit cutbacks. Politicians have an abundant supply of excuses for putting off the day of reckoning. One expedient is to forecast a buoyant economy that will liquidate the deficit; another is to announce deficit-cutting moves but to retreat in response to public protests or a lessening of public attention. An OECD study of governmental responses to macroeconomic crises in eleven countries concluded that political leaders did "not seriously tackle the root cause of their problems until the situation approached crisis conditions and the need for remedial action . . . became evident and broadly accepted by the unions and the population at large." According to the OECD findings, only when the existing course of action became "unsustainable" did democratic governments reluctantly alter their policies.[2]

This explanation puts all democratic governments into the same category. Surely, however, some countries acted more expeditiously than others, and some were more determined or effective in recasting fiscal policy. Arguably, no matter how onerous the task, some political arrangements may make accomplishing it a bit easier, while others throw up additional obstacles.

Priority Setting and Institutional Design

A more discriminating interpretation would link effectiveness in dealing with the deficit to the effects of political institutions on government capabilities. I will focus primarily on setting and maintaining government priorities, both because loss imposition is the subject of another chapter

2. OECD, *Why Economic Policies Change Course: Eleven Case Studies* (Paris, 1988), pp. 9, 12.

in this volume, and because the case studies presented in this chapter suggest that the three countries tried to minimize direct loss imposition, two of them portraying their policies as bestowing economic gains.

The concern here is not with maintaining existing priorities in the absence of external challenge—that is something that comes easily to most governments. It is instead with how governments ration scarce resources and attempt to balance resources and commitments when external constraints call into question the continuation of established policies. Policy conflicts are rife in budgeting, especially when the economy is in disrepair. In these circumstances, the government may have to choose between a larger deficit or lower taxes or between cutting spending or increasing taxes. It may have to decide whether inflation or unemployment should be its most important fiscal concern. A cohesive government may be able to act in a more decisive and constant manner than one that has to worry about holding a multiparty coalition together or about bridging the political distance between the White House and Capitol Hill.

Institutional effects on government priority-setting capabilities may be of several kinds. What the introductory chapter of this volume called the "first tier" of explanation attempts to explain differences in government capabilities in terms of differences between parliamentary systems and the U.S. separation-of-powers system. From a parliamentarist perspective, the fusion of executive and legislative powers offers several advantages for government priority setting. A cabinet offers a centralized forum for discussing and resolving disputes over priorities and for imposing resource constraints. The U.S. system, in comparison, is characterized both by decentralization within Congress and by the absence of definitive mechanisms for resolving conflicts between executive and legislative priorities. Frequently in recent years, the president's annual budget—the closest thing to a priority-setting exercise in the United States—has been declared "dead on arrival" in Congress, but Congress has been unable to put together a coherent alternative. Moreover, when a reordering of priorities involves proposals for loss imposition, the multiple veto points in the U.S. system help potentially disadvantaged interests to ward off losses.

A presidentialist perspective, on the other hand, suggests that the institutional advantages of a parliamentary system in providing a centralized forum for priority setting and government cohesion are likely to be largely illusory. Even in the centralized forum of a cabinet, pressures from program constituencies, incremental norms, and reluctance to cut colleagues' programs lest the same principle be applied to your own department (norms of reciprocity) suggest that the ability to reorient priorities is likely to be quite limited—especially when doing so means imposing losses on some constituencies. This is especially important when cabinets are multiparty coalitions or when cabinet ministers have political standing independent of the prime minister and are closely identified with specific interests or regions.

Both the parliamentarist and presidentialist perspectives suggest a degree of homogeneity among parliamentary systems that seems highly exaggerated, however. Weaver and Rockman's second tier of explanation stresses differences among parliamentary and presidential systems, especially the former. In particular, one can distinguish between parliamentary systems where multiparty coalitions are the modal pattern of cabinet formation, those where there tends to be alternation (although not necessarily with great regularity) between two parties holding parliamentary majorities (the party government model), and the more unusual occurrence of single-party dominance—with either a majority or near-majority—for very extended periods. As the introductory chapter notes, these "regime types" are highly dependent both on electoral rules (proportional representation versus single-member district) and cleavage patterns. Which governmental type is likely to have the greatest ability to set and maintain priorities? One reasonable hypothesis is that the cohesion of decisionmaking elites and the absence of effective veto points are at least as important as the existence of a centralized decisionmaking forum. On this dimension, single-party majority governments seem likely to have an advantage over coalitional and minority governments. However, party governments that are subject to frequent alternation in power may find that their clear priorities are reversed or muddled considerably after an election; single-party-dominant systems are likely to show the greatest capacity to maintain new priorities once they have been adopted.

Important differences can also occur across countries and over time in presidential systems. One such difference—again depending heavily on factors such as electoral rules—is the frequency of divided party control of the legislature and executive. Divided government is certainly not inherent in presidential systems, but it has come close to being institutionalized in the United States over the past twenty years. Not only has this division between the two political branches persisted for almost an entire generation, but politicians in both parties appear to behave as if it will continue for many more years. While divided government has radiated to many areas of national policy, in none has the effect been more pronounced or protracted than the budget. Divided government clearly can reduce elite cohesion and increase the likelihood that mutual vetoes will lead to stalemate, exacerbating difficulties in priority setting that are inherent in the separation of powers. I will argue later that divided government unquestionably has impaired the capacity of the United States to deal effectively with budget deficits in the 1980s.

Third-tier institutional features such as bicameralism and federalism may also affect government capabilities. A bicameral legislature will presumably have two distinct sets of priorities and will have to adopt compromises between them. The impact of federalism is less clear, however. If changing priorities and program retrenchment require approval or aid in implementation from subnational governments, then federalism may make these tasks more difficult. But federalism may also make it easier for a central government to foster retrenchment in programs that are centrally funded but delivered by subnational governments, since any public anger at cutbacks is likely to be concentrated at the level of government that delivers the service.

Institutions and Budgets: Some Preliminary Evidence

Table 1 shows the general government financial balances of thirteen OECD countries, with the countries divided into distinctive categories of executive-legislative relationships and modal patterns of government formation. Several patterns are evident from the data. First, there was a general decline in the financial balance as a percentage of GDP between 1970–74 and 1985–89. All but two countries (Norway and the United Kingdom) of the thirteen had a decline in financial balances; the average decline was 2.5 percent of GDP. However, ten of the thirteen countries (excepting only Italy, France, and the United States) showed improvement in 1985–89 over the immediately preceding (1980–84) period. All three case study countries experienced a decline over the twenty-year period. Sweden's decline was more severe than that of the other two countries, but it began from a healthier base and its recovery was stronger than that of the Netherlands or the United States. The increase in financial deficit was greatest in the Netherlands, which tracked U.S. performance fairly closely until 1978, but then began a decline that was somewhat more severe than that of the United States.

Some very crude patterns of institutional effects also emerge from the data in table 1. While the small and uneven number of cases in each category should make one very cautious in generalizing about the effects of institutional arrangements, the semipresidential systems (France and Finland) and single-party-dominant systems (Japan and Sweden) seem to do better at balancing budgets on average than party government systems, the U.S. system of full separation of powers, and systems where coalitional government is the norm. Countries with the same pattern of executive-legislative arrangements and modal pattern of government for-

Table 1. *General Government Financial Balances in Selected Countries, by Type of Regime, Selected Periods, 1970–89*[a]
Percent of GDP

Regime type and country	Average annual balance				Change, 1970–74 to 1985–89
	1970–74	1975–79	1980–84	1985–89	
Party government					
Australia	1.9	−2.4	−2.7	−0.6	−2.5
Canada	0.7	−2.4	−4.7	−4.5	−5.2
United Kingdom	−0.7	−4.1	−3.1	−0.7	0
Coalitional					
Denmark	3.9	−0.9	−6.1	0.7	−3.2
Germany	−0.1	−3.3	−2.9	−1.2	−1.1
Italy	−6.8	−10.4	−10.8	−11.2	−4.4
Netherlands	−0.5	−2.7	−5.9	−5.5	−5.0
Norway	4.5	1.7	5.4	5.0	0.5
Single-party-dominant					
Japan	0.7	−4.1	−3.5	0.6	−0.1
Sweden	4.1	1.1	−4.8	1.6	−2.5
Semipresidential					
Finland	4.6	2.5	−0.1	0.9	−3.7
France	0.7	−1.4	−2.1	−2.1	−2.8
Full separation of powers					
United States	−0.6	−1.4	−2.5	−2.6	−2.0

Sources: Organization for Economic Cooperation and Development, OECD Economic Outlook, no. 47 (June 1990), table R-14; and OECD Economic Outlook, no. 48 (December 1990), table R-14.

a. This table consolidates all units of general government, using accounting standards devised by international organizations.

mation may have very different experiences with budget deficits, however. Comparing party government systems, for example, Britain has had a fairly strong record of deficit reduction, while Canada's record has been especially weak in the 1980s. Among parliamentary systems where coalitions are the norm, Germany and Norway have strong records, whereas Italy and the Netherlands have particularly weak records. Moreover, countries and regime types that do very well in some periods may do quite poorly in others—Sweden being the foremost example.[3]

3. If the criterion is simply the best balance at the end of the period or the average deficit over the 1980–89 period, then Sweden is clearly the best performer, with the United

The data suggest, in short, that political institutional effects are likely to be important, but that one must look simply beyond the modal pattern of government formation (what Weaver and Rockman call the "regime type") to the governing relationships in effect at particular times (for example, minority, coalitional, or single-party majority government).[4] This argument about institutional effects on success in dealing with budget deficits is consistent with the approach taken in a series of recent articles by Nouriel Roubini and Jeffrey Sachs, who found a predictable relationship between changes in the ratio of public debt to GDP and governing arrangements. The authors conclude that "*differing institutional arrangements* in the political process in the various OECD economies . . . help to explain the markedly different patterns of budget deficits in the different countries."[5]

The key Roubini-Sachs argument is that the weaker the government, the less able it is to put together a majority in support of tough deficit-reducing actions. The authors construct an index of political cohesion based on the type and duration of government. The most cohesive governments are parliamentary systems in which a single party constitutes the government and presidential regimes in which the same party controls both the legislative and executive branches. "Small coalition" governments consisting of only two like-minded parties or governments in

---

States second and the Netherlands third among the three countries. If the criterion is instead change in performance between the first and last periods, the ranking is different: the U.S. budget imbalance grew by 2.0 percent of GNP from 1970–74 to 1985–89, Sweden's budget balance fell by 2.6 percent of GNP, and the Netherlands' budget deficit mushroomed by 5.0 percent of GNP. If the criterion used is improvement in 1989 (the last year for which data are available) over the lowest year of the deficit "trough," then Sweden wins hands down: an improvement of 12.1 percent versus 1.9 percent for the Netherlands and 2.1 percent for the United States. Not surprisingly, if the criterion used is instead the size of the fall from 1970s peak year of budgetary balance to the 1980s trough year, the ratings are reversed: the United States fell 4.4 percent, the Netherlands 7.7 percent, and Sweden an astounding 12.3 percent.

4. Three obvious factors to consider here are (1) the maturity of a country's contributory pension scheme: such programs produce large surpluses before they reach maturity; (2) the dependence of some countries on fluctuating oil and natural gas revenues; and (3) the effects of particular government types at specific points in time—for example, whether a particular coalition government contains a broad array of parties with different interests and whether the coalition has a majority.

5. Nouriel Roubini and Jeffrey D. Sachs, "Political and Economic Determinants of Budget Deficits in the Industrial Democracies," *European Economic Review*, vol. 33 (May 1989), pp. 903–38, quote at p. 905 (emphasis in original); and Roubini and Sachs, "Government Spending and Budget Deficits in the Industrial Countries," *Economic Policy*, vol. 4 (April 1989), pp. 100–32.

which presidential and legislative power are held by different parties are somewhat less cohesive. Even less cohesive are governments consisting of "large coalitions" with three or more parties, and the weakest type appears when the government lacks a majority in parliament.

Roubini and Sachs find that the relationship between governing arrangements and budget outcomes is asymmetric. Weak governments maintain reasonable budget balance when the economy is strong, but they are much less able to do so under adverse conditions. The authors surmise that coalition partners can block spending increases in good times and spending cuts when conditions become unfavorable. They also suggest that when a weak government is unsure of its tenure, its member parties may be unwilling to take steps that would, by reducing the deficit, make things easier for the next government.

The data and arguments presented by Roubini and Sachs are highly relevant to the issues under consideration in this chapter. On the whole, their conclusions are consistent with the hypothesis advanced earlier that political cohesion is the key ingredient in determining a government's capacity to arrest deficit spending. However, their study is limited in two important ways. First, it reduces all political institutions to a simple classification, and in so doing, it ignores substantial differences among governing systems. For example, both France and the United States are classified as presidential systems, but there is a big difference between the French hybrid and the U.S. system of checks and balances.

A second shortcoming of the Roubini-Sachs study is one that besets many cross-national comparisons and is especially troubling in comparing governmental performance with respect to the budget deficit. The authors follow conventional practice and measure the trend in the debt of general government. Thus they consolidate the debt of all units and levels of government in a single measure. For many purposes, such as comparing aggregate fiscal restraint, this is an appropriate and necessary measure. But in analyzing policies that produce deficits, consolidating all governments in a single measure can lead to erroneous conclusions. Although the institutional characteristics that concern Roubini and Sachs pertain to the national government, not to municipalities or provinces, their measure of fiscal performance spans all levels of government. This method yields misleading measures of U.S. performance in controlling public debt. Roubini and Sachs give the United States one of the highest success ratings in the 1980–85 period, higher, in fact, than Japan or Germany. According to their data, net public debt rose in the United States from 19.8 percent of GDP in 1979 to 27.1 percent in 1985, an average annual increase of only 1.2 percentage points. But during the same period, the public debt of the federal government rose from 26 percent of GDP to 38 percent, an annual average increase of 2.0 percentage points, much higher than the Roubini-Sachs rate.[6] If only federal results were used, as should be the practice when comparing the performance of national institutions, the United States would drop from being one of the best performers to being one of the worst. (Although table 1 of this chapter uses figures for all levels of government, the remaining tables are generated from country sources and, therefore, classify data in the manner that they are shown in the various budgets.) In short, the work of Roubini and Sachs is a good starting point for thinking about the influence of institutions on fiscal outcomes. But one must look more closely at both institutions and outcomes before drawing conclusions on how they interact.

Case Study Countries

Big, seemingly intractable, deficits have not been exclusively the problem of the United States. A number of parliamentary democracies, such as Ireland and Italy, have experienced extreme fiscal imbalance. But there also are some countries that have had considerable success in restoring budget balance. Sweden was chosen as a country to study because of such fiscal success. It offers one of the most dramatic cases of a reversal of budgetary shortfalls among the industrial countries. The Netherlands was selected as the third case study because it has had less success than Sweden in curtailing its deficits and has governing arrangements that are sufficiently differentiated from both Sweden's and the United States' to make for productive comparisons.

The Netherlands and Sweden are similar in important ways. They rank first and second, respectively, among OECD countries in total governmental outlays as a proportion of GDP. Both have large public sectors that dispense "cradle to grave" benefits to most of the population. Both are relatively small countries with open economies heavily dependent on international trade. The two countries rate first and second among the wealthier OECD countries listed in table 1 in terms of imports and exports as a percentage of GDP.[7] But they also have important differences: the Netherlands already had overall budget deficits by the

6. *Budget of the United States Government, Historical Tables, Fiscal Year 1992, Historical Tables*, table 7.1.

7. In 1987, imports and exports totaled 85.5 percent of GDP in the Netherlands and 53.4 percent in Sweden. The U.S. economy is much less dependent on trade. Its imports and exports combined for only 15.3 percent of GDP. See "Basic Statistics: International Comparisons," in OECD, *OECD Economic Surveys: Netherlands, 1988/1989.*

1970–74 period, while the Swedish budget had overall surpluses through this period (table 1).

Although both Sweden and the Netherlands are parliamentary regimes, there are important institutional differences between the two countries. Both countries elect legislators on the basis of proportional representation, but the latter has a single national list while the former divides the country into multimember districts, each with its own list. Sweden has had a dominant political party since the 1930s, while the Netherlands has been governed for generations by multiparty coalitions. The Swedish cabinet is characterized by a high degree of integration; the Dutch by a high degree of heterogeneity.[8] In Sweden, the ministries are unusually small and within easy walking distance of one another;[9] in the Netherlands, some ministries are very large and they are more separated geographically. In Sweden, the ministers usually are all of the same party and they meet with extraordinary frequency; in the Netherlands, key ministers often are from different parties and their meetings tend to be less frequent and more formal.[10] Sweden has an encompassing labor movement with strong ties to the dominant political party; the Netherlands has long been a segmented society in which social cleavages are patched over through "the politics of accommodation."[11] However, both countries were more politically cohesive than the United States during the 1980s, a decade during which the Republicans controlled the presidency and the Democrats controlled one or both houses of Congress.

My choice of two parliamentary systems where electoral rules of proportional representation are used does not allow direct extension of arguments to party government systems, but I will suggest later that issues of elite cohesion are equally relevant to these countries.

8. See Rudy B. Andeweg, "Centrifugal Forces and Collective Decision-Making: The Case of the Dutch Cabinet," *European Journal of Political Research*, vol. 16 (1988), pp. 125–51.

9. The Swedish government is compartmentalized into ministries, which are supposed to be the policymaking organs, and agencies, which are supposed to implement those policies. The typical ministry has perhaps a hundred or so employees. All the ministries are located in downtown Stockholm, and most or all are linked by underground passageways, which foster contact.

10. In 1981–82, a key period for making budget policy, the Dutch inner cabinet (called "the Pentagon") had leaders from three political parties. The prime minister was from one of the coalition parties; the minister of social affairs, his political rival, was from a second party; and the minister of economic affairs headed a third party.

11. The term is taken from the title of a renowned book on Dutch politics. See Arend Lijphart, *The Politics of Accommodation: Pluralism and Democracy in the Netherlands* (University of California Press, 1975).

From Expansion to Restraint: Fiscal Policy in the OECD Countries

The postwar growth era, stretching in most industrial democracies from the 1950s to the early 1970s, was characterized by widespread improvements in productivity and in the overall standard of living and by low rates of inflation and unemployment. Economic expansion gave rise to incremental budgeting, which concentrated governmental attention and policy decisions on the size and allocation of spending increases. Cyclical downturns usually were brief and shallow. Moreover, during a period dominated by expectations of continuing growth, it was deemed appropriate to spend according to the potential of the economy. Accordingly, actual budgetary balance was abandoned as the operative norm in most industrial countries: balancing the economy was considered more important than balancing the government's finances. Nevertheless, economic vigor ensured that deficits (when they occurred) were modest and manageable. Although public-sector growth generally outpaced the growth trend in the economy—total outlays in the OECD community averaged about 35 percent of GDP in 1974, compared with only 28 percent in 1960—there was widespread support during the expansive postwar years for allocating a rising share of national income to public programs.

Economic growth was accompanied by political stability. Even in countries that experienced high government turnover (such as Italy), the expansionary policies established by one regime were continued by the next. A broad consensus on the role of government in ameliorating the financial distress of old age and disability led to increased social expenditure and to steep escalation in transfer payments.[12] The consensus was much weaker in the United States than in most European democracies—note the failure to enact national health insurance and the battle over the Employment Act of 1946—but even here the national government settled into an expansionary pattern.

It was easy for politicians in those heady times. Politics entailed the allocation of gains. Government had more to spend, and so too did most households. Despite rising tax burdens, real per capita disposable income rose steadily in the United States and elsewhere. Choices still had to be made among competing claims on limited resources, but they generally revolved around how the economic largess should be parceled out.

---

12. The growth of government in OECD countries is analyzed by Peter Saunders and Friedrich Klau, *The Role of the Public Sector: Causes and Consequences of the Growth of Government* (Paris: Organization for Economic Cooperation and Development, 1985).

Economic and political stability were jarred, however, by the first oil crisis (1973–74), which brought in its wake stagnation, soaring inflation and unemployment, and a slowdown—a halt in some countries—in the productivity gains that had made it possible for both public expenditures and disposable incomes to rise. At first, some industrial countries responded to the oil shock as if it were an ordinary cyclical occurrence. They tried to reflate their economies through job creation (or preservation) schemes and tax relief, and they accepted the upsurge in budget deficits as a normal cyclical response. But recovery generally was short-lived and sluggish. Caught in the grip of stagflation, various democratic governments came to see big deficits as a structural problem that would not go away once economic growth resumed.

In a weakened economic condition, most OECD countries recognized that unless they changed course, the weight of past decisions, especially indexed entitlement and other commitments, would compel persistent deficits as well as the continued enlargement of the relative size of the public sector. These concerns solidified into government policies in the early 1980s after the second oil crisis (1979) further unsettled national economies. Still reeling from the aftereffects of the previous shock only five years earlier, most industrial countries concluded that they could not respond with standard countercyclical prescriptions. They could not afford the costs, and they were no longer confident that the old formulas would work. Instead, they shifted gears from expansionary policies to constrictive budgets.

A key step in this adjustment was the announcement of restrictive fiscal norms to guide budget policy. Governments in most OECD countries pledged to curtail their budget deficits by implementing constrictive policies that would reduce or stabilize public expenditures and tax burdens. Most established specific fiscal targets for the years immediately ahead, such as the amount by which the deficit would be reduced relative to GDP or the percentage by which real spending would be changed.[13] The most popular target was a reduction in the ratio of the deficit (the public debt, in some countries) to GDP. Fourteen of the nineteen countries participating in an OECD study on the control of public expenditure

---

13. A 1987 OECD report characterized the early 1980s as a period during which " 'top-down' constraints were gradually imposed much more effectively on the 'bottom-up' demands of spenders, their clients and supporters. . . . All countries taking part in the study now publish some form of summary objectives or targets for fiscal policy. These usually include a target for expenditure. Many governments publish their budgetary targets to stimulate public discussion. Often this is seen as a way to further build consensus about fiscal policy goals and means to meet them." OECD, *The Control and Management of Government Expenditure* (Paris, 1987), p. 21.

announced their determination to reduce the relative size of the deficit. Another four countries undertook to curtail the amount of the budget deficit.

It is hard to discern any relationship between political conditions in the various countries and the establishment of fiscal targets. Governments to the left and to the right of center embraced these norms, as did assorted cabinet and presidential governments. The homogeneity of government behavior was partly due to the pervasiveness of the fiscal crisis, and partly to the symbolic character of the announced objectives. The norms typically were formulated outside regular budgetary channels, and often without serious consideration of their attainability or of their impact on the economy and government programs. Moreover, they usually did not lock the government into a specific course of action. They were political statements designed to put interest groups and others on notice: after years of soaring growth, the government was entering a period of consolidation.

Announcing targets and achieving them are quite different political operations. Because the targets were stated in highly aggregated terms, they did not mention the specific revenue or spending actions required to implement them. At the targeting stage, the losses that would likely be generated by deficit-reducing policies were veiled from public view. Only the good things were publicized—such as stabilization of the economy and amelioration of the debt burden. A broad array of political interests, including some that might have objected if they had known how the bad news was to be distributed, could thus come together in embracing the targets. But once governments moved to implement the targets, they could no longer avoid difficult questions, such as precisely which programs were to be retrenched and whose taxes were to be raised. At the implementation stage, governments also faced conflicting objectives, such as the relative priority of lowering tax burdens or reducing the deficit. It was at this stage, when specific budget decisions were made, that political characteristics came into play and differentiated those countries that were able to carry out deficit-reduction plans from those that were not.

Battling the Deficit: Two Disappointments, One Success

The budget deficit dominated government policy in many industrial countries during the 1980s. Revenue and spending decisions were framed in terms of their effect on the deficit, and program issues were often debated almost wholly in terms of whether they would widen or narrow the fiscal imbalance. The size of the deficit became a measure of overall government performance, and success was measured in terms of whether deficit targets had been met.

In assessing government effectiveness in dealing with a deficit, I offer no judgment as to what the appropriate relationship between revenue and spending should be. Instead, I take the actions of government at face value: if a government has endorsed a specific deficit target, this target is then taken as the yardstick for gauging fiscal success or failure. The three countries selected for comparison all adopted deficit targets in the 1980s.

Before proceeding with review of the policy objectives and results in each of the countries, a few comments are in order. First, this analysis is bounded by the 1980s. Although a decade is an arbitrary time period, the 1980s provide a common point of reference for the three countries under review. The decade began shortly after the second oil crisis, which, as noted earlier, drove home the message that the deficit was a structural problem that would not be remedied by economic recovery alone. Each country replaced its government shortly after the decade started, and the new government (or a successor with a similar political orientation) remained in office through the rest of the 1980s. Thus each country offers a case study of policy changes initiated early in the 1980s and continued for an extended period of time.

Second, the analysis focuses principally on the actions of central governments, because their capabilities form the subject of this chapter. The three countries differ markedly in the relationship between the central and provincial, or in some cases municipal, governments. The United States is a federal system; Sweden and the Netherlands have unitary systems. Swedish local governments raise the bulk of their funds by imposing an income tax that piggybacks the national income tax. In the Netherlands, by contrast, most local money comes from funds controlled by the central government. The three countries have relatively independent social security sectors, though the Dutch government makes annual contributions to these funds and also makes frequent adjustments in social security benefits and premiums. Although the discussion here focuses on the central government, it will sometimes be appropriate to consider the consolidated public sector.

Finally, this chapter generally relies on each country's own data, rather than the uniform comparisons published by various international organizations. The data produced by each country provide a better picture of how it sees its budget predicament and what it purports to be doing about the deficit. For example, the Netherlands typically reports the size of the deficit as a proportion of net national income. While this measure is not used in the other countries, it is integral to examining what the Netherlands has done to control its budget deficit.

United States: Big Deficits, Small Deficit Reductions

Federal budgeting began and ended the decade with deficit-reduction agreements negotiated by presidential aides and congressional leaders. The first summit took place in March 1980, shortly after Jimmy Carter disowned the budget he had submitted only one month earlier. At the time, the projected deficit (for the 1981 fiscal year) was puny—only $16 billion—but it was accompanied by soaring interest rates and near panic in financial markets. The last summit of the decade occurred in April 1989, shortly after George Bush took office. It culminated in an agreement that the president and congressional leaders hoped would avert a Gramm-Rudman-Hollings sequester for the looming fiscal year. In between the two summits, the White House and congressional Democrats repeatedly fought over budget policies and what should be done about the deficit.

The year 1980 was important for another innovation that sought to reduce the deficit. It was the first time that the reconciliation process established by the 1974 budget act was used.[14] Reconciliation quickly became a regular part of the budget landscape. With the exception of 1983 and 1985 (when legislative action on reconciliation was not completed until the next year) and 1988 (when the need for reconciliation was obviated by a two-year deficit-reduction package negotiated the previous year), Congress enacted a reconciliation bill every year during the decade. These measures varied greatly in scope, but all purported to shrink the budget deficit. By the end of the decade, the reconciliation bill was popularly referred to as the deficit-reduction bill.

The first summit and the first reconciliation bill established a pattern that persisted throughout the decade. Steps were announced to reduce the deficit, and some were implemented. The president (and sometimes Congress as well) projected a declining deficit in the years ahead, but the actual deficit generally turned out much higher. In 1981, when Jimmy Carter's original budget showed a $16 billion deficit, the summit turned this into a projected $16 billion surplus, but the actual deficit for the fiscal year was $74 billion.

Table 2 compares the deficit outcomes with the president's initial

---

14. The procedures and early use of this process are discussed in Allen Schick, *Reconciliation and the Congressional Budget Process* (Washington: American Enterprise Institute for Public Policy Research, 1981).

Table 2. *Comparison of President's Budget, Congressional Budget, and Budget Outcome, Fiscal Years 1980–89*
Billions of dollars

Item	1980	1981	1982	1983	1984	1985	1986	1987	1988	1989
Receipts										
President's budget	503	600	650	666	660	745	794	850	917	965
Congressional budget[a]	509	614	658	666	680	751	796	852	933	965
Actual receipts[b]	517	599	618	601	667	734	769	854	909	991
Outlays										
President's budget	544	634	712	773	863	940	974	994	1,024	1,094
Congressional budget[a]	532	614	695	770	851	932	968	995	1,041	1,094
Actual outlays[b]	591	678	746	808	852	946	990	1,004	1,065	1,144
Deficit										
President's budget	41	34	62	118	203	195	182	144	108	130
Congressional budget[a]	23	0	38	104	172	181	172	143	108	130
Actual deficit[b]	74	79	128	208	185	212	221	150	155	153
Actual deficit excluding social security	73	74	120	208	186	222	238	169	194	211

Sources: *Budget of the United States Government*, various fiscal years; Conference Report on the Congressional Budget Resolution, various fiscal years; and *Budget of the United States Government, Fiscal Year 1990, Historical Tables*.

a. Before the 1983 fiscal year, Congress adopted two budget resolutions; the figures reported for 1980–82 are taken from the first resolution. In subsequent years Congress adopted only one resolution.

b. Actual amounts are based on current accounting practices, which may differ from the practices at the time the budget request was made.

estimates and the amounts set forth in congressional budget resolutions.[15] It shows recurring overruns on the deficit. Nevertheless, the situation was markedly different during the first part of the decade than during the second. The deficit climbed steadily during the first half of the 1980s. At $221 billion in 1986, it was almost three times higher than it had been five years earlier. In the next few years, the deficit receded somewhat, ending the decade about $50 billion below the peak, but still well above targeted levels. The buildup of the deficit during the first half of the decade was principally due to the tax and spending legislation enacted in 1981 and to the recession that followed shortly thereafter. The lower but still persistent deficit later in the decade was due to economic trends, a prolonged budgetary impasse between the president and congressional Democrats, and the Gramm-Rudman-Hollings law.

The 1980 summit was the calm before the 1981 budget blitzkrieg. Within half a year after taking office, Ronald Reagan obtained congressional approval of major reductions in taxes (estimated at the time at almost $750 billion over five years) and a big reduction in domestic spending (estimated at $130 billion over three years). While the spending cuts were sizable, they fell far short of the reductions requested by the president, and in subsequent years, Congress added back some of the funds it had cut in 1981.[16] This shortfall was only part of the reason for the extraordinary gap that opened up in the early 1980s between Ronald Reagan's budget scenario and the conditions that actually unfolded. As shown in table 3, instead of the balance promised by Reagan, the budget toppled into a huge, seemingly intractable deficit. The combined deficit for 1982–86 was almost $1 trillion more than the president had projected when he submitted his ambitious economic program to Congress in February 1981.[17] Political observers will undoubtedly argue for years over whether Reagan engineered the deficit to exert downward pressure on federal expenditures or merely exploited the opportunity once the imbalance became entrenched. But whatever his intent, the policy errors of 1981 shaped federal budgeting for the remainder of the decade.

15. As noted in table 2, the estimated and actual deficits may not be strictly comparable. The estimates in the president's budget and the congressional budget resolution are based on the accounting rules in effect at the time they were made; the actual deficits are drawn from the *Historical Tables*, which retroactively conform past data series to current accounting rules.

16. See David A. Stockman, *The Triumph of Politics: How the Reagan Revolution Failed* (Harper and Row, 1986) pp. 395–411, for a discussion of the estimation and policy errors in the 1981 economic plan, and for data on Congress's restoration of funds in subsequent years.

17. See Message of the President to Congress, *America's New Beginning: A Program for Economic Recovery* (Government Printing Office, February 18, 1981), p. 9.

Table 3. *Comparison of Reagan Budget Plan and Budget Outcome, Fiscal Years 1982–86*
Billions of dollars

Budget item	1982		1983		1984		1985		1986	
	Plan	*Outcome*	*Plan*	*Outcome*	*Plan*	*Outcome*	*Plan*	*Outcome*	*Plan*	*Outcome*
Receipts	651	618	710	601	772	666	851	734	942	769
Outlays	696	746	733	808	772	852	844	946	912	990
Balance	−45	−128	−23	−207	1	−185	7	−212	30	−221

Sources: The planned amounts are taken from *A Program for Economic Recovery*, February 18, 1981, table 4; the outcomes are taken from *Budget of the United States Government, Fiscal Year 1990, Historical Tables*, table 1-1. The accounting basis for computing the 1981 plan may differ from the basis used in the historical series.

One reason for the unbudgeted deficit was that the economy fell into a severe recession shortly after Reagan's far-reaching program was enacted in 1981. The recession robbed the government of revenue, added to spending, and, because it was accompanied by still-high interest rates, added substantially to the cost of financing the burgeoning public debt. The revenue base also was eroded by a much faster than expected fall in inflation and, consequently, much lower nominal GNP. The sharp drop in inflation—consumer prices rose less than 2 percent in 1986, compared with more than 10 percent in 1981—meant that the value of the 1981 tax cuts was much higher than had been planned and the value of the spending cuts was somewhat lower than had been estimated.

The 1981 budget actions and the subsequent recession bequeathed a sizable deficit, which has persisted despite economic expansion. In 1990 the United States was in its eighth consecutive year of growth—a peacetime record. Yet the nominal deficit remained well above the last recession's level.

Efforts to make deep inroads in the deficit were stymied by protracted conflict between the president and Congress. After 1981, the president typically asked for annual increases in defense spending, large cutbacks in domestic programs, and only minor adjustments in federal revenues. Congress usually gave the president less than he requested for defense, yet spending on this part of the budget was still about 50 percent higher in real terms at the end of the decade than it had been at the start. Neither branch tried very hard to rein in spending on entitlements—though there was an annual ritual of cutting medicare spending below an inflation-adjusted baseline—and real spending on transfer payments climbed approximately 30 percent during the decade. Just about all of this increase was due to prescribed cost of living adjustments and to mandated increases in the volume of services, not to new budget decisions. Congress refused to go along with Reagan's repeated demands for additional cutbacks in discretionary domestic programs—hence, the media's verdict that his budgets were dead on arrival—and it sometimes gave this part of the budget more than was necessary to keep pace with inflation.[18] Both branches had to accom-

18. The effect of congressional actions on discretionary domestic expenditures is a matter of dispute. While official statistics show modest real increases after 1982, they did not fully recover the 1981 cuts. Some observers argue, however, that after 1982 Congress supplemented domestic appropriations with user charges and other means of financing that do not appear in the computations of budget authority. With these nonconventional sources included, they argue, Congress substantially increased many domestic programs. See John F. Cogan and Timothy J. Muris, "Domestic Discretionary Spending in the 1980s," Working Papers in Economics E-90-19 (Stanford University, Hoover Institution, July 1990).

modate steadily rising interest charges, which quadrupled from $43 billion in fiscal 1979 to $169 billion a decade later.

When the books were closed on the 1980s, both revenues and expenditures had approximately the same share of GNP that they had at the start of the decade. During the decade, Congress enacted a dozen revenue increases, but these became increasingly smaller as the decade progressed and the impasse between the two branches deepened. Less than two-thirds of the receipts forgone in 1981 were restored. According to Office of Management and Budget estimates, almost $300 billion was sliced from fiscal 1989 revenues by the tax legislation enacted in 1981, but the cumulative effect of all the measures enacted in the following eight years added less than $200 billion back.[19]

The stalemate on the budget prevented reconciliation legislation from living up to its billing as the deficit-reduction bill. In fact, as the decade wore on, the yield from reconciliation actions steadily declined, so that by the end of the decade these measures tended to be coveted mainly for the extraneous legislation tucked into them.[20] It would be misleading to accept at face value the official estimates of deficit reduction made at the time the reconciliation bills were debated. The amounts were vastly overstated, and they included a variety of gimmicks such as postponing or accelerating federal payments, removing items from the budget, counting the receipts from asset sales, and repeatedly taking credit for temporary savings.

The same deceptive practices characterized the budget summits. The 1987 summit claimed some $76 billion in deficit reduction over a two-year period. But much of the new revenue was to come from tougher Internal Revenue Service enforcement and extension of expiring provisions, while more than half of the outlay savings were to come from asset sales and holding increases in defense spending and other appropriations below the inflation-adjusted baseline. To be sure, there was some genuine deficit relief, but it made little more than a dent in the structural problem facing the federal government. The 1989 summit brought even less real deficit reduction, as representatives from both branches acknowledged that the $24 billion of reported savings consisted mostly of bookkeeping tricks, such as removing the Postal Service from the budget and writing off spending that would not have occurred anyway.

The failure of the summits to deal effectively with the deficit was not

19. *Budget of the United States Government, Fiscal Year 1990*, pp. 4–15.

20. The declining use of reconciliation as a deficit-cutting measure is documented in Allen Schick, *The Capacity to Budget* (Washington: Urban Institute Press, 1990), especially chap. 4.

surprising. What the warring branches could not accomplish through routine give-and-take on the budget, they would not be able to do through extraordinary bargaining at the summit. The summit ratified the political impasse on the budget; it did not do away with interbranch conflict.

The final piece of the U.S. budget puzzle in the 1980s was the Gramm-Rudman-Hollings law enacted in 1985. The legislation was a by-product of protracted stalemate between the two branches. What the president and Congress could not agree to do on their own would be done through the automatic sequester process. At least this was the script writ into law, though it did not quite work out as planned. Although the sequester was automatic, hardly anything else about the process was. The cutbacks could be averted by forecasting a vigorous economy that would pare the deficit down to target; the targets could be changed, as happened in 1987;[21] false savings could substitute for real ones; spending could be loaded onto the previous year, for which the Gramm-Rudman-Hollings threat was no longer operative, as happened in 1989 when a big chunk of the cost of rescuing the savings and loan industry was added to spending for the year in progress; or additional spending could be removed from the budget, and thus from the reach of Gramm-Rudman-Hollings as well, as happened in 1989 with respect to the future cost of the savings and loan bailout.[22] In an era of extended budget conflict, the two branches managed to agree principally on one thing: that it is better to lie about the budget than to take the bitter medicine of deficit reduction.

In coming to this harsh conclusion, one must acknowledge that modest progress was made in easing the deficit. Much of that, however, was due to two factors: the extended economic recovery and the buildup of social security reserves.[23] Undoubtedly Gramm-Rudman-Hollings and budgetary stalemate made it difficult to enact new programs, but even

21. The original Gramm-Rudman-Hollings law set the maximum deficit for the 1988 fiscal year at $108 billion; in 1987, Congress reset the target to be $144 billion. The revised deficit targets for the 1988–91 fiscal years totaled $228 billion more than the original targets. *Overview of Entitlement Programs: 1991 Green Book; Background Material and Data on Programs within the Jurisdiction of the Committee on Ways and Means*, House Committee on Ways and Means, Committee Print, 102 Cong. 1 sess. (GPO, 1991), p. 1588.

22. Under the rule in effect from 1985 (when Gramm-Rudman-Hollings was enacted) through the 1990 fiscal year, a sequester occurred only if the deficit estimated at the start of the fiscal year exceeded that year's target. Actions taken later in the fiscal year did not trigger a sequester, even if they caused the deficit to exceed the target. The rules were changed beginning with the 1991 fiscal year to provide for sequesters during the fiscal year in progress.

23. The annual surplus in the social security funds rose from $17 billion in fiscal 1986 to $51 billion in fiscal 1989. This surplus accounted for more than half the drop in the unified budget deficit between 1986 and 1989. *Budget of the United States Government, Fiscal Year 1992, Historical Tables*, table 13.1.

so policymakers did little to come to grips with the deficit problem in the 1980s.

In 1990 the president and congressional leaders negotiated a much larger deficit-reduction package than had been considered during any previous budget summit. The package, which was enacted after further modification by Congress, projected that almost $500 billion would be pruned from the baseline deficit over a five-year period—from fiscal 1991 through fiscal 1995. The package also altered the Gramm-Rudman-Hollings process to shift emphasis from controlling the deficit to controlling expenditure levels and revenue legislation.

The framers of the 1990 agreement projected a steep decline in the budget deficit by fiscal 1995. However, the agreement had a number of loopholes and exceptions—increases in the deficit or in spending due to economic conditions, emergencies, and "technical reestimates" were exempt from the new controls—and it is unlikely that the 1990 summit and reconciliation measures will accomplish what previous efforts failed to do.

The Netherlands: Combating the "Dutch Disease"

On January 10, 1980, the Dutch government inaugurated a decade-long battle against the budget deficit by announcing an austerity package that included a temporary wage freeze and plans for new cutbacks in public expenditure. These emergency measures were prompted, in part, by a projected surge in the general government deficit to 7.5 percent of net national income (NNI), far above the level targeted in the 1980 budget. This was not the first cutback package unleashed in the Netherlands and it would not be the last. Like those that preceded it and some that followed, it was put forth during a period of rapidly deteriorating economic conditions, and it signaled the government's determination— hope might be a better word—to combat what had come to be known as the "Dutch disease."[24]

Dutch disease refers to a country's living well beyond its means. The disease gestated during the postwar period of industrialization and improvement in the country's economic condition. Revenue from the sale of natural gas pumped up both public and private consumption. Despite progressive deterioration in the competitiveness of the manufacturing sector, wage gains generally outpaced the rise in productivity. The growing symptoms of economic distress were partly masked by low inflation

---

24. This discussion of the "Dutch disease" is adapted from OECD, *OECD Economic Surveys: Netherlands 1985/86* (Paris, March 1986), p. 8.

and a strong currency, but they were evident in the steep expansion of the public sector. Each year during the growth era of the 1960s and 1970s, public revenue and spending grew relative to NNI. In the standardized OECD national accounts, government outlays soared from 34 percent of GDP in 1960 to 58 percent in 1980, an average increase of more than 1 percentage point a year. Much of the year-to-year rise in expenditure was concentrated in the social security sector, which came to claim a larger share of GDP than in any other OECD country.[25] Old-age pensions, unemployment compensation, and other payments were indexed to private wages, as were the salaries of civil servants. All this made for extraordinarily rigid budgets. A 1980 study by the Ministry of Finance found that only 3 percent of public expenditure was truly flexible in the year immediately ahead, 39 percent was wholly inflexible, and the remainder was partly inflexible.[26]

Indexed social expenditures and wages, and the resulting budgetary inflexibility, were rooted in postwar compacts between the "social partners"—the major trade unions and employers' associations.[27] The compacts, which were redefined and expanded from time to time, allowed all sectors—workers, employers, and the government—to share in the fruits of affluence and linked them in a common economic fate. The social understanding was forged in the expectation that there would be gains to be allocated, and so there were, even though the trend in wages exceeded that in productivity and the tax burden climbed steadily. Part of the shortfall was made up by natural gas revenue (especially after the first oil crisis when energy prices soared), and part by a chronic public-sector deficit.

During the growth era, deficit spending was justified by a structural budget norm that pegged public expenditure to the productive potential of the economy. This norm permitted a steady rise in the relative size of the public sector, especially because performance regularly fell short of potential. By the mid-1970s, however, the utility of this norm was vitiated by deficits that were almost double the level allowed by the structural rule. Moreover, the acceptability of structural policy was weak-

---

25. In 1980 social security transfers amounted to 26 percent of GDP in the Netherlands, higher than in any other OECD country. See OECD, *Historical Statistics: 1960–1987* (Paris, 1989), tables 6.3, 6.5.

26. See L. J. C. M. LeBlanc and Th. A. J. Meys, "Flexibility and Adjustment in Public Budgeting: The Netherlands Experience," *Public Budgeting and Finance,* vol. 2 (Autumn 1982), pp. 53–64, especially p. 57.

27. The term "social partners" appears frequently in official documents. The evolution of this arrangement is discussed in Steven B. Wolinetz, "Socio-Economic Bargaining in the Netherlands: Redefining the Post-War Policy Coalition," *West European Politics,* vol. 12 (January 1989), pp. 79–98.

ened by the spiral in the "collective burden" (taxes, social security premiums, and certain nontax revenues). In 1975 the government adopted a "1 percent" rule, which would have permitted the collective burden to rise by no more than 1 percentage point a year. It also undertook the first of what was to become a series of deficit-reduction packages.

However, these plans were overtaken by worsening economic conditions, a larger-than-budgeted deficit, and a large continuing rise in the collective burden. In a futile attempt to arrest these developments, a new government unveiled "Blueprint 81" in 1978. This multiyear plan called for a halt to the rise in the collective burden, the stabilization of public expenditure, and a reduction of the public-sector financial deficit to 4–5 percent of NNI within three years. The government imposed cash limits on spending and introduced "stringent budget rules" to trigger compensatory cutbacks when projected spending threatened to exceed budgeted levels. The key to these rules was that "any overstepping of a limit will be compensated for."[28] These moves were accompanied by yet another cutback package.

Despite austere norms, and seemingly strict controls, the government was unable to meet its budget targets. The chief problem was a shortfall in the economy that spread to the budget. Unemployment soared from 117,000 in 1973 to 700,000 a decade later. There were breakdowns in collective bargaining between the unions and employers' groups, as well as widespread resistance to the government's demand for wage restraint. With a severe decline in manufacturing, many firms were forced to operate at a loss, while worsening terms of trade led to a current account deficit (rare for the Netherlands).

1980–82: BUDGETARY AND POLITICAL INSTABILITY. Although the signs of economic distress were plentiful in the late 1970s, it was difficult for the Dutch government to take decisive action. Its resolve was weakened by the fact that it was supported by barely half (77 of 150) of the members of the Second Chamber, and that the center-right coalition was riven by conflict over spending cuts.[29] The 1980 budget was prepared with these constraints in mind. It provided a modest stimulus for employment and accepted a deficit—4 percent of NNI for the state budget, 5.5 percent for the consolidated public sector—above the level authorized in the medium-term plan. The budget acknowledged the need for reducing the deficit, but also that "the socio-economic problems and the

28. The fourteen "stringent budget policy" rules are set forth in *The Netherlands Budget Memorandum 1979* (Amsterdam: Ministry of Finance), sec. 5.6.

29. The Second Chamber is the more powerful of the two legislative bodies. Unlike the First Chamber, whose members are selected by provincial councils, members of the Second Chamber are directly elected.

concomitant problems of budgeting are so great that it is impossible to reduce the financing deficit in 1980 much below the 1979 level."[30]

The enfeebled course of action was continued a year later when the 1981 budget settled for another small cutback package in lieu of more far-reaching changes. "The alternative," the budget averred, "would be a general reduction in the disposable incomes that are formed and trans-ferred in the public sector."[31] The 1982 budget was prepared in an at-mosphere of political and economic crisis. The governing coalition broke up over economic policy, and the budget was the work of a caretaker government. The public-sector deficit, which had been estimated at 5.25 percent of national income in the preceding year, was projected to swell to 7.75 percent, and even this estimate turned out to be lower than the outcome. The deficit would have been much higher were it not for an upsurge in public revenue from natural gas. To compensate for the grow-ing fiscal imbalance, the 1982 budget proposed a slightly larger cutback package than in the previous year. But this budget was never put into effect. Elections were held in 1981, the ensuing government survived only five weeks, and its successor barely made it into the next year, when new elections became necessary.

The Dutch government consistently failed to meet deficit targets in the 1980–82 period. This failure occurred despite repeated cutback drives. On average, there were at least two rounds of budget cuts in each of these years, sometimes more. As a consequence, none of the budgets (or their revisions) were implemented as planned. As happened in other countries during this turbulent period, the budget and the government were hostage to the economy.

It is impossible to gauge the actual value of the cuts announced during this period. Some savings were announced but never carried out; others were trimmed back in the give-and-take between the government and parliament. There were offsetting moves that diminished net savings. Some cuts did little more than shift costs from the state (central) budget to the social security sector or to local governments. Some cutbacks were real, but they were relatively small and did not amount to more than 1–2 percent of total expenditure. More important, the cuts did not curtail the underlying pressure on the budget.[32]

The minimalist character of the cuts was attributable to several factors: the precariousness of the economy and concern that sterner measures

30. *The Netherlands Budget Memorandum 1980* (Amsterdam: Ministry of Finance), p. 8.

31. *The Netherlands Budget Memorandum 1981* (Amsterdam: Ministry of Finance), p. 37.

32. The cutbacks and one of the methods used in computing them are discussed in OECD, *OECD Economic Surveys: Netherlands, 1982–1983* (Paris, January 1983), pp. 39–43.

would further erode real incomes and stir social unrest; the fragility of the government and its inability to marshal a coalition behind more forthright actions; and conflicts among policy objectives, especially between the desire to rein in the deficit and the goal of easing tax burdens. The 1983 OECD survey on the Netherlands economy summed up the period by noting, "It is unlikely that a reduction of the deficit and a reduction of the tax burden . . . can be attained simultaneously in the short run. A policy choice will therefore have to be made."[33] However, the government was too divided and too weak to choose. It aimed for a smaller deficit and a smaller tax burden. It got nothing of the former and very little of the latter.

1982–89: POLITICAL STABILITY, FISCAL DIFFICULTY. The 1982 elections brought a reorientation of government from center-left to center-right. The two-party coalition (Christian Democrats and Liberals) was put together with remarkable dispatch, and the coalition agreement—which in the Netherlands takes the form of a detailed contract between the governing parties—announced the government's determination to reverse the burgeoning public-sector deficit and the spread in social expenditure while stabilizing the collective burden. Headed by Ruud Lubbers, the coalition acted more boldly than its predecessors had, and it also showed remarkable staying power. The Lubbers government was returned in 1986, and more than half of its ministers were retained in the new government. Prime Minister Lubbers also formed the government established after the 1989 elections, but a shift in the composition of the Second Chamber and friction between the Liberals and Christian Democrats induced him to go left of center for a coalition partner.

When it took office in November 1982, the Lubbers government faced a public-sector deficit that was projected in some quarters to reach 12 percent of NNI. The coalition agreement set forth a phased reduction in the deficit over the four years of the government's term, to 7.4 percent of NNI by 1986. This measure encompassed the central government and local authorities, but not the social security funds. The new government pledged to stabilize the collective burden, so that the brunt of bringing down the deficit was to be entirely borne by public expenditure. In fact, spending cuts were proposed in each of the 1983–86 budgets, and the level of these cutbacks was significantly higher than in the previous period. More important, the cuts sought to reverse the incessant rise in transfer expenditure. Perhaps the most drastic move was suspension of the indexation of certain social benefits and public-employee wages. The replacement ratio of various social payments was lowered from 80 percent

33. OECD, *OECD Economic Surveys: Netherlands 1982–1983*, p. 65.

of previous wages to 70 percent, and eligibility criteria were tightened for unemployment schemes and some other social programs.[34]

As the first Lubbers government drew to a close, the deficit was only slightly higher than the level targeted by the coalition. The collective burden had been moderated, but substantial overspending offset some of the budgeted cutbacks. Overspending picked up momentum as the coalition agreement aged and the next election approached and as the government responded to new demands. "Better control of open-ended schemes remains a necessity," the 1986 budget cautioned. It also urged that future governments should "err on the side of caution in order to reduce the risk of setbacks."[35]

One such setback was a sharp reversal in energy prices. While the 1982–86 government benefited from an increase in natural gas revenue, its successor saw that source of finance cut to less than half—a loss equal to about 3 percent of NNI. This forced the second Lubbers government to lower its sights for the 1987–90 period. In continuing the cutback drive, the coalition aimed at reducing the deficit to 5.5 percent of NNI. While this appeared to be significantly below the previous 7.4 percent target, it was not. The new deficit measure covered only the central government deficit; it did not include the finances of local authorities, which often incurred deficits of 1 percent of NNI or more. Thus the drive for deficit relief actually slowed in 1987 and beyond.

The new coalition agreement continued the freeze on public-sector wages and on the minimum wage (to which certain social payments were linked) and also called for substantial spending cuts in each of the next four years. Although further reforms were anticipated in the social security and tax systems, the government was forced by economic circumstances to accept a rise in the deficit for 1987. It did try, however, to return the 1988 and 1989 budgets to the fiscal path set in the coalition agreement. Each of these budgets had a cutback package, and each promised a lower deficit than the previous year's.

Nevertheless, the May 1989 OECD survey of the Dutch economy estimated the combined central-local deficit to be 7.7 percent of NNI in 1988, about the same as in 1985, and 6.5 percent or higher in the next year (see table 4). Moreover, the collective burden was higher in 1988 than it had been at mid-decade. The OECD survey concluded that "the extent to which expenditures have been reduced has been disappointing when compared to some other OECD countries. Fiscal correction has

34. Data on the 1983-86 cutbacks are presented in OECD, *OECD Economic Surveys: Netherlands, 1982–1983*, pp. 32–34.
35. *The Netherlands Budget Memorandum 1986* (Amsterdam: Ministry of Finance), p. 31.

Table 4. *The Netherlands' Public-Sector Deficits, Collective Burden, and Debt, 1980–88*[a]
Percent of net national income

Item	1980	1981	1982	1983	1984	1985	1986	1987	1988[b]
Financing requirement									
State budget	−5.6	−7.6	−9.4	−10.1	−9.0	−7.1	−6.4	−7.7	−6.5
Local authorities	−2.1	−1.6	−0.5	−0.5	−0.1	−0.8	−1.4	−1.4	−1.2
Social security	0.2	−0.4	−0.7	0.9	0.5	0.9	0.0	0.4	0.9
Collective burden	52.4	52.6	53.2	54.3	52.9	52.8	52.9	54.8	55.1
Central government debt	32.8	37.5	43.8	51.1	56.6	60.7	61.9	64.9	66.2
Central government interest payments	2.3	2.8	3.6	4.2	4.8	5.2	5.5	5.5	5.3

Source: Organization for Economic Cooperation and Development, OECD *Economic Surveys: The Netherlands 1988/1989* (Paris, 1989), table 5.

a. The collective burden includes taxes, social insurance premiums, and certain other receipts, such as revenue from the domestic sale of natural gas.
b. Preliminary.

been hampered by the decline in gas revenue, but spending overruns and constraints placed by distributional concerns have also slowed the pace of reduction of the deficit and of the collective burden."[36]

Why, despite all the strain and repeated cutbacks, were the results in the Netherlands so limited? They were limited by the amount of loss Dutch leaders were willing to impose on their society. They took a gradualist approach, reasoning that a little belt tightening each year would be more acceptable than trying to take big strides. Because fiscal restraint was half-hearted, the targets established in both the 1982–86 and 1987–90 coalition agreements forced a continuing rise in both the public debt and interest charges. To be sure, the rise was more moderate than before, but it was nonetheless relentless. After soaring from 33 percent of NNI in 1980 to 51 percent in 1983, the central government debt continued to climb to 66 percent in 1988. Interest payments followed the same trend, rising from 2.3 of NNI in 1980 to 4.2 percent in 1983 and 5.3 percent in 1988.

What is important about the fiscal gradualism is that it did not appear gradual to the affected constituencies. Workers saw a drop in real incomes and public employees suffered a decline in real wages. The fact that each budget emphasized the cuts being made stimulated public awareness of the losses that were incurred. By the time the second Lubbers government was installed, there was a noticeable drop in support for further cutbacks. While the percentage of Dutch citizens favoring cutbacks had risen from 34 percent in 1979 to 63 percent in 1983, it receded to only 47 percent in 1986.[37]

Gradualism and the shift in public sentiment took a toll on the coalition. There was increased sniping among the coalition partners of the second Lubbers government, as the Christian Democrats grew more eager to satisfy public demands and the Liberals generally stood to their pro-market stance. Although a dispute over a minor tax matter brought down the government prematurely in 1989, the strains ran much deeper.

Gradualism was rooted in the government's need to balance conflicting objectives. Easing the collective burden had to go hand in hand with lowering both the deficit and public expenditure. Unable to clearly spell out its priorities, the government was not able to commit itself to one course of action.

Finally, gradualism led to cuts that saved money but did not significantly alter the structure of the public sector. The scope of government

36. OECD, *OECD Economic Surveys: The Netherlands: 1988/1989* (Paris, 1989), pp. 22, 23, 81.

37. The Netherlands Social and Cultural Planning Office, *Social and Cultural Report 1986*, table 11.11.

and its tasks were not curtailed. Instead, the emphasis was on making it more efficient and trimming excess at the margins. The number of persons receiving social assistance continued to rise, and so also did the pressure on public finances.[38] The "dependency ratio"—the ratio of recipients to workers, which was high in the Netherlands relative to other countries—was about the same level in 1987 as it had been four years earlier.

Establishment of a center-left coalition in 1989 did not end fiscal stress, but it did close the books, at least temporarily, on recurrent cutback drives. The third Lubbers government continued to endorse deficit reduction and stabilization of the collective burden, but it subordinated these fiscal norms to other public objectives. Thus it launched an expensive environmental program and conditionally relinked certain social security benefits and public-sector wages to private wages. These initiatives will likely exert upward pressure on public expenditure in the 1990s, as will the aging of the population and the accumulated debt burden. Even if the economy grows robustly in the new decade, the Dutch disease will continue to afflict the budget in the form of chronic deficits and a high collective burden.

Deficit Reduction the Swedish Way

Sweden entered the 1980s in economic and political distress. The "Swedish way"—a unique amalgam of socialist egalitarianism and capitalist productivity—was in trouble. After governing for forty-four consecutive years, the Social Democratic party, the architect of the Swedish economic model, was ousted by the three "bourgeois" parties (the Liberals, the Center party, and the Moderates) in 1976. These parties retained control in 1979, but by a narrow margin. The bourgeois hold on government was weak, however. The coalition was sundered by friction over nuclear power in 1978 and tax policy in 1981. Both coalition splitups were followed by periods of minority government. All told, the country had six governments during a six-year period (1976–82).

Political turmoil was accompanied by economic difficulty. Sweden's economic performance during the 1970s was inferior to that of virtually every other industrial power.[39] Real GDP advanced less than 20 percent over the decade, less even than ailing Britain's. Sweden's exports lagged behind those of its European trading rivals, and its share of world trade

---

38. OECD, *OECD Economic Surveys: The Netherlands 1986/1987* (Paris, 1987), p. 30.

39. Sweden's economic performance is compared with that of other industrial countries in OECD, *OECD Economic Surveys: Sweden* (Paris, June 1981), p. 19.

declined steeply. Its 1980 share of the world market was barely 75 percent of what it had been a decade earlier.[40] Deteriorating terms of trade put the current account in deep deficit. Although the unemployment rate was low by just about everybody else's standards, as it edged toward the 3 percent mark in the early 1980s (it would have been higher if hidden unemployment masked by labor market programs had been included), Sweden's capacity to make good on its commitment to full employment was tested.

The country responded to adverse economic conditions by increasing public consumption and expenditures. The public sector accounted for a rising share of total employment—30 percent in 1980, compared with 21 percent a decade earlier—and total public outlays ballooned during the decade from 43 percent of GDP to 62 percent. A weak economy and an expansive public sector combined for gargantuan budget deficits. Through most of the 1970s, the central government ran a small deficit, which was more than offset by the surpluses accumulated in the social security funds. By the end of the decade, however, the central government deficit was about 10 percent of GDP and the public sector as a whole had an imbalance amounting to about 5 percent of GDP.

1980–82: THE BOURGEOIS PARTIES IN GOVERNMENT. One might suppose that the economic mess of the 1970s and early 1980s gave the three bourgeois partners license to prove that the Swedish way was the wrong path. Now that their time had finally come, they could begin to undo the social democratic legacy by scaling back the public sector and freeing the market to work without government intervention. As things turned out, however, the bourgeois parties were in the wrong place at the wrong time. They could neither dismantle the welfare state nor distance themselves from the budgetary implications of past commitments and current expectations.

Out of power, the Social Democrats were vigilant and vigorous critics of any move that deviated from the commitment to full employment or threatened the benefits that Swedes had come to expect. As unemployment rose, the bourgeois parties had to demonstrate their own fealty to full employment. They did so by investing prodigious sums on declining industries, such as shipyards and ironworks (see the chapter by Ellis Krauss and Jon Pierre). At their apogee in 1979, industrial subsidies amounted to more than 5 percent of GDP. When these costly schemes failed to turn the tide, the bourgeois government was left with the *force majeure* nationalization of weak or dying companies. Ironically, the Social Democrats had abjured state nationalization during their decades in power;

40. OECD, *OECD Economic Surveys: Sweden: 1981–1982* (Paris, July 1982), p. 27.

now that the bourgeois parties were running things, they embraced this most un-Swedish approach.

The bourgeois budgets were burdened by the weight of past decisions as well as some of their making. In 1976, the year they took power, a previously enacted reduction in the retirement age from 67 to 65 took effect, as did the entitlement of certain workers to pensions. These mandated expansions added tens of thousands to the pension rolls and billions of kronor to social expenditure. But they were only part of the central government's mandatory expenditure. In the early 1980s, some form of automaticity was built into more than 80 percent of total expenditure.[41] Significantly, one area that would have been controllable—industrial subsidies—was one of the places where the government decided to throw good money after bad.

The government did move cautiously to slow the rise in spending. It imposed a rule that gave agencies 2 percent less than a full adjustment for inflation for operating expenditures. The budget bill presented in early 1980 established an explicit objective of reducing the central government deficit by 1 percentage point in each of the next few years without adding to the tax burden.[42] This target could be reached, the government hoped, without much pain and without reconsidering basic policies. "It should be emphasized," the 1981–82 budget reassured Swedish voters, "that what is required is a slower growth of public expenditure, not an absolute reduction."[43]

During the 1980–82 period, the bourgeois governments mounted four cutback drives. The first, in late 1980, called for a Skr 6 billion reduction in the deficit. The next budget (presented in January 1981) pledged to curtail the deficit, but it was short on details because the coalition partners could not agree on what should be done. Further deterioration forced the government's hand, however, and in February it proposed another cutback package that relied mostly on reductions in grants to local authorities and on assorted revenue enhancements. A bolder package, produced in September of the same year, included spending cuts, devaluation of the krona, a temporary price freeze, and a reduction in the value-added tax rate. The bourgeois parties' final cutback plan came in the

41. See Björn Eriksson, "Sweden's Budget System in a Changing World," *Public Budgeting and Finance*, vol. 3 (Autumn 1983), p. 70.

42. This and later efforts to curtail the deficit are recounted in Rune Premfors, "Coping with Budget Deficits in Sweden," *Scandinavian Political Studies*, vol. 7 (June 1984), pp. 261–84.

43. *The Swedish Budget 1981/82* (Stockholm: Ministry of Economic Affairs and Ministry of the Budget, 1981), p. 35.

draft budget submitted in January 1982. Its cuts were estimated to be Skr 13 billion on a full-year basis.[44]

The various cuts gave the Social Democrats campaign fodder for the 1982 elections. They promised to roll back some of the most controversial cuts, including an increase from one to three waiting days for hospital insurance, removal of the effects of energy price increases from cost of living adjustments, and reductions in state assistance for child care facilities. These and other cutbacks put the bourgeois parties in a difficult predicament. On the one hand, the savings were too small to curtail surging budget deficits (see table 5). In the first three budgets of the 1980s, the actual deficit exceeded the budgeted level. On the other hand, the cuts were sufficiently large to enable the Social Democrats to portray their opponents as parties that would, if given the chance, take away the benefits built up over decades of prosperity.

The Social Democrats emerged from the 1982 election in control of the government but with a budget out of control. The central government budget deficit was approaching 13 percent of GDP, the national debt had skyrocketed from Skr 139 billion at the start of the 1979–80 fiscal year to Skr 320 billion only three years later, and interest charges had doubled during this period from Skr 13 billion to Skr 28 billion.

THE SOCIAL DEMOCRATIC "THIRD WAY. " Six years in opposition gave the Social Democrats ample opportunity to ponder the course they would take once back in power. This period had been one of intense debate within the party between those (mostly trade unionists) who wanted to continue the Social Democratic mission of making Swedish society more egalitarian, and those (mostly professionals) who believed that the austere economic circumstances dictated a more cautious approach in social policy.[45] The differences were patched up in the 1981 party platform, but after the election, key positions (especially the Finance Ministry) were entrusted to those who favored a more restrained policy.

Despite intraparty divisions, the Social Democrats moved with lightning speed to tackle the looming economic crisis and demonstrate that they were in command. The centerpiece of their crisis program was a 16 percent devaluation of the krona, the fifth devaluation since 1976.

44. The cuts were detailed in *The Swedish Budget 1982/83* (Stockholm: Ministry of Economic Affairs and Ministry of the Budget, 1982), pp. 52–60.

45. Hugh Heclo and Henrik Madsen provide an insightful account of policy disputes in the Social Democratic party and its allied labor movement in *Policy and Politics in Sweden: Principled Pragmatism* (Temple University Press, 1987). See chap. 2 and the readings accompanying it.

Table 5. *The Swedish Central Government Budget: Comparison of Budget and Outcome, 1980–81 to 1989–90*
Billions of Swedish kronor

Fiscal year	Revenue		Expenditures excluding interest		Interest		Total expenditure		Balance	
	Budget	Outcome	Budget	Outcome	Budget	Outcome	Budget	Outcome	Budget	Outcome
1980–81	148	155	130	191	18	24	148	215	−55	−60
1981–82	158	167	199	207	26	28	226	235	−68	−68
1982–83	169	191	212	230	39	48	252	278	−83	−87
1983–84	204	221	238	238	57	60	294	298	−90	−77
1984–85	224	261	240	254	65	75	305	329	−81	−69
1985–86	257	275	249	255	71	67	320	322	−64	−47
1986–87	287	320	265	272	71	64	336	335	−49	−15
1987–88	309	333	283	283	63	53	346	338	−37	−4
1988–89[a]	341	365	299	300	54	54	353	354	−12	−11
1989–90	375	n.a.	317	n.a.	58	n.a.	375	n.a.	0	n.a.

Source: *The Swedish Budget*, various fiscal years. Amounts may not add due to rounding.
n.a. Not available.
a. Provisional outcome, as reported in the revised budget bill presented in April 1989.

Unlike the previous ones, this time the government decreed that wage earners and pensioners would not be compensated (through indexation) for the ensuing price increases. It was risky for a bourgeois government to promote actions that eroded worker incomes while stimulating corporate profits. But the Social Democrats did, and they got away with it. Party leaders leaned on their trade union allies to accept modest, below-inflation wage settlements in the year following devaluation. The crisis program also rescinded most of the cuts made by the previous government, most notably the additional waiting days for health insurance, and added funds for job retraining and expanded labor market schemes. These additional expenditures were financed by a hike in the VAT rate and new taxes on capital gains.[46]

This was the only big bang in fiscal policy from 1982 through the remainder of the decade. Gone were the spasmodic cutback packages that had unsettled previous budgets and unnerved voters. Although they retained power after the 1985 and 1988 elections, the Social Democrats settled for quieter, more routine measures. Substantial savings from elimination of the industrial subsidies were incrementally plowed back into expanded social programs, such as day care facilities, family allowances, and pension improvements. The increments tended to be a bit larger in election years, but there were sweeteners for Social Democratic constituencies in just about every budget.[47]

Although it was applied calmly, fiscal restraint became a recurring budgetary theme. Every budget from 1983–84 through 1989–90 made a case for continuing restraint. Again and again, the budget warned that there was no margin for big reforms.[48] To drive home the point that the budget was tight, the Social Democrats retained the 2 percent rule, which squeezed agency finances.

The routine manner in which they went about their budget work did not mean that the Social Democrats were indifferent to deficits. Big

46. The main features of the crisis program are spelled out in OECD, *OECD Economic Surveys: Sweden, 1983/1984* (Paris, 1984), pp. 21–22.

47. For example, the 1985 budget proposed the largest-ever increase in the child allowance and also increased unemployment benefits, housing allowances, and assistance to the disabled. The budget presented in 1988 (the next election year) noted that success in managing the economy "has created room for urgent social reforms, such as greatly improved health insurance and increased efforts for pensioners and families with children." See *The Swedish Budget, 1988/89* (Stockholm: Ministry of Finance, 1988), p. 48.

48. Thus, although the 1989–90 budget estimated that the deficit would be eliminated during the fiscal year, it emphasized that "a strong economy can soon be weakened by reckless budget policies. . . . Reckless additions to Government expenditure would worsen the national economy." *The Swedish Budget 1989–90* (Stockholm: Ministry of Finance, 1989), pp. 50–51.

deficits were to be avoided for two reasons: they called into question the government's competence in steering society, and they robbed the government of the resources to reform and perfect society.[49] In accordance with the party's aversion to big deficits, the 1984 medium-term plan approved by the Riksdag aimed to restore financial balance by the end of the decade. The plan further indicated that budget policy in the years ahead should be largely based on unchanging tax pressure.[50] Inasmuch as this target covered the consolidated public sector, the government's hope was that continuing deficits in the state budget would be offset, as had occurred in the past, by social security surpluses.

The government surpassed the planned target from almost its first budget (see table 5). Moreover, the 1989–90 central government budget had a positive balance, the first time this had happened in almost three decades.[51] What most needs explaining is how the government accomplished this without frequent austerity drives. An important clue is a phrase that ran as a thread through Social Democratic budgets in the 1980s. Referred to as the "third way," it had more than a fair share of puffery and was conceived with sensitivity to the growing fissures on economic policy within party ranks.[52] Stripped to its essentials, the third way was one in which economic recovery would be led by a vigorous rebound in private enterprise and the government would therefore once again have sufficient resources to finance its social ambitions. The third way was a throwback to the postwar Social Democratic program that sought to reshape society in an egalitarian direction while allowing private enterprise to flourish. Devaluation accommodated this objective by giving Swedish firms an immediate price advantage in world markets. With profits booming, businesses added workers, unemployment abated, and the government had more buoyant tax revenue.

Some of the progress made in restoring budgetary balance was due to the revenue derived from increased economic activity. Much came, however, from a source that the government sought to quash—persistent

49. Heclo and Madsen argue that the Social Democrats "have successfully interpreted the national identity as one of an ever-reforming welfare state. . . . In the Social Democratic vision, politics is a kind of therapeutic exercise. Its mission is the slow, careful eradication of disease and the establishment of a regimen of good health in society." *Policy and Politics in Sweden,* p. 27.

50. See *The Swedish Budget, 1985/86,* pp. 18–19.

51. Updated estimates presented in a revised budget statement for 1989 indicated that the 1988–89 budget had a substantial balance.

52. The "third way" was unveiled in the first budget submitted by the Social Democrats after their return to power. See *The Swedish Budget, 1983/84* (Stockholm: Ministry of Finance, 1983), pp. 13–14.

inflation. The problem was a familiar one to Social Democratic doc-trine—how to reconcile the commitment to full employment with mod-eration in wage demands.[53] The party's fiscal experts knew that past inflationary wage settlements had eroded Sweden's competitiveness and caused its loss of world markets. Within a few months after the 1982 crisis program was launched, the government began an annual ritual of trying to jawbone down wage settlements and price developments. At first, the government was moderately successful, but as the decade pro-gressed, "wage drift" (local wage increases in excess of those agreed to in national negotiations) became more pronounced, as did the upward spiral in prices.[54] Happily for the government, however, these unwel-come developments produced revenue surges and deficit reduction above those anticipated in the annual budget. The increase from the 1982–83 budget's share of revenue in GNP to the 1986–87 share was almost 5 percentage points. Part of the spiral was due to economic growth, part to wage inflation, and part to numerous tax increases imposed by the government. Revenue increases accounted for at least half the deficit reduction achieved during the 1980s. Thus, by the end of the decade, Sweden had successfully achieved a balanced budget.

Despite this achievement, however, the economy and the party system were floundering by the late 1980s. Although unemployment remained low, the rate of economic growth was well below the OECD average and inflation was much higher. The current account deficit surged, and productivity improvement was sluggish. "The 'third way' has failed," *The Economist* announced in a 1990 survey of the Swedish economy; "the country is on the brink of a cost crunch, horribly similar to that of the late 1970s."[55]

The political situation also deteriorated for the Social Democrats. Their share of the vote dropped in both the 1985 and 1988 elections, as did the number of their seats in the Riksdag. The schisms between traditionalist and more market-oriented leaders deepened as the decade progressed and inflation soared. In 1990, the party's proposal for a two-year wage and price freeze was rejected by the Riksdag, and the finance minister (who had led the drive for tax reform and more austere budget policies) re-

53. A typical statement, variants of which appeared in every Social Democratic budget during the 1980s, is: "Full employment is the primary goal of economic policy." *The Swedish Budget 1984/85* (Stockholm: Ministry of Finance, 1984), p. 19.

54. Wage drift in Sweden is discussed in Robert J. Flanagan, David W. Soskice, and Lloyd Ulman, *Unionism, Economic Stabilization, and Incomes Policies: European Experience* (Brookings, 1983), chap. 6, especially pp. 312–15.

55. "The Swedish Economy," *The Economist*, March 3, 1990, p. 1.

signed. The party's standing also slumped in the public opinion polls, with barely one-third of Swedish respondents supporting it.[56] Despite the party's success in balancing the budget and holding down unemployment, it could not accommodate other national objectives, such as maintaining low inflation and reducing the tax burden. In 1991 the Social Democrats had their worst postwar showing at the polls and thus had to surrender control of the government.

A splintered party could not do what the Social Democrats had done so well during their long hold on power before 1976 and after they repossessed the government in 1982. It could not sort out the conflicting objectives buffeting the government, and it could not, therefore, maintain a stable, consistent set of fiscal priorities. Low unemployment remained the overriding objective, but the government could not agree on an effective response to the adverse by-product of this policy—principally, rising inflation and a current account deficit.

Political Capacity

The budget is a continuing story; its last chapter is never completed. One cannot be certain that the slice of time reviewed here fairly represents the capacity of each country to control budget deficits. Yet the 1980s offer useful clues to a nation's political capacity in meeting fiscal crisis; the three countries examined responded quite differently to seemingly similar problems. Sweden allowed tax revenue to drift upward and boosted various taxes, including the value-added tax rate, while exercising mild but prolonged spending restraint. The Netherlands sought to reduce the tax burden, while mounting periodic cutback drives. The United States chopped taxes and spending in a far-reaching policy shift at the start of the decade, then spent the next nine years making partial restoration in both. By the end of the 1980s, Sweden had eliminated its budget deficit, while the United States and the Netherlands had substantial deficit problems. On the basis of these cases, one can draw a number of conclusions about both the governmental capacities needed to lower budget deficits and the institutional and noninstitutional factors underlying those capacities.

1. *The different budget results were not principally due to variances in economic performance.* Each country shaped its own budget destiny by taking

56. The Social Democrats won 166 seats in the 349-seat Riksdag in the 1982 elections. In 1988 their share slipped to only 156 seats.

the course of action it did. High inflation in one country and low inflation in another did not just happen; they were in large measure due to policy choices. Similarly, the deficits resulted from policy actions. Real GDP grew an average of almost 4 percent a year in the United States during the 1983–89 expansion; yet the deficit persisted at a high level throughout this period. Sweden's growth rate averaged only about 2.5 percent a year, but it liquidated the budget deficit.

2. *Government capacity to impose losses is not a major determinant of differences in budgetary outcomes.* At the start of this chapter, it was suggested that the capacity to impose losses is one possible determinant of a government's capacity to subdue deficits. The reasoning was that deficit reduction would have to be accompanied by tax hikes or program shrinkages. But the three cases presented in this chapter offer little support for this hypothesis. In the United States and Sweden, political rhetoric emphasized the benefits that would flow from vigorous government action. Both Reagan's 1981 economic program and the Social Democrats' third way spoke the language of gains. In both countries, this upbeat posture was more than an effort to beguile naive voters. Whether as a matter of expedience or out of doctrinaire views, Reagan and his fellow supplysiders were confident that the country would be made more prosperous by trimming taxes and downsizing domestic government. The Social Democrats exuded their own brand of confidence that came from being in charge through so many prosperous years. Only in the Netherlands was the need for austerity and sacrifice repeatedly emphasized. Yet, though they tried harder than the Americans and the Swedes, the Dutch had much less to show for their efforts.

The Dutch experience suggests another difficulty of explaining budget outcomes in terms of loss-inducing capacity. Loss is not easy to measure; there is no uniform metric for comparing the benefits forgone or the additional taxes borne in the three countries. The losses were not all equal. Its bounty in natural gas meant that when revenue from this source plummeted, the Netherlands may have had to disadvantage its citizens more, even though it accomplished less.

3. *No democratic government can remain in a loss-imposing mode for very long.* Each of the country cases offers evidence of how difficult it is for modern democracies with attentive publics to parcel out losses. Sweden's Social Democrats returned to power in 1982 with a promise to restore the entitlement cutbacks made by the bourgeois parties. The big devaluation made in that year exported the losses to Sweden's trading rivals. The many calls for restraint in the budgets presented during 1983–89 were not matched by deeds because the government substituted social expenditure for industrial subsidies and skillfully inserted relatively low-

cost "sweeteners"—program enhancements—in the budget.[57] Shortly after the close of the 1980s, the Social Democrats verged on action that would have imposed considerable loss on a broad swath of the population. It proposed a wage and price freeze that, if adopted, would have prevented workers and producers from recouping losses due to inflation. The fact that the Riksdag rejected the proposal shows how difficult it is for a single-party government to impose losses if it lacks a parliamentary majority.[58]

The ruling coalition in the Netherlands targeted modest losses at public-sector employees and at persons whose social security benefits were linked to the minimum wage. The country's low rate of inflation meant that the losses resulting from deindexation were relatively modest—as were, therefore, the savings accrued by the government. Bite-size losses comported with the government's gradualist strategy, but the affected groups felt that they had been cheated of promised benefits and they campaigned to get back what had once been theirs. With the conditional reindexation of wages and benefits near the end of the decade, one of the most conspicuous losses was restored.

Blitzkrieg tactics in 1981 enabled the newly installed Reagan administration to trim many social benefits. But shock is not the standard operating procedure of democratic governments, nor is it an approach that gains from repetition. Once congressional Democrats and affected interest groups recovered from the onslaught, they incrementally restored many of the losses. Even in 1981, the cutbacks were less, David Stockman confessed to William Greider, than met the eye.[59] The "magic asterisk"—unidentified future cutbacks—veiled the gap between future revenue and expenditure and magnified the perceived size of the cuts. Reagan's policies were marketed by the White House as a boon for Americans and as the path to a more prosperous country. Moreover, the losses on the spending side were amply compensated for by highly publicized gains on the tax side. Public awareness of budgeted losses would

57. A small item in the 1989–90 Swedish budget suggests how difficult it was for the Social Democrats to impose losses. The provision updated old-age pensions by an amount equal to approximately $100 to compensate pensioners "for the amounts they relinquished to enable the 1982 devaluation to have the desired effect." *The Swedish Budget 1989–90,* p. 79. Seven years after imposing modest losses, the government gave back the money in order to expunge the stain of having disadvantaged its citizens.

58. The parliamentary defeat was less due to a split in Social Democratic ranks than to opposition by Communist legislators (who usually side with the Social Democrats). The party was also hurt by a progressive decline in its voting strength in the Riksdag and by its low standing in public opinion polls.

59. William Greider, "The Education of David Stockman," *Atlantic Monthly,* December 1981, pp. 27–54.

undoubtedly have been much greater if the program cuts had been accompanied by tax hikes.

   4. Ability to set clear priorities among economic objectives is critical to effective deficit reduction. Grappling with the budget deficit brought into play another of the policymaking capabilities identified by Weaver and Rockman in the introductory chapter: the ability to set priorities among conflicting objectives. Abating the deficit is never a country's only economic concern. With one eye on the budget, the government must cast the other on the real economy. It must guard against trying to balance the budget by unbalancing the economy, and it must constantly take account of the potential effects of its actions on jobs, prices, international trade, and other conditions. When it prepares to act, the government must consider how much growth and how many jobs it is willing to risk in the pursuit of its budget objectives. Further, it must balance one economic good against others: it may have to give up some price stability to get higher employment, or it may have to surrender some deficit reduction in order to keep the economy on a vigorous growth path.

   Within the realm of budgeting, there are layers of conflict that have to be sorted out. The government must decide whether to pursue budgetary balance through tax or expenditure policies. At a time when both the deficit and taxes are high, it must decide whether lowering the tax burden or ameliorating the deficit is the more urgent need. Finally, every budget poses tensions between the parts and the whole, that is, between pressure to enhance particular programs on the one hand and to lower total spending and taxes on the other.

   An inability to adjudicate among these conflicting pulls will lead to indecisive action and frequent policy shifts. Gradualism in the Netherlands and dissembling by American politicians stemmed from an inability of the governments in these countries to cast their lot firmly in support of a consistent set of priorities. The Dutch and American experiences are a sharp contrast to that of Sweden, which through years of fiscal stress never wavered in its commitment to full employment. As much as the Social Democrats may have wanted lower inflation, they were unwilling to sacrifice high employment in pursuit of this end.

   5. The U.S. system of separation of powers provides significant risks and few opportunities for effective setting of priorities. Conflict among objectives is ingrained in U.S. budget policy. Public opinion polls persistently show that Americans want lower taxes, smaller government, and bigger programs.[60] This contradiction in public opinion antedates recent budget

   60. See Royce Crocker, "Federal Government Spending and Public Opinion," *Public Budgeting and Finance,* vol. 1 (Autumn 1981), pp. 25–35.

developments and is not unique to the United States.[61] But the separation of powers is associated with two distinctive risks that follow from these contradictory attitudes. A first risk is that there will be a "bidding up" in program expenditures or tax cuts as legislation is considered, with the president and congressional leaders attempting to win credit with voters for taking actions that are more popular than those proposed by their rivals in the other branch.[62] The fact that the United States has lower central government expenditures than most other industrial democracies suggests that this phenomenon most often takes the form of relatively inexpensive "pork" rather than costly program initiatives. But the bidding-up phenomenon was clearly at work in two of the most important budget-imbalancing pieces of legislation in the past two decades: the social security benefit increase of 1972 and the tax cut of 1981. Thus while the risk of bidding up may usually be small, it is occasionally of major importance.

Stalemate is another risk associated with separation of powers. If the president and Congress are unable to arrive at a workable long-term compromise, existing policies and priorities are likely to be frozen in place. Stalemate is more likely to occur—and is likely to have particularly harmful effects on priority-setting capacity—when the budget is in deficit, and the president and Congress are wrangling over the allocation of losses, than when federal finances are in reasonably good shape and the two branches can dole out shares of a growing pie.

6. *Divided party control of the executive and legislative branches in the United States increases the risks of bidding up and stalemate, which inhibit effective priority setting.* The United States has now emerged from an extended period of divided government. From 1968 to 1992 the Republicans won every presidential election except the one tainted by Watergate; the Democrats have controlled the House for the past four decades and the Senate for all but a handful of the past thirty years. Divided government reflects the contradictions in public opinion over budgetary objectives. The American system of government allows voters to have it both ways in budget policy. Many vote for Republican presidential candidates because

---

61. On Sweden, see Axel Hadenius, *A Crisis of the Welfare State? Opinions About Taxes and Public Expenditure in Sweden* (Stockholm: Almqvist and Wiksell International, 1986). See also Richard M. Coughlin, *Ideology, Public Opinion and Welfare Policy: Attitudes toward Taxing and Spending in Industrialized Societies* (Berkeley: University of California, Institute of International Studies, 1980).

62. See John B. Gilmour, "Bargaining Between Congress and the President: The Bidding-Up Phenomenon," paper prepared for the 1990 annual meeting of the American Political Science Association.

they promise smaller government and for Democratic congressional candidates because they seek bigger programs.

Seen in this perspective, checks and balances throw up roadblocks to sorting out policy conflicts, and divided government increases the risks of bidding up and stalemate. The bidding up of both the 1972 social security reform and the 1981 tax cut occurred in periods of divided government. And interparty stalemate characterized budgeting during most of the 1980s: a Republican president wanted no tax increase and deep program retrenchments, while congressional Democrats wanted to raise additional revenue to finance their program ambitions. Throughout the 1980s, neither side was able to dislodge the other from its core positions. Periodic compromises lifted the impasse only to the extent needed to enable the government to complete essential budget tasks. The parties compromised by enacting modest revenue enhancements and (after 1982) constraining expenditure increases to a bit more than the rate of inflation. A little of one objective and a little of the other is an expeditious way of muddling through policy conflicts, but it does not ensure that the actions will accomplish any of the desired objectives.

While it is a matter of conjecture, I am convinced that the deficit outcome in the United States would have been different if either party had controlled both branches of government. Stronger measures would surely have been taken on the spending or revenue side, depending on the party in power. In the 1980s, the two parties repeatedly blamed one another for budgetary problems while conspiring to diffuse responsibility. Through extraordinary procedures, such as summit negotiations and omnibus reconciliation measures, politicians ensured that nobody was to blame because everybody was to blame. Each party's (and branch's) fingerprints were on the various deficit-reduction packages. The process enabled the two branches to patch over differences while avoiding blame, but it did not make for bold policies.

7. *Coalition governments in parliamentary systems pose risks to effective priority setting that are similar to those posed by separation of powers in the United States, while single-party-dominant parliamentary systems offer important opportunities for effective priority setting.* The policy conflicts that beset the U.S. Congress and the president were played out in the Netherlands among the coalition parties and in cabinet. Although the differences on budgetary matters were not as wide as in the United States, they nevertheless retarded the Dutch government's capacity to pursue budgetary objectives vigorously. The government wanted to reduce both taxes and the deficit, but the coalition partners differed in how they valued these objectives. During the years of center-right coalitions, the government tried for a bit of each but could not fully commit itself in one direction.

Coalitions are partnerships of convenience. The parties remain together only as long as it is advantageous for them to do so. Consider
the ease with which the Christian Democrats switched to a center-right
coalition in 1982 and back to center-left orientation after the 1989 elections. Partnerships of convenience breed conflict over objectives and
waffling over priorities, both of which characterized Dutch efforts to
control the budget deficit. These conflicts over priorities are likely to be
especially intense in periods leading up to elections, when coalition agreements are frayed and coalition partners are jockeying to improve their
electoral appeal.

Sweden also suffered from an inability to plot a determined course of
action early in the decade, when the bourgeois parties governed. There
were tax increases and tax cuts and spending increases to combat unemployment and spending cuts to combat the deficit. Out of power, the
Social Democrats went through much internal strife over the future
course of policy, but once back in government they managed to paper
over their differences with a reasonably consistent set of objectives that
they pursued for an extended period. On the most important of their
objectives, they had no doubts. Unemployment had to be liquidated,
and other economic objectives had to defer to this overriding goal. This
absolute position, along with the party's encompassing role in Swedish
politics, enabled the Social Democrats to put together a program that
boosted employment by stimulating industry and profits. They also had
a clear sense of how the budget's parts and whole were to be reconciled
in the drive for deficit reduction. The Social Democrats did not see a
conflict between spending and tax policy: expenditure restraint and tax
hikes would both have to contribute to deficit reduction. They welcomed
higher revenue (from increased economic activity, inflation dividends,
and higher tax rates) and, despite their historic commitment to expand
the welfare state, they also exercised modest restraint on spending.

The party's wholehearted embrace of full employment meant that
over time there would be increasingly serious imbalances in the economy.
As inflation escalated in the late 1980s and a current account deficit
reappeared, the fissures within the party that had been papered over
earlier deepened and the task of harmonizing policy conflicts became
more difficult. Moreover, support for the Social Democrats weakened
in elections and public opinion polls, and the party's lack of a majority
in the Riksdag made it increasingly vulnerable to internal strife and to
withdrawal of support by the Communists. The evidence from Sweden
suggests that even a one-party regime may be unable to reconcile conflicting objectives when policy differences are wide and the party's base
of support is shrinking.

8. *Efforts to employ institutional countervailing mechanisms to increase gov-*
ernmental priority-setting capabilities have not been successful. The split between the executive and legislative branches in the United States, and
the further decentralization of power within Congress, clearly makes
centralized establishment of a set of binding priorities more difficult.
Throughout the 1980s, policymakers tried a number of procedures—
notably reconciliation, budget summits, and automatic budget-cutting
mechanisms—to counteract these basic institutional characteristics of the
United States. With a few exceptions (notably the use of reconciliation
in 1981), these efforts to employ institutional countervailing mechanisms
in budgeting were a failure.

Perhaps the most serious effort to tighten the connection between
fiscal norms and budget actions in the United States was the Gramm-
Rudman-Hollings law, with its automatic sequestration procedure
for reducing expenditures if the projected deficit exceeds the preset
target.[63] On paper, at least, the law forces a tight connection between
fiscal norms and specific budget policies. The automatic sequester would,
it was hoped, enable the national government to do what the two quar-
reling branches could not get themselves to do: agree on a package of
program cuts or tax hikes that would ease the deficit crisis. The automaticity of the process did not suffice to overcome political divisions
between the two branches. After five years of the Gramm-Rudman-
Hollings law, the U.S. budget deficit was well above target and persisted
as a national problem.[64] In budget negotiations during the fall of 1990,
President Bush and congressional leaders essentially abandoned the Gramm-
Rudman-Hollings deficit targets and triggers for a new and less rigid set
of budgetary targets.[65]

In the Netherlands, the search for countervailing mechanisms to compensate for the inherent weakness of the cabinet as a priority-setting body
led, in 1981, to the establishment of a "reconsideration procedure" for
the review of selected programs. Reconsideration was a three-stage process, with political intervention required during the first and third stage
but barred during the second stage. During the initial phase, the cabinet,
often acting on the recommendation of the minister of finance, formally
selected programs for review. These reviews were conducted by inter-
departmental working groups assisted by the Ministry of Finance. In the

63. The law provides a $10 billion cushion; sequestration is triggered only if the pro-
jected deficit is at least $10 billion above the target.

64. The actual budget deficit exceeded the target in each of the first five fiscal years
(1986–90) of the Gramm-Rudman-Hollings process.

65. See George Hager, "One Outcome of Budget Package: Higher Deficits on the
Way," *Congressional Quarterly Weekly Report*, November 3, 1990, pp. 3710–13.

final stage, the cabinet authorized publication of various reconsideration reports.

The expectation was that this procedure would bolster the cabinet's capacity to rearrange government priorities. When this failed to occur, the government modified the reconsideration process to link it directly to the annual budget cycle. The results still were disappointing. As a countervailing mechanism, reconsideration failed in part because it violated a nonintervention norm of Dutch politics: ministers were not to interfere in matters within the cognizance of their colleagues.[66] Although they may have temporary success, countervailing mechanisms appear to be doomed to failure because they challenge embedded institutional norms and practices.

9. Differences in electoral rules exert an important influence on government priority-setting capability. The United States combines single-member districts with the separate election of the president and members of Congress. The first paves the way for majoritarian politics; the second for divided government. In some circumstances, the federal government can be poised to establish a national agenda and act on it; in others, the government can be hobbled by impasse. It was the misfortune of the United States to suffer the latter during a period of fiscal difficulty. Whether one accepts the argument advanced earlier that divided government has itself been a by-product of conflicts over budgetary policy, the record since 1982 suggests that once the government was divided, its ability to act decisively was weakened.

The Netherlands is one of the few democratic governments that combines a national list and proportional representation. It is also a country in which no party has ever won a majority in parliament. Multiparty coalitions are virtually inevitable, and the weakness of government is reflected in the tendency of ministers to go their own way. In the 1980s, the coalition parties joined hands in government but often broke rank on policy matters. The situation was not conducive to strong, determined action on the fiscal front.

Proportional representation is also a possible—but clearly insufficient—condition for the emergence of one-party-dominant systems like that of Sweden.[67] Sweden's system of proportional representation is cen-

66. For a discussion of reconsideration, see Frans van Nispen, "The Retrenchment Policy of the Dutch Government: The Reconsideration of Public Expenditures," paper prepared for Sixth APPAM Research Conference, October 1984; see also "Policy Review and Budgeting: Some Experiences with the 'Reconsiderations Procedure' in the Netherlands," discussion paper by the Netherlands, Organization for Economic Cooperation and Development, June 15, 1984.

67. T. J. Pempel, "Conclusion: One-Party Dominance and the Creation of Regimes,"

tered around multimember districts, not a national list. But it also has a relatively high threshold (4 percent) for party representation in the Riksdag. Hence it contains enough of an incentive for multipartyism to keep the established bourgeois opposition parties divided, but enough barriers to new entry to prevent fragmentation of the left vote by new parties, as occurred in Denmark.[68] In most elections, the outcome in recent years has been a Social Democratic government that lacks a majority in parliament but is able to govern with the abstention or support of the Left Party Communists. As the Social Democrats' share of the vote has declined, so too has its representation in the Riksdag.[69] If the voting trend continues, the party may face increased friction, and its capacity to speak for the national interest may diminish. The time may be approaching when the Social Democrats will be able to govern only in formal coalitions with other parties. If this were to occur, Sweden's priority-setting capacity could come to resemble that of other multiparty governments in Europe.

Electoral rules make a difference but not all of the difference. Single-member districts in the United States explain why electoral competition has been narrowed to two major parties, but not why one party is safely ensconced in Congress and the other more frequently controls the White House. Proportional representation drawn from national lists goes a long way to explain why the Netherlands lacks a majority party, but the existence of higher thresholds is not sufficient to explain why a dominant party emerged in Sweden. To explain the latter is beyond the scope of this essay. But clearly such an explanation must focus not just on electoral rules but also on how societal interests are articulated.

10. *An encompassing structure of interest articulation can exert a strong favorable influence on government priority-setting capabilities.* The three countries differ in their ability to mobilize interests in support of a consistent set of objectives. In sorting out the differences, Mancur Olson's distinction between narrowly based groups and encompassing organizations is relevant. Following Olson, I would argue that a pluralistic structure has

---

in Pempel, ed., *Uncommon Democracies: The One-Party Dominant Regimes* (Cornell University Press, 1990), p. 336.

68. See Pempel, "Introduction"; and Gosta Esping-Andersen, "Single-Party Dominance in Sweden: The Saga of Social Democracy," in Pempel, ed., *Uncommon Democracies*, pp. 19, 33–57.

69. Until the early 1970s, the electoral system gave the Social Democrats some bonus seats; under the current system, however, the distribution of seats in the Riksdag closely mirrors the national distribution of the vote. However, the current system is more advantageous to the Left Party Communists (on which the Social Democrats depend to maintain a working majority in the Riksdag) than the old system, because it limits under-representation of small parties once they reach the 4 percent threshold.

the weakest capacity to sort competing objectives into a consistent, durable set of policies; encompassing structures have the strongest capability.[70]

The United States is well known for the range and number of its organized interests. Interest groups' activity escalated on the federal level in the 1980s, as the threat of cutbacks made them more vigilant in protecting their programs.[71] Even if they shared the view that big deficits damage national interests, they could not agree on what should be done to cure the problem. The extraordinary procedures devised in the 1980s to deal with fiscal issues—budget summits, the reconciliation process, and Gramm-Rudman-Hollings rules—tried to bypass or weaken groups in making budget policies. But these special procedures lost much of their effectiveness as politicians and groups learned how to exploit or neutralize the new rules.

The Netherlands is often depicted as a country polarized by sectarian and (related) class divisions as well as a country bonded together by corporatist accommodation. Corporatism flourished in the postwar era as the social partners (the trade unions, employers' associations, and the government) forged an alliance that enabled them to share the fruits of economic growth. There is some evidence that consensus-building institutions were weakened by fiscal stress in the 1980s (now that there were losses rather than gains to divide) and by the government's austerity program, which was launched without consulting the unions and employers.[72] Steven Wolinetz has argued that this change gave the government more autonomy in charting its economic course. But freedom from having to bargain for the consent of corporatist partners came at a cost: the government was less able to mobilize unions and employers in support of more far-reaching measures.

Sweden has also been characterized as a corporatist society, but this label obscures two important differences between it and the Netherlands. One is the scope of interests represented in peak negotiations; the other is the role of the dominant political party in defining the social consensus. There is a big difference between a labor movement that encompasses

70. Encompassing groups are discussed in Mancur Olson, *The Rise and Decline of Nations: Economic Growth, Stagflation, and Social Rigidities* (Yale University Press, 1982), especially pp. 48–53, 89–92.

71. See Harold Wolman and Fred Teitelbaum, "Interest Groups and the Reagan Presidency," in Lester M. Salamon and Michael S. Lund, eds., *The Reagan Presidency and the Governing of America* (Washington: Urban Institute Press, 1984), pp. 297–329.

72. Wolinetz argues that "the Dutch government found it necessary to circumvent corporatist structures in order to orchestrate a response to economic change." "Socio-Economic Bargaining in the Netherlands," p. 95.

almost the whole of the working class and one that speaks for only a minority of workers.[73] Sweden's solidaristic wage policy would not be possible in the Netherlands. More important, no Dutch party has a role comparable to that of Sweden's Social Democrats. The Social Democrats are much more than a conventional, Western-style party. For half a century, they defined the terms of debate and the direction of social policy. This "Social Democratic hegemony"—the apt phrase is Heclo and Madsen's—meant that Social Democratic policy was very much Swedish policy.[74] Although it drew support from less than half of the electorate, the party saw itself as the custodian of the nation's well-being. The party's espousal of the need for a robust industrial sector manifested its encompassing role in Swedish society. In this role, the Social Democrats saw it as their responsibility to establish a comprehensive program for dealing with the fiscal crisis.

In short, the pronounced differences in the mobilization of interests exercised a major influence on government approaches to budgetary distress in the three countries. Pluralism in the United States sharpened the clash among interests and the disparate objectives they pursued; corporatism in the Netherlands broke down under the stress of widening disagreements among the social partners; and the encompassing role of the Social Democrats in Sweden facilitated forthright action to deal with the problem.

Concluding Thought

Although three countries and a single policy issue do not provide sufficient evidence to settle the argument, they do point in the direction of a strong relationship between institutional arrangements and policy outcomes. To emphasize the point, suppose that each of the countries had a different governing situation during the 1980s than the one it actually experienced. To begin with, speculate how U.S. budgetary out-

73. Less than one-third of the Dutch labor force was unionized in 1983. In the early 1980s, however, more then 90 percent of Sweden's blue-collar workers and more than 80 percent of its white-collar workers were union members. See OECD, *OECD Economic Surveys: The Netherlands 1984/1985* (Paris, February 1985), p. 1157. See also Peter Flora, ed., *Growth to Limits: The Western European Welfare States since World War II*, vol. 1: *Sweden, Norway, Finland, Denmark* (New York: Walter de Gruyter, 1988), p. 77.

74. Social Democratic hegemony, Heclo and Madsen write, "consists of the fact that almost everyone, knowingly or unknowingly, dances to the tune of the leading player. It is in this sense of preponderant influence . . . that one is justified in speaking of Social Democratic hegemony in Sweden." *Policy and Politics in Sweden*, p. 23.

comes might have been affected if one of the parties had firm control of both the legislative and executive branches. It is conceivable that a majority party might have been fractured by internal divisions and would have been unable to put together a cohesive budget package, but the much more probable outcome would have been either a Republican or a Democratic party acting to avoid being branded as fiscally irresponsible.

To carry the argument further, imagine that in the 1980s the governing conditions of Sweden and the Netherlands had been reversed. It is hard to envision that a Swedish government, weakened by coalition maneuvering and conflict among the coalition partners, would have embraced a budget policy that allowed revenues to rise 5 percentage points relative to GNP. It is highly likely that a cohesive Dutch government, unconstrained by the need to balance the clashing objectives of coalition parties, would have been able to cast its lot more decisively in favor of fiscal reform.

Speculation is a poor substitute for evidence, but it sharpens awareness of the enormous gaps in understanding the relationship between institutions and outcomes.

David Vogel

Representing Diffuse Interests in Environmental Policymaking

*A*ll democratic governments face the problem of ensuring adequate supplies of collective goods such as environmental protection, low prices for consumers, and civil liberties. Scholars such as Mancur Olson have long argued that such goods tend to be underprovided because of "free rider" problems. Individuals and groups tend not to mobilize on behalf of diffuse interests because they must share the benefits of such mobilization with those who have done nothing.[1] The political problem that societies face is to ensure that there is adequate representation of diffuse interests in the face of these discouraging incentives.

There are a number of ways around the collective action problem.[2] Equally important, the term *representation* can have two quite distinct meanings in this context. First, interest groups representing diffuse interests can enjoy *access* to the political process. This does not mean that they will be successful in actually influencing policy outcomes, however. Second, there may be incentives for officials to be *responsive* to diffuse interests in their decisions, even if interest groups have difficulties forming or interest group access is quite limited. Political entrepreneurs and parties may represent diffuse collective interests in the hopes of reaping political benefits from voters.

The purpose of this essay is to examine the extent to which differences in political systems, and especially differences between parliamentary systems and the U.S. system of separation of powers, affect both types of representation of diffuse interests. For example, it is possible that parliamentary systems may be more responsive to diffuse interests in

1. Mancur Olson, Jr., *The Logic of Collective Action: Public Goods and the Theory of Groups* (Harvard University Press, 1971).

2. For example, organizations may offer "selective benefits"—those from which non-participants can be excluded—to strengthen support for their cause.

237

terms of policy outputs, even if they offer groups representing these interests less access to the political process. Correspondingly, a system of checks and balances may provide groups representing diffuse interests with greater political access, but may also be less likely to implement their preferred policies.

This chapter focuses on environmental politics and policies during the postwar period in the United States, Great Britain, and Japan. Britain and Japan have parliamentary systems, while the U.S. system is based on the separation of powers. If the U.S. system exhibits capabilities that differ from those found in the other two countries, it might be reasonable to conclude that the separation of executive and legislative power is at least one of the factors that influences governmental ability to represent diffuse interests. Alternatively, if either of the two parliamentary systems represents diffuse interests in about the same way as the United States, yet there are differences between those two systems, the implication is that the structure of executive-legislative relations has less influence on governments' capacity to represent diffuse interests than do other institutional or noninstitutional factors. This inference also is appropriate if there is no discernible difference in the capacity to represent diffuse interests across the three countries.

Institutions and Diffuse Interests

Several types of political institutions may affect the ability of a political system to represent diffuse interests, and of equal importance, to resist concentrated interests. Institutional effects need not, therefore, emanate exclusively or even mainly from the parliamentary-presidential distinction.

In Weaver and Rockman's first-tier distinction, the parliamentarist position stresses the potential disjunction between access and responsiveness. This view emphasizes that parliamentary systems are likely to have a superior capacity to represent diffuse interests because the government is in a strong position to resist the entreaties of concentrated interests (such as polluting industries) and to exclude them from the decisionmaking process. Since it is more difficult to escape blame for failing to keep commitments in a parliamentary system than under a separation-of-powers system, governments in a parliamentary system are also more likely to be held accountable for electoral pledges on issues of collective goods (such as aiding the environment) than are political leaders in a separation-of-powers system.

Alternatively, a presidentialist position implies that the separation-of-powers system is better able to represent diffuse interests precisely because it offers numerous opportunities for interest groups to shape policy formation and implementation. Congress provides multiple points of access in the U.S. political system. Accordingly, there is a greater likelihood that interest groups to whom the executive branch is hostile or indifferent will be able to find other authorities willing to respond to their concerns. By contrast, if the political leadership of a parliamentary system decides not to represent diffuse interests, it is unlikely that those interests will be represented effectively.

Not all parliamentary systems are alike, however. Second-tier factors such as electoral rules and the norms and rules affecting the formation of governments can also have important effects on the capabilities of individual parliamentary systems to represent diffuse interests. Single-member constituencies promote single-party-majority governments by reducing the number of competing parties; these party governments, in turn, are most able to control and resist concentrated interests, but they may also have the least incentive to be responsive to diffuse interests. This is especially true where electoral rules combine with political conditions to allow a single party to hold majority power for an extended period (as in Japan), rather than alternating with another party. Durable majority-party governments are likely to see little reason to alter their electoral coalition and redistribute the prevailing pattern of policy payoffs. They are therefore unlikely to respond to diffuse interests unless groups and supporters of such interests already have become part of the coalition.

In contrast, proportional representation presents relatively low barriers to the formation and parliamentary representation of small parties. Thus it offers diffuse interests a different path to access—establishment of a distinct party. The European "Greens," for example, have taken this route. By cutting across existing ethnic, regional, and class cleavages, these parties are in a good position to be either partners in a governing coalition or members of the opposition. In either case, they can use their bargaining position to gain responsiveness to their agenda.

These hypotheses are at best rough expectations about how differences in electoral rules might affect the representation (or absence thereof) of diffuse interests across parliamentary systems. They do, however, suggest that explanations of variability in the capacity to represent diffuse interests that rest only upon the parliamentary-presidential distinction are likely to be too simplistic.

Third-tier institutional factors also may have important effects on governmental responsiveness to diffuse interests. An independent judiciary, for example, gives adherents of diffuse interests another channel through which to seek access. The same is true of subnational governments in a federal system. However, federalism also may lead to nonuniformities in responsiveness to diffuse interests across a nation. In addition, competition among state governments to attract business investment may lead state political leaders to avoid providing collective goods out of fear that imposing increased costs on firms will lead them to relocate elsewhere.

Noninstitutional third-tier factors, such as the norms and culture influencing the accountability of government and the breadth of participation in policy decisions, also can influence representation of diffuse interests. In the United States, for example, nonelectoral citizen participation tends to be high and is therefore likely to further the mobilization of nonpartisan causes. The relative insulation of the ruling coalition in Japan, however, and the responsiveness of that coalition to concentrated interests inhibit the formation of broad public movements. In comparison with the United States, Japan has much lower norms of nonelectoral political participation and governmental accountability to some encompassing public interest.

Case Study Countries

Using the cases of Japan, Great Britain, and the United States to test the hypothesis that a nation's system of executive-legislative relations is an important determinant of capacity to represent diffuse interests has both advantages and disadvantages. Great Britain and Japan represent a useful, if challenging, test of the hypothesis precisely because they differ in so many other important respects. Indeed, their parliamentary systems are among the few features they have in common. Most obviously, during the postwar period Japan has grown more rapidly than any constitutional democracy, while Britain's economic performance has been among the poorest in the industrialized world.

In addition, while Britain's democratic, constitutional system has deep historical roots, a constitutional democracy was imposed on Japan by the U.S. occupation forces after World War II. As a result, norms of governmental accountability and public participation are more deeply imbedded in British than in Japanese political institutions and cultures. Moreover, the former's political system places a high value on consultation, the latter's on consensus. Finally, students of comparative political economy generally place Britain and Japan at opposite ends of the political continuum in terms of the relative strength of their respective states.[3] Britain is usually classified as a weak state with relatively little institutional capacity for shaping the structure and priorities of civil society. By contrast, Japan virtually epitomizes the ideal type of a strong state with considerable institutional and political capacity to shape structure and priorities.[4] If representation of environmental interests is similar in Japan and Britain despite these great societal differences, while the U.S. pattern is quite different, it greatly strengthens the argument that differences in executive-legislative relations are a major determinant of the way that governments deal with diffuse interests.

Japan and Britain also have some important similarities in governmental structure that affect their usefulness in exploring the effect of fusion of legislative and executive powers on government capabilities. Among parliamentary systems, Japan and Great Britain are relatively distinctive in eschewing proportional representation: Britain uses a single-member-district system, and Japan uses a unique multimember-district system. Electoral rules in both countries have promoted essentially two-party political systems. Britain does have a number of political parties (including a Green party), but for all practical purposes only the Labour and Conservative parties are in a position to form a government. In Japan, only the Socialist party competes with the Liberal Democratic party (LDP) in both national and local elections. There are significant differences between the two electoral systems and the types of governments that they have produced, however: the LDP has been in power in Japan continuously since the mid-1950s, the most stable single-party dominance of any democratic nation in the postwar period. By contrast, Britain's Labour and Conservative parties have periodically alternated in office since the end of World War II. Both the Japanese and British patterns are quite different from the coalitional pattern common among systems with proportional representation. One should be careful about generalizing from the Japanese and British cases to all parliamentary systems.

Finally, Japan and Great Britain also differ from the United States with respect to the way political power is organized geographically.

---

3. See, for example, Peter J. Katzenstein, ed., *Between Power and Plenty: Foreign Economic Policies and Advanced Industrial States* (University of Wisconsin Press, 1978).

4. For a classic statement of this position, see Chalmers Johnson, *MITI and the Japanese Miracle: The Growth of Industrial Policy, 1925–1975* (Stanford University Press, 1982). However, for contrasting perspectives, see David Friedman, *The Misunderstood Miracle: Industrial Development and Political Change in Japan* (Cornell University Press, 1988); and Karel Van Wolferen, *The Enigma of Japanese Power: People and Politics in a Stateless Nation* (Knopf, 1989).

Britain and Japan are both unitary political systems in which the authority of local governments is limited. By contrast, the United States is a federal system in which state and local governments exercise important political power. As it happens, environmental policy is an area in which local political institutions and local political movements have historically played an important role. As a result, it is possible that at least some of the observed differences between British and Japanese environmental policy on the one hand and the United States on the other may be due not to the presence or absence of separation of powers, but rather to the contrasts between a unitary and federal system.

Comparing Environmental Policies

Environmental protection represents an important example of a diffuse interest: the reduction of air and water pollution, the conservation of wilderness areas, the protection of endangered species, and the proper disposal of toxic wastes are all policy goals promising current or future benefits for large numbers of people. For the most part, the benefits provided by these policies tend to be collective rather than divisible. In many, though by no means all cases, relatively few individuals are likely to benefit either specifically or disproportionately from environmental regulations. And those that benefit will do so whether or not they participate in the political process.

By contrast, those who benefit from the nonrepresentation of environmental interests not only tend to be well organized, but the interests they usually represent, namely industry and labor, typically enjoy a privileged political position in capitalist polities. All capitalist democracies have powerful bureaucracies whose officials seek to promote the interests of industry, while business generally enjoys a close relationship with politicians from the more right-of-center political party. Similarly, while the political influence of trade unions varies considerably, they invariably have at least a close relationship with the major left-of-center political party.

Protecting the environment has become a widely accepted responsibility of the governments of industrialized nations only during the last twenty-five years. Yet in this period this policy area has assumed major importance: not only have environmental issues come to occupy a permanent place on the political agenda in virtually all democratic nations, but they have also become an increasingly important dimension of international politics. Scores of governments now are forced to take positions on issues including the burning of fossil fuels, trade in endangered species, and the production of chemicals that threaten the ozone layer.[5]

At the same time, environmental regulation presents a number of shortcomings as a test of the capacity of different national institutional configurations to represent diffuse interests. Both the magnitude of environmental problems in general as well as the importance of specific environmental issues vary from nation to nation. For example, the British have traditionally placed a high value on protecting their countryside from blight and preserving wild animals and birds. By contrast, environmental issues in Japan have primarily focused on protecting the health of the public. Americans appear concerned with both protecting public health and preserving wilderness areas. Accordingly, at least some of the contrasts in the effectiveness of environmental regulation in the three countries may be due to the different priorities of their elites and citizenry.

Moreover, the cross-national assessment of the effectiveness of environmental regulation presents some unique measurement difficulties.[6] It is of course possible to compare national environmental standards. But in contrast with other policy areas, the effectiveness of government policy depends in large measure on decisions made by the private sector. Consequently, the relationship between the promulgation of public policy and its implementation may well be problematic: there are invariably implementation gaps that are not always easy to measure. Alternatively, one can compare the actual quality of the physical environment in different political systems. But the state of a nation's physical environment is dependent on a large number of factors other than government regulation, including its rate of economic growth, the geographic dispersion of its industry, and the nature and level of its energy consumption.

Finally, the politics of environmental regulation in the United States, Great Britain, and Japan have changed considerably, and in some cases dramatically, since the end of World War II. As a result, comparing environmental policies and politics in these countries over the entire period is likely to yield conclusions with rather limited significance. This essay therefore will assess the role played by national political institutions in representing environmental values and interest groups in the United States, Great Britain, and Japan during three distinctive time periods:

5. See David Vogel, "Environmental Policy in Europe and Japan," in Norman J. Vig and Michael E. Kraft, eds., *Environmental Policy in the 1990s: Toward a New Agenda* (Washington: CQ Press, 1990), pp. 257–78.

6. For a discussion of some of the methodological problems raised by cross-national studies of environmental regulation, see David Vogel, *National Styles of Regulation: Environmental Policy in Great Britain and the United States* (Cornell University Press, 1986), pp. 147–53.

1945–67, 1968–74, and 1974–88. This should lead to a more balanced assessment of the relative importance of public opinion, environmental group access, and institutional design in affecting the representation of environmental groups and the effectiveness of environmental regulation.

1945–67

From the end of World War II through the mid-1960s, the nation whose political system was most effective at both representing environmental values and providing political access to environmental interest groups was Great Britain. The nation least effective on both counts was Japan, and the United States fell somewhere in between.

GREAT BRITAIN. During the first two decades of the postwar period, the British made more progress in both controlling land use and reducing air pollution than any other industrial nation.[7] The Town and Country Planning Act of 1947 was among the most important pieces of legislation enacted by the Labour government of Clement Attlee. This statute effectively nationalized control over land use. Various local governmental units were designated as local planning authorities, and no private development could take place without their permission. Two years later, Parliament enacted another major piece of environmental legislation, the National Parks and Access to the Countryside Act. This legislation established a system of national parks in which commercial development would be restricted, allowed the government to designate "areas of outstanding beauty," created a governmental body to establish, maintain, and manage Britain's nature reserves, and facilitated public access to the British countryside.

Britain's parliamentary system of government contributed to the rapid passage of both these far-reaching statutes. The Labour government was elected in 1945 with a broad mandate to bring about a number of major reforms in British society, most of which significantly expanded the scope of government controls over economic activity. Given its electoral mandate, the government was in a position to enact its preferences, including active governmental involvement in the control of land use.

Moreover, the conservation statutes of the Attlee government both reflected and reenforced the influence of the British conservation movement. Significant segments of the British landed gentry had been active in efforts to conserve Britain's countryside and stately homes since the closing decades of the nineteenth century. The National Trust was officially recognized by Parliament in 1907, and the Royal Society for the

7. See Vogel, *National Styles of Regulation.*

Preservation of Birds received a royal charter a few years later. A number of national and local environmental organizations were formed during the 1920s.

By the 1940s, Britain had a more extensive network of environmental organizations—many enjoying quasi-official status—than any other industrial nation. Equally important, the Town and Country Planning Act, by giving citizens a means of participation in determining the physical future of their communities, encouraged the formation of a large number of community-based amenity groups throughout Great Britain during the following two decades.

The other major development in British environmental policy during this period followed a rather different dynamic. Since the beginning of the industrial revolution, the quality of Britain's air had steadily deteriorated, primarily because of the burning of coal by both industry and households. The Coal Smoke Abatement Society was formed around the turn of the century for the purpose of pressuring Parliament and local authorities into establishing "smokeless zones."

Although the Clean Air Society (as it came to be known) grew in membership, its efforts met with little success; indeed, in 1936 Parliament expressly forbade local authorities from prosecuting householders for smoke emissions. Why were these efforts so unsuccessful? First, no British government was willing to do anything to hurt the nation's severely depressed domestic coal industry. Secondly, the British public was ambivalent about domestic burning of coal: while many urban residents were upset about the poor visibility of the air, many citizens were reluctant to allow the government to interfere with what had become an important English tradition, the "pokeable, companionable fire."[8] Thus, unlike the areas of conservation and land use, where the Labour government felt it had a clear mandate to bring about a substantial policy change, neither the Attlee government nor the Conservative governments that held office both before and after it were either capable of or interested in challenging the power of the coal lobby.

The political environment changed dramatically in the winter of 1952, when an "unusually nasty" fog settled over London. It virtually eliminated visibility for nearly four days and led to 4,000 deaths. Six months after this "killer fog," the government agreed to establish a committee of inquiry; six months later the committee issued its report. Concluding that "air pollution on the scale with which we are familiar in this country today is a social and economic evil which should no longer be tolerated,"

8. Eric Ashby and Mary Anderson, *The Politics of Clean Air* (New York: Oxford University Press, 1981), p. 54.

the committee recommended a number of restrictions on the burning of coal and emissions of smoke.[9] Parliament subsequently enacted them in the summer of 1956.

Britain's parliamentary system does not appear to have played an important role in either facilitating or retarding the government's responsiveness to the problem of air pollution. It clearly took a major crisis to overcome the entrenched power of Britain's coal producers and their employees, and even then three and one-half years elapsed before the British government approved legislation that simply allowed communities to decide for themselves whether they wished to ban coal burning. Evidently, in the absence of a clear public mandate and in the presence of determined opposition, parliamentary systems can find it just as difficult to act as constitutional systems based on the separation of powers.

Still, the British government did finally respond to what was clearly a major public health problem. Moreover, the passage of the Clean Air Act in 1956 led to an increase in both private and public expenditures for pollution control. This in turn contributed to a significant improvement in air quality in a number of British industrial cities, including London, where smoke emissions declined by 76 percent between 1956 and 1966.[10]

JAPAN. The politics of pollution control policy in Great Britain during the 1950s and 1960s contrast sharply with that of another parliamentary democracy, Japan.[11] Japan's pollution problems were much more severe than Britain's. Not only was Japan's rate of industrial growth substantially higher, but it was much more concentrated geographically: three-quarters of its industrial production took place on only 1 percent of its land. The 1960s witnessed a doubling of carbon monoxide emissions, a threefold increase in hydrocarbons, and a sixfold increase in nitrogen oxides. Air pollution was so severe in Japan's major cities that many school children were issued masks, while a substantial portion of the fish caught in and around Japan could not be eaten because of the widespread dumping of industrial wastes into the rivers and the sea.

In addition to the "usual" types of pollution associated with industrial growth in general and coal burning in particular, the residents of various communities became inflicted with a number of pollution-related diseases. Many thousands of Japanese became visibly deformed and phys-

9. Quoted in Ashby and Anderson, *Politics of Clean Air*, p. 107.
10. See Vogel, *National Styles of Regulation*, pp. 38–39.
11. The best overall account of Japan's environmental problems during this period is Norie Huddle and Michael Reich with Nahum Stiskin, *Island of Dreams: Environmental Crisis in Japan*: (Cambridge: Schenkman Books, 1987). See also T. J. Pempel, *Policy and Politics in Japan: Creative Conservatism* (Temple University Press, 1982), pp. 218–36.

ically impaired due to mercury poisoning (Minamata disease), cadmium poisoning (itai–itai disease), and Yokkaichi asthma, a lung ailment caused by soot and smoke emissions.

During the 1950s and 1960s, many of those suffering from various pollution-related diseases tried to seek redress: they filed lawsuits and sought to persuade both national and local governmental officials to crack down on the companies whose emissions were causing them physical harm. They also sought financial compensation for the injuries they had suffered. But, unlike the British government, which finally did respond to what had evidently become a clear public health hazard, the Japanese government was completely unresponsive to the grievances of its citizens. It made no effort to solicit the views of citizen groups interested in environmental issues. Nor did it establish any administrative mechanisms comparable to the British public inquiry that allowed the public's views to be consulted before industrial sitting decisions were made.

While the British government established a highly respected commission to examine the health effects of smoke emissions, in Japan industry and government worked closely together during the 1950s and 1960s to suppress the release of scientific studies that demonstrated a connection between particular industrial emissions and various diseases or fatalities. The firm whose emissions were linked with Minamata disease falsified its test results and hired thugs to break up residents' protest meetings. Compounding their difficulty, the victims of pollution-related diseases in a number of communities were regarded by their neighbors employed at local factories as "troublemakers who were putting their own interests before the economic and social well-being of the community."[12] In contrast to Britain, where both major political parties included a number of politicians who were interested in environmental issues—and thus could help apply pressure on the government—in Japan neither major political party was interested in the plight of the victims of pollution. The LDP had close ties with Japanese industry, and the Socialist party had close links with organized labor and was obsessed with the evils of "monopoly capital."

Unlike Britain, where a national conservation movement had existed since the late nineteenth century, Japan never developed a network of grass-roots organizations that were interested in environmental issues; in contrast to their counterparts in Britain, Japan's landed gentry placed a low value on preserving the Japanese countryside. English culture ven-

12. Susan J. Pharr and Joseph L. Badaracco, Jr., "Coping with Crisis: Environmental Regulation," in Thomas K. McCraw, ed., *America versus Japan* (Harvard Business School Press, 1986), p. 241.

erated flora and fauna, while Japanese culture tended to be indifferent to them. In Britain the efforts of the central government to control air and water pollution dated from the mid-nineteenth century: Parliament had approved the world's first pollution control law in the 1860s. But in Japan, the Meiji politicians and bureaucrats who led Japan's industrial revolution were uninterested in ameliorating the effects of rapid industrial growth on either health or amenities. Indeed, on various occasions during the latter part of the nineteenth century the protests of farmers injured by emissions from local industry were violently suppressed.

The Japanese experience in the 1950s and 1960s clearly suggests that having a parliamentary system does not make a political system any more capable of representing diffuse interests. Rather, the striking differences in the politics of environmental protection in Japan and Great Britain during this period can be understood as a continuation of the policies and decisionmaking practices that had prevailed in both political systems since the mid-nineteenth century. Moreover, economic factors likely played a role as well: during the first two postwar decades, Britain was more affluent than Japan and thus was in a better position to devote more resources to environmental protection.

UNITED STATES. The ability of the American political system to represent diffuse interests during the 1950s and 1960s falls somewhat between that of Great Britain and Japan.[13] Like Britain, the United States had a relatively long history of citizen interest in issues of conservation and pollution control. Both the Sierra Club and the Audubon Society were established around the turn of the century. During the Progressive Era, a number of cities in the industrialized Northeast enacted statutes to control air pollution, and the administrations of both Theodore and Franklin Roosevelt enacted several important conservation measures.

Yet through the mid-1960s the American environmental movement was less well organized and politically influential than its counterpart in Britain: it had virtually no access to policymakers at the national level, and its role in shaping conservation and pollution control policies at the local level varied widely. In all but a handful of cities and states, citizen organizations interested in environmental issues confronted the determined and influential opposition of local business interests. Various American cities did have a number of pollution "scares," a few of which

13. This section is primarily based on Walter A. Rosenbaum, *The Politics of Environmental Concern* (Praeger, 1973). For a more detailed discussion of the politics of clean air regulation during this period, see David Vogel, "The Political Impact of the Large Corporation: A Legislative History of Federal Clean Air Policy, 1963–1981," in Betty Bock and others, eds., *The Impact of the Modern Corporation* (Columbia University Press, 1984), pp. 315–22.

were similar in severity to London's, but these produced little policy change.

On the other hand, when compared with the government of Japan, the American government, at both the federal and local level, was more effective at representing environmental interests. By 1967 more than two-thirds of the state governments had established agencies responsible for controlling air pollution within their boundaries, even though their standards were weak and poorly enforced. Moreover, during the first half of the 1960s, both pollution and conservation issues did make their way onto the national political agenda. Faced with growing evidence that air pollution, particularly from automobiles, had become a serious public health problem in a number of American cities, Congress approved air pollution control legislation in 1960 and again in 1965. In 1963, President John F. Kennedy signed into law the Clean Air Act of 1963—its name taken from the British statute enacted nearly a decade earlier—which marked the beginning of a federal role in the control of air pollution from stationary sources.

There are two reasons diffuse interests were less effectively represented in the United States than in Great Britain. First, in the United States there was a much greater presumption in favor of state, rather than federal, regulation. Although this did mean that local governments were, in principle, freer than those in Britain to control pollution within their jurisdictions, in practice it resulted in much weaker regulations since few state governments were willing to challenge the prerogatives of local firms and plants. Moreover, the American tradition of states' rights effectively precluded an expanded federal role in either pollution control or land use planning, policy areas that had historically been controlled by local governments.

Second, business and industry enjoyed considerably more political influence in the United States than in Britain.[14] One source of this strength was ideological. Given the strength of the ideology of free enterprise, as well as the existence of widespread public skepticism about the virtues of government intervention in the economy, it was all but inconceivable that any U.S. president during this period would have seriously proposed a program of public controls over industrial location and development decisions comparable to that put forth by the Attlee government following the election of 1945. In sum, the prevailing ideological consensus in American society between the mid-1940s and the mid-1960s allowed far

14. For the sources and extent of business political influence during the 1960s, see David Vogel, *Fluctuating Fortunes: The Political Power of Business in America* (Basic Books, 1989), chap. 2.

less room for the representation of diffuse interests than was the case in Britain.

To be sure, both the Kennedy and Johnson administrations did propose a number of policies that significantly expanded the role of the federal government in American society. Indeed, following his landslide election victory in 1964, Johnson had a mandate to enact a much more interventionist political agenda, which included a more active federal role in environmental regulation. But while much of the Great Society was enacted into law, the administration's efforts in the area of pollution control foundered. The American business community was able to use its influence in Congress to exercise a virtual veto power over the nation's environmental policies. In fact, the Clean Air Act Amendments of 1967 actually restricted the ability of the Department of Health, Education, and Welfare to regulate sulfur emissions.

The U.S separation of powers, which enables members of the legislature—even from the president's own party—to define their own political priorities, clearly weakened the ability of the American government to respond to diffuse interests in this period, as did the federal nature of the American political system. In a sense, during the 1950s and 1960s the American system of "interest group liberalism" functioned as the counterpart of the bureaucracy-LDP alliance that prevented the representation of diffuse interests in Japan.[15] However, the same institutional fragmentation of political power that hindered a coordinated effort to address environmental issues in the United States also served to make it possible for environmental issues to become a part of the political agenda.

1968–73

Beginning in the late 1960s and continuing up to the recession of 1974–75, environmental policies and politics became transformed in virtually every democratic capitalist nation: environmental issues moved to a much more prominent position on the political agenda, environmental organizations expanded in size and influence, and a number of important new environmental laws were enacted. Nonetheless, there was considerable variation in nations' responses to this global upsurge of interest in environmental issues.

In both Japan and the United States, environmental policies changed dramatically, although since Japan had previously done so little in the area of environmental protection, the magnitude of its policy changes

15. See Theodore J. Lowi, *The End of Liberalism: The Second Republic of the United States* (Norton, 1979).

was greater. Japan suddenly went from the industrial democracy with the weakest environmental controls to the one that allocated a higher proportion of its GNP to pollution control than any other industrial nation. American public policy also changed significantly: the ability of industry to veto major environmental initiatives weakened considerably and, as a result, the regulatory statutes passed by Congress in the late 1960s and early 1970s were the strictest and most comprehensive in the world.

In Great Britain, the membership of environmental organizations also increased dramatically, and both major political parties enacted new regulatory legislation when they were in power. However, because Britain already had an extensive system of pollution and land use controls in place—and because it was less affluent—it embarked on fewer substantive policy changes than did Japan or the United States.

What brought about such a significant policy departure in both Japan and the United States? What undermined the influence of the LDP-bureaucracy alliance in the former nation and the power of interest group liberalism in the latter?

JAPAN. One critical change that took place in Japan involved the political mobilization of its citizenry.[16] Although the tradition of civic activism is far weaker in Japan than in either Great Britain or the United States, large numbers of its citizens have participated in protest movements from time to time. The late 1960s through the early 1970s was such a period. Between 1970 and 1973 the number of citizen groups in Japan formed to protest environmental pollution increased tenfold. By 1973 there were approximately 3,000 such groups, most with 500 or fewer members. However, in contrast to groups in both the United States and Great Britain, Japanese environmental organizations were strictly local in scope and exclusively concerned with issues of public health: their members were united only by their place of residence or a common infliction from pollution from a particular source.

The LDP, which effectively controlled access to the Japanese political system, was unresponsive to environmental groups' concerns because of its close ties with industry and continued commitment to rapid economic growth. Thus these groups were forced to rely upon political strategies that went outside normal political channels. One of the most important of these mechanisms was the media. In part because Japan's pollution

16. See Ellis Krauss and Bradford Simcock, "Citizens' Movements: The Growth and Impact of Environmental Protest in Japan," in Kurt Steiner, Ellis S. Krauss, and Scott C. Flanagan, eds., *Political Opposition and Local Politics in Japan* (Princeton University Press, 1980), pp. 187–227. See also Pempel, *Policy and Politics in Japan*; and Huddle and Reich, *Island of Dreams.*

problems had grown so severe, the press, which had hitherto ignored the issue, now began to provide substantial coverage of the complaints of local groups; during the second half of the 1960s, pollution problems received more attention in the Japanese press than any other social issue. As a result, the demands of the victims of pollution for compensation from Japanese industry attracted increased public sympathy and support.

Second, citizen groups began to apply increased pressure on local governments. Between 1969 and 1971, local governments received almost 75,000 pollution-related complaints, nearly double the number they had received only two years earlier and quadruple the amount in 1966. By 1973 more than 10,000 local disputes about pollution had sprung up in Japan. Attracted by the sudden popularity of this issue, Japan's left-wing opposition parties began to attack the LDP for its close ties with Japanese industry. Socialist candidates began to run for office on environmental platforms, and Communist party members became active in mobilizing citizen demonstrations. Although the LDP's power in the Diet remained secure, Socialists were elected to office in a number of local governments, including the municipality of Tokyo.

The election of a number of Socialist party officials at the local level, combined with a sudden increase in community opposition to industrial expansion, placed business on the defensive in many communities. A number of local plants entered into "voluntary" agreements with local government officials and citizen groups to abate their pollution. In addition, a number of localities enacted pollution control standards that were far stricter than those issued or in some cases even permitted by the national government. The high point of these local political initiatives was the passage of the Tokyo Metropolitan Environmental Pollution Control Ordinance in 1969. Approved under a Socialist municipal administration, it was the strictest pollution control law enacted to date in Japan.

The judicial system was the third critical ingredient in the change in Japanese environmental policy.[17] Historically, Japanese courts, like those of most parliamentary systems, have played a relatively minor role in the policy process; in sharp contrast with those in the United States, they rarely become involved in political issues. Nonetheless, during the mid-1960s, four cases were filed by groups of individuals seeking damages from various companies for injuries from emissions. These trials received extensive media coverage, and suddenly the public became aware of the

17. Julian Gresser, Koichiro Fujikura, and Akio Morishima, *Environmental Law in Japan* (MIT Press, 1981), especially pt. 2. See also Frank K. Upham, *Law and Social Change in Postwar Japan* (Harvard University Press, 1987), pp. 28–77.

magnitude of the lack of concern of both business and industry for the health of the Japanese public. Even more important, between 1971 and 1973 the courts ruled in favor of the plaintiffs in all four cases. All Japanese corporations now found themselves financially liable for emissions that they had previously regarded as a normal part of doing business. Not surprisingly, this served to considerably weaken their opposition to spending substantial resources on abatement.

In 1967 the Diet had approved Japan's first major pollution control law. While it did represent the first formal recognition on the part of the Japanese government that it was responsible for protecting the citizenry from environmental harm, the statute also represented a major capitulation to the nation's powerful economic ministries and business federations: it contained no emission standards and did not provide any mechanism for the compensation of pollution victims. However, the combination of continuing media coverage, the LDP's steady electoral losses at the local level, and the increasing mobilization of citizen activists all finally forced Japan's ruling politicians and administrators to act.

The result was a special session of the Japanese parliament in 1970.[18] The "pollution Diet," as it came to be known, passed fourteen major pieces of environmental legislation, providing Japan with environmental standards in many cases comparable to those of the United States. Nor was this response simply a stopgap measure. During each of the following five sessions of the Diet, another major piece of environmental legislation was approved. One of the most important of these statutes established the world's first—and only—administrative system to compensate the victims of toxic substance pollution.

Elements of the Japanese bureaucracy also became less sympathetic to industry: in the fall of 1972 Japan's newly established Environmental Agency issued a set of automobile emission standards that were among the strictest in the world. The Japanese automobile industry had bitterly objected to these regulations when they were first proposed, and the majority of the Diet opposed them as well. But Buichi Oishi, a physician who headed the Environmental Agency, held firm and, "in the climate of the times, no one in the party was in a position to challenge him."[19]

Ironically, the very same factors that had enabled the Japanese government to all but ignore environmental concerns during the preceding two decades now enabled it to act decisively. Once Japan's political elites had decided that the problem of pollution control was one that Japanese

18. For the changes in Japanese environmental policy, see Pempel, *Policy and Politics in Japan*; and Pharr and Badaracco, "Coping with Crisis."
19. See Pharr and Badaracco, "Coping with Crisis," p. 246.

industry should address, they had relatively little difficulty in changing national priorities. During the first half of the 1970s the same system of "administrative guidance" that had helped Japan achieve the world's highest rate of economic growth during the 1950s and 1960s now began to emphasize the reduction of the pollution produced by that very growth. In addition to both imposing and enforcing strict pollution control requirements on industry, the Japanese government provided loans to companies to enable them to invest in pollution control technology.

The resulting change in business priorities was dramatic. Between 1970 and 1975, corporate expenditures for pollution control in Japan increased by an average of 40 percent.[20] By 1975 Japanese industry was devoting 4.6 percent of its total investment to pollution control—more than any other industrial nation.[21] Japan became a world leader in the development of sulfur oxide control technologies, employing five times as many scrubbers as any other industrial nation.

As a result, Japan made substantial progress in reducing pollution levels during the 1970s. Japan's sulphur oxide emissions declined by more than 50 percent between 1970 and 1975.[22] Just as the British Clean Air Act led to the disappearance of the London fog during the 1960s, so the air pollution control regulations enacted in the early 1970s made it possible for Mount Fuji to be seen several days a year from downtown Tokyo. By the end of the decade, the quality of Japan's water no longer constituted a serious health hazard, and swans could once more survive in the moat around the Imperial Palace.

UNITED STATES. American environmental policies also changed significantly beginning in the late 1960s.[23] As in Japan, the public's interest in environmental issues increased rapidly in a relatively brief period of time: "Alarm about the environment sprang from nowhere to major proportions in a few short years."[24] A survey taken in December 1970 reported that Americans now considered pollution to be "the most serious problem" facing their communities. An estimated 20 million Americans participated in Earth Day, April 22, 1970, in order to demonstrate

20. See Pempel, *Policy and Politics in Japan*, p. 233.

21. The comparable figure was 3.4 percent for the United States and 1.7 percent for Great Britain. This amounted to 1 percent of Japan's GNP, compared with 0.44 percent for the United States and 0.29 percent for Great Britain. Barry Eichengreen, "International Competition in the Production of U.S. Basic Industries," in Martin Feldstein, ed., *The United States in the World Economy* (University of Chicago Press, 1988), p. 330.

22. Organization for Economic Cooperation and Development, *The State of the Environment, 1985* (Paris, 1985), p. 25.

23. This section draws on Vogel, *Fluctuating Fortunes*, pp. 64–82.

24. Hazel Erskine, "The Polls: Pollution and Its Costs," *Public Opinion Quarterly*, vol. 36 (Spring 1972), p. 120.

their support for public policies designed to improve environmental quality.

The overall membership of American environmental organizations increased by one-third during the early 1970s. Between 1967 and 1971, enrollment in the Sierra Club increased from 48,000 to 130,000, while the membership of the National Audubon Society more than doubled. Several new, more politically militant environmental organizations were formed. As in Japan, the press coverage of environmental issues also increased. American press coverage both reflected and reenforced the importance of an issue that had become, in words of *Time* magazine, a "national obsession."[25] The press was filled with stories of environmental trauma, such as the burning of a river in Ohio, an air pollution alert in New York City, and the blowout of an oil well off the coast of Santa Barbara that released 235,000 gallons of crude oil. Various activists predicted "ecocatastrophe" by the end of the decade.

In Japan environmental protection was initially identified with the opposition Socialist and Communist parties, but in the United States the cause of environmentalism was, from the outset, bipartisan. It was embraced by numerous members of Congress from both parties, whose more affluent and educated constituents were now demanding stricter environmental controls. It was also supported by the White House, occupied by a Republican president with relatively liberal views on domestic policy. The National Environmental Protection Act, which declared improvement of the quality of the environment to be a major national priority and required all federal agencies to consider the impact of their decisions on the environment, was passed unanimously and signed into law by Richard Nixon in January 1970. A few months later the president, by executive order, established the Environmental Protection Agency (EPA), thus bringing under one agency all the federal government's employees responsible for pollution control.

As in Japan, the interest of the nation's politicians in improving the national environment extended beyond one legislative session: important new environmental laws were also approved in 1971 and 1972. However, unlike the 1970 act, these laws were subject to considerable debate in Congress: lobbyists from industry, concerned about the costs of compliance, worked hard to weaken them, although they did recognize that the passage of some additional regulatory legislation was all but inevitable. But, in sharp contrast to their strong influence during the 1960s, their efforts were relatively unsuccessful. Suddenly the same politicians who had been extremely responsive to the needs and demands of industry

25. "Issue of the Year: The Environment," *Time*, January 4, 1971, p. 21.

became fearful of being attacked by their opponents as favoring pollution. And in contrast to the 1950s and 1960s, environmental organizations were now well represented in the halls of Congress.

In the case of automobile emissions, federal standards became significantly stricter as air pollution control legislation worked its way through the legislative process. Senator Edmund Muskie, who chaired a powerful Senate committee with responsibility for environmental legislation, was a leading candidate for the Democratic party's 1972 presidential nomination. Anxious to prevent Muskie from making environmental regulation into a campaign issue, Richard Nixon became a strong supporter of stricter pollution control standards. In order to recapture the political initiative from Nixon, Muskie proposed a set of automotive emission requirements far stricter than anyone, even environmental lobbyists, had demanded. Given the widespread unpopularity of "Detroit," the president was unwilling to oppose the standards contained in Muskie's bill. The automobile manufacturers thus found themselves caught in the middle of a battle between two ambitious, powerful politicians. As a result, the Clean Air Act, passed in 1970, represented a major political setback for one of America's most important industries.

Not only were environmentalists well represented in Congress, but they also had access to the policy process through the judicial system.[26] The National Environmental Protection Act, the Clean Air Act, and the Clean Water Act of 1972 all contained provisions that allowed environmental organizations to sue government agencies, and in some cases industry, for noncompliance. The courts interpreted these statutes as giving organizations representing the public interest the same access to the judicial process that property interests had historically enjoyed. This was an extremely important development. In response to this opportunity, environmental organizations developed sophisticated legal staffs, and a number of environmental law firms were established.

In Japan the suits filed by citizen plaintiffs were confined to issues involving health and pollution, and the defendants were all private firms, while in Great Britain the courts played virtually no role in shaping either the making of environmental policy or its enforcement. Both contrast sharply with the American experience. In the United States environmental litigants were able to affect a wide range of both private and public policy decisions, including the construction of dams and canals, the status of wilderness areas, and the geographic dispersion of industry.

26. For the role played by the courts in shaping American environmental policy, see Frederick R. Anderson, *NEPA in the Courts: A Legal Analysis of the National Environmental Policy Act* (Johns Hopkins University Press, 1973); and R. Shep Melnick, *Regulation and the Courts: The Case of the Clean Air Act* (Brookings, 1983).

Thus on balance, thanks to the U.S. separation of powers, environmental interests now enjoyed more access to the policy process than in either Japan or Britain.[27]

Between 1970 and 1972, most major sectors of the American economy increased their investments in pollution control by 25 to 35 percent.[28] By the early 1970s several of the nation's largest industrial polluters were spending a significant amount of their total capital expenditures on pollution control equipment. The result was a measurable improvement in air quality for most urban residents as well as enhanced water quality in many parts of the United States during the 1970s.[29] For example, total emissions of the five major air pollutants declined by 21 percent (by weight) between 1970 and 1980.[30] Although Japan did devote more resources to controlling pollution, the United States made greater progress in protecting wilderness areas from commercial development, protecting endangered species, and reducing pesticide use. The areas designated as national wilderness (excluding Alaska) more than doubled between 1970 and 1980.[31]

GREAT BRITAIN. Environmental issues also became more salient in Britain.[32] As in the United States, public concern increased through a series of dramatic and highly publicized environmental disasters, most notably the destruction of the giant oil tanker *Torrey Canyon* off the coast of Cornwall in 1966, which spilled 60,000 tons of crude oil onto the beaches of Great Britain and France, and the death of 50,000 to 100,000 seabirds in 1969 following the massive dumping of the toxic chemical PCB into British rivers. The membership of both local and national environmental organizations increased substantially during the latter part of the 1960s and the first half of the 1970s, as did press coverage of environmental issues.

As in the United States, both major political parties competed with each other to demonstrate their commitment to improve the quality of Britain's physical environment. One journalist noted in 1972, "The environmental lobby has succeeded in creating a 'halo effect' for the conservationist cause; today it is a bold politician who risks its disapprobation."

27. See David Vogel, "The Public Interest Movement and the American Reform Tradition," *Political Science Quarterly*, vol. 95 (Winter 1980–81), pp. 607–27.
28. Rosenbaum, *Politics of Environmental Concern*, pp. 17–18.
29. For the American record on environmental quality, see Vogel, *National Styles of Regulation*, pp. 153–62.
30. Norman J. Vig and Michael E. Kraft, "Environmental Policy from the Seventies to the Eighties," in Vig and Kraft, eds., *Environmental Policy in the 1980s: Reagan's New Agenda* (Washington: CQ Press, 1984), p. 17.
31. Vig and Kraft, "Environmental Policy," p. 14.
32. This section is based on Vogel, *National Styles of Regulation*, chap. 1.

Another observed that "the environment as a general issue has risen to a dominant position among political concerns."[33]

Following the election of a Conservative government in 1970, the queen, in her annual address to Parliament, promised that her ministers would "intensify the drive to remedy past damage to the environment and . . . seek to safeguard the beauty of the British countryside and the seashore for the future."[34] The government subsequently established a Department of the Environment and in 1972 secured the passage of the Water Act, "as radical a policy shift as can be cited in post-war Britain."[35] Both these policy initiatives considerably centralized and strengthened the administration of pollution control in Britain. In 1974 a newly elected Labour government enacted another major administrative reform, the Control of Pollution Act. This statute marked "the first formal recognition of the environment as a single entity" and represented "a major step forward in the administration of pollution control in the U.K."[36]

However, the actual content of pollution and land use control regulations changed less in Britain than in either the United States or Japan. Britain, for example, was the only one of the three to continue to allow the use of lead in gasoline. Britain also devoted a smaller share of its resources to controlling pollution than the other two countries, although it was more effective than Japan in protecting scenic areas from industrial or mineral development and in preserving wildlife. (The United States and Britain are among only a handful of nations that have devoted at least 5 percent of their land areas to conservation purposes.) Nevertheless, Britain did make progress on improving the quality of its environment in a number of ways during the 1970s. The fact that it devoted fewer resources to this effort had less to do with its constitutional or political system than the fact that it was poorer and had less severe environmental problems.

In sum, during the late 1960s and early 1970s, neither a parliamentary system nor one based on the separation of powers proved any more or less capable of representing diffuse interests; rather, the critical deter-

---

33. Roy Gregory, "Conservation, Planning, and Politics: Some Aspects of the Contemporary British Scene," *International Journal of Environmental Studies*, vol. 4 (October 1972), p. 37; and William Solesbury, "The Environmental Agenda," *Public Administration*, vol. 54 (Winter 1976), p. 379.

34. "Queen's Tribute to Army in Ulster," *London Times*, July 3, 1970, p. 7.

35. J. J. Richardson and A. G. Jordan, *Governing under Pressure: The Policy Process in a Post-Parliamentary Democracy* (Oxford: Martin Robertson, 1979), p. 47.

36. Graham Bennett, "Pollution Control in England and Wales: A Review," *Environmental Policy and Law*, vol. 5 (June 1979), p. 95.

minant was the degree of public pressure. To be sure, the way each nation went about formulating its new policy initiatives varied. Because of the U.S. constitutional system, Congress enjoyed more influence over the shaping of environmental legislation than either Parliament or the Diet. For example, no member of the national legislature in either Japan or Great Britain who was not a member of the government had as much influence over the making of pollution control policy as Senator Muskie of Maine. The Clean Water Act of 1972 was enacted over the veto of President Nixon—something that obviously would be impossible in a parliamentary system. Likewise, the U.S. constitutional system made it possible for the judiciary to play a much more important role in shaping environmental regulation than was the case in either Japan or Great Britain. Thus, on balance, the U.S. system of separation of powers contributed to the strengthening of the representation of diffuse interests during the late 1960s and early 1970s. Indeed, the fact that Congress and the presidency were controlled by different political parties during this period may well have led American pollution control statutes to be stricter than they might otherwise have been.

On the other hand, the Japanese parliamentary system also proved an important asset in enabling public policy to change rapidly. Once the prime minister, as well as senior LDP politicians and bureaucrats, had decided Japanese industry should make a significant effort to reduce pollution, there was no difficulty in securing Diet adoption of a far-reaching pollution control program. Moreover, both the political strength of the bureaucracy and its relative independence from the Diet enabled the Japanese government to use its administrative flexibility to target pollution control expenditures by the private sector and to resist the efforts of some LDP politicians to reduce regulatory standards. Thus the same centralization of decisionmaking that had made Japan into the world's most polluted industrial nation during the 1960s also enabled it to devote more of its resources to pollution control than any other country during the first half of the 1970s.

1975–88

Since the mid-1970s environmental issues have become a permanent part of the political agenda in virtually every democratic nation: governments have come to accept their responsibility for protecting the health of their citizenry and preserving or improving the quality of the natural environment. Indeed, the representation of diffuse interests has become global in scope as the industrialized nations have begun to address issues such as the destruction of the ozone layer, trade in endangered

260   *David Vogel*

species, and global warming. At the same time, however, both the representation of diffuse interests in the policy process and the ability of organizations representing diffuse interests to participate in the policy process continue to diverge among different countries.

Beginning in the mid-1970s, in response to a slowdown in growth rates, all three nations relaxed some of their pollution control requirements. For example, both Japan and the United States delayed the introduction of the tough automobile emission requirements they had approved at the beginning of the decade. Overall investment in pollution control by private firms in Japan peaked in 1975; in 1981 firms were spending almost 40 percent less than they had allocated six years earlier.[37] As a percentage of GNP, pollution control expenditures in the United States were slightly lower in 1981 than they had been in 1975. (Unfortunately, no comparable British data are available, but other evidence points to some reduction in pollution control expenditures during this period, particularly in water pollution.)

UNITED STATES. However, important differences between the United States on one hand and Great Britain and Japan on the other began to emerge in the late 1970s. In essence, the American commitment to strong environmental regulation proved more durable and consistent.[38] The relaxation of automotive emission standards by Congress in 1977 proved exceptional rather than typical. Although the relative political influence of business in Congress increased between 1977 and 1980, to a significant extent this was counterbalanced by President Jimmy Carter's strong support for the representation of environmental interests. Carter appointed several environmental activists to key positions in his regulatory bureaucracy, and his leadership helped secure the enactment of two important environmental laws in 1980: the establishment of a "superfund" to clean up toxic wastes and an Alaskan lands bill.

Ronald Reagan was elected to the presidency in 1980 on a platform that included a promise to reduce government regulation of business. The officials he appointed to head the agencies and bureaus responsible for enforcing environmental policy were committed to a cooperative, rather than adversarial, relationship with business. The budgets of these regulatory bureaucracies, as well as the size of their enforcement staffs, were significantly cut, and fewer lawsuits were filed against companies. Consequently, the effectiveness of environmental regulation at the federal

37. Saburo Ikeda, "Risk Management Practices in Japan: Standards Setting Problems for Environmental Risks," paper prepared for U.S.-Japan Workshop on Risk Management, Tsukuba, Japan, 1984.

38. See Vogel, *Fluctuating Fortunes*, pp. 181–90.

level measurably declined during the Reagan administration's first two years in office.[39]

American environmental organizations responded to this dramatic erosion in their influence over the executive branch by remobilizing their supporters: after having remained stable, the Sierra Club's membership nearly doubled between 1980 and 1983, while other organizations reported an improved response to their direct mail campaigns for additional funds. Equally significant, while survey data had reported some decline in public support for environmental regulation during the second half of the 1970s, public attitudes became much more positive beginning around 1981—a trend that would continue through the remainder of the decade.[40]

The American separation of powers played a crucial role in maintaining the representation of diffuse interests in the United States during the early 1980s in the face of the election of a popular but unsympathetic president. Environmental groups were able to use their access to the courts and their influence in Congress to reduce the effects of the administration's program of deregulation. Congress not only refused to weaken the nation's environmental laws, it also repeatedly chastised the administration's appointees for not enforcing them. In 1983, amid strong and intense public criticism, the head of the EPA resigned in disgrace, and the secretary of interior was forced from office a year later.

The federal nature of the U.S. constitutional system also facilitated the representation of diffuse interests during this period. Local governments in the United States continued to play a much more important role in shaping environmental policy than their counterparts in Great Britain and Japan. During the 1950s, states' rights served to weaken the effectiveness of American environmental controls. But during the 1980s the opposite dynamic took place. Environmentalists were able to use their political influence in states and cities to secure the enactment of regulations stricter than those of the federal government and to reduce the effects of many of the Reagan administration's national deregulatory initiatives.

By the 1984 presidential election, the administration had abandoned Reagan's 1980 campaign promise to reduce the burdens of environmental regulation on business. After 1983 the budgets of environmental regulatory agencies began to increase again, and the agencies resumed filing

39. Vogel, *Fluctuating Fortunes*, chap. 9.

40. Riley E. Dunlap, "Public Opinion and Environmental Policy," in James P. Lester, ed., *Environmental Politics and Policy: Theories and Evidence* (Duke University Press, 1989), pp. 88–134.

lawsuits against firms that had violated rules and regulations. Moreover, throughout the decade Congress continued to pass new environmental statutes, in many cases strengthening the standards it had passed during the 1970s. On balance, the nation's air quality was better in 1986 than it had been in 1980, although for some pollutants the rate of improvement was slower than it had been between 1970 and 1979.[41] Performance with respect to water quality and the disposal of toxic wastes was mixed, although conservation policies remained quite effective. Beginning in the mid-1980s, the United States also began to take a leadership role in addressing global environmental issues, most notably ozone depletion.[42] A testament to the American public's continued strong support for environmental protection is the fact that in 1988 Republican presidential candidate George Bush campaigned on a pro-environmental platform.

GREAT BRITAIN. Like Ronald Reagan, British Prime Minister Margaret Thatcher came into office in 1979 on a platform that promised to reduce the scope of government controls over industry. However, in part because Britain is a parliamentary system, Thatcher, in contrast to Reagan, was better able to deliver on her pledge. Throughout most of the 1980s, she was generally unsympathetic to the concerns of Britain's active and well-organized environmental movement, referring to its leadership at one point as "the enemy within."[43] Anxious to promote the recovery of British industry, the government relaxed enforcement of environmental regulations. For example, the Department of the Environment made a determined effort to expedite the processing of applications for new industrial and commercial developments, thus weakening the effectiveness of some public controls over land use.

The result was some deterioration in the quality of Britain's physical environment. A large number of Britain's rivers and bathing areas remained below the European Community's standards for water quality, and the Community sued Britain for failing to comply with its standards for drinking water. On balance, Britain's rivers were dirtier in 1988 than they had been in 1980. Moreover, the government came under severe criticism for its indifference to the health hazards associated with a nuclear reprocessing facility located on the Irish Sea and for its support of the continued use of lead in gasoline. The British government also fought

41. Organization for Economic Cooperation and Development, *OECD Environmental Data: Compendium 1989* (Paris, 1989), pp. 17–39.

42. Richard Elliot Benedick, "U.S. Environmental Policy: Relevance to Europe," *International Environmental Affairs*, vol. 1 (Spring 1989), p. 94.

43. Quoted in Robin Herman, "An Ecological Epiphany," *Washington Post National Weekly Edition*, December 5–11, 1988, p. 19.

vigorously in the European Community for the least restrictive limits on the production of chlorofluorocarbons, emissions of sulfur, and radiation in food. However, while Britain was widely criticized for being the largest "exporter" of acid rain to the European continent, its emissions of sulfur oxides did decline steadily between 1980 and 1985. With respect to other air pollutants, the British record was more mixed.[44]

As the British economy began to recover somewhat during the mid-1980s, the public's unhappiness with the quality of its physical environment increased.[45] Thatcher responded with a highly publicized speech in which she stated that protecting "the balance of nature" constituted "one of the greatest challenges of the late 20th century."[46] The government subsequently announced a major reorganization of the administrative structure of British pollution control. It also committed itself to significantly reduce sulfur emissions from its coal-burning power plants over the next decade and to require the newly privatized water authorities to devote considerable resources to reducing water pollution. In addition, Britain's willingness to make its environmental regulations more consistent with EC standards and procedures has increased in a number of areas.

JAPAN. Both the visibility of environmentalism as a political issue and the political strength of Japan's environmental movement declined steadily between the mid-1970s and the late 1980s. During the second half of the 1970s, the number of community-based antipollution groups dropped significantly, the press coverage of environmental issues declined, the LDP improved its electoral fortunes at the local level, and most of the important suits by pollution victims were either settled or decided in favor of the defendants. Although environmental organizations remained active—and in some cases quite effective—in opposing various development projects at the local level, their national political influence was negligible. They had little access to the Diet and few ties with Japan's Environment Agency.

The Environment Agency also experienced a loss of political influence.[47] In 1984 it abandoned a four-year effort to secure Diet approval of legislation requiring environmental impact assessments for government projects, making Japan one of the few industrial nations without

44. OECD, *OECD Environmental Data*, pp. 17–39.

45. Richard Hudson, "Europeans Are Learning that Pollution Must Be Attacked in a Coordinated Way," *Wall Street Journal*, November 1, 1988, p. A24.

46. Herman, "An Ecological Ephiphany."

47. See Pharr and Badaracco, "Coping with Crisis," p. 251; and Pempel, *Policy and Politics in Japan*, p. 234.

such a requirement. The bill had been strongly opposed by a number of more powerful ministries, who wanted to defend their own power, and by the Japanese business community, which did not want to open to public review the process by which government projects were approved. A number of government ministries do perform environmental assessments for many public projects, but there is no mechanism to monitor them.

As in the case of Britain, there is some evidence that Japan's physical environment deteriorated during the 1980s.[48] For example, the number of smog alerts in Japan, after significantly declining during the 1970s, doubled between 1982 and 1983, and particulate matter as a source of air pollution increased during the mid-1980s. Although a 1982 survey conducted in fifteen cities revealed extensive groundwater deterioration, corrective action has been limited, and water pollution remains a serious problem for Japan's closed water borders as well as for many of its rivers. However, Japan's most conspicuous failing has been in the area of global environmental regulation.[49] "Despite her enthusiastic pledge of environmental good citizenship at the 1973 Stockholm Conference on the Human Environment, Japan has consistently taken anti-environmental positions in international negotiations," although during the second half of the 1980s, Japan's position, like that of Britain, did become more cooperative.[50] On the other hand, sulfur oxide emissions in Japan declined more rapidly than in either Great Britain or the United States, and Japan has become a world leader in the use of waste disposal technology.

It appears that in the case of both Japan and Great Britain, their parliamentary systems of government contributed to a decline in the access of environmental organizations to the policy process and to a weakening of the effectiveness of some environmental regulations. Given the indifference to environmental concerns of the political leadership that held office in both countries throughout this period (although the position of the British prime minister changed in 1988), environmental interests in these two countries had little chance of being effectively represented. They lacked the opportunities that their U.S. counterparts had—namely, to use the support of the White House when Congress became hostile and their influence in Congress when the White House became hostile, and to challenge agency decisions in the courts throughout the period.

48. See Vogel, "Environmental Policy"; and Pharr and Badaracco, "Coping with Crisis."

49. Neil Gross, "Charging Japan with Crimes Against the Earth," *Business Week*, October 9, 1989, p. 108.

50. Frank K. Upham, "Environmental Law in Japan," *Ecology Law Quarterly*, vol. 10, no. 1 (1982), p. 186.

Land use policymaking is more open to public participation in the United States than in Japan, and the opportunities for citizen access provided by the British system of public inquiries are less extensive than those offered through the U.S. federal courts.

Patterns and Explanations

This review of three nations' environmental policies in the post–World War II era suggests a number of conclusions about the influence of institutional and noninstitutional factors on government representation of diffuse interests.

1. *The content and intensity of public opinion have been more important than the structure of political institutions in determining cross-national and intertemporal differences in environmental policy.* During the 1940s, 1950s, and 1960s, there was a clear correlation between the interest of the citizenry of a nation in environmental issues and the extent and effectiveness of environmental regulation in that nation: Britain was the leader on both dimensions, followed by the United States and then Japan. Likewise, during the late 1960s and early 1970s, public demands for environmental regulation increased dramatically in all three nations, and all three governments responded by radically increasing the scope of their regulatory controls over business. Public unhappiness with the quality of the environment was greatest in Japan, which responded by devoting more of its resources than any other nation to pollution control; the United States was second on both dimensions, followed by Great Britain.

Since the mid-1970s, the American public has been consistently more concerned about environmental quality than have the citizens of the other two nations. According to a poll conducted in the late 1980s, the Japanese public trails behind that of other nations in realizing the importance of preserving the environment.[51] In Japan public interest in environmental issues rose for a relatively brief period during the late 1960s and early 1970s. In Britain public concern about the environment grew during the late 1960s and early 1970s, declined in saliency for approximately fifteen years, and then increased again toward the end of the 1980s. In contrast, public attitudes in the United States have been relatively stable since the late 1960s.[52]

51. "Poll Finds Japanese Lack Environmental Concern," *Japan Times*, May 10, 1989. There are no comparable data for the United States and Britain.
52. Dunlap, "Public Opinion and Environmental Policy."

During the twenty years after the end of World War II, Britain had the most well organized and influential environmental movement, followed by the United States and then Japan. However, since the late 1960s, the nation with the most well organized and influential environmental movement has been the United States, followed by Great Britain and then Japan. These differences were reflected in trends in environmental policy outputs.

2. *Each political system appears equally capable of responding to intense changes in the political preferences of large numbers of voters.* The leaders of both parliamentary and presidential systems must periodically face the electorate. If they believe that a group of voters large enough to determine the outcome of a national election holds strong views about a particular issue, such as pollution control, they will alter their public policies accordingly. This certainly explains the alacrity with which the political leadership in all three countries responded to the upsurge of environmentalism around 1970, as well as the "greening" of both Thatcher and Bush that took place toward the end of the 1980s. Low public interest in environmental issues also accounts for the relative lack of responsiveness on the part of Japan's political leadership to the "second wave" of environmentalism that emerged in the rest of the industrialized world during the second half of the 1980s.

3. *Independent legislatures and judiciaries allow diffuse interests to continue to influence the policy process even when their issues are not of high salience and they do not command sufficient support to influence the outcome of national elections.* Weaver and Rockman argue that institutional effects are best conceived of as "risks" and "opportunities" that are generally contingent upon the presence or absence of other conditions and variables across countries and time periods, rather than as mechanistic and uniform institutional advantages and disadvantages. Certainly this is true in the case of representation of diffuse interests. Separation of executive and legislative powers appears to offer three distinctive opportunities and one distinctive risk for this capability. Two of these opportunities are particularly characteristic during eras of low issue salience. First, separation of powers (and an independent judiciary as well) facilitates the political representation of groups representing diffuse interests by lowering the cost of access: it is not necessary to command the support of a significant number of voters in order to affect the decisions of a congressional committee or a panel of federal judges. U.S. presidents need the support of both the legislature and the judiciary in order to govern; these two branches regularly participate in both the making and implementation of public policy. The relative independence of both Congress and the

judiciary from executive control has been critical to the continued effectiveness of U.S. environmental policy since the beginning of the 1970s.[53]

A second opportunity afforded by the separation of powers is closely related to another policy capability—policy stability. Because the multiple veto points in the U.S. separation-of-powers system make it difficult to alter the statutory status quo, mechanisms of access and substantive policies favoring diffuse interests are unlikely to be repealed or to fall into disuse. Policymaking for diffuse interests is therefore more likely to be a "ratchetlike" phenomenon (advances that are difficult to reverse), rather than the "seesaw" (cyclical advances followed by equal declines) that often characterizes party government parliamentary systems.

In contrast, parliamentary systems pose two distinctive risks for representation of diffuse interests. First, without intense interest by significant numbers of voters, leaders are apt to pay little attention to the political representatives of diffuse interests, for the simple reason that they do not need their support in order to govern. Instead, they are apt to consult extensively with the representatives of concentrated interests, especially business. Environmental organizations will not necessarily be ignored, but they are apt to be consulted far less frequently, and on far less important matters, than organizations that represent traditional interest groups. This is what has occurred in Japan since the early 1970s and also took place in Britain from the mid-1970s through the mid-1980s. A second risk is that policy gains will be reversed, especially when there is a change in government or a decline in public interest.

One can generalize these arguments to other policy areas. Over the last quarter-century in the United States, interest groups representing a wide variety of diffuse interests, not all of which have commanded as much public support as the environmental movement, have had a substantial effect on public policy at the national level. In addition to environmental organizations, the women's movement, civil rights organizations, consumer organizations, and the American Civil Liberties Union have all benefited from America's unique constitutional system. A separation-of-powers system facilitates the political representation of in-

53. For an overall assessment of America's record in reducing pollution levels from the early 1970s through the mid-1980s, see Jeremy Main, "Here Comes the Big New Cleanup," *Fortune*, November 21, 1988, p. 102. For comparisons of the American and European record on environmental regulation, see Eckard Rehbinder, "U.S. Environmental Policy: Lessons for Europe?" *International Environmental Affairs*, vol. 1 (Winter 1989), pp. 3–11; and Benedick, "U.S. Environmental Policy," pp. 91–102. This independence of the branches has undermined the coherence of environmental policy, however. See, for example, Melnick, *Regulation and the Courts*.

tense, well-organized minorities, giving them opportunities to participate in the policy process on a day-to-day basis that are not generally available in at least some types of parliamentary systems. If they maintain an active organizational core, separation of powers enables them to continue to exercise effective group pressure—and thus to minimize policy retrenchment—even when the national salience of the issues that concern them diminishes.

4. *Control of the executive and the legislature by different political parties (divided government) has facilitated access and responsiveness to diffuse interests in the United States.* A third opportunity for representation of diffuse interests in separation-of-powers systems flows directly from divided government. It is what some analysts have called the "bidding up" phenomenon.[54] During the Nixon administration, when public interest in environmental issues was very high, interbranch partisan rivalries led presidential and congressional leaders from different parties to push for tougher legislation to ensure that they would not be portrayed as "soft on the environment" relative to their institutional and partisan rivals.

Divided government can lead to stalemate as well as bidding up, however (see Allen Schick's chapter). Stalemate may create opportunities for defense of diffuse interests, as noted earlier. In the Reagan administration, for example, continuing congressional support for environmental protection made it difficult to move as strongly as many officials would have liked to weaken the enforcement of environmental statutes. But stalemate may also create an important risk for representation of diffuse interests. Where defense of diffuse interests requires new government action rather than simply defense of the status quo, interbranch conflict and stalemate may weaken prospects for accommodation, as evident most clearly in the thirteen-year impasse preceding passage of the Clean Air Act of 1990 in the United States. Impasse is especially likely when there is no intense public pressure for action, when the legislature itself contains multiple veto points, and when there are strong regional divisions on an issue. All of these were in evidence in congressional consideration of a new clean air act. In contrast, one opportunity provided by a single-party-dominant system is that government can move expeditiously when public support for action is high: Japan changed environmental policy much more rapidly than either Britain or the United States.

---

54. On this phenomenon, see John B. Gilmour, "Bargaining between Congress and the President: The Bidding-Up Phenomenon," paper prepared for the 1990 annual meeting of the American Political Science Association.

5. *Parliamentary systems characterized by proportional representation and coalition governments offer advocates of diffuse interests greater opportunities for access and responsiveness than those generally found in other types of parliamentary systems.* In assessing the effect of constitutional systems on the representation of diffuse interests, it is important to distinguish among different kinds of parliamentary systems. In the absence of intense and widespread public support, organizations representing diffuse interests are likely to lack access to the policy process in Britain or Japan. But an electoral system based on proportional representation provides such organizations with an option that they do not have in either a presidential system or a Westminster-style parliamentary system, namely that of forming their own political party. Green parties emerged in a number of continental European countries during the 1980s.[55] As long as there are enough voters to allow an additional party to be represented in the national legislature, diffuse interests can effectively participate in the policy process.

In this context, it is worth noting that the three Western European nations with the most intense commitment to environmental protection—the Netherlands, Sweden, and the Federal Republic of Germany—all have electoral systems based on proportional representation. However, the environment may be an exceptional case: organizations representing other diffuse interests are less well represented in nations with proportional representation than they are in the United States.

Rather than simply distinguishing between presidential and parliamentary systems, it might be more appropriate to distinguish among several constitutional "regime types." Diffuse interests are likely to be best represented in a presidential system and least represented in a Westminster-style party government system or a single-party-dominant parliamentary system. Parliamentary systems with proportional representation appear to fall somewhere in between.

6. *The U.S. federal system helps to preserve group access when issue salience declines and one or more branches of the federal government have become unsympathetic. But federalism also creates problems of jurisdiction, competition, and implementation.*

Federalism enabled organizations representing diffuse interests to take advantage of their political support at the local level to participate in national politics and to shape policy at the local level during the 1980s, when the Reagan administration was unsympathetic to their

---

55. Sara Parkin, *Green Parties: An International Guide* (London: Heretic Books, 1989).

objectives.[56] But federalism has also had negative effects on representation of environmental interests. In the period before the growth of
public interest in environmental issues, federalism increased state and
local officials' fears that aggressive environmental policies would cause
them to lose investment to neighboring areas. More recently, the entrenchment of subnational governments in the implementation structure
for environmental legislation has made implementation more cumber-
some and inefficient in many states and cities.[57]

7. *Other factors, such as economic resources and bureaucratic strength, also
influence the degree to which diffuse interests are represented when public interest
wanes.* In the United States there has been a strong relationship between
the access of environmental organizations and the effectiveness of environmental policy throughout the entire postwar period. But this relationship has been less strong for both Britain and Japan during the
1980s. Since the mid-1970s environmental organizations in Britain have
enjoyed substantially greater access than those in Japan, yet the effectiveness of environmental regulation has not been greater in Britain. The
decline in the political strength of environmental groups in Japan between
1975 and 1988 far exceeded the reduction in the effectiveness of Japanese
environmental regulation.

This suggests that other factors may be needed to account for the
relative effectiveness of environmental regulation in Great Britain and
Japan in recent years. Among the most obvious is the significant difference in the performance of the two economies: Japanese bureaucrats
presumably have faced fewer economic constraints than their counterparts in Great Britain. In addition, the relative strength of the Japanese
state means that Japanese bureaucrats are more likely to be able to impose
their preferences on industry than their counterparts in Great Britain. In
a sense, environmental regulation has become institutionalized in Japan.

Conclusion: Evaluating Institutional Opportunities and Risks

Institutional effects on government capability to represent diffuse interests are neither uniform nor unidirectional. A constitutional system

56. For a general argument along these lines, see Richard P. Nathan, "The Role of the
States in American Federalism," in Carl E. Van Horn, ed., *The State of the States* (Washington: CQ Press, 1989), pp. 15–32, especially p. 17.

57. See Terry M. Moe, "The Politics of Bureaucratic Structure," in John E. Chubb
and Paul E. Peterson, eds., *Can the Government Govern?* (Brookings, 1988), pp. 267–329,
especially p. 318; see also Gary C. Bryner, *Bureaucratic Discretion: Law and Policy in Federal
Regulatory Agencies* (New York: Pergamon Press, 1987).

based on the separation of powers, for example, creates both important opportunities and risks for representation of these interests. But an overall evaluation of the environmental case suggests that on balance a separation-of-powers system is likely to be more responsive to organizations representing diffuse interests than parliamentary systems, at least those of the single-party-dominant and party government varieties. U.S. environmental policy has been decisively shaped by the access of environmental organizations to the political process. Moreover, because the U.S. system provides multiple points of access, a highly motivated minority of citizens has a greater opportunity to be heard. However, unless they are heard, they are likely to be ignored. By contrast, in most parliamentary systems regulatory officials are more likely to be shielded from direct pressures by environmental interest groups. Precisely because they enjoy more autonomy, they may choose to represent diffuse interests— although at the same time they are also freer not to do so.

Richard Gunther and Anthony Mughan

Political Institutions and Cleavage Management

*T*he effective management of political cleavages based upon economic, linguistic, religious, cultural, or ethnic divisions in society is vital to the functioning of political regimes and to their long-term stability. This task is particularly complex and demanding in democratic political systems, where the legitimacy of competition is formally recognized and even considered desirable. Democracies acknowledge the existence of varied and conflicting interests in a society (eschewing notions of a single "general will"); they guarantee the rights of groups to organize to advance their respective interests; and they provide institutions to accommodate competition between organized groups.

Accordingly, democratic regimes require the maintenance of a careful and often difficult balance between conflict and consensus. Conflict has to be directed into the proper institutional channels and expressed in accord with a commonly accepted set of rules. At the same time, however, for the system to be fully democratic, rights of citizenship must be extended to all segments of the population, all major political offices must be responsible (directly or indirectly) to the electorate, and no political options can be effectively excluded from competition over those offices.[1]

The central question addressed in this chapter is the extent to which political institutions—in particular, presidential or parliamentary forms of government—serve to improve or undermine the capacity of democratic regimes to manage political conflict, especially when that conflict involves deep social divisions. We analyze the experiences of four Western

---

1. See Juan J. Linz, "Totalitarian and Authoritarian Regimes," in Fred I. Greenstein and Nelson W. Polsby, eds., *Handbook of Political Science*, vol. 3: *Macropolitical Theory* (Reading, Mass.: Addison-Wesley, 1975), pp. 182–83.

industrialized societies—the United States, the United Kingdom, Belgium, and Spain—that vary significantly in their governmental structure, patterns of political conflict, and histories of democratic stability. After providing a brief overview of the structure of political cleavages and history of democratic stability in each of the four countries, we assess systematically how three aspects of political institutions—presidential or parliamentary structures of government, electoral laws, and federalism—have contributed to their differing patterns of democratic stability.

Identifying Failures of Conflict Management

The failure of a democratic regime to manage political conflict—or in terms more frequently used, to maintain "democratic stability"—manifests itself in three different ways. The first is the suppression of political competition.[2] For a regime to conform satisfactorily to our procedural definition of democracy, all sectors of its population must have an equal opportunity to advance their legitimate interests in the democratic marketplace. Departures from this criterion may take several forms, the most obvious of which is the legal exclusion of a particular group from full rights of citizenship. The institution of slavery in the United States before the Civil War or denial of political rights to blacks in South Africa are clear examples of *de jure* denial of civil and political rights. *De facto* exclusion from the enjoyment of full citizenship rights, another subversion of this fundamental democratic criterion, would include the cynical manipulation of voter registration requirements (such as literacy tests or poll taxes in the American South before the mid-1960s), intimidation of would-be voters by local notables, or outright electoral fraud. A third departure involves institutions or procedures that render participation by certain groups meaningless, despite the absence of overt restrictions on citizenship rights. For example, electoral laws may persistently underrepresent some groups and effectively exclude them from the governmental decisionmaking process. Catholics in Northern Ireland found themselves in such a position when governed by the Protestant-dominated Stormont until its abolition in 1972.

The other two manifestations of the failure of conflict management involve political instability. One type of instability is evident when a regime is beset by violent and disruptive conflict. Democratic systems, by definition, must allow for the expression of conflict; but its expression must be peaceful, in accord with basic norms of mutual tolerance and

2. Robert A. Dahl, *Polyarchy: Participation and Opposition* (Yale University Press, 1971).

respect, and within the institutional channels explicitly designated as the proper forum for the articulation and reconciliation of competing group demands. The ineffectiveness of conflict management, therefore, can be measured by the frequency, scope, and intensity of violence.[3]

Finally, the inability to manage conflict can lead to challenges to the legitimacy of the regime itself. The ultimate manifestation of a regime's instability is its collapse and its replacement by another (usually authoritarian) regime. Short of that extreme outcome, a rough gauge of instability is the popular support mobilized by parties or movements opposed to the democratic system.

Institutional Mechanisms for Cleavage Management

Our starting point in exploring the relationship between political institutions and democratic stability is acknowledgment that the prospects for democratic stability are profoundly shaped by the number, depth, and pattern of interaction of political cleavages in a society. Other things being equal, the existence of deep social divisions in a society is conducive to the emergence of intense conflict and possibly violence that may undermine popular adherence to a regime, especially when those cleavages tend to reinforce rather than cross-cut each other. Such conflict may threaten the longer-run survival of the regime.

We contend that political institutions are a significant force facilitating peaceful regulation of conflict insofar as they encourage consensual rather than majoritarian patterns of elite interaction.[4] *Majoritarianism* refers to the election of governing elites by mere pluralities (or artificially contrived or manufactured majorities), in combination with winner-take-all rules for government decisionmaking. *Consensualism*, in contrast, can

3. Examples of this approach to the study of political instability are Lijphart, Rogowski, and Weaver's essay in this volume; and G. Bingham Powell, Jr., *Contemporary Democracies: Participation, Stability, and Violence* (Harvard University Press, 1982).

4. It should be noted that, although we are using the same terms as Arend Lijphart, our respective concepts are different. See Arend Lijphart, *Democracies: Patterns of Majoritarian and Consensus Government* (Yale University Press, 1984). Our definitions are narrower than those set forth in *Democracies*, which consist of two dimensions and eight components and mix the structure of governmental institutions and party systems, the number and nature of divisive issues in a society, and dominant cabinet-formation practices. Those models are of considerable heuristic value, but for the purpose of explaining cross-national differences in conflict management capacities, they are overaggregated: they mix causally distal factors (cleavages, or "issue dimensions") with intervening variables (government institutions) and with more proximal factors (such as elite coalition formation), thereby undercutting the ability to measure the impact of political institutions per se.

take two forms: a formal agreement on power sharing that allocates key posts proportionately among all significant political forces (as in full-fledged consociational democracies) or more limited, uninstitutionalized patterns of elite behavior designed to coopt representatives of all significant political groups into decisionmaking processes at crucial times and to guarantee veto power for these groups over important decisions.[5]

Several types of institutional arrangements may ameliorate or exacerbate basic cleavage patterns. Consistent with the "three tiers of explanation" set forth in the introductory chapter, we will focus on three sets of institutional variables: presidentialism versus parliamentarism, electoral laws, and federal versus unitary state structure.

The merits of presidential, as opposed to parliamentary, systems in managing political cleavages have become the subject of lively debate. One view is that parliamentary systems encourage majoritarianism—and hence may exacerbate conflict—because they tend to concentrate governmental power, sometimes in the leadership of a single party. Thus the opposition has few means of making itself heard in the making of public policy. Arend Lijphart, Ronald Rogowski, and Kent Weaver argue in the following chapter, for example, that the formal separation of powers defining presidential systems may prevent oppression of minorities by adding veto points that tend to limit the powers of any government. In the same vein, some analysts have argued that centrifugal regional divisions in Canada have been exacerbated by the parliamentary structure of the national government and a single-member-district electoral system. As a result, some regions of the country have sometimes had virtually no representation in the government. This underrepresentation of regional minorities, in combination with strict party discipline in the House of Commons, undermines the utility of the legislature as an arena for the expression and reconciliation of regional demands and increases regional alienation.[6] Conversely, the U.S. system of separated powers and weak party discipline allows effective representation of regional interests, increasing the legitimacy of the central government and lessening pressures for devolution of power to regional governments.

5. These practices are analyzed in Richard Gunther and Roger A. Blough, "Religious Conflict and Consensus in Spain: A Tale of Two Constitutions," *World Affairs*, vol. 143 (Spring 1981), pp. 366–412; and Richard Gunther, "Constitutional Change in Contemporary Spain," in Keith Banting and Richard Simeon, eds., *The Politics of Constitutional Change in Industrial Nations: Redesigning the State* (Macmillan, 1985), pp. 42–70.

6. See Alan C. Cairns, "The Electoral System and the Party System in Canada, 1921–1965," *Canadian Journal of Political Science*, vol. 1 (March 1968), pp. 55–80; and R. Kent Weaver, "Are Parliamentary Systems Better?" *Brookings Review*, vol. 3 (Summer 1985), pp. 22–23.

An additional negative consequence of majoritarianism within parliamentary systems, especially where single-party governments are the norm, is the possibility of radical policy alternation with each change in party control of government.[7] As the government rejects the opposition's right to influence contentious public policies, they remain recurring and salient foci of partisan conflict. In contrast, the multiple veto points in the American system militate against rapid or drastic policy change. When Congress and the presidency are dominated by different parties, the establishment of broad interparty consensus is usually necessary for the passage of important legislation. Thus policies are usually adjusted incrementally, and once-divisive political issues (such as the creation of the social security system) become so widely accepted that they cease to be the subject of partisan conflict.

The opposite ("parliamentarist") view is taken by Juan Linz, who argues that it is presidentialism, not parliamentarism, that is less conducive to effective conflict management. His essential thesis is that presidentialism entails a strong element of majoritarianism, not least because of the zero-sum, winner-take-all nature of competition over the most important political office. Moreover, this characteristic of electoral outcomes can combine with the "full claim to democratic legitimacy of the president, very often with strong plebiscitarian components, . . . the qualities of the head of state representing the nation, and the powers of the executive . . . [to create] a very different aura and self-image, and very different popular expectations than those of a prime minister."[8]

Finally, the frustration of losers is compounded by the fixed term of office of the executive:

> Winners and losers are defined for the period of the presidential mandate—a number of years in which there is no hope for shifts in alliances, broadening of the base of support by national unity or emergency grand coalitions, crisis situations that might lead to dissolution

7. Weaver points to the nationalization of the steel industry by a Labour government, followed by privatization under the Conservatives, followed by renationalization under Labour, followed by privatization under Margaret Thatcher. "Are Parliamentary Systems Better?" See Sven Steinmo, "Political Institutions and Tax Policy in the United States, Sweden, and Britain," *World Politics*, vol. 41 (July 1989), pp. 500–35.

8. Juan J. Linz, "Democracy: Presidential or Parliamentary. Does It Make a Difference?" 1989 revised draft of a paper originally presented at the Workshop on Political Parties in the Southern Cone at the Woodrow Wilson International Center for Scholars, Washington, 1984, p. 7. This paper will be published in Juan J. Linz and Arturo Valenzuela, eds., *Presidentialism and Parliamentarism: Does It Make a Difference?* (forthcoming). An abbreviated version of this essay has been published as "The Perils of Presidentialism," in *Journal of Democracy*, vol. 1 (Winter 1990), pp. 51–69.

and new elections, etc. The losers will have to wait four or five years without any access to executive power, and thereby to a share in the formation of cabinets and access to patronage.[9]

Overall, Linz suggests that "presidential systems have been as vulnerable, if not more vulnerable, to breakdown of democracy as parliamentary systems, and there is considerable evidence that the presidential system contributed much to a number of those breakdowns."[10] The very tentativeness of this conclusion, however, is ample testimony that the nature of the relationship between separation of powers and effective conflict management remains ambiguous.

Moving to Weaver and Rockman's second tier of explanation, electoral laws can encourage consensual or majoritarian patterns of behavior in either parliamentary or presidential systems. In general, proportional electoral systems tend to promote consensual elite behavior by reducing or precluding the possibility that a single party can receive an absolute majority of seats and form a government. Coalition governments are usually formed by multiple parties that do not always agree with each other on important questions of ideology or public policy. To the extent that the coalition partners do not find themselves on the same side of a major cleavage line, the formation and maintenance of multiparty governments demands a continuous process of interparty negotiation and compromise. By contrast, other electoral systems (especially those based on single-member constituencies) obviate the need for negotiation and compromise among elites by manufacturing legislative majorities that commonly overrepresent parties whose share of the popular vote barely achieves a majority, or in some cases clearly falls short of one. The government is thus in a position to ignore its parliamentary opposition and go about enacting the mandate on which it was elected, despite having been endorsed by only a minority of the voting population.

A third level of institutional arrangements, notably federalism, may also affect cleavage management capabilities. Governments vary widely in the extent to which their constitutions allocate specific powers to central and subnational governments or concentrate policymaking authority at the center. In a unitary arrangement, subnational governments are to all intents and purposes the agents of central government and have

9. Linz, "Democracy," p. 15.
10. Linz, "Democracy." Prima facie evidence in support of Linz's argument (but in the specific context of the third world) is presented in Fred W. Riggs, "The Survival of Presidentialism in America: Para-constitutional Practices," *International Political Science Review*, vol. 9 (October 1988), pp. 247–78.

no constitutionally guaranteed powers of their own.[11] Political power in a federal state is thus distributed among a larger number of actors than in a unitary one. Since dispersed power is more likely than concentrated power to promote negotiation and compromise, federalism is commonly associated with consensualism and unitarism with majoritarianism. That is, the larger the number of autonomous political actors who are involved in decisionmaking, the greater the likelihood that the outcomes will reflect a compromise among their individual preferences. In addition, federalism, by devolving authority to make and implement decisions upon local and regional government bodies, may remove potentially divisive issues from the policy agenda at the national level. In principle, this allows local and regional minorities to formulate policies consistent with their own interests and to reduce the possibility of discrimination or, more generally, unfavorable treatment at the hands of the national majority.

The Cases: Cleavage Management in Four Democracies

One major obstacle to evaluating the effects of presidential versus parliamentary forms of government is that the universe of Western democracies includes only one example of presidentialism, the United States. This presents a daunting methodological problem of separating the unique from the general. Nor would it circumvent this problem to look also at the larger number of third world countries with presidential systems of government, since that would complicate matters even further by introducing a wide variety of additional, potentially important, explanatory variables. The difficulty can be alleviated somewhat, however, by undertaking both cross-national and longitudinal analyses, the latter taking advantage of variation in both the independent and dependent variables over time. Thus we have chosen two countries (the United States and the United Kingdom) that have shown remarkable institutional continuity and two (Belgium and Spain) that have experienced substantial institutional change in recent years.

The United States

The United States is the only Western democracy to have a presidential system of government characterized by separated powers within federal

11. See Ivo D. Duchacek, *Comparative Federalism: The Territorial Dimension of Politics* (Holt, Rinehart, and Winston, 1970).

and state governments as well as between them. Its political cleavage structure is also unique. Although its population is ethnically and linguistically heterogeneous and divided by the inevitable socioeconomic cleavages, the society is relatively free of deep, enduring political divisions among subgroups. In this regard, it is a heterogeneous society with a homogeneous political culture. This culture has facilitated moderation in partisan conflict: ideological differences between Democrats and Republicans are muted, and neither party even remotely questions the legitimacy of the social, economic, and political principles by which the country is governed. Because of this widespread agreement on fundamental principles, the political culture of the United States is often described as "consensual," as opposed to the "adversarial" culture found in democracies where political divisions are deeper and more enduring.[12]

America has enjoyed a remarkable degree of political stability over its more than 200 years of existence. Regional differences were responsible for the one glaring exception to this generalization, the Civil War of the 1860s. While bringing an end to the institution of slavery, this war introduced other elements of instability into the Republic by not settling, especially in the South, the question of the place of black citizens in American society. Racial exclusionism remained the norm in the southern states for almost a century as blacks were effectively disenfranchised through manipulation of such devices as literacy tests and poll taxes. The electoral exclusion of blacks was effectively brought to an end only by the 1965 Voting Rights Act and other federal legislation. But by this time, black frustration had reached a boiling point in the country at large, partly as the result of the political system's persistent failure to pass majority-backed civil rights legislation over the determined opposition of southern Democratic congressmen.[13]

The consequences of this failure to address racial tensions in American society came most obviously to the fore with the massive outburst of

12. Some of the classic works addressing the explanation of America's exceptionalism in this regard are Robert A. Dahl, "The American Oppositions," in Dahl, ed., *Political Oppositions in Western Democracies* (Yale University Press, 1966); Louis Hartz, *The Liberal Tradition in America: An Interpretation of American Political Thought since the Revolution* (Harcourt, Brace, 1955); Seymour Martin Lipset, *The First New Nation: The United States in Historical and Comparative Perspective* (Basic Books, 1963); and David Morris Potter, *People of Plenty: Economic Abundance and the American Character* (University of Chicago Press, 1954). Lipset has recently returned to this question in "American Exceptionalism Reaffirmed," in Byron E. Shafer, ed., *Is America Different? A New Look at American Exceptionalism* (Oxford University Press, 1991).

13. For the role of race in Southern politics, see V. O. Key, Jr., *Southern Politics in State and Nation* (Knopf, 1949).

violent protest in many cities in the 1960s. The destabilizing effect of this outburst was compounded by the almost simultaneous emergence of vocal and violent opposition to U.S. involvement in the Vietnam War. Although racial conflict persists to this day, the clearer representation of black interests through the Democratic party, together with the large increase in the number of elected black officials, reflects a substantial change from the past.[14] Thus, to the extent that the institutionalization of conflict makes it more manageable by normal democratic processes, race no longer poses the same threat to U.S. political stability.

The record of conflict management in the United States, then, is mixed. On the one hand, the democratic political system has remained profoundly stable insofar as its legitimacy has rarely been questioned by any significant group in the population. Even blacks for the most part want only their fair share of the American dream, not its radical redefinition. On the other hand, their failure to achieve this limited goal has been a persistent source of ephemeral instability, taking the form of civil unrest and the suppression of political competition, even as late as the second half of the twentieth century.

United Kingdom

Like the United States, the United Kingdom has the reputation of being one of the world's oldest and most successful democracies. It differs sharply from the United States in being a unitary state and an archetypal example of majoritarian, winner-take-all parliamentarism. Like all Western democracies, the United Kingdom has an inegalitarian class structure, but it is also heterogeneous in that it comprises four nations—England, Northern Ireland, Scotland, and Wales—and a growing nonwhite racial minority made up primarily of Asians and West Indians. This heterogeneity, however, has not been reflected in the political cleavages that have dominated national political life for most of the country's history as a democratic state. Rather, social class has been its dominant political division for most of the twentieth century, and it has given rise to a party system that, since the end of World War II, has produced single-party governments led by either the predominantly middle-class Conservative party or the predominantly working-class Labour party.

Britain's political life is more sharply polarized along class lines than

14. The changing nature of racial politics in the United States is explored in Edward G. Carmines and James A. Stimson, *Issue Evolution: Race and the Transformation of American Politics* (Princeton University Press, 1989).

that of the United States.[15] This is not to say that it has been markedly less stable. Indeed, for most of the postwar period it has generally been regarded as the model parliamentary democracy. With the leadership of both the Conservative and Labour parties reaching a consensus on the broad parameters of public policy, government was interventionist and generally held in high public regard. Political stability was high. The franchise may have been extended more gradually in Britain than in the United States, but when it did come it left no stragglers behind. There was little evidence of a sense of estrangement from the political system on the part of any significant group, and manifestations of public discontent, in such forms as support for antisystem parties or political violence, were virtually unknown.

This picture of a model democracy began to fray at the edges as a result of two important changes that occurred around 1970. The first of them was the onset of the "Troubles" in Northern Ireland in 1969. By that time the province had been governed for almost fifty years by a popularly elected and largely autonomous (at least in domestic affairs) parliament known as the Stormont. The assembly was dominated by the province's Protestant population by virtue of its 2 to 1 majority in the population at large. Catholics saw this as an unassailable majority being used to monopolize political power and to discriminate against them in the public and private provision of such necessities as jobs and housing. In the words of the official commission of enquiry into Catholic grievances, these "social and economic grievances or abuses of political power . . . were in a very real sense an immediate and operative cause of the demonstrations and consequent disorders."[16] Protestant distrust of the province's Catholics stemmed from its conviction that they accorded primary loyalty to an overwhelmingly Catholic Eire constitutionally committed to reclaiming the six counties in the Protestant north. After partition in 1920, successive governments in London simply ignored the political situation in Northern Ireland. Catholic resentment eventually surfaced in 1969 in the form of peaceful civil rights protest marches. The government in Westminster tried belatedly to overcome Protestant intransigence and impose various power-sharing measures on

15. For the role of class conflict in structuring mass voting behavior, see Robert R. Alford, *Party and Society: The Anglo-American Democracies* (Rand McNally, 1963); and for its impact on parliamentary voting patterns, see Samuel H. Beer, *British Politics in the Collectivist Age* (Knopf, 1965). Beer's book appeared in Britain under the title *Modern British Politics* (London: Faber, 1965).

16. Quoted in Christopher Hewitt, "Catholic Grievances, Catholic Nationalism and Violence in Northern Ireland During the Civil Rights Period: A Reconsideration," *British Journal of Sociology*, vol. 32 (September 1981), p. 363.

the province. These measures failed in the face of unyielding Protestant resistance. The Stormont was abolished in 1972, and direct rule from London was imposed. But decades of British complicity in Protestant domination had undermined Catholic confidence in the impartiality of the government. Direct rule also weakened Protestants' confidence that London would continue to be attentive to their interests. The conflict polarized and soon escalated into deadly terrorist warfare, mainly pitting the Catholic Irish Republican Army against the British army. The conflict has claimed the lives of some 2,500 people and remains unresolved to this day.[17]

The second important change was the crumbling of the consensus that had shaped postwar British political life.[18] Although it had fallen into disrepute by 1970, this consensus evaporated only with the election and reelection of Margaret Thatcher's Conservative party in the 1979, 1983, and 1987 general elections. With large parliamentary majorities—manufactured by the first-past-the-post electoral system rather than deriving from majority support among voters—she eschewed consensus politics and declared herself a "conviction politician" whose goal was to kill off socialism (and, by implication, its principal purveyor, the Labour party) as a force in British politics. The "caring state" would be less in evidence. Displacing the collectivist state and an overpowerful trade union movement, the market was to be restored to its rightful position as the principal determinant of the distribution of costs and benefits of membership in society. Inequalities were encouraged to widen as a necessary stimulus to economic growth. The inevitable result was intensification of political conflict on a number of fronts: racial tensions escalated and riots unprecedented in number and ferocity occurred in several British cities; a sense of marginalization and hostility to government grew in Scotland, Wales, and parts of England; and the government found itself confronting determined trade union and popular resistance to its economic and social policies. If consensus had been abandoned, so too had a degree of social peace and harmony.[19]

17. See Richard Rose, *Governing Without Consensus: An Irish Perspective* (London: Faber and Faber, 1971); and Paul Arthur and Keith Jeffery, *Northern Ireland Since 1968* (Oxford: Basil Blackwell, 1988).

18. The flavor of this decade is captured in Samuel H. Beer's *Britain Against Itself: The Political Contradictions of Collectivism* (Norton, 1982). See also Dennis Kavanagh and Peter Morris, *Consensus Politics from Attlee to Thatcher* (Oxford: Basil Blackwell, 1989); and Patrick Seyd, *The Rise and Fall of the Labour Left* (Basingstoke: Macmillan Education, 1987).

19. See Peter Jenkins, *Mrs. Thatcher's Revolution: The Ending of the Socialist Era* (Harvard University Press, 1988); and Dennis Kavanagh, *Thatcherism and British Politics: The End of Consensus?* (Oxford: Oxford University Press, 1987).

The United Kingdom, then, is a society that has become more unstable in the last decade or two. Conflict has not been suppressed, but there has been an escalation of political violence in both Northern Ireland and on the mainland. Economic decline and "conviction" politics have combined to sharpen racial, nationalist, and class tensions. This suggests that Britain does not enjoy the same degree of consensus as the United States on the social, economic, and political formula for governing the country. The persistence of adversarial politics is the legacy primarily of social class antagonisms nurtured by a system of structured inequality rooted in the nation's feudal past and compounded by the industrial revolution.

Belgium

Belgium was created in 1830 as a highly unitary state with a parliamentary system of government, but its deep political divisions have obliged it to modify significantly the majoritarian, winner-take-all character of its political system over the course of the twentieth century. It is a deeply divided society, at least in part because the three cleavages that shape its political life—religion, social class, and language—are mutually reinforcing, so that the same groups tend to be pitted against each other on more than one politically salient front.[20]

The Belgian population comprises two large linguistic communities: Dutch speakers in the region of Flanders, and French speakers in the Walloon region. Dutch speakers have always constituted the majority of the population, but the country's political life was shaped almost exclusively by French speakers until the 1960s. The vehicle of francophone domination was the unilingual state created at independence. Dutch did not become the second official language of the state until the turn of the century, and it was not until the 1930s that a monolingual Dutch-speaking university was created. Despite the Dutch-speaking majority's longstanding economic, social, and political subordination, however, language has only recently come to polarize national politics. Belgian political life in the nineteenth century was dominated by the antagonism between Catholics, located disproportionately in rural Flanders, and freethinking Liberals, residing primarily in industrializing Wallonia. After a

---

20. The best historical treatment of Belgium's cleavage structure is Val R. Lorwin's "Belgium: Religion, Class and Language in National Politics," in Dahl, ed., *Political Oppositions in Western Democracies*, pp. 147–87. More detailed, but stopping too early to give full credit to the importance of the language conflict in postwar Belgian politics, is E. H. Kossman, *The Low Countries, 1780–1940* (Oxford: Oxford University Press, 1978).

long period of alternating, highly divisive single-party governments in the second half of the century, the emergence of the class cleavage from about 1875 on produced the first significant dilution of the majoritarian principle in Belgian politics: the introduction of a proportional representation electoral system in 1899. Overlapping religious and class cleavages then dominated the country's political life until the 1960s. The profound mutual hostility of the rival subcultures that emerged constantly threatened the stability of the Belgian state. This threat was averted by the practice of consociational democracy: that is, leaders of the rival subcultures acted not to inflame hostilities but to institutionalize cooperation and thereby counteract the immobilizing and destabilizing effects of cultural fragmentation. It is a form of democracy that is perhaps best summarized as governance by elite cartel.[21]

Flemish resentment at their subordination became politicized in the last quarter of the nineteenth century. The movement that emerged had two broad goals. The first of them was to guarantee the integrity of Flanders' language and culture by making the region officially unilingual. This was largely achieved by the early 1930s except for the question of the future of Brussels, Belgium's French-speaking capital city physically located in Flanders. The second goal was to reclaim francophone Brussels by stopping its spread into, and "pollution" of, the surrounding Flemish countryside and legislating the equality of the Dutch language in the city to halt the gallicization of Flemings living there. In the early 1960s a linguistic frontier was defined and an "iron yoke" permanently fixed around the capital city. Legislating the equality of the two languages in the national capital proved much harder to achieve since the nine-tenths of the city's inhabitants who were French-speaking by choice fiercely resisted Flemish attempts at what they perceived to be linguistic and cultural imperialism. Concessions to Flemish sentiment thus only served to alienate French speakers in both Brussels and Wallonia.

For the rest of the 1960s, linguistic tensions escalated to the point at which the country's established elites were forced to admit that the unitary state could not be maintained. The constitution was revised in 1970 to establish cultural councils for the language communities and to initiate

21. For the general consociational model, see Arend Lijphart, *Democracy in Plural Societies: A Comparative Exploration* (Yale University Press, 1977); and for its specific application to Belgium, see the same author's "Introduction: The Belgian Example of Cultural Coexistence in Comparative Perspective," in Arend Lijphart, ed., *Conflict and Coexistence in Belgium* (Berkeley: Institute of International Studies, 1981), pp. 1–12; and Val R. Lorwin, "Belgium: Conflict and Compromise," in Kenneth D. McRae, ed., *Consociational Democracy: Political Accommodation in Segmented Societies* (Toronto: McClelland and Stewart, 1974), pp. 179–206.

a longer-term commitment to a system of regional government in Belgium. The precise form that regionalization would take could not be finalized, however, since the two language communities could not agree on the future of Brussels. Dutch speakers advocated a two-region structure comprising Flanders and Wallonia, with a subordinate status for Brussels, whereas French speakers wanted Brussels to be treated equally in a three-region governmental structure. Their disagreement not only proved irreconcilable, it also intensified linguistic divisions so that the only way regionalization could proceed in 1980 was by ignoring Brussels. Elected regional governments were established for Flanders and Wallonia, while Brussels remained under central government tutelage pending an agreement on its status acceptable to all parties.[22]

Political stability in Belgium, then, shows a distinctive pattern. The escalation and polarization of linguistic conflict was not accompanied by any significant political violence. Instead, popular support for antisystem separatist parties grew in both language communities throughout the 1960s and 1970s, which helps to explain why the polarization of the linguistic cleavage has had such a profoundly destabilizing effect on Belgian politics over the last three decades. Although it brought about a "reform of the state," without which the centrifugal strains on national unity would likely have been even greater than they were, even this reform has not eliminated these strains. Continued disagreement over the regional status of Brussels means that the future integrity of the Belgian state cannot be taken for granted.

Spain

Spanish society is deeply divided along several cleavage lines, the most divisive of which today is language; over 40 percent of the population lives in regions characterized by considerable linguistic pluralism. Reinforcing this linguistic diversity are political cultures with very different conceptions of how the Spanish state should be organized. Indeed, conflict between the centralizing tendencies of the Castilian Spanish state and the desire of minorities on the periphery of Iberia (especially Basques

22. See John Fitzmaurice, *The Politics of Belgium: Crisis and Compromise in a Plural Society* (London: Hurst, 1983), pp. 111–38, 237–44; Anthony Mughan, "Belgium: All Periphery and No Centre?" in Yves Mény and Vincent Wright, eds., *Centre-Periphery Relations in Western Europe* (London: Allen and Unwin, 1985), pp. 273–99; and Martine De Ridder and Luis Ricardo Fraga, "The Brussels Issue in Belgian Politics," *West European Politics*, vol. 9 (July 1986), pp. 376–92. A more recent account is Frank Delmartino, "Regionalisation in Belgium: Evaluation of an Ongoing Institutional Crisis," *European Journal of Political Research*, vol. 16 (July 1988), pp. 381–94.

and Catalans) to retain political autonomy, as well as linguistic and cultural distinctiveness, culminated in five civil wars: in 1640, 1700–15, 1833–40, 1872–76, and 1936–39.[23]

Religion is another source of division. Although the Catholic church had previously served as a unifying symbol during several hundred years of Spanish history, anticlerical opposition to the state religion had emerged by the nineteenth century and intensified during the short-lived democratic regime of the Second Republic (1931–36). This religious cleavage was prominent among the causes of the 1936–39 civil war.[24]

In the first half of the twentieth century, Spain was also deeply divided along lines of social class and political ideology. Aside from the usual class polarization that accompanies the first decades of industrialization, the rural sector of society in the south featured a great chasm between extraordinarily affluent absentee (often aristocratic) landlords and an impoverished *lumpenproletariat* of landless day laborers. Reflecting this deep socioeconomic division, the political ideologies that took root in Spain in the late nineteenth and early twentieth centuries polarized Spaniards considerably. During the Second Republic, antisystem parties and ideologies could be found on both left and right, and even the behavior of those in the middle could often be regarded as semiloyal. Anarchism received considerable support among agricultural workers in the latifundist south; anarchosyndicalism was the largest workers' movement in the industrial districts of Cataluña; and even the Socialist party's trade union embraced a radicalism that led (in 1934) to a violent insurrection in the industrial and mining areas of the north. Political extremists on the right included fascist and ultraconservative Catholic and Spanish nationalist parties. Rancorous verbal exchanges among elites were accompanied by increasingly frequent outbursts of political violence as the civil war approached. In light of these deep and sometimes reinforcing social and political cleavages, it is not surprising that Spain's previous democratic experience met with dismal failure.[25]

The violent collapse of the Second Republic stands in sharp contrast to Spain's consolidated constitutional monarchy today. With the excep-

23. See Juan J. Linz, "Early State-Building and Late Peripheral Nationalisms: The Case of Spain," in S. N. Eisenstadt and Stein Rokkan, eds., *Building States and Nations* (Beverly Hills: Sage, 1973), pp. 32–116.

24. See Stanley G. Payne, *Spanish Catholicism: An Historical Overview* (University of Wisconsin Press, 1984).

25. Among the best of the numerous explorations of the origins of the Spanish civil war are Gerald Brenan, *The Spanish Labyrinth: An Account of the Social and Political Background of the Civil War* (Cambridge University Press, 1971); Stanley G. Payne, *The Spanish Revolution* (Norton, 1970); and Edward E. Malefakis, *Agrarian Reform and Peasant Revolution in Spain: Origins of the Civil War* (Yale University Press, 1970).

tion of the Basque region, all politically significant parties fully support the current democratic regime. At the national level, political options range from a moderate Eurocommunism to a Spanish version of Thatcherite conservatism. The rancorous exchanges of the past have given way to mutual respect, tolerance, and cordial personal relations among political opponents. No groups are excluded from full participation, and there is relatively little political violence or widespread mass protest.[26]

The Basque region, Euskadi, is the highly significant exception. Up to one-quarter of Basques favor secession from Spain and creation of a Basque nation-state straddling what is now the French-Spanish border. About one-sixth of the votes cast in Euskadi are regularly cast for an explicitly antisystem party, Herri Batasuna, which supports the terrorist activities of ETA (Euskadi ta Askatasuna). And ETA's violent activities have resulted in the deaths of about 700 persons to this date.[27]

Nonetheless, the contrast between the success of Spain's most recent transition to democracy and the violent collapse of its previous democratic experiment is dramatic. It is also fortuitous in that it enables us to undertake a comparative analysis over time, holding some important variables constant (most social cleavages, as well as a parliamentary form of government) and allowing us to focus on others that change over time.

Political Institutions and Democratic Stability

The United States, the United Kingdom, Belgium, and Spain vary widely in their records as stable democracies. They range from full stability to civil war, from full democratic participation to substantial exclusion of minorities, and from full legitimacy and over two centuries of regime survival to regime collapse and replacement by an authoritarian system. But to what extent are these differences in performance attributable to their political institutions? An examination of the political histories of these four countries suggests several conclusions.

1. *The effect of basic institutional structures on effective conflict management is not direct, automatic, or unidirectional, but is mediated through the goals and*

26. See Richard Gunther, Giacomo Sani, and Goldie Shabad, *Spain After Franco: The Making of a Competitive Party System* (University of California Press, 1986).

27. See Juan J. Linz, *Conflicto en Euskadi* (Madrid: Espasa Calpe, 1986); and Goldie Shabad, "After Autonomy: The Dynamics of Regionalism in Spain," in Stanley G. Payne, ed., *The Politics of Democratic Spain* (Chicago Council on Foreign Relations, 1986), pp. 111–80.

behavior of political elites. Institutional structures themselves do not dictate how elites respond to conflict. Institutions change little over time, whereas elite behaviors can vary markedly—witness the transition to "conviction politics" in Thatcher's Britain. Institutions do, however, determine to some extent the context within which representative elites interact and mobilize their supporters. They do this by creating structures of incentives and disincentives to pursue certain types of goals in certain ways, or, as Weaver and Rockman would put it, they present elites with both risks and opportunities. This conclusion is not surprising. Political elites are not one-dimensional beings. They are affected by a multiplicity of concerns, objectives, and constraints.

2. *There is no consistent pattern linking effective conflict management to either presidential or parliamentary institutions.* Over time, presidential and parliamentary systems alike have varied in their ability to contain conflict within appropriate institutional channels. The United States has been presidential for over two centuries, but this did little to prevent the country from lapsing into civil war, practicing racial exclusionism until the mid-1960s, and experiencing a substantial and prolonged outburst of political violence in the 1960s. Neither is parliamentarism a panacea for effective conflict management. Belgium appears to have had some success in channeling linguistic conflict into institutional channels so that it does not take the form of political violence or represent the same pressing threat to national unity in the 1990s that it did in the 1970s. Britain, in sharp contrast, has failed over some twenty years even to halt political terrorism in Northern Ireland, let alone move Catholics and Protestants toward accommodating their differences. Spain makes this point even more starkly. Both the Second Republic and the present constitutional monarchy adopted parliamentarism, and yet one democratic regime collapsed in civil war while the other has become stable and consolidated.

3. *Majoritarian behavior is at least intermittently possible in separation-of-powers systems, especially when electoral rules in such systems are strongly majoritarian.* Consensual elite behavior is the product of compromise among power holders. A separation of governmental powers would seem to be better suited to promoting such behavior, since it distributes political influence among numerous political actors who need each other's cooperation and consent to govern.[28] A president, however, can stake a claim to political preeminence as the only national politician with a man-

---

28. Perhaps the best summary statement of this governing philosophy is Neustadt's observation that the "constitutional convention of 1787 is supposed to have created a government of 'separated powers.' It did nothing of the sort. Rather, it created a government of separated institutions *sharing* powers." See Richard E. Neustadt, *Presidential Power: The Politics of Leadership* (Wiley, 1960), p. 33.

date to govern from the whole people. But this mandate can be as much an artifact of the electoral system as the single-party majorities in first-past-the-post elections to the British House of Commons. For example, Ronald Reagan claimed to have received a popular mandate for radical change in his 1980 presidential election victory, based on his 489–49 majority in the Electoral College vote. This majority, however, bore little resemblance to his bare majority of 50.9 percent in the popular vote.[29]

It might be countered at this point that, contrived majorities notwithstanding, U.S. presidents are constrained to be consensual insofar as they need to accommodate other powerful political actors, particularly Congress. This observation is undoubtedly accurate, but the importance of Congress as a check on presidential power can be overstated. Reagan's aggressively majoritarian behavior during his first two years in office helped him achieve his goals of reducing personal and corporate taxation, cutting benefit programs for the poor, and increasing defense spending, all policies opposed by the Democratic majority in the House of Representatives. His success, however, was due to more than just the mandate to which he successfully laid claim. Reagan's highly partisan style and extensive campaign efforts on behalf of his party's candidates contributed to a Republican gain of over thirty House seats and a majority in the Senate for the first time in twenty-six years.[30] These gains were made possible in part by majoritarian election laws and simultaneous presidential and congressional elections. In the space of two years, however, the president's relations with his congressional party colleagues had cooled, his personal popularity was on the decline, and the Republican party lost most of its 1980 House seat gains in the 1982 off-year election. Reagan's majoritarian behavior and congressional successes were not replicated after the enactment of his 1981 legislative program.[31] The point is that a U.S. president faced with a Congress that is, for whatever reason, compliant is capable of majoritarian behavior. This will be particularly true when an ambitious president is of the same party as the majority in both houses of Congress.

4. *The separation of powers can worsen relations between rival partisan elites, leading to governmental stalemate.* Even steadfast congressional opposition to a president, usually because he is from the other major party, is no

29. See Robert A. Dahl, "Myth of the Presidential Mandate," *Political Science Quarterly*, vol. 105 (Fall 1990), pp. 355–72.

30. See Charles O. Jones, "Ronald Reagan and the U.S. Congress: Visible-Hand Politics," in Charles O. Jones, ed., *The Reagan Legacy: Promise and Performance* (Chatham, N.J.: Chatham House, 1988), p. 33.

31. Jones, "Ronald Reagan and the U.S. Congress," passim.

guarantee that consensual, accommodative behavior will ensue. Indeed, recent American history has generally seen a Republican president pitted against a Democratic Congress; the presidential response has increasingly been to go over the head of Congress and appeal directly to the public for support. This strategy of "going public" is designed precisely to obviate the need to build the consensual coalitions traditionally required for effective government in the United States.[32] A powerful president "endowed with popular legitimacy [and] with a tendency toward ple-biscitarian legitimation" may succumb to the temptation to question the motives and challenge the legitimacy of congressional opponents on the grounds that their defense of particularistic "special interests" runs counter to the wishes of "the people." Accordingly, the president is "likely to define his policies as reflecting the popular will and those of his opponents as representing narrow interests rejected by the people."[33]

Although U.S. presidents have sometimes opted for this ploy, it is relatively rare in a consolidated democracy like the United States where the defense of parochial interests is widely seen as a legitimate and proper role for Congress to play. "Imperial" U.S. presidents who have sought to bypass or nullify congressional opposition by whatever means may have threatened political destabilization by undercutting the pragmatic adjustment of competing interests that the system of separated powers is intended to facilitate. One-longer term consequence of Johnson's and Nixon's imperial presidencies may indeed have been to undermine mutual trust between the executive and legislative branches of government, with the result that there is stalemate on important and contentious national problems, such as reduction of the budget deficit.

The argument we are making, then, is not that the separation of powers is unrelated to the adoption of consensual behavior on the part of competing elites; it is rather that there is no simple relationship between the two. The winner-take-all method of electing the U.S. president is eminently capable of generating artificial majorities that enable the victorious candidate to claim to have received a popular mandate that is in turn instrumental in allowing him to bypass or ignore opposition to his policies. A distinct element of majoritarianism can thus be introduced into a presidential system of government. But even a majoritarian president cannot always impose his will on congressional opponents, so that pragmatic adjustment can give way to a clash of wills and some degree

32. See Samuel Kernell, *Going Public: New Strategies of Presidential Leadership* (Washington: CQ Press, 1986).

33. Linz, "Democracy," p. 25.

of governmental paralysis, with all its attendant risks for popular commitment to the regime and its long-term stability.

5. *Electoral laws can critically affect the choice of consensual versus majoritarian elite behavior in parliamentary systems.* If presidentialism cannot be equated simply with consensual elite behavior, neither can parliamentarism be equated simply with majoritarian elite behavior. Parliamentary systems of government give rise to very different conflict management styles, ranging from the adversarial majoritarianism found in Britain to the consociational consensualism characteristic of Belgium. But if parliamentarism per se contributes little to the explanation of this variation, its interaction with national electoral laws contributes powerfully to it. Majoritarian behavior and the subsequent exacerbation of conflict are fostered by the combination of a parliamentary system with an electoral law that manufactures legislative majorities, enabling governing parties to neglect or ignore the legitimate concerns of their partisan rivals.

Spain provides a good case study of the consequences of electoral laws for elite behavior. Both the Second Republic and its present constitutional monarchy adopted a parliamentary system, but they had very different electoral laws. Under the Second Republic, the electoral law was intended to manufacture artificial parliamentary majorities and thereby facilitate the formation of governments with majority support in the Cortes. It permitted voters in each district to cast as many votes as constituted a "majority" of seats in that district. This gave parties or local coalitions receiving a plurality of popular votes between 75 percent and 80 percent of the seats in most districts. The second largest party or coalition received the remainder of the seats. Parties finishing third (or lower) were denied parliamentary representation regardless of how closely they had finished behind the two victorious parties.[34] One result was that governments enjoying substantial artificial majorities did not need the support of opposition parties to pass legislation. Moreover, by so distorting the parliamentary representation of each political group, it created the illusion within the Cortes of an overwhelming mandate for the policy proposals of the victorious coalition when, in fact, the governing parties may have received a bare plurality of the popular vote.[35] Thus the electoral law

34. In the Madrid municipal district, for example, there were seventeen seats, and each voter could cast thirteen votes. In the 1933 election, this meant that the Socialists, with 175,000 popular votes, won thirteen seats. The conservative coalition received 170,000 seats but was allocated only four seats, while the Left Republicans and Radicals, with 100,000 votes, received no parliamentary representation at all.

35. In the 1936 election, for example, the Popular Front coalition received only 47.2 percent of the popular vote but controlled 263 out of 474 seats in the Cortes.

encouraged majoritarian behavior by members of parliament in much the same way that more conventional single-member constituency systems do. One consequence was the adoption of a constitution in 1931 that contained language (especially explicit anticlerical provisions) unacceptable to important political and social groups. Accordingly, the very act of writing a democratic constitution generated a significant challenge to the legitimacy of the new regime and contributed decisively to its eventual collapse and the onset of civil war.[36]

The electoral law of the current constitutional monarchy provides a better fit between the distribution of votes and seats in the Congress of Deputies.[37] The two largest parties in each district continue to be somewhat overrepresented, but minority groups are no longer denied parliamentary representation. Moreover, in only two of Spain's five parliamentary elections has a single party received an absolute majority of seats. Thus the single-party minority governments of 1977–82 were dependent on the support of other parliamentary groups to enact legislation, making interparty negotiations and dialogue a necessary component of the legislative process. Most important, Adolfo Suárez's first Union of the Democratic Center government chose to adhere closely to consensual principles in the writing and enactment of a new democratic constitution. While this decision was motivated by a variety of factors,[38] it was facilitated by the absence of a parliamentary majority. As Suárez himself stated, "If I had an absolute majority in the parliament, I probably would not have succeeded in writing the constitution I wanted—a constitution regarded as valid by everybody. There was a dogmatic attempt inside my own party to impose . . . [a more partisan and one-sided constitution on Spanish society]."[39] Thus the electoral law and the resulting structure of the party system help explain why Spain's two parliamentary regimes presented elites with very different institutional incentives to engage in majoritarian or consensual behavior, which in turn affected the capacity of the two regimes to manage potentially divisive conflict.[40]

36. See Gunther and Blough, "Religious Conflict and Consensus in Spain."

37. See Richard Gunther, "Electoral Laws, Party Systems and Elites: The Case of Spain," *American Political Science Review*, vol. 83 (September 1989), pp. 835–58.

38. For a more complete discussion, see Gunther, Sani, and Shabad, *Spain After Franco*, especially chap. 4.

39. Interview with Richard Gunther, June 1983.

40. A more recent example of this phenomenon can be seen in the Basque country, where mass-level political violence has been widespread since before the death of Franco, and where the legitimacy of Spain's current regime has been challenged by several important

This longitudinal comparative study does not imply a mechanistic relationship between type of electoral system and style of elite behavior: elite fragmentation, institutional stagnation, governmental inefficiency, and ideological polarization can also result from the adoption of proportional electoral systems, as the widely cited cases of the Weimar Republic and the Fourth French Republic would indicate. Our point is that certain types of electoral systems may facilitate certain kinds of elite behavior, but whether elites actually behave in accord with the incentives implied by these institutional relationships is a function of a variety of other variables, most of which involve elite political culture, calculations, tactics, and ultimate objectives.[41] The regime failures of Weimar and the Fourth Republic were rooted as much in the determination of antisystem parties commanding significant parliamentary support to bring the regime down as in the multipartism and coalition governments typical of stable as well as unstable parliamentary democracies.[42]

6. *The choice of electoral rules can itself reflect elite culture and aspirations.* The crucial role that these factors play in mediating the relationship between the electoral law and effective conflict management is more subtly apparent in the different reaction of the governing classes in Belgium and Britain to the politicization of the social class cleavage in the last quarter of the nineteenth century. Both countries had, to that point, used single-member-district plurality electoral systems in their parliamentary elections, but Belgium switched to a proportional system at the turn of the century and Britain retained its original system.

Belgium became independent in 1830. After a short period of cooperation to stave off potential Dutch reconquest, its Catholic and Liberal (anticlerical) elites lapsed into a period of bitter, ideological conflict. "The extremes of opposition were not in electoral tactics but in attacks on the

---

parties. Following a schism within the Basque Nationalist party (PNV), a multiparty coalition government became necessary, given the existing electoral law. For a variety of reasons, the PNV chose to enter into a regional coalition government with the Spanish Socialist party—the party of government in Madrid. Almost immediately, the forced interdependency between the two parties led to a depolarization within the region, to more vigorous Basque government efforts to contain terrorism, and ultimately, in January 1990, to the PNV's formal acknowledgment (for the first time) of the legitimacy of the Spanish constitution. Under a majoritarian electoral system (in which this coalition would not have been necessary), this depolarization and increased legitimation of the regime might not have occurred.

41. See Gunther, "Electoral Laws, Party Systems and Elites."

42. See Giovanni Sartori, "European Political Parties: The Case of Polarized Pluralism," in Joseph LaPalombara and Myron Weiner, eds., *Political Parties and Political Development* (Princeton University Press, 1966), pp. 137–76.

intimate beliefs and social relationships of Liberals and Catholics."[43] The electoral growth in the 1890s of the reformist and anticlerical Socialists, largely at the expense of the Liberals, made the Catholic party fearful of the potentially destabilizing consequences of a government-opposition duel with the Socialists alone. It therefore introduced proportional representation in 1900 to preempt the polarization of political conflict along reinforcing class and religious lines. Britain, by contrast, had a well-developed tradition of moderate, relatively nonideological political conflict by the time the reformist Labour party emerged as an electoral force in the early 1900s. Political opposition was not feared for its disruptive consequences. Instead, there had existed since the late nineteenth century "a consensus, especially among political leaders, about the general nature of the rights, privileges and duties of the Opposition, which makes the propriety of opposition as integral a part of the constitutional structure of conventions and understandings as the authority of government."[44] The result was a confidence that working-class reformism could be accommodated within the existing institutional structure, just as other political divisions had been in Britain's relatively peaceful transition from a feudal aristocracy to a representative democracy. The reformist socialist threat, then, was similar in both countries, but entrenched elites perceived its larger consequences for the political system differently and acted accordingly.

One important factor explaining the contrasting patterns of elite behavior in Spain, Belgium, and Britain involves the basic values and perceptions of the relevant elites. Some of these are rooted in political culture: the difference, for example, between the cooptive paternalism of Britain's established elite in the late nineteenth and early twentieth centuries and the rancorous and polarizing rhetoric and behavior of party leaders in Spain's Second Republic can help to explain the different patterns of political stability in the two countries.[45] The values, calculations, and objectives of key individuals at critical junctures—rooted or not in the broader elite political culture—can also play an important role in regulating conflict, as has been demonstrated in the Spanish case.[46]

The cases of Belgium and Spain also reveal that the causal relationships

---

43. Lorwin, "Belgium: Religion, Class and Language in National Politics," p. 154.

44. Allen Potter, "Great Britain: Opposition with a Capital 'O'," in Dahl, ed., *Political Oppositions in Western Democracies*, p. 3.

45. Compare Beer, *British Politics in the Collectivist Age* (or *Modern British Politics*), passim., and Payne, *The Spanish Revolution*, pp. 90–92.

46. See Gunther, "Constitutional Change in Contemporary Spain"; and Gunther and Blough, "Religious Conflict and Consensus in Spain."

between political institutions and effective conflict management may be quite complex: elite concern over the consequences of a majoritarian electoral system in these highly divided societies culminated in the selection of institutional forms designed to mitigate conflict. Thus the electoral law functioned at one point as a dependent variable. But, once adopted, the electoral system returned to its more accustomed role as a causal variable (in our analysis) affecting the intensity of conflict in Belgium and Spain.

7. *Unitary political arrangements may encourage majoritarian political behavior, but federalism does not necessarily encourage consensual behavior.* As with the association between type of electoral system and style of elite behavior, there is a seductive plausibility in equating the territorial structure of government with such behavior styles. In the case of the United States, for example, the potential majoritarianism inherent in electing a president and the House of Representatives by a single-member-district plurality electoral system is moderated by the existence in the federal government of a powerful and prestigious Senate, where each state has two members regardless of population size. Each state also has its own popularly elected government with constitutionally protected powers, including, most important, the power to raise and spend taxes. A plausible case can also be made that unitarism contributed to the majoritarian conflict management style common to the United Kingdom, pre-1977 Spain, and pre-1970 Belgium. In the name of national unity, central governments in all three countries long ignored territorially defined demands for some degree of meaningful self-government, contributing to the emergence and rapid electoral growth of separatist ethnic nationalist parties.[47]

Care must be taken, however, not to overstate the determinacy of this relationship. The relationship is indeterminate because it is asymmetric. Federalism may not always be conducive to consensual elite behavior—witness the U.S. Civil War—but unitarism has historically been more commonly associated with majoritarian elite behavior. The basic reason for this difference lies in the origins of the two types of states. Federations are commonly a voluntary union of existing territorial units enjoying a degree of political autonomy, whereas unitary states— of which Britain and France are the archetypal examples—grew "slowly and over a long period of time from some nuclear, germinal or core-area" principally through the involuntary mechanisms of bribery, inter-

---

47. Anthony Mughan, "Modernization and Regional Relative Deprivation: Towards a Theory of Ethnic Conflict," in L. J. Sharpe, ed., *Decentralist Trends in Western Democracies* (London: Sage, 1979), pp. 279–312; and Shabad, "After Autonomy."

marriage, and military conquest.[48] This pattern of state building has led to a deep-rooted equation of national integration and unity with a centralized, unitary state structure. Thus, for example, the 1974–79 British Labour government's modest proposals to create popularly elected assemblies with very limited powers in Scotland and Wales were hotly condemned by opponents as the first step on the "slippery slope" to the break up of the United Kingdom.[49] Similarly, the leaders of Belgium's traditional parties initially responded to linguistic separatism by granting it no legitimacy and then, when it became clear that the conflict would not just "go away," by granting minimal concessions in an effort to defuse its popular appeal.[50]

8. *Federalism may exacerbate group conflict rather than moderate it and may increase majoritarian behavior at the regional level.* When subnational territorial boundaries and the distribution of competing groups largely coincide, there can be no guarantee that federalism will promote consensual elite behavior. There are several reasons why this is so.

First, causality can flow either way in the relationship between governmental structure and style of elite behavior. Territorial politics are usually seen as a threat to stability, since the issue arises most commonly when subnational divisions coincide with the reform aspirations of territorial groupings in unitary states. As with the Scottish and Welsh in the United Kingdom and Flemings and Walloons in Belgium, such groupings demand some redefinition of the territorial distribution of power to meet their aspirations for a greater degree of control over their own affairs. This redistribution may take the form of devolution, federalism, or even redefinition of the state. The important point is that federalism is seen as an answer to the problem, as a means of regulating territorially defined conflict that may threaten the integrity of the state.

48. N. J. G. Pounds and S. S. Ball, "Core-Areas and the Development of the European State Systems," *Annals of the Association of American Geographers*, vol. 54 (March 1964), p. 14.

49. Much of the strongest opposition to the proposals came from inside the Labour party itself. See, for example, the book by Scottish Labour M.P. Tam Dalyell, *Devolution: The End of Britain?* (London: Cape, 1977). The "unionist" Conservative party all but unanimously rejected the devolution proposals. For a general discussion, see Vernon Bogdanor, *Devolution* (Oxford: Oxford University Press, 1979).

50. See Anthony Mughan, "Accommodation or Defusion in the Management of Linguistic Conflict in Belgium?" *Political Studies*, vol. 31 (September 1983), pp. 434–51; and Mughan, "Belgium: All Periphery and No Centre?" That the linguistic parties were never accorded full legitimacy by Belgium's established party elites is also indicated by the former's limited representation in Belgian cabinets since the reform of the state was begun in 1970. See André-Paul Frognier, "The Mixed Nature of Belgian Cabinets Between Majority Rule and Consociationalism," *European Journal of Political Research*, vol. 16 (March 1988), pp. 207–28.

The decentralization of some degree of governmental power promises a happy compromise between the political status quo and regional secession. A case in point is regionalization in Belgium.

The less common side of this coin, however, is that federal arrangements can greatly facilitate the emergence and escalation of territorial conflict should the marriage, no matter how old, between the constituent units cease to prove convenient for one or more of them. In encouraging diversity, federalism tends to promote and ossify regionally distinctive cultural and political identities and traditions, as well as economic, social, and political concerns and priorities. Moreover, the distinctive traditions and preoccupations of a particular region do not always coincide with those of other regions in the federation or, indeed, of the federation itself. Under these circumstances, federal arrangements can facilitate the emergence and escalation of territorial conflict. The economic, cultural, and political distinctiveness of America's southern states, for example, made their unilateral declaration of secession that much easier to contemplate. Moreover, these same characteristics outlasted the Civil War and play a great part in explaining the federal government's inability to address for over a century the issue that has been the country's most consistent source of political instability in the twentieth century, racial discrimination.[51] Federalism, in short, may foster parochial loyalties and endow regional elites with a set of institutional resources they can mobilize to buttress their own power vis-à-vis the central government.[52] Territorial conflict under these circumstances becomes very difficult to manage since the measures acceptable to disaffected regional elites will probably be unacceptable to their counterparts in other regions of the country. For want of a shared will to maintain the federation, the ultimate manifestation of political instability, national disintegration, becomes a real possibility.

Another reason the decentralization of governmental power need not always lead to consensual elite behavior is that the structure of regional power and the uses to which it is put can themselves generate serious political conflict. Subnational governments can contribute to conflict

51. Key, *Southern Politics*, pp. 317–84.

52. This argument has been made of French-speaking Quebec in its efforts to free itself of its perceived domination by English-speaking Canada. See Richard Simeon, "Regionalism and Canadian Political Institutions," *Queen's Quarterly*, vol. 82 (Winter 1975), pp. 499–511; and Donald V. Smiley, "Territorialism and Canadian Political Institutions," *Canadian Public Policy*, vol. 3 (Autumn 1977), pp. 449–57. Both argue that one important consequence of federalism is to put in place incentives that encourage regional politicians and bureaucrats to seek to strengthen the regional government at the expense of the central government. Under normal political circumstances, such competition should promote consensual behavior, but when regional elites seriously question the continuing worth of the federation, the likelihood of its disintegration is enhanced.

management by equitably dispensing goods and services within a given territory, as well as through their interaction with the central government. They can thus help to deepen popular commitment to the larger regime by being responsive and accountable and affording citizens more opportunities for political participation. But conversely, they can use their political autonomy to discriminate against minority groups, thereby exacerbating intergroup conflict at both the national and subnational level of government.

This situation occurs most commonly when a region's population is divided along ethnic lines. A group that may or may not be a minority of a country's total population is dominant within a particular region and uses its institutional position within a federal system to discriminate systematically against other groups in that region. The well-documented, institutionalized discrimination against blacks in America's southern states immediately springs to mind here, although this is not the only example. The British grant of a measure of self-government to Northern Ireland after its creation in 1920 went hand in hand with an abandonment of responsibility for overseeing the actions of the built-in Protestant majority even after the Protestant Unionist party had removed the provisions for proportional representation built into the 1920 settlement. The single-member-district plurality electoral system was then supplemented by gerrymandering to institutionalize majoritarian behavior on the part of the Protestant elite, and the Catholic minority was effectively deprived of political influence and subjected to systematic discrimination over the course of almost fifty years. Similar behavior can be seen in Spain: the recent decentralization of the state may have more or less satisfactorily met the demands of Basque and Catalán nationalists (thereby playing a crucial role in the consolidation of the constitutional monarchy), but it does not necessarily preclude majoritarian behavior on the part of the regional governments vis-à-vis minority linguistic groups falling in their own jurisdictions.[53]

Thus, as with electoral laws, federalism's effect on the style of elite behavior is neither simple nor direct. Much depends on the manner in which subnational governments are structured and on the ultimate political objectives of governing regional elites. If decisionmaking is retained primarily at the center and regional elites are guaranteed influence there through, for example, overlapping membership in regional and central governments or through an institution like the U.S. Senate, federalism requires and probably fosters accommodative behavior on the part of

53. Goldie Shabad and Richard Gunther, "Language, Nationalism and Political Conflict in Spain," *Comparative Politics*, vol. 14 (July 1982), pp. 443–77.

elites. If, by contrast, regional elites choose to use their political power to engage in systematic discriminatory behavior that is not condoned or practiced at the national level, there is likely to be a failure of conflict management in the form of either polarization between national and regional governments or undemocratic repression of conflict within the region in question.

Conclusion

We conclude that political institutions do affect a democratic regime's prospects for successful conflict management, primarily by providing incentives for elites to engage in either majoritarian or consensual behavior. However, this statement is subject to two caveats. First, the prospects for democratic stability are greater in societies not deeply divided by social cleavages, regardless of the dominant pattern of behavior among political elites. Polities with shallow or few divisions may be able to sustain majoritarian, winner-take-all behavior without experiencing significant political instability. Conversely, in deeply divided societies rigorous adherence to consensual, accommodative behavior may be required to maintain stability. Second, a regime's stability is more at risk during its crucial formative period than after its consolidation. During a regime transition, for example, accommodative patterns of elite interaction are likely to be necessary if newly emerging political institutions are to be accepted as legitimate.[54] After a regime has been consolidated, however, elite and mass acceptance of its legitimacy may make room for majoritarian practices. Thus both societal and temporal contexts help to determine the political consequences of the patterns of elite interaction.

Our second conclusion is that the effects of political institutions on democratic stability cannot be adequately understood in terms of a simple presidential-parliamentary dichotomy. Questions involving the capacity of governments to regulate conflict are inherently complex and multivariate. The extent to which the separation of powers affects a regime's capacity to manage conflict depends greatly upon the manner in which presidential or parliamentary institutions interact with a variety of other key institutions in the political system, especially electoral laws and the territorial division of governmental authority. Other things being equal (and, as we have argued, they usually are not), centralized systems are more conducive to majoritarianism than federal systems; majoritarian electoral systems often "manufacture" artificial majorities that enable

54. See John Higley and Richard Gunther, eds., *Elites and Democratic Consolidation in Latin America and Southern Europe* (Cambridge University Press, 1991).

single-party governments to ignore the opposition; and party-government parliamentary systems seemingly lack the incentive for consensualism inherent in separation-of-powers systems.

But this argument is still not entirely adequate, since elite behavior is more than a response to institutional incentive structures alone. It is also influenced by a wide variety of programmatic, symbolic, and personal objectives, as well as by norms of behavior rooted in a particular political culture or set of historical memories. Thus the calculations that guide elite behavior may be at odds with the incentive structures inherent in the institutional framework of a particular regime.

A clear example of institutional indeterminacy is Britain, which possesses all three of the political institutions normally conducive to majoritarian behavior: parliamentarism, a majoritarian electoral system, and a highly centralized state. This incentive structure is consistent with the polarization of British politics resulting from the sometimes rancorous majoritarianism of the Thatcher governments, but it leaves unexplained the "collectivist consensus" that characterized British politics in the 1950s and 1960s. These institutional relationships *made possible* majoritarian forms of behavior, and yet in modern times only Margaret Thatcher took advantage of that possibility. During the 1950s and 1960s a broad consensus among leaders of the two dominant parties ("Butskellism") reduced the number of divisive partisan issues. Thus a complete explanation of conflict management in Britain would have to examine the historical, cultural, or personal origins of this elite convergence.

Majoritarian behavior by the Thatcher governments also underscores the importance of the caveats set forth above. We pointed out that success or failure in conflict management is very much a function of the initial depth of cleavages dividing a society. With the exception of Northern Ireland, British society is devoid of the same kinds of deep and potentially explosive divisions present in Belgium and Spain. Thus Britain can tolerate the polarizing consequences of majoritarianism better than those other countries. Consistent with this line of argument, in the one region of the United Kingdom where religious and class cleavages are deep and mutually reinforcing—Northern Ireland—political conflict has been extraordinarily violent. Our second caveat pertained to the age of a regime or stage of development of a political system. Britain is almost unique in that its parliamentary institutions were consolidated three centuries ago—well in advance even of the extension of the suffrage to the overwhelming majority of its citizens.[55] Given the legitimacy of these insti-

---

55. See Michael G. Burton and John Higley, "Elite Settlements," *American Sociological Review*, vol. 52 (June 1987), pp. 295–307.

tutions and the restraining influence of a common set of behavioral norms inculcated into British elites over centuries, Britain has been able to tolerate majoritarianism to a much greater extent than could a new and unconsolidated democracy.

Finally, it should be pointed out that institutional incentives can effectively influence behavior of elites only if they are playing the same game according to the same set of rules. No constitutional formula, regardless of how decentralized the governmental system it establishes, will placate regional elites doggedly committed to separatism. Spain's grant of a considerable degree of self-government to the country's regions, for example, may have met the demands of most regional nationalists, but it did not satisfy those Basques committed to outright independence. The Basque antisystem party, Herri Batasuna, fields candidates for national elections, but its elected deputies' refusal before 1990 to take their seats in the Cortes indicated their implacable hostility to the regime. Their desire to secede and create an independent state far outweighed the participatory incentives offered by the new Spanish democracy.[56] Whether one looks at nationalist elites in Belgium and Spain or Catholic terrorists and Protestant Unionists in Northern Ireland, the simple point is that where politically significant elites are not committed to reconciling their differences for the sake of regime viability, institutional tinkering will most likely fail to stave off profound instability.

The analysis overall, then, points to the primacy of political elites in the management of conflict in democratic systems. The necessary, but not sufficient, condition of democratic stability is that competing elites must want to make prevailing political arrangements work. This is not to claim that they are free agents, able to act as they see fit. Their actions are clearly constrained by the cultural and institutional framework in which they operate; they ignore this framework at their own risk. Elites may, and do, try to shape this institutional framework to their own advantage over the long term. In the short term, however, it exerts a systematic but not deterministic influence on their behavior and their prospects for success in managing conflict.

56. See more generally Sartori, "European Political Parties," passim.

Arend Lijphart, Ronald Rogowski, and
R. Kent Weaver

Separation of Powers and Cleavage Management

*M*anagement of political cleavages is one of the most important, and potentially most difficult, challenges for any government. The term *cleavages* denotes not merely political and social differences and diversity, but divisions that are deep and lasting, usually between clearly defined ethnic, racial, or religious groups in a society. In the United States, for example, a racial cleavage between blacks and whites has long been an important political divide. Regional cleavages between North and South and, at the local level, less profound ethnic cleavages (for example, between Irish-Americans and Protestants or between citizens of Italian and of East European origins) have also been politically significant.[1]

This chapter, like the one that precedes it, examines how differing institutional arrangements affect governments' ability to manage cleavages peacefully. We give particular attention to how well democracies with separation-of-powers systems, and the U.S. separation-of-powers system in particular, handle the problem of deep political cleavages compared with democracies characterized by nonseparation or "fusion" of powers. While the Gunther-Mughan chapter uses a comparative case study approach of four countries, our investigation relies upon a com-

We gratefully acknowledge the many helpful comments of the other participants in this project and of John M. Carey, Thomas E. Cavanaugh, Philip Klinkner, Mathew D. McCubbins, Matthew S. Shugart, and Thomas Sugrue.

1. On cleavage structures in the United States, see, for example, Richard Franklin Bensel, *Sectionalism and American Political Development, 1880–1980* (University of Wisconsin Press, 1984); Edward G. Carmines and James A. Stimson, *Issue Evolution: Race and the Transformation of American Politics* (Princeton University Press, 1989); and Robert Huckfeldt and Carol Weitzel Kohfeld, *Race and the Decline of Class in American Politics* (University of Illinois Press, 1989).

bination of macroquantitative methods and a more intensive discussion of one case, the United States.

Political Institutions and Cleavage Management

In examining the record of political institutions in managing cleavages, we begin with Lijphart's proposition that nonmajoritarian decisionmaking mechanisms that restrain majority rule by sharing, dispersing, delegating, and limiting power are more suitable for plural societies than are mechanisms that concentrate power in the hands of the political majority.[2] Lijphart defines plural societies as "societies that are sharply divided along religious, ideological, linguistic, cultural, ethnic, or racial lines into virtually separate subsocieties with their own political parties, interest groups, and media of communication."[3] The historical and time series evidence concerning the relationship between the needs of these societies and nonmajoritarian mechanisms is quite strong. Many countries with sharp cleavages and increasing conflict have turned to nonmajoritarian mechanisms—especially power-sharing executives, minority autonomy, and proportional representation—in order to manage these cleavages. In addition to the cases discussed in Gunther and Mughan's chapter, striking examples include cultural autonomy and power sharing in Canada during the period of the United Province from 1840 to 1867; the 1917 Dutch "peaceful settlement" based on religious autonomy and proportionality; the Lebanese "National Pact" of 1943, which provided for power sharing, religious-cultural autonomy, and proportionality; the establishment of a fully power-sharing, four-party executive in Switzerland in 1943; the formation of the *Grosse Koalition* in Austria in 1945; the establishment of the interethnic Alliance government in Malaysia in 1955; and the institution of Liberal-Conservative *alternación* in the presidency in Colombia in 1958.

Among parliamentary systems, there is a strong cross-national and historical linkage between systems with deep cleavages and proportional representation electoral rules.[4] One of the main reasons for the intro-

2. Arend Lijphart, *Democracy in Plural Societies: A Comparative Exploration* (Yale University Press, 1977).

3. Arend Lijphart, *Democracies: Patterns of Majoritarian and Consensus Government in Twenty-One Countries* (Yale University Press, 1984), p. 22.

4. The cross-national relationship would be considerably stronger if it were not for the strong influence of the Westminster model of democracy on countries with a British political heritage. For instance, Canada is pulled in the direction of nonmajoritarian institutions by its linguistic pluralism but, through its British-inspired single-member-district electoral

duction of proportional representation from the end of the nineteenth century on was to cope with the problem of deep cleavages. Stein Rokkan writes:

> It was no accident that the earliest moves toward proportional representation (PR) came in the ethnically most heterogeneous European countries. . . . In linguistically and religiously divided societies majority elections could clearly threaten the continued existence of the political system. The introduction of some element of minority representation came to be seen as an essential step in a strategy of territorial consolidation.[5]

The same reasoning can be found near the end of the twentieth century in the recent report of the Royal Commission on the Electoral System in New Zealand. The commission was deeply concerned about the problem of ethnic diversity, especially the need for the Maori minority to be "fairly and effectively represented in Parliament"; more generally, the commission argued that "New Zealand society is steadily developing in a more diverse way and is no longer as homogeneous as it once was." On the basis of these considerations, the commission recommended the replacement of New Zealand's plurality electoral system by a system of proportional representation.[6] In a 1992 referendum New Zealand voters

---

system, is pulled even more strongly in the majoritarian direction. Without the interference of these traditions, Canada's institutional arrangements would probably have been much more nonmajoritarian. Of course, Canada's formal majoritarianism is mitigated by several informal mechanisms, such as the tradition of alternating between anglophones and francophones in the leadership of the Liberal party and hence in the prime ministership in Liberal cabinets, in the office of governor general, in the speakership of the House of Commons, and in the position of chief justice of the Supreme Court. See Kenneth D. McRae, "Consociationalism and the Canadian Political System," in Kenneth D. McRae, ed., *Consociational Democracy: Political Accommodation in Segmented Societies* (Toronto: McClelland and Stewart, 1974), pp. 238–61.

5. Stein Rokkan, *Citizens, Elections, Parties: Approaches to the Comparative Study of the Processes of Development* (Oslo: Universitetsforlaget, 1970), p. 157.

6. Moreover, the commission's hope was that proportional elections would make New Zealand politics less majoritarian in other respects, by encouraging the development of a multiparty system, ethnic minority parties, and coalition cabinets, as well as a more balanced executive-legislative relationship. Royal Commission on the Electoral System, *Report of the Royal Commission on the Electoral System: Towards a Better Democracy* (Wellington, N.Z.: V. R. Ward, Government Printer, 1986), pp. 11, 19. See also Arend Lijphart, "The Demise of the Last Westminster System? Comments on the Report of New Zealand's Royal Commission on the Electoral System," *Electoral Studies*, vol. 6 (August 1987), pp. 97–103.

supported a move to a two-ballot system, similar to Germany's, to increase proportionality in their electoral system.

Efforts to manage political cleavages through institutional reform do not necessarily succeed; for instance, the British government's attempt to solve the Northern Ireland problem in 1973 by introducing proportional representation and a power-sharing executive was brought down by the inflexible and uncompromising Protestant majority after only a few months. It is significant, however, that the British government—in spite of its strong promajoritarian bias—decided that these nonmajoritarian mechanisms were necessary in order to deal with the deep divisions in Northern Ireland.[7]

Not all arrangements to limit majority rule work in the same way, however, and specific institutional arrangements have distinctive implications for how groups are represented and the types of policies that are likely to be produced to respond to the grievances of various cleavage segments. Moreover, specific mechanisms operate best under differing social conditions. Thus individual mechanisms may offer what Weaver and Rockman term distinctive opportunities and risks for dealing with some kinds of cleavage patterns. Cleavage management strategies for limiting majority rule can be categorized into four types, and specific institutional mechanisms are usually associated with each strategy.[8] However, the lines between these strategies are not always clear in practice, and specific institutional mechanisms may fit in several categories.

Consociational strategies attempt to encourage bargaining among elites of relatively well organized cleavage segments. Proportional representation electoral systems, norms or rules requiring representation of all major cleavage segments in the cabinet, and oversized coalitions are among the specific institutional mechanisms used to facilitate this bargaining. Consociationalism is less likely to work well where cleavage lines are more fluid, there are rivalries among leaders of individual cleavage segments, and masses in each cleavage segment are unwilling to give their elite leaders substantial leeway to bargain in their interests or are unwilling to accept bargains once they are made. A major risk of a consociational strategy is that it will produce a stalemate if leaders are unable to agree or unable to implement their agreement.

Delegatory strategies, on the other hand, attempt to allow each cleavage segment to govern its own affairs with limited interference from gov-

7. Lijphart, *Democracy in Plural Societies,* esp. pp. 25–52, 119–29, 134–41, 147–53.

8. For a more extensive development of this framework and an application to the case of Canada, see R. Kent Weaver, "Political Institutions and Canada's Constitutional Crisis," in Weaver, ed., *The Collapse of Canada?* (Brookings, 1992), pp. 7–75.

ernments or other groups. Federalism is the foremost institutional mechanism used in this strategy, but group autonomy can also be increased within a particular area on a nongeographic basis.[9] Federalism also shows the limitations of a delegatory strategy: if cleavage segments are interspersed and interdependent, it will be difficult to give them autonomy over their own affairs without creating aggrieved minorities at the regional level. Moreover, federalism carries with it certain risks: if regional autonomy is quite high and unchecked by the national government, regional majorities (which may or may not be national majorities) may use that autonomy to oppress regional minorities.

Arbitral strategies attempt to restrain majority rule by placing political authority in the hands of officials who have limited (or no) direct accountability to either political majorities or minorities. Examples include judicial review by an autonomous judiciary or executive officials with life or extended tenure. Such strategies also have limits and risks, however. Citizens are unlikely to entrust too many policy decisions to officials who need not be responsive, and arbitral institutions that take firm sides on divisive issues may lose popular legitimacy. Moreover, authority that is not held accountable may become tyrannical.

Finally, *limited-government* strategies attempt to limit majority rule not by encouraging broad inclusion of interests, but by making some or all government decisions difficult—by forbidding them outright (such as constitutional prohibitions against entrenchment of a specific church), by requiring supermajorities, or by putting in place multiple veto points (such as bicameralism and independent executives with veto authority).[10] Since minority veto powers and supermajority rules require broad coalitions for decisions to be made, they may serve as potent incentives for consensual decisionmaking when governmental inaction is widely regarded as undesirable. But a limited-government strategy also has important limitations and risks. Institutional mechanisms that limit government are unlikely to be effective in resolving disputes where one group has a heavy stake in the status quo—especially if that group is the majority—because that group is unlikely to agree to changes and is likely to be able to block them. The associated risk, of course, is that societies may be stalemated and may thus fail to respond to such policy challenges, increasing the level of societal conflict.

9. In the Canadian provinces of Quebec and Ontario, for example, there are separate publicly financed Catholic and Protestant (in practice, secular) school boards operating in the same localities.

10. The French Third and Fourth Republics paralleled the United States in use of the limited-government strategy. David R. Mayhew, *Congress: The Electoral Connection* (Yale University Press, 1974), pp. 160–64.

Cleavage Management: A Macroquantitative Evaluation

Our basic approach in this section will be to compare the cleavage management performance of the American system with that of the other twenty long-term and stable systems that have been democratic without interruption since approximately the end of World War II.[11] Most of these other democracies are West European countries: Austria, Belgium, Denmark, the Federal Republic of Germany, Finland, France, Iceland, Ireland, Italy, Luxembourg, the Netherlands, Norway, Sweden, Switzerland, and the United Kingdom. In addition, six non-European countries are part of the universe of long-term democracies: Japan, Israel, Australia, New Zealand, Canada, and the United States itself. Because the French system of government changed fundamentally in 1958, we treat the Fourth and Fifth Republics as two separate cases of democracy. At least initially—we discuss some exclusions in an appendix to this chapter—this gives us twenty-two cases for our comparative analysis.

These democracies are similar in several important respects: in addition to having long records of democratic rule, they are all highly industrialized and prosperous; and, with one exception (Japan), they are part of the Western Judeo-Christian cultural world. These are the constants for the purpose of this chapter's analysis. Their differences—independent variables—are the depth and intensity of their political cleavages and their particular forms of democratic government.

As a first step, we explore the relationship between presidential or parliamentary government and the management of cleavages. The independent variable is separation of powers or presidential government— terms that we shall use interchangeably. In the set of twenty-two long-term democracies, parliamentary forms of government predominate, and there is only one unambiguous case of presidentialism: the United States. However, three political systems may be classified as exhibiting semi-separation of powers: the French Fifth Republic, Finland, and Switzerland. They are presidential in some respects and parliamentary in others. In France and Finland, a popularly elected president coexists with a prime minister who is subject to parliamentary confidence.[12] The Swiss federal

11. We shall use the data on these countries for the period from about 1945 to 1980 reported in Lijphart, *Democracies*.

12. In the Fifth Republic, the key question is: who is the real head of government, the president or the prime minister? Most of the time since 1958 the president has clearly been the chief executive. Only during the two years of "cohabitation" from 1986 to 1988, when the president lost his majority in the National Assembly, did the prime minister become the true head of government. When the president is the head of government, the system is mainly presidential, but when the prime minister assumes this role, the system shifts to

executive is partly parliamentary (it is a collegial body, elected by the legislature) and partly presidential (it is elected for a fixed term and not subject to parliamentary confidence).[13] Common to all three systems is an important convention that places the presidency in some sense "above politics." The president (or, in Switzerland, the plural executive) avoids identification with any particular political tendency and seeks to embody the elusive "national interest."[14] That role, well played, permits the presidential authority to serve as trusted arbiter among contending social groups. The remaining eighteen democracies are unambiguously parliamentary systems.[15]

Explaining Failures in Cleavage Management

The most promising way to define and operationalize our dependent variable, the management of deep political cleavages, is to focus on the failures; these are more visible and measurable than the successes. Gunther

---

parliamentarism. We are inclined to classify the Fifth Republic as mainly, albeit not fully, presidential. We defer, however, to the prevalent view that it should be labeled a semi-presidential regime. In Finland, power is shared, rather than alternated, between the president (elected by an electoral college roughly comparable to that of the United States) and the prime minister. G. Bingham Powell, Jr., argues that "the Finnish system is very much like the standard parliamentary system in domestic affairs, but the directly elected president has special authority in foreign policy." Powell, *Contemporary Democracies: Participation, Stability, and Violence* (Harvard University Press, 1982), p. 56. Especially under President Urho Kekkonen (1956–82) the president's powers also extended to domestic politics; but we agree that Finland is less presidential than France. The best solution is to call both systems semipresidential.

13. Members of the Swiss plural executive—the Federal Council—are elected for four-year terms of office and cannot be removed by parliament. In fact, by long custom federal councillors are reelected so long as they wish to serve. See George Arthur Codding, *The Federal Government of Switzerland* (Houghton Mifflin, 1961), pp. 89–90.

14. The early Mitterrand presidency is the exception that proves the rule. After emerging as too combative a politician, Mitterrand lost parliamentary elections and endured the years of "cohabitation." Having learned to play more convincingly the role of apolitical statesman, he was triumphantly returned to the Elysée.

15. Three other democracies in our set—Austria, Ireland, and Iceland—have popularly elected presidents and, on the basis of this characteristic, they are sometimes called semi-presidential (for instance, by Duverger). But Duverger also correctly points out that, in spite of the popular election of the president and (in the Icelandic case) strong presidential powers specified in the constitution, the president in these three countries is in practice a figurehead. Maurice Duverger, "Which Is the Best Electoral System?" in Arend Lijphart and Bernard Grofman, eds., *Choosing an Electoral System* (Praeger, 1984), pp. 31–40. The real head of the government is the prime minister, and according to all three of the basic criteria these three countries qualify as parliamentary.

and Mughan suggest several indicators. We focus here on two of these indicators of the failure to maintain political order: riots and deaths from political violence.[16] These indicators are not ideal. Deaths from political violence may reflect the efficiency (or ruthlessness) of the police as much as the level of discontent. Efforts to ameliorate cleavages may in fact stimulate violence in the short run as consciousness of "relative deprivation" and frustration over the pace of change grow among a group that has been discriminated against.[17] Moreover, violent acts may be caused by factors other than the deep, lasting, and group-based divisions that are the subject of this chapter. They may be prompted, for instance, by economic shortages or by opposition to the government's foreign policy. On the other hand, when a democratic society with deep ethnic or other cleavages experiences severe tensions, these are highly likely to be related to the societal cleavages. Since no better indicators are available, we are inclined to use them, albeit with caution—and not to expect extremely high correlations with our explanatory variables.[18]

In an appendix to this chapter, we present the numbers of riots and deaths from political violence in the twenty-two democracies (table A-1) and the averages for these countries, adjusted for population size, by their type of government (table A-2). In this first look at the relationship between our principal independent and dependent variables, the evidence is rather ambivalent and contradictory. The fifteen parliamentary systems have, on average, fewer riots, but the United States has fewer deaths from political violence. For both these indicators of dysfunction, the intermediate semi-separation-of-powers systems show the best performance. These results must still be regarded as tentative, however, since there are other obvious explanations for the failure of cleavage management that should be controlled for.

16. On the use of violence as an indicator of failure in a democracy, see Powell, *Contemporary Democracies,* p. 20.

17. This point was perhaps first made by Tocqueville: "It is not always when things are going from bad to worse that revolutions break out. On the contrary, it oftener happens that when a people which has put up with an oppressive rule over a long period without protest suddenly finds the government relaxing its pressure, it takes up arms against it. . . . Experience teaches us that, generally speaking, the most perilous moment for a bad government is when it seeks to mend its ways." Alexis de Tocqueville, *The Old Regime and the French Revolution,* trans. Stuart Gilbert (Doubleday Anchor Books, 1955), pp. 176–77.

18. Powell also uses a third indicator: the suspension or replacement of democracy at the national level. This measure does not work well for our set of twenty-two democracies since these are defined as long-term, stable democratic regimes; hence there is no variation with regard to the interruption of democracy.

Controls: Degrees of Pluralism and Majoritarian Democracy

The first control that must be instituted is the degree of social pluralism, that is, the degree to which the countries have cleavages to manage. It is obviously more difficult to contain political cleavages when
these are salient and intense than when they are relatively mild; in other
words, one should expect the indicators of failure of cleavage management to be correlated with the degree of pluralism. We distinguish here
among plural, semiplural, and nonplural societies. Nonplural societies
are not necessarily "homogeneous" societies: they may be quite diverse,
but they do not have sharply defined separate groups with their own
separate organizations.

A second possible control is the electoral system: is it characterized
by relatively "pure" proportional representation, by a plurality or majority system of the Anglo-American type, or by some hybrid of these
two systems? In our set of countries, Australia, Canada, France V (for
the most part), New Zealand, the United Kingdom, and the United
States are classified as plurality or majority; Ireland and Japan are hy-
brids;[19] all others employ proportional representation. As noted above,
proportional representation provides significant opportunities for ameliorating the conflicts of plural and semiplural societies by providing
fuller representation.

The third control involves a broader set of institutional mechanisms
that may influence cleavage management capabilities. We employ Lijphart's distinction between majoritarian mechanisms, which concentrate
political power in the hands of the majority, and consensual mechanisms,
which try to share, disperse, and limit power in a variety of ways. Lijphart
further categorizes majoritarian and consensual institutions along two
separate and unrelated dimensions, which are conceptually independent
of separation of powers: (1) majoritarian characteristics of parties and
executives and (2) unitary—as opposed to federal—rule. Since Lijphart
argues that consensus and federal mechanisms are better suited to plural
societies than their opposites, we expect that majoritarianism and unitary
government will be positively related to the indicators of the failure of
cleavage management.

The results of our regression analysis are shown in appendix tables
A-3 and A-4. As one would expect, plural societies experienced significantly higher rates of political deaths and riots; and, controlling for the

19. Ireland uses the single transferable vote, Japan the single nontransferable vote. In
both countries, districts elect too few members to afford much proportionality.

presence of such cleavages, unitary mechanisms seem to weaken societies' abilities to avoid violence. More surprisingly, neither majoritarianism nor presidential government appears to have any effect on either measure of political violence. It seems, however, that proportional representation may significantly reduce political deaths, even after one controls for the degree of pluralism, and that semipresidential rule as practiced in Finland, post-1958 France, and Switzerland may work to reduce the number of political riots.

To see more clearly the possible connection between riots and semi-separation-of-powers regimes in plural societies, we display our full set of data as a cross-tabulation in figure 1. Among the semiplural societies, there is little difference in the average (population-adjusted) number of riots between the lone separation-of-powers system (the United States) and the four parliamentary ones, but there is quite a large difference between either of those and the two semi-separation-of-powers, semi-plural systems (Finland and the French Fifth Republic). Similarly, among the five plural societies, semi-separation-of-powers Switzerland has a markedly lower level of riots than all but one of the parliamentary regimes.

The point becomes even clearer if—as seems proper in light of their similarities of means and effects—we merge the plural and the semiplural categories. The parliamentary regimes then exhibit a population-adjusted average of 919 riots; the United States, as the only separation-of-powers regime, 861; and the three semi-separation-of-powers regimes, 421. It is perhaps equally remarkable that all of the nonplural societies have parliamentary regimes and all of the separation-of-powers and semi-separation-of-powers regimes are in plural or semiplural societies. Separation of powers and semi-separation of powers appear to be options to which only plural and semiplural societies are drawn.

The "semipresidential" forms of Finland, France, and Switzerland are associated with significantly lower levels of intercommunal conflict even when the effects of pluralism and unitary government are controlled for. Why should the semi-separation of powers play so important a role? To put the matter more sharply, why should the Finnish, French, and Swiss forms of rule significantly suppress intercommunal violence, while the pure American form of separation of powers does not?

One possibility—and it is little more than that—is that these are all successful arbitral regimes: the president (or, in the Swiss case, the collective Federal Council) manages to stand above politics and to serve in significant measure as the trusted neutral referee of intercommunal competition. In the Finnish and French cases, the arbiter is assisted in his role

Figure 1. *Riots in Nineteen Democracies, by Type of Regime and Type of Society*[a]

Type of society	Separation of powers	Semi-separation of powers	Parliamentary
Plural (average 765)		Switzerland 265	UK 1,294 Belgium 1,199 Austria 926 Netherlands 140
		(average 265)	(average 890)
Semiplural (average 808)	USA 861	France V 540 Finland 459	Italy 1,615 France IV 1,367 Germany 474 Canada 340
	(average 861)	(average 500)	(average 949)
Nonplural (average 339)			Ireland 1,132 Japan 374 Sweden 292 Denmark 277 Australia 170 New Zealand 74 Norway 52
			(average 339)
	(average 861)	(average 421)	(average 648)
(Average, plural and semiplural)	861	421	919

a. Numbers adjusted for population size as in table A-1.

by the presence of a political prime minister who is free to play a more partisan role.[20] In Switzerland, the Federal Council dispenses with such assistance but enjoys an independence and prestige—and a term of office—that resemble those of the U.S. Supreme Court. In their arbitral aspect if in no other, these semipresidential regimes may be compared to the system that prevailed so durably in Yugoslavia so long as Marshall Tito remained alive and played the role of referee among that country's many nationalities.

The U.S. separation-of-powers system is obviously different. Despite the system's many nonmajoritarian features and multiple veto points, the powerful U.S. president is emphatically a combative politician and, often enough, one who stands distinctly on one side of a major ethnic, regional, or religious cleavage.[21]

Although it is not evident that institutional features account for the markedly lower number of riots in the semipresidential systems, it should be pointed out that Switzerland, France, and Finland have not been blessed with less social conflict than the United States. Switzerland, like the United States, fought a civil war (in which the Protestant cantons quickly defeated the Catholic ones) in the nineteenth century; and religious conflict long remained bitter.[22] From the revolution of 1789 to today, the religious cleavage in France between Catholic and secular

20. To be sure, the Fifth Republican presidency rapidly evolved into a stronger policymaking institution than de Gaulle had originally foreseen; yet both the general and his successors have taken great care to portray themselves as "above parties." Philip M. Williams and Martin Harrison, *Politics and Society in de Gaulle's Republic* (Doubleday, 1972), chap. 10. As Giscard d'Estaing put it in a representative utterance before the European elections of 1979: "[The president's] role is to remind people what, in these circumstances, is the position of France . . . but not to indicate a choice or a preference between lists of candidates." J. R. Frears, *France in the Giscard Presidency* (London: George Allen and Unwin, 1981), pp. 37–43, quotation at p. 41.

21. Nie, Verba, and Petrocik have traced the path by which most African-Americans, beginning during the New Deal, came to support Democratic presidential candidates. Ronald Reagan, as surveys consistently revealed, was widely perceived among this group as actively antiblack. Between the Civil War and the New Deal, of course, Democratic contenders were widely seen (in an infamous but telling slur) as representatives of "rum, Romanism, and rebellion," that is, of urban immigrants and the defeated South. Republican presidents symbolized WASP (and, especially after 1896, industrial) hegemony. Norman H. Nie, Sidney Verba, and John R. Petrocik, *The Changing American Voter* (Harvard University Press, 1976), pp. 226–29. See also Gerald D. Jaynes and Robin M. Williams, Jr., eds., *A Common Destiny: Blacks and American Society* (Washington: National Academy Press, 1989); and Patricia Gurin, Shirley Hatchett, and James S. Jackson, *Hope and Independence: Blacks' Response to Electoral and Party Politics* (New York: Russell Sage Foundation, 1989).

22. See, for example, Codding, *Federal Government of Switzerland,* pp. 30–31, 115, 120.

forces has overshadowed all other influences on political loyalties.[23] And the bitter and bloody Finnish civil war of 1919–20 left class tensions that Americans can hardly imagine.[24]

Institutions and Cleavage Management in the United States

We find, in short, that the U.S. form of separation of powers has no advantages in the management of profound social cleavages; and, compared with semi-separation of powers, it may have disadvantages. Why this should be so is not obvious, given that the U.S. system, in consonance with its Madisonian origins, embodies not only the separation of executive and legislative powers but a number of other nonmajoritarian mechanisms that should safeguard minorities.

There are at least two possible explanations for this finding, and the evidence provides some support for both of them. The first is that, viewed in comparative perspective, U.S. institutions are in fact more majoritarian than they seem on the surface. Majoritarian institutional arrangements that bear no necessary connection to the separation of powers are more important for effective cleavage management than is the executive-legislative relationship. Many of these institutional arrangements have tended to concentrate power in the hands of the majority rather than encourage cooperation and consensus across cleavage lines.

A second reason is suggested by our argument at the beginning of this chapter: that nonmajoritarian arrangements have risks as well as opportunities for effective cleavage management and can promote stalemate and continued majority oppression as well as consensus. Limited-government mechanisms, for example, are most likely to be effective at

23. As late as the presidential elections of 1988, only 18 percent of regularly practicing Catholics pronounced themselves ready to vote for either the Socialist or Communist candidate; among those who professed no religion, 60 percent intended to vote Socialist or Communist. Reported in William Safran, *The French Polity,* 3d ed. (New York: Longman, 1991), p. 92. Social class has always mattered far less. See Alain Lancelot, "Opinion Polls and the Presidential Election, May 1974," in Howard R. Penniman, ed., *France at the Polls: The Presidential Election of 1974* (Washington: American Enterprise Institute for Public Policy Research, 1975), pp. 192–93. For a thorough and convincing analysis of the relative weights of religion and class in French voting, see Guy Michelat and Michel Simon, "Religion, Class, and Politics," *Comparative Politics,* vol. 10 (October 1977), pp. 159–86.

24. "The civil war was over after only a few months, but it was marked by terrible cruelty on both sides and it left lasting scars." Thousands were killed in battle, 125 of the defeated Reds were executed, and "many more were sentenced to varying terms of imprisonment." F. L. Carsten, *The Rise of Fascism* (University of California Press, 1967), pp. 161–69; quotations at p. 163.

mitigating conflicts where minorities find the status quo acceptable. Where redress of minority grievances is required to promote social peace, mechanisms that require consensus or near-consensus may actually inhibit effective cleavage management by allowing "minorities of the majority" to block such redress. Delegatory strategies—notably federalism—may allow regional majorities to take especially oppressive steps against regional minorities.

American institutions are a complex mixture of majoritarian and non-majoritarian arrangements, as the scores of individual institutions on Lijphart's cross-national index indicate (see figure 2 and table A-5). Some institutional mechanisms are highly majoritarian, notably the reliance on single-party cabinets and electoral rules that produce a small effective number of political parties. Equally important, the nonmajoritarian elements—absence of executive dominance, bicameralism, and lack of constitutional flexibility—are primarily of the limited-government variety. There are almost no consociational elements at all. Instead of measures to promote elite consensus and cooperation, majorities are constrained primarily by mechanisms that make any change from the status quo difficult. The American system also contains important arbitral elements (judicial review) and delegatory elements (federalism).

These institutions, were, of course, designed in large measure to respond to the concerns of the late eighteenth century about the management of cleavages (most notably divisions between populous and less-populous states and between a slavery-based, largely agricultural southern economy and a free-holding northern economy), as well as concerns about executive tyranny. They were not designed to respond to the concerns of blacks, who were almost totally excluded from political participation; indeed, they were intended to facilitate that exclusion. And they preceded the development of highly institutionalized political parties that facilitated (and were in turn further stimulated by) proportional representation electoral rules in other countries. This institutional legacy has nevertheless critically shaped current cleavage management strategies.

America's racial cleavage is quite distinctive. In particular, this cleavage has been and continues to be reinforced by inequality and discrimination. It also has a marked (although changing) geographic basis. Although minorities in other countries have been economically disadvantaged and regionally concentrated—Flemings in Belgium and francophones in Quebec, for example—the U.S. case is extreme. The ancestors of most African Americans came to the United States in slavery, and after emancipation the great majority of blacks remained a poor and dependent class of

sharecroppers and tenant farmers in the South. Several waves of migra-
tions to northern cities in the twentieth century radically changed the
demographic profile of the country's black population.[25] The black population became overwhelmingly urban, and the percentage of blacks
employed in white-collar occupations has grown.[26] But blacks remained
far poorer than white Americans; by the early 1980s, social scientists
were worrying about the development of a black "underclass" concentrated in central cities that was socially isolated not only from job-growth
areas and from white society but also from middle-class blacks.[27]

The characteristics of America's institutions and its racial cleavage have
had several related implications for the country's cleavage management
agenda and for the kinds of strategies most likely to be successful in
easing tensions. First, the long history of discrimination and economic
disparity confronting blacks has meant that black concerns have not been
limited to securing adequate representation and equalization of opportunities and political and civil rights. Societal redress and equalization of
economic outcomes have also been central, and highly controversial,
issues. Second, American institutions that limit government and delegate
power to regional majorities have provided numerous opportunities for
opponents of increased representation and redress for blacks to block
such initiatives and impose white hegemony. Institutional arrangements
that, under other conditions, might have increased minority autonomy
(such as bicameralism, federalism, and absence of executive dominance)
have tended instead to facilitate oppression by regional majorities. We
will examine the record of institutional mechanisms associated with each
of the four cleavage management strategies, beginning with those where
U.S. institutions are least majoritarian.

25. In 1900, 89.7 percent of American blacks lived in the South. This had fallen to 78.7
percent by 1930, 59.9 percent by 1960, and 53.0 percent by 1970. Daniel M. Johnson and
Rex R. Campbell, *Black Migration in America: A Social Demographic History* (Duke University
Press, 1981), pp. 73–155. On the northern migration, see Carole Marks, *Farewell—We're
Good and Gone: The Great Black Migration* (Indiana University Press, 1989); and Nicholas
Lemann, *The Promised Land: The Great Black Migration and How it Changed America* (Knopf,
1991).

26. In 1939, 42.5 percent of black men and 16.0 percent of black women were employed
in agriculture; by 1984 the percentages were 3.4 percent and 0.5 percent, respectively. In
1939, 3.1 percent of black men and 5.0 percent of black women employees were categorized
as professionals, proprietors, managers, and officials. In 1984, the corresponding percentages were 14.3 percent and 19.1 percent. Jaynes and Williams, eds., *A Common Destiny*,
p. 273.

27. On the forces generating these patterns, see, for example, Stanley Lieberson, *A
Piece of the Pie: Blacks and White Immigrants Since 1880* (University of California Press, 1980);
and William Julius Wilson, *The Truly Disadvantaged: The Inner City, the Underclass and
Public Policy* (University of Chicago Press, 1987).

Limited-Government Mechanisms

Lijphart measures three institutional attributes consistent with a limited-government strategy for constraining majority rule: level of executive dominance, level of dominance by one chamber of the legislature, and difficulty of amending the constitution. The U.S. score on all three attributes is highly nonmajoritarian.[28] But it is far from clear that these institutional arrangements have in fact contributed to more effective cleavage management.

Lack of executive dominance is a direct and obvious consequence of the separation-of-powers rule: the absence of the vote of confidence makes the legislature more independent and more the equal of the executive. For our purposes, lack of executive dominance has a twofold significance: it adds veto points, making rule by simple majorities more difficult (consistent with a limited-government strategy), and it may also provide opportunities for access and representation in the legislature for groups that are underrepresented in the executive.

The U.S. Congress is a strikingly powerful legislative body compared with the parliaments of all of the parliamentary systems considered here.[29] Switzerland is roughly on a par with the United States with regard to the equilibrium between executive and legislature; and, significantly, Switzerland is also characterized by the absence of the vote of confidence. Finland can be placed in the same category. And only the Fifth Republic's semi-separation-of-powers system is exceptional in that the executive clearly dominates the legislature, mainly as a result of the president's special constitutional powers and the presidential prerogative to dissolve the legislature.[30] As a result, the average score of the three semi-sepa-

28. For most of the countries, the measure of executive dominance is based on "hard" data: cabinet durability serves as the indicator of executive dominance, on the assumption that cabinets that stay in power for a long time are likely to be dominant vis-à-vis the legislatures and vice versa. Unfortunately, this measure works for parliamentary systems only. Hence subjective judgments on the relative powers of executives and legislatures were necessary in all of the separation- and semi-separation-of-powers cases; see Lijphart, *Democracies*, pp. 80–81, 212.

29. Jean Blondel has suggested that about a third of the rule-making function is still "the prerogative of the U.S. Congress" in contrast with the "not more than perhaps 4 or 5 per cent of the rule-making [that] can be ascribed to the British parliament or to most parliaments of Western Europe." Jean Blondel, *An Introduction to Comparative Government* (London: Weidenfeld and Nicholson, 1969), pp. 355–56.

30. In Anthony King's words, "The French legislature has, if anything, become even more subordinate to the executive than the British." Anthony King, "Modes of Executive-Legislative Relations: Great Britain, France, and West Germany," *Legislative Studies Quarterly*, vol. 1 (February 1976), p. 21. Note, however, that King's statement was made at a

ration-of-powers systems is not as low as that of the United States, but it is still clearly on the nonmajoritarian side (see table A-5).

But has the balance of executive and legislative power in the United States actually aided in promoting political representation and economic and social redress for black Americans? For the first three-fifths of this century, the answer would have to be that it did not. The fragmentation of power in Congress that facilitated legislative independence, in combination with seniority systems used to select committee chairmen in Congress and the one-party character of southern politics during most of that period, provided an institutional power base for southerners within the national government. Southern congressmen used committee chairmanships to delay civil rights and voting rights legislation and to delay and limit social legislation (on issues such as educational aid, child benefits, and old-age pensions) that would have disproportionately aided African Americans.[31] Even relatively liberal presidents, such as Franklin Roosevelt and John Kennedy, were reluctant to press for legislation in these areas for fear of losing the support of southern Democrats for other aspects of their programs that they valued more highly. In short, the risks associated with this limited-government characteristic were dominant: separation of powers did prevent change from the status quo.

The answer for the last part of the twentieth century is more ambiguous, however, because of the potential for separation of powers to allow groups underrepresented in the executive branch to exercise power through the legislature. Black representation in the House of Representatives has increased dramatically, from only five members in the 90th Congress (1967–68) to twenty-five in the 102d (1991–92) and thirty-eight in the 103d (1993–94). Blacks remain underrepresented in Congress and, until the Clinton administration, were generally underrepresented in presi-

---

time when all cabinets under the Fifth Republic had been of the same political persuasion as the president.

31. Senator James O. Eastland, chairman of the Judiciary Committee from 1955–1978, and Representative Howard Smith, chairman of the House Rules Committee from 1955–1966, were notable examples of committee chairmen who blocked civil rights bills. See Charles and Barbara Whalen, *The Longest Debate: A Legislative History of the 1964 Civil Rights Act* (New York: New American Library, 1985); and Robert Bendiner, *Obstacle Course on Capitol Hill: What Happens to a Bill in Congress* (McGraw-Hill, 1964), pp. 140–56. Southern legislators opposed inclusion of domestic and agricultural workers within the old age insurance (social security) system and a national benefit standard and uniform national administration for the means-tested old age assistance program during the New Deal because they feared that federal transfer payments might undermine their control of black agricultural labor in the South. See Jill Quadagno, *The Transformation of Old Age Security* (University of Chicago Press, 1988).

dential cabinets. But self-selection norms for all but the most exclusive committees allow black members to concentrate on committees where they can have the most influence on programs of interest to minorities, such as Education and Labor. Black representatives are beginning to accumulate substantial seniority that has already carried some into committee and subcommittee chairmanships of particular importance to minority constituencies. These incumbency advantages should increase in future years, because most black members of the House come from black-majority, inner-city districts that are safer than the norm for all House members. In an executive-dominated parliamentary system, the influence of these committee and subcommittee chairmanships on policymaking would almost certainly be less important.

The United States receives the lowest possible (that is, least majoritarian) scores on two other attributes of limited-government institutions: unicameralism and constitutional flexibility. But again, it is not clear that these features have been positive on the whole for the protection of minority rights or for effective cleavage management. Bicameralism, and in particular equal representation for all states in the Senate, has protected the rights of small states. But it has also made it more difficult to redress minority grievances that go against the wishes of conservatives. And the use of statewide majority elections to the Senate has made it extremely difficult for ethnic minorities to win election there: in the 103d Congress, the Senate had only one black member, one American Indian, two Asian Americans (both from Hawaii), and no Hispanics.[32]

The effects of a fairly rigid constitutional structure are even more complex. Clearly, the rigid requirements for revision of the U.S. Constitution (two-thirds of both congressional chambers plus three-quarters of the states), combined with the entrenchment of numerous constitutional rights, make it more difficult for national majorities to revise the Constitution in ways that discriminate against minorities.[33] But they also make it difficult to entrench new rights that protect minority interests. Significantly, most of the major extensions of constitutional rights to be entrenched in the Constitution during the last 150 years took place during the Civil War and Reconstruction—when the opposition of white south-

32. Norman J. Ornstein, Thomas E. Mann, and Michael J. Malbin, eds., *Vital Statistics on Congress, 1989–1990* (Washington: Congressional Quarterly, 1990), p. 35; and John R. Cranford, "The New Class: More Diverse, Less Lawyerly, Younger," *Congressional Quarterly Weekly Report*, November 7, 1992, p. 8. The nonvoting delegates of the District of Columbia and U.S. territories to the House are excluded from this count.

33. There is also the formal possibility of amendment by constitutional convention, but this has never been used.

erners was institutionally weakened. The failure of the Equal Rights Amendment to win approval in the state legislatures is a recent manifestation of this decidedly mixed constitutional provision.[34]

Delegatory Mechanisms

Delegatory mechanisms attempt to promote minority rights by allowing groups or regions—usually the latter—to govern themselves. The United States has substantial geographic decentralization of power due to its federal system. Only West Germany, Canada, and Switzerland have a lower ratio of central government tax receipts to total tax receipts (Lijphart's measure of decentralization). However, the federal system has not helped minority representation and minority autonomy a great deal because ethnic and racial cleavages generally cut across, rather than coincide, with state boundaries (with the partial exception of Hawaii).[35] Thus, rather than protecting the rights of national minorities who are regional majorities (such as francophones in Quebec), federalism in the United States historically served as a mechanism for politically dominant groups in the South to exclude blacks entirely from the political process, using their autonomy to continue social and political practices (notably the "Jim Crow" laws) different from those prevailing in most of the rest of the country.[36]

Arbitral Mechanisms

Arbitral mechanisms, such as judicial review and presidents who are above politics, are intended to protect minorities by insulating decision-makers from majority opinion. Of course, there is no guarantee that minorities will in fact be protected, and there is a potential risk that insulated power will be abused by those who hold it. The U.S. experience suggests that the first concern, at least, is a legitimate one. It is clear that

34. On the fate of the Equal Rights Amendment, see in particular Gilbert Y. Steiner, *Constitutional Inequality: The Political Fortunes of the Equal Rights Amendment* (Brookings, 1985); and Jane Mansbridge, *Why We Lost the ERA* (University of Chicago Press, 1986).

35. No U.S. state has an African-American majority (although the District of Columbia and the Virgin Islands do). In even more decentralized Switzerland, by contrast, almost half the comparable units (cantons and half-cantons) have Catholic majorities and almost a quarter are predominantly francophone; both groups are minorities nationally.

36. The differences between northern and southern white opinion should not be overstated, however. C. Vann Woodward argues that northern white opinion on racial matters became more conservative toward the end of the nineteenth century, "so that at no time were the sections very far apart on race policy." Woodward, *The Strange Career of Jim Crow* (Oxford University Press, 1957), p. 52.

judicial review has been an important element in extending minority rights in areas such as voting rights, school desegregation, and access to public facilities. Court extensions of civil and voting rights beginning in the 1950s took place precisely because the courts are *not* consensual institutions, but rather relatively autonomous arbitral ones that are able to act against the will of regional and even national elected officials—and in the case of school desegregation, in the face of massive resistance from regional elites.[37]

It should be noted, however, that the courts in the United States have not always played a positive role in advancing or even preserving minority rights. The Supreme Court's *Plessy* v. *Ferguson* decision, for example, legitimated "separate but equal" public facilities for more than half a century. Equally important, the Supreme Court in the late nineteenth century permitted the evisceration of voting and civil rights guarantees under the Fourteenth and Fifteenth Amendments.[38] Showing once again that courts may not be as protective of minorities as congressional majorities, in 1990 Congress tried to enact a civil rights bill precisely to overturn six court decisions that had limited minority rights in the area of employment discrimination. The bill was vetoed by President Bush.

Consociational Mechanisms

Consociational arrangements attempt to promote organization and legislative representation through bargaining among elite representatives of distinct societal segments. A number of institutional mechanisms can be used to promote this approach, most notably electoral rules based on proportional representation or reservation of some seats for minority groups. These rules, in turn, tend to promote a multiparty system, a close match between party vote shares and legislative representation, and a multiparty sharing of executive authority—three of the subdimensions in Lijphart's index. The U.S. score on all three characteristics is strongly majoritarian.

37. See, for example, Numan V. Bartley, *The Rise of Massive Resistance: Race and Politics in the South During the 1950's* (Louisiana State University Press, 1969). The freedom of courts from changes in public opinion should not be overstated, however. For a review of the evidence on this issue, see Gregory A. Caldeira, "Courts and Public Opinion," in John B. Gates and Charles A. Johnson, eds., *The American Courts: A Critical Assessment* (Washington: CQ Press, 1990), pp. 303–34.

38. See John Braeman, *Before the Civil Rights Revolution: The Old Court and Individual Rights* (New York: Greenwood Press, 1988); and Woodward, *The Strange Career of Jim Crow*, pp. 53–54.

POLITICAL PARTY FORMATION. American electoral rules strongly discourage the formation of separate parties representing minority interests. The United States has a smaller average effective number of parties than any of the other twenty-one democracies—1.9—reflecting the postwar dominance of the Democrats and Republicans and the fact that one of these parties usually had a clear majority in the House of Representatives.[39] This number is lower than New Zealand's average of 2.0 effective parties, the British average of 2.1, and the Canadian average of 2.4. What these four countries have in common is the plurality single-member-district method of election, which tends to favor the larger parties, discriminate against the smaller ones, and produce a basically two-party system. There are several special reasons why the United States has developed an almost pure two-party system. One is that the influence of the electoral system is reinforced by presidentialism: the two major parties are given even greater advantages over the smaller ones, because only their candidates can be serious contenders in a contest in which there can be only one winner.[40] The second reason is the use of primary elections—an almost uniquely American phenomenon. Primaries make it more attractive for nonmainstream aspirants for political office to seek nomination within the major parties instead of forming or joining third parties. Third, American state laws strongly discriminate against small parties by making it very difficult for new parties to get on the ballot for a particular election and, if this attempt is successful, to stay on the ballot in subsequent elections.[41]

Presidentialism and primaries protect and promote not only the two-party system but also the lack of cohesiveness of the two major parties, however. In parliamentary systems, reasonably disciplined and cohesive parties are required to support cabinets in office; in presidential systems, parties can afford much greater laxness with regard to organization and programs. This characteristic is reinforced by primaries, which take away

39. The "effective number of parties" weights the parties according to their respective strengths. For instance, in a two-party system with two exactly equal parties, the effective number of parties is 2.0. With three exactly equal parties, the effective number is 3.0; but if one of the three parties is considerably weaker than the other two, the effective number will be about 2.5. For each country, the score is the average effective number of parties represented in the lower house after legislative elections in the 1945–80 period. Markku Laakso and Rein Taagepera, "The 'Effective' Number of Parties: A Measure with Application to West Europe," *Comparative Political Studies*, vol. 12 (April 1979), pp. 3–27.

40. The unit rule for awarding electoral college votes for the presidency—that is, all of the state's votes go to the candidate with a plurality of the state's popular vote—further exacerbates the majoritarian characteristics of presidential elections.

41. Kay Lawson, "How State Laws Undermine Parties," in A. James Reichley, ed., *Elections American Style* (Brookings, 1987), pp. 243–47.

the parties' ability to control their organizational and ideological unity by means of the nomination process. As a result, while the United States has a much purer two-party system than any other Western democracy in the sense that significant third parties are usually entirely absent, minority representatives in Congress have substantial autonomy to represent their constituents' interests.

ELECTORAL DISPROPORTIONALITY AND MINORITY REPRESENTATION. A closely related characteristic of political systems, also heavily influenced by electoral rules, is electoral disproportionality. Disproportionality is measured here in terms of the average deviation between vote and seat shares of the two largest parties in elections to the lower house of the national legislature. Figure 2 shows that the United States is only moderately majoritarian in this regard. For the U.S. House of Representatives in the period 1945–80, the mean index of disproportionality was the same as for Australia, but lower than in any of the other four countries with plurality or majority electoral systems (Canada, the United Kingdom, New Zealand, and the French Fifth Republic). The principal explanation for the comparatively low degree of disproportionality of congressional elections is the unusual nature of the American two-party system, discussed above. In other two-party systems, the two major parties do not predominate to the same degree. Their indices of disproportionality tend to be higher because their minor parties are systematically underrepresented. Since the United States has almost no minor parties, their degree of underrepresentation is much smaller.[42]

In fact, this index greatly understates the degree of minority underrepresentation in American government. As mentioned earlier, there were thirty-eight black members of the House of Representatives (8.7 percent) after the 1992 election, about 80 percent of their share of the voting age population. There was only one black senator. Although there have been massive gains in the number of minority elected officials at most levels in the United States since passage of the Voting Rights Act of 1965, a still-paltry 2 percent of elected officials were black and 1 percent were of Hispanic origin in 1987.[43]

42. Arend Lijphart, "The Pattern of Electoral Rules in the United States: A Deviant Case Among the Industrialized Democracies," *Government and Opposition*, vol. 20 (Winter 1985), pp. 25–27.
43. "Elected Officials Proliferate, Census Bureau Study Shows," *New York Times*, January 25, 1989, p. A6. On gains under the Voting Rights Act, see J. Morgan Kousser, "The Voting Rights Act and the Two Reconstructions," and Hugh Davis Graham, "Voting Rights and the American Regulatory State," in Bernard Grofman and Chandler Davidson, eds., *Controversies in Minority Voting: The Voting Rights Act in Perspective* (Brookings, 1992), pp. 135–76, 177–96.

Figure 2. *Majoritarian and Nonmajoritarian Aspects of U.S. Political Institutions*

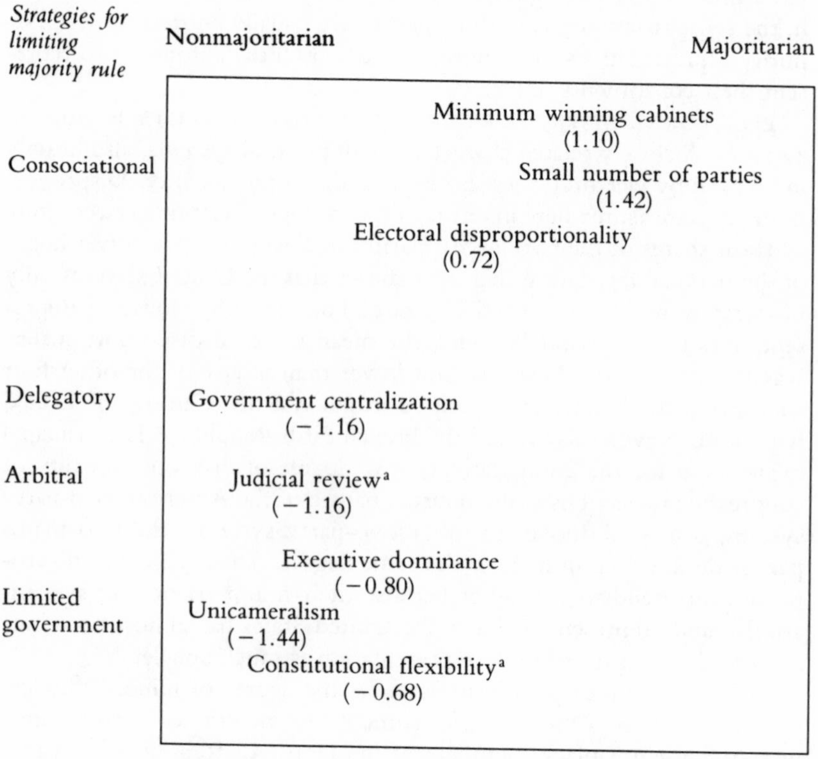

Strategies for limiting majority rule	Nonmajoritarian	Majoritarian
Consociational		Minimum winning cabinets (1.10)
		Small number of parties (1.42)
	Electoral disproportionality (0.72)	
Delegatory	Government centralization (−1.16)	
Arbitral	Judicial review[a] (−1.16)	
Limited government	Executive dominance (−0.80)	
	Unicameralism (−1.44)	
	Constitutional flexibility[a] (−0.68)	

a. See table A-5. Lijphart's constitutional flexibility score is disaggregated into a separate judicial review score and a constitutional flexibility score (in the narrower senese of how easy it is to amend the constitution).

Separate election of political executives in the United States contributes to a further underrepresentation of minorities not fully captured by Lijphart's index of disproportionality. Elections to a single office are intrinsically highly disproportional: proportional representation obviously cannot be used, and the only available methods are plurality and majority choice.[44] Presidential elections are strikingly disproportional in terms of minority representation. So far, women, blacks, and Hispanics have had exactly

44. This argument parallels that of Juan Linz, discussed in the chapter by Richard Gunther and Anthony Mughan in this volume. We disagree, however, with Linz's con-

0 percent representation in the presidency. Moreover, ignoring the Reconstruction era, it was not until 1989 that a black politician was elected governor in any of the fifty states.

Countries with proportional representation have a record superior to plurality and majority systems in representation of religious and ethnic minority groups.[45] Many of these democracies have explicitly religious or ethnic political parties—most of the Belgian parties and the Swedish People's Party in Finland offer particularly good examples of the latter—and here the minorities in question can be said to be represented with full or close to full proportionality.

While minority underrepresentation in government in the United States seems destined to continue for the forseeable future, it should be pointed out that the 1982 amendments to the Voting Rights Act of 1965 and judicial interpretations of that statute have reduced that underrepresentation significantly in the House of Representatives, as well as adding the closest thing to a "consociational" element as can be found in the American political system.[46] The 1982 amendments added a "results" test that allows challenges to electoral measures (such as congressional district boundaries or at-large elections to county councils) that dilute minority voting strength and prevent minorities from electing candidates of their choice. As interpreted by the courts, this has meant that where "majority minority" congressional and state legislative districts can be drawn, they must, under certain conditions, be drawn.[47] This is consis-

---

tention that this barrier to minority representation is a necessary concomitant of the separation-of-powers system, since, as we shall argue shortly, plural executives are possible.

45. Plurality and majority systems also tend to underrepresent women. In the early 1980s, the percentage of women in the U.S. House of Representatives was 4.1, close to the average of the six democracies with plurality and majority systems. In the proportional representation countries, the average was 13.6 percent, with a high of 27.7 percent (Sweden) and a low of 5.0 percent (Iceland). Wilma Rule, "Electoral Systems, Contextual Factors and Women's Opportunity for Election to Parliament in Twenty-Three Democracies," *Western Political Quarterly*, vol. 40 (September 1987), p. 483.

46. See Armand Derfner, "Vote Dilution and the Voting Rights Act Amendments of 1982," in Chandler Davidson, ed., *Minority Vote Dilution* (Howard University Press, 1989), pp. 145–63. Conservative critics have argued that the courts' interpretation of these statutes has gone beyond the legislative intent of their congressional framers and has led to the twin presumptions that only minorities can represent minorities and that representational schemes that do not maximize minority representation are prima facie unfair. Most notable among the conservative critics is Abigail M. Thernstrom, *Whose Votes Count? Affirmative Action and Minority Voting Rights* (Harvard University Press, 1987).

47. The conditions, outlined in the Supreme Court's 1986 *Thornburg* v. *Gingles* decision, include a large and geographically compact minority, a history of voting along racial lines, and a record of minority candidates being defeated by white bloc voting.

tent with the consociational principle that minorities should be allowed to choose their own representatives.

The 1982 amendments had a profound effect on the most recent (1991) round of redistricting, leading not only to an increase of more than 50 percent in the number of African-American members in the House of Representatives in the 1992 election, but also to a 70 percent increase in the number (from ten to seventeen) of Hispanic representatives. The effects of the voting rights amendments are not unambiguous, however. Redistricting conflicts in many cases have pitted white Democrats against alliances of black Democrats and Republicans, with the Republicans hoping to pack enough Democratic-voting minorities into "majority minority" districts that Republicans will be able to make net gains by picking up additional seats in the other, less Democratic districts.[48] Moreover, the Voting Rights Act does not ensure that there will be consociational bargaining among group representatives.

SINGLE-PARTY CABINETS. With respect to the concentration or sharing of executive power, the accepted American pattern is to have one-party rather than coalition cabinets. This pattern has developed in spite of the constitutional requirement that the Senate give its advice and consent for cabinet appointments; the unwritten rule is that advice is almost never asked and that, with very few exceptions, consent is routinely given. If anything, the majoritarian score assigned to the United States may once again be too low, for it is based merely on the concentration of power in one party. However, there is a crucial difference between parliamentary one-party cabinets, which are always collegial although the prime minister is *primus inter pares,* and presidential one-party cabinets in which the president is necessarily *primus* but the other cabinet members are advisers rather than *pares.* Obviously, the concentration of executive power in one person is even more majoritarian than concentration of power in one party.

This characteristic of presidentialism means that the minority community is likely to have a voice in selecting its own representatives—or failing this, that the minority representatives will at least reflect the minority's opinions, attitudes, and interests—only when political forces friendly to that community control the presidency. The president's virtually unrestricted appointing power tempts him to rely on what has

48. See James A. Barnes, "Minority Mapmaking," *National Journal,* April 7, 1990, pp. 837–39; James A. Barnes, "Minority Poker," *National Journal,* May 4, 1991, pp. 1034–39; and Peter Bragdon, "Democrats' Ties to Minorities May Be Tested by New Lines," *Congressional Quarterly Weekly Report,* June 2, 1990, pp. 1739–42.

been called "descriptive representation."[49] This view holds, for instance, that a black person "represents" blacks simply by being black, regardless of any correspondence between his or her opinions and those of most other blacks.[50]

INSTITUTIONAL CHANGE AND MINORITY REPRESENTATION. While it is clear that blacks are underrepresented in American governmental institutions, institutional remedies are less clear. Adopting proportional representation in the House of Representatives is one (albeit highly unlikely) electoral reform consistent with consociational principles, but even its effects are highly uncertain. These effects would depend on (1) whether blacks chose to form a separate political party and how successful it would be in attracting electoral support from both blacks and whites; (2) the effects of the formation of such a party on the intensity of the racial cleavage and the strategic and policy choices of other parties; and (3) whether black leaders were able to form alliances with other groups to advance their interests or were politically marginalized.

Certainly proportional representation would lessen barriers to formation of a separate black-oriented political party.[51] It would not eliminate them, however. Because such a party could not hope to field a successful candidate for the presidency or for most Senate seats (assuming the electoral system for the Senate remained the same), many voters would not see it as a serious political vehicle. How attractive a separate black political party would turn out to be for black (and white) voters is difficult to predict in advance.[52] Calculations of the potential effects

---

49. Hannah Fenichel Pitkin, *The Concept of Representation* (University of California Press, 1967), pp. 60–61.

50. Referring to both cabinet and noncabinet appointments made by Presidents Richard Nixon, Ronald Reagan, and George Bush, black columnist Carl Rowan comments: "What all these Republican presidents have had in common is their callous willingness to use black nobodies . . . to destroy programs that they didn't like while leaving a halo hanging over the White House. Reagan set a record for drumming up blacks so bereft of qualifications that they gave 'affirmative action' a bad name, or blacks so lacking in conscience that they became the agents of destruction of programs critical to the well-being of 30 million black Americans." Carl Rowan, " . . . Expected Something Better from Bush," *San Diego Union,* July 26, 1989, p. B7.

51. For a discussion of the opinions of black elites on formation of a separate political party, see Ronald W. Walters, *Black Presidential Politics in America: A Strategic Approach* (State University of New York Press, 1988), chaps. 1–2, 6.

52. In Canada, however, voters have frequently supported parties—notably Social Credit, the Parti Quebecois, the Cooperative Commonwealth Federation and the New Democratic Party—in federal or provincial elections that had no prospect of winning power at the national level. And in many countries with proportional representation, voters persist in supporting very small parties that completely lack any "coalition potential," that is, any serious chance of being included in a governing coalition.

328   *Arend Lijphart, Ronald Rogowski, and R. Kent Weaver*

of a proportional representation system on black representation in the House, with each state as an election district having the same number of seats as its 1990 and 1992 House delegations, are shown in table 1.[53] The most recent round of redistricting dramatically reduced the difference between the number of African Americans actually elected to the House and those that might be elected under optimistic assumptions about proportional representation. The additional seats produced by proportional representation fall from nineteen in 1990 to only nine in 1992. The change is especially dramatic in the South, where blacks gained twelve House seats in the 1992 election, but where they remain most seriously under-represented.[54]

Formation of a separate black-oriented party also carries with it the risk that such a strategy would lead to a heightening of racial cleavages and to a decline in efforts by white politicians to attract black voters. The latter risk is especially apparent in the South. Southern Democratic congressmen have increasingly moved toward the mainstream of the national party in the last twenty years.[55] This change reflects increasing black voting in the South in the wake of the Voting Rights Act of 1965; the recognition by Democratic politicians in the South that unless they took positions that were attractive to blacks, that group would not bother to vote; and that if they did not vote, many southern Democrats would lose their seats. Proportional representation would give more seats in the South to Republicans and might lower the incentives of southern (as well as northern) Democrats to be responsive to the interests of black voters, potentially lowering these voters' influence on policymaking. The more general (and unanswerable) question is whether other political parties would continue to nominate blacks under such a system and to represent black interests, or whether they would forgo such appeals to concentrate

53. Black voters as a percentage of the voting-age population are multiplied by the number of seats in each state's delegation to determine the likely number of seats to be obtained by black candidates, assuming that all blacks vote for black candidates and non-blacks for nonblacks, and that members of each group vote in equal percentages. These are of course overly simplistic assumptions, but they provide a reasonable upper bound on the prospects for a black-oriented political party.

54. A national-level system of proportional representation would produce exactly the same maximum estimate for a black-oriented political party of forty-seven House seats, based on a 1990 Census Bureau estimate that blacks form 10.885 percent of the voting age population in the fifty states. Department of Commerce *News*, Release CB91-177, May 16, 1991.

55. Party unity scores for southern Democrats, which averaged slightly more than 50 percent in the late 1960s, approached 80 percent in the late 1980s; the gap in party unity between southern Democrats and all Democrats dropped precipitously. Ornstein and others, eds., *Vital Statistics on Congress, 1989–1990*, p. 199.

on their political base. Recent European experience, on the other hand, suggests that where proportional representation has permitted the emergence of new parties representative of intense minorities (such as the Greens), traditional parties have usually hastened to preempt the interlopers' appeal by altering their own programs. In earlier periods, wherever ethnic or religious minorities formed their own parties (for example, in the Netherlands, Norway, Switzerland and even pre-1918 Germany), governments eventually made fundamental concessions.

A final issue raised by the prospect of a separate black political party under proportional representation is whether it would bring African Americans into the political mainstream or marginalize them further. Certainly such a party would be small and at or near the left end of the American political spectrum. We can imagine at least two quite different scenarios about its fate. If it drew votes largely from the Democrats (as seems likely), and the Democratic and Republican parties did not split further under a system of proportional representation, the Democrats and Republicans would be placed in rough parity in the House, with our putative African-American party holding the balance between them. The likeliest development under these conditions, based on similar experiences ranging from Labour in the United Kingdom during World War I to the Greens in various German states, is that parties of the center and left—here the Democrats and a new African-American party—would coalesce to organize the House. In such an event, black representatives would likely increase their influence with their newly independent organization and gain significant leverage to advance its legislative objectives.

Quite a different scenario is indicated where a center party becomes aware that such a coalition costs it votes. That has happened often enough, for example, between Socialists and Communists and, in some quite recent cases, between Socialists and Greens. Then, center and right collaborate to marginalize the "extremists" of the left. In the U.S. case, the enormous tensions between black and white Democrats over employment discrimination legislation, and the latter's fear that Republicans are successfully using the issue of racial hiring quotas to lure white working-class voters away from the Democratic party suggests that an alliance between "rump Democrats" and an African-American party is not a foregone conclusion.[56] If Democrats and Republicans (or some center-

56. On the political tensions created by the civil rights bill, see, for example, Joan Biskupic, "Behind the Fight Over Quotas Lie Divisive Racial Issues," *Congressional Quarterly Weekly Report*, June 1, 1991, pp. 1442–45. For broader discussions, see Carmines and Stimson, *Issue Evolution*; and William Julius Wilson, "Race-Neutral Policies and the Democratic Coalition," *American Prospect*, vol. 1 (Spring 1990), pp. 74–81.

Table 1. Potential Black Seats in the U.S. House of Representatives under a State-Level Proportional Representation System[a]

State	Blacks as percent of voting age population, 1990	1990				1992			
		House seats for state	Potential black seats using PR	Seats won by blacks	Additional black seats using PR	House seats for state	Potential black seats using PR	Seats won by blacks	Additional black seats using PR
South									
Alabama	22.73	7	2	0	2	7	2	1	1
Arkansas	13.73	4	1	0	1	4	1	0	1
Florida	11.42	19	2	0	2	23	3	3	0
Georgia	24.59	10	2	1	1	11	3	3	0
Louisiana	27.87	8	2	1	1	7	2	2	0
Mississippi	31.63	5	2	1	1	5	2	1	1
North Carolina	20.07	11	2	0	2	12	2	2	0
South Carolina	26.93	6	2	0	2	6	2	1	1
Tennessee	14.37	9	1	1	0	9	1	1	0
Texas	11.22	27	3	1	2	30	3	2	1
Virginia	17.58	10	2	0	2	11	2	1	1

Northeast/middle Atlantic

Connecticut	7.44	6	0	1	−1	6	0	1	−1
Maryland	23.45	8	2	1	1	8	2	2	0
New Jersey	12.36	14	2	1	1	13	2	1	1
New York	14.73	34	5	4	1	31	5	4	1
Pennsylvania	8.47	23	2	1	1	21	2	1	1
Midwest									
Illinois	13.45	22	3	3	0	20	3	3	0
Indiana	7.05	10	1	0	1	10	1	0	1
Michigan	12.76	18	2	2	0	16	2	2	0
Missouri	9.71	9	1	2	−1	9	1	2	−1
Ohio	9.77	21	2	1	1	19	2	1	1
West									
California	7.02	45	3	4	−1	52	4	4	0
Total	10.89[b]	...	44	25	19	...	47	38	9

Source: Authors' calculations based on Mike Mills, "Voters Elect Record Numbers of Women and Blacks," *Congressional Quarterly Weekly Report*, November 10, 1990, p. 3835; John R. Cranford, "The New Class: More Diverse, Less Lawyerly, Younger," *Congressional Quarterly Weekly Report*, November 7, 1992, p. 8; and Department of Commerce News, Release CB91-177, May 16, 1991.

a. States where no black representatives were elected in either 1990 or 1992 and where state-level proportional representation is unlikely to change this result are omitted from the table. To give a likely upper bound for representation for an African-American-oriented political party, a very liberal assumption is made that a remainder of 0.50 or greater when multiplying a state's voting age population would be needed to elect a representative using proportional representation system. Under most proportional representation allocation formulas, a higher remainder would in fact be required. If a remainder of 0.60 were used, the likely upper boundary for the number of seats won by a black-oriented party would decline by three in 1990 and four in 1992.

b. For all fifty states.

right coalition if those parties split further) worked together, a separate black party could be deprived of precisely the committee and subcommittee chairmanships that have begun to expand African-American influence in government.[57]

It is, in short, quite plausible that blacks would not choose to form a separate political party even if the United States adopted a system of proportional representation for House elections; and it is possible that their access to power might not be increased if they did form a separate party. What is clear is that the nature of intergroup relations and group demands and the political dynamics that follow from them are at least as important as political institutions in determining minority group access to political power.

Patterns and Explanations

This analysis suggests several general conclusions about the roles that political institutions play in cleavage management.

1. *Both majoritarian and nonmajoritarian cleavage management strategies have distinctive advantages, limitations, and associated risks.* The disadvantages of majoritarian strategies are widely known, but this chapter shows that specific nonmajoritarian stratgies—which we have here labeled consociational, delegatory, arbitral, and limited government—also have important limitations and risks.

2. *The effect of specific institutional arrangements on the capacity of governments to manage cleavages peacefully depends on both the exact nature of the institutions and the way that they interact with particular cleavage structures.* Federalism, for example, can be a useful mechanism to grant autonomy to ethnic or linguistic minority groups who live in a geographically distinct area, but it does little to help geographically dispersed minority groups, such as African Americans in the United States, who do not form a majority in any major political subdivision. In fact, federalism may increase the ability of regional majorities to engage in discriminatory behavior and policies.

Similarly, for consociational mechanisms to work, elites from each cleavage segment must be able to act with some autonomy from their followers, must cooperate to lessen stresses, and must make cleavage management a top priority. None of these conditions has consistently held in the United States. Historically, both white elites and white masses

57. By far the least likely result, all comparative evidence suggests, is a coalition between the right and left, that is, between Republicans and a separate African-American party.

have been divided for and against political, social, and economic integration of blacks; blacks have, to a lesser extent, also been divided about whether it was more fruitful to pursue an integrationist or nationalist strategy.[58]

3. *The separation of powers per se appears to have little independent effect on government capability for cleavage management.* Separation of powers can have both positive and negative effects on cleavage management. In the United States, presidentialism has in theory weakened the ability of majorities to discriminate against minorities; but, because of splits within the white majority on racial issues, legislative autonomy has probably weakened the ability of presidentially led coalitions to redress minority grievances. On the other hand, it has provided black members of Congress with national positions of influence. Semi-separation-of-powers systems' apparent success at cleavage management owes less to the fact that legislative and executive power are separated than to the arbitral (politically neutral and relatively insulated) character of political executives in these countries.

4. *The absence of consociational mechanisms in the U.S. system has inhibited minority participation in government.* Concentration of executive power in a single party, electoral disproportionality, and a small number of effective parties all inhibit effective minority representation. Minorities are at a serious disadvantage in presidential and senatorial elections, and in presidential cabinets they are likely to be only weakly and "descriptively" represented.

The issue of minority representation is powerfully symbolic, but it also has direct policy consequences. The principle of informal representational norms or even rigid quotas—for example, in the distribution of cabinet posts and even some governmental expenditures—in proportion to major ethnic, racial, and religious groups' share of the population has come to be widely accepted in plural societies that rely heavily on consociational mechanisms. In each historical case, this acceptance has grown out of a first step toward population-proportional political representation of each group and thence out of the recurrent need to bring groups into governing, or broader social, coalitions.[59]

---

58. See, for example, the discussion in Gary Orfield, "Race and the Liberal Agenda: The Loss of the Integrationist Dream, 1965–1974," in Margaret Weir, Ann Shola Orloff, and Theda Skocpol, eds., *The Politics of Social Policy in the United States* (Princeton University Press, 1988), pp. 313–55.

59. The classic example is the Netherlands; see Arend Lijphart, *The Politics of Accommodation: Pluralism and Democracy in the Netherlands,* 2d ed. (University of California Press, 1975), esp. pp. 103–21, 127–29. For a more critical comparative perspective on quotas, see Thomas Sowell, *Preferential Policies: An International Perspective* (William Morrow, 1990).

That the issue of quotas remains so contentious in the United States may in part reflect the absence of consociational mechanisms to ensure minority political representation. Of course, quotas in the United States face other significant obstacles as well. They conflict with widely held beliefs about the potential for individual mobility and the illegitimacy of group claims.[60] In addition, quotas (and more frequently, informal affirmative action goals) have become more contentious as they have been applied more broadly and where they have been perceived by other groups as involving "affirmative discrimination" against them.[61]

5. *Most U.S. political institutions are neither majoritarian nor consensus-seeking in intent or practice, but are rather a distinctive limited-government type.* Lijphart has presented a single dichotomy between two types of mechanisms for resolving disputes across cleavage lines: majoritarian mechanisms that allow the majority group to govern with few constraints and consensual mechanisms that encourage the groups to work together across cleavage lines. But the evidence presented here suggests that this dichotomy is too simple. The American system is—consistent with the intent of the Founders—riddled with veto points that impede decisive government action. These institutional mechanisms—separation of powers, bicameralism, decentralization within Congress, and rigid rules for constitutional revision—have often discouraged rather than encouraged consensus-seeking behavior.

6. *Many of the limited-government characteristics of the U.S. system have inhibited effective cleavage management.* The multiple veto points described above may hinder explicit legislative discrimination against minorities at the national level, but they also have allowed "minorities of the majority" to frustrate decisive action in favor of integrating blacks into the mainstream of American society. Indeed, much of the progress made in improving the status of blacks has occurred during a few isolated "majoritarian" outbursts—notably the Civil War and Reconstruction and the "Second Reconstruction" of the early 1960s—against practices that most whites clearly found offensive. After each of these outbursts, however, there has been a relapse into a limited-government mode of cleavage management, in which the racial cleavage was given less explicit attention and efforts at further reforms were stalemated by the system's many veto points.

7. *Arbitral political institutions appear to play a generally useful role in*

60. See, for example, Nathan Glazer, *Affirmative Discrimination: Ethnic Inequality and Public Policy* (Basic Books, 1975).

61. See, for example, Thomas Byrne Edsall with Mary D. Edsall, "Race," *Atlantic* (May 1991), pp. 53–86.

cleavage management, both in the United States and in semi-separation-of-powers systems. The only institutional feature of the American system that appears to have had a net positive effect on amelioration of the racial cleavage is an independent judiciary. The courts, and in particular the Supreme Court, have done more than other institutions to ameliorate and resolve profound racial divisions since World War II. But this institutional feature fits easily into neither the majoritarian or consensual categories. In most of its actions advancing civil rights, for example, the judiciary played an arbitral role, acting without checks to evade the institutional roadblocks that American institutions presented to securing equal rights for blacks. In so doing, the Court was able to draw on its legitimacy as a trusted, neutral arbiter of institutional conflicts. By taking a more activist role in setting social policy, especially in contentious areas such as school busing, the courts have, however, undercut their own legitimacy as neutral arbiters with some segments of the public.[62] Conflicts over civil rights have also become an issue in judicial appointments, most notably in the rejection of Robert Bork's nomination to the U.S. Supreme Court. For the most part, legislative efforts to curtail the courts' role have been rejected. Arbitral institutions need not always be more protective of minorities than elective institutions, moreover. As noted earlier, Congress in recent years has been more protective of minority rights than has the Supreme Court.

Interestingly, it is in precisely these arbitral aspects, where the United States most resembles the semi-separation-of-powers regimes (Finland, the French Fifth Republic, and Switzerland), that it has performed best in the management of racial and ethnic cleavages. We have already noticed a similarity between the Swiss Federal Council and the U.S. Supreme Court. What these institutions have in common is not only that they are trusted, but also that they are relatively insulated from electoral or appointive political pressures that compel responsiveness to constituents. They require not agreement by political leaders across cleavage lines, but simply the acceptance of a decision by a neutral arbiter. Of course a government relying primarily on arbitral mechanisms (Tito's Yugoslavia might be an example) would not be democratic at all.

8. *It is not necessary to abandon separation of powers in order to increase minority influence over policymaking.* One possible alternative is the adoption of state-level proportional representation for elections to the House of Representatives. Such a shift might increase black representation in the House, but it is not without significant risks for effective represen-

---

62. We owe this point to Thomas Cavanaugh.

tation of black interests.[63] Maurice Duverger, who is opposed to proportional representation and the multipartism it tends to produce for parliaments that have to sustain a cabinet in office, argues that proportional representation can do no harm, and even has definite advantages, in presidential systems.[64] Arguably, proportional representation is the only way of satisfying all of the criteria that the Supreme Court has enunciated, beginning with *Baker* v. *Carr,* for equality of voting rights.[65] The adoption of proportional representation would almost certainly increase the number of parties in the U.S. political system.[66] It would also eliminate the incentives for "strange bedfellow" alliances between minority groups and Republicans in redistricting fights, in which the former seek to increase the number of black-majority districts and the latter seek to concentrate black voters to increase the prospects that Republicans can win more of the remaining (less heavily Democratic) districts.

On the other hand, since proportional representation tends to produce multipartism, it also greatly increases the probability that the president's party will lack a majority in the legislature, that is, there will be divided government and hence frequent executive-legislative conflict and deadlock.[67] Moreover, it is far from clear that blacks would choose to form a separate political party even if the United States adopted a system of proportional representation for House elections; nor is it clear that doing so would increase their bargaining leverage in Congress.

Neither the concentration of executive power in one person nor a single-party presidential cabinet is a necessary feature of separation of

63. A combination of proportional representation and separation of power has numerous precedents. Most Latin American presidential systems use proportional representation for their national legislative elections. Ronald H. McDonald and J. Mark Ruhl, *Party Politics and Elections in Latin America* (Westview Press, 1989), pp. 12–14. Moreover, Switzerland and Finland use it, and even the French Fifth Republic used it for one of its National Assembly elections (in 1986).

64. Duverger, "Which Is the Best Electoral System?"

65. Ronald Rogowski, "Representation in Political Theory and in Law," *Ethics,* vol. 91 (April 1981), pp. 395–430.

66. Former House Speaker Thomas P. O'Neill is reported to have opined that "in any other country the Democrats would be four or five parties and the Republicans two or three." Cited in Walter Dean Burnham, "The Turnout Problem," in Reichley, ed., *Elections American Style,* p. 106. Under proportional representation, these latent "parties" would presumably emerge.

67. Scott Mainwaring argues that this is the main explanation for the problems of Latin American presidential regimes. Mainwaring, "Presidentialism in Latin America," *Latin American Research Review,* vol. 25, no. 1 (1990), pp. 167–69. Their failures have been especially striking in the areas of economic development and control of the military, but their performance with regard to managing ethnic and racial cleavages is much more positive.

powers, moreover. In Switzerland's separation-of-powers system, for example, the executive is independent of the legislature (although elected by it); yet the Swiss executive is a collegial seven-member body. The Uruguayan *colegiado*, which operated from 1952 to 1967, was a nine-member "presidential" body that was both popularly elected and not subject to a legislative vote of confidence.[68] It is worth noting in this connection that the collegial nature of the Swiss executive has served the purpose of broadly representing not only all the major Swiss parties but also Switzerland's diverse religious, linguistic, and regional groups. Uruguay's *colegiado* was specifically designed to include both majority and minority party representatives. Although a collegial presidency may have serious problems of its own,[69] it is important to make the logical point that these alternative institutional designs do not conflict with the basic principle of separation of powers. It is not separation of powers as such that is inimical to effective minority representation, but rather single-member congressional districts and other barriers to black representation in the South, single-state plurality elections to the Senate, and plurality election to a unitary presidency.

Conclusions

Political institutions clearly affect governments' capabilities to manage political cleavages, but we would emphasize, as Richard Gunther and Anthony Mughan do in their chapter, that they do not determine success in managing cleavages peacefully. Both majoritarian political arrangements and various forms of nonmajoritarian institutions have associated risks as well as opportunities. Whether risks or opportunities are more in evidence depends in part upon choices made by elites, but also upon the structure of the cleavages themselves. Factors such as the degree of separation of groups, the level of economic disparity among them, whether their economic and cultural interests are compatible or in conflict, and whether they share common values that can bridge their differences play a critical role in determining which institutional mechanisms are used to regulate group conflict. They play an even more critical role in

68. Russell H. Fitzgibbon, "Adoption of a Collegiate Executive in Uruguay," *Journal of Politics*, vol. 14 (November 1952), pp. 620–22, 633–38; and Alexander T. Edelmann, "The Rise and Demise of Uruguay's Second Plural Executive," *Journal of Politics*, vol. 31 (February 1969), pp. 119–39.

69. One potential concern is whether its decisionmaking procedures would meet the requirement for quick crisis response that accompany the United States' role as a super-power.

determining the effects of those mechanisms once they are called into play.

Appendix: Quantitative Data

Table A-1 presents the number of riots and deaths from political violence in twenty-two democracies, both actual and adjusted for population size (that is, the latter numbers for all countries other than the United States represent the number of riots and deaths they would have experienced if their populations had been as large as that of the United States).[70]

Table A-1 also classifies each country according to its degree of social pluralism,[71] and shows each country's score on Lijphart's indices of majoritarianism and unitary government.[72]

70. Powell discusses the question of the appropriateness of adjustment for population size at some length. He sounds ambivalent: "On the one hand, it seems clear that an intensive burst of rioting, such as that which shook France in 1968, counts in some absolute sense, and should not be buried by being divided by population size. On the other hand, it seems plausible that 27 riots in tiny Uruguay do indicate more severe discontent, a more serious failure of democratic performance, than the similar numbers of riots in Japan and France." Powell, *Contemporary Democracies*, p. 21. In practice, however, he chooses the adjustment option, either by using per capita figures or by using population size as a control variable in multiple correlation and regression analysis. Following Powell, we shall employ only the adjusted numbers of riots and deaths. In the case of deaths from political violence, it seems particularly obvious that unadjusted data would be meaningless for cross-national comparisons. These adjustments do not "disadvantage" the smaller countries by artificially inflating their deaths and riots. In fact, the correlations between population and adjusted deaths and riots are slightly—and not significantly—positive: 0.04 and 0.27.

71. With one exception, our classification is taken from Lijphart, *Democracies*, p. 43. The exception is the United Kingdom. Because Northern Ireland is but a small part of the United Kingdom, it is classified as nonplural in *Democracies*. Given, however, that most of the violence in the United Kingdom is related to Northern Ireland, the United Kingdom must be placed in the plural category for the purpose of this chapter. Powell employs the *World Handbook*'s index of ethnic fractionalization rather than the threefold classification of pluralism used here. See Charles Lewis Taylor and Michael C. Hudson, *World Handbook of Political and Social Indicators*, 2d ed. (Yale University Press, 1972), pp. 271–73. This index performs much worse than our measure in explaining riots and political deaths.

72. The correlations in our sample are as follows: separation of powers with majoritarianism, 0.23; with unitary rule, −0.36; semi-separation of powers with majoritarianism, −0.36; with unitary rule, −0.07. The majoritarianism dimension is based on five basic aspects of the party and electoral systems and the arrangement of executive power: the differences between majoritarianism and consensus on this dimension are bare-majority (minimal winning) cabinets versus broad coalition cabinets, executive predominance over the legislature versus executive-legislative balance of power, a two-party versus a multiparty system, parties that differ from each other mainly with regard to left-right issues versus a

Table A-2 shows the simple bivariate relationship between the average number of deaths and riots and the type of government—separation of powers, semi-separation, or parliamentary. We show two averages for the parliamentary democracies: one for all eighteen parliamentary systems and one for fifteen of them, excluding three for which the data are insufficiently comparable: Israel (because of its international situation), and Luxembourg and Iceland (because of their very small size).[73] The rest of our analysis omits these three countries.

We used preliminary regressions employing all five explanatory variables to eliminate those that appeared to have no significant effect on the two dependent variables of political deaths and political riots and to combine categories of the same variable that appeared to have similar effects.[74] Tables A-3 and A-4 give parameter estimates for the variables that emerged as significant in each case.

Plural societies had, on average, 1,210 more deaths from political causes than did semiplural or nonplural societies; countries lacking a pure proportional representation electoral system had, even controlling for their degree of ethnic pluralism, 1,082 more deaths;[75] and for each full unit of increase in the score for unitary rule, there were 508 more political deaths (table A-3).

Majoritarianism appeared to have no significant effect on political riots, and although a preliminary regression suggested that the "semi-

---

larger number of issue dimensions, and a high degree of electoral disproportionality versus proportional representation. The federal-unitary dimension comprises the differences of centralized versus decentralized government, unicameralism versus bicameralism, and flexible versus rigid constitutions.

73. Israel's extremely high adjusted numbers of deaths from political violence and riots—the highest numbers reported in table A-1—are to an important extent the result of international, not domestic, conflict. We therefore omit Israel from our set of democracies. At the other extreme, we also exclude Luxembourg and Iceland, for which no riots and deaths from political violence are reported. Such events may have been underreported in these very small and often neglected countries. More important, the adjustment for their small population size is meaningless since zero remains zero even when multiplied by the adjustment factor. Powell also omits these two small countries from his analysis, since he uses a population of 1 million as the minimum criterion for inclusion.

74. The characteristics of presidentialism, semipresidentialism, pluralism, semiplural-ism, proportional representation, and "hybrid" electoral systems appear in these analyses as dummy variables; the measures of majoritarianism and unitary government are treated as continuous. Obviously, since the electoral system is one component of the broader measure of majoritarianism, the two are highly correlated: between majoritarianism and the dummy variable for plurality or majority electoral system, $r = 0.71$. Hence at no point in the subsequent analysis do we permit both to enter a regression equation.

75. Lijphart's broader measure of majoritarianism predicts less successfully: $t = 1.63$, the overall adjusted $R^2 = 0.23$.

Table A-1. *Riots and Deaths from Political Violence and Measures of Political Power in Twenty-two Democracies, 1948–77*

Country	Riots	Riots (adjusted)[a]	Deaths from political violence	Deaths from political violence (adjusted)[a]	Degree of pluralism[b]	Majoritarianism[c]	Unitary government[d]
Australia	10	170	0	0	nonplural	1.01	−0.97
Austria	36	926	10	257	plural	0.88	−0.39
Belgium	60	1,199	81	1,619	plural	−0.49	0.08
Canada	34	340	12	120	semiplural	1.55	−1.18
Denmark	7	277	14	555	nonplural	−0.62	0.35
Finland	11	459	4	167	semiplural	−1.26	0.33
France IV[e]	115	1,367	26	309	semiplural	−1.73	0.45
France V[e]	92	540	138	810	semiplural	0.37	0.23
Germany	143	474	61	202	semiplural	0.24	−1.70
Iceland	0	0	0	0	nonplural	−0.17	0.88
Ireland	18	1,132	50	3,143	nonplural	0.79	0.38
Israel	80	6,320	84	6,636	plural	−1.28	1.87
Italy	444	1,615	259	942	semiplural	−0.85	−0.07

Japan	195	374	60	115	nonplural	0.17	−1.07
Luxembourg	0	0	0	0	plural	0.42	0.63
Netherlands	9	140	13	202	plural	−1.20	0.20
New Zealand	1	74	0	0	nonplural	1.37	1.79
Norway	1	52	1	52	nonplural	−0.10	0.10
Sweden	12	292	6	146	nonplural	0.03	0.07
Switzerland	8	265	0	0	plural	−1.44	−1.52
United Kingdom	372	1,294	1,463	5,087	plural	1.31	1.09
United States	861	861	434	434	semiplural	1.02	−1.55

Sources: Author's calculations based on data in Charles Lewis Taylor and David A. Jodice, *World Handbook of Political and Social Indicators*, 3d ed. (Yale University Press, 1983), vol. 2: *Political Protest and Government Change*, pp. 33–36, 48–51; and Arend Lijphart, *Democracies: Patterns of Majoritarian and Consensus Government in Twenty-One Countries* (Yale University Press, 1984), pp. 61, 83, 99, 122, 130, 160, 178, 193, 212–14.

a. Adjusted numbers of riots and deaths from political violence are the numbers per 185,111.50 people (the average population of the United States in 1948–77, calculated using the populations of each country in every fifth year from 1950 to 1975). Statistical Office of the United Nations, Department of Economic and Social Affairs, *Demographic Yearbook, 1957*, pp. 124–31; *1977*, pp. 158–62.

b. A threefold classification based on the degree to which countries are divided along cultural, ethnic, or racial lines into separate subsocieties with their own political parties, interest groups, and media of communication.

c. Standardized averages of standardized scores on five characteristics of party and electoral systems and of the arrangement of executive power.

d. Standardized averages of standardized scores on three characteristics: government centralization, constitutional flexibility, and bicameralism versus unicameralism.

e. France IV covers 1948–58; France V covers 1959–77. Both were proportionally increased to make them comparable to thirty-year span. Data for France IV from Charles Lewis Taylor and Michael C. Hudson, *World Handbook of Political and Social Indicators*, 2d ed. (Yale University Press, 1972), pp. 94–95, 112–13.

proportional representation" category of countries had a significantly higher incidence of riots—some 692 more than in "pure" proportional representation or majoritarian systems—on reflection we regard that association as spurious. No theoretical link between the variables comes readily to mind; and one must consider that the only two members of this category, Ireland and Japan, are unusually riot-prone for other reasons.

Table A-4 includes the three variables that attained both substantive and (in one case borderline) statistical significance. We see (a) that non-plural societies had on average 851 fewer riots than plural or semiplural ones; (b) each unit increase in a country's score for unitary government raised the number of riots by 182; and (c) in our first clear effect of regime type, semi-separation of powers is associated with 495 fewer riots than either pure separation of powers or parliamentary government. As the R^2s suggest, these naive regressions express a seriously underspecified model. Nonetheless, the t-scores obtained for the individual variables strike us as demonstrating the likely presence of some basic relationship.

Table A-5 shows standardized scores (with a mean of 0 and a standard deviation of 1) for the United States and the semi-separation-of-powers systems and parliamentary systems on Lijphart's indices of majoritarianism and unitary rule and on the individual components of those two indices.[76]

76. In figure 2, we examine only those subdimensions that are especially institution-focused. Lijphart's "number of issue dimensions" subdimension, which is not an institutional variable, is eliminated from our discussion. We also disaggregate constitutional flexibility and judicial review in figure 2.

Table A-2. *Average Numbers of Riots and Deaths from Political Violence in Nineteen Democracies, by Type of Government*[a]

Type of government	Riots	Deaths from political violence
Separation of powers[b]	861	434
Semi-separation of powers[c]	421	326
Parliamentary[d]	648	850
All 18 parliamentary systems[e]	891	1,077

Source: Based on the data in table A-1.
a. Numbers adjusted for population size as in table A-1.
b. United States.
c. Finland, France V, Switzerland.
d. Australia, Austria, Belgium, Canada, Denmark, France IV, Germany, Ireland, Italy, Japan, Netherlands, New Zealand, Norway, Sweden, United Kingdom.
e. All of the fifteen countries above, plus Ireland, Israel, and Luxembourg.

Table A-3. *Deaths from Political Violence Regressed on Pluralism, Absence of Pure Proportional Representation, and Unitary Government*[a]

Independent variable	Dependent variable (deaths from political violence)		
	Coefficient value	Standard error	Probability
Constant	61.7	. . .	. . .
Pluralism	1,209.9 (2.1)	586.7	0.057
No proportional representation	1,082.1 (2.1)	522.8	0.0561
Unitary government	508.4 (1.9)	275.7	0.083

a. Numbers in parentheses are t-statistics. Summary statistics: $R^2 = 0.417$; $\overline{R}^2 = 0.3$.

Table A-4. *Riots Regressed on Semipresidentialism, Pluralism or Semipluralism, and Unitary Government*[a]

Independent variable and summary statistics	Coefficient value	Standard error	Probability
		Dependent variable (riots)	
Constant	325.5	. . .	. . .
Semipresidentialism	−494.5	277.7	0.0952
	(1.8)		
Pluralism or	635.7	215.1	0.0093
Semipluralism	(3.0)		
Unitary government	141.8	107.9	0.2086
	(1.3)		

a. Numbers in parentheses are t-statistics. Summary statistics: $R^2 = 0.401$; $\overline{R}^2 = 0.281$.

Table A-5. *Majoritarianism and Unitary Government in Nineteen Democracies, by Type of Government, 1945–80*[a]

Variable	Separation of powers[b]	Semi-separation of powers[c]	Parliamentary[d]	All 18 parliamentary systems[e]
Majoritarianism	1.02	−0.78	0.16	0.07
1. Minimal winning cabinets	1.10	−1.33	0.18	0.16
2. Executive dominance	−0.80	−0.44	0.22	0.12
3. Small number of parties	1.42	−1.03	0.20	0.09
4. Small number of issue dimensions	1.63	−0.87	0.10	0.05
5. Electoral disproportionality	0.72	0.56	−0.08	−0.13
Unitary government	−1.55	−0.32	−0.06	0.14
6. Government centralization	−1.16	−0.60	0.07	0.16
7. Unicameralism	−1.44	−0.15	−0.10	0.10
8. Constitutional flexibility	−1.04	.00	−0.10	0.06

Source: Based on the data in table A-1.

a. The values of the eight variables are standardized scores (with a mean of 0, a standard deviation of 1, and majoritarianism assigned a positive sign). The values of majoritarianism and unitary government are the averages (again standardized) of the relevant variables.

b. United States.

c. Finland, France V, Switzerland.

d. Australia, Austria, Belgium, Canada, Denmark, France IV, Germany, Ireland, Italy, Japan, Netherlands, New Zealand, Norway, Sweden, United Kingdom.

e. All of the fifteen countries above, plus Iceland, Israel, and Luxembourg.

Helen Milner

Maintaining International Commitments in Trade Policy

*T*he economic environment of the advanced industrial countries has changed dramatically since the early 1970s. Although the 1950s and 1960s were a time of stability and growth, the period since has been marked by economic shocks and slowing growth. All industrial countries have experienced these difficult changes, which include the abrupt end of an international regime of fixed exchange rates (the Bretton Woods system), its replacement by an unstable flexible exchange rate mechanism, the two oil shocks of the 1970s and 1980s and the consequent inflation in energy and raw material prices, the rapid changes in comparative advantage as Japan and the newly industrialized countries (NICs) moved into international markets in manufactures, and the dramatic opening of these countries' markets through the Kennedy and Tokyo rounds of the General Agreement on Tariffs and Trade (GATT). The effect of these changes was a series of economic problems: rising unemployment, surplus capacity in industry, sluggish growth, and surging imports. These problems, in turn, gave rise to intense pressures to protect domestic firms and workers from international competition. Governments faced the difficult choice of upholding their international commitment to trade liberalization, symbolized by GATT and the European Community, or abandoning it to satisfy domestic interests.

This chapter examines the effect of political institutions on several governments' ability to maintain international commitments—specifically a commitment to a free trade regime—in the face of internal protectionist pressure. Much theoretical work in the field suggests that

I would like to thank Andrew Cortell, I. M. Destler, Peter Lange, Maureen Molot, the participants at the Duke University seminar on political economy, and those at the Brookings Institution conference "Assessing the Effects of Institutions" for their help.

individual countries should respond differently to international economic challenges. This assertion is based on the assumption that countries have distinctive economic and political traditions and institutions. Thus an economic shock would affect each nation differently. What may appear to be a similar type of economic challenge across countries is actually felt dissimilarly by each. Even when the shocks are similar, the response of each country will differ since their institutions and past responses for dealing with such problems are unique.[1]

This chapter explores whether these theoretical predictions can explain the foreign trade policies of three advanced industrial countries, Great Britain, France, and the United States, since the early 1970s. By trade policy, I mean all commercial policies, such as import quotas, tariffs, and nontariff barriers (NTBs), which affect the relative prices of exports and imports. Various industrial policies (including export subsidies) are not explicitly covered; other chapters examine them. Also, my focus is limited to trade policy for *manufactured* goods.

I sort trade policies into two categories. First, without attempting to understand policymakers' intentions, I classify policies as either protectionist or trade liberalizing in effect. If a policy alters prices (or restricts quantities) so as to discourage imports or encourage exports, it is considered protectionist. If a policy has neutral or trade-promoting effects, then it is liberal.[2] Second, trade policies can be seen as varying in their coherence in furthering broad national interests rather than particularistic ones. Since protectionism slows the adjustment of certain domestic sectors to international economic developments and imposes costs on other sectors, one might conclude that protectionist policies of any sort fail to provide coherent or effective means to pursue the national interest. But such a conclusion is too sweeping. In pursuing long-term developmental goals, states may wish to promote certain industries at the expense of others; a commercial policy that consistently forwarded these aims could be in the national interest, broadly construed. By contrast, a set of trade policies that protected industries on an ad hoc basis—that is, without any strategic rationale for their choice and with little attention to their effects—would be judged incoherent.

Hypotheses about how domestic institutions affect policymaking abound; this chapter focuses on those relating to the division of responsibility between the executive and legislature, the variations across party

1. Peter J. Katzenstein, "Introduction: Domestic and International Forces and Strategies of Foreign Economic Policy," in Katzenstein, ed., *Between Power and Plenty: Foreign Economic Policies of Advanced Industrial States* (University of Wisconsin Press, 1978), p. 3.

2. While not all policies fit easily into these two categories (some may have both effects or no effect at all), this simple categorization is useful.

and electoral systems, and the bureaucratic structures of each state. Institutional arguments imply that capabilities flowing from political institutions shape policy outputs. That is, in some discernible way policies reflect institutional capabilities. I believe this emphasis is overdrawn. Institutions may not always live up to their capabilities because other factors intervene, such as governing elites having protectionist goals. Thus, the gap between capabilities and policies may be serious.[3] To possess independent explanatory power, however, institutional arguments must show that the capabilities of different institutions can shape policies in some rough but systematic way, despite other influences. The cases examined here show this contention to be difficult to support. I therefore argue in this chapter that differing political institutions in Great Britain, France, and the United States have not led to major differences in their ability to make and maintain international commitments in the trade sector. Policy responses were similar for three interrelated reasons— common external problems, common internal interest group pressures, and common international institutions.

Institutions and Capabilities

State capacity to make and maintain international commitments combines several of the capabilities discussed elsewhere in this volume— notably the abilities to impose losses on powerful groups, represent diffuse interests, and maintain policy stability.[4] These intertwined capabilities are especially important in trade policy. Trade policies exert differential effects on domestic and international actors. Protectionism benefits the protected industry but hurts other industries and (generally unorganized) consumers; it also hurts foreign industries who lose sales to the protected market. Trade-liberalizing measures tend to improve overall national welfare but hurt the once-protected industries; liberalization may also benefit foreign producers. As a result, pressure from powerful interest groups may grow, with them demanding protection

3. The conclusion of one important institutionalist study of foreign economic policy recognizes the importance of political elites and their goals. But, like other institutionalist analyses, it does not discuss how to reconcile the influence of elites and institutions when they conflict. See Katzenstein, "Conclusion: Domestic Structures and Strategies of Foreign Economic Policies," in Katzenstein, ed., *Between Power and Plenty*, pp. 295–336.

4. For a more extended discussion of institutional influences on government capacity to impose losses and represent diffuse interests, see the chapters by Pierson and Weaver and by Vogel in this volume.

and opposing the adoption of policies promoting the welfare of the majority and that of foreign countries.

Differences in political institutions may mean that similar problems are manifested differently, that interests are aggregated in unique fashions, and that past commitments exert distinct influences on the policy process. I begin by comparing executive-legislative arrangements, Weaver and Rockman's "first tier" of explanation, and examining their effects.

In traditional arguments—referred to in this volume as the "parliamentarist position"—parliamentary systems with power centralized in the prime minister and cabinet and with strong party discipline are presumed to have a stronger capability to make and maintain international commitments than the U.S. separation-of-powers system. Because legislators in parliamentary systems must follow the party line and because the policymaking structure is highly centralized in the cabinet, powerful groups outside the cabinet may not be able to obtain access to or influence over policymaking. It is unlikely, for example, that a parliament could block a treaty once the cabinet had given its assent. Nor could individual legislators or committees initiate policies contrary to international commitments made by the cabinet. The cabinet thus may be able to pursue policies—including those made pursuant to international commitments—that impose losses on otherwise powerful groups and that promote the majority's welfare over particularistic interests. In the U.S. separation-of-powers system, however, the Senate may refuse to ratify presidentially negotiated treaties.[5] In addition, Congress may enact policies that undercut international commitments.

"Presidentialist" defenders of the separation of powers argue that although the system's multiple veto points can make it difficult to get unpopular commitments adopted by Congress, they also make it relatively difficult to undo them. Once the president has obtained Senate ratification of a treaty, for example, it is unheard of for Congress to renege. In a parliamentary system, by contrast, a change in government can lead to a reversal of all international commitments made by the prior government.

Parliamentary systems do not all operate in the same way, however. Furthermore, individual presidential and parliamentary systems differ over time in the way they operate. These differences (equivalent to Weaver and Rockman's "second tier" of explanation) result in large measure from varying electoral laws and from different norms and rules for gov-

5. The failure of the U.S. Senate to ratify President Wilson's decision to join the League of Nations and its failure to ratify the SALT II treaty are frequently cited as exemplars of congressional restrictions on treaty-making power. See Lloyd N. Cutler, "To Form a Government," *Foreign Affairs*, vol. 59 (Fall 1980), pp. 126–43.

ernment formation. Some effects of electoral rules are fairly direct—for instance, single-member-district systems are usually seen as prone to local pressures, especially when party discipline is weak—but others are indirect. Multiparty governments, for example, which most often occur in countries with proportional representation, are likely to be less cohesive and may have more internal veto points than those with single-party majorities. Coalition parliamentary governments may be more vulnerable to pressure from specific interests to protect particular industries and localities. Majority governments, on the other hand, may be most prone to dramatic policy reversal when a new party wins control of the government, such as renouncing a commitment to enter into the European Economic Community or some other trade-liberalizing agreement. In the United States, the ability to maintain international commitments may vary according to whether the two branches are controlled by different parties. In a situation of divided government, maintaining international commitments may be difficult. Legislative majorities may use unpopular presidential commitments as an opportunity to direct blame at the executive and may defeat those initiatives and even enact contrary legislation over a presidential veto. Electoral differences among systems, however, remain insufficient as an explanation of trade policy; further examination of other governmental institutions is needed.

Additional hypotheses about the effects of political institutions on a state's capacity to maintain international commitments can be derived from Weaver and Rockman's "third tier" of explanation, especially the role of governmental administrative structures. Much literature has argued that in a modern political economy the influence on policy of legislatures, political parties, and elections has diminished as society and its problems have grown more complex. Bureaucracies and civil servants have become the primary means of dealing with these problems, especially economic ones.[6] The key issue, then, becomes how autonomous the governmental administration is from political and social pressure. When policymaking structures are highly professionalized, insulated from the legislature and interest groups, centralized, and possessed of a cohesive agenda, then policy will be coherent and broadly based. Such a state apparatus will be "strong" relative to its domestic social base.[7] It

6. See the literature on corporatism: for example, Gerhard Lehmbruch and Philippe C. Schmitter, eds., *Patterns of Corporatist Policy-making* (London: Sage, 1982); Gerhard Lehmbruch and Philippe C. Schmitter, eds., *Trends Toward Corporatist Intermediation* (London: Sage, 1979); and Peter J. Katzenstein, *Small States in World Markets: Industrial Policy in Europe* (Cornell University Press, 1985).

7. For examples of the literature on "strong" and "weak" states, see Katzenstein, *Between Power and Plenty*; John Zysman, *Governments, Markets, and Growth: Financial Systems*

will be able to resist powerful domestic groups, represent broad interests, and maintain foreign commitments when they are desired. "Weak" states will lack these capacities. Since states' administrative structures vary, their policymaking capabilities and hence their policies should also differ. In conclusion, differences in the structure of government bureaucracies combine with differences in executive-legislative relations and electoral laws to affect policy outcomes through the differential capabilities they produce.

The Making of International Policy in Three Nations

Great Britain, France, and the United States are appropriate case studies of government's capability to maintain international commitments because they differ in the three tiers of institutional structure: legislative-executive arrangements, electoral rules, and bureaucratic institutions.[8] The three countries do share some similarities, which means that certain external influences can be controlled for and potential institutional influences can be highlighted. All three countries are advanced Western industrial states with long-standing democratic practices. Each is well integrated into the world economy, although the United States is the least so. All are members of a common international trade regime, GATT. Moreover, both France and Great Britain belong to the European Community (EC), which assumes primary responsibility for the definition of many of their trade policies. In addition, all three have faced similar economic dilemmas since the early 1970s.

A comparison of Great Britain, France, and the United States, however, has its limitations. First, only Great Britain has a parliamentary system (France is a hybrid presidential-parliamentary one); therefore, testing second-tier hypotheses about differences among parliamentary systems is virtually impossible. Examining the effects of divided versus unified government in the United States is also problematic since control of the executive and the legislative branches was split during much of the 1970s and 1980s. Second, France and Great Britain may not be independent economic actors. Since the early 1970s, the EC has exerted increasing control over their trade policymaking. This common insti-

---

and the Politics of Industrial Change (Cornell University Press, 1983); and Eric A. Nordlinger, *On the Autonomy of the Democratic State* (Harvard University Press, 1981).

8. Often links among the three tiers of institutions are implied. Usually "weak" states (ones with weak administrative structures) are ones with a divided executive-legislature relationship, as in the United States. No logical link is proposed for this; it is historical. See Katzenstein, "Conclusion."

Figure 1. *Hypothesized Institutional Effects on Trade Policy Outcomes*

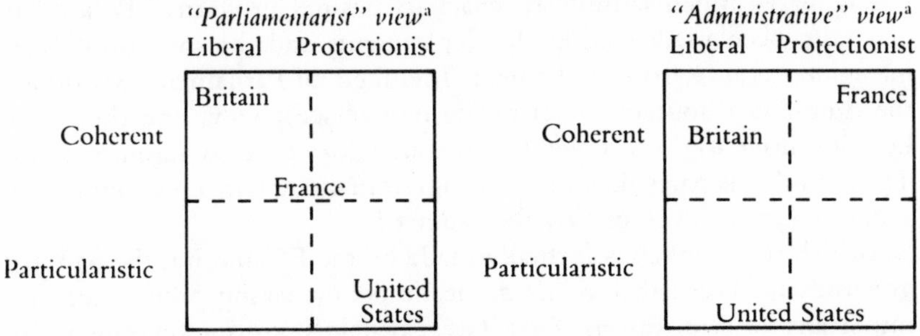

a. The parliamentarist view considers the effects of parliamentary or presidential differences and those of differing electoral rules. The administrative view considers the effects of bureaucratic institutions.

tutional pressure has led to a growing convergence in their policies, thus damping the effects of their distinct political institutions.

Confronted by similar economic problems but possessing distinct political institutions, how did the states respond in terms of their trade policies? In terms of the first two tiers of explanation, a parliamentarist perspective would predict that Great Britain should have the most coherent and liberal trade policy; the United States should have the most incoherent and protectionist one; and France should fall somewhere in between, on both measures. The expectations generated by the third tier (the bureaucracy), however, differ from those of the first two. France's commitment to statism suggests that it should have the most coherent—but also highly protectionist—policies; the United States should have the most incoherent but also the most liberal; and Great Britain should fall in between, being both fairly liberal and fairly coherent. These hypothesized relationships are summarized in figure 1. To understand this characterization requires a detailed knowledge of trade-policymaking institutions in the three countries.

Representative Institutions and Trade Policymaking

Great Britain is a parliamentary system, based on single-member districts and plurality electoral rules. Until recently, two large parties (Conservative and Labour) have been the only serious competitors for governmental power. For most of the postwar period, one of these parties has held a clear majority without the need for coalition partners. Governing responsibility has been vested mainly in the prime minister and his or her cabinet, although power has depended ultimately on a majority in Parliament. Strong party discipline has traditionally existed, constraining expression of local interests. This has tended to give the governing party much latitude to enact its desired program.[9] Policy has generally been made within the departments and the cabinet without great interference from Parliament. Members of Parliament (MPs) lack the time and resources to formulate or oversee policy, and they have little incentive to do so given the pressures for voting with one's party. Thus, while the party does devise programmatic statements about issues, actual policy is developed by the cabinet.[10]

British trade policy is formally made by the EC and not the national government. Nevertheless, its domestic policymaking process remains important for two reasons. First, Great Britain's position on trade issues at the EC is decided upon domestically. Second, much trade policy, other than tariffs, has been a product of national policies. Decisions about British trade policy fall under the jurisdiction of two departments, those of Trade and Industry. Separated throughout most of the 1970s, these departments have been united in the Department of Trade and Industry since 1983. It was hoped that this superministry would provide the requisite coordination in trade policy that had been missing in the 1970s.[11] Other departments, too, have been involved in trade policy, especially the Treasury, with its control over finances, and the Foreign Office, with its interest in preserving good foreign relations.[12]

9. The rise of a third party, the Liberal–Social Democratic Party (SDP) alliance, beginning in the early 1970s weakened these traditional patterns. In Parliament, increased dissent by members has been registered, and party discipline has eroded to some extent. H. Drucker and others, eds., *Developments in British Politics 2*, rev. ed. (St. Martin's Press, 1988), pp. 67–69. But by 1990 the successor to the alliance, the Social and Liberal Democrats, had lost much support and hardly played the role of third party. The SDP is disbanding and two-party competition has returned. Relative to French and American democratic institutions, the British system still features a strong prime minister supported by tight party discipline.

10. There is increasing debate over whether the cabinet or the prime minister devises policy, which reflects the tendency of recent prime ministers to develop their own institutions to create policy. See Drucker and others, eds., *Developments in British Politics*, pp. 92–101, 356–57; and Peter A. Hall, *Governing the Economy: The Politics of State Intervention in Britain and France* (New York: Oxford University Press, 1986), pp. 127–29. In economic policy, this is apparent in the creation of the prime minister's Economic Policy Unit, which was designed to give the prime minister a means to counterbalance the influence of the Treasury Department. See Anthony King, ed., *The British Prime Minister*, 2d ed. (London: Macmillan, 1985), pp. 53–54.

11. Drucker and others, eds., *Developments in British Politics*, p. 99; William Wallace, *The Foreign Policy Process in Britain* (London: Royal Institute of International Affairs, 1975), pp. 72–73; and Stephen D. Cohen, *The Making of United States International Economic Policy: Principles, Problems, and Proposals for Reform* (Praeger, 1977), pp. 121–25.

12. Cohen, *Making of U.S. International Economic Policy*, pp. 121–25.

From a "parliamentarist" perspective, Britain's party government system allows trade policy to be made in a highly centralized and politically insulated environment. This system should be able to resist interest group pressures for protection and to enact a trade policy that represents the broad national interest. One would expect the majority party, once in power, to be able to pursue its trade policy program without significant interference, and the departments, which are relatively insulated from parliamentary pressure, to be able to formulate and implement policies coherently.

Democratic institutions in the United States should lead to the opposite outcome. Though a strong two-party system, the United States has separate executive and legislative institutions with independent electoral mandates. The president and an independent legislature elected from single-member districts vie for control over policymaking. This checks-and-balances system is seen by the parliamentarist perspective as creating a divided and weak policymaking structure. The president, while potentially strong, is checked by Congress, which in addition to being independently elected has control over certain major functions, such as the tax and budgeting process. Congress and the presidency are often controlled by different parties, exacerbating the political stakes of institutional rivalry. Party discipline is also weak, since members of Congress can get elected without much party support. Unlike the British Parliament, Congress with its entrepreneurial members and elaborate committee system can be an independent force in the policy process.

Indeed, in the trade policy area Congress has rightful control through its constitutional authority over taxation and appropriations. Before the Great Depression, trade policy was wholly made in Congress, in the House Ways and Means Committee and the Senate Finance Committee. This pattern of control gave interest groups great access to and influence over the process. Dependent upon their local constituencies for reelection, members of Congress were keenly attuned to satisfying local interests, and trade policy allowed each member to do so through the logrolling process.[13] In this way, the United States developed a strongly protectionist policy that hurt both its domestic welfare and its relations with foreign countries.

In 1934 this structure was altered. Congress delegated some authority over trade to the president, for limited periods and restricted actions. Throughout the postwar period, Congress and the executive have shared formal control over trade, with various semi-independent organiza-

13. E. E. Schattschneider, *Politics, Pressures, and the Tariff* (Prentice-Hall, 1935).

tions—that is, the International Trade Commission and the U.S. Special Trade Representative—playing a role as well.[14] De facto jurisdiction over trade policy has been a contested terrain between the two branches. About every five years, control is renegotiated, with Congress affixing new terms to its delegation of authority to the president.[15] While some have argued that the delegation of authority to the executive has completely changed trade policymaking institutions, this is questionable.[16] Delegation to the executive has been strictly limited in time and substance. In each renegotiation, the executive has had to relinquish something in exchange. Under such an arrangement, then, according to the parliamentarist position, trade policy should be driven more by powerful interest groups that possess multiple access points to policymaking than by a consistent and national welfare-maximizing program or by foreign obligations and interests.

French representative institutions fall between those of the United States and Great Britain. The French have a multiparty system linked to single-member majority electoral rules, and their parties tend to be weakly institutionalized and faction-ridden. The system has coalesced into a four-party regime: two parties—the Gaullists and Republicans—on the right, and two parties—the Socialists and Communists—on the left.[17] In its structure, the Fifth Republic combines presidential and parliamentary institutions. Both are elected in separate elections, but the two are mutually dependent. Constitutionally, the president dominates the prime minister; he can appoint and dismiss the prime minister and dissolve the parliament. But the president lacks his own bureaucracy and has few advisers. He depends upon the prime minister for policymaking and for access to the bureaucracy and the National Assembly. The prime minister's office is "not only the main executive arm of government and the overall director of the administration, but also has critical policy functions in developing new initiatives."[18] The prime minister thus formulates and

14. Cohen, *Making of U.S. International Economic Policy*; and I. M. Destler, *American Trade Politics: System under Stress* (Washington: Institute for International Economics, 1986).

15. Helen Milner, "The Political Economy of U.S. Trade Policy: A Study of the Super 301 Provision of U.S. Trade Law," in Jagdish Bhagwati and Hugh T. Patrick, eds., *Aggressive Unilateralism: America's 301 Trade Policy and the World Trading System* (University of Michigan Press, 1990), pp. 163–80.

16. Destler, *American Trade Politics*; and Stephan Haggard, "The Institutional Foundations of Hegemony: Explaining the Reciprocal Trade Agreement Act of 1934," *International Organization*, vol. 42 (Winter 1988), pp. 91–120.

17. Philip Cerny and Martin Schain, *French Politics and Public Policy* (London: F. Pinter, 1980), pp. 13–18.

18. Douglas E. Ashford, *Policy and Politics in France: Living with Uncertainty* (Temple University Press, 1982), p. 51.

implements policy through his or her cabinet. The French system is complex; it features a division of authority, as in the United States, but one that is much less formal. It also creates a fusion of authority in the interdependence of the president and prime minister. The 1958 constitution attempted to combine parliamentary power with an independent executive, and "in the resulting lengthy text confusion competed with contradiction and ambiguity with obscurity."[19]

In this system, policymaking is more centralized than in the United States. The French legislature since 1958 has been weak. Strict constitutional limits circumscribe both the National Assembly's legislative jurisdiction and the duration of its sessions. Moreover, the government sets its own agenda and has a variety of mechanisms at its disposal to curtail debate and induce legislative assent to its proposals.[20]

In contrast to that of Great Britain, however, the French cabinet is also weak. It is an informal and flexible structure—"selecting a cabinet is a delicate political act."[21] Ministers tend to be more autonomous and divided than in Britain, and the prime minister has less control over them, in part due to his or her dependence on the president. French ministers have their own sizable cabinets, and because of the party system, ministers often represent different parties or political factions within the prime minister's own party. The lack of party discipline and the coalitional basis of French government have meant that the ministers possess more independence than in Great Britain and that centralized control is more difficult to achieve.

As in Britain, formal trade policy in France is in the hands of the EC, though the structure of French policymaking remains important. Unlike the process in the United States, trade policymaking in France takes place within one set of institutions, the ministries, in particular the Ministry of Foreign Trade and Industry. (As in Britain, these two departments, trade and industry, have at times been constituted as separate bodies.) The key player in the combined ministry is the Directorate of External Economic Relations, which was once part of the Finance Ministry and is now part of the Foreign Trade Ministry.[22] Being in charge of the government's finances, the Finance Ministry still plays a role in trade

19. Vincent Wright, *The Government and Politics of France* (New York: Holmes and Meier, 1978), p. 23.

20. John Frears, "The French Parliament: Loyal Workhorse, Poor Watchdog," *West European Politics*, vol. 13 (July 1990), pp. 32–51.

21. Ashford, *Policy and Politics in France*, p. 54.

22. Cohen, *Making of U.S. International Economic Policy*, pp. 131–36; and Helen V. Milner, *Resisting Protectionism: Global Industries and the Politics of International Trade* (Princeton University Press, 1988), pp. 264–89.

policy, as do the Foreign Ministry and various committees on European foreign policy coordination.

Although control over national trade policy seems centralized, as in Great Britain, this has depended on a unique situation in French politics: between 1958 and 1986, the president's party also led the National Assembly, ensuring more coordination than otherwise possible. In the divided system of the 1986–88 period, when the president and prime minister came from opposite ends of the political spectrum, trade policy looked more decentralized. The president claimed control over international issues, while the prime minister claimed economic ones. Where did trade policy fall? During a longer period of cohabitation, national trade policymaking might come to resemble a divided system, as in the United States.

The fusion of parliamentary and presidential systems in France, combined with the centralization of policymaking in the ministries, suggests a policy outcome between the American and British ones. The greater the extent to which the French president's party can control the parliament, the more like the British system it should become. The more divided control becomes, both between the president and the Assembly and within the Assembly, the more likely trade policy will be an incoherent and interest group–driven issue area, in the American style.

Administrative Institutions and Trade Policymaking

While France's representative institutions have advantages and disadvantages for maintaining international commitments in trade policy, its bureaucratic institutions are seen as highly distinctive. Among Western industrial democracies, France is often viewed as the quintessential "strong" state.[23] It is said to possess a highly centralized and unified policymaking apparatus, embodied in the trade arena in the dominant influence of the Ministry of Foreign Trade and Industry. France's bureaucracy is said to be professional, independent from other political and social actors, and bound by a strong esprit de corps. Its administrative structure has also been blessed with control over numerous instruments for affecting trade, ranging from central planning to customs outposts in Poitiers. Finally, it is manned by civil servants who have a strong ideological predisposition toward an active policy—a mercantilist bent—and a coherent set of policy goals, which are widely shared. This structure has supposedly given the bureaucracy great capacity to shape and implement integrated policies in pursuit of "the national interest," albeit through protectionist measures.

23. See Milner, *Resisting Protectionism*, pp. 274–88.

As one scholar concludes, "[Its] state bureaucracy, partially able to shelter itself from parliament and to influence the industrial sector directly, has been able to maneuver to protect national interests in an economically interdependent world . . . [and has] succeeded in its basic task of promoting rapid growth and the modernization of industry and commerce."[24] According to this argument, one would expect the French to have a coherent trade policy that promoted "state-led" transformations of industries to enhance their competitiveness.

The United States is described in terms directly opposite to those of France. It is the paradigmatic "weak" state,[25] with a decentralized and divided policymaking structure, and Congress and the president vying for control over trade. The U.S. bureaucracy is staffed with political appointees who change frequently; top-level administrators are not professional, long-term civil servants. The number of policy instruments is limited, since selective firm- or industry-level intervention is not practiced. Finally, the bureaucracy is immobilized by a liberal, antistatist ideology that sings the virtues of free markets.[26] This structure, it is claimed, undermines attempts at coherent policymaking directed at broad national interests. It promotes the influence of powerful domestic groups that press their own agendas. Policy, especially regarding trade, is likely to be ad hoc and particularistic as a result.[27] As Stephen Krasner predicted for the period after the early 1970s,

> Because of the weakness of the U.S. political system, that is, the ability of private groups to check state initiatives, public officials were constantly faced with domestic political constraints. These constraints were more apparent in the area of commercial policy, where decisions involved Congress and executive agencies susceptible to societal influences. . . . The decline of America's external power, which became

24. John Zysman, "The French State in the International Economy," in Katzenstein, ed., *Between Power and Plenty*, pp. 291–92.

25. See Milner, *Resisting Protectionism*, pp. 274–88.

26. Stephen D. Krasner, *Defending the National Interest: Raw Materials Investments and U.S. Foreign Policy* (Princeton University Press, 1978). Krasner, in discussing another policy area, suggests that the U.S. state is stronger in part because of its Lockean liberal ideology. In trade, this would suggest that the United States has greater capacity to resist protectionist appeals, no matter what its institutions look like. His argument in the Katzenstein volume about trade policy seems to differ, however.

27. For an analysis of why trade policy may be more fragmented than other policy areas, see Joanne Gowa, "Public Goods and Political Institutions: Trade and Monetary Policy Processes in the United States," *International Organization*, vol. 42 (Winter 1988), pp. 15–32. But this argument should apply cross-nationally, no matter what political institutions exist.

evident in the mid-1960s, was accompanied by growing demands for protection as more sectors of the American economy were adversely affected by foreign trade. This has led to increasing *incoherence* in U.S. policy.[28]

British bureaucratic institutions are "stronger" than their American counterparts, but "weaker" than in France. Hence British trade policies should exhibit characteristics of each. As noted above, the British administrative apparatus is centralized and unified, perhaps even more so than the French system. The Department of Trade and Industry holds responsibility for trade policy, and the strong cabinet system may force more coordination in the policymaking process. The British civil service, like France's, is highly professional and boasts a strong esprit de corps. It too has the potential to be highly autonomous from Parliament and special interests. On two other dimensions, however, British institutions resemble American ones. The British lack the full panoply of policy instruments, especially a selective industrial policy capacity, that the French supposedly have. In the mid-1960s and early 1970s, the British tried to establish such a planning and industrial policy capacity, but much of this effort was abandoned by the Thatcher government in the 1980s.[29] The British also lack an activist ideology; pragmatism and a concern for the maintenance of a liberal international economy seem to have guided policy.[30] In the British case, a centralized and insulated policymaking structure is unaccompanied by a coherent set of goals and policy instruments. Thus the two former characteristics should lend coherence to trade policy, while the latter should make policy more liberal.

In light of these arguments about bureaucratic institutions, trade policy should be most coherent though also highly protectionist in France, most incoherent but also fairly liberal in the United States, and both liberal and fairly coherent in Great Britain. This set of expectations generates a different pattern of outcomes than did the more limited "parliamentarist" focus on democratic political institutions alone. According to that perspective, Britain should have a more coherent as well as more liberal policy than France, and U.S. policies should be protectionist as well as particularistic.

28. Stephen D. Krasner, "U.S. Commercial and Monetary Policy: Unravelling the Paradox of External Strength and Internal Weakness," in Katzenstein, ed., *Between Power and Plenty*, p. 51. (Emphasis added.)

29. Hall, *Governing the Economy*, pp. 52, 91–93; and Vincent Cable, *Protectionism and Industrial Decline* (London: Hodder and Stoughton, 1983), pp. 222–23.

30. Katzenstein, "Conclusion," pp. 308–14.

Patterns of Trade Policy

The previous sections have suggested how these nations, because of their individual political institutions, might have systematically different trade policies. The issue addressed in this section is whether British, French, and American policies in fact differed in the 1970s and 1980s and, if so, how?

This discussion adopts a high level of generalization in its analysis. It asks if broad institutional structures have affected overall policy outputs. It does not delve into detail about the policy process for two reasons. First, if institutions matter in policymaking, there should be systematic differences in policy outcomes, and institutional effects should show up in aggregate measures of policy outcomes. Second, an overall view of trade policy is desirable since specific processes for making policy vary significantly by product and over time. In most advanced industrial countries, no single process for formulating trade policies exists. Often, how policies are made for different sectors differs as much within a country as across them. To discuss any one case may mislead about others.

Aggregate statistics hold perils of their own, however. For example, measures of nontariff barriers usually do not account for the intensity of their restrictiveness. Thus, for two voluntary export restraints (VERs) on automobiles that prevent the respective entry of 5 percent and 95 percent of the cars that otherwise would have been imported, simple measures of the percentage of trade covered by NTBs would not differentiate between the two.[31] A second methodology for estimating nontariff barriers compares actual import levels for various countries with those predicted by a model that controls for natural barriers to trade such as transportation costs. This method has problems of its own, however.[32]

While aggregate statistics clearly should be used with caution, they nevertheless show interesting patterns and trends. Most striking, the trade policies pursued by Great Britain, France, and the United States over the past two decades appear quite similar. All three have reduced their tariffs on manufactured goods to negligible levels, as they agreed to do in the GATT negotiations. By 1987, these tariffs averaged between 4 and 5 percent for the three states.[33] While tariff protection declined,

31. Indeed, countries with highly restrictive nontariff barriers may be listed as quite unrestrictive as measured by conventional statistics, since each protected sector will account for a very small share of total trade. This problem affects other trade measures as well.

32. See Luca Barbone, "Import Barriers: An Analysis of Time-Series Cross-Section Data," *OECD Economic Studies*, no. 1 (Autumn 1988), pp. 155–68.

33. Joan Pearce and John Sutton with Roy Batchelor, *Protection and Industrial Policy in Europe* (London: Royal Institute of International Affairs, 1985), p. 33.

Table 1. *Measures of Trade Restrictiveness in Three OECD Countries,*
Selected Years
Percent

Study and item of interest	Year	Share of sectoral imports affected by nontariff barriers		
		France	Great Britain	United States
Page				
Manufactures	1981	16.2	17.4	21.0
Kelly and others				
Manufactures	1981	11.2	10.2	11.7
	1986	15.4	12.8	17.9
Laird and Yeats				
All nonpetroleum products	1981	15.7	11.2	11.4
	1983	18.8	13.4	13.7
	1986	18.6	12.8	17.3
Barbone[a]				
Total imports	1974–84	−0.190**	0.087	−0.027
		(0.043)	(0.045)	(0.062)
Manufactured goods	1974–84	−0.139*	0.290**	0.163
		(0.066)	(0.067)	(0.951)
Nonmanufactured goods	1974–84	−0.167**	0.065	−0.089
		(0.056)	(0.058)	(0.080)

Sources: S. A. B. Page, "The Revival of Protectionism and its Consequences for Europe," *Journal of Common Market Studies*, vol. 20 (September 1981), p. 29; Margaret Kelly and others, *Issues and Developments in International Trade Policy* (International Monetary Fund, 1988), p. 122, table A8; Sam Laird and Alexander Yeats, *Quantitative Methods for Trade Barrier Analysis* (New York University Press, 1991); and Luca Barbone, "Import Barriers: An Analysis of Time-Series Cross-Section Data," *OECD Economic Studies*, no. 1 (Autumn 1988), p. 163.
*Confidence at 5 percent level.
**Confidence at 1 percent level.
a. Data are country dummies. Numbers in parentheses are standard errors.

nontariff barriers rose; antidumping investigations, safeguard measures against imports, and voluntary export restraints grew substantially.[34] Indeed, the level of "managed trade" (that is, the percentage of traded goods affected by nontar f controls) for manufactured goods increased in the two decades. It rose from less than 1 percent in 1974 to almost 20 percent by the 1980s.

A summary of recent data on cross-national trends in trade restrictions is presented in table 1; it draws on both of the methodologies discussed above and suggests several conclusions. The first point, which is striking, is that direct measures of NTB protection appear roughly equivalent in

34. Pearce and Sutton, *Protection and Industrial Policy in Europe*, pp. 41–44; Judith Goldstein, "The Political Economy of Trade: Institutions of Protection," *American Political Science Review*, vol. 80 (March 1986), pp. 161–84; and Judith Goldstein, "Ideas, Institutions, and American Trade Policy," *International Organization*, vol. 42 (Winter 1988), pp. 179–217.

the three countries. In part, these data reflect the broad similarities among the states—they are advanced, industrial, Western democracies. Nevertheless, by a number of the measures in the table, Britain appears slightly less protectionist. This may provide some support for the idea that its political structures make it less prone to internal and external pressures to insulate its industries. But the data cannot sort out whether Britain's relative liberalism arises from its parliamentary system, as "first-tier" arguments suggest, or from its "second-tier" party government institutions.[35] Also, the two methods for assessing nontariff barriers outlined above produce different results. Models of import "deficits" or "surpluses" suggest that France is more protectionist in both manufactured and nonmanufactured goods. Yet direct measures of nontariff barriers, which do not control for the intensity of restrictions, do not support the notion of France as a protectionist outlier—indeed, the United States was the more protectionist by the mid-1980s. Finally, levels of protection have been rising in all three countries, especially in the late 1980s. This growth was greatest in the United States and least in Great Britain. Consistent with the parliamentarist argument, this finding suggests that parliamentary systems may do better at enabling elites to maintain their international commitments against strong domestic forces. The aggregate data, then, may provide some support for institutionalist arguments, despite the strong similarities they reveal.

Similarities in the three states' policies extend beyond the overall levels of trade protection. Each of the countries has protected the same types of industries. Textiles and clothing, steel, shoes, automobiles, electronic goods, and shipbuilding have been the most protected sectors in all three.[36] As one assessment of Great Britain and France, together with West Germany, concluded, "By and large the three governments have tended to promote the same 'strategic' sectors and defend the same problem sectors, with aerospace, electronics and nuclear energy in the first group, and coal, shipbuilding, textiles and steel (and increasingly cars) in the second."[37] This assessment could easily be extended to the United States. Both first-tier and second-tier arguments about institutions suggest that the pattern of protection across the countries should vary. A parliamentary system coherently promoting the broad national interest

35. An alternative explanation could be the strength of its international banking and trading sectors, which are antiprotectionist.
36. Margaret Kelly and others, *Issues and Developments in International Trade Policy* (International Monetary Fund, 1988), pp. 25–28; and Pearce and Sutton, *Protection and Industrial Policy in Europe*, pp. 41–44.
37. Roger Morgan and Caroline Bray, *Partners and Rivals in Western Europe: Britain, France, and Germany* (Brookfield, Vt.: Gower, 1986), p. 49.

should choose to support different sectors than a divided checks-and-balances system responding to interest group pressures. Likewise, a "strong" administrative system should develop a different pattern of protection than a "weak" one. These expectations of trade policy variance, in levels as well as products, are not well supported by the extant data.

Explaining Trade Policy

Trade policies in the three countries have resembled each other. Although their timing has differed, they have protected the same industries at about the same levels in the same rather incoherent fashion. This suggests two conclusions. First, the common outcomes derive from some powerful, general forces at work across the three countries. Second, insofar as institutions influence capabilities to make and maintain international commitments, these effects are probably contingent on the existence of other factors and may vary over time. The evidence provides strong support for the first of these conclusions and some support for the second.

1. *Common crises faced by the three countries promoted similar policy responses.* Over the past two decades, Britain, France, and the United States confronted three jarring economic changes. In the early 1970s, the United States abruptly ended the fixed exchange rate system that had provided a stable international monetary environment over the postwar period. This system was replaced by one of floating exchange rates, which produced great exchange rate instability. Planning became more difficult as flux predominated. Trade flows were affected too. Imports flooded countries when their exchange rates were seriously overvalued (for example, Great Britain in the 1980s and the United States in 1981–85) and generated great pressure for protection. In addition, the two oil price shocks, accompanied as they were by an increase in raw materials' prices in the 1970s and a collapse of both sets of prices in the 1980s, produced a second economic upheaval affecting the three countries. Trade flows were reshaped to some extent, and industries faced decreased profitability. Moreover, the need to export manufactured goods to pay for increased imports rose. Finally, the countries saw their competitive advantages altered dramatically. As East Asian and Latin American NICs and East European nations entered industrial markets, the three countries experienced rapidly increasing import penetration in manufactured goods, especially mass-produced consumer goods. But the countries, especially Britain

and France, also were beset by rising competition in high-technology products, largely from Japan. For each nation, import penetration grew in the same sectors. Loss of competitiveness and high uncertainty characterized the new environment.

High levels of unemployment, slower growth, rising imports, and periods of currency instability developed in all three countries. Protecting industries under economic pressure seemed a natural response. (Indeed, one of the best predictors of the cross-sectional level of protection in all three countries has been the level of import penetration.)[38] Unemployment levels also influenced protectionist sentiment. Industries idling large numbers of workers and facing import surges were the most likely to get help: steel, autos, textiles, and consumer electronics are the obvious cases.

Institutional arguments suggest that the countries' individual political structures should shield them from these internal and external pressures to differing degrees. In general, the two European states should be more able to manage these pressures and develop coherent policies. Yet all three states remain deeply intertwined in the international economy, and changes in the international economy have large effects on their domestic markets. Trade has become an increasingly important part of their economic activity, accounting for roughly 20 percent of gross national product (GNP) by the 1980s.[39] The Europeans are more involved than the Americans; estimates for Britain, for instance, place its ratio of total trade to GNP at almost 50 percent by the late 1970s.[40] With this factor in mind, the United States, with its lower trade dependence and large size (relative to the world economy), should be the most able to resist external pressures, since they will be less compelling. Nevertheless, the similar economic policy responses of the three states seem to reflect the common external problems confronted by the three. Despite their differences, none could escape from these external pressures.

2. *Politicians in the three countries faced similar electoral pressures and similar reliance on domestic industries.* Although international economic events exerted common pressures, each political system absorbed the difficulties in its own way. To note the likeness of policies does not imply that domestic politics made no difference; rather, it points to *similarities* in the domestic process that require exposition.

38. Cable, *Protectionism and Industrial Decline*, p. 47; Robert E. Baldwin, *The Political Economy of U.S. Import Policy* (MIT Press, 1985); and Goldstein, "Ideas and Institutions," especially pp. 195, 213.

39. Morgan and Bray, *Partners and Rivals in Western Europe*, pp. 36–37; Cable, *Protectionism and Industrial Decline*, p. 22; and Milner, *Resisting Protectionism*, p. 266.

40. Roy Jenkins, *Britain and the EEC* (London: Macmillan, 1983), p. 91.

The political leaders in Great Britain, France, and the United States face recurrent votes of confidence in the form of elections. Voters' decisions in these elections are substantially based on their economic situations.[41] Poor economic performance by a government (a record of high unemployment or inflation) is likely to cause electoral losses. Thus political leaders in all three states must respond to economic problems if they want to stay in office. Bureaucrats, too, respond to economic pressures. Even if the bureaucracies are insulated from partisan politics and relatively autonomous from the legislature, they still rely on interest groups for information, advice, implementation, and, sometimes, future jobs, giving these groups privileged access to state institutions. In addition, state bureaucracies may find that their best weapon in bureaucratic fights with other agencies is an alliance with societal groups. For these reasons, bureaucrats may depend on interest groups as much as politicians do.

The similarities in British, French, and American trade policy seem to result from the patterns of interaction between policymakers and domestic social groups. In the U.S. case, few analysts puzzle over the role of interest groups; most agree the political system is porous to domestic pressures. The U.S. checks-and-balances system and its "weak" administrative structure allow interest groups multiple points of access and prompt officials to be responsive to their problems.[42] Surges in import penetration, rising unemployment, and downward pressure on profitability tend to lead to demands for protection by certain industries and to protectionist policy responses. By contrast, the desire for a liberal trade policy among internationally oriented firms can help explain the more liberal aspects of U.S. trade policy.[43]

The British have achieved a somewhat more liberal policy than Americans; they do, however, remain vulnerable to domestic pressures despite their more centralized institutional structure. In part, the trade policy process is not as immune to political influence as the institutional arguments suggest. First, quarrels among bureaucratic departments reduce the coherence of decisionmaking and improve societal groups' access to policymakers. In trade policy, there have been "unavoidable problems

41. While controversy reigns over exactly how these evaluations are made (retrospectively or prospectively, subjectively or objectively, for the individual or for the nation), there is agreement that economic performance affects who wins elections.
42. See Krasner, "U.S. Commercial and Monetary Policy"; Zysman, *Governments, Markets, and Growth*; and Milner, *Resisting Protectionism*, especially chap. 8.
43. Milner, *Resisting Protectionism*; I. M. Destler and John S. Odell, *Antiprotection: Changing Forces in United States Trade Politics* (Washington: Institute for International Economics, 1987); and Jagdish Bhagwati, *Protectionism* (MIT Press, 1988).

of reconciling conflicting goals within a large and complex field. The British government's ability to identify and to choose among divergent goals . . . has not always been high. Part of the explanation for this lay in the compartmentalized structure of Whitehall, part in the secrecy which . . . clouds the policy-making process; but part also lay in the limited perspectives of ministers as well as civil servants."[44] Others point out that this structure favors protectionist interests because "the style of decision-making in Britain . . . shields the costs and benefits of trade measures from close public scrutiny."[45]

Second, the influence of Parliament is understated. Its role is to transmit societal pressures to the bureaucracy, just as in the United States. Although "Parliament has no direct means of formulating trade policy, . . . few MPs in marginal seats would risk being accused of not defending the livelihood of their constituents, and almost all, including those in safe seats, would consider it a duty to speak up for local industries."[46] MPs do not attempt to legislate trade policy, but they do exert indirect influence on policymaking in support of particular interest groups.[47]

In addition to Parliament, interest groups have gained access to trade policy through the party system.[48] Policy decisions at the highest levels of government can reflect the influence of domestic groups through the party system. The Labour party, supported by the Trade Union Congress, has since the early 1970s pushed for a strongly protectionist policy, while in the 1980s the Conservatives, backed by the Confederation of British Industry, favored a more mixed policy.[49] Some have speculated that a Labour party victory in the 1980s would have meant a significant turn to protectionism. If so, this casts doubt on the parliamentarist argument: a change in the party controlling government, reflecting shifting societal interests, might have led to changes in policy. This also could have been the outcome in the United States if the Democrats had won control of the presidency in the 1980s.

Finally, British industries themselves have been intimately involved in trade policymaking within the bureaucracy. They have played a large

44. Wallace, *Foreign Policy Process in Britain*, p. 162.
45. Cable, *Protectionism and Industrial Decline*, pp. 262–63.
46. Cable, *Protectionism and Industrial Decline*, p. 218.
47. Cable argues that "overall, the role of MPs is important, but the importance lies not only in mobilising and reflecting 'public opinion' but also in bringing pressure to bear upon ministers in their capacity as heads of departments; and ministers are, after all, usually ambitious and eager to please. The main part played by MPs, then, in relation to pressure groups, is helping them to unlock the door of the passage leading to Whitehall." Cable, *Protectionism and Industrial Decline*, p. 219.
48. Hall, *Governing the Economy*, pp. 64–65.
49. Cable, *Protectionism and Industrial Decline*, pp. 12–15.

role because of their hold over critical information, their ability to implement policy, and policymakers' own views of the legitimacy of their influence.[50] For example, British industries have tended to negotiate VERs on their own. The Official White Paper of 1981 on Trade Policy states that " 'industry to industry discussions' are commended as a means 'to resolve specific structural trade problems.' "[51] The government has in effect delegated part of trade policy to industry.

The formulation of British interests in trade also appears driven by domestic forces. As one scholar describes it, "to a considerable extent, the 'national interests' which the British government is promoting and defending abroad *are* those of British finance and industry. . . . In most sectors governmental success is measured by its ability to promote and protect particular interests."[52] Thus, despite its formal institutional arrangements, the British trade policy process is enmeshed in bureaucratic politics, subjected to political pressures from Parliament and parties, and dependent upon industries for policy formulation and implementation. It is no wonder that this system produces fairly incoherent policies responsive to industries' immediate economic problems, especially import competition.

In France, the centralized structure of policymaking is also penetrated by political and domestic social forces. Many scholars see the French bureaucracy as fraught with internal conflicts and closely allied with domestic societal groups.[53] The state's fractiousness reflects the extreme fragmentation of French society;[54] political differences have been embedded in the policy process. Since French parties are factionalized and governing majorities have traditionally been coalitions, ministries have been staffed at the top level by individuals representing different factions or

50. Wallace, *Foreign Policy Process in Britain*, p. 180.

51. Paul Henderson, "Trade Policies: Trends, Issues and Influences," *Midland Bank Review* (Winter 1983), p. 13.

52. Wallace, *Foreign Policy Process in Britain*, p. 160.

53. For example, see Jack Hayward, *The State and the Market Economy: Industrial Patriotism and Economic Intervention in France* (New York University Press, 1986); Milner, *Resisting Protectionism*, especially chap. 8; Sonia Mazey, "Public Policy-Making in France: The Art of the Possible," *West European Politics*, vol. 9 (July 1986), pp. 412–28; Harvey B. Feigenbaum, *The Politics of Public Enterprise: Oil and the French State* (Princeton University Press, 1985); and Ezra N. Suleiman, *Private Power and Centralization in France: The Notaires and the State* (Princeton University Press, 1987).

54. "The ministers directly responsible for economic policy were patently divided, and this was probably inevitable, since they defended different departmental interests, belonged to different ideological trends within the Socialist Party, and were political rivals." Howard Machin and Vincent Wright, *Economic Policy and Policy-making under the Mitterand Presidency, 1981–1984* (St. Martin's Press, 1985), p. 15.

parties. This contributes to bureaucratic turf battles, which allow societal interests access to the state as ministers use them to support their positions. It also leads to an "acute problem of imposing coherence and coordination" on trade policy.[55]

Furthermore, as in Britain, industries in France are deeply involved in trade policymaking. The political structure encourages this. Since French "groups cannot rely on political parties to achieve their aims, nor does parliament have the power to protect their interests, . . . the relationships between groups and policymaking [are], in some ways, more direct than in the Anglo-Saxon parliamentary model."[56] Industries are directly involved in negotiations over trade policy in France. They provide essential information to policymakers, help carry out policies, and play a large role in shaping the conception of French interests.[57] That French trade policy therefore reflects the demands of its distressed industries is not surprising, given bureaucratic divisions, political influences, and industry involvement in the policy process.

3. *Similar trade policy outcomes were induced by common international regimes (the norms, rules, institutions, and procedures for trade policymaking) in which the three states were embedded.* As contracting members of GATT, all three countries are obliged to conform to its norms and rules. The benefits brought by the liberalization of trade through GATT, plus other less tangible benefits, such as the lowering of transaction costs and the provision of information, are reasons why these states mostly meet their GATT obligations. At times, though, the three have violated their commitments when protectionist interests became irresistible. But no systematic difference in their levels of violation appears, as their similar levels of "managed trade," which are inconsistent with GATT, reveal.[58]

For the most part, though, GATT commitments have been kept and have bolstered the trade-liberalizing forces within these states. Fears of retaliation by other countries and loss of face internationally have discouraged these countries from breaking their commitments. As one scholar noted about Great Britain, "Another factor in the choice of [trade policy]

55. Machin and Wright, *Economic Policy*, pp. 9–10.

56. Ashford, *Policy and Politics in France*, pp. 59–60.

57. For more details, see Milner, *Resisting Protectionism*, chaps. 5, 8.

58. The United States may be more in violation in some areas; see Robert E. Hudec, "Thinking About the New Section 301," in Bhagwati and Patrick, *Aggressive Unilateralism*, pp. 113–59. The United State's new section 301 may also lead to massive violations of the spirit of GATT; see Milner, "Political Economy of U.S. Trade Policy" in the same volume, pp. 163–80.

instruments is the role of international trade rules and the force of likely international reaction."[59] The French, too, have been susceptible to these external pressures. "Some dissatisfaction with VERs on imports from Japan is discernible in France; . . . these [reservations] stem from the fact that VERs are becoming internationally less respectable."[60] Similar sets of international rules and norms embodied in GATT have exerted further pressure for convergent policies in the three states.

Finally, British and French policy have converged because of the EC's growing role in trade issues. By law, trade policy, at least in the form of import restrictions, is not controlled by London or Paris, but by Brussels.[61] Since Britain joined in the early 1970s, the two countries' trade policies have converged. The EC's policy has involved the same trends as discussed for each country: lower tariffs and higher nontariff barriers.[62] Although each country retains a measure of de facto control over its trade policies, the EC has been expanding its jurisdiction in large part because the states have desired it. The more integrated European market envisioned by the 1992 process reflects, and will propel, growing EC control and will push countries' policies even closer together. A part of the pressure for this internal trade liberalization has come about because of the effects of common external threats and domestic pressures. The stiff competitive challenge posed by U.S. and Japanese producers made European industries and states realize that a more unified European market was essential to their future competitiveness.[63] The increasing weight of the EC's common trade policy has thus engendered further similarities in French and British policies.

4. *Britain's party government parliamentary system aided the Thatcher government in resisting protectionist pressures in the 1980s, but only in concert with other factors, such as a strong commitment from the Conservative government.* The British did marginally better than the French or American governments at keeping their markets open. As the parliamentarist argument claims, Britain's system may have given political leaders the opportunity *not* to respond to certain domestic pressures. But

---

59. Cable, *Protectionism and Industrial Decline*, p. 236. A desire to live up to international commitments in foreign economic matters has been adduced as a central factor in the shaping of British postwar policy in general. See Stephen Blank, "Britain: The Politics of Foreign Economic Policy, the Domestic Economy, and the Problem of Pluralistic Stagnation," in Katzenstein, ed., *Between Power and Plenty*, pp. 89–137.

60. Pearce and Sutton, *Protection and Industrial Policy in Europe*, pp. 62–63.

61. Pearce and Sutton, *Protection and Industrial Policy in Europe*, p. 40.

62. Pearce and Sutton, *Protection and Industrial Policy in Europe*, p. 12.

63. Pearce and Sutton, *Protection and Industrial Policy in Europe*, p. 84; and Wayne Sandholtz and John Zysman, "1992: Recasting the European Bargain," *World Politics*, vol. 42 (October 1989), pp. 95–128.

in general, political institutions do not seem to provide consistent advantages for making and maintaining international commitments; instead institutional effects are better conceptualized as opportunities and risks that are only actualized in concert with noninstitutional factors. Britain's relatively insulated parliamentary system may have facilitated governmental resistance to protectionist pressures, but it was not in itself sufficient to explain the relatively modest increases in NTBs in the 1980s. The Conservative government's attachment to a free market ideology was also an important factor. In addition, the relative strength of Britain's antiprotectionist banking and trading sectors, compared with those in the United States or France, helps account for its ability to maintain its international commitments.

Conclusion

The economic crises and changes of the 1970s and 1980s elicited similar trade policy responses in Great Britain, France, and the United States. Constrained by high levels of international economic interdependence and a turbulent world economy, the three countries reacted in rather incoherent ways, protecting and promoting basically the same group of distressed industries. None of the countries seems to have fashioned a policy that was substantially more liberal or coherent than the others. The electoral pressures common to competitive democracies, the bureaucratic divisions and overlap in complex organizations, and policymakers' reliance on economic actors for information and policy implementation have necessarily infused the policy process with politics. Consequently, the raw capabilities that institutions provide may not be transformed into policy outputs; other factors can intervene and prove decisive. A focus on institutions alone provides a limited understanding of trade policy in advanced industrial countries. The nature of domestic interest groups, the goals of political elites, and the constraints of the international system have stronger effects on trade policymaking than do institutions; they seem to mediate the institutional effects that are visible. Nonetheless, the argument about the advantages of certain parliamentary systems is supported to some extent by the marginally superior performance of the British party government system. Other factors, however, are also important in explaining this case. The cases and data presented here do not enable one to sort out definitively the effects of first-tier institutional factors either from second-tier ones or from other noninstitutional influences. A comparison among more cases is needed to assess systematically the influence of these different factors.

Edward A. Kolodziej

Nuclear Weapons and Policy Stability

*T*his chapter compares the effects of parliamentary and separation-of-powers systems on policy stability and resource targeting as they apply to making and implementing strategic nuclear policies in the United States, Britain, and France. All three countries receive high marks for stability of operational policies despite wide variations in the levels of conflict over nuclear policy that they have experienced and their very different mechanisms for resolving these conflicts. The French Fifth Republic has proved the most successful in building consensus on nuclear policy among otherwise sharply divided political factions and parties. In contrast, Britain's postwar party and societal divisions became progressively polarized over nuclear policy and the policymaking process, but governmental policy nevertheless remained stable. The United States is somewhere between the other two in its level of conflict, but its institutions and decision processes have shown considerable flexibility and adaptability in managing internal divisions.

The United States has, however, been considerably less efficient than the other countries in targeting its resources effectively. Redundant nuclear capabilities have multiplied, and competing offensive and defensive systems, based on conflicting strategic rationales, have been simultaneously supported as national nuclear policy. Inefficiency has been part of the price of maintaining policy stability to accommodate competing groups urging major shifts in U.S. nuclear policy. Partly because they have fewer economic and technological resources, Britain and France have been forced to be more efficient in building their nuclear systems. These are much smaller than those of Washington and Moscow, but still formidable in their ability to destroy adversary cities and industrial centers.[1]

1. For a description of U.S., British, and French strategic nuclear capabilities, consult International Institute for Strategic Studies, *The Military Balance: 1992–1993* (London:

Political Institutions and Government Capabilities

Many policies require substantial stability to be effective. Stability is particularly important in nuclear weapons policies. For deterrence to work, adversaries must have confidence in each other's intentions. And developing new weapons systems is extraordinarily expensive and requires a very long lead time.

Political institutions may affect policy stability in a variety of ways. From a "parliamentarist" perspective, the major risk associated with the U.S system of separation of powers is the constant jockeying for policy influence between the president, executive agencies, and various subunits of Congress. As political tides shift, so may policy. This is particularly the case in foreign and security policy, where the necessity of presidential leadership is almost universally recognized, but where the power of Congress to modify or even reverse presidential initiatives is also beyond dispute.[2] From a "presidentialist" perspective, the multiple veto points in the U.S. separation-of-powers system make it difficult to drastically revise a policy once it has been enacted. The risk of a dramatic reversal—or a series of such reversals—in policy is potentially much higher in a parliamentary system, although this difference has not been prominent in nuclear policy, especially with respect to the strategic doctrines and operational policies of the three states under examination.

The distinction between parliamentary and separation-of-powers systems may disguise important differences in regime and government types within those systems. The British-style party government model is perhaps the parliamentary type most likely to lead to significant policy reversals because changes in party control of government usually involve a complete transfer of power between two major party contenders.[3] Major policy change may be less likely in single-party-dominant and multiparty coalitional regimes because there is rarely wholesale turnover in the parties forming the government.[4] But when it does occur, of course, it may be significant. The biggest risk in a coalitional system,

Brassey's, 1992), pp. 231–321. For an analysis of British and French nuclear forces, see Edward A. Kolodziej, "Modernization of British and French Nuclear Forces: Arms Control and Security Dimensions," in Carl G. Jacobsen, ed., *The Uncertain Course: New Weapons, Strategies, and Mind-Sets* (Oxford University Press, 1987), pp. 239–54.

2. Of course, the exact boundaries of legitimate and desirable action by each party are open to debate, most notably in conflict over the War Powers Act.

3. Sven Steinmo, "Political Institutions and Tax Policy in the United States, Sweden, and Britain," *World Politics*, vol. 41 (July 1989), pp. 500–35.

4. Ronald Rogowski, "Trade and the Variety of Democratic Institutions," *International Organization*, vol. 41 (Spring 1987), pp. 203–23.

however, is that such systems may never be able to establish any clear policy baseline if coalition partners are riven by disagreements. The same sorts of arguments might be made about change in the U.S. system: development of a clear policy baseline and substantial policy change are least likely in periods of divided party government, and most likely when party control of the presidency and Congress change at the same time—a very rare event of late. Oscillations in party control of the presidency or one or both houses of Congress do not appear to have had any appreciable effect on the stability of U.S. nuclear policy, which has maintained a remarkable consistency since the 1960s. In contrast, the mixed presidential-parliamentary system of the French Fifth Republic was designed to insulate presidential responsibility for national defense and nuclear policy from divisive parliamentary party politics and from the precarious legislative coalitions of the Fourth Republic—a design that proved remarkably workable in fostering stable nuclear policies.

"Third-tier" factors may also affect policy stability. For example, where bureaucracies are stable and relatively independent of elected politicians, policy will presumably be more stable. The experience of the French Fifth Republic suggests, however, that this generalization may not hold when a volatile fractionalized political process creates opportunities for bureaucratic intervention in pursuit of organizational and elite objectives. Bicameralism adds additional veto points to block policy change. Among noninstitutional factors, policy inheritances may have an especially important effect. Policies that distribute benefits widely, giving a variety of groups a stake in the status quo, will be particularly difficult to break; policies that distribute benefits narrowly or resist participation of opposing groups may be especially easy to modify under the pressure of external change or of major shifts in electoral preferences. And supranational commitments are an institutional constraint that may be especially important in making foreign policy: political elites may be reluctant to break commitments in trade and defense treaties, for example, regardless of their own views of the merits of those agreements. Conversely, in response to domestic constraints, international arms control accords may be cast in such broad terms—witness SALT II—that the signatory governments have considerable flexibility in managing internal conflict over treaty interpretations.

Hypotheses about institutional effects on governments' abilities to target resources effectively have already been discussed in detail in the chapter by Ellis Krauss and Jon Pierre, so only a brief reprise is needed here. A parliamentarist perspective suggests that parliamentary governments with tight party controls tend to limit group access and legislators' ability to campaign for local interests, while a presidentialist perspective suggests that the greater centralization of allocative activity in parliamentary systems simply leads to a different pattern of allocation rather than a more efficient one. Electoral rules that make legislators responsive to constituency pressures hinder efficient targeting, while autonomous and expert bureaucracies presumably are better at making targeting decisions. This expectation may not be realized where governmental units with overlapping responsibilities block efforts to coordinate their activities; an example is interservice rivalry over nuclear policy in the United States.

These generalizations, which have some empirical basis in other policy areas, need to be modified with respect to U.S. nuclear policy, especially concerning efficient resource targeting and elite consensus. The division of power between Congress and the president and its diffusion within the executive branch and the military services create an institutional setting and political process that favor coalition building more than care for cost or coherence in responding to external threats. U.S. institutions and a decentralized process of bargaining and decisionmaking have aided the domestic proliferation of nuclear weapons.

The Cases

The United States, Britain, and France—the three nuclear powers among Western industrial democracies—have a number of important institutional differences that influence policy stability and effective targeting of resources. Britain's parliamentary regime, based on single-member electoral districts, fosters a system of two dominant parties. In the post–World War II era, one of these parties has usually formed a single-party majority government. France, on the other hand, has had two quite different political regimes in the postwar era. Before 1958 it had a parliamentary system in which most governments were weak multiparty coalitions. The Fifth Republic initiated a "semipresidential" system based on direct election of the president. The president nominates the prime minister and can dissolve the legislature. The constitution assigns the president, who is also commander of the French armed forces, special status in overseeing security affairs. The nationalization of French elections, through the creation of a popularly elected president and a system of two-round majority elections to the National Assembly in single-member districts, has encouraged the consolidation of multiple party affiliation, characteristic of the Fourth Republic, into a four-party system—two of the right and two of the left.[5] In general, the president has been able to appoint prime ministers from his own bloc, if not party. The period of cohabitation between a Socialist president and Gaullist premier from 1986 to 1988 did not fundamentally upset these institutional arrangements. The United States, of course, has a pure separation-of-powers system with substantial periods of divided government.

Policy Stability and Weapons Procurement: The U.S. Case

Despite persistent conflict over nuclear strategies and weapons programs and the resultant appearance of policy instability, U.S. operational nuclear policies, particularly those affecting long-range nuclear weapons, have been remarkably stable in the past three decades. At the strategic level, they are keyed to what may be termed a "MAD-plus" posture, supported by elaborate weapons acquisition and modernization programs and complex nuclear targeting options. The mutual assured destruction (MAD) element of the formula was first defined by Secretary of Defense Robert McNamara as the ability of the United States to destroy one-third of the population and three-quarters of the productive resources of the Soviet Union in a second strike.[6] This constituted the commitment of the United States to deliver an unacceptable retaliatory blow against the Soviet Union in the event of an attack against U.S. territory or vital interests. The "plus" signified the actual targets and targeting plans devised by the United States to execute its nuclear policies.

The Stability of U.S. Nuclear Policies

After the early 1960s, U.S. nuclear targeting plans and long-range nuclear warheads were principally aimed at the corresponding nuclear capabilities of the Soviet Union and its war-fighting assets.[7] These targets are incorporated into the single integrated operational plan (SIOP), which also identifies available weapons and options for how they might be

5. The 1985 elections were conducted under a proportional representation system. France also has an indirectly elected Senate. See John Frears, "The French Parliament: Loyal Workhorse, Poor Watchdog," *West European Politics*, vol. 13 (July 1990), pp. 32–51.

6. Paul P. Craig and John A. Jungerman, *Nuclear Arms Race: Technology and Society* (McGraw-Hill, 1986), pp. 42, 51.

7. For early targeting plans, see David Alan Rosenberg, "The Origins of Overkill: Nuclear Weapons and American Strategy, 1945–1960," *International Security*, vol. 7 (Spring 1983), pp. 3–71.

employed by responsible political and military officials.[8] Although the SIOP has been constantly updated as weapons capabilities and political and strategic needs have evolved, the MAD-plus strategy survived persistent efforts to revise it. The same cannot be said for the dramatic December 1992 nuclear accord signed by Russian Federation President Boris Yeltsin and President George Bush. If both countries eventually succeed in lowering their strategic warhead totals to around 3,000 and eliminating their ground-based multiple warhead systems and increasingly shift to invulnerable sea-based systems to underwrite nuclear deterrence, these significant cuts will require a revision of the SIOP and major adjustments in force postures and deployments, but in ways that are still too early to tell. These exterior-driven changes do not, however, affect the generalizations developed below about how the U.S. nuclear policy process operated during the cold war.

Nuclear war-fighting and bargaining criteria rationalized the generation of MAD-plus capabilities. These criteria included sufficient nuclear forces to support extended deterrence, damage limitation, escalation control and dominance, quick termination of hostilities, and continuing bargaining leverage in the wake of a nuclear exchange. More and better nuclear weapons are needed to fulfill these criteria than would be needed to meet a simple MAD formula.[9] But the weapons cannot guarantee a

8. Desmond Ball and Robert C. Toth, "Revising the SIOP: Taking War-Fighting to Dangerous Extremes," *International Security*, vol. 14 (Spring 1990), p. 65.

9. It would be misleading to suggest that U.S. nuclear targeting does not change or that new criteria for deciding upon targets do not arise in SIOP planning. For example, nuclear planning in the middle of the 1970s and into the 1980s was extended to targets whose destruction would have seriously hampered, and perhaps irretrievably precluded, the socioeconomic and political recovery of the Soviet Union after an all-out nuclear exchange. These missions have since been downgraded, with targeting again concentrated largely on the Soviet Union's nuclear forces and leadership centers. The leading reference guide for the targeting plans of the nuclear states is Desmond Ball and Jeffrey Richelson, eds. *Strategic Nuclear Targeting* (Cornell University Press, 1986). Especially informative is Ball's chapter, "The Development of the SIOP, 1960–1983," pp. 57–83, and his *Can Nuclear War Be Controlled?* Adelphi Paper 169 (London: International Institute for Strategic Studies, 1981), and *Targeting for Strategic Deterrence*, Adelphi Paper 185 (London: IISS, 1983). Additional commentary can be found in Anthony H. Cordesman, *American Strategic Forces and Extended Deterrence*, Adelphi Paper 175 (London: IISS, 1982); Jeffrey Richelson, "PD-59, NSOD-13, and the Reagan Strategic Modernization Program," *Journal of Strategic Studies*, vol. 6 (June 1983), pp. 125–46; and Edward A. Kolodziej, "Nuclear Weapons in Search of a Role: Evolution of Recent American Strategic Nuclear and Arms Control Policy," in Paul R. Viotti, ed., *Conflict and Arms Control: An Uncertain Agenda* (Westview Press, 1986), pp. 3–23. The collapse of the Soviet Union would suggest the need for a fundamental overhaul and revision of the SIOP, but at this writing there is no accessible public information that these adaptations to radically different strategic imperatives in the post–cold war environment are being, or have been, made.

winning strategy because invulnerable long-range nuclear weapons, primarily sea-based strategic forces, preclude the ability of the United States
to disarm the nuclear forces of the CIS, and principally those of the
Russian Federation, in a first strike. Despite this shortcoming, U.S.
announced policy retains a first-use option, even in responding to a
conventional attack, notwithstanding efforts in the early 1980s by some
prominent members of the U.S. security community to gain public and
elite support for abandoning this commitment.[10]

Several factors should be kept in mind, quite apart from the U.S.
policy process that is the concern of this chapter, in attempting to explain
the evolution of U.S. nuclear forces and the adoption of a SIOP driven
by a MAD-plus strategy. First, U.S. perceptions of the Soviet nuclear
threat were critical. The gradual emergence of superpower nuclear parity
and the continued buildup and modernization of Soviet nuclear capabilities, especially heavy ground-based missile forces, furnished a powerful
impetus through most of the 1970s and 1980s for the expansion of U.S.
nuclear forces. Many in the United States believed that the Soviet Union
was bent on gaining nuclear superiority and implementing a war-fighting
strategy. (As a mirror image, the Soviet buildup may be partly explained
as a response to perceptions by Kremlin policymakers of U.S. efforts to
achieve nuclear ascendancy.)[11] Second, the United States, unlike its nuclear allies, had the economic and technoscientific means at its disposal
to choose either an all-out war-fighting posture, a MAD-plus posture,
or simply a MAD posture. Thus motive and means conditioned the
choice to pursue a MAD-plus stance since the late 1960s.

But the mere existence—even expansion—of Soviet nuclear capabilities and growing U.S. concern for the strategic implications of these
developments did not themselves dictate specific U.S. nuclear responses.
One would also have to examine U.S. global political and strategic aims,
including what were assumed by policymakers to be alliance obligations,
as well as widely held doctrinal views about the requirements of deterrence and the alleged bargaining leverage afforded by nuclear weapons,
to fully explain the U.S. nuclear capabilities and deterrence doctrine. A

10. The challenge to first use, launched by McGeorge Bundy and others, failed. See
McGeorge Bundy and others, "Nuclear Weapons and the Atlantic Alliance," *Foreign Affairs*,
vol. 60 (Spring 1982), pp. 753–68. It remains in place despite critics who were encouraged
by President Bush's fall 1991 nuclear proposals. See Morton H. Halperin, "What's the Use
of 'First Use'?" *New York Times*, September 28, 1991, p. A23.

11. For a magisterial review of the difficulty of estimating Soviet intentions, see Ray-
mond L. Garthoff, *Détente and Confrontation: American-Soviet Relations from Nixon to Reagan*
(Brookings, 1985).

discussion of these factors falls outside the scope of this discussion, although their importance is difficult to exaggerate.[12]

What is important here is to identify the contribution made by institutions and decisionmaking processes to the observed stability of U.S. nuclear policies. The diffusion and decentralized structure of these institutions and processes, prompted and sustained by the separation of powers between Congress and the president, has supported U.S. operational nuclear strategic policy and war-fighting targeting plans. Multiple access points exist within the policy process for the partisans of a war-fighting or a MAD-plus posture to press their claims. Bolstering these pressures are those of groups with narrower concerns associated with the acquisition of specific weapons or components. These various interests have converged on the policymaking process in successful efforts over the past three decades to increase spending for new weapons or to expand and perfect those systems already deployed or under development.

Proponents of nuclear weapons systems or partisans of a broad and varied nuclear posture—signified by the nuclear triad of sea-based and ground-based intercontinental ballistic missiles and long-range bombers—are not limited to the military services. Nor can an explanation of the triad be attributed solely to weapons contractors and their congressional and executive branch supporters. Support for expanded nuclear capabilities also extends beyond the military-industrial complex or the "iron triangle."[13] In the two major buildups of the postwar period, in the early Kennedy and Reagan years, the president, cooperating with congressional partisans and appointed civilian officials (most notably Secretaries of Defense Robert McNamara and Caspar Weinberger), pressed for more and better nuclear weapons systems in excess of the nuclear requirements then defined by the military services in their official spending requests. In the context of what appeared to be a clear, present, and enlarging Soviet danger, first in the late 1950s and again in the late 1970s,

12. Several books trace the evolution of U.S. strategic doctrine and weapons systems programs: Lawrence Freedman, *The Evolution of Nuclear Strategy*, 2d ed. (St. Martin's Press, 1989); Gregg Herken, *The Counsels of War* (Knopf, 1985); and Fred Kaplan, *The Wizards of Armageddon* (Simon and Schuster, 1983).

13. For a balanced, general review of the weapons procurement process, see Thomas L. McNaugher, *New Weapons, Old Politics: America's Military Procurement Muddle* (Brookings, 1989). Also relevant are Richard A. Stubbing, *The Defense Game: An Insider Explores the Astonishing Realities of America's Defense Establishment* (Harper and Row, 1986); Gordon Adams, *The Iron Triangle: The Politics of Defense Contracting* (Council on Economic Priorities, 1981); and J. Ronald Fox, *Arming America: How the U.S. Buys Weapons* (Harvard University, Graduate School of Business Administration, 1974).

the very diffusion of power centers between and within the two branches facilitated the promotion and maintenance of multiple nuclear systems. Out of this process of pulling and hauling over favored weapons systems, the dominant players in the security community gradually reached a consensus on a nuclear triad that has not been seriously challenged since.

The diffusion of power also extends to executive branch decision-making. Nuclear weapons decisions are compromises arrived at as much by horizontal or legislative bargaining among bureaucratic elites in different agencies as by vertical or hierarchical decisionmaking. These untidy processes seem to favor the initiation of innovative weapons programs responsive to national strategic imperatives more effectively than a hierarchical bureaucratic system associated with authoritarian political regimes.[14] And presidents and their secretaries of defense have been more successful in urging expansion of nuclear capabilities on this agency sprawl than in checking or reducing them once they have been authorized and funds have been appropriated.[15]

Secretaries of defense can command the military services to do their bidding on a few important nuclear issues, especially if they enjoy backing from a politically strong president. Otherwise, they have to bargain with the services and even with their own civilian secretaries within the Office of the Secretary of Defense (OSD). By most accounts, Robert McNamara, the most energetic and ambitious of postwar secretaries of defense, had mixed success in imposing his preferences on the services. In announcing his support for a counterforce strategy in the early years of his tenure, he primed the services to enlarge their force requirement requests to implement the new strategy.[16] The air force more than doubled the request he expected, forcing him to limit the service to 1,000 Minuteman missiles. In the resulting bargaining between OSD and the air force, McNamara reportedly added 50 Minutemen to his previous ceiling as partial compensation for his canceling the air force's Skybolt program.[17] On another occasion, he relented in authorizing an additional nuclear carrier for the navy that he was disposed to reject; "One can slay only so many dragons each day," he explained.[18]

14. Samuel P. Huntington, *The Common Defense: Strategic Programs in National Politics* (Columbia University Press, 1961). On bureaucratic politics, standard sources include Graham T. Allison, *Essence of Decision: Explaining the Cuban Missile Crisis* (Little, Brown, 1971); and Morton H. Halperin, *Bureaucratic Politics and Foreign Policy* (Brookings, 1974).

15. Stubbing, *Defense Game*, pp. 259–398, surveys the different conceptions that successive secretaries of defense have had of their roles.

16. Stubbing, *Defense Games*, pp. 72–74; and Herken, *Counsels of War*, pp. 141–62.

17. Stubbing, *Defense Game*, p. 73.

18. Quoted in Stubbing, *Defense Game*, p. 79.

The tendency to initiate nuclear programs and then resist terminating them is also illustrated by the B-1 bomber and the MX missile programs. At least two presidents, Kennedy and Carter, attempted to end the follow-on bomber to the B-52. With the help of allies in Congress and in the aerospace industry, the air force and its allies in and out of Congress frustrated both efforts. President Kennedy was forced to accede to congressional demands, focused in the House Armed Services Committee, that impounded funds for the then RS-70 program be released. President Carter actually terminated the B-1 as redundant to the secret development of the Stealth (B-2) bomber and the modernization of the other components of the triad. The B-1 survived under various research and development accounting headings until it could again be politically rehabilitated by the Reagan administration.[19]

The long and frustrating search for a workable ground-based missile system that would be less vulnerable to a surprise Soviet attack provides an even more pointed illustration of how the U.S. political process has favored weapons initiatives and discouraged the termination of existing programs. Support for a favored weapon system can be generated anywhere in the security policymaking process. To meet MAD-plus requirements and to solve the problem of vulnerability to a Soviet first strike, the air force and its partisans championed the MX missile in the 1970s and 1980s. The MX, which was designed to meet SALT II limits, is extremely accurate, reacts quickly, and can destroy enemy hard-target missile sites.[20] More than thirty basing modes were considered for the missile. Both the Carter and Reagan administrations proposed several iterations of how such a system might be constructed, including a mobile system with 200 missiles and 2,000 warheads, a "dense pack" with 100 missiles and 1,000 warheads, and, finally, the replacement of 100 Minuteman systems with 100 MX missiles. Alternatives to the MX, such as Midgetman or a fleet of B-52 bombers armed with air-launched cruise missiles and short-range attack missiles, descendants of the canceled Skybolt program, were also proposed. The air force, the Joint Chiefs of Staff, and the Pentagon preferred the MX; the Midgetman enjoyed considerable support in Congress, where proponents touted its mobility, invulnerability, and single-warhead design as contributions to nuclear stability between Washington and Moscow.

Since strategic doctrine and nuclear deterrence theory cannot precisely

---

19. Nick Kotz, *Wild Blue Yonder: Money, Politics, and the B-1 Bomber* (Pantheon, 1988).

20. Strobe Talbott, *Deadly Gambits: The Reagan Administration and the Stalemate in Nuclear Arms Control* (Knopf, 1985), p. 209ff. The congressional battle over the MX and several other nuclear systems between 1969 and 1988 is covered in James M. Lindsay, *Congress and Nuclear Weapons* (Johns Hopkins University Press, 1991).

define the weapons capabilities required for deterrence, capabilities are shaped by compromises among those associated with diffuse power centers within the government or castellating them.[21] The U.S. nuclear arsenal cannot be satisfactorily explained as simply an objective response to a single shared perception of the Soviet threat. The domestic bargaining power, skill, and commitment of those in the security community, whose shifting alliances cut across institutional and party lines, frame strategic choices and specific decisions on weapon systems and arms control postures.

The experience of the special blue-ribbon commission impanelled by President Reagan to resolve differences between Congress and the executive branch over nuclear modernization furnishes a useful look at how the process works. The commission advised spending for MX *and* Midgetman, but at levels that were too low to meet the damage limitation requirements of those pressing for a thick, war-fighting MAD-plus strategy based on the MX but too high to satisfy advocates of a thin MAD-plus stance, qualified by arms control aims, based on Midgetman. The debate had still not subsided when the Bush administration assumed office in 1989.[22] In a compromise, Congress authorized 50 MX missiles (with 500 hard-kill warheads), not the 100 sought by the Pentagon, and appropriated funds for Midgetman over the objections of the air force, which preferred an MX deployed on railcars.

A more centralized, parliamentary system of government might well have pursued the same policies and proliferated nuclear capabilities no less energetically. If it cannot be definitively shown that political pluralism promotes nuclear proliferation, it can at least be argued that the diffusion of the U.S. decision centers did not impede the development of nuclear capabilities in support of MAD-plus. Partisans of nuclear disarmament, a freeze on weapons acquisitions, or a simple MAD posture had little effect on weapons choices. Ironically, a diffuse policymaking

21. This discussion has deliberately sidestepped the debate between strategists and academic theorists over nuclear deterrence. The debate has generated a vast literature that cannot be summarized easily or satisfactorily. For the strategic debate among policy analysts and those close to the policy process, see notes 12 and 13; and Robert A. Levine, *The Arms Debate* (Harvard University Press, 1963). For the academic debate consult, among others, two symposia on deterrence, viewed, respectively, from the perspective of a rational actor and from a psychological perspective: "The Rational Deterrence Debate: A Symposium," *World Politics*, vol. 61 (January 1989), pp. 143–237; and "Beyond Deterrence," *Journal of Social Issues*, vol. 43 (1987). For an overview, see Patrick M. Morgan, *Deterrence: A Conceptual Analysis*, 2d ed. (Beverly Hills: Sage, 1983).

22. Talbott, *Deadly Gambits*, p. 300, describes the compromises orchestrated by partisans of rival strategic policies on the president's commission headed by General Brent Scowcroft.

process effectively narrowed options so that extremes—either a nuclear war-fighting posture or unilateral efforts to cut the U.S. nuclear arsenal—were excluded from serious consideration.

Rather than choose among potentially competing nuclear systems, the policy process chose them all: MX, Midgetman, B-52s, B-1s, B-2s, F-111s, ground-, sea-, and air-launched cruise missiles (ALCMs, SLCMs, and GLCMs), short-range air missiles (SRAMs), Trident submarines and C-4 and D-5 missiles, aircraft-carrier-launched nuclear capabilities, and antiballistic missile programs. Each leg of the triad is expected to meet the minimal test of simple MAD; together they add up to MAD-plus. Even the army temporarily joined the ranks of the nation's strategic forces: its Pershing II missile positioned in West Germany was capable of hitting targets in Eastern Europe and western Russia. If strategic nuclear systems are defined as those capable of attacking an opponent's homeland, then the army, until the INF Treaty was signed in 1987, was as much an arm of U.S. strategic might as the air force and navy.

The decentralization of power centers biases decisions on weapons systems in at least two significant ways. First, it provides multiple sources for weapons proposals and multiple access points for intervening in support of a program. Under what was perceived as a mounting Soviet threat and the necessity for readily mobilized resources to meet that threat (and pressures to create military forces that could underwrite an ambitious foreign policy), diffuse centers of decision prompted new proposals and provided political and financial assistance to keep them alive. In particular, Congress, quite apart from urging from the armed services, and sometimes over presidential objections, helped expand nuclear programs. Its support for the Kennedy administration's expansion of nuclear systems in the 1960s, for example, was anticipated in repeated congressional efforts at the end of the 1950s to surmount the resistance of the Eisenhower administration to increased defense spending for ICBMs, SLBMs, and bombers.[23]

Second, the decentralization of the U.S. power centers also has a "ratchet" effect once nuclear systems are set in motion toward development and production. Sunk costs, ample service reserves of unobligated funds to support a program in lean years, implicit service compromises (having Trident, the navy had little incentive to challenge the air force's MX or B-1 and B-2),[24] lucrative weapons contracts, and congressional

---

23. This struggle is reviewed in Edward A. Kolodziej, *The Uncommon Defense and Congress: 1945–1963* (Ohio State University Press, 1966), pp. 253–324.

24. Nevertheless, when resources are tight, service rivalries can still erupt if choices have to be made between competing weapon systems. See, for example, the B-36 hearings,

constituency interests have conspired to protect nuclear programs of interest to weapons proponents from cancellation or reduction.[25] On-going programs create incentives for politicians seeking votes to support a particular weapon or a strategic position associated with increased spending on nuclear systems. President Nixon, for example, reportedly shaped his campaign strategy in California by promoting the expectation that his election would ensure development of the B-1 bomber and the continued flow of aerospace contracts to the state.[26]

More generally, the commitment to a nuclear triad and to multiple weapon systems has essentially banalized and bureaucratized nuclear weapons decisions. These nuclear institutions have allies among the military services and intelligence community and the Office of the Secretary of Defense and other executive agencies, as well as in Congress, the arms industry, and technoscientific centers, particularly the nuclear weapons laboratories and think tanks associated with defense. The secrecy as well as technological and military expertise associated with nuclear weapons furnish policymakers with privileged access within the nuclear weapons establishment to promote their interest in maintaining and modernizing their arsenals. These interests can effectively resist efforts to weaken their hold on nuclear policies, while their privileged access enhances their self-interested claims.[27]

Managing Political Conflict and Targeting

Just as there are many ways to intervene in the policy process to lobby for more and better weapons and for a greater range of nuclear options, so there are many ways to voice criticism and to accommodate threat, use, and control strategies and associated weapons and arms limitation proposals that are at odds with official governmental policies. Neither apparent strategic coherence nor (and much less so) efficiency in allocating economic and technoscientific resources are the controlling aims in nuclear decisionmaking. Achieving political cohesion among elites holding widely differing points of view, however uneasy or provisional the consensus, counts for a great deal among those within the security com-

---

which were partially prompted by a revolt of naval officers who objected to the Truman administration's decision to favor the air force before the outbreak of the Korean War. Kolodziej, *Uncommon Defense and Congress*, pp. 33–70.

25. Although analysts differ sharply in their evaluation of the strategic, political, and economic implications of this conclusion, there appears to be more accord on the factual basis for the evaluation. See the studies cited in note 13.

26. Kotz, *Wild Blue Yonder*, pp. 103–04.

27. Kotz, *Wild Blue Yonder*, pp. 103–04; and the studies cited in notes 13 and 20.

munity. In arriving at an evolving calculus of consent to American nuclear policies among competing elites, an elaborate and exhaustive process of decisionmaking has been fashioned within which nuclear choices as much *emerge* as are *made* by elected officials. Even when conflict was intense and the consensus strained, as during the first Reagan administration, those whose efforts to limit weapons development and to promote arms control and disarmament negotiations had been stalled continued to act on the expectation that their views would prevail by adhering to the implicit rules and norms of the security decisionmaking process rather than seeking to circumvent or reform it.

The seeming paradox, on the one hand, of an operational MAD-plus posture, with the ceaseless modernization of the American nuclear arsenal, and, on the other, of the contentious expression of differing strategic perspectives, accompanied by the adoption of competing weapons systems and arms control stances, can be partially reconciled by distinguishing between operational and announced policy. Announced policies address a wider number of interests and constituencies than operational policies. Every American governmental pronouncement on nuclear weapons is received simultaneously by three audiences that can influence governmental nuclear policies and procurement programs: real or perceived adversaries, like the former Soviet Union; allies whose security interests are directly affected by U.S. policies; and domestic elites and the public on whose support an administration's policies ultimately depend. Threatened adversaries aside, the history of U.S. nuclear policies indicates that it has been impossible to develop doctrinal statements covering the threat, use, and control of nuclear weapons and their corresponding procurement programs that have simultaneously satisfied administration partisans and foreign allies and domestic critics.

Announced nuclear strategy may thus be understood as the product of the political demands of allies and domestic elements and the equilibrium struck among these elements within the executive branch over the requirements of responding to adversary threats, underwriting diplomatic bargaining with nuclear weapons, and seizing opportunities for cooperation for arms control accords with the then Soviet Union. These announced shifts in policy, however, masked an unwavering operational commitment to MAD-plus targeting plans.

Announced nuclear policies are sensitive to new or emerging pressures for change or to shifts in an administration's strategic priorities. When the Soviet threat was thought to be expanding, announced strategic doctrine emphasized a more threatening U.S. posture to deter its military or political intervention abroad or reassure allies and domestic critics clamoring for a tougher U.S. stand. At times of superpower détente, arms control and disarmament were stressed. Similarly, when allies or domestic opponents were more disturbed than reassured by administration pronouncements keyed to assuring rather than threatening the Soviet Union, announced policies (such as the Carter administration's presidential directive PD-59) were reformulated to emphasize resolve in threatening to use nuclear weapons and determination to fight a limited nuclear war. With the end of the cold war, announced U.S. nuclear policy has assumed a more conciliatory tone, but despite coming cuts in U.S. nuclear capabilities, operational targeting policies were still guided by MAD-plus.

EVOLUTION OF ANNOUNCED USE AND THREAT STRATEGIES. The adaptability of U.S. nuclear strategic policies to competing pressures can be illustrated by the evolution of announced U.S. strategic doctrine and the conflicting functions served by arms control as a key component of nuclear strategy during the cold war.[28] Growing opposition to the Korean War and U.S. military intervention abroad and public concern with high defense spending urged President Eisenhower to adopt a doctrine of massive retaliation.[29] Capitalizing on the provisional but passing U.S. nuclear monopoly, the administration proposed to respond to communist expansion by relying more on nuclear threats than on conventional arms and intervention. The burden for the nonnuclear defense of the West was correspondingly shifted to allies. European partners, most particularly West Germany, were expected to provide most of the conventional forces for their defense.

The end of the U.S. nuclear monopoly, dramatized by the launch of Sputnik in October 1957 and communist expansion in the developing world, prompted a revision of U.S. strategy, as a critical element of an overall policy appraisal to meet what was widely perceived as a growing communist challenge. The Kennedy administration's strategy of flexible response required increased nuclear and nonnuclear forces and substantially greater defense expenditures for reasons as much to do with stimulating the economy through increased government spending as with matching perceived Soviet capabilities. Flexible response, as announced U.S. strategy, proved a malleable concept that successive Washington administrations of different partisan persuasions used to adapt nuclear policy to changing strategic imperatives, alliance needs, and domestic pressures, alternately pushing and pulling for more or fewer weapons or for raising or lowering arms control priorities.

28. For a historical review of U.S. nuclear policies, see McGeorge Bundy, *Danger and Survival: Choices about the Bomb in the First Fifty Years* (Random House, 1988); and Freedman, *Evolution of Nuclear Strategy.*

29. Kolodziej, *Uncommon Defense,* pp. 180–252.

The ambiguity inherent in the concept of flexible response and, accordingly, its political utility in signaling either a more or a less threatening nuclear posture is suggested by the contradictory meanings attached to the term over the years—a shorthand for war fighting, a code word for MAD, or an emphasis on nonnuclear forces. McNamara himself used the term to cover a counterforce or war-fighting posture and then MAD and MAD-plus.[30] The term was also useful to redefine the nuclear debate between the United States and its NATO allies. It allowed the United States to oppose in the early 1960s but then to accept, at the NATO Ottawa meeting in 1974, independent European nuclear forces as contributions to the Western deterrent. It also prepared, albeit with only mixed results, the expansion of U.S. and European nonnuclear capabilities in the 1960s and 1970s to meet a perceived growth in communist threats to NATO and to Western interests in the developing world, threats that Washington argued could not plausibly be deterred by nuclear weapons.

In the late 1960s and early 1970s, when opposition to U.S. intervention in Vietnam grew and resistance to defense spending mounted, U.S. nuclear policy under Presidents Johnson, Nixon, and Ford gradually shifted to emphasize nuclear parity between the superpowers and agreements to limit defensive and offensive strategic weapons. Vietnamization, U.S. withdrawal from Vietnam, and cuts in military programs and expenditures were accompanied by the ratification in 1972 of SALT I, restricting the development and deployment of antiballistic missiles. An interim accord with the Soviet Union on offensive weapons eventually became the SALT II Treaty. The resumption of direct U.S. contacts with Communist China was of a piece with the priority assigned to nuclear stability and the hope of real disarmament and the pursuit of détente. These efforts also resulted in the Berlin accords of 1971, essentially eliminating the city as a cold war issue, and in the Helsinki accords of 1975, establishing the Conference on Security and Cooperation in Europe (CSCE).

Nuclear policies within the United States again hardened between the mid-1970s and mid-1980s. Domestic and allied pressures mounted for an expansion of offensive and defensive nuclear capabilities to match what again appeared to be a rising Soviet military and political threat. These concerns centered on the deployment of heavy SS-18 missiles

30. His thinking and speeches are traced by one of his key advisers in William Kaufmann, *The McNamara Strategy* (Harper and Row, 1964). On the other hand, "flexible response" is often criticized as the opposite of a minimal nuclear deterrent. See, for example, Robert Jervis, "Why Nuclear Superiority Doesn't Matter," *Political Science Quarterly*, vol. 94 (Winter 1979–80), pp. 617–33.

aimed at U.S. ground-based systems (the so-called window of vulnerability), the development of SS-20 missiles targeted against NATO bases in Europe, and increased Soviet influence in the developing world, culminating in military intervention in Afghanistan. By the end of the Carter administration, military expenditures, including spending for new nuclear systems, were increased to levels that approached those of the early Reagan administration. Presidential Directive 59 assigned greater priority to military and civilian leadership sites as targets and to fighting an extended nuclear war.[31] Approval was also given in December 1979 to deploy Pershing II and cruise missiles in Europe to modernize NATO's long-range nuclear forces. Meanwhile, the SALT II Treaty was withdrawn from Senate consideration to protest Soviet aggression in Afghanistan.

The first Reagan administration aggressively pursued the nuclear buildup and the emphasis on war-fighting capabilities. Defense expenditures for nuclear and nonnuclear forces climbed to $300 billion annually. In line with the expansion of U.S. nuclear forces, Washington rejected any moratorium on nuclear testing. The ceilings on nuclear deployments set by SALT II were exceeded. The strategic defense initiative (SDI) was proposed in 1983 to strengthen U.S. antiballistic capabilities, placing U.S. adherence to SALT I in jeopardy. Finally, the deployment of Pershing II and cruise missiles in Europe went forward. Despite rising European opposition to the deployment, especially in the United Kingdom and along NATO's northern tier, and despite the protests of domestic critics pressing for a freeze on nuclear weapons, the Reagan administration advanced on all these nuclear fronts, encouraged by continued overall domestic public support for the president.

With the resumption of START talks and growing signs of Soviet interest in returning to nuclear arms control negotiations, the administration adjusted its language to fit the times. Allied and domestic pressures to cap U.S. military expenditures and to hold the line on nuclear weapons development, partly to exploit renewed Soviet interest in cuts, prompted the administration to signal greater interest in arms control. President Reagan even allowed at the Reykjavik summit in September 1986 that it was desirable in principle and conceivable in practice to eliminate all ICBMs. This concession was never tendered at the Iceland meeting since it depended on Soviet willingness to accept the Reagan administration's interpretation of its SDI program as consistent with SALT I. For most allies, eliminating superpower strategic ground-based systems went too far, and the administration was prevailed upon to return to a tougher

---

31. Richelson, "PD-59, NSOD-13, and the Reagan Strategic Modernization Program."

bargaining stance.[32] But despite these oscillations, the INF treaty banning all nuclear missiles with ranges between 500 and 5,000 kilometers was signed, and new impetus was given to nuclear and nonnuclear arms talks.

EVOLUTION OF U.S. ARMS CONTROL POLICIES. As the later Reagan years suggest, U.S. arms control policies also evidence an adaptability to incorporate seemingly contradictory strategic perspectives and weapons interests. On the one hand, the evolution of actual arms control agreements since the 1960s can be viewed as a rationalization of U.S. nuclear modernization and as a way to manage domestic and allied opposition to operational U.S. nuclear policies. The Partial Test Ban Treaty actually led to an increase in underground nuclear testing, partly because of Kennedy administration compromises with the military services and the Joint Chiefs of Staff to gain their support for the treaty.[33] SALT II ceilings on the development of new offensive weapons were set high enough to permit both superpowers to deploy more and more powerful nuclear systems. Soviet deployment of SS-18 and SS-20 missiles did not violate the letter of the treaty, nor did SALT II preclude new U.S. systems. Similarly, the counting rules of the START treaty, which progressively fell under the control of the Defense Department and the military services, limited reductions to approximately 20 percent of U.S. and Soviet warhead and bomb totals, not the 50 percent cut that has been widely publicized,[34] and legitimated the modernization of U.S. nuclear forces. Partisans of expanded U.S. nuclear capabilities in Congress, the executive branch, and among arms producers and interested parties inside and outside the nuclear policy process have been able to use their influence to bargain hard for compromises that have essentially reinforced the MAD-plus posture. If the current post–cold war climate prevails, more cuts in strategic forces than covered by START can be expected. The success of these initiatives will almost certainly require the full support and high priority of the president, as suggested by the proposals for cuts in short-range ground-based nuclear systems after the attempted Soviet coup. On other critical nuclear issues, like testing, U.S. policy has not essentially shifted since the late 1970s.

But it would be misleading to say that no checks have been placed

32. See the press release of the British Embassy (Washington, D.C.), November 15, 1986.

33. Glenn T. Seaborg, *Kennedy, Khrushchev, and the Test Ban* (University of California Press, 1981); and Steve Fetter, *Toward a Comprehensive Test Ban* (Cambridge, Mass.: Ballinger, 1988).

34. For a review of START I counting rules, see Edward A. Kolodziej, "Arms Control, Disarmaments, and Budgetary Implications of Start," in Serge Sur, ed., *Disarmament Agreements and Negotiations: The Economic Dimension* (Aldershot: Darmouth, 1991), pp. 17–32.

on the development of nuclear offensive and defensive capabilities. A broad spectrum of opinion opposed to war-fighting policies has been vented through the arms control process. Arms control advocates in the 1960s won the fight for the Partial Test Ban Treaty and set in motion a process for imposing stiffer limits on civilian and military nuclear testing. Partly in response to congressional objections, they also impeded development of antiballistic programs, preparing the way for the ratification of SALT I.[35] The Reagan administration also felt impelled to quiet protests against Pershing and cruise missile deployments by proposing a so-called zero option. If the Soviet Union dismantled its long-range regional systems, the United States would do likewise. The administration was also compelled to accept a reduced number of MX missiles (as noted earlier), the development of the Midgetman, and arms talks with the Soviet Union on the basis of a "build-down" of strategic systems (until negotiations were abruptly suspended by Moscow in the wake of U.S. Pershing II deployments in Germany).[36] Congress and the public also began to pressure the administration to observe SALT II limits, engage in INF and START talks, retard development of antisatellite systems, curb SDI spending, challenge the application of a broad interpretation of permissible research and development to the SALT I Treaty, slow nuclear testing, and open discussions with the Soviet Union for the creation of risk-reduction centers.[37]

Announced U.S. nuclear policies have been sensitive to a wide range of strategic viewpoints and weapons programs. They have adapted to shifts in the U.S. bargaining stance brought about by changing perceptions of the Soviet threat and allied and domestic demands, for more or fewer nuclear weapons and for a firmer or more flexible negotiating stance toward Moscow. At the same time, below the surface of these seemingly turbulent shifts in nuclear aims and strategic priorities, operational policy was remarkably consistent in its pursuit of a MAD-plus targeting strategy.

It is also important to recognize that since World War II the battle lines between coalitions with opposing nuclear policies have not been drawn simply along institutional boundaries, separating the Congress

35. Alton Frye, *A Responsible Congress: The Politics of National Security* (McGraw-Hill, 1975).

36. "Unlike the freeze, the build-down would have permitted each side to modernize its nuclear weapons but only so long as a number of warheads were retired for each new warhead deployed." See Barry M. Blechman, "The New Congressional Role in Arms Control," in Thomas E. Mann, ed., *A Question of Balance: The President, the Congress, and Foreign Policy* (Brookings, 1990), pp. 109–45, quote at p. 125.

37. Blechman, "New Congressional Role," especially pp. 110–11.

and the executive branch, nor, for that matter, have they consistently conformed to partisan or party differences. Although it is certainly true that the separation of powers has been an invitation to Congress and the president to compete for the control of foreign and security policy, divisions along nuclear policy lines have not conformed to those marked by the separation of powers. Nor have the president or even the military services in the executive branch been the most vociferous supporters of expanded nuclear capabilities at all times or of an aggressive nuclear doctrinal stance. The political equilibrium of opposing forces between and within each branch of government has favored an operational strategy of MAD-plus. The equilibrium point for announced nuclear policies has wavered more, tilting at times in the direction of war fighting and on other occasions toward arms control and a more modest (but still impressive) MAD-plus posture.

In the late 1950s and 1970s, for example, congressional pressures mounted on the president to increase U.S. nuclear preparedness. In the early 1970s the shared congressional-presidential priority for SALT I and SALT II and for détente with the Soviet Union also accommodated interests favoring expanded nuclear options for the president. Within the executive branch, the so-called Schlesinger doctrine, named after Defense Secretary James Schlesinger, called for new nuclear capabilities, principally the MX and longer-range, more accurate sea-launched ballistic missiles, to provide the president choices between all-out nuclear war or policy paralysis and inaction in the face of a Soviet challenge to U.S. interests. In this vein, Senator Henry Jackson, a Democrat and recognized congressional authority in security policy, succeeded in attaching an amendment to the Nixon administration's proposed SALT I treaty, insisting that any future agreements "not limit the U.S. to levels of intercontinental strategic forces inferior to the limits provided for the Soviet Union."[38] This meant that SALT II would have to hold both superpowers not only to equivalent numbers of launchers but also to equivalent throw weight or megatonnage, the destructive power that each was able to launch.

If differences over nuclear policy do not fall neatly along institutional or party lines, the decentralization and diffusion of power within the two branches of government and within parties allow partisans of divergent interests to carry on their battles even as they struggle to adapt to new challenges to U.S. security interests. The process also allows for contesting views about the political utility of nuclear weapons and the potential dangers that nuclear arms races and large inventories pose.

There is, of course, a price that has had to be paid for a policy process

38. Quoted in Talbott, *Deadly Gambits*, p. 216.

at perpetual odds with itself, as rival forces capture temporary control of centers of decisionmaking. As Samuel Huntington suggests, the decentralization of the process encourages the promotion of new weapons systems.[39] Partisans and opponents are then engaged in ceaseless debate and jockeying to determine whether these programs will be approved, at what level of support, for how long, and with what implications for U.S. threat, use, and control strategies.

Opponents of new weapons initiatives or those who want to slow the nuclear arms race and cut existing arsenals can also claim victories. Post–cold war spending cuts will effectively limit new weapons programs and foster incentives for arms control accords, such as a comprehensive test ban treaty and renewal of the non-proliferation regime. While group and personal differences of policymakers are almost always sharp and sometimes bitter, the process, framed by the separation of powers between Congress and the executive branch, provides multiple forms of access and accommodation, however temporary and provisional, that encourage dissensus without necessarily precluding long-term policy stability.

Policy Stability and Conflict Management: The British and French Cases

Policy stability also marks the nuclear policies of Britain and France under the Fifth Republic. But the decisions to develop nuclear forces and to stay the course in the nuclear arms race were by no means inevitable. Canada, Italy, and other states with nuclear know-how and fissionable materials at their disposal did not exercise their options. French and especially British leaders in the early postwar years were moved by powerful domestic and external considerations, most notably their perception of being big powers in the international system, to pursue the development of nuclear forces. Their limited resources, however, dictated construction of much smaller, but still formidable, nuclear forces than those of the superpowers. Neither sought to match the size or sophistication of the Soviet arsenal. Instead each sought to develop an invulnerable nuclear capability sufficient to destroy Soviet material and human resources in excess of any gain that Moscow might have expected in attacking their vital interests. Viewed within the context of the American debate over nuclear weapons, resources limited both states to a MAD posture based on an idea of proportional deterrence or what the French

---

39. Huntington, *Common Defense.*

prefer to call "the deterrence by the weak of the strong" (*la dissuasion du faible au fort*).[40]

Policy Stability in France

The French case is particularly interesting. It enables a comparison of policy outcomes as a function of institutional change since two regimes, the Fourth and Fifth Republics, had to address the same nuclear policy issues. Styled on traditional parliamentary lines, the Fourth Republic was headed by a prime minister, whose cabinet was responsible to a majority of the National Assembly. Through its brief life, it was ruled by constantly shifting party coalitions. While the governments proved unstable because they repeatedly lost the confidence of the legislature, a small group of party leaders reappeared in successive cabinet shuffles. This small but critical element of ministerial stability permitted a few cabinet officials to sustain a nuclear weapons program at crucial periods during the 1950s despite the opposition of their cabinet colleagues.

No Fourth Republic government was sufficiently strong or coherent enough to openly avow its support for a nuclear weapons program. In its formative years, France's nuclear weapons work was secretly advanced by a small but determined clique of nuclear scientists, military officers, and civilian bureaucrats. The National Assembly and most cabinet members were either kept uninformed or were misled into voting for what they believed were nonmilitary nuclear programs. Only in 1958, in the closing months of the Fourth Republic, did Prime Minister Felix Gaillard officially authorize the test of a nuclear device, although the government, and the regime itself, did not survive long enough to approve his decision.[41]

40. For a thorough review and evaluation of French nuclear strategic doctrine, see David S. Yost, *France's Deterrent Posture and Security in Europe, Part I: Capabilities and Doctrine*, Adelphi paper 194 (London: International Institute for Strategic Studies, 1984); and Yost, *France's Deterrent Posture and Security in Europe, Part II: Strategic and Arms Control Implications*, Adelphi paper 195 (London: IISS, 1984).

41. Fourth Republic nuclear policies are discussed in Lawrence Scheinman, *Atomic Energy Policy in France under the Fourth Republic* (Princeton University Press, 1965); and Wilfrid L. Kohl, *French Nuclear Diplomacy* (Princeton University Press, 1971). Scheinman's analysis was later confirmed by the bureaucrats who shepherded the nuclear program through the Fourth Republic despite strong governmental and parliamentary opposition. See the seminar sponsored by the Université de Franche-Comté and the Institut Charles de Gaulle, *L'Aventure de la Bombe: De Gaulle et la Dissuasion Nucléaire, 1958–1969* (The adventure of the bomb: De Gaulle and nuclear deterrence, 1958–1969) (Paris: Plon, 1985). Indispensable, too, are three books by Bertrand Goldschmidt that trace the French nuclear program from its origins to the present: *L'Aventure Atomique: Ses Aspects Politiques et*

The principal charge raised against the Fourth Republic by Charles de Gaulle, the first president and architect of the Fifth Republic, was the alleged political incompetence of the Fourth Republic to address France's security problems and to project its power abroad in the continuing service of French interests.[42] As early as June 1946, even before the constitution of the Fourth Republic was formally adopted, de Gaulle had already rejected the notion of a weak president and parliamentary preeminence that was enshrined in the constitutions of the Third and Fourth Republics.[43] Given the divisions within French society, the location of power in the parliament invited division among parties in deciding national defense policy and devolved the power of the state into the hands of party officials and weak coalition governments. De Gaulle looked instead to a constitution based on a separation of legislative, executive, and judicial powers in which an independent executive, with its own powers derived from the constitution, could arbitrate party and class divisions, assume full responsibility for defense policy, and exercise emergency powers during crises.

According to de Gaulle, parliamentary and party politics favored partisan considerations and advantages (low politics) over foreign policy interests and national security imperatives (high politics). The prime minister, beholden to the changing party coalitions of the National Assembly, had to focus on piecing together fragile and internally flawed majorities to stay in power rather than mobilize national power to meet external needs.

Unstable party governments, according to de Gaulle's reckoning, weakened the state's power, blurred security and foreign policy choices by filtering them through incessant party conflicts and domestic strife, and undermined France's bargaining position abroad. No one in the government was specifically charged with the nation's defense. Not only were these inevitably short-lived ruling coalitions incapable of pursuing effective foreign and security policies, but they also purportedly failed to exploit opportunities for increasing France's power and influence—

Techniques (The atomic adventure: Political and technical aspects) (Paris: Fayard, 1962); *Les Rivalités Atomiques, 1939–1966* (Atomic rivalries, 1939–1966) (Paris: Fayard, 1967); and *Le Complexe Atomique: Histoire Politique de L'Energie Nucleaire* (The atomic complex: Political history of nuclear energy) (Paris: Fayard, 1980).

42. See Charles de Gaulle's critique of the Fourth Republic and party government in *Mémoires d'Espoir*, vol. 1: *Le Renouveau, 1958–1962* (Memories of hope: The renewal, 1958–1962) (Paris: Plon, 1970).

43. See his Bayeux speech in *Discours et Messages*, vol. 2: *Dans L'Attente, Fevrier 1946–Avril 1958* (Speeches and messages: In expectation, February 1946–April 1958) (Paris: Plon, 1970), pp. 5–11.

its *grandeur*. Ever-changing prime ministers could not assert control over national security and foreign policy since they were subject to the vicissitudes of party compromise. National and foreign policy interests were, therefore, hostage to the delicately balanced and provisional bargains of cabinet members, drawn from rival parties, whose support was needed by the government to retain the confidence of the National Assembly.[44]

On his return to power in 1958, de Gaulle fashioned the Fifth Republic constitution to suit his conception of presidential power. The constitution invested the president, not the parliament, with primary responsibility for the nation's security and based presidential power on universal suffrage and popular election.[45] In an emergency the president, as *garant* (guarantor) of the state, was to enjoy special powers to act without the consent or a vote of confidence of the National Assembly. In normal times, day-to-day governance was to be left to a prime minister, chosen by the president, and to a cabinet formed by the president's appointee. This government was to be responsible to the National Assembly, much as the British prime minister and his cabinet are answerable to Parliament.

De Gaulle directly linked his presidency and the institutions of the Fifth Republic to the adoption of an independent nuclear deterrent. No clearer or more publicly proclaimed link between a nation's nuclear policy and its policy process and governmental institutions appears in the postwar experience of the three Western nuclear states. During the early years of the Fifth Republic, the de Gaulle governments deliberately risked defeat in the National Assembly—and a national crisis—in pushing through the *force de frappe* over strong parliamentary opposition. Since the 1960s, French nuclear capabilities have been developed through a series of five-year plans, designated as so-called law programs. These have created a triad of nuclear forces composed, in accumulating succession, of a Mirage IV bomber force, eighteen intermediate-range ballistic missiles, and six nuclear submarines equipped with sea-launched ballistic missiles. De Gaulle's risky gambit worked. An independent nuclear deterrent is now supported by all political parties and is broadly sustained by French public opinion.

Would France have had nuclear forces if the Fourth Republic had

44. Historical support for the Gaullist critique of the Third and Fourth Republics is supplied by William L. Shirer, *The Collapse of the Third Republic: An Inquiry into the Fall of France in 1940* (Simon and Schuster, 1969); and Edgar S. Furniss, *France, Troubled Ally: De Gaulle's Heritage and Prospects* (Praeger, 1960).

45. The Fifth Republic constitution initially elected the president through a college of notables, distantly akin to the U.S. electoral college. De Gaulle later submitted an amendment requiring the direct popular election of the president to a referendum, which overwhelmingly voted in favor.

survived? It is difficult to say conclusively. Despite the absence of governmental and legislative approval, a nuclear weapons program steadily, albeit secretly, progressed under the Fourth Republic. By the end of the regime, France was at the threshold of an atomic test and had already begun work on the Mirage IV bomber to deliver nuclear weapons. Bureaucratic secrecy and dissembling protected against both public and legislative attack. Sufficient parliamentary support might eventually have been marshaled for a nuclear weapons test, but much time, patience, and delicate political bargaining would have been required for even a determined prime minister to cobble together a stable ruling coalition favoring a national nuclear force. The president, aided by parliamentary majorities reoriented by the institutional reforms of the Fifth Republic toward national and presidential politics and away from a concentration on coalition building within the National Assembly, was able to join the issue of nuclear weapons and bring it to successive votes for legislative approval. The presidential system of the Fifth Republic also succeeded in basing the *force de dissuasion* on broad public support, an option that was neither pursued nor available to Fourth Republic prime ministers.[46]

Policy Stability in Britain

British governments have been no less focused in developing nuclear weapons than has the leadership of France under the Fifth Republic. Since World War II British governments have consistently pursued two interdependent strategic aims: British possession of nuclear weapons and close military and foreign policy cooperation with the United States.[47] For a little more than a decade after World War II, the two policies had to be pursued separately because the U.S. McMahon Act prohibited military nuclear collaboration with any other state, notwithstanding the important

46. The gradual enlargement of public support for the French *force de frappe* is traced in Michael M. Harrison, *The Reluctant Ally: France and Atlantic Security* (Johns Hopkins University Press, 1981). For recent, supporting commentary, see John G. Mason, "Mitterrand, the Socialists, and French Nuclear Policy," in Philippe G. Le Prestre, ed., *French Security Policy in a Disarming World* (Boulder, Colo.: Lynne Rienner, 1989), pp. 49–84.

47. For the early period of decision on nuclear weapons, see Margaret Gowing, *Independence and Deterrence: Britain and Atomic Energy, 1945–1952*, vol. 1: *Policy Making* (London: Macmillan, 1974). Also useful is Andrew Pierre, *Nuclear Politics: The British Experience with an Independent Nuclear Force* (London: Oxford University Press, 1972). For updates, see Lawrence Freedman, *Britain and Nuclear Weapons* (London: Macmillan, 1980); and John Simpson, *The Independent Nuclear State: The United States, Britain, and the Military Atom*, 2d ed. (London: Macmillan, 1986). For a general review of British defense policy, consult John Baylis, *British Defence Policy: Striking the Right Balance* (Basingstoke: Macmillan, 1989).

contributions Britain had made to the development of the atomic bomb. Rebuffed but not dissuaded, the British persevered in developing their own program, leading in the 1950s to fission and fusion bombs and to the construction of a V-bomber force to deliver nuclear weapons against Soviet targets, principally major Soviet population and industrial centers, with Moscow heading the list.[48] The success of the British efforts induced revision of the McMahon Act, enabling U.S.-British nuclear cooperation to recommence. Since the 1950s, Washington and London have collaborated closely in nuclear weapons development, and it is hard to imagine that the British program could have survived without critical U.S. nuclear assistance.

Whereas the French sought to influence U.S. nuclear policy through their independence, British officials pursued the same objective by multiplying and strengthening the political and strategic relations between the two countries. Nuclear cooperation was designed not only to gain access to U.S. assistance and know-how but also to help ensure close policy coordination across a broad range of shared strategic and foreign policy aims. These policy aims led to the Polaris accord, which permitted British access to U.S. nuclear submarine technology and Polaris missiles. U.S. assistance was extended in the 1980s when the British adopted the Trident submarine system and D-5 missile. In exchange for U.S. help, Britain pledged its nuclear forces to NATO and agreed to coordinate targeting with the United States, subject to a right of withdrawal to protect British vital interests in the case of extreme national emergency. This understanding remains in place.

Throughout the postwar period, Labour and Conservative governments have weathered serious challenges to the pursuit of a nuclear weapons program and close defense ties with the United States. The first major challenge came in the 1950s from those who wished to renounce the British nuclear weapons program. The Labour party became one of the principal arenas of the struggle, and in 1960 the party convention adopted a resolution favoring unilateral nuclear disarmament. Hugh Gaitskell, the Labour party leader who initially failed to defeat this plank, subsequently turned Labour opinion around. By 1964 the party, headed by Harold Wilson, entered the elections reconciled to Polaris. Once in power, Wilson affirmed the nuclear policies of his Conservative party

48. The so-called Moscow criterion has been central to British targeting policy since the inception of its nuclear deterrent forces. See Lawrence Freedman, "British Nuclear Targeting," in Ball and Richelson, *Strategic Nuclear Targeting*, pp. 84–108. The introduction of the Trident system makes the Moscow criterion somewhat moot because Britain will have far more weapons at its disposal than would be needed just to destroy Moscow.

predecessors, amending the accord with the United States only marginally by reducing the number of British Polaris submarines from five to four.

Public and party opposition to Anglo-American nuclear cooperation and pursuit of an independent British nuclear force persisted throughout the 1970s. This did not prevent Wilson from secretly approving the Chevaline program. The deployment of Soviet antiballistic missiles around Moscow raised doubts about the penetrability of British Polaris missiles, then armed with only one warhead. At risk was the Moscow criterion, which was at the center of British targeting plans. To ensure penetration, the British undertook the Chevaline program to develop a new bus for its Polaris missiles that would increase the number of warheads aimed at Soviet targets and, through the use of concealment and decoys, would offer greater chances for penetrating antiballistic missile defenses around Moscow. The program came to light only after the Labour party left office in 1979. Outrage within the party's ranks and reforms of party governance to preclude such secret decisions if Labour were to assume power again had no effect on the Thatcher government's determination to complete Chevaline.

The next major challenge to the British nuclear program and policy coordination with Washington was the Thatcher government's decision in the early 1980s to build Trident and to adopt the D-5 missile. It defeated the efforts of the Labour party and the Social-Democratic-Liberal party alliance to block the modernization program. Although the Conservative party won only a plurality of the votes in the elections of 1983 and 1987, it nevertheless garnered a substantial majority of the seats in Parliament, thanks to Britain's system of single-member districts. Declining electoral support for the Social Democrats, the reconciliation of Labour's party leadership to Trident, and the Conservative party's electoral victory in 1992 suggest that this latest assault on British nuclear policies and on U.S.-British cooperation will also be frustrated.

Managing Political Conflict in Britain

Of the three political systems under examination, the British system polarizes public opinion on nuclear policy the most. Party politics and the time-honored debating and questioning procedures of Parliament foster sharp differentiation of official positions between the parties instead of the compromises across party and legislative-executive lines characteristic of the U.S. system. Ideological and party differences in Britain also inform the public discussion of nuclear policy. The deep splits within the British security policy community and public are suggested by the considerable body of opinion since the 1950s that has been committed to less extensive nuclear capabilities than those preferred by the government in power, if not to abandoning an independent nuclear deterrent altogether. This opposition to official British policies has also been associated with deemphasizing the special Anglo-American relationship in contrast to setting an independent national course or one committed to greater integration into the European community.[49]

National security considerations, the need for discretion in dealing with Washington, and the necessity of managing the partisan struggle and public opposition have all encouraged British prime ministers to avail themselves of the broad discretion that they enjoy under British governing traditions. They have been able to define nuclear policy without having first consulted their parliamentary parties or Parliament and often without the knowledge of many of their cabinet colleagues. Whereas French nuclear policy under the Fifth Republic was thrust on the National Assembly and populace at de Gaulle's insistence, successive Labour and Conservative British prime ministers retreated behind closed doors with only a handful of advisers and cabinet ministers to make the most important decision that any government can make—the security of the nation. Although membership on these prime ministerial committees varied somewhat over the years, normally the secretaries for defense and foreign affairs and the chancellor of the exchequer were consulted. Their decisions, however, were still binding on the cabinet as a whole. Some committees were so secret that their existence was never reported. The conventional wisdom that the prime minister and cabinet are responsible to Parliament has to be qualified if the evolution of British nuclear policy is carefully reviewed.[50]

Whereas France's military nuclear program under the Fourth Republic was pursued in spite of the government, Britain's efforts to build a bomb were authorized in secret at the highest levels of government by a small group of determined men. At the close of World War II, Prime Minister Clement Attlee and his closest cabinet advisers had few doubts about their decision. Foreign Secretary Ernest Bevin swept aside the strategic and economic reservations raised at the meeting of GEN 75, the prime minister's special committee to consider the decision: "We've got to have [the bomb]. . . . I don't want any other Foreign Secretary of this country to be talked to or at by a Secretary of State in the United States as I have just had in my discussions with Mr. Byrnes. We have got to have this

49. See Roger Ruston, *A Say in the End of the World: Morals and British Nuclear Weapons Policy, 1941–1987* (Clarendon Press, 1989).

50. For a succinct but informed examination of these decisions at the cabinet level, see Peter Hennessy, *Cabinet* (Oxford: Basil Blackwell, 1986), especially pp. 123–62.

thing over here whatever it costs."[51] Similarly, the decisions associated with achieving close nuclear cooperation with the United States were largely decided *in camera* and, accordingly, pursued with circumspection to minimize adverse partisan and public opposition. Neither the cabinet nor the voting public, much less the opposition, was consulted.

On practical grounds, as Labour Prime Minister Harold Wilson observed in explaining his closed-door approach to nuclear decisionmaking, "It isn't a question of not trusting. It's a question that the more people you have, the more people can be got at." In the short run, secrecy helped control dissidents within the cabinet and party, frustrated foreign adversaries, and minimized frictions in allied bargaining. In justifying the Trident decision taken by the prime minister's cabinet committee, former Defense Permanent Undersecretary Sir Frank Cooper summarized an attitude shared by Labour and Conservative prime ministers: "The Government's perfectly entitled to take decisions in any way it wants."[52]

British prime ministers and aspirants to the post assume that once in power their policies will be carried out by the ministries even though the policies may dramatically depart from prevailing practices and override entrenched interests. If Labour had won the 1987 election, the new prime minister, Neil Kinnock, could have been expected to implement the party's manifesto embracing unilateral disarmament, to which he was publicly committed. Because of the latitude in policymaking accorded a prime minister in this domain, anxieties inevitably arose in Washington policy circles when Labour embraced a unilateralist position. In reply to a question about whether Whitehall would support a radical shift in Britain's nuclear policy if Labour were elected, Kinnock expressed surprise that his party's platform would not be implemented by the civilian and military ministries:

> I think you do both the Chiefs of Staff and junior officers and senior civil servants and their juniors a disservice in believing that they are so prejudiced against the ideas of government—an elected government—as to try and frustrate its will especially in an important area of activity [abandonment of Polaris and Trident]. So I don't think they would change the habit of a lifetime, which . . . is . . . admired throughout the world, for the purpose that you suggest.[53]

51. Quoted in Hennessy, *Cabinet*, pp. 126–27.
52. Wilson and Cooper are quoted in Hennessy, *Cabinet*, p. 123.
53. Quoted in Hennessy, *Cabinet*, p. 157.

Managing Political Conflict in France

In contrast, no one would dispute that French presidents are the major force determining French nuclear policy: they exercise the final say in resolving disputes over weapons and strategy. This does not mean that they can escape being pressured or lobbied by special interests. Until recently, all the services were equipped with nuclear arms and assigned a role in the state's deterrent strategy. This policy can of course be explained on grounds of perceived strategic imperatives, but it also suggests that, since nuclear weapons are at the center of French strategic policy, all the services had to be placated. The army's acquisition of tactical nuclear weapons lends some support for this view. The limited range of these weapons, now scheduled for elimination, posed as much a threat to Germany, France's NATO ally, as it did to the now defunct Warsaw Pact. In any event, special pleaders must go *through* the French president; unlike the American system, they cannot go *around* him.

That de Gaulle's successors have essentially accepted his conception of the presidential office, particularly with respect to decisions on nuclear weapons, is suggested by the title of one of the few probing analyses of French foreign-policy decisionmaking available, *The Nuclear Monarchy*.[54] Socialist President François Mitterrand assumed the full powers of the constitutional office bequeathed to him by de Gaulle, although he and most of his Socialist colleagues had voted against the creation of a presidential office based on popular election and had strongly opposed the *force de dissuasion*.

The French and British have also rejected the idea of establishing a separate government agency to be concerned with arms control. In contrast, the creation of the U.S. Arms Control and Disarmament Agency (ACDA) can be partially traced to the political incentives arising from the separation of powers and the struggle between Congress and the president for power over foreign and security policy. Congressional supporters of ACDA argued that a separate organization, presumably dedicated to arms control and disarmament and independent of other executive branch agencies, particularly the Department of Defense, had a better chance of advancing these policy preferences than if it were simply a subordinate unit within one of the established agencies. ACDA afforded congressional interests favoring disarmament and arms control yet another way to intervene in executive branch bargaining over strategic

---

54. Samy Cohen, *La Monarchie Nucléaire: Les Coulisses de la Politique Étrangère sous la Ve République* (The nuclear monarchy: The corridors of foreign policy under the Fifth Republic) (Paris: Hachette, 1986).

nuclear policy.[55] What some ACDA supporters did not anticipate—witness the Nixon and Reagan years—was that the agency could be captured by partisans of expanded nuclear capability and neutralized in the bureaucratic infighting of the executive branch.

Traditional conceptions of diplomatic practice precluded the creation of separate French and British agencies for arms control and disarmament issues. French and British decisionmakers do not sharply distinguish between arms control and nuclear deterrence, both of which presumably support national foreign policy and security aims. These leaders have concluded that competing choices over threat, use, and control strategies were better resolved by relying on their Ministries of Defense and Foreign Affairs instead of creating yet another agency that would complicate the coordination and implementation of policy.[56] Thus nuclear policy, viewed under the guise of threat or use, was allotted a higher organizational status in both governments during the cold war than arms control and disarmament considerations.[57]

Finally, like the British Parliament, the French National Assembly has little leeway in revising government plans and defense budget requests short of overturning the government. Power over defense policy, weapons procurement, and military budgets has clearly shifted from the National Assembly under the Fourth Republic to the presidents and their chosen prime ministers under the Fifth. Under the Fourth Republic, budgets were voted sometimes for only a few months at a time (fifty-four were voted in the last ten years of the Fourth Republic). This short-term and unstable system of policymaking was as much attributable to France's continuous state of war in Indochina and Algeria and economic

55. Duncan L. Clarke, *Politics of Arms Control: The Role and Effectiveness of the U.S. Arms Control and Disarmament Agency* (Free Press, 1979).

56. For a sketch of British and French arms control decisionmaking, see Nicholas A. Sims, "The Arms Control and Disarmament Process in Britain," in Hans Guenter Brauch and Duncan L. Clarke, eds., *Decisionmaking for Arms Limitation: Assessment and Prospects* (Cambridge, Mass.: Ballinger, 1983), pp. 97–130; Jean François Bureau, "Decisionmaking for Arms Limitation in France: Past Experience, Prospects, and Suggestions," in Brauch and Clarke, eds., *Decisionmaking for Arms Limitation*, pp. 71–96; and Scilla McLean, *How Nuclear Weapons Decisions Are Made* (Basingstoke: Macmillan, 1986); Hugh Miall, *Nuclear Weapons: Who's in Charge?* (Basingstoke: Macmillan, 1987); and Patrick Burke, ed., *The Nuclear Weapons World: Who, How and Where* (Westport, Conn.: Greenwood Press, 1988).

57. With the end of the cold war and progress in superpower nuclear disarmament, a new emphasis on arms control and disarmament may be anticipated. See "Sélection Hebdomadaire," *Le Monde*, May 30–June 5, 1991, pp. 1–2. Concern for arms control is exhibited in France's departure from previous policy in agreeing with the other members of the UN Security Council to share information on arms transfers to the Middle East. See Craig R. Whitney, "U.S. and 4 Other Big Arms Makers Adopt Guidelines on Sales," *New York Times*, October 20, 1991, p. 11.

upheaval as to the instability of party coalitions in parliament. The result was, as one commentator noted, a "patchy and incoherent military policy."[58]

In the Fifth Republic the executive tightly controls the National Assembly's examination of the five-year law programs and the budget process with respect to the timing of debates, the information that will be supplied to the parliament, and amendments to the budget. Hearings by the Committee on National Defense and the Armed Forces and the Committee on Finances and the Economy provide useful information about the government's defense plans, but these inquiries are heavily dependent on the government's cooperation. French legislators have few means of evaluating defense programs independently of the assessments channeled through official sources or of making cuts without prior government consent. These committees are also limited by the constitution in their capacity to amend government defense bills. Only amendments that have been discussed in committee can be considered on the floor; the amendments cannot raise or lower expenditure authority; and even if they are passed, the government can ignore them if it chooses since the parliament has no effective way to insist on its will short of overturning the government.

If the government engages the confidence of the National Assembly, legislators are hard-pressed to defeat a proposal. Censure requires an absolute majority of the National Assembly. Only the votes of parliamentarians who are present are counted, so those absent or not voting essentially endorse the government's position. This procedure was used on two occasions in the early de Gaulle years to pass the 1960–64 law program and to authorize supplementary appropriations to cover overruns at the isotope separation plant at Pierrelatte.[59] A challenge to the president on defense policy is not assumed lightly by legislators. And the challenges that have been made were unsuccessful and threatened their continued stay in office. Given these risks, opposition tends to be expressed through temporary coalitions that register displeasure with prevailing policies but stop short of precipitating a government crisis.

French legislators have apparently adjusted to their limited influence

58. Wolf Mendl, *Deterrence and Persuasion: French Nuclear Armament in the Context of National Policy, 1945–1969* (London: Faber, 1970), pp. 86–87, quote at p. 109; see also David S. Yost, "French Defense Budgeting: Executive Dominance and Resource Constraints," *Orbis*, vol. 23 (Fall 1979), p. 593.

59. Only once since 1958 has the National Assembly met the censure requirement. It rejected de Gaulle's plan for the direct election of the president. But in a subsequent referendum the public resoundingly endorsed a proposed constitutional amendment to allow direct election.

on defense policy and generally seem less interested in defense issues, although former Defense Ministers Joel le Theule and Charles Hernu and a few other legislators have developed successful legislative careers by becoming defense experts.[60]

Patterns and Explanations

Alexis de Tocqueville was among the first to argue that democracies differ from other forms of government in their foreign and security policies. His argument that popularly based systems were slow to go to war and, by extension, unwilling and ill equipped to pursue consistent and coherent policies to prevent or prepare for war have been echoed through the years by many distinguished observers.[61] Insofar as nuclear policies are concerned, however, it would appear that the American, French, and British democracies belie this age-old belief. Below the surface of often contentious public debates and the pull and haul of powerful elites supporting different nuclear programs and strategic postures, each democracy has sustained nuclear programs characterized more by continuity than by rapid changes or even by slow and uneven development. The U.S. separation of powers, British party government, and the French Fifth Republic's presidential parliamentarism have created remarkably stable nuclear policies against the backdrop, particularly prominent in the United States and Britain, of persistent elite and party attacks on the nation's nuclear security policies and procurement programs. Only the Fourth Republic deviates from this pattern, and its demise can be partially

---

60. Le Theule explained the disincentives of following such a career pattern: "Parliament no longer knows the distribution of program authorizations for main programs, has no means to modify the major choices when the budget is voted, and cannot even be assured that the execution of the budget will be entirely compatible with what was foreseen. Having little to do with defense policy and with how its objectives are attained, parliament is losing interest in these problems. . . . Parliament hardly enters into the definition of this policy." Joel le Theule, "L'Opinion Publique, le Parlement, et la Défense," *Défense Nationale* (August–September 1977), p. 46. This assessment may be too pessimistic: some legislators continue to develop their careers as security experts, and efforts, largely frustrated to date, to increase parliamentary oversight persist. For example, Jean-Michel Boucheron, chairman of National Defense and Armed Forces, and François Fillon are exceptions.

61. For example, George F. Kennan and Walter Lippmann, however much they otherwise disagreed on the approach of the United States to the Soviet Union in the immediate postwar period, shared the same skepticism with respect to the capacity of democracies to pursue long-term foreign policies. See George F. Kennan, *American Diplomacy*, rev. ed. (University of Chicago Press, 1984); and Walter Lippmann, *The Cold War: A Study in U.S. Foreign Policy* (Harper and Row, 1947).

attributable to its institutional inability to develop a consistent nuclear policy.

This is not to argue that institutional arrangements are irrelevant to promoting policy stability—the Fourth Republic is an important exception—but rather that institutional effects, particularly in matters of national security, are contingent on real and widely shared perceptions among elites and the public of military threats. Within this larger international setting, each system has its own particular checks to guard against major swings in nuclear policy. The following institutional opportunities and risks are evident in these case studies.

1. *In nuclear policymaking the U.S. system of decentralized power encourages significant dissent, which is aired and subsequently accommodated in part in announced policies; however, the diffusion of power also acts to check the erosion of operational policy.* If one distinguishes between announced and operational nuclear policies, the United States has been the most robust of the three Western nuclear states in managing conflicting strategic viewpoints and competing special interests. U.S. arms control policy illustrates the adaptability of announced policy to changing perceptions of the Soviet or communist threat or, conversely, to domestic and allied fears that nuclear arms races may have themselves contributed to cold war tensions and the destabilization of the balance of terror. Superpower arms control agreements, most notably the Partial Test Ban Treaty, SALT II, and the START I Treaty, rationalized nuclear modernization and managed domestic and allied opposition to strengthening the war-fighting capabilities of the U.S. nuclear arsenal. These accords reconciled and legitimated the seeming contradiction between the development of new weapon systems that provided greater options for the president in using or threatening to use nuclear weapons and announced arms control and disarmament objectives.

Multiple sources of policy initiative in the executive and legislative branches have been able to generate a proliferation of nuclear weapons programs since World War II and to rationalize them into a MAD-plus posture without incurring a fundamental rift among elites close to the policy process. But these multiple sources have also acted as veto centers, preventing any significant dismantling of the U.S. strategic nuclear arsenal or its guiding doctrine of MAD-plus. The nuclear arsenal was ratcheted forward with the introduction of each new system. As a new weapon became operational, the arsenal as a whole was held in check by the ratchet effect of the policy process, which defined just how much nuclear power was enough.

Each tooth of the ratchet may be conceived of as a compromise be-

404   Edward A. Kolodziej

tween rival groups advancing divergent nuclear proposals inside and outside the formal governmental policy process. These understandings set limits for the size of the arsenal and define its composition and quality. MAD-plus was the operational result of these compromises. Nuclear policy has proven stable, but at the same time, those who consider nuclear arms and arms races as fundamentally disruptive have been able to have a voice in the process. On the other hand, in the absence of internal division within the U.S. security community, which elicits compromises and sets ceilings, albeit high ones, on nuclear capabilities, the U.S. arsenal might well have been larger than it is.

Tactical concessions to the adversaries of MAD-plus have not essentially undermined the persistence of this strategic posture. The U.S. process has been remarkably successful in containing the opposed pressures of sharply split participants in the security decisionmaking process. But MAD-plus opponents are provided public forums, especially within Congress, to pursue their efforts to revise U.S. nuclear policies and procurement programs. If MAD-plus has triumphed as operational policy, partisans of MAD or of deep cuts in U.S.-Soviet nuclear capabilities have never relented in their struggle for major changes and a reformulation of the public consensus on U.S. nuclear policy. The U.S. policy process, which begins with ideological splits, institutional division, and scattered centers of decisional power, works toward operational consensus, while policy pronouncements are keyed to blur differences even as the public debate appears to be placing the pronouncements under constant and serious attack. The process is testimony to the aphorism that the more things change, the more they remain the same.

2. *The British party government system has stimulated party polarization at the risk of policy reversal, but policy stability has been facilitated by elite autonomy.* The British parliamentary system, which presumes internal unity between the government and Parliament, has tended to polarize nuclear positions between the parties and to project these divisions on the public. Yet the system has also been decisive in persistently pursuing a nuclear weapons policy and close ties with the United States. Both the high level of partisan disagreement and policy stability require explanation: strong partisan disagreement is inconsistent with Downsian assumptions that parties tend to converge on policy in the effort to maximize votes, while policy stability seems inconsistent with such great divergences. That the two should exist together is especially surprising.

Partisan disagreement over nuclear policy has several roots, of which the most important is perhaps the strong role played by disarmament proponents among Labour party activists in league with a broadly based peace movement committed to unilateral nuclear disarmament. In the

1980s these activists pushed Labour into positions far to the left of the median British voter, despite the misgivings of some leaders of the party's parliamentary wing.[62]

The greater secrecy surrounding British nuclear policymaking than is the case in the United States, and to a lesser extent France, would also appear to have contributed to the dissensus on nuclear policy. Collective responsibility has continued to operate in British nuclear policy but not collective cabinet knowledge of what it is responsible for. If the cabinet has been kept in the dark, the opposition and public have had even less knowledge of what policies the government was actually pursuing or when key decisions were taken. Intraparty differences over nuclear policy have not been regularly thrashed out in the cabinet nor have interparty differences been regularly debated and aired within Parliament, as they have been within the American and French systems. Public and partisan debates tend to assume a sharper either-or form in the British system than in the American system or the presidential system of the French Fifth Republic.

Elite autonomy and cabinet secrecy have also been critical to maintaining policy stability in Britain, and again the role of Labour has been critical. Although antinuclear activists have had a strong influence on Labour party positions and manifestos, they have had little ability to influence Labour governments in power. Prime Minister Harold Wilson ignored the Labour party's official position by continuing purchase of Polaris, for example, while Wilson and Callaghan pursued the Chevaline program in complete secrecy.[63] After three successive electoral losses to the Conservatives between 1979 and 1987, partly attributable to Labour's inflexible stand on nuclear weapons, Neil Kinnock, as shadow prime minister and head of the parliamentary party, moved Labour toward the

62. For discussions of public opinion on nuclear issues in Britain, see Robbin Laird and David Robertson, "'Grenades from the Candy Store': British Defense Policy in the 1990s?" *Orbis*, vol. 31 (Summer 1987), pp. 193–205; and Catherine Marsh and Colin Fraser, eds., *Public Opinion and Nuclear Weapons* (Basingstoke: Macmillan, 1989). Labour party reforms that increased the role of party activists relative to the parliamentary party and the exodus of many right-wing Labour politicians into the Social Democratic party exacerbated the isolation of Labour on defense issues. See the discussion in Dennis Kavanagh, *Thatcherism and British Politics: The End of Consensus?* (Oxford University Press, 1987), chap. 6. On the role of Labour party activists, see also George Tsebelis, *Nested Games: Rational Choice in Comparative Politics* (University of California Press, 1990), chap. 5. As Ivor Crewe notes, the divergence of positions between the Labour party and the electorate (including the working-class electorate) on many issues is due in large measure to changes in working-class opinion and interests rather than to extreme positions taken by Labour. See Ivor Crewe, "The Labour Party and the Electorate," in Dennis Kavanaugh, ed., *The Politics of the Labour Party* (Allen and Unwin, 1982), pp. 9–49.

63. See Laird and Robertson, " 'Grenades from the Candy Store.' "

center of popular preferences for the retention of nuclear weapons in some form and for continued close security ties with the United States. Neither of these fixed elements of British security policy were at issue in the 1992 elections.

3. *Multiparty coalitional regimes risk policy instability, especially where polarization develops among coalition partners.* The French Fourth Republic illustrates this rule of thumb. Beset by internal and external pressures beyond its capacity to control, the Fourth Republic failed to confront the nuclear issue. Its weak coalitional form of government, centered on a prime minister who acted more as a compromiser and temporizer than as an arbitrator and leader, had, as de Gaulle argued, the ironic effect of fostering division and polarization in nuclear and foreign policy and, accordingly, of producing parliamentary indecision and paralysis. On the other hand, it proved too weak to control the unauthorized behavior of officials in the military and civilian bureaucracies who laid the groundwork for the construction of a French bomb.

The change of regimes leading to the Fifth Republic is a necessary if not sufficient element of any satisfactory explanation of France's embrace of an independent nuclear policy. Under the Fifth Republic, France has more successfully integrated divergent party positions on nuclear policy than have the United States or Britain, thanks partly to the concentration of national nuclear policymaking and operational authority in the office of a popularly elected president. The Fifth Republic not only fixed decisions about nuclear weapons squarely in the presidency but also freed the office from day-to-day political demands. Coping with urgent and pressing issues is left to a prime minister, subject to a qualified vote of confidence of the National Assembly. The combination of a president with political authority over nuclear policy, an independent popular electoral base, and freedom from the daily exigencies of office has fostered both policy stability and public and elite support for an independent nuclear force. It cannot be argued that these constitutional changes assured harmony of interests, but the Fifth Republic regime did dismantle many of the impediments and dissolve many of the partisan incentives working against national consensus on nuclear weapons, simply by confronting them head on.

4. *The executives in all three countries have been aided by support from the legislative and executive branches and by the subsequent inexorable bureaucratization of nuclear weapons and their institutionalization in strategic and foreign policies.* Ruling coalitions within the legislatures of these countries have steadfastly supported their governments' operational nuclear policies. If Congress has played an important role as a vehicle for dissent, its crit-

icisms and revisions of administrations' nuclear proposals and programs have never seriously threatened the U.S. nuclear triad or MAD-plus. As in the late 1950s and again in the late 1970s, Congress has usually given impulses to movements to expand and modernize the nation's nuclear arsenals. And although Prime Minister Margaret Thatcher's Conservative party parliamentary majorities never commanded more than a plurality of the electoral vote, they were sufficient to frustrate all of the attempts of Labour, Liberals, and Social Democrats to revise or defeat the Trident program. The Gaullist party worked on larger margins. It commanded solid majorities throughout the 1960s and early 1970s and easily defeated legislative attempts to block the creation of an independent French nuclear deterrent.

Once in place, weapons systems are difficult to eliminate. Opposition to weapons galvanizes around the decision to produce them, and less so around the question of eliminating them once they have been produced. The Fifth Republic's nuclear policies have received little effective opposition on either score. The MX and the B-2 appear to be partial exceptions in U.S. policymaking, but the intense controversy prompted by these systems still did not preclude production of limited numbers. In Britain, controversy over the nuclear deterrent mounted as Whitehall decided to replace the aging Polaris system. Yet between the early 1960s and early 1980s, there was relatively little debate or controversy over the Polaris system itself, and now the Trident system appears to be following the same pattern.

The military bureaucracies responsible for nuclear planning and operations are also resistant to major changes in weapons. Once systems are put at the disposal of the services, the politics of nuclear weapons is transformed into the planning and operational use of them. The weapons tend to disappear from view as they are shrouded from public scrutiny by the claims of national security. The U.S. single integrated operational plan is simply not open to discussion or to legislative and electoral vote. Nor are the targeting plans and operational control systems of French and British forces. Nuclear systems have been gradually institutionalized and routinized as commonplace items within the nation's military arsenal. This has had the effect of deadening interest and weakening opposition to their incorporation. Controversy has centered more on developing and constructing these weapons than on reducing or eliminating them. And arms control accords—with the INF treaty and START as exceptions—have served more to contain than to expand pressures to cut arsenals, particularly during the cold war.

5. *The separation of powers, lack of party discipline in Congress, constitu-*

ency-oriented legislators, and a large and decentralized elite security decision-making process anchored by institutionalized military services and industrial interests hinder the efficient targeting of resources in weapons procurement decisions in the United States. Although perceptions of external threats frame and elicit strategic weapons decisions, they do not by themselves dictate what those decisions should be. The policy process and pulling and hauling of contesting groups over strategic doctrine, operational planning, and weapons requirements shape the numbers and kinds of offensive weapons actually procured. But as the arsenals of the CIS, especially the Russian Federation, grow more invulnerable with the introduction of sea-based systems and progressively smaller, the American arsenal becomes in effect larger than it need be to destroy these targets. The number of weapons needed to eliminate the CIS and promptly destroy well over half their populations in a nuclear attack is a mere fraction of the approximately 9,000 warheads that will remain in the U.S. nuclear arsenal after START I is implemented.[64] Even START II will afford the United States greater destructive power than needed to meet MAD requirements. In principle, the difference between operational capability to meet the purported strategic aims of MAD-plus and that needed to meet simple MAD constitutes (however much one may debate the specific number of warheads and weapons systems) an inefficient use of resources.

The nature of the policy process does not fully account for this inefficiency. It has, however, been an important conditioning factor, facilitating the proliferation of nuclear systems. The effort to centralize weapons procurement in the Office of the Secretary of Defense under Robert McNamara ultimately failed because it would have forced choices and, strategic relevance aside, would have probably encouraged more efficient allocation of resources.

However, the forces favoring more and better nuclear weapons are formidable and might not have been resisted even within a more centralized decisionmaking system. Technological change and the availability of technoscientific resources encouraged weapons purchases to meet what was viewed as a growing Soviet (and Chinese) nuclear threat. Doctrinal debates were settled provisionally by procurement decisions that were biased toward proliferation. That bias was subsequently incorporated, not resisted, in arms control accords that facilitated nuclear modernization. Arms control ceilings offered stability (Midgetman) as the carrot to opponents of MAD-plus and increased and more effi-

64. "Estimated Strategic Forces under START," *Arms Control Today Fact Sheet* (December 1991).

cient nuclear capabilities (B-1, B-2, SDI, and MX) to partisans of war fighting during the cold war.

Service and industrial interests that are tied closely to specific weapons systems reinforce the tendency toward proliferation. A weapons system is advocated as an end in itself even though the terms of the strategic debate might change around it. The histories of the B-1 and B-2 exemplify the mission flexibility of these systems to meet shifting attacks on their procurement. Meanwhile, the ratchet effect of the policy process holds the nuclear arsenal in place and leaves the SIOP intact. This is not to suggest that the ratchet can never be moved downward. Shocks like those of the aborted Soviet coup and current anxiety in U.S. nuclear policy circles about political implosion and decreasing control of nuclear weapons among the CIS can slip the ratchet down several notches. They have already done so, in the form of the Bush-Yeltsin accord of December 1992 and congressional pressures to cut defense spending, including funds for offensive and defensive nuclear systems.

In contrast to U.S. practices, British allocation practices appear to be extremely cost efficient. Despite widespread political turmoil and sharp party splits, successive Labour and Conservative governments have steadfastly pursued an independent nuclear capability without costly starts and stops in program development and operations. The cost to British taxpayers has been considerably less than the cost of the French independent program because the British program has been substantially underwritten by the United States. The British are obliged to pay for only 5 percent of the cost of the research and development associated with the Trident submarines, which are superior to French submarines as platforms for sea-launched missiles and for the size and accuracy of the missiles and warhead payloads. An exception to this pattern was the Chevaline program, built by the British themselves and reported to have considerably exceeded initial cost estimates. Still, the program was partly devised to lengthen the life of the Polaris submarine system and to maintain an independent British capability in warhead design that purportedly was of some interest to U.S. scientists and engineers as yet another tie that would bind the two weapons communities together.

The French triad and tactical nuclear systems for the army may, on the surface, appear to support the proposition of inefficient resource targeting. The vulnerability of the aircraft and ground-launched missile components of the strategic deterrent and the army's Pluton and Hadès systems appear to be examples of profligacy. But unlike the British, the French received little material assistance from the United States in building their nuclear arsenal. Forced to develop the needed technology, the Fifth Republic created, in successive five-year programs, the Mirage bombers, ground-based intermediate-range ballistic missiles, and submarine-based missile systems in an order roughly corresponding to its control of the relevant technologies. With modest resources, the French developed formidable nuclear capabilities, although they had to do so at the expense of conventional forces to remain below the cap on defense spending that has progressively slipped as a percentage of GNP. It is now below 4 percent of GNP and declining.[65]

The distribution of tactical nuclear weapons to the French army has proven difficult to rationalize in strategic terms and bears some of the marks of interservice rivalry and the need to respond to army demands to be a part of the French nuclear deterrent posture. Recent governmental decisions effectively take the army out of the nuclear business. The British did not feel the need to pay for consensus among the military service in the coinage of nuclear weapons. Nevertheless, France is much closer to Britain than to the United States in the efficient allocation of scarce resources for its nuclear systems. Pressures to decrease defense spending and progress between Moscow and Washington in nuclear weapons reductions have encouraged cutbacks in French plans for tactical and strategic nuclear modernization. These cutbacks in previously announced nuclear systems will ease some of the problems confronting French policymakers in allocating an ever declining defense budget to competing service needs.

Conclusion

Do institutions count in nuclear policymaking? The clearest evidence for an affirmative response arises from French experience. Do they always count? Here the response has to be more shaded and nuanced. All three countries have produced stable nuclear policies, whether one agrees with them or not. The American system evidences continued public tension and discord, especially when new systems are introduced, but a basic consistency in operational policy, if at some cost in the efficient targeting of resources. In the elections of 1983 and 1987 the British system posed the issue squarely of whether the nation should continue as a nuclear power. The British electoral system aided policy continuity. Labour party defeats and the sunk costs of the Trident program have gradually modified party opposition. This kind of moderating process has tended to

---

65. "Sélection Hebdomadaire," *Le Monde*, September 5–11, 1991, p. 8. Military spending, as a percentage of GNP, will fall from 3.92 percent in 1981 to 3.36 percent in 1992.

emerge more gradually but surely within the American system as frictions at the margin are addressed almost immediately through compromises on specific weapons and arms control measures among rival viewpoints. In contrast, the linkage of the Fifth Republic's constitution and presidential power to an independent nuclear deterrent forced a social compact on nuclear weapons in France that still prevails today, although under strain as Paris adapts to the post–cold war environment that has deemphasized the role of nuclear weapons, at least among the superpowers.

Davis B. Bobrow

Military Security Policy

Military security has been a central preoccupation of U.S. government and politics for the last forty years. Both policy and process
have been the subject of abundant criticism. In particular, the incoherence, volatility, and inefficiency of policy have been attributed to basic
characteristics of the U.S. system of government, such as the division
of powers between the executive and legislative branches. These policy
defects allegedly follow from a need to cater to the numerous special
interests that are encouraged by fragmented political authority.

The central question of this chapter is whether differences in fundamental governing structures make for differences in the effectiveness of
military security policy. The vehicle is a comparative examination of
Japanese and U.S. military security policy, centering on abilities to manage international commitments and to target limited resources effectively.
Any comparison of the Japanese and U.S. cases obviously must recognize
fundamental differences in what the two policy systems have been trying
to achieve and in the importance each has given to the military instrument. Those differences are far less a function of fundamental governing
structures than of other factors.

During the cold war period, America has sought to be the manager
of a global military security order. To perform this role, it has made
extensive commitments. It has attempted to have the forces, both existing
and planned, to deter others and, as needed, to achieve success in war.
By contrast, Japan's primary military policy objectives have been to
secure homeland defense and deter attack by relying on U.S. protection,
with a future option of independent military power. American security
policy has given primacy to the military instrument. Japanese security

policy has given it only a modest role. Comparisons are further complicated by the uniqueness of U.S. military security objectives in the second half of the twentieth century. It alone among contemporary democracies has pursued a superpower role.

These profound differences in military policy objectives and the centrality of military institutions to national security reveal the weight of diverse policy histories. The United States was substantially affected by its victorious experience in World War II, the lack of domestic damage from that conflict, and its consequent abundance. The lessons Japan drew from its disastrous experience became a set of "never agains" that defined military security policy in very restrictive rather than very broad ways.

Security policy in Japan and the United States has been shaped more by differences in national circumstances and choices than by differences in fundamental governing structures. The distinction between presidential and parliamentary systems does not appear to have been crucial in explaining either the choices made or their implementation. To a greater extent, those choices have differed because of differences between the two countries in political history, tangible resources, and international context. Beyond the effects of those situational and contextual differences, however, more subtle features of the respective political systems become significant. Especially important among these features are the stability of legislative majorities and thus of party organs, and the influence of the civilian bureaucracy on military institutions.

A Useful Comparison?

While experts differ on matters of degree and pace, it is now widely recognized that U.S. military policy needs to accommodate to a set of imperatives far different than those of the cold war. This is especially true with regard to managing international commitments—making them and obtaining them—and to targeting resources. With respect to commitments, the United States faces imperatives to reduce what it contributes to the military security of others and to increase their contributions. It is also beginning to place a greater value on contributions to U.S. economic security as the quid pro quo for military commitments. Targeting resources efficiently is becoming more complex and urgent on a variety of grounds. Some types of targeting may be useful to bolster international competitiveness, meet domestic social and physical infrastructure needs, and cope with macroeconomic policy imperatives. Others call for military investment appropriate to coalition defense, industrial mobilization capacities, and, especially, advanced technologies that hold extraordinary military potential (a "long shadow posture").

From this perspective, one parliamentary system provides an extreme example of success: that of Japan.[1] Japan's self-restraint on military matters is now in its fifth decade.[2] Its share of financial and human resources devoted to military consumption has been dramatically low compared with that of most other countries.[3] Yet military hardware assets and the military potential provided by the national industrial-technological base have become very substantial in the context of both extraordinary economic growth and advanced dual-use technology yielding commercially competitive, profitable products.[4] Military burdens that primarily benefit

1. Davis B. Bobrow and Steve Chan, "Understanding Anomalous Success: Japan, Taiwan, and South Korea," in Charles F. Hermann, Charles W. Kegley, Jr., and James N. Rosenau, eds., *New Directions in the Study of Foreign Policy* (Unwin, Hyman, 1987), pp. 111–30.

2. The security perspective of Japan's early postwar doctrine fits with the "comprehensive security" rhetoric of the late 1970s and early 1980s, which reemerged a decade later. See John W. Dower, *Empire and Aftermath: Yoshida Shigeru and the Japanese Experience, 1878–1954* (Harvard University Press, 1979); Shigeru Yoshida, *The Yoshida Memoirs: The Story of Japan in Crisis*, trans. Kenichi Yoshida (London: Heinemann, 1961); Donald C. Hellman, "Japanese Security and Postwar Japanese Foreign Policy," in Robert A. Scalapino, ed., *The Foreign Policy of Modern Japan* (University of California Press, 1977), pp. 321–40; J. W. M. Chapman, R. Drifte, and I. T. M. Gow, *Japan's Quest for Comprehensive Security: Defence—Diplomacy—Dependence* (St. Martin's Press, 1982); The Comprehensive National Security Study Group, *Report on Comprehensive National Security*, trans. (Tokyo: Prime Minister's Office, July 2, 1980); and Davis B. Bobrow, "Playing for Safety: Japan's Security Practices," *Japan Quarterly*, vol. 31 (January–March 1984), pp. 33–43.

3. Measures of military spending (per capita), ratio to GNP, ratio to government spending, and military personnel in relation to population are all comparatively low even when adjusted to foreign conventions. See *Comparative Economic and Financial Statistics, Japan and Other Major Countries, 1989* (Tokyo: Bank of Japan, Research and Statistics Department, 1989), p. 86; *The Military Balance, 1988–1989* (London: International Institute for Strategic Studies, 1988); Japan Defense Agency, *Defense of Japan 1988*, trans. Japan Times (Tokyo: Japan Times, 1989); and Davis B. Bobrow, "Eating Your Cake and Having It Too: The Japanese Case," paper prepared for 1990 annual meeting of the International Studies Association.

4. Japan's defensive naval and air systems compare favorably with those of major European powers. The military budget, with the aid of a strong yen, is the world's third largest. Relevant technological capabilities outstrip those of the European members of NATO or the Soviets in many areas and of the United States in some. See U.S. Department of Defense, *Critical Technologies Plan*, report submitted to the Armed Services Committees, March 15, 1990, p. 11; Steven K. Vogel, *Japanese High Technology, Politics, and Power*, University of California, Berkeley Roundtable on the International Economy, Research Paper no. 2 (March 1989), pp. 5–49; and Defense Science Board, *Defense Industrial Cooperation with Pacific Rim Nations* (Office of the Under Secretary of Defense for Acquisition, October 1989).

other countries have been nonexistent for practical purposes, while the United States has borne the bulk of the costs of providing military security for Japan.[5]

It is hard to dispute the reasonableness of looking at Japan for insights into institutions that work for a post–cold war world. That is especially the case because Japan has succeeded in standard security terms. Without waging war or incurring any military casualties, Japan has regained territory and increased national autonomy and international power. As a major modern military power, Japan has had to deal with the policy management challenges associated with its military budget (large in absolute terms but small in relation to the size of its economy) and its advanced military technology.

There are two common objections to the relevance for other countries of Japanese institutions and achievements in military security. The first is that of cultural uniqueness. Some Japanese and some Western writers on Japan treat Japanese behavior as if it were almost organically predetermined, rather than being a matter of voluntary policy choice and political bargaining. It follows that others cannot emulate Japan because they lack its culture. This argument is not persuasive. In an earlier period, the Japanese pursued a far different military policy that culminated in war in the Pacific; and their current policies and policy process have followed less from a common inherent culture and more from political competition, economic interests, and organizational proclivities.

The second objection—that Japan received U.S. security protection and burden bearing—is harder to dismiss. Japanese security alternatives clearly would have been far different without the U.S. military umbrella, and no other country could have provided analogous protection. Yet other parliamentary systems that received similar protection did not act in the same way as Japan. The provision of protection by one superpower against another may well be of declining importance. Evolution in U.S.-Soviet relations may lessen requirements for strategic homeland deterrence and a balance of terror. Thus Japanese policies and institutions that evolved in one set of circumstances may become appropriate for other countries in a far different context.

---

5. Japan's record high payment of 40 percent of the direct annual costs of U.S. Forces (Japan) is generous by the standards of the European members of NATO. Yet it understates the costs to the United States by omitting investment spending (R&D and procurement) and the continuing costs of relevant capabilities not part of U.S. Forces (Japan). For a comparative treatment, see Ito Kobun, *Toward Bilateral and Multilateral Burdensharing in the Western Alliance* (Tokyo: National Institute of Defense Studies, 1985).

Policy Capabilities and their Determinants

The subsequent discussion deals with only two of the government capabilities raised in the introductory chapter: managing international commitments and targeting resources. Those must be specified in ways that are appropriate both to nations that are not superpowers and to the new security imperatives facing the United States.

Managing International Commitments

The relevant capability for nations that are not superpowers has been less one of making and honoring international commitments than that of securing commitments from others while dodging, delaying, and diluting commitments others would extract from them. For example, U.S. allies in Europe have tried rather successfully to avoid non-European commitments imposed by the United States, total subordination to U.S. commanders, and overwhelming defense industrial dependence on the United States. Admittedly, these allies have had to wrestle with significant domestic opposition to military commitments to the United States. Even so, the question is one of emphasis and justification. By and large, the allies' priority has been to get commitments from the United States while justifying their own commitments as the minimum price that had to be paid. In contrast, the United States has concentrated on making commitments. That difference matters, even if it may be masked by the U.S. quest for commitments by foreigners, such as military base and overflight rights, that in turn enable it to become committed. The strategy of managing one's protector differs from that of providing protection.

Japan has preserved the U.S. security commitment (and solidified it in the later 1970s and early 1980s) and avoided reciprocal collective security obligations to send forces abroad.[6] It has with equal success avoided

6. The government made international commitments in the face of substantial opposition and direct action protests in the security treaty revision of 1960 and renewal of 1970. Both avoided obligations to do more than defend Japan. The extensions of responsibilities in the 1980s covered only U.S. forces associated with the defense of Japan, seas and straits bordering Japan, and ocean transit areas within 1,000 miles of Tokyo. Under the U.S.-Japan "guidelines" of 1975, a "joint system" emerged with numerous joint exercises, joint studies, and substantial information exchange. For details on the joint system, see the annual white paper, *Defense of Japan*. For relatively recent developments, see Aurelia George, "Japan and the United States, Dependent Ally or Equal Partner," in J. A. A. Stockwin and others, eds., *Dynamic and Immobilist Politics in Japan* (London: Macmillan, 1988), pp. 237–96. On earlier periods, see Martin E. Weinstein, *Japan's Postwar Defense Policy,*

the autonomy losses of an integrated command structure or dependence on the United States for most military production.[7]

Targeting Resources

Resources can be targeted to secure the most effective forces in the short run or to optimize the cost-effectiveness of current weapon system procurement. This sort of microeffectiveness has been an American preoccupation at least since the McNamara-Kennedy period in the early 1960s, albeit not one at which the United States has been notably successful. Japan and many other U.S. allies have often resisted possibilities for military specialization of functions and the economies of scale that could result from reliance on procurement from a common national source. Rivalries in tank and fighter development are illustrative. Although notable instances of cooperation, such as in fighter coproduction, have been more efficient than autarchic policies, they have been more costly than single, common-source procurement. In short, Japan's "national champion" defense production policies have led to avoidable high unit costs for defense equipment and duplicative research and development (R&D) efforts. Its independent high-technology programs have generally not produced reliable and efficient operational military systems. Even the exceptions to this have usually reflected less urgency in Japan than in the United States about pushing the frontiers of military technology and quickly fielding systems that will anticipate Soviet military capabilities.

The content of effective resource targeting changes, however, if seen from a larger security perspective. National military effectiveness in the short term becomes less important than two other yardsticks. One is that of long-run self-sufficiency in the national military industrial-technological base. Japan and other U.S. allies, such as France and Israel, have repeatedly accepted gross microeconomic inefficiencies in exchange

---

1947–1968 (Columbia University Press, 1971); and Makato Momoi, "Basic Trends in Japanese Security Policies," in Scalapino, ed., *Foreign Policy of Modern Japan*, pp. 341–64.

7. There are forums for discussion and facilities where U.S. and Japanese military personnel both sit, but no integrated command structure. The foreign share of Japanese military procurements has ranged from 10 to 20 percent for the last thirty years, with a clear convention to protect the domestic market. Interviews with staff of the Keidanren Defense Production Committee, 1983; interviews with Defense Agency officials, 1982, 1983, and 1989; Reinhard Drifte, *Arms Production in Japan: The Military Applications of Civilian Technology* (Westview Press, 1986), p. 22; and annual editions of *Defense of Japan*.

for a higher degree of defense industrial self-sufficiency.[8] The second yardstick is a security guarantor's military commitment and economic tolerance. That overarching benefit may far outweigh the ineffectiveness of a dubious purchase from a guarantor country. Japanese behavior has on occasion reflected this calculation.[9] In contrast, the United States has been very reluctant to purchase either military systems or components from its allies unless they could more than match its own in performance and cost.

A far more fundamental interpretation of targeting resources effectively leads well beyond the military arena. Suppose long-run military security effectiveness depends far more on national economic strength, technological prowess, and regime legitimacy than on existing military forces. What happens in the military domain is not very important, then, compared with national investment in the technoindustrial civil base and domestic consensus. Here the U.S. government has at best been inattentive and at worst, irresponsible. Japan has excelled. Obvious examples lie in the exceptionally large share of government R&D spending the United States has devoted to the military and its resistance to the use of commercial, off-the-shelf components.

There are five sets of factors that underlie the governmental capabilities of managing international commitments and targeting resources: historical legacies, security givens, party and electoral systems, administrative institutions, and the defense part of the private business sector. What are the consequences of each for these capabilities, and to what extent can their operation be attributed to the framing institution of a parliamentary system? Have they been different because of it? Would their workings and effects on capabilities have been different in a presidential system?

8. Full indigenous development and production, licensed coproduction, or even codevelopment are two to three times more expensive than direct purchase of finished military products from abroad, but the last provides no technology transfer or indigenous production base. Rough magnitudes of the cost differentials have not changed in recent years. "Japanese Industry Reaches for Its Gun," *The Economist*, December 18, 1982, p. 72; and interviews with Japanese defense journalist, 1989.

9. The F-15 procurement is the best known case; the FSX, the most salient recent example. See Sungjoo Han, "Japan's PXL Decision: The Politics of Weapons Procurement," *Asian Survey*, vol. 18 (August 1978), pp. 769–84; "The FSX Project: Changing the Nature of Defense Technology Transfers," *JEI Report*, no. 21B, May 26, 1989, pp. 8–9; Otsuki Shinji, "Battle Over the FSX Fighter: Who Won?" *Japan Quarterly*, vol. 35 (April–June 1988), pp. 139–45; Shinji, "The FSX Controversy Revived," *Japan Quarterly*, vol. 36 (October–December 1989), pp. 433–43; and Masaru Kohno, "Japanese Defense Policy Making: The FSX Selection, 1985–1987," *Asian Survey*, vol. 29 (May 1989), pp. 457–79.

Historical Legacies

"Never again" resolves drawn from bitter historical experience differ across nations in the content of their military security policy, yet they have a common implication. Politicians incur great risks to themselves and their parties by being linked to military security policies associated with past disasters. Bureaucrats and agencies risk similar dangers.

Since Japan regained independence forty years ago, its military security policy has taken place within the context of four inheritances from the Pacific war and the period that led up to it. First, never again rely on the military instrument as the primary means to achieve desired domestic or international economic goals. Second, never again let the homeland experience mass destruction bombing, to say nothing of nuclear attack.[10] Third, never again allow military institutions or officers to exercise a veto on public policy or to confront civilian politicians, bureaucrats, or business leaders with life-threatening ultimatums or political-military fait accompli.[11] Fourth, never again slight the importance of superior technology and the capacity to produce large quantities of high-quality advanced weapons (what some call the "imperial military legacy").[12]

The first two resolves have led to a host of self-imposed restraints: the "peace constitution" (the renunciation of war and use of the military provided for in Article 9); the three non-nuclear principles (possession, manufacture, and transit); the military "nonexport" principles; and for-

---

10. As late as 1969, 40 percent of Japanese had experienced war as a soldier or through air raids. Akio Watanabe, "Japanese Public Opinion and Foreign Affairs: 1964–1973," in Scalapino, ed., *Foreign Policy of Modern Japan*, p. 111. The Hiroshima and Nagasaki experiences are kept salient; for example, they are taught about in the public schools.

11. "The disasters of the Pacific War were not just a military experience, they were an experience with militarism." Interview with academic security expert, 1989. See also Jun-ichi Kyogoku, *The Political Dynamics of Japan*, trans. Nobutaka Ike (University of Tokyo Press, 1987), p. 17. Right-wing extremists have attacked Liberal Democratic party prime ministers, as well as senior officials of the opposition parties. The LDP-connected mayor of Nagasaki was recently subjected to an assassination attempt for attributing some war responsibility to the late emperor. Ami Miyazaki, "Mayor Broke Political Taboo by Criticizing Late Emperor," *Japan Times*, January 19, 1990, p. 3.

12. The imperial period initially featured catching up, but then emphasized substituting will and fervor for industrial-technical capacity. Defeat ensued. Interviews with Keidanren official, 1986, and senior military strategist, 1989. As a defense counsel at the Tokyo war crimes trial remarked, "No one but a Don Quixote would start to conquer the world with a handful of aircraft—not in this day and age." Quoted in Masao Maruyama, *Thought and Behavior in Modern Japanese Politics*, ed. Ivan Morris (Oxford: Oxford University Press, 1969), p. 86.

midable conventions to limit military budgets (to 1 percent of GNP) and uses of national technologies.[13] Selective violations of these restraints are tolerated if their legitimacy stands. The violations need to be sold as regrettably necessary to avoid a wholesale jettisoning of the restraints.

The third resolve follows from the widespread view that the real victims of the Pacific war were the Japanese people. Military institutions and officials betrayed their responsibilities. Wrapped in a cloak of strategic romanticism and mystical nationalism, they not only misled the people, but in the last days of their dominance behaved with great selfishness. This resolve has had profound institutional consequences that will be discussed later. The fourth resolve has legitimated the pursuit of a highly advanced, militarily relevant technological-industrial base, but in ways that seem compatible with the other "never agains."[14]

The "never again" resolves do not amount to a posture of military innocence, complete abstention, or principled pacifism. They do limit the acceptability of alternative policies for dealing with military security vulnerabilities and externally set circumstances. They also motivate the definition and pursuit of particular capabilities with respect to international commitments and targeting resources.

Nations differ in the legacies that motivate security objectives, define desirable policy capabilities, and generate institutional emphases. Consider how the Japanese resolves differ from those of a U.S. political culture marked by memories of Pearl Harbor, Munich, the "loss" of China and Eastern Europe to communism, and success as the arsenal of democracy. The U.S. imperatives imply alertness to and deterrence of surprise attack, political firmness based on military strength rather than appeasement, active containment through large standing forces and forward defense presence, and self-confidence about military industrial and technological supremacy. American legacies emphasize the resolve never again to do too little militarily or to be too passive about posing military threats and making international commitments.

These profoundly different legacies are not consequences of whether the countries possess parliamentary or presidential institutions. Diverse

13. Article 9 states, "The Japanese people forever renounce war as a sovereign right of the nation and the threat or use of force as a means of settling international disputes. . . . Land, sea, and air forces, as well as other war potential, will never be maintained. The right of belligerency of the state will not be recognized." On the other limitations, see George, "Japan and the United States."

14. Emphasis is on dual-use technology and production capacities, not military ones, and nonweapons exports. This may require sophistry about what is a military export. Drifte, *Arms Production in Japan*, pp. 73–79; and Marie Söderberg, *Japan's Military Export Policy*, Japanological Studies 6 (University of Stockholm, 1986).

legacies, once established, lead to differences in security policy capabilities. They do so directly by providing policy principles or norms and
indirectly by shaping the particulars of military security organizations
and policy processes.

Security Givens

Whatever its legacies, each nation also has to deal in security policy
with givens provided by relatively fixed matters of geography, demog-
raphy, and identity (racial, religious, and ethnic). At any time, governments also have to deal with the security orientation of other nations.
The craft of higher security policy emphasizes creatively synthesizing the
constraints from security givens with those from historical legacies.

Japanese Vulnerability

Japanese security givens have emphasized the country's inherent vulnerability—its small size, lack of resources, and lack of close, empathic
ties with others.[15] In the narrow military sense, the increasingly extreme
concentration of people, economic assets, and leadership institutions in
a few urban areas makes Japan vulnerable to a small number of weapons
of mass destruction. The coastal proximity of those concentrations of
resources makes tactical warning times extraordinarily short, even by
the standards of the missile age.[16] Soviet forces are close by, unbuffered
by the territory of others.

In a broader sense, the fundamentals of food and energy and the
exports to pay for them depend on the behavior of others and on ocean
transit. The sea routes are not just long but studded with choke points.
Thus relevant threats are posed not only by established enemies, but can
also come from the political instability of formerly reliable suppliers or
nations bordering key straits. They can also come from shifts in policy
priorities by friendly governments whose military forces have been as-

---

15. Morinosuke Kajima, *A Brief Diplomatic History of Modern Japan* (Rutland, Vt.:
Charles E. Tuttle, 1969); and Seizaburo Sato, "The Foundations of Modern Japanese
Foreign Policy," in Scalapino, ed., *Foreign Policy of Modern Japan*, pp. 367–89.

16. Endicott's findings of the mid-1970s have been made even more alarming by
technological advances. John E. Endicott, *Japan's Nuclear Option: Political, Technical, and
Strategic Factors* (Praeger, 1975). Even small numbers of conventional weapons could have
disastrous consequences. Motofumi Asai, *Nihon Gaikō, Hansei to Tenkan* (Diplomacy of
Japan, reconsideration and turnabout) (Tokyo: Iwanami Shoten, 1989).

suring safe passage. The sources of threat are many, and the locales for pressure are often distant from Japan.[17]

The combination of inheritances and vulnerabilities would seem to impel Japan to strive for external relations free of enemies. Indeed, for several decades after the Pacific war, publicly available Japanese defense policy documents did not identify any enemy. Among the elite there was substantial advocacy for nonaligned diplomacy and a separation between external economic and political relations. As the nature of other national needs made that too costly, impossible, or premature, there seemed to be a need for some alternative to the unilateral military strength prohibited by the "never again" resolves. Since the early postwar period, mainstream Japanese opinion has given great weight to several reasons for pursuing such an "unavoidable" second-best course—a course embodied in the U.S.-Japan Security Treaty.[18]

For Japan's initial economic and political recovery and subsequent economic prosperity, it was essential to secure good treatment from the United States. U.S. policy focused on strategic containment of the Soviet Union (and, for a period, China), and Japan had value to Washington as an asset for such containment. That value gave Japan bargaining leverage to regain automony and secure economic benefits.[19] Japanese leaders well knew its attractiveness to military institutions and elites influential in Washington.

Economic, cultural, and military security considerations made it essential for Japan to reestablish and sustain good relations with other Asian governments (including the ASEAN states, South Korea, and, if possible, China). In the postwar years those relations would have suffered if other Asians had perceived Japan's revival as a serious military threat. Those relations benefited from their perception that Japanese military capability

17. Nobutoshi Akao, ed., *Japan's Economic Security* (St. Martin's Press, 1983); Davis B. Bobrow and Robert T. Kudrle, "How Middle Powers Can Manage Resource Weakness: Japan and Energy," *World Politics*, vol. 39 (July 1987), pp. 536–65; and Chapman and others, *Japan's Quest for Comprehensive Security*, pp. 143–230.

18. Jitsuo Tsuchiyama, "Alliance in Japanese Foreign Policy: Theory and Practice," Ph.D. dissertation, University of Maryland, 1984.

19. "[For the United States] there were three considerations. First, there was Japan's geopolitical position, second, its potential industrial power, and third, its potential military power. The question of what would happen if Japan were to remain in the American sphere or were to join the Soviet sphere was considered, and this resulted in the recognition of Japan's value, militarily speaking. Japan's position thus changed from that of a former enemy to a future ally." Kyogoku, *Political Dynamics of Japan*, pp. 13–14. See also Davis B. Bobrow and Steve Chan, "Assets, Liabilities, and Strategic Conduct: Status Management by Japan, Taiwan and South Korea," *Pacific Focus*, vol. 1 (Spring 1986), pp. 23–55.

was effectively limited by U.S. security commitments to Japan and the U.S. military presence in the area.[20]

Soviet intentions and capabilities seemed to pose genuine and substantial dangers to Japan. Historic concerns with Soviet military power were joined by bitterness about the opportunistic and "unprovoked" Soviet role at the end of World War II, the delayed repatriation of Japanese nationals after it ended, and continued Soviet retention of the portion of the Kuriles known as the Northern Islands. Soviet verbal threats and military activities conveyed ability to attack the home islands.[21]

Deterrence of Soviet military pressure on Japan, and diversion of Soviet military resources to other fronts and targets, has thus been a security imperative. Only the United States could have provided that sort of deterrence and diversion. The U.S. military presence conveyed to the Soviets that any attack on Japan would be tantamount to an attack on the United States. American views of Japan as a major asset for global U.S. strategy also ensured both a military presence and a strategic umbrella. That of course implied Japan's compliant adaptation to shifts in U.S. strategy toward the Soviet Union, a tolerable if sometimes irritating task so long as it did not involve Japan in posing direct, unilateral offensive threats to Moscow.[22]

Japan's commitment to export-led economic growth and dependence on distant suppliers for raw materials brought about a need for some military capabilities to ensure safe passage. The relevant sorts of military forces had to be able to operate far from Japan. They had to be substantial

20. Non-Japanese Asians have persistently lobbied the United States to maintain its military presence and to enjoin Japan to limit military projection capacities. With waning East-West tension, some senior Japanese foreign affairs experts are arguing for quieting Asian concerns as the major external reason for continuation of the security treaty regime. (Interview with former Ministry of Foreign Affairs official, 1989.)

21. Japanese public opinion toward the Soviet Union has been extraordinarily negative. Davis B. Bobrow, "Japan in the World: Opinion from Defeat to Success," *Journal of Conflict Resolution*, vol. 33 (December 1989), pp. 571–604. The Northern Islands issue continues to be treated as a litmus test of Soviet intentions. Kenichi Ito, "Japan and the Soviet Union—Entangled in the Deadlock of the Northern Territories," *Washington Quarterly*, vol. 11 (Winter 1988), pp. 35–44. For Soviet air and naval activities and declaratory policy, see the annual issues of *Defense of Japan*, and Research Institute for Peace and Security, *Asian Security* (London: Brassey's).

22. Japanese practices (such as nonencrypted air defense communication) almost ostentatiously ensure that the Soviets need not fear unilateral military initiatives and show substantial respect for Soviet territorial sovereignty. Many unilateral Japanese practices resemble confidence-building measures in Europe associated with the Helsinki process, such as providing ample notice of military exercises.

and expensive and, like those needed to deter the Soviets, had to provide an inherent military threat to other Asians. By even the most lenient interpretation, such forces would pose domestically provocative violations of the peace constitution. The U.S. provision of forces located outside Japan was the obvious solution.

Perhaps less obviously, the alignment with the United States justified some Japanese military effort as a necessary, but modest, form of dues. American "demands" for a growing Japanese military capability had three advantages. First, they shifted the domestic perception of such steps; rather than a violation of the inherited resolves, they became an unavoidable compromise to avoid major rearmament in the face of Soviet threats. Second, the U.S. demands abetted steps to satisfy the elite and public minorities advocating a national military capability as a matter of prudence and a symbolic corollary of being an advanced and independent nation ("not being like a man with one arm and one leg").[23] Third, steps toward military capabilities presented as tokens of good faith could also make the United States more manageable. Japan would seem increasingly important to matching forces with the Soviet Union, increasingly able to provide or withhold militarily relevant advanced technology, and increasingly able to choose whether to be a third military-technological giant. Good relations could not be taken for granted with a Japan that might not say yes and could eventually say no.[24]

The Economic Context

Economics is of course intertwined with military security policy. Growth rates affect the ability to make increased allocations to policy claimants, including the military. Technology and human capital shape the availability and opportunity cost of military equipment. Economic sluggishness or even recession and depression can motivate government spending in the military area, as in others. Demographically related labor shortages or underemployment affect personnel aspects of military policy. The military share in the national economy, and in the sales of major indus-

23. This "standing tall" view has always had minority support from the public and from important elements of the ruling party. Interview with Japanese defense journalist, 1989.

24. By the early 1980s, foreign affairs commentators talked of leverage. Interviews, 1982. The merits of the capacity to say no appear in Akio Morita and Shintaro Ishihara, *The Japan that Can Say "No": Why Japan Will Be First Among Equals* (Simon and Schuster, 1991).

tries, affects the role of military policy choices in macroeconomic management, firm profitability, and regional (that is, constituency) economic vitality and employment.

The economic context for Japanese military security policy has had several key features: remarkable growth in the size of the economy and the level of technology; crucial economic relations with the United States; subordination of defense spending to broader macroeconomic emphases;[25] and civilian R&D, production, and sales volumes that dwarfed those of the military sector.[26]

As a result, military spending increases became possible even though military security had a stable or declining national priority. The technological level of defense equipment could increase without special major investment. That is, militarily useful technologies came to "spin forward" from the civil sector to the military rather than "spin off" from the military to the civil. By the time the military adopted them, the technologies were relatively well understood and problems of efficiency and quality control had been resolved. The rewards of civil production lessened the temptation for business and politicians to emphasize military products and thus stake their own survival on military business.

U.S. Differences

The security givens facing the United States, at least until the 1970s, were very different. Its fixed national characteristics were held to be ones of immensity—in size, resources, and the potential affinity of others for the United States. The Soviet threat provided a central focus for security policy and broader foreign policy. Because other countries were held

25. Aggregate defense spending changes have been driven by general macroeconomic policies and by relations with the United States. Davis B. Bobrow and Stephen R. Hill, "Non-Military Determinants of Military Budgets: The Japanese Case," International Studies Quarterly, vol. 35 (March 1991), pp. 39–62.

26. In fiscal year 1987, defense agency funds accounted for less than 1 percent of national R&D expenditures, and in fiscal 1989 for about 5 percent of government R&D spending. Indicators of Science and Technology, 1989 (Tokyo: Science and Technology Agency, 1989), p. 22; and Ministry of International Trade and Industry, Agency of Industrial Science and Technology, AIST, 1989 (Tokyo, 1989), p. 4. In fiscal 1986, the value of defense procurements amounted to less than 1 percent of total industrial production. Defense of Japan, 1988, p. 317. In fiscal 1986, the top ten defense contractors who received almost 66 percent of JDA procurement funds were on average dependent on JDA for only 8 percent of their total sales, and only one of them for as much as 20 percent. Eduardo Lachica and Masayoshi Kanabayashi, "Growing Arsenal: Japan's Arms Builders Openly Vie for Orders after Long Hesitancy," Wall Street Journal, August 19, 1987, p. 1.

to need the United States for both military protection and economic recovery far more than it needed them, U.S. military strength was perceived as a public good. Its economic strength was natural and inherent, so the United States could readily afford to provide economic benefits in exchange for military followership. The policies that followed had consequences for the United States just as did those in Japan, yet the policies and their consequences were radically different in the two countries.

Several consequences merit special mention. First, the adequacy of U.S. military spending and forces depended primarily on what the Soviets did, not on what U.S. allies did. Second, America's own security came to be seen as fluctuating with the degree to which others followed it militarily. Since that followership was said to hinge on the credibility of U.S. security guarantees, it was imperative to make the military effort that would give others confidence in those guarantees. Third, the resulting budgetary emphases created extraordinary self-interest among business and politicians in defense spending. That self-interest, combined with the historical legacies discussed above, made the adequacy of defense effort a major political litmus test in national elections (examples include the Kennedy missile gap, McGovern's electoral defeat, and Reagan's "present danger").

In turn, the emphasis on national strength centered in military effort came to have consequences of its own for political controversy involving military matters. These have recurrently involved tensions between the costs of military effort and other aspects of national well-being. The most dramatic have been over the costs of wars, such as those in Korea and Vietnam. Equally familiar have been several quests for "peace dividends." Most recently, such tensions have involved the compatibility of military emphases with building national industrial and technological strength. The givens and legacies work to create situations of tension that keep military security policy at the heart of recurring debates over national priorities.

Security givens, like historical legacies, cannot be attributed to broad political institutions. Their most visible consequences are for less basic patterns of politics and policy, including narrower institutions (ones that do not inherently derive from differences between a separation-of-powers system and a parliamentary system). Yet it still may be the case that the treatment of legacies and givens will differ because of framework institutions. Grappling with that possibility requires that one look at the narrower institutions and practices and then consider whether those would be very different with alternative framework institutions.

Party and Electoral Systems

Central to Japanese politics are the protracted rule of the Liberal Democratic party (LDP), an electoral system that rewards attentiveness to local district benefits, and the self-conception of the major opposition party, the Japan Socialist party (JSP). None of these features is generic to parliamentary systems.

Protracted LDP rule has made its internal institutions—including the organs related to national security, military policy, and military bases—far more important than the committees of either house of the legislature.[27] The party organs and groupings focused on military matters may not get their way within the LDP, but their opposition will probably doom any departure from the status quo. That includes initiatives supported by a prime minister.

The LDP's long tenure has led to extraordinarily intimate relations between the bureaucracy, including the Japan Defense Agency (JDA), and internal LDP organs and individual legislators. Preconsultations on military policy are the norm on budget levels, matters of concern to the United States, constituency tangibles, and possible bad press. Good connections with the LDP have significance during a bureaucrat's career.[28] The LDP Diet ranks contain a substantial number of former bureaucrats, even a few from the military. LDP legislators tend to stay on the military-

27. That is not only true for military matters. See Francis R. Valeo and Charles E. Morrison, eds., *The Japanese Diet and the U.S. Congress* (Westview Press, 1983). Relevant LDP organs are parts of the Policy Affairs Research Council (PARC), including a division for national defense, and several military-related groups among its numerous research commissions and special committees. LDP Diet members automatically join the PARC division that covers the same jurisdiction as the Diet standing committee to which they belong, and they can join as many as two others. Division chairmen matter: they usually carry the burden of advocacy as proposals move up the internal LDP hierarchy. The prime minister does not have full control of the membership of various levels in the policy clearance hierarchy. The divisions' lack of substantive staff, the often large number of members, and ease of joining all give more importance to smaller, more informal clusters or "tribes" (*zoku*). *Zoku* members include the pertinent division chair, former holders of the pertinent cabinet portfolio, ex-officials from the pertinent bureaucracy, and issue-committed specialists. See Takashi Inoguchi and Tomoaki Iwai, *"Zokugiin" no Kenkyū: Jimintō Seiken o Gyūjiru Shuyaku-tachi* (A study of "zoku" representatives: main actors controlling Japanese politics) (Tokyo: Nihon Keizai Shinbunsha, 1987).

28. For military matters, politicians have been important to bureaucrats because of domestic political sensitivity and foreign attention. That sensitivity made bureaucrats politically attuned, and politicians dependent on bureaucrats for reliable information and discretion. See Yung H. Park, *Bureaucrats and Ministers in Contemporary Japanese Government* (University of California Press, 1986).

related party organs and thus build up substantial expertise.[29] All heads of the JDA have been LDP Diet members, often far from the end or peak of their career. These alumni provide a cadre of senior politicians with military security policy credentials and connections. As a party that supports development and business, the LDP also has had close, mutually financially beneficial relations with large firms. Those firms dominate the Federation of Economic Organizations (Keidanren) and its Defense Production Committee (DPC).

The LDP has supported amending the constitution to modify the limits on military forces, the security alignment with the United States, national military Self-Defense Forces (SDF) with a substantial budget and advanced weapons, close relations with South Korea, and a massive domestic nuclear energy industry. Each of these positions has direct relevance to military security policy. Although distinctions eroded in the 1980s, these issue positions have distinguished the LDP from the principal opposition parties, in particular the one with most seats in the legislature, the Japan Socialist party. If the LDP has been the party of the security alignment with the United States, the JSP has been the party of the peace constitution.[30]

The LDP's lengthy dominance has perpetuated an electoral system that ensures the party a much larger share of Diet seats than its share of the popular vote. It also has led other parties to see themselves as a permanent opposition, or at best minor members of an LDP-centered coalition. Short of a breakup of the LDP, opposition exists to temper LDP actions, not to provide alternative rulers.[31] Thus one would expect

29. The longevity of membership on the LDP defense division exceeds the average for all divisions. Multiterm Diet members with an issue interest may well know more than higher civil service generalists on two- or three-year job rotation assignments. That is particularly true for the JDA because of the importance of loaned officials from other agencies. That sort of tribal history may also be conducive to informal networks with career military officers.

30. On the political parties, see Gerald L. Curtis, *The Japanese Way of Politics* (Columbia University Press, 1988); Ronald J. Hrebenar and others, *The Japanese Party System: From One-Party Rule to Coalition Government* (Westview Press, 1986); and J. A. A. Stockwin, "Parties, Politicians, and the Political System," in Stockwin and others, eds., *Dynamic and Immobilist Politics in Japan*, pp. 22–53. Contrasting positions on these military-related issues were summarized in "Opposition Focuses on 3% Consumption Tax," *Japan Economic Journal*, October 7, 1989, p. 7, and emphasized repeatedly in 1983 and 1989 interviews with LDP and JSP Diet members.

31. Legitimate opposition has its own imperative of indifference to power-maximizing compromise. Kyogoku, *Political Dynamics of Japan*. The opposition may either lose legitimacy or seem irrelevant to governance. The LDP has more to fear from an opposition that poses a credible governance alternative than from a voice of pure rejection. The latter only constrains policy; the former could threaten office.

extreme centralization of military security policy authority in the LDP, with the concomitant policy capacity to make bold moves. That expectation would be wrong.

The LDP is a coalition of factions. Factional strength is key to career advancement for individual politicians. Maintaining a coalition of factions is crucial for ascendancy to the presidency of the party and the prime ministership. Ministerial positions are primarily allotted on the basis of faction size and a politician's seniority (number of terms in the Diet) within a faction. Party leaders benefit from maximizing the number of cabinet plums to distribute, which leads to very short terms at the head of most cabinet-level bureaucracies (including the JDA).[32] The factions have no clearly distinct position on most issues, including those related to security. They are more important for the electoral process, including slate making and campaign financing, than the central party machinery.

All of the lower house, and a substantial fraction of the upper house, achieve office through a district-based, multimember electoral system without proportional representation.[33] That is, members of the LDP, even of the same faction, can be in the position of running against each other. Thus a premium is placed on what the individual member, using the vehicles of faction and party, can provide at the district level. Interest groups have numerous points of access, given locally based politicians, competing factions, and busy internal party organs. The politics of the LDP basically involve hammering out agreements that are tolerable to affected parties, providing tangible benefits, and dealing with foreign pressures. LDP politics are not about cost-effective, systematic policy and program design.

Military security issues seldom distinguish LDP candidates from each other in their election campaigns, although the LDP umbrella shelters a wide variety of views from approximately the center of European democratic socialism to right-wing conservative politics. Within the LDP, competitors for the party presidency and prime ministership may emphasize differences on military matters when that seems useful.[34]

32. From November 1964 until July 1987, twenty-one individuals headed the JDA with an average tenure of less than a year. Stockwin, "Parties, Politicians, and the Political System," pp. 42–43.

33. The basic features are hardly new: see Nathaniel B. Thayer, *How the Conservatives Rule Japan* (Princeton University Press, 1969); and Gerald L. Curtis, *Election Campaigning, Japanese Style* (Columbia University Press, 1971). A major data source is Seizaburo Sato and Tetsuhisa Matsuzaki, *Jimintō Seiken* (The Liberal Democratic party) (Tokyo: Chuo Koronsha, 1986).

34. In the late 1970s, LDP leadership competitor Masayoshi Ohira adopted a security policy position that placed him in the middle between the two other candidates. Interview

Ministerial portfolios especially useful for benefiting constituents are ones other than the JDA, and major stepping-stones to party leadership do not include the JDA directorship. Not surprisingly, therefore, the LDP organs whose members favor the military tend to be composed of politicians with limited party standing. Some others with far greater clout may be sympathetic and highly knowledgeable, but they are often frying bigger fish.[35] In effect, most LDP legislators treat military security as a "residual" policy area rather than a primary one. It is not one most legislators find worth bearing substantial costs to advocate. They are fully aware of the lack of affection for the ruling party and their thin electoral margins and relatively low incumbent reelection rate (compared with U.S. legislators).[36]

Keeping the costs of military advocacy high has been a primary mission of the JSP. Its self-styled guardianship of the "never again" resolves and the associated policy principles has served to maintain sufficient legislative seats to block any amendment of the peace constitution. More pervasively, it has kept the LDP on constant notice that any major departure from established military policy will receive substantial publicity and tie up parliamentary deliberations for a significant length of time.

Because the LDP has the ultimate power of denial, however, pragmatic considerations have led to a set of informal conventions enabling the substantial military security steps Japan has taken. The JSP will tolerate incremental and implicit violations of avowed military limitation, so long as the LDP continues to avow adherence to those limits. In 1984, Masashi Ishibashi, then chairman of the JSP, wrote: "While the JSP considers the Self-Defense Forces and the Japan-U.S. Security Treaty to be unconstitutional, it has no intention of immediately doing away with either should it come to power. Our refusal to recognize the SDF and the security pact

---

with LDP Diet member, 1983. In the mid-1980s, Yasuhiro Nakasone clearly traded on the "special relationship" his promilitary activism helped build with President Reagan.

35. Inoguchi and Iwai measured the popularity of the defense division in the LDP compared with other divisions during 1964–83. It was consistently below average, with a gap smallest in the mid-1960s. Takashi Inoguchi and Tomoaki Iwai, "The Growth of *Zoku*: LDP Politicians in Committees, 1964–1984," paper prepared for the 1984 annual meeting of the Association for Asian Studies, p. 44a. Hideo Otake emphasizes the diversity of views among the Diet "defense club" and points out how the most politically influential have taken other factors into account. Otake, "The Politics of Defense Spending in Conservative Japan," Peace Studies Program Occasional Paper, no. 15, Cornell University, February 1982.

36. The "residual" label and the comparative perils of reelection are from Kent E. Calder, *Crisis and Compensation: Public Policy and Political Stability in Japan, 1949–1986* (Princeton University Press, 1988), pp. 66–69, 411. The LDP last received a majority of the popular vote in a national election for either house in 1963.

on constitutional grounds is solely a conceptual matter; we see no contradiction in recognizing their existence."[37] In effect, the majority of the ruling party has been able to rest on a centrist position supporting the current security system against extremes posed by the JSP and military enthusiasts in the LDP.[38]

The ruling party has needed extraordinary incentives and self-confidence to take actions that would open up debate on military security and remove it from backburner status. Indeed, the major disruptions of the postwar period, involving mass turbulence and breakdown of parliamentary decorum in 1960 and 1970, were associated with raising salient public issues about security matters. The LDP survived and retained control, but the involved prime ministers paid a substantial price. For two decades, that sort of confrontation has been avoided.[39] The ruling party has been creative about, and the opposition tolerant of, stratagems that avoid serious parliamentary debate on military strategy and requirements. Military policy thus has been kept in a "windless" zone of comfort and familiarity for Japanese politicians and bureaucrats. The rule about limiting military spending to 1 percent of GNP, officially breached in 1986, has been resurrected. The 1976 defense program outline, with its vague goals of "defensive defense," has stood as the central policy document for fifteen years.[40] The United States has had reasons to tolerate

37. "The Road to Unarmed Neutrality," *Japan Quarterly*, vol. 31 (April–June 1984), p. 144. As early as 1980, the JSP explicitly made a commitment to avoid any precipitous change. In 1987 it signaled sticking with the 1 percent rule and defensive defense. Zen'ichiro Tanaka, "Domestic Politics in Contemporary Japan," in Robert A. Scalapino and others, eds., *Asia and the Major Powers: Domestic Politics and Foreign Policy* (University of California Press, 1988), pp. 91–92.

38. Direct conflict became "subtle collusion." The JSP de facto accepted the security relationship with the United States while criticizing it publicly; the LDP center of gravity accepted much of the security status quo, while occasionally calling for more spending and national pride. Tetsuya Kataoka and Ramon H. Myers, *Defending an Economic Superpower: Reassessing the U.S.-Japan Security Alliance* (Westview Press, 1989), pp. 18–20.

39. The months since this was written have seen the Iraqi invasion of and expulsion from Kuwait, the subsequent passage (on June 15, 1992) of a bill permitting the participation of Japanese military units in United Nations peacekeeping operations, and dispatch of units to Kampuchea. Although these decisions represent an important breach in restraints on the use of the Japanese military, the general analysis put forward in this paper stands. The bill was passed in a very severely restricted form more than a year and a half after being first introduced. It limits the number of personnel to 2,000 and their role to noncombat activities under UN (not U.S.) command. Further legislation is required should self-defense require the use of small arms. The parliamentary process required for passage was arduous and conflictful. A public opinion poll immediately following passage showed positive support from only 15 percent of the national sample. "U.N. Peacekeeping Support Bill Becomes Law," *JEI Report*, no. 23B, June 19, 1992, pp. 5–7.

40. The 1 percent principle was resurrected in the cabinet-approved budget of December

only limited LDP military cooperation, given the alternative of JSP rule.

Major contrasts with the U.S. experience are obvious. Japanese senior politicians have had substantial experience with the management of international commitments, not with the management of national military forces. Military matters have not been a good basis for advancing careers. Political risk to the ruling party and thus to personal careers would lie in making defense issues electorally central and challenging the legacies. JSP opposition politicians would risk whatever political base they had by deviating from a policy of military minimization. The sheer reliability of party cleavages on military policy lines has led to remarkable policy continuity and regularity. Yet it is hard to attribute these patterns primarily to parliamentary institutions. They seem to result far more from the particulars of party and electoral systems in the context of particular legacies and security givens.

Administrative Institutions

Japanese administrative institutions specializing in military security may seem rather similar at first glance to those of the United States. The United States has a largely civilian Office of the Secretary of Defense headed by a political appointee; Japan has the Defense Agency, also headed by a political appointee, and its internal bureaus. The United States has three large uniformed services—the army, navy, and air force—and Japan has the ground, maritime, and air Self-Defense Forces. Even the names of some bodies are similar: the U.S. Joint Chiefs of Staff and National Security Council and the Japanese Joint Staff Council and National Defense Council.

In reality, Japan differs from the United States and from many parliamentary systems in two major respects: the subordination of the defense ministry to other ministries and the extremely limited standing of the uniformed military. These differences are hard to attribute to framework institutions. At the same time, they have profound bearing on national policy capabilities to target resources away from the military, to minimize the role of military interests in international commitments, and to skirt domestic political cleavages on military matters. Military policy becomes the servant of others' policy agendas.

1989. Many of the conventions are matters of euphemistic language. Glenn D. Hook, *Language and Politics: The Security Discourse in Japan and the United States* (Tokyo: Kurioso Syuppan, 1987), pp. 25–45, 67–81.

Japan differs from the United States but resembles most parliamentary systems in the almost total absence of political appointees and the power and prestige of its corps of elite civil servants. These characteristics may well follow from a parliamentary system and may serve to check the ability of elected officials to influence military policy.

In its civilian internal bureaus, the JDA is a colonized bureaucracy in which key positions are often held by persons on assignment from far more important ministries.[41] The Ministry of Finance controls the key budget position; the Ministry of Foreign Affairs, that for international affairs; and the Ministry of International Trade and Industry (MITI), that for procurement. Officials from the police are not unusual. Except for police and some Finance assignees, the JDA is often but one stop on a longer road, a road best traveled by attentiveness to the concerns of the bureaucrat's home ministry. Currently detailed personnel and their predecessors form important and active networks.[42] The loaned civil servants bring back to their home ministries considerable sophistication in the military security aspects of foreign affairs, technology and production, and finance.[43] Those major home bureaucracies have higher domestic standing, better legislative connections, and more staff presence around the prime minister than does the JDA. Several of them can do infinitely more for the private sector.

The power lesson is clear: the JDA and its career civilians gain by being helpful to the agendas of its colonizers and suffer by hindering them. For the Ministry of Foreign Affairs, that has primarily involved being helpful to the agenda of the North American bureau. For MITI, it has involved being helpful in alleviating trade friction with the United States and helping modestly with some industries. For the Ministry of Finance, it has involved some accommodation to general constraints on government personnel and spending. If the many colonizers happen to be at cross-purposes, the JDA has to either wait or hope that friendly party elders will produce a resolution. And if a major colonizer changes its views, the JDA is expected to follow, barring LDP tribal intervention.

41. For details, see Katsuya Hirose, *Kanryō to Gunjin: Bunmin Tōsei no Genkai* (Bureaucrats and soldiers: the limits of civilian control) (Tokyo: Iwanami Shoten, 1989), pp. 5–11.

42. For example, MITI alumni of the Weapons Bureau directorship meet monthly with the incumbent from MITI.

43. In former years, officials of the colonizing agencies had direct experience with military matters as soldiers or defense industry managers. On the Foreign Ministry, see Haruhiro Fukui, "Policy-Making in the Japanese Foreign Ministry," in Scalapino, ed., *Foreign Policy of Modern Japan*, p. 32; on MITI, see Chalmers Johnson, *MITI and the Japanese Miracle: The Growth of Industrial Policy, 1925–1975* (Stanford University Press, 1982).

In ancillary policy matters related to military security, the Defense Agency is at best a minor player. For example, primary responsibility and authority for arms control, weapons exports, controls on technology transfer, and space development all lie elsewhere.[44]

Elite JDA civil servants are drawn from the same high-status institutions as the rest of the higher career civil service.[45] Nevertheless, recruitment and morale suffer from lesser status and promotion opportunities than at the Finance, Foreign Affairs, International Trade and Industry, and Home ministries. For those with aspirations toward political or commercial second careers, the JDA also suffers relative to, for example, the Construction and Transportation ministries.

The military components of the JDA are career services, except for some lower enlisted ranks. There are almost no opportunities except within one's parent service. In spite of a now common undergraduate education, interservice rivalry is extremely bitter. The joint staff organization proceeds only by unanimity. Interservice rivalry strengthens the influence of civilian officials and induces the services to seek U.S. public- and private-sector support for their equipment preferences. Relations are probably more cooperative between particular U.S. and Japanese sister services than between the Japanese services. The service struggles lead to marked inefficiency in mission integration, complementary procurements, support services, and even planning about threats, doctrines, and tactics.[46] Tight restraints lead to military silence on all major matters of security policy, including its adequacy and realism.[47] Military officers are usually absent from high-level government deliberations, although retired ones may be in close contact with some LDP legislators.[48]

44. The key institutions are the Ministry of Foreign Affairs, MITI, and, for space, the Science and Technology Agency.

45. On the elite service, see B. C. Koh, *Japan's Administrative Elite* (University of California Press, 1989).

46. Matters have not improved since a Japanese diplomat wrote in 1980, "The SDF lacks a strategy and an organization for integrated operations between the three branches. Their missions and strategies are not well coordinated, nor are force structures and weapon systems designed to meet the requirements for integrated operations." Yukio Satoh, "The Evolution of Japanese Security Policy," *Adelphi Papers*, no. 178 (London: International Institute for Strategic Studies, 1982), p. 19. In the late 1980s, the services differed about the primary geographic front of military threat.

47. Senior officers have taken early retirement after public statements on lack of readiness and aspects of Soviet threats. Others have been criticized for statements that implied acceptance of a government whose leadership did not come from the LDP.

48. The chairman of the Joint Staff does not deal directly with the prime minister. Nakasone was viewed as exceptional among JDA directors in calling on military officers other than service heads for papers and briefings. Connections with retirees are illustrated by LDP elder Shin Kanemaru's sponsorship of the Japan Center for Strategic Studies.

The status problem affects the quality of officer personnel and the quality and quantity of enlistments in an all-volunteer force.[49] It leads to a great desire to avoid notice and controversy, which is achieved through self-limitation on training and public expression. Senior military officers receive lower pay and benefits than senior civilian public officials. Mission restrictions make a military career rather uninteresting and parochial. A military career is not a good launching pad for a subsequent political career or lucrative private-sector opportunities. Retired senior officers are retained by defense industrial firms, but usually only for marketing purposes and even then only on a short-term basis.[50]

In sum, both the civilian and military parts of the JDA are defensive and subordinated. Attention usually bodes difficulties. They are in no position to make demands or threaten to arouse criticism of prevailing policies. They fare best when taken for granted and when seen as useful for more important actors' objectives, which have included managing relations with the United States. In important ways, they have been dependent on Washington as their primary lobbyist.

There are obviously substantial transaction costs for reaching agreements among the services, internal bureaus, and colonizing agencies. To minimize those costs, a multiyear framework is generated that at least presents the facade of some policy agreement and perhaps reduces the intensity of the annual fray with the opposition political parties over military matters. In the early years of the JDA, that framework took the form of several multiyear defense buildup plans (for fiscal years 1958–60, 1962–66, 1967–71, and 1972–76). Subsequently, in the context of the national defense program outline, three mid-term defense program estimates (*chugyo*) were adopted (for fiscal years 1980–84, 1983–87, and 1986–90).

None of the buildup plans or *chugyo* have met their targets.[51] What

---

Largely composed of senior ex-officers, it prepares position papers on defense matters for circulation under the aegis of Kanemaru and several other members of the "defense tribe."

49. Enlisted quotas, especially in the army, have long failed to meet the totals allowed (*Defense of Japan*, various years). Many enlisted personnel see military service as a way station to a civilian career. The quality of officer candidates is expected to decline with the general tightness of the labor market associated with an aging society and a strong economy.

50. For data on defense industry employment of high-ranking retirees, see Drifte, *Arms Production in Japan*, pp. 27–28; and Vogel, *Japanese High Technology*, p. 75. The sense of being cut off from serious corporate activity and of employment only for the next contract is from interviews with current and former military officers (1983, 1989).

51. Drifte, *Arms Production in Japan*, pp. 14–16; and Hirose, *Kanryō to Gunjin*, pp. 182, 222.

they have done is to create future funding imperatives through small down payments on major procurements. The future spending necessary to complete procurements has come to be an increasingly substantial amount relative to current-year spending. That sort of budgetary bow wave can be contained, but only through inefficient procurement stretch-outs or paring other parts of the defense budget. The JDA has done both.[52] Further, the *chugyo* come up from the services before being trimmed to fit budget limits. Despite signs to the contrary, the system lacks mechanisms to maximize cost-effectiveness across the Self-Defense Forces or to carry out sustained, substantively based multiyear force structure and acquisition strategies.

Again, the contrasts with the United States are profound. They also are very substantial with parliamentary systems that emphasize military policy (such as Israel), elitism (such as France), or mass participation (such as Switzerland). Postwar practices in the United States make it exceedingly difficult to minimize international military commitments, to avoid directing resources to the military, and to keep military matters and individuals with military credentials out of domestic political contests. Japanese administrative institutional practices have the opposite effects. However, Japanese military institutions are not particularly different from those in the United States, and are perhaps even worse, in interservice rivalry and procurement inefficiency. In the Japanese case, that may be because the stakes have been so small; in the U.S. case, because they have been so big.

Defense Private Sector

Much discussion of the need for institutional reform in the United States focuses on an "iron triangle" among the military services, Congress, and the defense industry. That coalition supposedly eludes control by the president and the cabinet. Looking at comparable institutions in Japan, I have already established the weakness of the JDA compared with other administrative institutions and of the Diet compared with the LDP. What of the third element—the defense private sector?

The defense industry in Japan is constrained by the "never again" resolves and their policy manifestations. Individual firms tend to avoid

52. From fiscal years 1976 through 1985, the out-year burden increased from 34 percent to 74 percent of the current defense budget. Hirose, *Kanryō to Gunjin*, p. 212. Retirement ages were raised to avoid separation payments, and personnel-related amenities were underfunded.

high visibility for their defense-related activities. The limited size of the domestic market and export restraints combine to limit the stature of defense production in the business community, compared with more dynamic and open civil product lines. Most public demands for increased military resources are made by the aggregated peak interest group association, the Defense Production Committee, which contains the firms that do the bulk of defense business.[53]

JDA procurement practices resemble those of much of the Japanese public sector. A largely stable set of major suppliers has JDA assurances of substantial profit (about 10 percent) and of their continued market share.[54] A very large share of procurement and R&D is noncompetitive.[55] Major systems usually involve consortia in which all of the few relevant firms negotiate funding shares. The limited numbers of units of any one type lead to demand for and funding of successor systems to maintain the industry. Because the JDA has only a modest share of science and technology funding, there is a tendency to use technology that has been debugged by applications in the private sector or by the U.S. government and U.S. firms.[56] The JDA and the defense firms have an interest in portraying the resulting products as free of disappointment, although their interests are not fully identical.[57]

53. The DPC was quick to seize on FSX-related tensions to justify increased investments in domestic capabilities. Interview with DPC staff, 1982–83; "Mitsubishi to Develop Defense Software," *Japan Economic Journal*, May 20, 1989, p. 20; and "Keidanren Urges Japan to Boost Defense R&D," *Japan Times*, May 17, 1989, p. 2. Other umbrella business interest groups are the Japan Weapons Industry Association (*Nihon Heiki Kōgyōkai*), the Defense Equipment Association (*Bōei Sōbi Kyōkai*), and the Export Council (*Yusyutsu Konwakai*). Major organizations also exist along general industry lines, such as the aircraft and electronics industries.

54. Major contractors have been funded to develop a production base with capacities far greater than needed for current or prospective orders. Profit and capacity information are from interviews with MITI, JDA, and industry officials. Others suggest that the profit percentages are somewhat lower.

55. In a typical year in the mid-1980s, 44 percent of the total number of contracts carrying 85 percent of the total value were awarded through "optional contracts," that is, where the JDA specified a sole bidder. Another 55 percent of the total number of contracts and 15 percent of the value went through "designated competition contracts," that is, where the JDA specified a small number of eligible bidders. Kiyoshi Aikawa, "Procurement Policy, Plan and Procedures," in Kuni Sadamoto, ed., *The Arms and Defense of Japan* (Tokyo: Survey Japan, 1987), pp. 95–96. This is particularly pronounced in aircraft cases, such as the FSX. Interviews with JDA and MITI officials, 1989.

56. The amount of local content is often overstated in claims by Japanese firms. JDA officials and nongovernment experts often attribute the companies' ability to complete tasks on cost and on time largely to avoiding cutting-edge, first-time-out technology.

57. Many institutions would be implicated in any mistake. Firms and service staffs sold the system to the internal bureaus, all of them dealt with MITI and Ministry of Finance

The military users often would prefer technologies tested for realistic performance elsewhere, albeit with Japanese quality of manufacture.[58] The relatively high costs of indigenous systems, often two or three times as much as imports, clearly limit the numbers that can be purchased. Yet shared interests dominate, given little likelihood of obtaining sufficient personnel to man a much larger inventory of military systems.[59] More realistic training or an emphasis on the ammunition and parts associated with fighting a war would only lead to adverse publicity. The JDA is the only available market for completed weapons systems. Both the JDA and firms are more likely to secure funds when projects can be presented as responsive to broader American desires and can transfer advanced technology to Japan. The appearance and reality of a substantial indigenous defense industry provide JDA officials with at least some important domestic friends. They also can bolster bargaining power with U.S. firms through the carrot of flowback technology and the stick of threatened self-sufficiency. More parochially, the JDA's own technological bureaucracy would have little to do without advanced Japanese private-sector military R&D and production.[60]

The Japanese do not have a quasi-autonomous "iron triangle" of the defense industry, the military bureaucracy, and legislators. Relevant firms can often find much larger and less controversial sources of government or private funding to pursue their dual-use technology interests. The conventional wisdom is that LDP politicians do not get involved in source selection for big-ticket military purchases, except those seen to be im-

---

reviewers, and the National Defense Council ultimately approved the procurement. Evidence of poor performance would be used by numerous critics and funding competitors in other services, internal bureaus, external ministries, and even in the companies involved. Problems with airplanes, most recently the T-4 trainer that supposedly warranted a fully indigenous FSX, are often handled by reducing demands on the aircraft.

58. Interviews with JDA officials, 1982, 1983, and 1989.

59. The Ministry of Finance has kept a very tight lid on military personnel. Plans are now under way in the JDA to reduce personnel in the face of demographic changes in Japan as a whole.

60. Technology transfer for ostensibly solely military purposes from the United States has a long history. See J. R. Phillips, "A History of Hi Tech Exchange: Japan and USA," paper prepared for the 1986 Asian-Pacific Strategy Symposium, Taipei, Taiwan; and *Defense of Japan, 1988*, p. 331. Transfer policy was avowedly one-way from 1967 until 1983, when there was an exchange of notes enabling Japanese transfer to the United States (*Defense of Japan, 1988*, pp. 180, 325–28). While little has flowed since then from Japan to the United States, the bargaining uses are clear, so long as the reliance on foreign content and know-how seems modest and declining. Vogel, *Japanese High Technology*; and Drifte, *Arms Production in Japan*. JDA's Technical R&D Institute strongly supports a strong, world-leading indigenous defense industry. Generalists in JDA are far more skeptical of company capability claims, and even of those certified by the institute. Interviews, 1989.

portant for general relations with the United States. A minority view claims that major source selections have been politically directed to the degree that there have been early resignations of uncooperative high-ranking military officers. Also, it may be significant that the political appointee heading the JDA at the time of major aircraft selection decisions has been from a major faction in the coalition around the current LDP president and prime minister.[61]

In contrast with the United States, Japan has a relatively unimportant defense industry that accommodates itself to imperatives of the ruling party and nonmilitary administrative institutions. It also rarely challenges national military institutions. The results are poor in terms of absolute or comparative short-term efficiency. Yet they do provide formidable technological and industrial long-term benefits for only a modest share of national wealth. The key lies in continuing investment in the modernization of military technology and manufacturing capacity. There are obvious advantages for a nation that wants to avoid war and at the same time have substantial deterrent potential.

Conclusions and Speculations

The central contextual features shaping Japan's military security policy since 1950 have been a particular set of historical legacies, security givens, and profound economic and technological successes. The crucial institutions have been a factional but enduring ruling party of highly opportunistic bent, an opposition party and major media with an *idée fixe* about military matters, subordinated military institutions within an able and politicized higher civil service, and a protected and financially secure defense industry of modest importance in the national political economy. These factors are for the most part not inherent in parliamentary systems per se, but they also differ radically from features of cold war America.

Japan's rather modest and nationally productive military security goals

61. Lack of procurement intervention is a repeated theme in interviews with officials in the Ministry of Finance, JDA, MITI, and the Ministry of Foreign Affairs (1982, 1983, 1986, and 1989). Even those who argue this general position find it caused more by lack of interest than by institutional constraint, and they note aircraft as an exception. For example, see Otake, "The Politics of Defense Spending." The aircraft industry is exceptionally dependent on JDA funds. Direct participants provide ample evidence of repeated intervention in aircraft procurement. Interview with former JDA official, 1989. Similar stories have appeared about a domestic lead firm for licensed missile production. Kazuo Tomiyama, "Who Makes Defense Policy Decisions?" in Sadamoto, ed., *Arms and Defense of Japan*, p. 49.

have been made relatively easy to achieve and difficult to depart from. The country has made major adaptations to changing circumstances in its rhetoric, technology, and international relationships, but has shown great staying power and resilience in the basic principles that limit its military security policy. Major challenges in the early 1970s and late 1980s lost momentum in the face of international changes, LDP scandals, and military accidents that took civilian lives.[62]

Four decades of military security policy have given Japan international leadership in the capacity to cast an economically and politically sustainable "long shadow" in military technology for deterrence and coalition bargaining.[63] That is puzzling because Japanese institutions do not appear to possess the capabilities that much Western public policy thinking associates with a strong, bold policymaking apparatus. Two different solutions to the puzzle yield very different lessons for policy capability.

First, Japan's success results not from policy capabilities and institutions, but from circumstances, including U.S. and Soviet policy tendencies, secular features of the world economy and of technology innovation cycles, and even racial homogeneity and addiction to work.

The second lesson is that Japan made deliberate choices, especially about administrative institutions and the defense private sector. The effects of circumstances on outcomes followed from conscious acts to exploit those circumstances. Those acts in turn led to further success and support for continuing established policies and policy process arrangements.

This perspective can be expanded to include conscious decisions to maintain an electoral system and types of political parties (both ruling and opposition) in the face of numerous proposals to change them into forms found more commonly in parliamentary systems. Rejection of change surely had narrow, special-interest motivations. However, it also has followed from a view of politics and public policy that emphasizes efficient investment and explicit, authoritative management less than policy latitude, tangible material benefits, situational political opportunism, principled opposition, blurred innovation and continuity, and ad-

62. Proposed versions of the fourth build-up plan (1972–76) explicitly emphasized "autonomous defense" and envisioned a doubling of defense expenditures. They were withdrawn. A collision between a maritime Self-Defense Forces submarine and a civilian sport fishing boat in the summer of 1988 was widely viewed as a blow to the defense buildup and the image of the military. More than a year later, it was still an ongoing issue in the Diet and press, rich with coverup allegations.

63. In late 1989 numerous Japanese officials admitted to having a de facto strong "long shadow" posture, while emphasizing that no one had planned such an outcome. Interviews with MITI, JDA, and Science and Technology Agency officials, 1989.

aptation to foreign developments and concerns. Given this perspective, state organs are more concerned with status and resources than program content.

Were parliamentary institutions essential to nurture the capabilities attributed to Japan? It probably would have been much harder for Japan to walk so many military security policy tightropes and balance so many external and domestic factors without senior, influential, extraordinarily experienced Diet members; tight links between ruling-party politicians and the higher civil service; and an elitist and sectional higher civil service determined to subordinate military institutions. The first two factors require prolonged one-party rule and an elder oligarchy within that party that serves many terms, but not parliamentary institutions. Parliamentary institutions may benefit the third, but not more so than broad consensus on military subordination.

More speculatively, what difference would presidential institutions have made? It seems likely that some narrower institutional features would have been different, such as LDP cohesion, the path to prominence in the party, and the electoral system. Campaigns might have focused more on national issues, including military ones.[64] The tissue of military security ambiguities and discrepancies might not have survived.

There is little reason to believe that an alternative framework institution would have changed the policies and capabilities central to military matters. The historical legacies and security givens argue otherwise. For at least the past twenty years, Japanese public opinion overwhelmingly and consistently has favored the prevailing course of policy. Ambiguity and adjustment are endemic in Japanese public- and private-sector operations and are hardly limited to military matters or the ruling party. Even if the LDP had split or the JSP had come to office, the differences between the parties would have emphasized nonmilitary matters. Even with a presidential system, it is hard to imagine a JSP victory without departure from its single-issue focus.

In sum, the enviable Japanese performance provides no general brief for the superiority of parliamentary institutions. Nor does it support the contention that framework institutions directly determine policy capabilities.

64. The single-member district has long been on Japanese institutional reformers' menus. Opposition parties have resisted it on grounds that it would tend to increase LDP dominance. So have many LDP members bothered by its potentially adverse implications for their careers and autonomy. It is not obvious that a stronger, more centralized LDP would have been better for Japanese military security policy in the past or will be in the future. The possible consequences of a presidential system were called to my attention by Professor Yoshinobu Yamamoto, Tokyo University.

Thus it is hard to see how a "parliamentary remedy" for the United States could suffice to avoid the intense political and economic competition and maneuvering associated with a policy area that consumes a substantial share of national resources. The big stakes associated with being a military superpower make military policy extraordinarily important to interest groups and politicians. Concerns that might otherwise be directed toward other policy topics are focused on military matters. That is true for would-be presidents trying to assemble electoral and legislative majorities, for legislators seeking constituency employment, and for firms seeking contract revenues. The relative abundance of resources in defense budgets creates incentives to put all sorts of matters under the aegis of defense institutions, for example, the role of the Defense Advanced Research Projects Agency in high-technology industrial policy. At the same time, incentives flourish to attack defense institutions and military policies in order to free resources for other areas of government spending. In short, the scale of a policy area within a national political economy has inherent implications that may be adverse for some policy capabilities.

Skepticism about the role of framework institutions is supported by even the briefest reflection on the contemporary experience of other parliamentary systems. Britain and France have managed far larger allocations of national wealth to military purposes than have Canada and Italy. The latter two have shunned involvement in distant conflicts and the former two have pursued it, especially in traditional areas of empire. Britain has not succeeded at maintaining an economically efficient, modern defense apparatus and an advanced technology base, while Israel has done extraordinarily well, given its resources. Direct threat to the homeland provides stronger explanation than do framework institutions for the British, French, and Dutch capacity to cut losses by withdrawing from controlled territories and the Israeli inability to do so.

Some critics of the U.S. separation-of-powers system argue that separation imposes undesirable constraints on the bold and decisive use of military power. This argument is suspect on many grounds. The experience of Israel in Lebanon in 1982 and France in Algeria during the Fourth Republic suggests that parliamentary systems are not always able to engage in or sustain the bold and decisive application of force. Other instances suggest that even when they do, it may not be wise. There are some who envy Prime Minister Thatcher's pursuit of the Falklands campaign. Yet it would have been much less expensive for Great Britain to have provided every Falklander with a handsome lifetime annuity and comfortable relocation for each of them (and their sheep) in New Zealand.

As for the United States, it is not obvious that the major inhibitions on boldness in its application of military power (as seen, for example, in Vietnam, Korea, Lebanon, Angola, and Central America) have resulted primarily from its framework institutions. The United States took the lead in making massive military commitments to the Persian Gulf in 1990–91 despite congressional opposition—hardly evidence of institutional paralysis. Even the often-mentioned War Powers Act has in fact imposed little in the way of binding constraint. In any event, those who argue the need for bolder uses of force must demonstrate that quicker, larger, more escalatory, and more sustained U.S. military involvement in many of those situations would have been in the nation's interest.

These patterns of performance are hard to explain without emphasizing differences in historical experiences, the existence and stability of single-party legislative majorities, external security threats, and the preferences of allies.

As the United States attempts to meet its security challenges, it could benefit from emulating Japanese practices, including institutional arrangements. Those benefits, however, would involve changes that would not hinge on the establishment of a parliamentary system. The United States cannot readily change its history, but it can emphasize different elements of it. This means two changes in political focus. One is to emphasize a legacy preceding World War II, indeed going back to George Washington's farewell address. The other is to learn from the nation's economic and industrial-technological performance in recent decades. The first argues for rejecting the role of global security architect or policeman. The second argues for deemphasizing the role of military institutions and professionals, especially of military industry and technology relative to their civilian counterparts. More concretely, this would involve major revisions in the distribution between military and civilian bureaucracies of status, career benefits, budgets, programs favoring industry, and influence within the executive branch and with Congress and the public. These changes would follow from a shift in national priorities and would also lead to public policy consistent with different priorities.

There is a certain conceptual appeal to the arguments of those who call for replacing a presidential system with a parliamentary system. Such a bold and general act would provide a basically different structure through which political life would be conducted. It resembles the school of urban renewal that emphasizes destroying existing buildings to put up far different ones. Yet political systems and their associated policy capabilities rest less on neatly layered hierarchical structures than they do on webs of shared experiences, established conventions, and working coalitions.

Those are hard to uproot, and if destroyed are not quickly replaced by the stroke of a pen or by a constitutional convention. Far more predictable and timely benefits can be achieved through the equivalent of urban renewal that stresses rehabilitation. Like houses, political systems can be substantially improved without discarding their basic structure.

American opportunities for selective and timely improvement lie elsewhere. The basis for particular changes lies in the increasing recognition of nonmilitary security needs. The imperatives of economic strength—competitiveness in industry and technology based on a capable work force and sound macroeconomic policy—are coming to rival military matters in public debate. Nonmilitary threats to the environment and public health are assuming a high place on lists of widely shared concerns.

Thus the nation may become receptive to two sets of steps. The first is to bolster the resource claims of the nonmilitary sectors of the economy. Like Japan, the United States could adopt a national investment concept that makes the military only the second-order beneficiary or consumer of accomplishments pursued for civil reason. As a corollary, military institutions and problems would become of secondary importance and attractiveness to the best and the brightest civil servants, to those seeking government support, and to politicians. The result would be a redistribution within the national government of competence, budgets, and departmental political clout to more closely resemble the Japanese pattern. What bears emulating is not Japan's form of government, but its priorities.

R. Kent Weaver and Bert A. Rockman

When and How Do Institutions Matter?

*A*t the beginning of this book, we asked whether political institutions affect the capacity of government to function effectively. It is easy to answer this question in the affirmative, but this answer does not necessarily make political institutions the most important element affecting governing capacity. Ascertaining which institutions matter, and when and how they affect governmental performance, is a complex matter. Effective governance is multidimensional: it involves tasks as diverse as targeting resources efficiently, imposing losses on powerful organized groups, coordinating conflicting objectives, and managing deep societal cleavages.

The case study chapters suggest that most of the governance problems of the United States are shared by all industrial democracies, most of which have similar difficulties in addressing those problems. Very few countries succeed in targeting resources on behalf of an effective industrial policy, for example. Problems with balancing budgets are ubiquitous. All elected (and most unelected) governments are reluctant to impose losses on pensioners. Ethnic, racial, and linguistic conflict is all too common. Particular institutional arrangements do not cause these governance problems; they are inherent in complex societies and in democratic government. Groups inevitably want more from government than government is able to provide, and they want above all else to be protected from losing ground. Therefore policy failings in the United States should not be blamed exclusively, or perhaps even mainly, on the structure of American governmental institutions.

Nevertheless, some governments do perform at least some of these tasks better than others, and political institutions do affect government capabilities and policy outcomes. But the institutional influences on governmental capabilities are also complex. The distinction between parliamentary systems and the U.S. system of checks and balances, which is often seen as a crucial influence on governmental effectiveness, captures only a small part of potential institutional influences on governmental capacity. Consequently, we have added two additional "tiers" of possible institutional effects on governing capabilities. The second tier includes such features as the electoral rules and norms leading to the formation of different types of governments (such as alternating single-party majorities, durable single-party dominance, or multiparty coalitions in parliamentary systems). The third tier includes other institutional forces, some stemming from constitutional architecture or tradition (federalism, bicameralism, and judicial review, for example) and others from institutional rules or political organization (such as forms of parliamentary voting and party discipline). Further, the third tier of explanation includes noninstitutional factors such as a society's political culture and its structure of social and political divisions.

Some institutional influences are strong, direct, unidirectional, and consistent over time and across policy sectors. Most are subtle or indirect and are contingent in strength and direction upon the presence of other factors. In this chapter, we sort through these institutional influences on governmental effectiveness and attempt to arrive at some general conclusions about their scope and importance. We begin by outlining some very general conclusions about institutional effects on government capabilities. We also look at the effects of particular sets of institutional arrangements on specific government capabilities. These substantive conclusions set the stage for the final chapter, in which we examine the implications of these findings for the design of political institutions.

Overall Patterns Of Institutional Influence

Some firm conclusions can be reached about the overall influence of political institutions on government capabilities.

1. *Although institutions affect governmental capabilities, their effects are contingent.* Specific institutional arrangements are insufficient to guarantee a high or low level of a specific capability, but they may exacerbate failures of governance or help to make societies more manageable. Even where institutional arrangements do contribute to overall differences in specific capabilities, moreover, these effects usually are strongly mediated by other institutional and noninstitutional factors. Thus, instead of speaking of the sufficiency of certain institutional arrangements, it is more appro-

priate to speak of opportunities they provide for strong capabilities when other conditions are present to facilitate those opportunities. For example, party government–style parliamentary systems are most likely to provide opportunities for policy innovation when the governing party has a strong majority and cohesive political leadership and faces weak electoral threats from a divided opposition. Similarly, one may speak of the risks of weak capabilities created by specific combinations of institutions and social and political conditions. For example, the risk that separation of powers will lead to unclear policy priorities and big budget deficits is likely to be greatest when there is divided partisan control of government and the public holds inconsistent preferences on taxing and spending.

2. *Specific institutional arrangements often create both opportunities and risks for individual governmental capabilities.* The effects of specific institutional arrangements on government capabilities and policy outcomes are rarely unidirectional. David Vogel's chapter on environmental policy showed, for example, that single-party-dominant parliamentary systems may insulate politicians from at least some short-term political pressures, but politicians may use that insulation to exclude relatively diffuse interests *or* to respond to them. The tendency of party government systems to concentrate both power and accountability may give governments the resources they need to impose losses yet simultaneously make them more afraid to do so, as Pierson and Weaver's review of Canadian pension policy suggests.

Because institutional opportunities and risks are contingent upon political and social conditions, they are subject to variation over time. Institutional characteristics that give party government regimes a high capability to impose losses in one set of conditions (a majority government in its first year in office) may lead to a weak capability under other conditions (minority government or a government facing election in the near future). Very crude estimates of the risks and opportunities associated with the U.S. system of checks and balances and with three parliamentary regime types are summarized in table 1. Each regime type is evaluated for the opportunities and risks for each capability. Both significant opportunities and risks are associated with most regime type–capability pairs.

3. *Policymaking capabilities may also differ substantially across policy areas within a single political system.* Such variations may occur either because somewhat different institutional arrangements have come into being in different policy areas (a topic to be discussed below as "countervailing mechanisms") or because similar institutions operate differently across these areas. For example, the risk of policy instability in the U.S. system

Table 1. *Capabilities of Regime Types*[a]

	Regime type							
	Separation of powers		*Coalitional*		*Party government*		*Single-party-dominant*	
Capability	*Level of risk*	*Level of opportunity*	*Level of risk*	*Level of opportunity*	*Level of risk*	*Level of opportunity*	*Level of risk*	*Level of opportunity*
Concentrated power better								
Policy innovation	--	+	*	*	*	+	*	+
Loss imposition	--	*	-	*	-	++	*	++
Priority setting	--	*	--	*	*	+	-	++
Targeting resources efficiently	--	*	--	*	?	?	-	+
Coordinating conflicting objectives	--	*	*	*	-	+	*	++
Policy implementation	-	*	*	*	-	+	*	+
No difference								
Maintaining international commitments	*	*	*	*	*	*	*	*
Concentrated power worse								
Representing diffuse interests	-	++	*	+	--	+	-	+
Cleavage management	-	+	-	++	--	*	x	x
Policy stability	-	++	-	++	--	*	*	++

a. Ratings are risks and opportunities associated with various regime types vis-à-vis mean of all regime types.
Scores:
++ Significantly higher than average opportunities.
+ Significant opportunities.
* Minor or nonexistent opportunities or risks.
- Significant risks.
-- Significantly higher than average risks and limitations.
x Unlikely regime type when policy challenge is significant.
? No data or unclear from data.

of separation of powers and bicameralism is likely to be highest in cases such as synthetic fuel development, where it is difficult to build a stable logrolling coalition by spreading benefits broadly.

4. *Institutional effects on government capabilities are channeled through governmental decisionmaking characteristics.* Five decisionmaking characteristics are especially important: elite cohesion, multiple veto points, elite stability, interest group access, and elite autonomy from short-term political pressures.

Of course, particular decisionmaking attributes have a greater effect on some capabilities than on others and also are more directly affected by institutional structures than are others. The existence of multiple veto points, for example, is very important in inhibiting the ability to impose losses and to set and maintain a consistent set of priorities. Parliamentary systems with single-party majority governments usually have fewer veto points than do separation-of-powers systems. However, parliamentary systems with coalition governments may have equally complex, if less formal, veto systems than the United States.

Similarly, stability of decisionmaking elites is likely to be especially important for ensuring that policies are implemented as intended and that the policies themselves remain stable. Newcomers to political office may not have the same stake in policies as their predecessors, and may (especially in the case of electoral change) even be committed to a different set of policies. Among parliamentary systems, there is great divergence in elite stability across regime types. Single-party-dominant systems like Japan often exhibit substantial circulation of elites among top posts, but the cast of players remains largely the same over time. Executive and legislative leadership in party government parliamentary systems usually turns over completely when a governing party is turned out of office. Executive stability in systems where coalitions are the norm tends to be between that for the other two parliamentary regime types—and probably closest to the American separation-of powers-system. The U.S. system, however, seems to have crosscutting effects on elite stability. There is less stability in the executive because of the personalized nature of the presidential office, its term limits, and reliance on noncareerists in the top reaches of the executive branch. However, third-tier features in the legislative branch encourage elite stability in Congress: weak parties and campaign finance laws that benefit incumbents lessen the probability that there will be a change in party control, and seniority rules further enhance prospects for continuity in committee leadership positions.

5. *Second-tier institutional arrangements influence government capabilities at least as much as do the separation or fusion of executive and legislative power.* Differences in electoral rules and in rules and norms guiding the for-

mation of governments distinguish the three main types of parliamentary systems: Westminster-style party government regimes, single-party-dominant systems, and systems in which coalition governments are the norm. These differences are visible first, and most notably, in the number of veto points (single-party majority governments in party government systems are likely to have fewest); second, in the cohesiveness of the leadership stratum (single-party majority governments in party government systems are likely to have the most cohesion); third, in the resistance of politicians to short-term political pressures (single-party-dominant governments are apt to be most resistant); fourth, in the stability of the leadership stratum over time (single-party-dominant governments tend to be most stable); and fifth, in the amount of access enjoyed by interest groups (single-party majority governments tend to grant less).

As a result, parliamentary institutions do not have a uniform effect on governing capabilities. Instead, the Westminster and single-party-dominant systems tend to concentrate power while coalitional systems tend to diffuse it, as does the U.S. separation-of-powers system. The U.S. separation-of-powers system tends to cluster closely with the co-alitional parliamentary regime types in terms of its associated risks and opportunities, while party government and single-party-dominant systems also tend to cluster together on most capabilities (table 1). Systems within the two clusters are not identical in their decisionmaking attributes or in their government capabilities, as we will show when we discuss individual capabilities, but their effects tend to be in the same general direction.

The similarities in capabilities between the U.S. system and coalitional regimes should not be surprising, given that they tend to resemble each other and to differ from most party-government and single-party-dominant regimes in most of the second-tier decisionmaking attributes. Both the U.S. and coalitional systems are likely, for example, to have less elite cohesion than the other parliamentary regime types, and both are more likely to have significant continuity in elected policymaking elites after elections.

Of course, there also are important differences between coalitional systems and the U.S. separation-of-powers system that affect some capabilities. Because the U.S. system relies more upon multiple veto points rather than inclusion of minorities to limit majority rule, for example, it often discourages rather than encourages consensus-seeking behavior. This has implications most obviously for the ways that cleavages are managed, but also for other capabilities such as policy innovation.

6. *Neither "parliamentarist" nor "presidentialist" arguments offer satisfactory explanations of capabilities.* One of the simplest, and most common,

ways of formulating institutional effects on governmental capabilities is to ask, Are parliamentary systems better? Parliamentarist arguments suggest that the U.S. system, unlike most parliamentary systems, poses a number of obstacles to effective government policymaking. Given a reasonably comparable set of challenges, therefore, parliamentary systems should exhibit stronger performance on most capabilities. Presidentialist arguments, on the other hand, suggest that few, if any, differences should be evident in the performance of parliamentary systems and the U.S. checks-and-balances system. The United States should be near the median level of governmental performance on most capabilities. The evidence in this volume suggests that the question "are parliamentary systems better" is too simplistic. It assumes that generalizations can be made about the capabilities of parliamentary systems across regime and government types. It assumes that the risks and opportunities associated with a particular set of political institutions will be the same regardless of different societal conditions (homogeneity versus heterogeneity of populations, for example). And it assumes that the set of desirable institutional capacities is the same in all countries. None of these assumptions is valid.

7. *Divided party control of the legislative and executive branches of government in the United States exacerbates some problems of governance, especially the problem of setting priorities.* Divided government affects several of the decisionmaking attributes outlined here and thus influences several capabilities. Divided government obviously lowers elite cohesion and increases the importance of the multiple veto points that inhere in the U.S. system. It also reinforces short-term electoral pressures for leaders of the executive and legislative branches of government to generate blame against the other. But the policy consequences of divided government are more complex than the inevitable stalemate portrayed by some critics of divided government.

The evidence in Allen Schick's chapter on how governments in Sweden, the Netherlands, and the United States have coped with the problem of reducing budget deficits strongly suggests that the combination of lower elite cohesion and multiple veto points characteristic of divided government presents formidable obstacles to setting clear priorities.[1] Divided government may also increase incentives for Congress to micromanage policy in ways that make it difficult to implement programs effectively, because especially under these conditions Congress does not

---

1. See also the discussion in Gary W. Cox and Samuel Kernell, eds., "Conclusion," in Cox and Kernell, eds., *The Politics of Divided Government* (Westview, 1991), pp. 239–47.

trust the executive to do what legislative majorities prefer. With respect
to the capability of policy innovation, however, divided government
may lead either to stalemate or to a "bidding up" process. The latter can
produce significant innovation, as was the case with environmental legislation in the Nixon administration and tax cuts in the first year of the
Reagan administration. Stalemate is more likely when the ideological
distance between the parties and leaders of the two branches is high,
interest group pressures conflict sharply with one another, and budget
scarcity makes policy conflict into a sustained zero-sum game. When
these conditions operate under unified government, their effects are likely
to be less sharp.

8. *There are direct trade-offs between some institutional capabilities.* Institutional arrangements whose decisionmaking attributes facilitate some
capabilities tend to inhibit others. For example, institutional arrangements that promote capabilities for innovation in policymaking by limiting veto points, such as party government parliamentary systems, also
are likely to create risks of policy instability for exactly this reason.
Institutional arrangements that increase elite cohesion tend to increase
governmental capacities to set and maintain priorities and to coordinate
conflicting objectives, but these arrangements are also likely to limit
capabilities to represent diffuse interests. And when elite cohesion is
gained by narrowing the representativeness of government in a highly
divided society, the effects on cleavage management can be disastrous.

9. *Governments gain some room to work around basic institutional arrangements by generating countervailing mechanisms.* In a number of the case
studies, policy outcomes seem to be strongly influenced by institutional
adaptations that directly counteract the limitations and risks associated
with basic institutional mechanisms. In the United States, legislative
power frequently is delegated to the executive (in the trade sector, for
example) and to independent regulatory commissions, giving them broad
policymaking discretion so long as they do not offend legislative majorities. In turn, politicians are shielded from local political pressures
arising from the distributive decisions these agencies make.

Westminster-style parliamentary systems, on the other hand, sometimes develop mechanisms to weaken centralized power. These may be
implicit, such as the use of broad consultations, or explicit, such as the
devolution of power to regions. Systems in which multiparty coalitions
are the norm also have developed mechanisms to counteract the potential
for exceptionally weak minority governments or deadlocked coalitions.
Perhaps the most important of these arrangements are inclusive corporatist and consociational links between government and interest groups

associated with the smaller North European democracies. Through formal oversized coalitions, inclusive governments help implement these arrangements.

While it is often difficult to know whether the countervailing mechanisms were the product of a conscious decision to strengthen specific capabilities, we do observe in some of our case studies a strong tendency for both parliamentary systems and the U.S. system of checks and balances to adjust at least marginally for perceived institutional weaknesses. These adjustments may be sectoral or systemwide, and they may be formal (statutory or imbedded in constitutions) or informal. They also may be designed to deal with a set of problems or represent an ad hoc response to an immediately pressing one. However, countervailing mechanisms usually cannot completely eliminate strong institutional limitations and risks.

Institutional Influences on Specific Capabilities

Because we have used a comparative case study approach to study the relationship between institutions and governing capacity, we have very few countries, and very few policy areas, on which to base generalizations about specific capabilities. We know that specific institutional arrangements may provide both opportunities and risks for any given capability, but we cannot be certain that the exact balance between institutional opportunities and risks that we observe in our intensive, yet necessarily limited, set of case studies is representative of all countries and sectors sharing those institutional arrangements. This, we conclude, provides some limits around our confidence in the connections we draw between institutional arrangements and specific government capabilities. Still, the case studies provide us with sound evidence, allowing us to see how policy influences are shaped by institutional and other factors. The inferences we draw from the evidence at hand are reasonable but not irreversible.

Types of Capabilities and Regimes

The capabilities that we have focused on in this book can be characterized by three very broad categories. The first are the steering functions of government: policy innovation, resource targeting, loss imposition, priority setting, coordination of conflicting objectives, and policy implementation. The ability of governments to decide and to steer a course of action seems to depend on their ability to generate sufficient authority. A second set of capabilities seems to coincide generally with the maintenance functions of government. The ability to stand by what has been done in the past, however, requires relatively little new decisionmaking energy. It does require generating strong inertial effects behind policies once made or at least discouraging radical disruption. These maintenance functions include sustaining policy stability and maintaining international commitments. A third set of capabilities might best be thought of as political, having to do with representing and reconciling diversity, managing conflict, and representing new interests. The capabilities of cleavage management and representation of diffuse interests seem to accord reasonably with these political functions.

The effects of specific institutional arrangements, we have argued, are neither uniform or unidirectional. Those arrangements that concentrate power (single-party-dominant and party government parliamentary systems) tend to perform better at the steering tasks of government than at those that diffuse power. At the same time, the systems that concentrate power tend to do less well at other tasks. A more specific portrait of the relationship of institutional arrangements to particular capabilities is found in table 1. Following the format of the table, we first discuss capabilities for which opportunities appear to outweigh risks in systems that concentrate power. This is followed by one capability where few differences seem to flow from institutions. Finally, we look at those capabilities that are aided by institutions that check centralized power (the U.S and coalitional systems).

CONCENTRATED POWER IS BETTER. The chapter by Feigenbaum, Samuels, and Weaver on energy policy draws a number of conclusions about institutional capacity for policy innovation. Not surprisingly, elite cohesion, autonomy of elites from short-term political pressures, and the absence of multiple veto points all provide important opportunities for innovation. The creation of the national energy program in Canada's party government system is a classic illustration of this opportunity for comprehensive policy innovation—and also of the attendant risk of policy reversal when political forces shift. The analysis of energy policy paints a portrait of sufficient complexity that it transcends the straightforward notion of parliamentary institutions having greater innovative capacity than the U.S. system. It is possible, indeed for minority governments to provide important, albeit limited, opportunities for innovation, despite their susceptibility to short-term pressures and multiple veto points. For example, the short-term political vulnerability of Trudeau's minority Liberal government in 1973 contributed to the creation of Petro-Canada.[2] Similarly, the existence of multiple veto points in the U.S. system generates a lot of policy innovation, too, because the system induces policy entrepreneurship from disparate sources. The policy innovation produced in the U.S. system, however, tends to be at the piecemeal level of individual programs rather than comprehensive, sectorwide policies. Moreover, such innovation tends to resist imposing heavy concentrated costs. Finally, the innovative capacity of Japan and France in the energy sector has more to do with their industrial structure and their bureaucracy, respectively, than with the nature of their legislative-executive relationships. In short, parliamentary institutions do not always concentrate power, and political institutions that concentrate power are far from sufficient for producing policy innovation.

Several chapters in this volume address governmental capability to impose losses on powerful groups in society. In their chapter on pension cuts in Britain, Canada, and the United States, Pierson and Weaver argue that the absence of veto points in party government parliamentary institutions provides important opportunities for loss imposition, but that increased concentration of accountability in those systems weakens that advantage. The first effect is probably stronger on average, but other factors determine which effect dominates in any particular situation. Among these factors are whether existing policies allow losses to be imposed with low visibility and whether an election is close at hand or far away. Lessened visibility and greater distance from elections can have a dramatic effect on strengthening the capacity to impose losses regardless of the system. Allen Schick argues in his chapter on budget deficits, though, that coalitional parliamentary governments are likely to find it particularly difficult to impose losses.

Systems that check power—coalitional and separation-of-powers governments—pose important risks for setting priorities. Interbranch conflict in the United States may give rise either to "bidding up" or to stalemate during the bargaining process, and divided party control increases the risks that this will occur. Coalition governments in parliamentary systems at least offer a more centralized forum for resolving conflicts, but risks remain substantial that there will be either stalemate or a "lowest common denominator" approach to setting priorities, leading to policy drift. This is especially true in the period before elections, when elite autonomy from short-term political pressures is likely to be lowest. The generally higher elite cohesion and minimal veto points of

2. For a related critique of the notion that minority governments are likely to be paralyzed and incapable of innovation, see Kaare Strom, *Minority Government and Majority Rule* (Cambridge University Press, 1990).

456 R. Kent Weaver and Bert A. Rockman

governments in party government and single-party-dominant systems offer important opportunities for—but no guarantee of—a strong priority-
setting capability.

Effective targeting of resources is one capability in which some parliamentary systems appear to have significant potential for superior capabilities. The potential is a limited and highly contingent one, however,
and it entails substantial risks. Ellis Krauss and Jon Pierre argue that
Japan's single-party-dominant parliamentary system provides a centralizing capability that makes a relatively effective industrial policy possible.
But they argue that these institutions alone are insufficient, as Sweden's
lack of success at industrial policy suggests. A political consensus on the
idea of having an industrial policy at all is the key factor that has contributed to Japan's success in this policy area. The exclusion of labor
representation from the governing coalition also played a role in Japan.
The lesson indicated here is that while parliamentary institutions may be
necessary for effective targeting, they are hardly sufficient to achieve that
purpose. American institutions may make governmental elites reluctant
to undertake interventions that they cannot manage effectively. But as
Edward Kolodziej's chapter on nuclear policy suggests, where interventions are undertaken, the need to distribute benefits broadly is intense.

Coordination of conflicting objectives is among the most difficult of
all capabilities. The chapter by Feigenbaum, Samuels, and Weaver supports the parliamentarist critique that the United States has difficulty
coordinating objectives because it has no central mechanism for resolving
such conflicts. The structure of the American political system gives politicians strong incentives to ignore or underplay trade-offs among goals,
because when trade-offs are explicit and highly visible more groups are
likely to become mobilized in an already complex bargaining environment. This poses the risk that groups will be able to prevent adoption
of any policies that cause them to lose, causing stalemate. Systems that
concentrate power by minimizing veto points and allowing relatively
cohesive elites to monopolize power (notably party government systems
and to a lesser extent single-party-dominant ones) run the opposite risk
of maximizing the goals that matter most to the elites while giving short
shrift to other goals.[3]

Concentration of power is also important for implementation of a
government's objectives and programs once they have been decided upon.
The most obvious obstacle to effective implementation is additional veto
points in the implementation process, which are most likely to involve

---

3. For a parallel analysis, see Sven Steinmo, "Political Institutions and Tax Policy in
the United States, Sweden and Britain," *World Politics*, vol. 41 (July 1989), pp. 500–35.

third-tier institutions such as subnational governments or courts. But first- and second-tier institutions affect implementation as well by leading to policies that are either more or less difficult to implement or more or less stable. If executive-legislative conflict and intralegislative squabbles in separation-of-powers systems lead to either "bidding up" or "splitting the difference" in policy design, serious implementation problems could result. Policies also may be adopted without adequate funding. Party government systems, on the other hand, run the risk that policies developed and adopted without adequate consultation will run into similar implementation difficulties or that policies may be reversed before they can be implemented. Political arrangements (notably single-party-dominant systems and, to a lesser extent, coalitional ones) that feature both a high degree of elite stability and a well-established consultation process are likely to be most conducive to effective implementation of government policies.

THE SYSTEM MAKES NO DIFFERENCE. There does not appear to be a clear institutional advantage for either parliamentary institutions or the U.S. system in maintaining international commitments, at least in trade. The general direction of policy pressures has been similar in all of the countries examined by Helen Milner, and all three countries—Britain, France, and the United States—have faced constraints from international policymaking regimes. In the trade sector, several forces have led to cross-national similarities in the level of special interest influence. Countervailing mechanisms have been employed in the United States. Delegation of authority to the president and to special agencies has undercut the ability of local and industry interests to dominate trade policy. Troubled industries in Britain and France, though, have found channels to exercise influence on governments despite the putatively greater insulation of these governments.

CONCENTRATED POWER IS WORSE. One capability for which the U.S. system and coalitional systems appear to create a significant opportunity is the representation of diffuse interests. However, as Vogel points out in his review of environmental policy in Japan, Britain, and the United States, this opportunity is far from uniform over time. When public opinion is highly mobilized, differences between parliamentary systems and the U.S. system tend to disappear. Under conditions of single-party majority government, parliamentary systems *can* be more responsive to diffuse interests because actions taken in those systems will not become entangled in interbranch wrangling. Such governments often *choose* not to be responsive, though, because they normally have weak incentives to consider the preferences of groups outside their own party constituencies. The multiple channels of access afforded to environmental interest groups in the U.S. system make it more likely that their interests will be taken into account, while parliamentary systems with proportional representation electoral rules facilitate the direct entry of relatively diffuse interests (notably environmentalists and taxpayers) into the formation of political parties.

Management of political cleavages is one area in which separation of powers per se appears to have little effect on government capabilities. Separation of powers poses both significant risks and potential for improved outcomes. Separation of powers may allow groups that are excluded from executive power to hold power in the legislature, but such a system may also lead to stalemate between the legislature and the executive. Both decentralization of power in the legislature and bicameralism may enhance the role of intransigent legislative groups hostile to minority concerns, as the long odyssey of civil rights legislation in the United States shows. Overall, though, electoral laws that encourage or discourage representation of minority interests and elite responsiveness to minority concerns appear to be far more important than separation or fusion of legislative and executive powers in determining effectiveness in cleavage management. Electoral laws that turn plurality preferences into legislative majorities are likely to be especially disastrous in highly divided societies, as Richard Gunther and Anthony Mughan note.

Finally, several of the chapters suggest important conclusions about policy stability. The chapter on energy policy by Feigenbaum, Samuels, and Weaver, for instance, notes that the downside of party government systems' high innovative capacity is the risk of major policy reversals when control shifts between two parties with highly polarized views on an issue. This risk may be lowered, Kolodziej's discussion of British nuclear policy suggests, if strong mechanisms are in place to protect party leaders from activists with more extreme views, there is consistent bureaucratic support for a particular policy direction, and party leaders are able to negotiate interparty agreements as binding long-term commitments. Yet there is no enforcement mechanism in party government systems to ensure that interparty commitments will not be broken, as illustrated by Margaret Thatcher's reforms of earnings-related pensions in Britain. The three other regime types pose somewhat less risk of policy instability, although for somewhat different reasons. The U.S. separation-of-powers system (because of its plethora of veto points) and coalitional and single-party-dominant systems (because of their high degree of elite stability) all have stronger inertial tendencies than do majority party governments.

Other studies confirm these findings on policy stability. Sven Steinmo's study of tax policy in Britain, Sweden, and the United States, for example, suggests that the U.S. system is likely to have greater policy stability than party government systems where there is alternation in office between two class-based parties, as in Britain.[4] Another study of the same three countries similarly found that one of the essential conditions for the stability of housing policy in Sweden was that dominant political forces (the Social Democratic party) also were stable, allowing policy direction to be maintained.[5]

Third-Tier Effects

This book principally compares the effects on government capabilities of the U.S. separation-of-powers system and several types of parliamentary regimes. Our attention, therefore, has been mainly on the effects of the first- and second-tier institutions. From the cases of policymaking examined in this book, however, it is evident that third-tier institutional variables, such as judicial review, federalism, and bicameralism, also shape governing capabilities, as do noninstitutional variables, such as policy inheritances. Because our cases were not selected to provide a systematic examination of third-tier variables, we will not attempt to provide a comprehensive review of their effects. These factors can nevertheless be seen to operate, as our general framework suggests, through the five decisionmaking attributes outlined above (see point number 4, page 449). They provide important risks and opportunities for governing capacity, but are rarely unambiguous in their effects.

Most of the lessons that we derived from analysis of presidential and parliamentary systems apply equally to third-tier factors, such as federalism. Like parliamentary systems, federalism is a generic label that masks a variety of institutional arrangements that create distinctive risks and opportunities for governing capabilities. Federal and provincial governments may have the authority to intervene in a policy area without permission from the other level of government. This tends to provide strong incentives for policy innovation as each level of government tries to control a policy jurisdiction before the other does. However, this type of federalism also runs the risk that different levels of government will impose conflicting programs, raising implementation costs and making the problem of coordinating objectives even more difficult. Alternatively, federalism may be structured to require the approval of both affected subnational governments and the federal government for any deviation

---

4. Steinmo, "Political Institutions and Tax Policy."
5. Bruce Headey, *Housing Policy in the Developed Economy: The United Kingdom, Sweden and the United States* (London: Croom Helm, 1978), especially chaps. 3, 9.

from the status quo. These arrangements, noted in the case of nuclear plant construction, add veto points and inhibit implementation.

Noninstitutional factors also raise risks and opportunities. Policy inheritances, as Pierson and Weaver's chapter on pension retrenchment shows, affect the number and effectiveness of veto points operating in a particular policy sector. Policy inheritances also help to determine who has access to policymaking. Perhaps, most obviously, intense societal cleavages are likely to undermine elite cohesion. Certainly, they are apt to decrease elite insulation from short-term constituency pressures. Alternatively, broad encompassing social organizations help generate elite cohesion and buffer elites from short-term pressures.

Conclusions

We set out in this book to ask how political institutions affect government capabilities. They do so, we conclude, in important but often complex ways. Although our findings confirm some conventional wisdom about the shortcomings of the U.S. system, they also provide important correctives to some of the received wisdom. The most important of these correctives concerns the contingency and frequent bidirectionality of institutional effects; these findings led us to reconceptualize advantages and disadvantages of institutions as risks and opportunities. Institutions that in one set of political conditions may provide risks for a given capability can provide important opportunities under other conditions. For example, concentrated power may lead both to elite insulation from interests outside the governing coalition and to expeditious response when their demands become politically compelling. This seems to be the story of Japanese responses to environmental pressures. A second needed corrective is the relative unimportance of first-tier (presidential versus parliamentary) institutional effects. The U.S. system does not stand out from all parliamentary systems in its pattern of capabilities, but rather tends to cluster with coalitional systems on many of those capabilities. A third needed corrective is suggested by our findings on loss imposition in the United States; the problem of the U.S. system is not so much that accountability is lacking, but rather that it is divided and targeted effectively at individual politicians, who have little institutional insulation from the blame-generating activities of political opponents. Finally, our findings suggest that divided government need not be (and is not) consistently stalemated. Both stalemate and "bidding up" of program initiatives may occur under divided government, even during the same presidency.

These findings have implications both for researchers and for political actors—especially proponents of political reform. In discussing the very real governance shortcomings of the United States, it is important to compare it with other advanced industrial democracies rather than with some theoretical ideal. It is also clear that effective governance does not consist of choosing a single "best" set of institutions valid for all countries. Instead, it requires matching political institutions to a set of problems that determine which capabilities are needed most and to political and social conditions (for example, strong or weak cleavages) in a country that determine whether particular institutional arrangements are likely to enhance or inhibit a specific capability. These potential opportunities, in turn, must be offset by risks posed for other capabilities that are presently being satisfactorily met but could be weakened in a blizzard of reforms that fail to take into account how various institutional arrangements affect different capabilities. The contingent nature of institutional reform has implications especially for practitioners who seek to change institutions or who are faced with building a new set of institutions when an old political order has collapsed. What, if anything, can we say to them, based on the findings of this volume? The final chapter speaks to these concerns.

R. Kent Weaver and Bert A. Rockman

Institutional Reform and Constitutional Design

*T*he preceding chapter summarizes the findings of the case studies and draws some generalizations about the effects of political institutions on government capabilities. Now we explore how and to what degree these findings might be helpful in considering institutional reforms to enhance governmental effectiveness. Some institutional changes require constitutional alteration. Others, such as changes in legislative voting rules, do not. Because constitutional change faces such enormous obstacles, whatever its potential payoffs, this route to reform is least likely to succeed.

We begin by outlining some general questions and cautions that institutional reformers need to consider. We then address the need for institutional reforms to improve governmental performance in the United States and the feasibility of any such reforms.

Questions for Institutional Reformers

Issues of constitutional reform and institutional design are very complicated. What are the conditions under which reforms might work? What are the specific consequences of particular reforms? What are the trade-offs in values that reforms require? And what are the feasibilities of various reforms? Proponents of institutional reform should be able to provide answers to the following questions.

1. *What capabilities should be increased?* Not all capabilities can be maximized at the same time, so priorities must be clear.
2. *What other values should be risked and potentially sacrificed to obtain the desired capabilities?* In order to get more of some desirable government

capabilities (priority setting, for example), other capabilities may have to be sacrificed (for example, policy stability or responsiveness to diffuse interests). The enhancement of government capabilities, moreover, is not the only value that should be considered in designing political institutions. Other values, such as the legitimacy of established arrangements, democratic access, and accountability to the governed, also need to be considered in making reform proposals.

3. *Are facilitating conditions present to maximize the prospects of attaining the desired capabilities?* Institutional reform alone is likely to have only a limited effect on most government capabilities. The functioning of current institutions is influenced by the historical and societal contexts in which they developed, evolved, and have operated. These contexts also are apt to influence how institutional reforms would work.[1] Even with the most wildly optimistic assumptions about the political feasibility of institutional change and behavioral responses to those changes, a healthy dose of skepticism that all institutional reforms would have their desired effects is necessary.

4. *Are facilitating conditions present that will minimize risks for the preferred capabilities and other values?* Institutional reforms can have harmful as well as beneficial effects. Not all reforms travel well or are applicable at all times. Centralizing power, for example, may threaten the political order in a country with deep ethnic or religious divisions if one group perceives itself to be excluded from power and threatened by another group.

5. *Can these objectives be achieved by ad hoc sector-specific measures rather than general institutional reforms?* In designing capacity-enhancing responses to policy failures, sector-specific countervailing mechanisms should usually be a first resort and general institutional reforms a last resort. Different specific capabilities may be required across policy sectors, and sector-specific mechanisms are less likely to have broad-scale, adverse, unanticipated consequences. Custom tailoring thus may be both more suitable and also more feasible than broad-scale institutional redesign.

1. Moreover, using institutional reform to increase specific government capabilities may simply bring other, previously latent, institutional obstacles to the fore. Attempts to increase innovative capacity by making legislatures more responsive to the will of political majorities, for example, may lead to more judicial review or to lack of executive implementation. The effect might be to alter the form, while preserving the reality, of minority veto power. See, for example, the discussion of shifting veto points in Ellen M. Immergut, "The Rules of the Game: The Logic of Health Policy-making in France, Switzerland and Sweden," in Sven Steinmo, Kathleen Thelen, and Frank Longstreth, eds., *Structuring Politics: Historical Institutionalism in Comparative Analysis* (Cambridge University Press, 1992), pp. 57–89.

6. *Is the proposed reform politically feasible?* Institutional changes that make almost everyone in a society better off presumably would be relatively easy to make, because few would object to them. But such reforms are rare. Much more often, proposed reforms are redistributive in that they are likely to make some segments of a society or some institutional officeholders better off and others worse off.[2] Political opposition thus arises. Even groups likely to benefit from institutional change in the short term may object to it because they fear the uncertainty of its long-term consequences. Reforms that enhance the power of political majorities, for example, are attractive only to those who are certain they will be part of the majority for a long time. Actors in any political system are more likely to want to minimize their losses than to maximize their gains under conditions of uncertainty. Thus risk aversion presents a powerful barrier to institutional change that goes beyond short-term winners and losers. Finally, frequent institutional change tends to delegitimize the entire institutional framework, putting at risk the interests of virtually all leaders.

Given the risks of institutional change and its redistributive impact, the frequency of such change and the types of changes adopted are likely to reflect the ease with which rules can be altered as well as the specific historical experiences that prompted the rules. Most democratic polities place severe restrictions on changing the rules of the political game—the nature of the electoral laws, the powers of the different branches or different levels of government, and the rights of individuals vis-à-vis the state. In very heterogeneous societies, such restrictions tend to be especially onerous. They may include requirements for supermajorities or concurrent majorities and ratification by successive sessions of the legislature.

The most obvious route to institutional change is a massive failure in governance. The choice in France to have a strong independent executive clearly flowed from the instability of the Fourth Republic. The relatively strong role accorded to the Länder (states) in the Federal Republic of Germany—both in implementing federal policies and in having the power to delay Bundestag actions through the Bundesrat (where the Länder governments are directly represented)—reflected a fear of centralized power stemming from the Nazi period. Other features of the contemporary German system (notably the requirement of a constructive vote of no confidence and the 5 percent hurdle that parties must meet to win

2. See George Tsebelis, *Nested Games: Rational Choice in Comparative Politics* (University of California Press, 1990), chap. 4.

seats in the Bundestag) result from the earlier failings of the Weimar period.

Without massive institutional failure, institutional rules usually are changed either because newly empowered elites want to consolidate political power or because old elites, fearing a loss of power, want to manipulate the rules to hang on.[3] The Swedish move to proportional representation came about for the latter reason: the Conservatives saw proportional representation as a way to preserve a minority role for themselves in the face of probable extinction under the old single-member-district system.[4] Without a severe crisis or failure, changes in institutional arrangements are most likely to come about when the rules providing for their modification are relatively lenient.

General Caveats about Institutional Reform

The case studies in this volume suggest five general caveats that should guide initiatives for institutional reform as well as theories about the process of reform. First, even when some type of institutional reform is assured, either because the old order has lost its legitimacy (as in Eastern Europe) or because some important societal interest demands a renegotiation, there is little guarantee that high priority will be given to increasing government capabilities. During constitutional reform negotiations, the problems of the country tend to take a back seat to the problems of the people at the negotiating table.[5] Politicians may feel that they have to posture and take intransigent positions favored by their constituents, especially if they face political threats from more radical forces. Equally important, even when formal reforms of institutions do occur, they may have little effect when they conflict with the interests of those who have political and economic power. This is clearest in the case of empty constitutional guarantees for individuals, such as the wide

3. Institutional reform may also occur if elements of an old ruling coalition and members of the former opposition form a coalition in order to further their joint interests. See Tsebelis, *Nested Games*, p. 111.

4. See, for example, Leif Lewin, *Ideology and Strategy: A Century of Swedish Politics* (Cambridge University Press, 1988), pp. 82–86. See also Tsebelis, *Nested Games*, pp. 223–31, for a discussion of electoral rule reform in the French Fifth Republic.

5. See Keith G. Banting and Richard Simeon, *Redesigning the State: The Politics of Constitutional Change* (Toronto and Buffalo: University of Toronto Press, 1985); and Edward McWhinney, *Constitution-making: Principles, Process, Practice* (Toronto and Buffalo: University of Toronto Press, 1981), for discussions of the constitutional reform process in several countries.

citizen protections stipulated in the old Communist Soviet and East European constitutions or the failure of the Civil War amendments (especially the Fourteenth and Fifteenth amendments) to aid African Americans in the American South before the 1960s.

Second, even major constitutional reforms rarely resolve the societal conflicts that are usually a contributing factor in failures of governmental performance. As Keith Banting and Richard Simeon noted in their cross-national study of constitutional reform, "Outcomes are less likely to 'resolve' the conflicts than they are to register a truce among contending forces with the struggle likely to continue, sometimes in constitutional and sometimes in other forums."[6]

Third, there is no single optimal set of institutions that can be applied to all countries at all times.[7] Effective institutional reform necessarily involves a careful matching of an individual country's policy problems, the societal conditions that influence how institutions will function, and the institutions themselves. Where a country is torn by severe ethnic, religious, or linguistic divisions, top priority must be given to devising an institutional design for managing these cleavages. Under these circumstances, capabilities such as innovation and priority setting are likely to seem less important.

This caveat is especially important in considering institutional reforms for newly democratizing countries. Because countries vary dramatically in their problems and societal conditions that facilitate or limit specific institutional arrangements, these arrangements need to vary accordingly. It is best to temper prescriptions with country-specific knowledge. Whether a newly democratizing country should adopt such institutional arrangements as the separation of powers or federalism depends on the nature of its problems.

A fourth caveat is that, given the uncertainties and risks of redesigning institutions, the case for reform should be very strong before it is undertaken. In any given setting, it is hard to prove that proposed reforms would improve governmental effectiveness because claims must be either counterfactual or based on evidence from other countries that lack exactly equivalent social and political conditions. It is impossible, in other words, to provide "proof" of institutional effects for institutions that do not yet exist. These complications should not stifle a lively debate among policymakers and the public about institutional innovation, but they ought

6. Keith G. Banting and Richard Simeon, "Introduction: The Politics of Constitutional Change," in Banting and Simeon, *Redesigning the State*, p. 6.

7. See Donald L. Horowitz, *Ethnic Groups in Conflict* (University of California Press, 1985), chap. 14.

to provide a note of caution about the likelihood that an institutional fix will be successful.

A final caveat is that constitutional amending rules should not be too inflexible. This follows from the third caveat that proper institutional design requires a careful match between a country's problems, its political and social conditions, and its institutions. As problems and political conditions evolve over time, institutions need to do so as well. Making institutions extremely difficult to change (the amending formula in the U.S. Constitution being a good example) can be a good practice if it fosters reverence for the political order. However, if institutional change is frustrated because veto points lurk everywhere, conflict and frustration may fester with no prospect of resolution. Alternatively, of course, having the constitutional "rules of the game" constantly under renegotiation creates feelings of uncertainty that can be quite destructive of a polity. It also increases the risk that political majorities will be able to discriminate against minorities and erode constitutional protections afforded them.[8] The proper balance between constitutional flexibility and rigidity must, therefore, vary with the intensity of a country's political cleavages. The more intense the political cleavages, the greater the need to protect rights and to make constitutional reform difficult.

Institutional Reform in the United States

There is widespread agreement that major deficiencies in American governing capacities exist. There is even some agreement on the types of capabilities that need to be increased. In particular need of strengthening are the capabilities of the American system to tackle large problems in a coherent and coordinated fashion and to set priorities. Moreover, evidence suggests that U.S. governing institutions make the problem of bringing agreement from diversity worse than it otherwise might be.

These deficiencies are not the simple or direct consequence of the country's governing arrangements, however. Governing the United States, a diverse society of 250 million people, is not equivalent to governing Sweden or even Japan, for example: both are far more homogeneous and geographically compact societies whose cultures emphasize collective interests to a far greater degree. The heterogeneity of the United States suggests that adapting a British Westminster-style system probably would

8. See in particular Arend Lijphart, *Democracies: Patterns of Majoritarian and Consensus Government in Twenty-One Countries* (Yale University Press, 1984), chap. 11.

produce a political system more like Canada's, with its severe regional cleavages and frequent minority governments, than that of the United Kingdom.

Decisiveness in making public policy is not to be equated with bringing agreement from diversity. Indeed, institutions that facilitate decisiveness may work against acceptance of policies that are adopted and induce hostility against the institutions that adopted them. The capacity of government to manage conflict must be weighed against its capacity to steer and direct policy change.

Institutions clearly facilitate or impede different types of policy capabilities, but the right set of political conditions can overcome most structural impediments. Above and beyond institutional arrangements, political leadership can influence policymaking. However, the possibilities for leadership also are shaped by institutional arrangements.[9]

The interaction between leadership and institutions can be quite complicated. Clear-cut majorities provide optimum conditions for the flexing of political will. Yet British institutions allowed Margaret Thatcher to make changes more sweeping (and more unpopular) than those made by her American soulmate, Ronald Reagan. The U.S. system frequently requires patching together piecemeal coalitions to accomplish anything at all and does not encourage taking comprehensive action or unpopular and risky steps. Such action does happen from time to time, of course, even in America, usually because leadership has overcome the institutional obstacles. The difference between what Thatcher and Reagan accomplished is a function of institutional arrangements, but the difference between the accomplishments of Reagan and George Bush or between those of Thatcher and Harold Wilson is largely a function of their leadership. Thatcher and Reagan were conviction politicians, and each accomplished what their respective systems would allow (more in Thatcher's case than Reagan's). Bush and Wilson were addicted to maintaining the status quo and a fragile equilibrium among their various party constituencies.

Possible Reforms

A wide variety of reform proposals have been suggested by critics of the U.S. system or can be derived from the experiences of other advanced industrial countries.[10] Table 1 lists a "menu" of reform possibilities for

9. See Bert A. Rockman, *The Leadership Question: The Presidency and the American System* (Praeger, 1984).

10. The most comprehensive and thoughtful review is James L. Sundquist, *Constitutional Reform and Effective Government*, rev. ed. (Brookings, 1992).

the American system, with the proposals categorized both by the "tier" of explanation from which they are derived and by the attributes of the policymaking process they would most affect. Particular decisionmaking attributes, we argued in the last chapter, are linked to specific government capabilities. If the goal is to increase institutional capacity for policy innovation, for example, reducing the number of veto points in the system is probably a desirable strategy. This can be done by first-tier reforms, such as abolishing or weakening presidential veto power, or through a combination of first- and second-tier institutional reforms, notably adopting a set of parliamentary arrangements and electoral rules likely to yield a single-party majority government. The number of effective veto points also can be reduced through third-tier reforms, such as limiting bicameralism. One might, therefore, seek to limit the authority of the Senate over ordinary legislation to that of merely a delaying veto,[11] or to abolish the Senate entirely. Policy innovation might also be stimulated by creating an alternative policymaking path, such as citizen-initiated referenda, to bypass the normal legislative process. This route, however, carries with it great risks and threatens a republican form of government.

Similar arguments can be made about the capacity of governments to impose losses. Although a number of decisionmaking attributes are relevant to this capability, perhaps the most important is the autonomy of elites from short-term constituency and electoral pressures. A variety of institutional mechanisms could enhance this autonomy within the present electoral context. These include longer terms for legislators, increasing the use of secret ballots in voting in the legislature, or delegating more decisions to nonelective bodies modeled after the Federal Reserve Board. Of course, these reforms pose serious challenges to other values that Americans hold dear, notably their ability to hold individual politicians accountable.

These same reform proposals also make clear just how hard it is to develop a set of proposals that address all of the questions and caveats posed earlier. Longer terms for legislators, for example, are unpopular with the public, which is more likely to favor term limits—at least for other peoples' representatives—rather than increased job security.[12] Similarly, few legislators would like to go on the record as favoring increased use of the secret ballot in legislative votes, since that almost certainly would be used against them by challengers in future elections.

11. The German Bundesrat has a delaying veto over legislation passed by the Bundestag, but maintains an absolute veto over changes in the Basic Law.
12. See Sundquist, *Constitutional Reform*, chap. 5.

Table 1. *Effects of Potential U.S. Institutional Reforms on Specific Decisionmaking Attributes*

	Decisionmaking attributes				
Elite cohesion	Multiple veto points	Stability of decisionmaking elites	Autonomy of elites from short-term pressures	Interest group access
First-tier reforms (differences between parliamentary and separation-of-powers system)				
Increase by adopting Westminster-style parliamentary system; allowing president to dissolve Congress for new elections; or allowing Congress to remove president in vote of no confidence	Decrease by adopting Westminster-style parliamentary system; abolishing presidential veto power; or giving president enhanced rescission authority Increase by allowing legislative veto; or giving president item veto authority		Decrease slightly by adopting Westminster-style parliamentary system	
Second-tier reforms (differences in electoral laws and rules and norms of government formation)				
Increase by enhancing central party control over legislative candidates, such as replacing individual constituencies with party lists; or forbidding presidential-legislative ticket splitting to lessen probability of divided government	Decrease by forbidding presidential-legislative ticket splitting to lessen probability of divided government	Decrease by adopting legislative term limitations	Increase by lengthening terms of office	

Third-tier reforms[a]

Increase by strengthening incentives for legislators to support party position; or making legislative candidates more dependent on central party organizations for financing	Decrease by ending or limiting judicial review of legislation; limiting power of upper chamber (Senate) to suspensive veto; limiting prerogatives and resources of legislative committees and subcommittees or abolishing them altogether; lowering votes required for congressional override of presidential veto; or using single ad hoc legislative committees instead of multiple referral for complex legislation	Increase by making fewer departmental positions political appointments	Increase by instituting secret ballot on some or all legislative votes; or giving more decision-making authority to nonelective bodies	Decrease by limiting role of political action committees in congressional elections Increase by easing rules for referendum initiatives

a. These include factors such as the extent of effective bicameralism, the independence of legislative committees, provisions of campaign finance laws, the extent of judicial review, and rules governing the independence of the bureaucracy.

Feasibility

The prospects for major institutional reforms in the United States are not promising. If major institutional reform is most likely when there is either a massive, visible institutional failure or when the rules for institutional change are quite permissive, then the prospects in the United States are dim, because neither condition exists. Whatever the problems facing the country, they seem less than a massive crisis of governance. Further, the rules on constitutional revision are perhaps the toughest of any democratic country. Since even narrow reforms in areas such as campaign finance and voter registration have been blocked, the outlook for broader-scale constitutional change must be considered bleak indeed. And even if the amendment route were a plausible one, it should be pursued cautiously because of uncertainty about the risks that most amendments pose were they to be adopted. Furthermore, such amendments would prove virtually impossible to rescind once they took effect.

Outlining a set of reform proposals inevitably requires making choices about the relative importance of values that have to be traded off. What emphasis, for example, should be placed on ensuring broad access to policymaking versus responding to pressing policy problems? Not only must choices be made between values, these value choices also have to be weighed against the prospects of adopting the proposed reforms and the likelihood of their actually working in a predictable manner. In short, embarking on the path of reform involves both value judgments and guesswork. In making these evaluations, reasonable people will differ.

Indeed, the findings in this volume are subject to two equally plausible interpretations. One plausible reading of this study in the context of current American politics is that institutional change alone will not create a consensus among policymakers on the taxing and spending priorities of the federal government, or, indeed, on any of the large problems the United States faces. Structural fixes guarantee nothing. Whether the separation-of-powers system is broken or not, it is unlikely to be replaced. More important, changing it is not going to solve the country's most serious problems. That requires leadership that is infused with the values of compromise and consensus building. Divided government is not inherently ineffective, nor does the restoration of united government offer any guarantee of effective government. Of course, some institutional repairs might be worthwhile. The key here, however, is to focus on feasible and specific remedies while realizing that reforms can be unpredictable and that, like lunches, they do not come free. This reading does not minimize problems but is skeptical that the answers can be institutionally derived.

An equally plausible reading, however, stresses that institutional complacency also has its risks. Although structural fixes guarantee nothing, policy problems are not independent of governing institutions, and the failure to consider serious structural reform channels immense popular discontent with existing institutions into vehicles that erode governing capacity, such as government by referendum, term limitations for politicians, balanced budget amendments, and independent presidential candidacies. Under this reading, the results of the study suggest that there are a variety of mechanisms short of abolishing the separation of powers that can be employed to increase the potential of critical governing capabilities.

In addition, this second reading stresses that skepticism about the feasibility of radical reform, although deservedly high, does not mean that reform should be excluded from public debate. If conditions warrant major institutional reform, there is little to be gained by shying away from discussing it, whatever its current feasibility. Moreover, reform opportunities often strike unexpectedly. Few people thought that comprehensive tax reform was a realistic probability in the 99th Congress, but it took place as a result of a conjunction of presidential and congressional credit-claiming ambitions and the reluctance of other players to take the blame for blocking a politically popular move. With distrust of politicians and political institutions at very high levels, political entrepreneurs may create opportunities for institutional reform. It is impossible to predict with confidence when these opportunities might arise or precisely what forms the reform proposals will take. But it is important that if such opportunities do occur, thoughtful options and analyses be available.

A Two-Track Strategy

Given the uncertainties over both the risks and the feasibility of large-scale constitutional experiments at the federal level, we propose a middle-ground reading of the evidence and a two-track strategy of institutional reform. One track is aimed at the federal level, the other at the states.

The first track involves institutional changes at the federal level that can be enacted without formal constitutional amendment, especially through changes in the rules of the two chambers of Congress. To be effective, however, such changes would have to meet several criteria. In addition to having relatively low barriers to adoption, reforms should not appear to give substantial overall advantages to one group or institution against another. If they do, they risk not being adopted at all. Since any *individual* reform meeting this criterion would by definition be inconsequential in its policy effects, the key here is to develop *packages* of reforms that offer something of value to all participants while requiring reciprocal concessions.[13] Thus such packages differ from presidents' repeated requests that they be given a unilateral line-item veto over the budget while offering Congress nothing in return. In addition, reforms should be reversible or subject to renegotiation relatively easily, so that participants do not feel that they may be trapped forever in a bad bargain; politicians (and especially legislators) are, after all, highly risk averse. Periodic renegotiations can also take account of changing institutional positions and bargaining powers, such as those that resulted from the shift from divided to united party control of government in the 1992 election. Finally, sector-specific countervailing mechanisms might be used to attain many of the desired changes in government capabilities without incurring the risks inherent in broad institutional changes. In seeking to increase the U.S. capability to set priorities, for example, changes focused on the budgetary process should be tried before considering broader institutional change.

What would such a package look like in concrete terms? An example of one possible agreement would be a change in congressional rules to weaken veto points and thus facilitate policy innovation, especially during periods of divided government and strong partisan division. House and Senate rules could be changed to allow the president to submit an alternative to a limited number of pieces of legislation (perhaps ten a year) immediately following a vote on final passage of that legislation. The chamber would then have a limited time to study the president's proposal, after which it would have to take a vote on substituting it for the legislation that had just passed. In exchange, the president would agree to sign previously vetoed legislation on any topic that was repassed by both chambers by a 60 percent majority (rather than the constitutionally sanctioned two-thirds majority). The rule granting automatic consideration of presidential alternatives could be written so that it would cease to have effect—either permanently or for that session of Congress—if the president failed to keep his part of the bargain, thus giving the president a strong incentive to cooperate.

Another device is the use of special ad hoc commissions, especially those with a bipartisan cast, whose recommendations would be guaranteed a place on the congressional agenda. This device is likely to be especially useful when politicians need to avoid blame while imposing

13. On the importance of reciprocal concessions, see Horowitz, *Ethnic Groups in Conflict*, chap. 14.

losses. At a minimum, such commissions can be used to develop detailed policy proposals in controversial areas, setting the policy agenda and allowing politicians to say that they were simply doing their distasteful duty by supporting the commission's proposals for the good of the country. It is possible to go even further, giving the commissions' recommendations the force of law unless Congress or the president specifically rejects their recommendations within a specified period of time and limiting politicians' ability to modify the recommendations.

This device has been used in areas such as congressional pay raises and military base closings. The record of such commissions in the 1980s suggests some important limits to their potential, however. First, politicians are unlikely to give away their ability to modify or overturn a commission's recommendations unless they are already largely agreed among themselves on the direction of needed policy change and are confident that a commission will echo these policy views. In these cases, politicians simply need a vehicle to shield themselves from blame. But such commissions have limits in shielding politicians. Where consensus is lacking, as in the social security financial crisis of 1981–83, commission recommendations are likely to be subject to a full congressional review. Second, where an issue has huge blame-generating potential (congressional pay increases, for example), ad hoc commissions are unlikely to succeed in sheltering politicians from blame.[14]

These examples of first-track reform mechanisms are intended simply to illustrate the broader set of principles that are essential to increase the governing capacity of the federal government. Reciprocal concessions by the president and Congress, relatively low barriers to adoption, relatively narrow focus, and opportunities for periodic renegotiation are essential elements of a reform package. What makes them particularly attractive is that they may be feasible.

The second track in our strategy is constitutional reform at the state level. The states have been hailed in recent years as "laboratories of democracy" for policy innovation.[15] There have been significant institutional experiments as well. Among these are deviations at the state level from the federal arrangement of a bicameral legislature elected in single-member districts. The state of Nebraska, for example, has a unicameral legislature, while other states, notably California, provide liberally for citizen initiatives as an alternative path to legislative enactment.

14. See R. Kent Weaver, "Is the Congress Abdicating Power to Commissions?" *Roll Call*, February 12, 1989, p. 5.

15. See David Osborne, *Laboratories of Democracy* (Harvard Business School Press, 1990).

A number of states have recently enacted term limitations for legislators. There is even greater diversity of institutional forms t the local level.[16]

Not all experiments are equal, of course. Unicameralism is especially deserving of further attention at the state level since the Supreme Court has, through its one-person, one-vote decisions, undermined the distinctive representational features of upper chambers in most state legislatures. Experiments at the state level with parliamentary forms of government and proportional representation electoral laws might also be worthwhile. The citizen initiative, on the other hand, is generally destructive because it is so open to manipulation by special (and especially moneyed) interests.[17] And the case that term limits will enhance governments' capacity to innovate, impose losses, or set priorities is dubious at best.[18]

Constitutional experimentation at the state level is easier to justify than amendments to the federal Constitution. First, it may provide more effective government where it is adopted. Second, any ill effects it creates will be more limited in geographic scope. Third, it may make alternative governance options available to an American public that is frequently unaware of foreign experience. If such experiments prove successful, they might later gain adoption at the federal level.

Institutional experimentation by the states may also be more possible than at the federal level, because state-level constitutional amending procedures are generally less stringent than those at the federal level.[19] This also allows for easier repeal at the state level of amendments that turn out to undercut governing capacity. Barriers to state-level experiments in the federal Constitution are also minimal. The Constitution does require the federal government to "guarantee . . . a republican form of

16. Some localities use professional chief executives such as city managers and have either figurehead elected executives or none at all.

17. For an assessment of the referendum device, see Thomas E. Cronin, *Direct Democracy: The Politics of Initiative, Referendum, and Recall* (Harvard University Press for Twentieth Century Fund, 1989).

18. For arguments for and against term limits, see, for example, James K. Coyne and John H. Fund, *Cleaning House: America's Campaign for Term Limits* (New York: Regnery Gateway, 1992); Bill Frenzel, "Term Limits and the Immortal Congress: How to Make Congressional Elections Competititive Again," and Thomas E. Mann, "The Wrong Medicine: Term Limits Won't Cure What Ails Congressional Elections," both in *Brookings Review*, vol. 10 (Spring 1992), pp. 18–25; and Charles R. Kesler, "Bad Housekeeping: The Case against Congressional Term Limitations," *Policy Review*, no. 53 (Summer 1990), pp. 20–25.

19. On amending procedures in the American states, see Sundquist, *Constitutional Reform*, pp. 325–26.

government" in the states (Article IV), and the Seventeenth Amendment allows the "executive authority" in the states to appoint replacements to the federal Senate when such an office falls vacant. Neither requirement would bar adoption of a parliamentary system, proportional representation, or unicameral legislatures at the state level.

Radical reform in the states faces many of the same political barriers as at the federal level, of course, including increased risks to incumbent politicians. Unicameralism would make these risks into a sure thing by eliminating some political positions altogether. With fifty potential laboratories for institutional reform, however, the odds that the barriers to reform can be overcome in some places increase significantly.

Institutional Reform and America's Central Policy Concerns

The caveats we have stipulated about the consequences and design of institutional reforms are sobering. But so too are the problems besetting American society. Three in particular stand out. First is the continuing irresolution over mammoth budget deficits that suffocate capital investment and crowd out the federal government's discretionary expenditures. Another is the failure of the U.S. health care system to provide universal coverage and to control its costs. The costs of the health care system not only suck up more and more of society's resources, they also frustrate the capacity of the system to extend coverage to those who presently lack it. A third festering crisis has to do with the growing economic marginalization and social disintegration occurring largely, if not exclusively, in the nation's cities. The list of important problems needing an effective governmental response could be easily extended. But listing problems is not our purpose here. Our objective is to try to discover the extent to which the inability to deal effectively with these problems can be remedied at least in part through institutional reforms flowing from the "first track" of institutional reforms at the federal level outlined above. We recognize that institutional reform is no panacea and that when the right set of political conditions appear, the prospects for overcoming the structural impediments designed into the American system of government are much better. We begin by identifying the capabilities that need to be strengthened to address the three large problems we have outlined. Then we examine specific institutional mechanisms to strengthen those capabilities. We give particular attention to proposals relevant to the new governing situation facing the country in 1993—the first period of united party control of government in twelve years.

Budget Deficits

Cutting budget deficits directly calls into play the policy capabilities of loss imposition and priority setting. Because budgets raise very directly the questions of who gets what and who pays for it, institutions matter a lot. Obviously, if there were a clear consensus as to how to bring the deficit under control, institutions would matter little. While there may be some agreement as to the general solution of deficit reduction, there is little agreement about the specifics of any such solution. Here the prevalence of veto points works against the U.S. system in being able to generate policy agreement precisely because budgets make both costs and benefits especially visible. Paying more to get less is not a popular formula anywhere. And the evidence of our empirical cases indicates that a parliamentary system by itself does not guarantee the ability of a system to tackle hard problems like budget deficits. Furthermore, much of the budget—so-called mandatory spending, including transfer payments to individuals and the medicare program—enjoys special protections from cutbacks.

A variety of changes have been tried over the past two decades to reduce deficits, including the Budget and Impoundment Control Act of 1974, enhanced use of reconciliation in the 1980s, the Gramm-Rudman-Hollings Act of 1985, and several budget summits. But the budget deficit shows no sign of coming under control. In fact, just the opposite is occurring.

Although the record suggests that one should not expect too much of institutional reform in deficit reduction, there are a few partial remedies that might be politically feasible. One, suggested in a slightly different form by budget scholar Allen Schick, would enhance the president's authority to rescind spending authority previously approved by Congress.[20] Currently, the president can propose rescissions, but Congress has no obligation to act on them; if Congress is silent, nothing happens. An enhanced presidential rescission authority would guarantee the president an up-or-down vote on a limited number of rescission packages per year within a certain number of legislative days. The president would clearly have an incentive to tailor those packages narrowly enough that they would have a strong possibility of passing, since he would be guaranteed expedited consideration of a limited number of them. What might allow Congress to accept this? A provision that legislative votes on these "enhanced rescission" packages be by secret ballot would shield legis-

20. See the statement of Allen Schick before the Subcommittee on the Legislative Process of the House Committee on Rules, September 25, 1992.

lators from constituency blame if they voted against programs or projects popular in their localities. Although the president would gain institutional power, he also would have to take increased responsibility and blame for any cuts. Congress would sacrifice some institutional power, but by gaining increased opportunities to avoid blame, it might be better able to make choices that are unpopular with narrow constituency interests.

A second reform, also proposed in a somewhat different form by Schick, would establish on a temporary basis a deficit reduction commission composed of presidential and congressional appointees. The commission could recommend a limited number of nonoverlapping deficit reduction packages organized by either policy area or likelihood of passing. The legislative rules governing this procedure would need to guarantee an up-or-down floor vote.

Health Care

The challenge of creating a health care system that limits cost increases while extending coverage also calls into play the capabilities of priority setting and loss imposition. However, it also requires the capability of policy innovation. Institutional arrangements that concentrate power do not guarantee that the capabilities to impose losses and set priorities will be attained. But institutional arrangements that diffuse power when operating under normal circumstances almost assuredly will block these capabilities. Unlike the budget problem, health care is not just a matter of subtracting and reallocating. It also requires putting together a coherent plan to do simultaneously things that do not naturally cohere—cutting costs and extending benefits.

Health care issues have tended to cleave along party lines, at least before they become established programs that provide benefits. The U.S. system encourages innovative policy proposals, but because of the prevalence of veto points, the system tends to stifle coherent policy innovation at the ratification stage. Indeed, the last great burst of health care policy innovation—medicare and medicaid legislation—was passed during one of those rare moments in American history when supermajorities prevailed in both chambers of Congress under a unified government. The policy dilemma today is, however, a more complicated one than it was in 1965 when policy innovation largely consisted of extending benefits. Now the issues of cost control are much more prominent, and these matters have come to the fore at a time when income growth has been stagnant.

The revival of unified party control of the presidency and Congress in the 1992 election removes one of the greatest stumbling blocks to serious innovation, namely, conflicting partisan approaches to health care reform. But there are still many disagreements, many interests with stark conflicts, and many roadblocks to achieving meaningful reform. The challenge is to gain a reasonable degree of lasting agreement across an institutional landscape that is more favorable to unraveling than cutting deals.

Revising America's health care system is a matter of such complexity that it demands presidential leadership, which has been notably lacking in recent administrations. It requires careful and detailed deliberation as it is being formulated, but also needs expedited consideration by Congress. It is neither appropriate nor realistic to expect Congress to sacrifice a meaningful role in developing such an immensely important policy initiative, but it is also neither appropriate nor realistic to expect a workable program to emerge from the rabbit's warren of committees with overlapping jurisdictions in the two houses of Congress. A possible solution is to have special committees appointed in the House (where the Speaker already has this power) and the Senate—or better yet, a single two-chamber committee, by the leaderships of the two chambers. The committee(s) could then consider the president's plan, issue a report, and have these plans considered under modified closed rules in their chambers to allow floor consideration of a maximum of three plans: the committee plan, a plan proposed by the minority party leader in the chamber, and a presidential plan if the president still wished to pursue an alternative. This procedure would enable a variety of proposals to be heard but also would permit the issue to reach the floor.

Economic Marginalization

The problems of economic marginalization and social disintegration that beset the nation's center cities seem so vast and complicated that, for now at least, institutions appear less immediately relevant to getting a grip on them. Not only is there no consensus as to what the solutions ought to be, there is dismayingly little consensus on what the actual problems are. Some see the problems stemming from poverty; others see them arising from a disconnection to mainstream culture. What comes first in the bundle of problems that fall under the loose rubric of "the crisis of our cities?" How can problems be disentangled when they seem intricately related to one another? And would the country be willing to bear the costs of a massive effort to regenerate areas caught up in a deadly cycle of economic hopelessness, crime, and social disintegration? There is no doubt that were agreement reached on the need for a full-scale attack on these problems, policymakers would have to identify clearly the problems that need to be addressed, set priorities in trying to address them, and bear the costs of doing so. For the time being, all of this seems highly unlikely whatever the character of our institutions, because of the presence of severe budget deficits and the political isolation of cities and their poor residents.[21]

Certainly there are some policies, especially those that enhance human capital, that can alleviate the problems of the cities. Some institutional reforms at the state and local level that expand the urban revenue base, such as metropolitan government and regional tax sharing, offer hope as well. But it is difficult to imagine institutional reforms at the federal level that could by themselves make a major contribution to addressing the problems of cities.

Conclusion

In sum, a brief look at a few of the most staggering problems confronting the United States today suggests, as we have said throughout, that institutions offer risks and opportunities, not certainties. There are no institutional fixes to these problems. But there may be institutional opportunities for dealing with them. Similarly, institutions alone do not deter responses to the problems, but they can make it harder to find solutions. There is no doubt that the recent state of American government has been discouraging. Evasive behavior has been dominant where difficult decisions were required. Deadlock and finger pointing prevailed where consensus building was needed. Surely, effective leadership has been absent. But America's institutions do not make it easy to lead.

One thing is certain: a continuing failure to address the country's major problems—whether because of deficiencies of institutional arrangements or because of deficiencies of leadership—will beget perverse demands for reform and populist responses likely to add to the problems of governing. Since efforts to remedy the worst failings of American governing institutions are unlikely to be successful in the near future, the topic of institutional reform in the United States is likely to be both timely and timeless.

21. On the political isolation of cities, see Margaret Weir, "American Social Policy and the Politics of Race and Localism," in Stephan Liebfried and Paul Pierson, eds., *Fragments of Social Policy: The European Community's Social Dimension in Comparative Perspective* (forthcoming).

Chapter Authors

Davis B. Bobrow *University of Pittsburgh*
Harvey B. Feigenbaum *George Washington University*
Richard Gunther *Ohio State University*
Edward A. Kolodziej *University of Illinois, Champaign-Urbana*
Ellis S. Krauss *University of Pittsburgh*
Arend Lijphart *University of California, San Diego*
Helen Milner *Columbia University*
Anthony Mughan *Ohio State University*
Jon Pierre *University of Gothenburg*
Paul D. Pierson *Harvard University*
Bert A. Rockman *The Brookings Institution* and *University of Pittsburgh*
Ronald Rogowski *University of California, Los Angeles*
Richard J. Samuels *Massachusetts Institute of Technology*
Allen Schick *University of Maryland, College Park*
David Vogel *University of California, Berkeley*
R. Kent Weaver *The Brookings Institution*

Other Conference Participants

with their affiliations at the time of the conference

Keith G. Banting *Queen's University*
E. Colin Campbell *Georgetown University*
I. M. Destler *University of Maryland, College Park*
Peter A. Hall *Harvard University*
Fen O. Hampson *Carleton University*
Hugh Heclo *George Mason University*
George A. Hoberg *University of British Columbia*
Peter Lange *Duke University*
Renate Mayntz *Max-Planck-Institut*
Thomas L. McNaugher *The Brookings Institution*
Maureen Appel Molot *Carleton University*
Sven H. Steinmo *University of Colorado, Boulder*
Deborah Stone *Brandeis University*
James L. Sundquist *The Brookings Institution*
Philip Williams *University of Pittsburgh*
Ernest J. Wilson, III *University of Michigan*
Graham K. Wilson *University of Wisconsin, Madison*

Index

Clark, Joe, 68, 126
Clarke, Duncan L., 400n
Clean Air Act Amendments of *1967*, 250
Clean Air Act of *1956* (Great Britain), 246, 254
Clean Air Act of *1963* (United States), 249
Clean Air Act of *1970* (United States), 256
Clean Air Act of *1990* (United States), 268
Clean Air Society, 245
Clean Water Act of *1972* (United States), 256, 259
Cleavage management: in Belgium, 283–85, 293–95, 296; failures of, 273–74, 308–10; in Great Britain, 280–83, 294, 296, 298, 300–01; and institutional structure, 287–90, 299–300, 314–15, 332–33, 458; institutions for, 274–78; in plural societies, 303–05; in Spain, 285–87, 291–92, 298, 301; strategies for, 305–06, 332; in United States, 278–80, 315–16
Clift, Eleanor, 2n
Cloud, Stanley W., 2n
Clugston, Michael, 126n
Coalition governments, 19–20, 22, 23, 24, 27, 48, 49, 160, 269, 349, 449–50; and budget deficits, 212–16, 217–19, 229–30
Coal Smoke Abatement Society, 245
Codding, George Arthur, 308n, 313n
Cogan, John F., 205n
Cohen, Samy, 399n
Cohen, Stephen D., 352n, 354n, 355n
Conflict management. *See* Cleavage management
Conklin, David W., 124n
Conradt, David P., 84n
Consensualism, 274–75, 310
Conservative party (Great Britain), 130–35, 144, 241, 280–82, 365, 368–69, 395–96, 407
Control of Pollution Act of *1974* (Great Britain), 258
Cooper, Frank, 398
Cordesman, Anthony H., 375n

Corrigan, Richard, 56n
Coughlin, Richard M., 228n
Countervailing mechanisms, 104, 149, 452–53
Courchene, Thomas J., 124n
Covell, Maureen, 34n
Coyne, James K., 476n
Cox, Gary W., 451n
Craig, Paul P., 374n
Crandall, Robert W., 59n, 63n
Cranford, John R., 123n, 319n
Crewe, Ivor, 35n, 405n
Crocker, Royce, 227n
Cronin, Thomas E., 476n
Crossman, R. H. S., 15n
Crozier, Michel, 5n
Curtis, Gerald L., 172n, 428n, 429n
Cutler, Lloyd N., 2n, 111n, 348n

Daalder, Hans, 3n, 29n
Dahl, Robert A., 11n, 273n, 279n, 283n, 289n, 294n
Dalyell, Tam, 296n
Davidson, Chandler, 323n, 325n
Davidson, Roger H., 34n
Davis, David Howard, 54n, 59n
Davis, Evan, 132n
Dawkins, William, 81n
Deakin, Nicholas, 131n
Debnam, Geoffrey, 4n
de Gaulle, Charles, 391–94, 397, 399, 401, 406
Delmartino, Frank, 285n
Democratic party (United States), pension policy, 118–21
Denmark, 23
Derfner, Armand, 325n
De Ridder, Martine, 285n
Derthick, Martha, 49n, 116n
Destler, I. M., 354n, 364n
Dillon, C. Douglas, 2–3
Di Palma, Giuseppe, 5n
Divided government, 2–3, 30, 38, 49, 268, 451–52; and budget deficits, 190–91, 228–29; and energy policy, 63, 100–01; and nuclear policies, 372; and pension policy, 145
Doern, G. Bruce, 43n, 66n, 67n, 68n, 69n, 71n, 74n